For my wonderful Cos... [barcode: SO-AZV-048] who is the real scholar ... family, Love, Cos... B...

"Balogh's splendid synthesis convincingly describes how the federal government unobtrusively shaped the growth of the nation. Along the way, he also reveals the vital relationship between high political theory and policy implementation in the making of the American state."
 – Richard Bensel, Cornell University

"In this pathbreaking book, Brian Balogh brings *into* sight the hidden wellsprings of national political authority in America's supposedly stateless nineteenth century. Combining revealing new historical research with a deft grasp of both historical and political science scholarship, Balogh not only untangles the mystery of how a national government so putatively weak could govern so powerfully in advance of modern bureaucracy; he also offers an extraordinary historical vista on the governing challenges of our own era."
 – Jacob S. Hacker, University of California, Berkeley

"Brian Balogh recasts our understanding of the role of government in the United States. His ambitious and elegant interpretation changes the plot line of American history, replacing fantasies of ungoverned freedom and iconoclastic reformers with a deeper story, cutting against some of the most enduring myths of American history."
 – Edward L. Ayers, University of Richmond

"Returning political history to a pride of place and combining rich assessments of federalism, political thought, territorial expansion, political economy, and judicial decision making, this synoptic inquiry convincingly solves a great mystery. By explaining why the vigorous activities of American federal governance were elusive and hard to credit despite the wide arc of public authority, this powerfully argued and deeply researched book puts to rest the myth of a weak nineteenth-century state."
 – Ira Katznelson, Columbia University

A Government Out of Sight

Although it is obvious that America's state and local governments were consistently active during the nineteenth century, a period dominated by *laissez-faire*, political historians of twentieth-century America have assumed that the national government did very little during this period. *A Government Out of Sight* challenges this premise, chronicling the ways in which the national government intervened powerfully in the lives of nineteenth-century Americans through the law, subsidies, and the use of third parties (including state and local governments), while avoiding bureaucracy. Americans have always turned to the national government – especially for economic development and expansion – and in the nineteenth century even those who argued for a small, non-intrusive central government demanded that the national government expand its authority to meet the nation's challenges. In revising our understanding of the ways in which Americans turned to the national government throughout this period, this study fundamentally alters our perspective on American political development in the twentieth century, shedding light on contemporary debates between progressives and conservatives about the proper size of government and government programs and subsidies that even today remain "out of sight."

Brian Balogh is an associate professor in the Department of History at the University of Virginia and Chair of the Governing America in a Global Era Program at the Miller Center of Public Affairs. He is author of *Chain Reaction: Expert Debate and Public Participation in American Commercial Nuclear Power, 1945–1975* and editor of *Integrating the Sixties: The Origins, Structures and Legitimacy of Public Policy in a Turbulent Decade*. He has published articles and essays about Progressive Era politics, the link between interest groups and public policy, and the legacy of Vietnam – some of which have appeared in the *Journal of Policy History, Studies in American Political Development*, and *Social Science History and Environmental History*. He also serves on the editorial board of the *Journal of Policy History* and *Studies in American Political Development*. Balogh is a frequent commentator on politics in the national media. He co-hosts a radio show, *Backstory with the American History Guys*, that is carried on several NPR-affiliated stations. Before receiving his Ph.D. in history at The Johns Hopkins University, Balogh ran several welfare programs for the City of New York and was an adviser to New York City Council President Carol Bellamy.

A Government Out of Sight

The Mystery of National Authority in Nineteenth-Century America

BRIAN BALOGH

*University of Virginia and the Miller
Center of Public Affairs*

CAMBRIDGE
UNIVERSITY PRESS

CAMBRIDGE UNIVERSITY PRESS
Cambridge, New York, Melbourne, Madrid, Cape Town, Singapore, São Paulo, Delhi

Cambridge University Press
32 Avenue of the Americas, New York, NY 10013-2473, USA

www.cambridge.org
Information on this title: www.cambridge.org/9780521527866

First published 2009

Printed in the United States of America

A catalog record for this publication is available from the British Library.

Library of Congress Cataloging in Publication data
Balogh, Brian.
A government out of sight: the mystery of national authority in nineteenth-century
America / Brian Balogh.
p. cm.
Includes bibliographical references and index.
ISBN 978-0-521-82097-4 (hbk.) – ISBN 978-0-521-52786-6 (pbk.)   1. United
States – Politics and government – 19th century.   2. Conservatism – United
States – History – 19th century.   3. Liberalism – United States – History – 19th
century.   4. Progressivism (United States politics)   5. Free enterprise –
United States – History – 19th century.   I. Title.
JK216.B33 2009
320.97309′034–dc22   2008054803

ISBN 978-0-521-82097-4 hardback
ISBN 978-0-521-52786-6 paperback

For CMB, JEB, DAB, and KC

Contents

Acknowledgments

I could not have written this book without the support of friends and colleagues. Several individuals stand out as both. Ed Ayers provided enthusiasm, encouragement, and insight when I most needed it. He even let me score a few points on a variety of sporting surfaces. Mel Leffler balanced Ed's optimism with keen critical skepticism. He, too, provided extraordinary levels of friendship and scholarly insight over the years, except after a loss by the New York football Giants. Ed Russell, like Mel and Ed, read multiple drafts of the manuscript and offered smart criticism and invaluable personal guidance during our weekly walks. Lou Galambos continued the wise, incisive guidance that he has now provided for more than twenty years. The late Steve Innes was a source of inspiration and insight. Were he still alive, I know that he would be urging me to push the story back, well into the sixteenth century.

As readers who venture into the footnotes will soon discover, the work of two other friends and colleagues at the University of Virginia provided the intellectual framework for a good portion of my argument. Peter Onuf's brilliant conceptualization of Jeffersonian democracy and Americans' shared developmental quest provided a foundation for *A Government Out of Sight*. Chuck McCurdy's inspired reinterpretation of the independent authority of the law informed my understanding of state-society relations throughout the last two thirds of the nineteenth century. Many other colleagues in the Corcoran Department of History served as guides to the nineteenth century. Gary Gallagher, Michael Holt, and Olivier Zunz read the entire manuscript and drew on their expertise to make this a better book.

I benefitted greatly from commentary provided by my readers at Cambridge University Press. Bruce Schulman drew upon his mastery of twentieth-century U.S. history to offer criticism and suggestions that I hope will resonate with readers in our field. Bruce illuminated many of the connections between the nineteenth and twentieth centuries. Few scholars know the nineteenth century better than Richard John. Richard spared no effort in sharing his knowledge with me. A small army of other scholars have read the entire manuscript or portions of it and offered valuable criticism and suggestions. I am grateful for the guidance offered by Alan Brinkley, Richard Bensel, Lis Clemens, Gareth Davies, Robin Einhorn, Mary Furner, Patrick Griffin, John Mark Hansen, Ira Katznelson, Sid Milkis, Bill Novak, Dorothy Ross, Herman Schwartz, and Jim Sparrow.

I have learned more from the graduate students I have worked with over the years than they have learned from me. Those who deserve special thanks for their intellectual contributions to this project include Christy Chapin, Derek Hoff, Meg Jacobs, Chris Loss, Andrew McGee, Paul Milazzo, Alan Miller, Andy Morris, Brian Murphy, Johan Neem, Chris Nichols, Laura Phillips, Taylor Stoermer, Andy Trees, Drew Van de Creek, and Rai Wilson. Graduate students have also provided timely research assistance. I would like to thank Michael Broome, Vanessa May, Peter Norton, and Drew Van de Creek, and I offer special thanks to James Lawson, who never met a fact that did not need checking or a quotation that did not need correcting. I also want to thank Jim for preparing the index.

The Miller Center of Public Affairs has been a crucial source of institutional support and intellectual stimulation. Former director Phillip Zelikow, interim director Gene Fife, and current director Gerald L. Baliles were unwavering supporters of this project. I would also like to thank the staff at the Miller Center and offer a special shout-out to Sheila Blackford, Sean Gallagher, George Gilliam, Sarah Graham, Mike Greco, Stephanie Hassell, Maurice Jones, Chi Lam, Wistar Morris, Mike Mullen, Anne Mulligan, Taylor Reveley, and Joseph Taylor. My colleagues in the Governing America in a Global Era Program and many of the Miller Center Fellows and their "dream mentors" have been a great source of intellectual stimulation. I would also like to thank the panelists and audiences at the following conferences and seminars, where I presented portions of the manuscript: the American Political Development Workshop, University of Chicago; the Institute for Social and Economic Research and Policy Twentieth-Century American Politics and Society Workshop at Columbia University; the University of Texas Department of History

Workshop on Politics and History; the Ecole Des Hautes Etudes En Sciences Sociales; and the Policy History Conference. I have received a generous fellowship from the Woodrow Wilson International Center for Scholars and generous research support from the National Endowment for the Humanities, the Bankard Fund for Political Economy, and the University of Virginia College of Arts and Sciences.

Frank Smith is a dream editor. Smart, *patient*, and extraordinarily well informed, he provided good counsel and valuable criticism from the inception of this project to its conclusion. The team at Newgen Imaging Systems made copy editing relatively painless and saved me from many errors. Thanks also to Cathy Felgar for overseeing the production process and to Jeanie Lee, for her assistance.

Friends also made this book possible. Among those who are scholars, I am indebted to Ed Berkowitz, Jack Brown, Bernie Carlson, Don Critchlow, Martha Derthick, Dall Forsythe, George Gilliam, Grace Hale, John Mark Hansen, Lisa Cobbs Hoffman, Phyllis Leffler, Doug Rossinow, Ed Sermier, Tom Sugrue, Julian Zelizer, and Jon Zimmerman. Among my friends who live in the fiscal year as opposed to the academic year, I would like to thank Robert Balogh, Greg Briehl, David Carley, Carol and Phil Cooper, David and Trish Crowe, Greg Doull, Claire Gargalli, Page Gilliam, Steve Golub, Thomas Hines, Dan Josephthal, John Muresianu, Karen Rockwell, Barbara Salisbury, Ted Small, and Marcy Wagner. I would also like to thank the entire team at *Backstory with the American History Guys* for making history fun as I drew near the end of this project.

If my family thought that writing these acknowledgments delayed the completion of the book for one minute, they would insist that I not bother. But having already bothered them for far too long, I want to thank Michael Balogh, Robert Balogh, Sonya Balogh, Julia Garcia, and Katie Tanaka. Dustin Balogh helped me turn three projected books into one real one. Jake helped me by promising to accompany me on a vacation when I finished the book. Carmen sat with me through many losing UVA football games, providing welcome relief from writing and editing. Kathy Craig, my wife, has been an enduring source of inspiration, even though the vast majority of her support was carefully hidden in plain sight.

I

Introduction: Why Look Back?

Why should Americans care about their past? After all, "what have you done for me lately?" is a question posed to politicians and public officials daily, and "what will you do for me tomorrow?" is an even more common demand. Why, when "that's so twentieth century" is already an insult, should Americans care about the nineteenth century?

Here's why: the stories we absorb about the past help frame the way we see ourselves today and influence our vision of the future. Fundamental assumptions about the national government's origins and history have influenced political debate and continue to do so. For progressives, the emergence of a more powerful national government during the first decade of the twentieth century was a blessing. A remarkably resilient interpretation of American political development, originally crafted by Progressive Era activist historians like Charles Beard, traced the continued growth of national authority, powered largely by bursts of presidentially inspired reform that crested during the twentieth century through the New Deal and the Great Society. These cycles of reform were the key to building a more powerful state. Progressives applaud these developments as a marked departure from the minimalist government of the nineteenth century. Some, like Arthur Schlesinger, Jr., even predicted precisely when the next cycle of reform would begin. Others hope that charismatic leaders, like Barack Obama, will jump-start that overdue cycle.[1]

---

[1] Arthur M. Schlesinger, Jr., *The Cycles of American History* (Boston, MA: Houghton Mifflin, 1986). As Schlesinger wrote, "At some point, shortly before or after the year 1990, there should come a sharp change in the national mood and direction – a change comparable to those bursts of innovation and reform that followed the accessions to office

Besides grousing about being relegated to decades without snazzy nicknames, conservatives do not dispute this interpretation of modern American politics. They do, however, question the premise that each growth spurt was beneficial for the nation. For them, morning in America shines brightest when the sun illuminates a society organized by the principles of *laissez-faire*. Oddly, both conservatives and progressives agree on one thing: nineteenth-century Americans embraced the free market and the principles of *laissez-faire*. Conservatives want to harness that past; progressives celebrate America's liberation from it and credit the growth of national administrative capacity for their victories. Neither ideological perspective takes seriously the possibility that Americans turned regularly to the national government throughout the nineteenth century, or that it played a crucial role in shaping what Americans then and now regard as the "natural" market.

But what if the basic historical premise upon which this debate has been waged is fundamentally flawed? What if the historical foundation for *both* progressive and conservative prescriptions for twenty-first-century public policy – more government/less government – is based on the wrong set of questions? What if modern-day progressives understood that the national government often proved to be most influential when it was least visible? And what if conservatives acknowledged the crucial role that the national government played in shaping both the market and the legal status of corporations that emerged as the key players in that market during the height of *laissez-faire*? What if the period that preceded the supposed rise of "big government" – the Gilded Age that stretched from Reconstruction through the early 1890s – was *exceptional*? What if the Gilded Age was anomalous in American history precisely because some public officials sought to do something that had never been done before – draw a hard and fast line between public and private activity?

Most significantly, what if our understanding of the nineteenth century allowed for the possibility that the United States governed *differently* from other industrialized contemporaries, but did not necessarily govern *less*? Existing rules, routines, and structures of power were always in place in nineteenth-century America – even at the national level. And those rules mattered. They influenced the life chances of millions of Americans. The challenge to those who wish to understand politics today, then, is to

of Theodore Roosevelt in 1901, of Franklin Roosevelt in 1933, and of John Kennedy in 1961." [47]

discern how these governing patterns operated and to identify the ways in which they endured and evolved.[2]

In the United States, a national government capable of mobilizing compatible resources in the private and voluntary sectors often yielded more impressive results than unilateral state power. Historically, that is exactly the way Americans preferred it. Where no intermediate institutions stood between citizen and national government, Americans consistently advocated energetic governance when it came to trade, security, and economic development. Where local and state government was up to the task, or where voluntary and private groups might fulfill public purposes, Americans preferred that the national government enable rather than command.[3]

The reader may well ask how it is possible that so many scholars, not to mention millions of Americans, could miss this important story. A partial answer begins with no less an expert on governance than Alexander Hamilton. In "Federalist 27," Hamilton pronounced that "A government continually at a distance and out of sight can hardly be expected to interest the sensations of the people. The inference is that the authority of the Union and the affections of the citizens toward it will be strengthened, rather than weakened, by its extension to what are called matters of internal concern."[4]

---

[2] Bruce Seely, "A Republic Bound Together," *Wilson Quarterly,* 17, no. 1 (Winter 1993): 19–40; Peter Baldwin, "Beyond Weak and Strong: Rethinking the State in Comparative Policy History," *Journal of Policy History,* 17, no. 1 (2005): 13; Robert O. Keohane, "International Commitments and American Political Institutions in the Nineteenth Century," in *Shaped by War and Trade: International Influences on American Political Development,* ed. Ira Katznelson and Martin Shefter (Princeton, NJ: Princeton University Press, 2002): 57–61; John Brewer, *The Sinews of Power: War, Money and the English State, 1688–1783* (Boston, MA: Unwin Hyman, 1989): xix–xx.
"Though the forms and instruments of government have changed substantially over the years," Orren and Skowronek insist, "America in the nineteenth century was no less fully governed than America in the twentieth." As one political historian put it recently, "States are ... qualitatively different, not merely stronger or weaker than one another." Regimes should be compared based upon their ability to achieve fundamental objectives, not simply based upon the size of their budgets or bureaucracies. Karen Orren and Stephen Skowronek, *The Search for American Political Development* (New York, NY: Cambridge University Press, 2004), 22–23. This way of looking at state capacity fits well with Michael Mann's conception of "infrastructural power." Mann, "The Autonomous Power of the State: Its Origins, Mechanisms and Results," *European Journal of Sociology,* 26, no. 2 (1985): 185–213, esp. 189, 209.
[3] Theda Skocpol, Ziad Munson, Andrew Karch, and Bayliss Camp, "Patriotic Partnerships: Why Great Wars Nourished American Civic Voluntarism," in Katznelson and Shefter, *Shaped by War and Trade,* 139.
[4] Alexander Hamilton, "Federalist No. 27," December 25, 1787.

What Hamilton failed to anticipate was a national government that was often *most* powerful in shaping public policy when it was hidden in plain sight. Such was the case when the national government created and nourished a corporate-driven market, stimulated expansion by subsidizing exploration and removing Indians, and influenced trade patterns through communication and transportation policies. The national government shaped internal development through an active foreign policy. All of these federal actions touched the day-to-day lives of Americans as much as Hamilton's more visible policies on the national debt or the Bank. Even in those instances where the national government entered the fray as a "Leviathan," its influence was quickly displaced by sagas of heroic settlers fighting back Indians or individually making their way west without assistance from the federal government. For good reason, Tocqueville noted that "in the United States, government authority seems anxiously bent on keeping out of sight."[5]

It is also important to note that many nineteenth-century specialists have *not* missed this story. In fact, I rely on their monographs to tell it. But I tell it in a way that will pique the interest of scholars who study the twentieth century and, I hope, inform citizens and political leaders as well. That is, I emphasize the role of *national* authority, even though nineteenth-century Americans were far more likely to encounter state and local power. I emphasize the *national* story because it illuminates the patterns that guided government during the twentieth century, and even today. My efforts to tease out these patterns will frustrate those who are seeking a narrative that moves in lock-step chronological order, especially in the first half of this account. Although we start in the mid-eighteenth century and end at the conclusion of the nineteenth century, the early chapters are organized thematically. This means that readers will find themselves back at the founding more than once, as we explore the broad world views that informed political debate among citizens (Chapter 2); the debate surrounding the Constitution and its ratification (Chapter 3); the battle over interpretations of national authority that were not made explicit in the Constitution (Chapter 4); and those, like postal delivery, that were (Chapter 6). Domestic and foreign policy

---

[5] The phrase "hidden in plain sight" was suggested by Ed Ayers. Ed also suggested the construction 'mystery of' national authority used in my subtitle, Alexis De Tocqueville, *Democracy in America*, ed. J. P. Mayer, trans. George Lawrence (New York, NY: Harper Perennial, 1989), 77, cited in Pauline Maier, "The Origins and Influence of Early American Local self-Government," in *Dilemmas of Scale in America's Federal Democracy*, ed. Martha Derthick (New York, NY: Cambridge University Press, 1999), 78.

merged in the early republic. It was at the intersection of the two, and often at or beyond the boundaries of the Union, that national authority was most pronounced – a theme explored in Chapter 5. Internally, legal discourse and the federal judiciary helped knit the nation together and forge a common understanding of the political economy. (Chapter 6). Because each of these chapters proceeds chronologically, within the designated theme, readers will find themselves circling back in time to understand the evolution of each of these themes. Chapters 7 through 9 proceed in a more straightforward fashion, chronologically. They examine the impact of the Civil War, pose the high point of Gilded Age *laissez-faire* as an exceptional moment in American history that many twentieth-century scholars have mistaken for all of nineteenth-century political development, and sketch the intellectual basis for a new liberalism that set the stage for the national associative order that emerged in the twentieth century.

WHY THE NINETEENTH CENTURY?

A Government Out of Sight draws on a growing body of historical work and a cluster of theoretical insights, culled from a literature that political scientists call American Political Development, to offer a narrative of nineteenth-century political history that revises many of the assumptions shared by progressives and conservatives alike. So familiar is the historical narrative that pits America's conversion from nineteenth-century *laissez-faire* to twentieth-century big government that the multiple, well-noted exceptions to this familiar story have been all but ignored. When noticed at all, they are regarded as anomalies, interesting sideshows to the "real" thrust of American history.[6]

Providing an alternative view of the nineteenth century, redirecting the lens through which the historical narrative is glimpsed, sharpens our collective conception of America's past. It provides perspective for events and actions that heretofore have been shunted aside or ignored. There is no better example of the power exerted by these framing devices than the history of African Americans and women. For close to a century of professional history, women and African Americans were all but ignored

---

[6] For an introduction to the APD literature, see Orren and Skowronek, *Search*. For a thoughtful review of the relationship between historians and political scientists in charting APD, see Julian E. Zelizer, "History and Political Science: Together Again?" *Journal of Policy History,* 16, no. 2 (2004): 126–36.

by scholars. But social challenges in the 1960s radically altered historians' conception of what, and who, mattered. Within a decade, women's history and African American history emerged as two of the most vibrant enterprises in the academy and remain in that position today. This, in turn, has dramatically altered what scholars now consider to be the central themes of American history, not to mention the complexion and gender of the faces on postage stamps.[7]

Acknowledging that government action is sometimes most powerful when it is least visible changes the stale debate that pits big vs small government and public vs private administration. Voters may begin to notice instances of *twenty-first-century* public-private collaboration, such as the laws and tax expenditures that subsidize the so-called private world of pension and health care benefits today or the more dramatic bailout of private financial institutions by the national government. They might well ask whether federal subsidies to tens of millions of middle-class beneficiaries through their employers or some of America's wealthiest CEOs should be classified as welfare and subjected to the same scrutiny as cash grants to the indigent. Understanding the variety of ways in which Americans have governed themselves in the past can change our understanding of who we *can* be, and how we should get there.

I focus on national governance for two reasons. First, it highlights a central dilemma in American political development – how to hold distant public officials accountable. Americans were far more amenable to energetic government at the local and state levels. One of the central challenges for those who crafted the new republic was overcoming hurdles posed by size and distance. Local government fit best with traditional conceptions of republics. That meant face-to-face government. *A Government Out of Sight* examines the challenge that did not neatly fit into this pattern – governance that spanned extensive territory and that delegated authority to distant agents.

---

[7] For a brief summary of this trend and a commentary on the ways in which it has affected political history, see my article "The State of the State Among Historians," *Social Science History*, 27, no. 3 (Fall 2003): 455–63. Perhaps the most dramatic example of such a paradigmatic shift is C. Van Woodward, *The Strange Career of Jim Crow* (New York, NY: Oxford University Press, 1974). Woodward demonstrated that segregation in the South was actually a relatively recent phenomenon, not a pattern indelibly rooted in Southern race relations. Coming at the very time that African Americans were challenging the existing racial order, Woodward's interpretation was emblematic of the notion that human relations were plastic – subject to change, especially through political intervention.

Second, I focus on the national government because that is the story most neglected by scholars and popularizers alike. The story of local "commonwealth" activity is well documented. Portions of it are available in popular understandings of nineteenth-century history: even high school students learn about the Erie Canal. While the same students rarely stop to think about the massive state power embodied in the slave codes, slavery itself, which was enforced at the state and local levels, is a staple of the most basic history texts. Hundreds of local laws regulating the use of liquor during the nineteenth century and the thousands of battles fought over these regulations nicely illustrate just how pervasive (and invasive) local government could be – another familiar part of the story. I incorporate elements of that local story into the narrative that follows, but do so primarily to provide context for a discussion of national authority.[8]

Virtually all accounts of federal governance, whatever the century, note the ways in which war expands the national government. I too address this phenomenon. Often neglected by scholars, however, are the numerous ways in which the national government's responsibility for day-to-day international relations and territorial governance shaped American lives. Defining foreign policy broadly and recognizing that the boundaries between foreign and domestic policy were fluid, casts the national government in a new light. *A Government Out of Sight* underscores the

---

[8] Terrence McDonald summed up the power of local (and to some degree, state) government well when he noted that the sense of "statelessness" that political scientists think that they found in the nineteenth century was to a great extent invented in the twentieth century. Once you get beyond the boss model and actually study points of contact between citizens and state, you see that the American state, like other states, had to extract resources, differentiate itself from society, obtain a monopoly on coercive force, and maintain its own political legitimacy. Terrence J. McDonald, "Reply to Professor Katznelson," *Studies in American Political Development*, 3, no. (1989): 51–55. On labor regulation, see Jonathan A. Glickstein, *Concepts of Free Labor in Antebellum America* (New Haven, CT: Yale University Press, 1991). On the laws of slavery, see Thomas D. Morris, *Southern Slavery and the Law, 1619–1860* (Chapel Hill, NC: University of North Carolina Press, 1996); for a good example, see James A Morone, *Hellfire Nation: The Politics of Sin in American History* (New Haven, CT: Yale University Press, 2003). For an important recent article that challenges many of the traditional interpretations about national authority, see William J. Novak, "The Myth of the "Weak" American State," *The American Historical Review*, 2008 (113:3): 752–772. See also Morton Keller's broad-guaged reperiodization in *America's Three regimes: A New Political History* (New York, N.Y.: Oxford Universeity Press, 2007). Eric Rauchway adds an important comparative perspective to the discussion of late nineteenth-century American Political development in *Blessed Among Nations: How the World Made America* (New York, N.Y.: Hill and Wang, 2006).

long-term changes in governance that often preceded crises and endured after the fighting stopped and the patriotism waned.[9]

Over the past fifty years, historians have significantly altered their interpretations of why the national government grew. Despite their many differences and the sharp disagreement between progressives and conservatives about the costs and benefits of government expansion, all these approaches share one important assumption – that the national government only began to exercise significant influence over the lives of most Americans in the early twentieth century. Looking back at the nineteenth-century history of governance from this vantage point is not unlike the *New Yorker*'s cartoon view of America as seen from New York City. Glimpsed from the perspective of a three-dimensional and variegated New York City, the rest of the country looks small, flat, and uniform, just like the conventional interpretation of the national government's role in the nineteenth century.[10]

---

[9] Chapter 3, for instance, argues that, in relative terms, the War for Independence probably had as great an impact on the domestic economy and state-society relations as any war in American history. Jack N. Rakove, review of *A Union of Interests: Political and Economic Thought in Revolutionary America,* by Cathy D. Matson and Peter S. Onuf, *Journal of Economic History,* 50, no. 4 (December 1990): 979. On the impact of war on the domestic economies in this period, see Brewer, *Sinews of Power.* On war and government expansion, see Robert Higgs, *Crisis and Leviathan: Critical Episodes in the Growth of American Government* (New York, NY: Oxford University Press, 1987); Katznelson and Shefter, *Shaped;* Richard Bensel, *Yankee Leviathan: The Origins of Central State Authority in America, 1859–1877* (New York, NY: Cambridge University Press, 1990). For a balanced discussion of some of the forces that blunt such expansion, see Aaron L. Friedberg, *In the Shadow of the Garrison State: America's Anti-Statism and Its Cold War Grand Strategy* (Princeton, NJ: Princeton University Press, 2000). See also Louis Menand, *The Metaphysical Club* (New York, NY: Farrar, Straus, and Giroux, 2001), preface. For an older European perspective, see Brewer, *Sinews of Power.*

[10] "View of the World From 9th Avenue" by Saul Steinberg was the *New Yorker* cover on March 29, 1976. Thanks to George Gilliam for identifying this citation.

Progressive interpretations, championed by scholars like Arthur Schlesinger, Jr., underscored waves of reform animated by powerful chief executives. This reform-powered, presidential-centered approach was undercut by the "consensus school" in the 1950s. Consensus historians like David Potter and Daniel Boorstin emphasized the pragmatic streak in Americans and explained the growth of government as a natural adaptation to changing circumstances. "Organizational approaches," best represented in the work of Louis Galambos, Samuel P. Hays, and Robert Wiebe, drew on the latest trends in social science in the late 1950s and early 1960s. This set of theories explained the way society benefited from modern practices, like bureaucratic authority, professional autonomy, or interest group (pluralist) representation. Prodded by the great social movements of the mid- 1960s, "New Left" historians like Gabriel Kolko brought class back into the story, but with a twist. The catalyst stimulating the growth of government, they argued, came from the corporate sector, which sought to impose costs on smaller competitors and to

CONNECTING NINETEENTH- AND TWENTIETH-CENTURY GOVERNANCE

The pages that follow revise that perspective. I challenge the standard story of a weak or hollow national government by exploring the variety of ways in which national public authority was exercised. In telling that story, it is worth asking how Americans conceived of the relationship between their polity and the key spheres of their lives – such as social and economic relations. What was the relationship, as they understood it, between the public and the private spheres? How rigidly were the public and private parts of their lives separated? Were there distinct boundaries

ensure a predictable market. Most recently, social scientists like Dan Carpenter, Theda Skocpol, and Steve Skowronek, have explored the factors that account for the growing autonomy of public officials, and the limitations of their power. While there is no magic bullet that explains the relative success or failure of any given agency, the degree to which state agents are able to adapt to the deeper underlying political structures (like constitutions, or the rules that determine how citizens can participate in politics), or the effectiveness of public officials in forging enduring ties to stable sources of political support (like interest groups), often determines the size and success of government programs, these scholars argue.

Even scholars who have presented impressive arguments for the Constitution's capacious authority during the early years of the republic, such as the author of *A Revolution in Favor of Government*, accept the standard account for the rest of the nineteenth century. As Max M. Edling sees it, "Left with powers and tasks that the Antifederalists had considered insignificant, the states in fact expanded the sphere of legitimate government activity beyond anything that the participants in the ratification debate had expected. Meanwhile, the era of free trade and free security reduced the importance of the national government and, for well over a century, it remained 'a midget institution in a giant land.'" Max M. Edling, *A Revolution in Favor of Government: Origins of the U.S. Constitution and the Making of the American State* (New York, NY: Oxford University Press, 2003), 228. I am deeply indebted to Edling's work on the Federalist period. Nor do I take issue with the crucial role played by the states during the heyday of the American "party period." But as the following pages make clear, I do not subscribe to Edling's embrace of the standard characterization of the national government's governing capacity as a "midget institution in a giant land".

Leonard White's account of the early War Department is representative of an older scholarship that has left a powerful legacy with the American public. Leonard D. White, *The Federalists: A Study in Administrative History* (1948; Westport, CT: Greenwood Press, 1978). According to the standard accounts, the national government went from little to nothing after the Jeffersonian "Revolution of 1800." More recent accounts continue the pattern. They, like Edling, characterize the early national government as a "midget institution in a giant land." John Murrin, "The Great Inversion, or Court versus Country: A Comparison of the Revolution Settlements in England (1688–1721) and America (1776–1816)," in *Three British Revolutions, 1641, 1688, 1776*, ed. J. G. A. Pocock (Princeton, NJ: Princeton University Press, 1980), 425, quoted in Richard John, *Spreading the News: The American Postal System from Franklin to Morse* (Cambridge, MA: Harvard University Press, 1995), 18.

between the polity and the voluntary sector? The answers to these questions changed significantly over the course of the long nineteenth century. *A Government Out of Sight* chronicles these shifts as it traces the evolution of national policy.[11]

For much of the eighteenth century, a classical republican vision submerged private interest. The world was viewed through a lens in which politics existed prior to social divisions. The nature of political systems, many educated Americans believed, determined social divisions. Social strife was the by-product of imperfectly formed political regimes. Centuries of social science, not to mention the more recent emergence of social history, have made it difficult for us to imagine a world in which governing arrangements, rather than economic interests, created basic social divisions. Nevertheless, before the American Revolution, most educated citizens entertained just such a conception of the polity. Recapturing this world view is an important reminder that conceptions of the relationship between the polity and the social spheres have changed dramatically over the course of American history and are subject to future shifts.[12]

From its inception, conditions in British North America that did not fit neatly into the world of classical Greek republics, or even the Enlightenment reconstruction of that world, clouded the republican outlook. The young nation faced a host of interstate rivalries, disorder on the frontiers, international threats to its security, competition for trade, and communications challenges. Self-interest was ubiquitous, and virtue in short supply. These problems plagued the Confederation and inspired calls for stronger central government. George Washington, for instance, noted that the citizens of the Confederation were "torn by internal dis-

---

[11] For two of the most recent challenges to this perspective, see Gautham Rao, "Sailor's Health and National Wealth: The Political Economy of the Federal Marine Hospitals, 1799–1860" (draft dissertation chapter, University of Chicago, October 29, 2005), 11, and generally; and Stefan Heumann, "The Tutelary Empire: State- and Nation-Building in the 19th Century United States," (Dissertation, Political Science, University of Pennsylvania, forthcoming).

[12] See Gordon S. Wood, "'The Rise of American Democracy': A Constant Struggle"; review of *The Rise of American Democracy: Jefferson to Lincoln,* by Sean Wilentz, *New York Times,* November 13, 2005, http://www.nytimes.com/. See also Sean Wilentz, *The Rise of American Democracy: Jefferson to Lincoln* (New York, NY: Norton, 2005). James G. March and Johan P. Olson argue that the "new institutionalism" returns to the ancient theme that "politics creates and confirms interpretations of life." March and Olson,"The New Institutionalism: Organizational Factors in Political Life," *American Political Science Review,* 78, no. 3 (September 1984): 741.

putes, or supinely negligent and inattentive to every thing which is not local and self interesting."[13]

Advocates of a developmental vision argued that a national perspective, embodied in a continental union, could counter these centrifugal forces. Rather than pitting local or sectional groups against each other, leaders believed, a common commitment to expansion and development of the West would create truly national interests capable of binding the states and sections together. By projecting trade and commerce westward, political tendencies toward disintegration would be reversed.[14]

Those who subscribed to this conception of relations between state and civil society explicitly acknowledged the overwhelming importance of self-interest. To justify and naturalize self-interest, they turned to a set of ideas, best represented in the work of Adam Smith and John Locke. Scholars have loosely labeled these ideas "classical liberalism." In the American context, classical liberalism was tempered by the moral restraints embedded in the nation's Protestant heritage. By the 1830s, most citizens believed that divinely inspired bounty and a powerful set of natural laws – illustrated by the market – ordered social actions and exempted Americans from the social turmoil that Europe had repeatedly experienced.

National governance remained hidden in plain sight because many of its activities were directed at the margins of the nation. Yet acquiring, exploring, surveying, and ultimately selling land were crucial to the nation's future. Pacifying Indians, whether through treaty or brute force, meant life or death for many; it affected the economic well-being of hundreds of thousands more. The assurance that property laws would be enforced throughout the land, even when that property was human, was an article of faith for some. Protecting existing borders, extending those borders, and guaranteeing trade routes touched virtually every American life.[15]

From today's perspective, American territorial expansion unfolded inexorably. Yet little could be taken for granted in the early national period.

[13] John Lauritz Larson, *Internal Improvement: National Public Works and the Promise of Popular Government in the Early United States* (Chapel Hill, NC: University of North Carolina Press, 2001), 15.
[14] Cathy D. Matson and Peter S. Onuf, *A Union Of Interests: Political and Economic Thought in Revolutionary America* (Lawrence, KS: University Press of Kansas, 1990), 79. At its most abstract level, the developmental vision substituted future integration for past competition and division.
[15] Bartholomew H. Sparrow, "U.S. Territorial Policy: Subsidy and Settlement, 1783–1898" (unpublished paper, 1999), 22.

For instance, it could not be assumed that settlers would remain loyal to the United States if trade opportunities did not beckon. Given Congress's failure to open navigation on the Mississippi, the words of one North Carolinian captured the growing frustration on the frontier: "We must ... be allowed to export our produce, for when a whole nation has a passion which is not fitted to their situation they will infallibly strive to alter their situation. If the liberty of trading is not given us, we must take it."[16]

While nature's bounty and willing citizens made growth possible, it could only be realized through properly structured *national* rules that ensured orderly development. This required the exercise of *national* authority to protect land titles, provide security, forge trading opportunities, and reinforce shared values regarding religion, education, and language. In short, it required a common vision of orderly economic development and the legal wherewithal to impose that vision on a mobile, diverse, and economically opportunistic population.

Land, however, only contributed to development if it was accessible. Both Federalists and Jeffersonian Republicans advocated national internal improvements toward this end. Governing Jeffersonians, it turned out, were more amenable to using the latent authority of the federal government than they had been when not in power. As Joseph Story, a Republican appointed by Madison to the Supreme Court in 1811, wrote, it should not be surprising "that the opposing parties shall occasionally be found to maintain the same system, when in power, which they have obstinately resisted when out of power." Probably thinking of Jefferson, Story continued, "Without supposing any insincerity or departure from principle in such cases, it will be easily imagined that a very different course of reasoning will force itself on the minds of those who are responsible for the measures of government, from that which the ardor of opposition and the jealousy of rivals might well foster." Most directly associated with Henry Clay of Kentucky, the American System called for the national government to act as a catalyst and coordinator in nurturing

---

[16] Extract of a letter from Davidson County, North Carolina, dated October 20, 1786, in *Virginia Journal*, February 15, 1787; quoted in Matson and Onuf, *Union of Interests*, 64. The situation was equally volatile in Kentucky. Under the leadership of James Wilkinson, some Kentuckians were prepared to negotiate with Spain for the right to trade on the Mississippi. They were even willing to consider "admission *to her protection as subjects*"; General Wilkinson's *Memorial* is the source quoted in William R. Shepherd, "Wilkinson and the Beginnings of the Spanish Conspiracy," *American Historical Review*, 9, no. 3 (April 1904): 501, cited in Thomas P. Slaughter, *The Whiskey Rebellion: Frontier Epilogue to the American Revolution* (New York, NY: Oxford University Press, 1986), 55.

an American market for agricultural products by creating demand for them in developing industrial centers. For Daniel Webster and the Whigs, internal improvements epitomized the kind of projects that required collective public action to promote the welfare of private citizens. Isolation posed the greatest challenge to citizens, the states they lived in, and the successful union of those states.[17]

In some policy venues, the national government – which contemporaries often called the "General Government," as will I – was the only game in town (foreign policy, for instance). Even at home, however, the General Government retained exclusive control and pursued its unilateral responsibilities vigorously by the standards of the time. The postal system was an impressive example of this. As one communications scholar put it, "No other branch of the central government penetrated so deeply into the hinterland or played such a conspicuous role in shaping the pattern of every day life." While the Federal Marine Hospital system did not reach as deeply into the lives of all Americans, it provided service nationwide, funding treatment by garnishing the wages of seamen. At least when it came to economic or political development, Americans were willing to seek federal help if other means were not available.[18]

There was little room for powerful centralized administrative structures in this vision, but plenty of room for states and localities to take the initiative. At the state and local levels, government was free to mingle public and private interests in endeavors known as "mixed enterprises" in order to nurture a dynamic economy that grew rapidly. State and local governments retained their commitment to advancing the common weal of the polity. At the same time, however, Americans who supposedly feared distant government subsidized a national postal service that dwarfed its European counterparts in its scope and capacity to carry the news at bargain prices. A national legal structure laid the foundation for integrated markets, transportation systems, and, eventually, the modern business corporation. Lawyers, though far from government functionaries in most instances, developed a discourse that was shared across the states, and influenced the very way that many Americans defined political issues. District federal courts served as mediators between this national

[17] Joseph Story, *Commentaries on the Constitution of the United States.* 5th edn., edited by Melvin Bigelow, 2 vols. (Boston, MA, Little Brown, 1891), 1:662, quoted in Theodore Sky, *To Provide for the General Welfare: A History of the Federal Spending Power* (Newark, NJ: University of Delaware Press, 2003), 222; Larson, *Internal Improvement,* 3.
[18] Larson, *Internal Improvement,* 4; John, Spreading, 4.

discourse and local practice. And an active foreign policy ensured that borders kept expanding, while territories remained loyal and were eventually incorporated into the growing nation. Both geological and human obstacles to expansion were tackled by the General Government. Most significantly, public decisions about federal land distribution reinforced the perception of divinely inspired development and market-fueled expansion at the very time they subsidized that development.

The seemingly "natural" balance that Americans subscribed to in the first half of the nineteenth century was undermined by crises that originated in both the public and private spheres. The public crisis that tore the union apart during the Civil War demonstrated that the myth of harmony was ephemeral at best. After the war, class stratification challenged the authority of those who insisted that the prophylactic power of America's exceptional past endured.

Fueled by wartime growth, key components of civil society – businesses, markets, networks of transportation, and the very understanding of these phenomena – began to outgrow the political jurisdictions that in some instances had helped to create them. The political system responded by hardening the boundary between public and private. Reaching its peak during the Gilded Age, this sharp demarcation – which had always been applied more forcefully to the General Government because of its political distance from its citizens – was now extended to state and local functions.

Thus, the Gilded Age is exceptional because it stands in sharp contrast to the eighteenth-century republican era, during which society was considered to be an extension of the state, and the "commonwealth" mingling of public and private interests that dominated the first half of the nineteenth century. Nor does it comport with the turn to explicitly statist solutions, most pronounced in the Confederate government during the Civil War and the Union government during Reconstruction. The Gilded Age *laissez-faire* ideal clashed most dramatically with the naked state power leveled at African Americans in the South and women across the republic for much of the nineteenth century.

Although most historical accounts extrapolate America's modern history from its supposed *laissez-faire* origins in the Gilded Age, no period in America's history was *less* representative of America's past than the brief era that stretched from the end of Reconstruction in 1877 through the panic of 1893. It was during the Gilded Age that political institutions, especially the Supreme Court of the United States, made a self-conscious and, ultimately, unsuccessful effort to establish strict boundaries between the public and private spheres. It was this ambitious initiative to parse public and private that proved exceptional, not the rich mixture of federal, state, voluntary, and private initiatives that characterized both nineteenth- and early twentieth-century political development.

The judiciary radically reshaped the legal standing of corporations between Reconstruction and the first decade of the twentieth century. Corporations were transformed from publicly crafted organizations granted special privileges in order to meet public service requirements, into natural outcroppings of the economy, protected under the constitution from state interference with Fourteenth Amendment due process rights. A series of decisions in the late nineteenth century confirmed that corporations really were more than just the sum of their parts. Nobody appreciated this early history better than Supreme Court Justice Louis Brandeis. Courts began to perceive corporations as bundles of contracts between private investors – not unlike partnerships – rather than as extensions of public authority. As Brandeis reminded his brethren in 1933, "The prevalence of the corporation in America has led men of this generation to act, at times, as if the privilege of doing business in corporate form were inherent in the citizen. ... Through the greater part of our history a different view prevailed."[19]

The General Government also fashioned a national market that ensured the predictable, stable environment essential to corporate growth. This laid the legal groundwork for a world inhabited by groups and associations, rather than individuals, a world in which individuals increasingly exercised their political and economic preferences through groups. The modern corporation, endowed with a full set of constitutionally protected rights, was first in line for this public recognition and protection.[20]

[19] Gerald Berk, "Constituting Corporations and Markets: Railroads in Gilded Age Politics," *Studies in American Political Development,* 4, no. 1 (1990): 141. However, corporations continued to offer investors limited liability.
   Santa Clara v. Southern Pacific Rail Road (1886) and its companion cases placed the nation's highest court squarely behind the principle that corporations were protected by the Fourteenth Amendment. Morton J. Horwitz, *The Transformation of American Law, 1870–1960: The Crisis of Legal Orthodoxy* (New York, NY: Oxford University Press, 1992), 66–71; James Willard Hurst, *The Legitimacy of the Business Corporation in the Law of the United States, 1780–1970* (Charlottesville, VA: University Press of Virginia, 1970), 65; *Santa Clara County v. Southern Pacific Railroad Company; California v. Central Pacific Railroad Company; California v. Southern Pacific Railroad Company,* 118 U.S. 394 (1886); *Louis K. Liggett Co. V. Lee,* 288 U.S. 517 (1933). Brandeis's dissent in *Liggett,* the 1933 Supreme Court case restricting the rights of a chain store in Florida is still one of the most, concise histories of the nineteenth-century transformation of corporate standing in the law.
[20] No distinction between public and private was drawn in the first American corporations: they were all "bodies-politic." Robert W. Gordon, "Legal Thought and Legal Practice in

In the immediate wake of the Civil War amendments, particularly the Fourteenth Amendment, the autonomous, rights-bearing individual stood at the center of the fray. By the dawn of the twentieth century, that individual had been replaced by the group, starting with the now-naturalized corporation. They were soon joined by a broad range of national associations. By embracing corporations as persons and vesting them with due process rights, the Court contributed materially to the radical shift in perception that occurred in the thirty years following the Civil War. By 1900, corporations were viewed as the product of market forces that required political protection only from those who dared to interfere with natural law. Remarkably, the active role that the federal judiciary played in this transformation was barely noticed. It remained out of sight, superseded by supposedly natural forces.[21]

While progressives will be pleased to learn that Americans consistently turned to the national government, and that efforts to parse private from public were the exception rather than the rule in American governance, my interpretation of "new liberalism," which provided the intellectual basis for the Progressive Movement at the end of the nineteenth century, will surely enrage them. The 1890s ushered in a transition in state-society relations heralded by the rise of new liberalism. New liberals explored nationally administered solutions to social problems. While a necessary precondition to the growth of the national government, new liberalism did not lead automatically to a central administrative state. Rather, it made possible, once again, the intermingling of public and private authority. What distinguished this latest phase of state-society relations from the "commonwealth" period, however, was that far more interaction now took place at the national level. New liberals embraced a broad range of national associations, including voluntary, religious, and even corporate organizations. They turned to the national government only as a "special" category of "associative action."[22]

---

the Age of American Enterprise, 1870–1920," in *Professions and Professional Ideologies in America*, ed. Gerald L. Geison (Chapel Hill, NC: University of North Carolina Press, 1983), 100. Corporations in the early republic were exceptions in a legal system built upon the individual's natural rights. Corporate rights were the product of political contest and subject to public regulation. Horwitz, *Transformation*, 75.

[21] Horwitz, *Transformation*, 105. It is this intellectual transformation, aided and abetted by the Supreme Court's unwavering endorsement of corporate personhood, that helps explain why many states chose to jump on the bandwagon started by New Jersey's relaxation of corporate regulation, rather than work collectively with the ample legal authority they already possessed, to influence, if not actually guide, the form that America's economy would take in the next century.

[22] E.J. James, "The State as an Economic Factor," *Science*, 7, no. 173 (May 28, 1886): 487.

Progressive Era intellectuals, Chapter 9 argues, advocated delegating national authority to associations, voluntary organizations, the professions, interest groups, and even commercial enterprises. Those intellectuals who challenged the Gilded Age *laissez-faire* regime, standard accounts tell us, turned toward national government and lay the groundwork for a federal administrative state in the Progressive Era. While economists like Richard Ely and sociologists like Albion Small did not rule out such national administration, they embraced a range of techniques that sought progressive ends through the vast array of *non*governmental associations that flourished in this era.

Perhaps the best evidence for the powerful ways in which the national government touched the lives of nineteenth-century Americans is the persistent strain of antistatism that has prevailed into the twenty-first century. Either Americans have been paranoid for two hundred years, or this sentiment remains powerful precisely because the national government was an important presence for much of American history. It shaped the daily lives of Americans through a variety of mechanisms. In doing so, it posed a real threat to those who would limit governmental actions by the strict boundaries of *laissez-faire*, inflaming antistatist sentiment, deepening and enriching this ideological and programmatic tradition. As we shall see, however, those who challenged national "consolidation" in some spheres were often the first to demand national solutions in other domains.

2

How Americans Lost Sight of the State:
Adapting Republican Virtue to Liberal Self-Interest

The republican ideas that informed leading thinkers resonate today in America's distrust of distant authority. Yet this vigilance was only one part of the compound known as republicanism. Lost today is an element in republican thought that supported an expansive view of governance. Indeed, from a republican perspective, vigilance was essential because the polity was all-encompassing. Granting so much authority to the government required extraordinary citizens. As long as those who governed remained virtuous, and citizens remained engaged, government could be trusted to carry out an ambitious agenda, enlightened British North Americans believed. This complex compound of authority and scrutiny worked best at the local level. Government was most active there, intervening in the economy and sharply proscribing the rights and prospects of women, not to mention slaves.

From this republican perspective, politics structured everything else. In the eyes of the founders, social divisions and economic relationships were the product of, not the foundation for, the political order. It is this republican conception of the relationship between politics and the rest of the society that students of American political development have neglected.

We should not judge contemporary scholars too harshly for ignoring what was at best, a fragile, idealized conception of governance. Even some of the founders who had embedded republican ideas in the Constitution narrowed their conception of the proper role of the central government by the early nineteenth century, going so far as to charge their Federalist counterparts with the Tory tendency to "consolidate" the executive and judicial branches of government. Men like Jefferson leveled these charges, laying the groundwork for more than two centuries of antistatist rhetoric.

Jeffersonians warned of "consolidation," even as they pursued bold national initiatives like the Louisiana Purchase. This temptation to categorize some national policies as consolidation (or in today's parlance, "big government" or "welfare"), while promoting other policies that had far greater impact on the lives of Americans yet were seen as perfectly legitimate was reinforced by the relative ease with which liberal ideas intersected with, and reinforced, selective elements in the republican world view.

Explicating that republican world view and charting its rapid demise in the last third of the eighteenth century helps us understand why many Americans lost sight of the central government, even as it extended its reach and influence. Because a republican world view that placed politics at the center of life gave way to social and economic constructions of human interaction, the polity was not only displaced; rather, its contribution to national development was all but ignored, and eventually forgotten. Most scholars did not rediscover the central government until it built new national administrative capacity in the early twentieth century. Indeed, the standard account of political development chronicles a "stateless" America, propelled, kicking and screaming toward that "patchwork" administrative state. Recapturing the primacy of the polity in the early republic turns this story on its head by concentrating on the ways in which civil society and a robust sphere of private activity were carved out of a world that previously had been viewed through political lenses.

Once restored, the course of American political development looks quite different. Starting from the perspective of virtuous citizens scrutinizing energetic governance exposes the many ways in which government structured state-society relations over the course of the nineteenth century. The central government retained a healthy partnership in many of these ongoing endeavors, ranging from communications to territorial expansion, not to mention national security and trade. In many instances, the central government served as a coordinator, as in the case of internal improvements – providing fiscal aid and a national perspective to state and local partners. It reinforced tendencies in civil society, providing crucial legal protection to, and increasingly assisting this evolution toward, the "private" status of corporations. Americans sought active governance at the federal level time and again over the course of the nineteenth century. Their efforts produced a variety of mechanisms, from debt assumption to Supreme Court decisions that undercut the health and safety prerogatives of states in the name of interstate commerce.

Republican ideas were overwhelmed by three distinctly American phenomena: social flux, easy access to land, and the sheer size of the "republic" to be governed. While republican distrust of authority was reinforced by liberal ideas, the prospect for representation in a republic as extensive as the United States soon gave way to demands that the voices of a growing number of citizens be heard directly through actual, rather than virtual, representation. Of even greater significance, the growing reach of the market justified individual choice, while liberalism equated the sum total of these choices with enlightened social policy. Social flux, abundant land, and extensive jurisdiction eroded the republican rationale for energetic governance, which had always depended on the intimate relationship between virtue, citizenship, and common welfare of the republic.

Yet, *A Government Out of Sight* is not a story of declension. Rather, my narrative chronicles the emergence of an alternative basis for public intervention – one that ultimately provided a far more enduring ideological foundation for *national* governance, precisely because it broadened the basis for citizenship and explicitly recognized divergent material interests. Consonant with the principles of classical liberalism, this developmental vision (elaborated in the next chapter) shifted the basis for energetic government from the obligations of citizenship to the aggregate self-interest of individuals who stood to benefit from their collective action.

Over the course of the late eighteenth century, the justification for collective action evolved – from virtuous service to the republic, to stimulating the economic and moral development of a nation in a manner that would directly benefit groups of citizens. Relying on liberal conceptions of individual rights and opportunities, this "developmental vision" nonetheless demanded more from the General Government than ever. Consistently understated or ignored by proponents of a classical liberal political economy were the actions of the central government, which, through its military and trade policy, carried out crucial developmental tasks, coordinated activities that crossed state boundaries such as interstate commerce, and subsidized the news.

The explicit role of the General Government, however, was overshadowed by social and economic emphasis on individual initiative and private interest. The role of the central government, as coordinator and direct developer, was eclipsed, if not actively hidden. Just as idealized visions of the republic had earlier denied the apparent self-interest of individuals, classical liberal ideology effaced the crucial role played by government in the national development.

The history crafted during the nation's infancy paved the way for the transition to a liberal framework by flattening the complex republican compound that had once encouraged energetic government, at the same time that it promoted vigilance. That interpretation, crafted by the Jeffersonians, pitted a nation of independent farmers against elite-inspired efforts to "consolidate" government and remove it from the people. As democratic participation flourished over the course of the nineteenth century, Americans embraced this dichotomy. So too did generations of professionally trained historians in the twentieth century. Nineteenth-century Americans, they argued, wanted as little government as possible, and when they had to have it, they preferred that it remain local where it could be watched carefully.

This chapter traces the intellectual conceptions that framed the debate about American political development from the late seventeenth century through the early nineteenth century. It does not replay the fierce internecine battle among scholars who pitted a republican founding against notions that "America was born liberal," or the more recent correctives that have documented the powerful role of commerce and self-interest that shaped political thought even before the Revolution. Rather, the chapter instructs students of American political development in the contest of ideas that resonated with those citizens who governed during this period.

Individual self-interest and the polity's claim on the allegiance of citizens had always existed in tension with each other. As the balance between interest and the common weal of the republic shifted toward the former, the republican basis for energetic government lost its hold. Just as advocates of the republican vision who denied self-interest treated the examples of it that surrounded them as exceptions, advocates of the classical liberal polity that emerged in the early nineteenth century regarded instances of energetic governance, which abounded, as exceptional.

"GOVERNMENT EVEN IN ITS BEST STATE IS BUT A NECESSARY EVIL": ONE HALF OF THE REPUBLICAN IDEAL

The half-life of one half of the republican tradition in America has been lengthy. Americans have long feared that their fellow citizens would lose their independence – that they would fall prey to political influence and be manipulated by others. Nor has this fear of concentrated power been limited to the government. By the late nineteenth century, broad social movements turned first to state government, and eventually to the General

Government, to break up concentrations of private power embodied in trusts and monopolies.

Fear of corruption and the fierce defense of an independent citizenry are the legacies of a set of ideas that scholars call "republican" ideology. Labeled "small r republicanism" to distinguish this political philosophy from the "capital R" political party that emerged in nineteenth-century America, the republican perspective was pervasive throughout the Atlantic world in the eighteenth century. British North Americans absorbed these ideas from late seventeenth and early eighteenth-century British critics of the Crown.[1]

Republican writers concluded that the crown sought to corrupt Parliament, the branch of government that best represented the public. The king had the wherewithal to achieve this through his placemen who

---

[1] British North Americans drew on "country party," or "Opposition" ideas that Britons had used for some time to temper the king's absolute power. Gordon S. Wood, *The Radicalism of the American Revolution* (New York, NY: Knopf, 1992), 96.

Republican thought was built upon foundational texts like James Harrington's *Commonwealth of Oceana* (1656). Harrington employed ideas recovered during the Italian Renaissance that popularized the perspective of Roman writers like Virgil, Cicero, and Tacitus. Commonwealths that balanced the authority of a monarch – who provided strong leadership – with nobles – who contributed wisdom, and with a popularly elected assembly that represented the citizens' collective wishes, offered the best prospect for enlightened, stable government. Montesquieu, another source of republican thought, systematically analyzed the benefits and disadvantages of republics and monarchies in the *Spirit of the Laws* (1748). He concluded that most modern states combined elements of both. James Harrington, *The Oceana and Other Works of James Harrington, With an Account of his Life by John Toland*, (London: printed for T. Becket, T. Cadell, and T. Evans, 1771) in Eighteenth Century Collections Online, (GaleGroup, 2003 [Gale Doc. No. CW103440112]), http://galenet.galegroup.com/servlet/ECCO/; Wood, *Radicalism*, 97–98; Charles de Secondat baron de Montesquieu, *The Spirit of The Laws*, trans. Anne M. Cohler, Basia C. Miller, Harold Stone (New York, NY: Cambridge University Press, 1989).

As eighteenth-century British monarchs sought to extend their control over parliament, opposition tracts like those published as *Cato's Letters* (1720–1723) celebrated mixed government. But they also warned of its inherent instability. The danger came from a powerful court capable of corrupting the parliament's independence. Through the use of politically motivated factions, the promise of property, and favors to the court rewarded in the coin of title and position, the crown undermined the delicate balance essential to effective governance. Lance Banning, *The Jeffersonian Persuasion: Evolution of a Party Ideology* (Ithaca, NY: Cornell University Press, 1978), chaps. 1–2. For cautionary advice on applying this thinking directly to British North America, see Joyce Appleby, *Liberalism and Republicanism in the Historical Imagination* (Cambridge, MA: Harvard University Press, 1992), Chap. 6. On mixed or "compound" government, see J.R. Pole, *The Gift of Government: Political Responsibility from The English Restoration to American Independence* (Athens, GA: University of Georgia Press, 1983), 31.

depended on the crown for their livelihood and status. As the British philosopher and essayist David Hume noted in 1741, when the king's property was combined with "the encreasing luxury of the nation, our proneness to corruption, together with the great power and prerogatives of the crown, and the command of military force, there is no one but must despair of being able, without extraordinary efforts, to support our free government much longer under these disadvantages."[2]

The republican perspective served as a powerful counterweight to the king. Public opinion informed by republican ideas tempered a nation's blind loyalty to the crown, Hume contended. "There has been a sudden and sensible change in the opinions of men within these last fifty years by the progress of learning and of liberty. Most people, in this island, have divested themselves of all superstitious reverence to names and authority." Chastened and properly prepared to fight encroachment, advocates of balanced government might prevail.[3]

Colonists in British North America burnished republican ideology into an effective revolutionary weapon directed at British rule. Mid-eighteenth-century British North Americans feared distant, centralized power. Opposition rhetoric resonated with colonists because it exposed the threat to liberty that arbitrary use of power and executive corruption posed at a time when the crown threatened their rights. They believed that liberty was the natural prey of distant authority. Power tended to expand and centralize, threatening the very local institutions, like juries and militias, that preserved liberty. British North Americans countered distant power with citizen supervision and surveillance of executive authority. Only determined and wise political vigilance could preserve the republic, they believed.[4]

Republican ideas were powerful in England, where the crown had an impressive array of inducements and threats to win over its opposition. In the American colonies, where such a formidable foe was distanced by

---

[2] David Hume, "Essay VII: Whether The British Government Inclines More to Absolute Monarchy, or to a Republic," in *Essays, Moral, Political, and Literary,* ed. Eugene F. Miller, Intelex Past Masters Series (Indianapolis, IN: Liberty Classics; University of Virginia Library Electronic Text Center, 1987), 49, http://library.nlx.com/.

[3] Wood, *Radicalism,* 95; Hume, Essay VII," 51.

[4] Max M. Edling, *A Revolution in Favor of Government: Origins of the U.S. Constitution and the Making of the American State* (New York, NY: Oxford University Press, 2003), 40–41; Joseph J. Ellis, *Founding Brothers: Stories from the Early Republic* (New York, NY: Knopf, 2000), 7; Andrew S. Trees, *The Founding Fathers and the Politics of Character* (Princeton, NJ: Princeton University Press, 2004), 1.

time and space, the fear of central power grew unchecked. There *was* no powerful court in British North America to entice or compel allegiance. Republican thought seeded antistatism in America. Thomas Paine, who served multiple terms as governor of Virginia, summed up this strain of republican thought best, declaring "government even in its best state is but a necessary evil."[5]

"HIS TIME AND TALENTS ... ALL BELONG TO HIS COUNTRY": THE COLLECTIVE HALF OF REPUBLICAN THOUGHT

Yet there was more to the republican vision than fear of corruption and dependence: republican thought also emphasized energetic governance. It did not acknowledge a distinction between state and civil society or, for that matter, public and private roles for citizens. It embodied a commonwealth tradition that thrived along with its citizens' vigilance. The commonwealth tradition stressed that the public good derived from placing the polity's interests ahead of the rights of individual citizens. Service to the republic disciplined self-interest in the cause of the commonweal of all citizens. In the hands of such virtuous leaders, government could be trusted to do a great deal.[6]

Leaders like George Washington worked tirelessly to preserve liberty, but they conceived of liberty as a corporate privilege to be enjoyed collectively by all of the republics' citizens. It was a blessing bestowed on the entire community rather than a privately held benefit distributed to rights-bearing individuals. In contrast to Paine, noted physician and Philadelphia reformer Benjamin Rush fashioned the boundary between public and private spheres in a manner that left little room for the latter. A citizen was "public property," Rush contended. As such, "his time and

[5] Gianfranco Poggi, *The State: Its Nature, Development, and Prospects* (Cambridge, UK: Polity Press, 1990), 57–76; James A. Morone, *The Democratic Wish: Popular Participation and the Limits of American Government* (New York, NY: Basic Books), 2; Charles Taylor, "Modes of Civil Society," *Public Culture*, 3 (Fall 1990): 101; Stanley Elkins and Eric McKitrick, *The Age of Federalism* (New York, NY: Oxford University Press, 1993), 24; Lance Banning, "Republican Ideology and the Triumph of the Constitution, 1789 to 1793," *William and Mary Quarterly*, 3rd ser., 31, no. 2 (April 1974): 177; Thomas Paine, "Common Sense" in *Complete Works* (Boston, MA: J. P. Mendum, 1859; University of Virginia Library Electronic Text Center, 1995), 19; http://etext.lib.virginia.edu/collections/, cited in Trees, *Founding Fathers*, 2.
[6] Ellis, *Founding Brothers*, 14. It was just such a conflation of the two that Paine challenged, writing, "Some writers have so confounded society with government, as to leave little or no distinction between them." Paine, "Common Sense," 19.

talents – his youth – his manhood – his old age – nay more, life, all belong to his country."[7]

This collective impulse in republican thought tempered market-oriented choices and promoted active government. As Washington wrote to Jefferson in 1784, "From Trade our Citizens *will not* be restrained, and therefore it behoves us to place it in the most convenient channels, under proper regulation, freed *as much as possible,* from those vices which luxury, the consequences of wealth and power, naturally introduce." For Washington, freedom did not mean *less* government. Rather, regulation might steer trade toward public benefits. He was responding to similar sentiment from Jefferson, expressed in a letter only two weeks earlier. Jefferson had argued, "Our citizens have had too full a taste of the comforts furnished by the arts and manufactures to be debarred the use of them. We must then in our own defense endeavor to share as large a portion as we can of this modern source of wealth and power." A well-maintained republic would guide commerce, trade, communications, and a host of other social interactions in ways that would benefit the entire commonwealth and serve the collective good.[8]

For republicans like Jefferson and Washington, faith in the capacity of the polity to provide for the common benefit of its citizens was simply taken for granted because they considered politics to be foundational. The polity encompassed, indeed, defined, the social and economic realms, leaving only a narrow spectrum of life outside its reach. Even in a world inexorably "becoming commercial," the primacy of politics demanded that leaders engineer public solutions to what today might be defined as private problems. Because the demands placed upon the commonwealth's leadership were high, only men of impeccable virtue could shoulder these responsibilities. Choosing wise leaders freed republics, even required them, to pursue energetically the collective good.

---

[7] John L. Larson, *Internal Improvement: National Public Works and the Promise of Popular Government in the Early United States* (Chapel Hill, NC: University of North Carolina Press, 2001), 20; Peter S. Onuf, "Federalism, Democracy, and Liberty in the New American Nation," (lecture, Expansion of English Liberty Overseas, Cincinnati, OH, November 1–3, 2007), 15–23; Benjamin Rush, "On the Defects of the Confederation," in *The Selected Writings of Benjamin Rush*, ed. Dagobert D. Runes (New York, NY: Philosophical Library, 1947), 31, quoted in Trees, *Founding Fathers*, 3.
[8] George Washington to Thomas Jefferson, March 29, 1784, in *The Papers of Thomas Jefferson*, ed. Julian P. Boyd et al., (Princeton, NJ: Princeton University Press, 1950), 7: 51, cited in Larson, *Internal Improvement*, 16; Jefferson to Washington, March 15, 1784, in Boyd, *Papers of Thomas Jefferson*, 7:26–27.

Republican thought was inextricably bound to a classical view of the world that was suspicious of change, particularly the kind wrought by commerce. The citizen's virtue – his public integrity – lay at the heart of this world view. The virtuous citizen was a disinterested citizen who threw himself into his public responsibilities. In this classical republican world, man was a political animal committed to the commonweal. It was through participation in politics that other objectives, like protecting individual rights, were secured. Revolution-era Americans conceived of rights inhering in the corporate associations to which they belonged. Regardless of differences in status and wealth, within this bounded context, citizens could imagine that they were equal. States and counties were the best examples of such corporate bodies, but there were many others, such as churches.[9]

Stringent requirements for independence, however, severely restricted the number and type of Americans who qualified for citizenship in the eighteenth century. The citizen in a republican government approximated Aristotle's ideal of the independent man. Servants and men who did not own property were excluded from this scheme of politics since they were considered dependent and easily corrupted. Women too were excluded, dismissed as far too dependent to be trusted with the public task of governance. Even among the propertied class of men, living up to the ideal was no easy task, as it required the subordination of private interest to public service at all times. Merchants, for instance, were too vested in their own profits to meet the stiff test imposed by citizenship in a republic. Pennsylvania Senator William Maclay warned of these limitations, cautioning that "it seems as difficult to restrain a Merchant from striking at Gain, as to prevent the keen spaniel from springing at Game, that he has been bred to pursue." Crucial to maintaining civic virtue was the proper alignment of independent citizenry and republican government.[10]

[9] Daniel T. Rodgers, "Republicanism: The Career of a Concept," *Journal of American History*, 79, no. 1 (June 1992): 19; Wood, *Radicalism*, 103–104; Onuf, "Federalism Democracy, and Liberty," 26–29.
[10] Banning, *Jeffersonian Persuasion*, 31, 46; *The Diary of William Maclay and Other Notes on Senate Debates*, ed. Kenneth R. Bowling and Helen E. Veit, vol. 9 of *Documentary History of the First Federal Congress of The United States of America 4 March 1789–3 March 1791*, ed. Charlene Bangs Bickford (Baltimore, MD: Johns Hopkins University Press, 1988), 69, quoted in Wood, *Radicalism*, 106. As Adam Smith put it, "The interest of the dealers ... in any particular branch of trade or manufactures, is always in some respects different from, and even opposite to, that of the publick." Adam Smith, *An Inquiry into the Nature and Causes of the Wealth of Nations*, ed. R.H. Campbell and A.S. Skinner

John Adams struggled with the challenge of independence for his entire life. Self-deceit, the young Adams wrote, was "the source of far the greatest ... calamities among mankind." Even society's most enlightened men were "often snared by this unhappy disposition in their minds, to their own destruction, and the injury, nay, often to the utter desolation of millions of their fellow-men." But Adams believed that the military and political obligations of citizenship, the honor that the virtuous citizens derived and the structural safeguards afforded by the proper mixture of aristocratic and democratic rule might prove sufficient to sustain republican governments. It was precisely such a mixture of virtue, citizenship, and governance that unified economic and military interests under the broader vision of the commonwealth.[11]

Getting governance right was a high stakes venture. Properly ordered government *produced* virtue: this essential resource was political, not social in its origins. "It is not true, in fact," Adams wrote in *Defense of the Constitutions of Government of the United Sates of America* in 1787–88 "that any people ever existed who loved the public better than themselves, their private friends, neighbors, & c. and there fore this kind of virtue, this sort of love, is as precarious a foundation for liberty as honor or fear." "It is the laws alone," Adams continued, "that really love the country, the public, the whole better than any part; and that form of government which unites all the virtue, honor, and fear of the citizens, in a reverence and obedience to the laws, is the only one in which liberty can be secure." Corruption, declining virtue, and social strife were symptoms, not causes of the poorly ordered republic.[12]

(Oxford, UK: Clarendon Press, New York: Oxford University Press, 1981), 1:265–67 [I. xi. p. 8–10].

[11] John Adams, "'On Self-Delusion,' for the *Boston Gazette*, 29 August 1763", in *The Works of John Adams*, ed. Charles Francis Adams (Boston, MA: Little, Brown, 1850), 2:433–35, quoted in Trees, *Founding Fathers*, 9. See also Lance Banning, "Republican Ideology and the Triumph of the Constitution, 1789 to 1793," *William and Mary Quarterly*, 3rd ser., 31, no. 2 (April, 1974): 174–75.

Neoclassical thinkers like Machiavelli and Harrington were not oblivious to private interest. Indeed, it was man's nature to attend to his selfish instincts. Machiavelli spent considerable time treating the problems caused by corruption and other evils. Leaders, Machiavelli warned, should "take for granted that all men are evil and that they will always act according to the wickedness of their nature whenever they have the opportunity." Niccolò Machiavelli, *Discourses on Livy*, trans. Julia Conaway Bondanella and Peter Bondanella, World Classics Series (New York, NY: Oxford University Press, 1997), bk. 1, chap. 3, p. 28.

[12] John Adams, *A Defence of the Constitutions of Government of the United States of America, Against the Attack of M. Turgot, in his Letter to Dr. Price dated the twenty second*

The obligation to serve trumped private interests. As Benjamin Franklin admonished one royal official recently retired from "Publik Busines" in 1750, "Let not your love of philosophical amusements have more than its due weight with you." Serving the nation came first, Franklin hectored. Even Sir Isaac Newton's discoveries paled by comparison to public service, Franklin noted. Had the great scientist been "Pilot but of a single common Ship, the finest of his Discoveries would scarce have excus'd or atton'd for his abandoning the Helm one Hour in Time of Danger; how much less if she had carried the Fate of the Commonwealth."[13]

Unlike monarchies, which mixed public and private interests quite regularly, there was little room for private interest in republics. Indeed, private interest represented one of the greatest threats to republican government.

day of March, 1778, 3 vols. (London: printed for John Stockdale, 1794) in Eighteenth Century Collections Online; GaleGroup, 2003 [Gale Doc. No. CW104438960]), 3:491, cited in Trees, *Founding Fathers,* 93.

As long as citizens were independent and property was dispersed, virtue provided the over-arching principle that ordered citizens' lives. This was especially true as theology loosened its hold on citizens. As Anthony Stoddard's 1716 sermon put it, "Interest bears great sway with men." "That what men can't be persuaded to, by any means, when they conceive their Interest may be served thereby, they will apply themselves to it whatsoever it may be." It fell to government to reconcile the tension between these individual interests and the greater happiness of the commonwealth's citizens. Anthony Stoddard, *An Election Sermon* (New London, CT, 1716) in Early American Imprints Series I (American Antiquarian Society and NewsBank, 2002 [doc. no.1856]), 3, http://infoweb.newsbank.com/, quoted in Pole, *Gift of Government,* 21.

For an important corrective to notions of unilateral decline in faith, see Jon Butler, *Awash in a Sea of Faith: Christianizing the American People* (Cambridge, MA: Harvard University Press, 1990), ch. 4.

[13] Benjamin Franklin to Cadwallader Colden, October 11, 1750, in *The Papers of Benjamin Franklin,* ed. Leonard Labaree, et al. (New Haven, CT: Yale University Press, 1959), 4:68, cited in Wood, *Radicalism,* 104.

The ability to assess virtue publicly was crucial in a society built upon a foundation of honor. Citizens took the measure of a man's "character," which was defined largely in public terms. Rather than implying intrinsic qualities, as the term came to suggest by the nineteenth century, reputation, or standing, determined character in the eighteenth century. At the time of the American Revolution, educated Americans spoke of "acquiring" a character. Treated as a possession, a man's character often proved to be his most valuable resource. It could be fashioned, preserved, and destroyed. In the view of statesmen like John Adams, the very fate of the nation depended upon the character of its citizens. "The Preservation of Liberty," Adams wrote in his diary in 1772, "depends on the intellectual and moral Character of the People. As long as Knowledge and Virtue are diffused generally among the Body of a Nation, it is impossible they should be enslaved." Trees, *Founding Fathers,* 2; *The Diary and Autobiography of John Adams,* ed. L.H. Butterfield, vol. 2, *Diary 1771–1781* (Cambridge, MA: Belknap Press of Harvard University Press, 1961), 58, cited in Trees, *Founding Fathers,* 86. See also Joanne B. Freeman, *Affairs of Honor: National Politics in the New Republic* (New Haven, CT: Yale University Press, 2001).

Patriotism, justice, and reason could all be distorted by private interest. As one American wrote in 1753, "there is such a bewitching Charm in Self-Interest, that the Mind, intoxicated by this delusive SYREN, is generally impervious to Truth and Reason. … A Man's personal Advantage gives so strange a Biass to his Reason, that he perceives not his own Injustice, where he would condemn the like Action in another, with high Disdain." By building the republic upon a foundation of independent men who demonstrated their virtue through self-denying dedication, the republic could be protected from the ravages of private interest.[14]

Even James Madison, author of "Federalist Number 10," which posited faction as one of the diseases "most incident to Republican Government," believed that the clash of interests could be mitigated. Rather than simply accepting what twentieth-century thinkers labeled pluralism, Madison's plan to protect republican government sought to preserve the leadership of those best qualified to govern. A larger republic, in this case, might actually strengthen republican government. Madison favored extending the scope of government to promote a "filtration of talent" that would be more likely to empower wise and able statesmen who were "proper guardians of the public weal." Extensive jurisdictions increased the odds that men untainted by local and private interest would lead the republic.[15]

This conception of the public good, so radically different from our own pluralist understanding of good government today, was only possible in a

---

[14] Wood, *Radicalism*, 252; William Livingston, "Remarks on a Petition," in *The Independent Reflector*, ed. Milton Klein, no. 10, February 1, 1753, 118, quoted in Cathy D. Matson and Peter S. Onuf, *A Union of Interests: Political and Economic Thought in Revolutionary America* (Lawrence, KS: University Press of Kansas, 1990), 14; Rodgers, "Republicanism," 18.

[15] Drew R. McCoy, *The Last of the Fathers: James Madison and the Republican Legacy* (New York, NY: Cambridge University Press, 1989), 43–44. The phrase "filtration of talent" used by McCoy was coined by Gordon Wood in *The Creation of the American Republic 1776–1787* (Chapel Hill, NC: University of North Carolina Press, 1998).

Jefferson embraced this reasoning, writing to a friend in 1795 that it would be easier to distinguish men "free from particular interests" on a national scale rather than in individual states. "The smaller the societies," Jefferson warned, "the more violent and more convulsive their schisms." Jefferson to François d'Ivernois, February 6, 1795, in *The Writings of Thomas Jefferson*, ed. Andrew A Lipscomb and Albert Ellery Bergh, 20 vols. (Washington, D.C.: Thomas Jefferson Memorial Association, 1903), 9:300, quoted in Onuf, *Jefferson's Empire: The Language of American Nationhood* (Charlottesville, VA: University Press of Virginia, 2000), 54. See also Wood, *Radicalism*, 251–53, 283.

Many of the advocates of this perspective were also the beneficiaries of inherited wealth. Adams pointed this out to John Taylor, who questioned Adams's view of aristocracy. Though Adams was the son of a father of middling wealth, Taylor inherited much of his wealth from his wife's side of the family. Ellis, *Founding Brothers*, 237.

world where citizens believed that politics ordered everything else. Social institutions that stood outside the polity paled by comparison. Glimpsed through the lens of republican ideology, economic life, for instance, served private, not public ends. The rights of citizens were not contracted for in a universal state of nature, as enlightenment thinkers had begun to argue. Rather, they were derived specifically from loyalty to the republic. The republic's safety and welfare, in turn, trumped individual rights when the two were in conflict.[16]

For a brief period in the life of British North America and the early years of the United States, power was conceived in political rather than in economic or social terms: politics, many citizens believed, guided economics and social relations. Consequently, when Massachusetts tavern keeper William Manning addressed "all the Republicans, Farmers, Mecanicks, and Labourers In Amarica" in 1798, he complained of the exclusion of producers from republican government, not their exploitation at the hands of their employers. Manning's *The Key of Liberty* assumed that proper governance protected laborers' welfare, providing that it was not controlled by the elite few. In the ensuing decades, labor would focus increasingly on exploitation at the point of production. The social structure and the irreconcilable clash between capital and labor eclipsed the polity as labor's nemesis.[17]

---

[16] Gordon S. Wood, "'The Rise of American Democracy': A Constant Struggle," Review of *The Rise of American Democracy,* by Sean Wilentz, *New York Times,* November 13, 2005, http://www.nytimes.com/; Appleby, *Liberalism and Republicanism,* 5; James Q. Wilson, "City Life and Citizenship," in *Dilemmas of Scale in America's Federal Democracy,* ed. Martha Derthick, (New York, NY: Cambridge University Press, 1999), 148.

[17] Christopher L. Tomlins, *Law, Labor, and Ideology in the Early American Republic* (New York, NY: Cambridge University Press, 1993), 1–16; William Manning, *The Key to Libberty: Shewing the Causes Why a Free Government has always Failed and a Remidy Against It,* ed. Samuel Eliot Morison (Billerica, MA: Manning Association, 1922), 3.

The progenitors of republican thought also understood that social disorder or the decline of moral order threatened balanced republics. By the mid-eighteenth century, the warning signs of corruption, all too familiar to British North Americans reared on republican thought, loomed large. They were visible in standing armies, patronage, social strife, and declining interest in the public good. Banning, *Jeffersonian Persuasion,* 46, 75.

For many, however, the solution only underscored the primacy of the political order. John Adams made it clear that it was the government and its laws that produced virtuous citizens. "It is the Form of Government which gives the decisive Colour to the Manners of the People, more than any other Thing," Adams wrote in 1776. The people, James Harrington wrote, are never "subject to any other corruption than that which derives from their government." Or, from the perspective of the citizen, "where the commonwealth is perfect," Harrington insisted, the citizen "can never commit any such crime as will render it imperfect or bring it to a natural dissolution." John Adams to Mercy Otis

The idealized polity accounted for only a small portion of political behavior, never reigned exclusively, and increasingly gave way to market-oriented conceptions of the public good that embraced self-interest as the most reliable guide to political action. Nevertheless, the possibility for energetic governance embodied in the commonwealth ideal remained a powerful force in the nation's political development. Men soon turned to government action for reasons far removed from honor and virtue, but they regularly relied on it nonetheless. It was not the willingness to employ the General Government that changed. Rather, it was the basis for government intervention that changed.[18]

THE LOCAL TRADITION

Fierce commitment to localism kept energetic government in check. British North Americans maintained their mother country's preference for strong local self-government, reflecting the republican celebration of small homogeneous polities. Popularly controlled institutions like juries, town councils, and militias offered a bulwark against centralized, distant power. It also ensured that citizens maintained a direct stake in their governance.[19]

Warren, January 8, 1776, in *Warren Adams Letters: Being Chiefly a Correspondence among John Adams, Samuel Adams, and James Warren.* Collection of the Massachusetts Historical Society series, vols. 72 and 73. (Boston, MA: Massachusetts Historical Society, 1925), 72:202, cited in Trees, *Founding Fathers*, 93; Harrington, *Oceana*, 178–79, cited in Banning, *Jeffersonian Persuasion*, 47.

[18] In fact, it inverts the pervasive belief that America was "born liberal." Louis Hartz, *The Liberal Tradition in America: An Interpretation of American Political Thought since the Revolution*, (1951; San Diego, CA: Harcourt Brace Jovanovich, 1991). For a thoughtful review of the enduring power of Hartz's argument, see James T. Kloppenberg, "From Hartz to Tocqueville: Shifting the Focus from Liberalism to Democracy in America," in *The Democratic Experiment: New Directions in American Political History*, ed. Meg Jacobs, William J. Novak, and Julian E. Zelizer (Princeton, NJ: Princeton University Press, 2003), 381–400. In discussing the "mind and sensibility" of the founding generation, Elkins and McKitrick point out that a society in which the significances of "private" and "public" are "so inverted from those we attach to them now, is a society sufficiently different from ours that ... we do not report what we see in the voice of easy recognition." Stanley Elkins and Eric McKitrick, *The Age of Federalism* (New York, NY: Oxford University Press, 1993), 5.

[19] Pauline Maier, "The Origins and Influence of Early American Local Self-Government," in Derthick, *Dilemmas of Scale*, 76; Edling, *Revolution in Favor of Government*, 41. Initially, legal authority was vested in the provinces (which were, in turn, dominated by the crown). However, responsibility for administering and funding the functions that touched the lives of most individuals soon devolved to local or county governments. In "Origins and Influence," Maier points out that Tocqueville got this sequence wrong [72].

While a passion for local governance was one of the few bonds that connected British North American colonists to each other, accommodating local preference allowed for great variation between, and even within, the colonies. Slavery was the most important of these distinctions. But attitudes toward taxation and the proper reach of government also varied widely. These too were indulged by the decentralized nature of local governance. It is tempting to label New England's "covenanted" society communally inclined toward more active local government, while Southerners' preference for lower taxes suggested a more libertarian bent. Yet slavery confounds this generalization. The slave-holding colonies used the state to intervene in civil society and the intimate affairs of slaves' religious and family life in a fashion that dwarfs the power of governments today. Southerners' fear of distant government underscored just how crucial closely held control was to the preservation of a slave society.[20]

Because local officials did not "report" to administrative superiors at the provincial level (or anywhere else) the links to more concentrated authority, so visible in the French bureaucracy, for instance, were nowhere to be found in America. While voters held officials accountable through frequent elections, provincial law was enforced through the judiciary. Tocqueville appreciated the political appeal of such a system. It was "all the more powerful, having that almost irresistible force which men accord to due process of the law." That central control remained "out of sight" strengthened the perception that the United States was a loose collection of local republics. This stood in stark contrast to the kind of unmediated relationship that revolutionary France, for instance, created between citizen and state. Karl Marx described this best, writing, "The centralised State power ... originates from the days of absolute monarchy ... Still, its development remained clogged by all manner of medieval rubbish. ... The gigantic broom of the French Revolution ... swept away all these relics ..., thus clearing simultaneously the social soil of its last hindrances to the superstructure of the modern state edifice."[21]

[20] James H. Henderson, "Taxation and Political Culture: Massachusetts and Virginia, 1760–1800," *William and Mary Quarterly*, 3rd ser., 47, no. 1 (January 1990): 91–93. Henderson's article, "Taxation," to which I am greatly indebted, is part of a much broader literature that uses this distinction. It works well, until slavery is entered into the calculus.

[21] It is instructive to compare French schooling and conscription during the nineteenth century, to their American counterparts, which were far more localized. Eugen Weber, *Peasants into Frenchmen: The Modernization of Rural France, 1870–1914* (Stanford, CA: Stanford University Press, 1976), chaps. 17–18; Alexis deTocqueville, *Democracy*

One conspicuous demand levied upon localities from afar was the tax assessment. But such levies were quickly rebuffed. As early as 1632, the Massachusetts Court of Assistants taxed the area west of Boston in order to finance a fortification. The citizens of Watertown wasted no time in responding. The town's minister and another town notable addressed their fellow citizens: "It was not safe to pay moneys after that sort, for fear of bringing themselves and posterity into bondage," they admonished. Watertown would not pay taxes to a body that made no provision for local representation. As this incident demonstrated, threats to local autonomy might come from sources far closer than the crown.[22]

Local government collected the majority of tax revenue. Even combined, local and provincial taxes were low in the quarter of the century before the Revolution, especially compared to those paid by the English. War-time taxation was the exception to this rule. In 1760, during the war with France, provincial taxes increased almost fourfold.[23]

In New England, local control was reinforced by covenants that joined family to church, church to town, and town to commonwealth. This "covenanted society" created a distinctive environment that fostered capitalist

---

in America, ed. J.P. Mayer, trans. George Lawrence (New York, NY: Harper Perennial, 1989), 77; Karl Marx, "The Civil War in France," 289, in Karl Marx and Friedrich Engels, *Selected Works in One Volume* (New York: International Publishers, 1968), quoted in Rogers Brubaker, *Citizenship and Nationhood in France and Germany* (Cambridge, MA: Harvard University Press, 1992), 48. Brubaker also offers a comparison of France to Germany, especially regarding the basis for citizenship (1–5).

[22] James Kendall Hosmer, ed., *Winthrop's Journal, "History of New England, 1630–1649,"* 1:74, quoted in T.H. Breen, "Persistent Localism: English Social Change and the Shaping of New England Institutions," *William and Mary Quarterly,* 3rd series, 32, no.1 (January 1975): 26. On the variety of tax mechanisms used and services provided at the local level, see Robert A. Becker, *Revolution, Reform, and the Politics of American Taxation, 1763–1783* (Baton Rouge, LA: Louisiana State University Press, 1980).

[23] Henderson, "Taxation," 93–94. The Massachusetts Town Act of 1635 demonstrates the range of authority delegated to the local level. Towns were to "dispose of their owne land, and woods," to "make such orders as may concerne the well ordering of their townes," and "to chuse their owne particular officers, as constables, surveyors of highways, and the like" to enforce and implement the laws. In Virginia, the governor and council ruled from the center as long as the population remained small. But as settlers crossed the York and Rappahannock Rivers, spreading along the Potomac, the rudimentary state of transportation and communication encouraged decentralization. Basic tasks, like registering deeds and probating wills, were soon administered at the local level. Massachusetts Town Act of 1635, cited in Kermit L. Hall, *The Magic Mirror: Law in American History* (New York, NY: Oxford University Press, 1989), 25, as quoted in David Grayson Allen, *In English Ways: The Movement of Societies and the Transferal of English Local Law and Custom to Massachusetts Bay in the Seventeenth Century,* (Chapel Hill, NC: University of North Carolina Press, 1981). On Virginia, see Maier, "Origins and Influence," 74–75.

economic development bounded by strong communal and religious ties. Until the middle of the eighteenth century, one of the most important functions of towns was to establish and regulate a marketplace. In the 1730s, Bostonians fought over the degree to which markets would be regulated. Established merchants backed a carefully regulated system. Wealthy merchant Peter Faneuil gave the City of Boston a grand hall, calculated to encourage municipal regulations that structured the market. Town officials surveyed stalls, enforcing local standards for weights and measures and licensing butchers. Town officials oversaw the quality of goods and the prices of these goods. When the carpenter who constructed the stocks in Boston charged an excessive fee, he became the first person clamped in his own handiwork.[24]

Economic regulation occurred less often in the Chesapeake. Even here, however, a stagnant economy convinced planters to submit to a system of public warehouses and inspection in order to ensure a standard product. Despite the commitment to low taxes, Virginia continued to levy taxes that supported churches until it entered the War for Independence.[25]

Local governance was premised on an intimate connection between voters and their representatives. Deference was the glue that held electoral politics together before the rise of political parties. Although there was little in the way of bureaucratic hierarchy in British North America, social and religious hierarchy dominated politics. Even the small percentage of male property holders who qualified to vote instinctively deferred to a set of gentlemen with the highest social standing. Elections were personal affairs. In Virginia, voters called out their choice. In response, the candidate, seated at the center of the action, would often rise and thank the voter. Authority in the colonies before the Revolutionary War was decentralized, diffuse, and localized: the practice of politics took place almost exclusively at or within the provincial level – often in a highly personalized fashion. Public opinion mattered, but only as a deliberative process that led to the selection of the polity's most virtuous leaders.

[24] Stephen Innes, *Creating the Commonwealth: The Economic Culture of Puritan New England* (New York, NY: Norton, 1995), 209; Jon Butler, *Becoming America: The Revolution Before 1776* (Cambridge, MA: Harvard University Press, 2000), 95; Hall, *Magic Mirror,* 25, 40.
[25] Hall, *Magic Mirror,* 41; Henderson, "Taxation," 105. Disestablishment came later in New England. For a detailed discussion of the relationship between churches, tax obligations, and evolving corporate law, see Johan N. Neem, "Creating a Nation of Joiners: Democracy and Civil Society in Early National Massachusetts," (Ph.D. dissertation, University of Virginia, March 17, 2006).

There was relatively little coordinated action between these local nodes of governance.[26]

Nor was the law handed down from a distant sovereign. Rather, the judiciary operated under the watchful eye of local communities. In the Commonwealth of Massachusetts, for instance, justices of the peace provided the foundation for the judicial system. They handled low-level civil cases and petty offences such as trespass. Before the Revolution, juries played a free-wheeling role in determining the common law. They operated with relatively few judge-imposed constraints, even if their interpretation of the law diverged from that of the judge.[27]

With a few exceptions, the law that these courts administered was the common law as received from England. Before the Revolution, this law had been applied in conformity with the community's sense of ethical practice, especially in the case of contracts. This reinforced the community's economic and social stability. It precluded exchanges that the community considered unfair – even if both parties to the contract freely agreed to the exchange.[28]

Where public safety was concerned, the rights of the community prevailed. This English common law precedent was vigorously upheld in the United States. As Chief Justice M'Kean of the Pennsylvania Supreme Court noted in a 1788 decision, "the safety of the people is a law above all others." M'Kean, who went on to become governor of Pennsylvania, even defended the right to tear down houses when they stood in the path of a fire.[29]

---

[26] Michael Schudson, *The Good Citizen: A History of American Civic Life* (New York, NY: Free Press, 1998), 20–21; Tomlins, *Law, Labor, and Ideology*, 51; Alexander Keyssar, *The Right to Vote: The Contested History of Democracy in the United States* (New York, NY: Basic Books, 2000), 3–25; Saul Cornell, *The Other Founders: Anti-Federalism and the Dissenting Tradition in America, 1788–1828* (Chapel Hill, NC: University of North Carolina Press, 1999), 78.

[27] William E. Nelson, *Americanization of the Common Law: The Impact of Legal Change on Massachusetts Society, 1760–1830* (Athens, GA: University of Georgia Press, 1975), 3–4, 15.

[28] Ibid., 6–8. These practices changed dramatically in the first third of the nineteenth century, as property was freed from such constraints. Becker, *Revolution, Reform*, 6.

[29] *Respublica v. Sparhawk*, 1 U.S. 357, 363 (Supreme Court of Pennsylvania, 1788), cited in William J. Novak, *The People's Welfare: Law and Regulation in Nineteenth Century America* (Chapel Hill, NC: University of North Carolina Press, 1998), 74–75. The Mayor of New York applied that rule liberally in fighting the Great Fire of 1835. With large portions of the City's central commercial district already in ruins, the mayor resorted to gunpowder. Blowing up buildings to create a fire break eventually contained the massive blaze. His reward? Lawsuits. Twenty years of litigation did little to undermine the

The laws that proscribed individual freedom most harshly were the slave codes enacted by provincial assemblies in the late seventeenth century. From Thomas Jefferson's perspective, it was precisely such self-governing communities, defending their corporate rights, that protected the liberties of all Americans. Nor was slavery, or the naked government authority required to enforce it, confined to the South. As late as 1755, for instance, 12 percent of Rhode Island's population was enslaved. British North Americans did not inherit these laws. Rather, they fashioned a system of human bondage and legal enforcement that provided the modern principles for state-sanctioned control of one person (and her offspring) by another, fears of concentrated authority aside.[30]

The provincial laws enforcing slavery serve as a vivid reminder that British North Americans had few qualms about designing and invoking energetic government – especially at the local level. The colonists far surpassed even Great Britain's capacity to bring the power of the state to bear on the lives of individuals.

In the case of slavery, British common law did not suffice. In fact, a 1772 case in England's highest common law court, *Somerset v. Stewart*, ruled that slavery was too odious for the common law to support. It would take positive law, such as those passed in America, to legitimate it. Virginia had been happy to oblige, more than a century before *Somerset*. Maryland followed Virginia's lead in 1663. In both colonies and in a host of others, the law codified black chattel slavery. Technically, this left the few free blacks, especially those who owned property, with the protections available to other British subjects. The colonies soon restricted these rights through statutory provisions that added "free blacks" to existing restrictions, such as freedom of movement and the right to assemble. By the early eighteenth century free blacks were also denied voting rights, the right to hold office, and other prerogatives available to whites of similar status.[31]

Nor did the rules weigh virtue or dedication to republican ideals when it came to the majority of the population. Divine will and natural

---

common law principle: a well-regulated society committed to the people's welfare had the right (some argued, the obligation) to place the public safety ahead of personal property rights, even when the owners of that property had done nothing wrong. Novak, *People's Welfare*, 71–79.

[30] Onuf, "Federalism, Democracy, and Liberty" 37; Butler, *Becoming America*, 41–42.

[31] *Somerset v. Stewart*, 98, English Reporter 499, reprinted at 20 Howell's State Trials 1 (King's Bench, June 22, 1772), http://medicolegal.tripod.com/somersetvstewart.htm#, cited in Rogers N. Smith, *Civic Ideals: Conflicting Visions of Citizenship in U.S. History* (New Haven, CT: Yale University Press, 1997), 64; Smith, *Civic Ideals*, 63–65.

traits determined the person's legal status. For Indians, slaves, blacks, and women, this meant that participation in public life was sharply curtailed or simply nonexistent. While colonists bridled at any efforts by the British to interfere with America's "peculiar institution," mother country and colonies were in agreement on the status of women: they had none – at least not in the public sphere. Coverture, based on the English common law, made daughters the legal property of their fathers. It made married women the property of their husbands. Some single women did procure independent legal standing, but the number of such women was small and their rights carefully circumscribed. Congregationalist minister John Cotton's dictum captured women's status as citizens: It was "good for the Wife to acknowledg all power and authority to the Husband, and for the Husband to acknowledg honour to the Wife."[32]

The laws that translated these prejudices into practice were among the most powerful interventions into the lives of British North Americans. In the case of women, these constraints were an extension of England's laws. In the case of African Americans, however, the supposedly liberty-loving colonies proved adept at crafting state-supported structures of restraint that far exceeded any imagined by the British Crown. In all cases, deference to local prerogatives reinforced public acceptance, and justified these powerful intrusions into the lives of Americans.[33]

"IT WILL NOT ENDURE UNASSISTED BY INTEREST": CHALLENGING THE PRIMACY OF POLITICS

A polity-dominated conception of society was rudely challenged from the start. Two elements in the republican compound that conceived of the world as politically ordered proved particularly unsuited to the social flux that buffeted British North America in the late eighteenth century. The first was republican attitudes about change. Republican ideology was permanently braced for decline. The classical cyclical view of history allowed no other possibilities. John Adams, despite his personal contributions to the Revolution, could not imagine a future that contained something new.

---

[32] Smith, *Civil Ideals*, 67–69; John Cotton, "Limitation of Government," in *The Puritans*, Perry Miller and Thomas H. Johnson, eds. rev. ed. (New York, NY: Harper, 1963), 214, cited in Smith, *Civic Ideals*, 67.

[33] On the politics of social regulation, see James A Morone, *Hellfire Nation: The Politics of Sin in American History* (New Haven, CT: Yale University Press, 2003).

Complaining that both political parties in 1812 had crossed the "boundaries of morality into the regions of ambition, selfishness, and rapacity,"
Adams instinctively turned to the script that he believed history drafted for
republics.[34]

Adams believed that republics were fated to fail. That his own republic was so extensive simply made the matter worse. "The lawgivers of
antiquity ... legislated for single cities," Adams worried, but "who can
legislate for 20 or 30 states, each of which is greater than Greece or
Rome?" Adams was all too familiar with the final act. He anticipated the
reestablishment of rigid ranks and orders. How could the outcome be any
different in a world where change was so precarious.[35]

The United States avoided dictatorship, but it could not avoid change.
The flux created by commerce proved far more threatening to republican
ideals than the counter-revolution anticipated by Adams. Although they
lacked the conceptual language of liberalism, republicans instinctively
distrusted the speculative interests promoted by the growth of commerce
and viewed them as threats to republican order.[36]

Republican conceptions also foundered because the basis for virtue
was democratized. Rather than serving as the crucial test of political wor-
thiness, virtue became just one of many potential political assets. There
was a powerful connection between property and virtue in republican
thought. Only men secure in their property could be virtuous. Land
ownership ensured personal independence and autonomy. Land was the
bulwark against the irrational lure of interest. But the egalitarian thrust
of the American Revolution and the availability of property in America
undermined this source of disinterestedness. More men qualified for citizenship, but the basis for their independence was less assured.[37]

[34] Appleby, *Liberalism and Republicanism,* 330; Adams to Benjamin Rush, July 10, 1812, in
The Spur of Fame: Dialogues of John Adams and Benjamin Rush, 1805–1813, ed. John
A. Schutz and Douglas Adair (San Marino, CA: Huntington Library, 1966), 231–32.

[35] Adams to Rush, July 10, 1812, quoted in Ellis, *Founding Brothers,* 8; Appleby, *Liberalism
and Republicanism,* 200. Adams, for instance, considered his fellow Federalist Alexander
Hamilton to be a potential American Napoleon, eager to build a standing army and crush
republican government. Ellis, *Founding Brothers,* 194.

[36] Appleby, *Liberalism and Republicanism,* 283. On the distinction between opposition to
commerce and opposition to speculative interests arising out of commerce see Matson
and Onuf, *Union of Interests,* 15.

[37] Appleby, *Liberalism and Republicanism,* 283; Matson and Onuf, *Union of Interests,* 12.
On the expansion of the franchise, see Joyce Appleby, *Inheriting the Revolution: The First
Generation of Americans* (Cambridge, MA: The Belknap Press of Harvard University
Press, 2000), 26–31.

Property in America came to represent just one more commodity, and those who owned it just one more interested party. Property no longer served as a platform that supported men who could discern the public good in a disinterested manner. Some European observers worried about conflating "the great distinction (the only one which is founded in nature between two classes of men) between landholders and those who are not landholders." Such distinctions, in their minds, were the basis for rights related to legislation and the administration of justice. Conditions in British North America flattened these distinctions and, along with them, the deferential style of politics that colonists had practiced. Citizens demanded direct oversight of their representatives – rejecting notions of virtual representation. Because of the extensive distances traveled to state capitals, those seats of government were moved from their original sites near the seacoasts to more central locations. Nine of the original thirteen colonies shifted their state capitals between 1776 and 1812 in response to the overwhelming demands for more direct representation. James Madison's quest to set the "practicable sphere of a republic" through the constitutional principle of federalism turned on his determination to find a "middle ground" between localism and concentrated distant authority that was unrepresentative of the people.[38]

Virtue was democratized. With relatively easy access to land, even those who had amassed large quantities of it could not count on the luxury of a steady income from tenants to subsidize the owner's republican commitment to public life. George Washington came closest to fulfilling the ideal of the virtuous citizen. Yet even he could not transcend a personal speculative interest in developing land along the Potomac at the very time he sought to found the nation's capital there. At the other end of the social hierarchy, the wide distribution of land produced "citizens" with rough manners and little education. "The knowledge, generally, necessary for men who make laws," an Anti-Federalist wrote, "is a knowledge

---

[38] Wood, *Radicalism*, 269; Letter From M. Turgot to Richard Price, March 22, 1778, in *Richard Price and the Ethical Foundations of the American Revolution*, ed. Bernard Peach (Durham, NC: Duke University Press, 1979), 219; Rosemarie Zagarri, *The Politics of Size: Representation in the United States, 1776–1850* (Ithaca, NY: Cornell University Press, 1987), 9, 18–20; Lance Banning, "The Practicable Sphere of a Republic: James Madison, the Constitutional Convention, and the Emergence of Revolutionary Federalism," in Richard Beeman, Stephen Botein, Edward C. Carter II eds., *Beyond Confederation Origins of the Constitution and American National Identity* (Chapel Hill, NC: University of North Carolina Press, 1987), 185. For a view favorable to expanding democracy through wider suffrage, see the writings of Tunis Wortman, reported in Cornell, *The Other Founders*, 258.

of the common concerns, and particular circumstances of the people." It followed that men from all classes could meet these criteria.[39]

Reality never kept pace with the ideal of virtuous leadership. Even that ideal collapsed in the wake of the Revolution. American colonists effectively used republican language to resist power. However, they failed fully to realize a republic founded on virtue – the kind of republic that could be trusted to carry out the collective ideals embodied in republican thought. Even George Washington, the military hero who epitomized these ideals, wrote from Valley Forge in April 1778, that the rhetoric of virtue and patriotism had no basis in "the rule of Action" that governed actual conduct: the "prospect of Interest or some reward." That virtue was not sufficient even during times of war, which stimulated commitment to the republic, did not bode well for the more pedestrian demands of citizenship. "Men may speculate as they will," Washington continued, "they may talk of patriotism – they may draw a few examples from ancient story of great achievements performed by its influence; but, whoever builds upon it, as a sufficient basis, for conducting a long and bloody War, will find themselves deceived in the end."[40]

---

[39] Wood, *Radicalism*, chap. 7, especially 113–14; Larson, *Internal Improvement*, 259; Letter from The Federal Farmer, XI, January 10, 1788, in *The Complete Anti-Federalist*, ed. Herbert J. Storing (Chicago, IL: University of Chicago Press, 1981), 2:292, quoted in Cornell, *The Other Founders*, 97. Democratizing virtue is a key theme in Appleby, *Inheriting the Revolution*.

[40] Washington to John Bannister, April 21, 1778, in *The Papers of George Washington* Digital Edition, ed. Theodores J. Crackel (Charlottesville, VA: University Press of Virginia, Rotunda, 2007), http://rotunda.upress.virginia.edu/pgwde/ cited in Diggins, "New Mythologies," 631, no. 63. See also Paul A. Rahe, *Republics Ancient and Modern: Classical Republicanism and the American Revolution* (Chapel Hill, NC: University of North Carolina Press, 1992); J.R. Pole, review of *Republics Ancient and Modern: Classical Republicanism and the American Revolution* by Paul A. Rahe, *English Historical Review*, 108, no. 428 (July 1993): 685–87; Joyce Appleby, review of *Republicans Ancient and Modern: Classical Republicanism and the American Revolution* by Paul A. Rahe, *American Political Science Review*, 87, no. 2 (June 1993): 840–41. On Washington, see also Ellis, *Founding Brothers*, chap. 4.

   Concern for the commonwealth clashed most consistently with naked interest when it came to tax policy. While all preferred that taxation remain local, and most agreed in principle that taxation should be based upon the "ability to pay," the disproportionate share of the tax burden fell upon the poor before the Revolution, and continued to do so afterwards. Becker, *Revolution, Reform*, especially 42–84; Wood, *Radicalism*, 229; John Patrick Diggins, "New Mythologies in American Historiography," *American Historical Review*, 90, no. 3 (June 1985): 630.

   What dropped out of practical politics was the "rhetoric of affirmation" embodied in the classical tradition exemplified in *Cato's Letters*. This principle required that citizens subordinate their "passions" to "the public" and "general welfare" in order that "they

Washington did not dismiss entirely the influence of patriotism. "I know it exists, and I know it has done much in the present contests," he wrote. "But I will venture to assert, that a great and lasting War can never be supported on this principle alone – It must be aided by a prospect of interest or some reward. For a time it may, of itself, push men to action – to bear much – to encounter difficulties; but it will not endure unassisted by interest." Washington anticipated a different basis for public action, one that admitted far more room for self-interest.[41]

"THE *Voluntary Choice* OF MANKIND":
THE SOCIAL ROOTS OF LOCKEAN LIBERALISM

During the last third of the eighteenth century, Lockean liberalism, with its emphasis on choice – both in the market as well as the political sphere – undercut the primacy of the polity as it shifted attention to the social and economic bases of political action. Politics still mattered, but as the young nation developed, fewer Americans believed that a well-ordered polity structured social and economic relations. Indeed, it was precisely such self-interested actions that shaped politics. Increasingly, politics was viewed as the venue in which interests battled for narrow advantage.[42]

Yet collective initiatives thrived in the first third of the nineteenth century. In fact, they increased in frequency, size, and scope. However, the rationale for such actions shifted dramatically, from virtuous citizenship to self-interest. Americans believed that self-interest could still produce outstanding public results. Although they rarely generalized about the principle, when it came to ventures that they were personally connected

may justly be esteemed virtuous and good." No. 39: "Of The Passions," (July 29, 1751) John Trenchard and Thomas Gordon, *Cato's Letters: or Essays on Liberty, Civil and Religious, and Other Important Subjects*, 3rd edn, (Berwick, 1754) in Eighteenth Century Collections Online (GaleGroup, 2003 [Gale doc. no. CW105261199]), 2: 39–40, cited in J.G.A. Pocock *The Machiavellian Moment: Florentine Thought and the Atlantic Republic Tradition* (Princeton, NJ: Princeton University Press, 1975), 471–72.

[41] Washington to John Bannister, April 21, 1778, in Crackel, *Papers of George Washington*.

[42] Appleby, *Liberalism and Republicanism*, 2. Appleby elaborates on the ways in which a society built around individual choice displaced older conceptions of the polity in *Inheriting the Revolution*. In this work, the possibility of individual choice, and the consequences of failure overshadow the bounties and other governmental assistance provided. Nonetheless, the shift in citizens' perspective still plays an important role in Appleby's argument. "Once the discipline of the market had been internalized," she writes in *Inheriting the Revolution*, "its workings appeared natural, a perception that discouraged purposeful intervention." [255].

with, they argued that public action was often the key to private success. Citizens discovered a multitude of issues that required cooperation
between disparate interests. They preserved some of the forms through
which the collective will was expressed, whether subsidizing public works,
or promoting improved communications via a powerful post office. The
vast majority of this cooperation occurred on the state and local levels.
Nevertheless, the national government was often solicited, as coordinator
and especially in the nation's external relations and matters that crossed
state boundaries, promoter.

The rationale for this activity shifted to one that emphasized the instrumental value of energetic governance in specific instances. Rather than
carving pockets of self-interested activity out of a polity that regarded
private interest with great skepticism, energetic governance came to be
regarded as the exception in an otherwise self-regulating society. The days
in which an Alexander Hamilton could proclaim that government hidden
from sight would never succeed were long gone by 1830. In fact, the most
effective governance was hidden from sight in a variety of ways.

Over time, the rhetoric of the market, the emphasis on citizens'
voluntary choice, and the insistence that such mechanisms were natural occluded the crucial role that government played in expanding the
nation's boundaries, creating a secure national market and protecting the
republic from powerful nation-states that dominated commerce beyond
its borders. The General Government did more than ever, but governing
effectively often meant minimizing its visibility and often retrospectively
denying its role. Elements of republican rhetoric lingered, of course, and
the vociferous calls for vigilance against corruption continues to this day.
But the notion that a citizen's first obligation was to the republic, not himself, gave way to the refrain, "what has government done for me lately."

Deteriorating British-American relations also pushed Americans
toward Lockean liberalism. Great Britain's continuous wars with France
reshaped the attitudes of British citizens toward their own nation-state.
A century during which Britons were more often than not at war with
a common enemy forged a shared identity among them. Britons were
unified, if only in the certainty that they were not French. By the last third
of the eighteenth century, however, Britons who lived in the metropole distinguished themselves from their brothers and sisters in the colonies.[43]

---

[43] Linda Colley, *Britons: Forging the Nation, 1707–1837* (New Haven, CT: Yale University
Press, 1992), 5.

This move toward English nationalism occurred at the very time that the American colonists identified strongly with Great Britain. Admiration and respect for the British constitution was one of the few bonds that many Americans shared. While allegiance to their provincial governments grew, British North Americans felt little attachment to their counterparts in other provinces: their affection for the larger empire was far greater. It was fueled by Britain's overseas victories between 1739 and 1763. Much to the Americans' chagrin, however, their growing sense of solidarity with their fellow Britons overseas was not reciprocated.[44]

In England, the term "American" increasingly signified inferiority and connoted provincial status. Americans were quick to sense their mother country's change in tone and policies. Disrespected by the English, Americans sought redress in principles that transcended their shared British heritage. American national identity was profoundly shaped by developments beyond its borders. Reacting to the Stamp Act in 1765, the young John Adams insisted that "We won't be their Negroes. ... I say we are as handsome as old English folks, and so should be as free." If Americans could not get a fair hearing in England due to their "Americanness," appealing to deeply held British values lost much of its luster.[45]

Liberal thought reinforced the egalitarian thrust of republicanism at the same time that it freed Americans from their now-burdensome British genealogy. Spurned by the English, some Americans eagerly grasped for the moral, rights-based justification of equality that Locke's philosophy offered. It promised to liberate them from the constraints of history and custom that, until recently, had constituted constructive bonds between them and the British. The appeal to liberalism, in other words, was a defensive strategy by colonists who lacked a common history beyond their British heritage.[46]

---

[44] Jack P. Greene, *Pursuits of Happiness: The Social Development of Early Modern British Colonies and the Formation of American Culture* (Chapel Hill, NC: University of North Carolina Press, 1988), 174–75; John M. Murrin, "A Roof Without Walls: The Dilemma of American National Identity," in Beeman, Botein, and Carter, *Beyond Confederation*, 338–39.

[45] Ellis, *Founding Brothers*, 10; T.H. Breen, "Ideology and Nationalism on the Eve of the American Revolution: Revisions Once More in Need of Revising," *Journal of American History*, 84, no.1 (June 1997): 29–31; Humphry Ploughjogger (John Adams), *Boston Gazette, and Country Journal*, 14, October 1765, issue 550, p. 3, in Early American Newspapers, Series I, 1690–1876 (Newsbank and American Antiquarian Society, 2004), http://infoweb.newsbank.com/.

[46] Breen, "Ideology and Nationalism," 36–37; Onuf, Jefferson's *Empire*, 6–7. On formation of national identities, see Benedict Anderson, *Imagined Communities: Reflections on the Origin and Spread of Nationalism*, 2nd edn (1983; New York, NY: Verso, 1991).

The formal principles of republican or liberal thought were far removed from the lives of most Americans. More accessible was a democratic impulse inspired by the Enlightenment and ultimately embodied in the French Revolution. Those captivated by this democratic impulse aspired to create "a political community considered without regard to bodies, ranks or classes." The conflict that might have pitted American aristocrats against democrats was subsumed in the collective alliance that both classes joined to thwart British tyranny. At a moment in history when elites on both sides of the Atlantic (and across Europe) were reasserting their corporate rights and privileges, American elites joined forces with their more middling neighbors. They embraced a democratic revolution in opposition to a more immediate threat to their freedom mounted by the British (who of course felt that they were merely reasserting their own privileges).[47]

Colonists practiced some of liberalism's principles before they had the language to articulate Lockean liberalism. Reconciling ubiquitous private interest to the public good, Americans developed a distinctive set of attitudes toward the size, shape, and scope of the political economy. Ultimately, any scheme of governance would be judged by its results. Struggling with the exigencies of economic, political, and social development, British North American colonists drew upon an amalgam of Protestant, Enlightenment, and republican ideas. What Enlightenment thinkers conceptualized as a "natural order," many colonists practiced in their daily social and economic relations. They enlarged the individual's role and forged a significant place for self-interest in the larger polity.[48]

The market loomed large in this process. As market relations and private interactions touched more lives, the conception of a politically ordered society – always frail at best – collapsed. To be sure, there was still a crucial role for politics when it came to ordering people's lives and promoting the commonweal. But fewer citizens assumed that the

[47] R.R. Palmer, *The Age of the Democratic Revolution: A Political History of Europe and America, 1760–1800*, 2 vols. (Princeton, NJ: Princeton University Press, 1959–1964), 1:268, cited in Peter S. Onuf, "Democracy, Revolution, and the Historiography of the Modern World" (English manuscript, 2007), 3; Onuf, *Jefferson's Empire*, 35; Onuf, "Federalism, Democracy and Liberty," 7.
[48] Innes, *Creating the Commonwealth*, 208; Cornell, *The Other Founders*, 65. On society as a natural order, see Joyce Appleby, "The Radical Recreation of the American Republic," review of *The Radicalism of the American Revolution* by Gordon S. Wood. *William and Mary Quarterly*, 3rd ser., 51, no. 4 (October 1994): 679–83. Appleby describes the way in which individualism takes shape "historically," in *Inheriting the Revolution*.

legitimacy of private conduct, economic intercourse, and social interaction was derived from the political order. Increasingly, politics came to be viewed as an adjunct to, even the exception to that order. By the end of the eighteenth century, self-interest, rather than virtue, was the principle that animated politics.[49]

Free trade arguments, which became increasingly popular by the late colonial period, were a good example. The free traders critiqued imperial politics and argued that it was merchants, not politicians, who best advanced the commonweal because merchants could anticipate the needs of consumers and citizens. The interplay of private interest, without the elaborate mercantilist apparatus, was the surest path to achieving the public good.[50]

It was not just merchants who were touched by the market. The expanding exchange of goods and broader justifications of economic development reached thousands of British North Americans. By the mid-seventeenth century, Puritans in New England, for instance, faced a tough choice between maintaining a devout workforce and pursuing economic development. The saga of the Leonard family is instructive. The Leonards were highly skilled iron workers. They were equally renowned for making trouble. Charges levied against the Leonards of Essex County, Massachusetts, included: armed robbery, rape, lewdness, and chronic drunkenness. Keeping pace with the men, female Leonards were charged with indecent exposure, singing bawdy songs, and contempt of authority. Despite flaunting the religious and legal conventions of their neighbors, the Leonards were not "harried out of the land." Their skills were too valuable. Indeed, they flourished, emerging as one of the colony's leading families.[51]

The American economy was transformed as more Americans were drawn into market relations. The Chesapeake, with its cash crop of tobacco led the way. But even in the middle and Northern colonies,

---

[49] Matson and Onuf, *Union of interests*, 15–16. British North Americans had plenty of opportunity to observe the interplay of interests in the dramatic expansion of the Atlantic economy over the course of the eighteenth century. Mercantilists, though happy to extend the state's regulatory apparatus to the market, hammered home the connection between the merchant's private interest and the public good. They questioned classical republican notions of a fixed organic polity. A nation, they argued, could expand its boundaries through the successful use of military power and commercial competition. American traders and many of their countrymen imbibed a mercantilist rationale that justified, even honored, the pursuit of private interest.

[50] Ibid., 23.

[51] Innes, *Creating the Commonwealth*, 256, 266–67.

increasing percentages of farmers dedicated a portion of their labor to production for the regional market or beyond. While subsistence farming remained a staple, by 1770 most farmers had a hand in the commercial market.[52]

The space carved out between the market and the political realm over the course of the eighteenth century encouraged a new, liberal conception of self. Public debate over economic and religious alternatives multiplied the opportunities for private choice, heightening the potential for individual assertiveness. One early example was John Colman's petition to establish a private land bank in 1739. Colman's scheme, designed to address a currency crisis, met with popular support that reached beyond elite circles, garnering subscriptions from farmers as well as artisans. When the Massachusetts General Court deadlocked over the proposal in September 1740, the Land Bank released paper bills without government authorization. The notes that it issued had no more intrinsic value than the market was willing to vest in them.[53]

While shocking to advocates of hard money, supporters of the scheme appealed to the reason of ordinary New Englanders. The author of *An Inquiry into the Nature and Uses of Money*, for instance, argued that the price of most objects was established by "accidental" value. "Every Article of Provision, Cloathing, or Lodging … have their Value or Estimation from the *voluntary Choice* of Mankind, guided either by Reason, or meer Humor & Fancy, in choosing one Thing and neglecting or refusing another."[54]

Money was no different. "It is not the Act of Government that gives value to our Bills of Credit in the Market; but the common Consent of the People." Individual decisions fueled the flux of the market, challenging the fixed nature of all that stood in its path. Government could not fix value; ultimately it was a series of individual choices that determined value. As Alexander Hamilton would soon argue, the market could hardly be the sole determinant of the value of money. A crucial role for politically sanctioned oversight and initiative remained. Nevertheless, the

---

[52] Butler, *Becoming America*, 2, 6, 54. For some graphic examples of the ways in which this affected the lives of farming families, see Appleby, *Inheriting the Revolution*, 66–68.

[53] T.H. Breen and Timothy Hall, "Structuring Provincial Imagination: The Rhetoric and Experience of Social Change in Eighteenth-Century New England," *American Historical Review,* 103, no.5 (December 1998):1415.

[54] Hugh Vans, *An Inquiry in to the Nature and Uses of Money; More Especially of The Bills of Publick Credit, Old Tenor,* (Boston, 1740) in Early American Imprints, Series I [document no. 4533], 2; Breen and Hall, "Structuring Provincial Imagination," 1422.

government held no monopoly on such decisions: the market and individual choices within that market prevailed. When Hamilton assumed the debt, he hoped to promote loyalty among bond holders by competing in the market against other investment opportunities, rather than fixing the value of those financial instruments through governmental edict.[55]

A very different kind of debate about the role of itinerant ministers in the 1740s demonstrates similar impulses that overturned fixed hierarchies by embracing individual choice. The Great Awakening challenged the theology of Congregational ministers across New England. Itinerant ministers, particularly "The Great Itinerant" evangelical preacher George Whitefield, captivated some congregants while threatening others. Itinerants offered the people a choice. Connecticut antirevivalist Isaac Stiles, for instance, lamented this development. "They are given to change in matters of Religion," Stiles complained. "They seem always as tho' they had their Religion to chuse, in regard they are never vix'd in any thing; but are for ever wavering like a wave of the Sea, driven to and fro and carried about with diverse and strange Doctrines."[56]

Defenders, on the other hand, celebrated these alternatives as likely to "draw the Attention" of complacent parishioners, defending the option of crossing parish boundaries as an "unalienable Right." "If a particular Church makes it a Matter of Offence or a censurable Evil," John Cleaveland declared," for any of their Members to seek their Edification in any other true Church, they not only practically say, that they are the only true Church ... but also make themselves a *Prison*, in which the *Rights, Liberties and Consciences* of their Members are fast bound in Chains." While few ministers would have disputed this assertion in principle, itinerants made such a choice practical, even convenient.[57]

---

[55] Vans, *Nature and Uses of Money*, 1–2, 32, quoted in Breen and Hall, "Structuring Provincial Imagination," 1422. On the ways in which Hamilton's financial innovations stimulated the general economy, see Richard Sylla, "Political Economy of Financial Development: Canada and the United States in the Mirror of the Other, 1790–1840," *Enterprise and Society*, 7 (December 2006): 657–59. See also Thomas K. McCraw, "The Strategic Vision of Alexander Hamilton," *The American Scholar*, 63 (Winter 1994): 31–57.

[56] Isaac Stiles, *A Looking-Glass for Changelings* (New London, CT, 1743), in Early American Imprints, Series I, (American Antiquarian Society and NewsBank, 2002 [document no. 5295]), 15, cited in Breen and Hall, "Structuring Provincial Imagination," 1428.

[57] "Draw the attention" is from Thomas Prince, Jr., ed., *The Christian History; Containing Accounts of the Propagation and Revival of Religion in England, Scotland, and America*, 2 vols. (Boston, MA, 1743–45), quoted in Breen and Hall, "Structuring Provincial Imagination," 1428; "unalienable Right" is from John Cleaveland, *A Short and Plain*

Itinerancy challenged some of the same "fix'd steady Principles" of social relations that were being eroded by paper currency. Bankers and silver schemers shifted toward a liberal means of constructing value. The "independent reasoned choice of individuals," not political or ecclesiastical prescriptions, increasingly prevailed. Nor was this turn of events ordained or even planned. Rather, it was the unintended consequence of burgeoning trade and increased social interaction among British North Americans. The implications were enormous: nothing short of the "elevation of a liberal self through appeal to an imagined provincial community of reasoning people."[58]

When a newly assertive English state intruded in colonial affairs after 1763, Americans were already well versed in the practice of debating their rights and liberties in response to a changing economy and shifting social relations. When Americans finally did begin to explain their views of governance using the language of Lockean liberalism, they did so because it best described the very economic and social relations that they had been practicing for some time. Recognition and celebration of the "liberal self" overshadowed the citizen's obligation to the well-ordered republic, even as many of these citizens called upon the government to enhance their prospects.[59]

"ONE CONTINUED LIE":
FORGETTING HALF OF THE REPUBLICAN LEGACY

"Who shall write the history of the American revolution?" Adams asked Jefferson in 1813. "Who can write it? Who will ever be able to write it?" The struggle over America's republican legacy began even before its spokesmen had retired from the scene. The correspondence between Thomas Jefferson and John Adams in the early nineteenth century is instructive. By then the Jeffersonian Republicans were firmly in control. Jefferson passed the torch of leadership to his trusted ally, James Madison; James Monroe waited in the wings. Adams had worried about

---

Narrative of the Late Work of God's Spirit at Chebacco in Ipswich, in the Years 1763 and 1764, (Boston, MA, 1767) in Early American Imprints, Series I [document no.10581]), 38, quoted in Breen and Hall, "Structuring Provincial Imagination," 1428.

[58] Breen and Hall, "Structuring Provincial Imagination," 1431–32.

[59] Ibid., 1438. For a compelling account of the transition from the republican world view to a liberal perspective, see Steven Watts, *The Republic Reborn: War and the Making of Liberal America, 1790–1820* (Baltimore, MD: Johns Hopkins University Press, 1987).

this problem for a long time, confiding to Benjamin Rush in 1790 that the "History of the Revolution will be one continued lie."[60]

Jefferson worried about history, too. For one thing, he believed that "one generation is to another as one independent nation to another." One of the few links that generations shared with their predecessors was their common history. But even among citizens of the same generation, Jefferson's "empire for liberty" drew its strength from self-conscious citizens who shared a commitment to "federal and republican principles." History transmitted these sentiments to the entire nation. The Revolution gave rise to a new kind of polity – the republican empire. Just as Jefferson believed that this empire would unfold across space, he was at pains to ensure that history linked each chapter of the nation's development to the Revolution's founding principles as the republic unfolded.[61]

Jefferson acknowledged the common origins that he and the now "Federalist" Adams shared. They had served together under the newly crafted constitution. But then, as Jefferson's version of the nation's history went, "we broke into two parties, each wishing to give a different direction to the government; the one to strengthen the most popular branch, the other the more permanent branches, and to extend their performance. "Here," Jefferson wrote Adams, "you and I separated for the first time."[62]

In predictable republican fashion, Jefferson attributed the distinction to timeless divisions between men and the forms of government they preferred. As he reminded Adams, "it appears that there have been differences of opinion, and party differences, from the first establishment of governments, to the present day; and on the same question which now divides our own country: that these will continue thro' all future time: that every one takes his side in favor of the many, or the few, according

---

[60] John Adams to Thomas Jefferson and Thomas McKean, July 30, 1815, in *The Adams Jefferson Letters: The Complete Correspondence between Thomas Jefferson and Abigail and John Adams*, ed. Lester J. Capon (Chapel Hill, NC: University of North Carolina Press, 1959), 2:451, cited in Trees, *Founding Fathers*, 8; Adams to Benjamin Rush, April 3, 1790, in *Old Family Letters: Copied from the Originals for Alexander Biddle, Series A* (Philadelphia, PA: J.B. Lippincot, 1892), 1:55, as quoted in Trees, *Founding Fathers*, 8.

[61] Jefferson to James Madison, September 6, 1789, in Boyd, *Papers of Jefferson*, 15:395, quoted in Onuf, *Jefferson's Empire*, 12; Jefferson to Spencer Roane, September 6, 1819, in Lipscomb and Bergh, *Writings of Thomas Jefferson*, 15:212, quoted in Onuf, *Jefferson's Empire*, 13. For Jefferson as a "sentimental nationalist," see Onuf, *Jefferson's Empire*, 14.

[62] Ellis, *Founding Brothers*, 231; Thomas Jefferson to John Adams, June 27, 1813, in *Adams Jefferson Letters*, 2:335–36, quoted in Ellis, *Founding Brothers*, 231.

to constitution, and the circumstances in which he is placed." By 1823, Jefferson's opinion of the two camps had hardened considerably. He wrote to his friend, the Marquis de Lafayette, complaining that "the sickly, weakly, timid man, fears the people, and is a Tory by nature. The healthy, strong and bold, cherishes them, and is formed a Whig by nature." For Jefferson, it could not be otherwise, as "the parties of Whig and Tory, are those of nature." Tories sought to "strengthen the executive and general Government." Whigs, on the other hand, cherished "the representative branch, and the rights reserved by the States, as the bulwark against consolidation." For Jefferson, Tory inclinations led inevitably back to monarchy and consolidation.[63]

Jefferson anticipated and contributed to the fundamental contours of political debate down to the present day. Jefferson, the man of the "many," stood guard against others, like Adams, who preferred governance by the few. Implicit in this framework was an even more powerful conceptual conflict between a nation of independent yeomen, who required little or no government hierarchy, and a state bent on "consolidation" for the benefit of a few, eager to "extend the performance" of the judiciary and executive.[64]

Though Jefferson won the war over how the founding should be framed, Adams fought a valiant battle for a more capacious understanding of the republican ideals that informed the founders. Adams rejected Jefferson's division of the founding into Whigs and Tories, and insisted that leaders like Washington and himself had fought for a more capacious republican vision – one that trusted an energetic national government kept honest by virtuous citizens. A government that served its citizens could not be an anemic government, Adams believed. As we will explore in greater detail in the next chapter, Adams and many Jeffersonians battled the Anti-Federalists, granting the central government significant authority through the Constitution.[65]

---

[63] Jefferson to Lafayette, November 4, 1823 in *The Writings of Thomas Jefferson,* ed. Paul L. Ford, 10 vols. (New York, NY: Putnam, 1892–99) 10: 281–82, cited in Wood, *Radicalism,* 97.

[64] On the historiographic battle over the role that the constitution played through Charles Beard's famous indictment of the constitution's origins, see Richard B. Morris, "The Confederation Period and the American Historian," *William and Mary Quarterly,* 3rd ser., 13, no. 2 (April 1956): 139–156.

[65] For a good summary of the evidence suggesting that Jefferson's framework endured, see Edling, *Revolution in Favor of Government,* 33–36.

Perhaps Adams's failure to salvage the historical memory of the republican rationale for energetic government could be attributed in part to poor political skills. More likely, it was doomed by the roiling possibilities grasped by individuals in a newly formed nation that was short on labor, long on land, and drawn to a rapidly emerging market economy. In either case, what Adams clumsily called the "monarchical principle" was defeated by the Jeffersonian "revolution" of 1800 in the contest to write the nation's history. No longer could a group of public officials, elected or otherwise, presume to stand for the long-term interests of the republic. Popular sovereignty gradually replaced deference. Interest replaced virtue as the legitimate basis for governing. Jefferson forged an historical interpretation that pitted the interests of the people – expressed at the ballot box – against the will of a small elite. It presumed that the people feared the central government and that leaders like Jefferson would resist consolidation. Jefferson laid the groundwork for a powerful narrative that has informed scholarship and popular history alike.[66]

Thus the Jefferson "revolution" of 1800 shaped more than the string of political successes that his Virginian disciples enjoyed and the public policies they enacted. It helped to fix a conception of the nation's history that equated republican ideas with a specific moment in the distinctly American evolution of those ideas, associating energetic national government with "the few." Defenses of the "monarchical principle" by fellow republican revolutionaries like Adams probably did not help the case for a more nuanced version of this story. The more fundamental problem, however, lay not with the past, but in the future.

Beginning with Jefferson's own administration, and continuing to the present, adjectives like "energetic," "active," "consolidated," and "big" government – or simply "the state" – were used pejoratively. They were euphemisms attached to federal efforts to carry out the collective will when it entailed extracting direct taxes, regulating individual behavior, or erecting permanent hierarchical organizations to administer national programs. They laid the foundation for America's antistatist ideology. Alexander Hamilton perceived the problem as early as 1792 when he warned that the "National government, once rendered odious, will be kept so by these powerful and indefatigable enemies." It was much "easier to raise the Devil," Hamilton chided, "than to lay him." Because its leadership was more directly accountable, local and state action drew

---

[66] Ellis, *Founding Brothers*, 204–205, 232.

far less criticism – even from Jeffersonian Republicans and latter-day Democrats.[67]

Controlling the way in which the central government's policies were framed, it turned out, could sometimes be more important than the actual impact of those programs, or the degree to which they penetrated the lives of citizens. Some powerful expressions of national authority escaped censure from would-be Jeffersonian republicans. Such policies ranged from the exploration, purchase, and protection of millions of acres of French territory, to the construction of a postal service that dwarfed continental counterparts, to policies that extracted precious fiscal resources and often penetrated deeply into state or local prerogatives and private lives. Partisan struggles often determined whether popular history would celebrate national action, as it did in the case of the Louisiana Purchase, or relegate it to the purgatory of "consolidation," as was the case of the Second Bank of the United States.

In many instances – as was the case with land distribution and the post office – *where* the federal government intervened, and *how* it intervened proved crucial to both political acceptance and historical judgment. Federal action at the margins of the nation extended through third parties, guided through the judiciary, and, in the case of taxes assessed indirectly at the nation's borders rather than at citizens' front doors, was smart politics. It did not overshadow the national story that eclipsed a good portion of the earlier republican vision – a society built upon the remarkable initiative of private citizens that remained vigilant against government consolidation. That story dominated the first quarter of the nineteenth century, at least at the voting booth, at the same time that an energetic central government promoted the economic well-being of independent farmers and enhanced the civic participation of independent white males in a variety of ways. Directly contradicting Hamilton's republican conception of the polity-centered society, the central government was most effective when its authority went unnoticed or remained hidden, or was quickly obscured.

---

[67] Alexander Hamilton to Edward Carrington, May 26, 1792, in *The Papers of Alexander Hamilton*, ed. Harold C Syrett et al., 27 vols.(New York, NY: Columbia University Press, 1961–87), 11:442.

3

Between Revolutions:
The Promise of the Developmental Vision

Although the ideal of autonomous individuals pursuing happiness through an expanding market while governing themselves locally displaced a polity-centered conception of citizenship, this objective was more easily conceived than realized in British North America. This chapter returns to the late eighteenth century to examine the ways in which Americans adapted ideas and practices to the political and economic challenges they faced in their daily lives. At times these obstacles were imposed by the British. On other occasions, it was the colonists who struggled to resolve political differences among themselves as they grappled with a wide range of demographic and economic differences. Whether uniting across class lines to demand rights from an imperial foe, or airing internal differences at the national level, the crucible of political struggle and the institutions and policies that these battles produced reinforced the premise behind a geographically extensive union. Even the political factions that eventually hardened into much-denounced political parties contributed to the process as they nationalized the debate in ways that underscored the extensive reach of issues like trade, national security, and expansion.[1]

---

[1] Karl-Friedrich Walling explores the tension between guaranteeing liberty at home and protecting the peace through a strong state by examining Hamilton's thought on these matters in *Republican Empire: Alexander Hamilton on War and Free Government* (Lawrence, KS: University Press of Kansas, 1999). For an outstanding example of the power of political conflict to define institutional legacies, and the impact of those institutions on democratic practice, see Robin L. Einhorn, *American Taxation, American Slavery* (Chicago, IL: University of Chicago Press, 2006).

Americans fought and won two revolutions between 1776 and 1790. The first, waged against the British Empire, was conducted in the name of liberty. How was liberty for individuals and local communities to be preserved in a world of power politics and mercantilist trade policy? Perhaps this balance was possible when Great Britain provided military and commercial protection to British North Americans without demanding much in return. But as Great Britain sought to consolidate its empire after the Treaty of Paris (1763), imposing new taxes and enforcing duties, British North Americans began to pay a high financial and political price for their provincial status. The growing threat of war, in turn, galvanized national sentiment, underscoring the one relationship (to Great Britain, not each other) most British North Americans shared in common up to that point.[2]

British North Americans struggled over how best to protect individual liberty while enforcing collective discipline. In key debates over military and trade policy, colonists wondered which, and whose, short-term freedoms to sacrifice in order to create a society that ensured lasting liberties for its citizens. How could they protect individual liberties while preserving the young republic's autonomy? Fighting the British required a disciplined army. Yet, the colonists worried that their army might come to resemble that of their imperial foe. Nevertheless, by the end of the war, they had produced a standing army motivated by the fear of living permanently under a standing army. British North Americans were willing to tap the military capacity of a central government, if only for the duration of the crisis. War forced British North Americans to get to know each other, but in many instances they did not like what they learned.

The second "revolution" was fought "in favor of Government," as the *Pennsylvania Gazette* put it. Like the first revolution waged against the British, advocates of the second revolution claimed to be fighting on behalf of liberty. The supporters of a new constitution contended that only an energetic government could protect that liberty in a dangerous

---

[2] Robert A. Becker, *Revolution, Reform, and the Politics of American Taxation, 1763–1783* (Baton Rouge, LA: Louisiana State University Press, 1980) 71–72; Christopher L. Tomlins, *Law, Labor, and Ideology in the Early American Republic* (New York, NY: Cambridge University Press, 1993), 50. On the impact of war on states generally, see Michael Mann, "State and Society, 1130–1815: An Analysis of English State Finances," *Political Power and Social Theory*, 1, (1980):165–208; Michael Mann, "The Autonomous Power of the State: Its Origins, Mechanisms and Results," *European Journal of Sociology*, 26, no. 2 (1985): 185–213.

world. Sustaining the collective will to fight the British was difficult enough, even with citizens' homes and livelihoods at stake. Once the patriotic ardor cooled, bounties, rather than virtue were required to meet conscription goals. Without that ominous external threat, maintaining national bonds seemed almost impossible, as an ineffectual Continental Congress scrambled for both funds and legitimacy.[3]

In the aftermath of the War for Independence, many thoughtful Americans worried about possible conflict between the colonies themselves. The fear that competing federations would form, as they had on the European continent, stimulated support for an extensive union. Nor could the continued loyalty of settlers be assured if their access to trade was denied. How best to preserve that union became the fundamental challenge, and ironically, the unifying theme of American politics.[4]

Debating that question helped to create the very nation that its citizens sought to preserve. It was sharp political differences among Americans after the Revolution, and the elaboration of these differences through partisan debate, that ultimately accelerated a sense of national identity in the last third of the eighteenth century. Many Americans who had opposed the constitutional convention eventually defended its product – insisting upon its strict construction in matters regarding the federal government. The Constitution became the touchstone for parsing federal/state responsibilities, and federalism the standard mechanism for parceling out responsibilities. While the view of strict constructionists clashed with the Federalists' more capacious interpretation of the Constitution, both nascent parties battled over how best to preserve a union that had not even existed a few decades before and that many expected to fracture within the next decade.[5]

[3] *Pennsylvania Gazette*, September 5, 1787, (Provo, Utah : Folio Corp., 1991) online at University of Virginia Etext Center, http://etext.lib.virginia.edu/accessible/pengaz/, quoted in Max M. Edling, *A Revolution in Favor of Government: Origins of the U.S. Constitution and the Making of the American State* (New York, NY: Oxford University Press, 2003), vii; Ibid., 7.

[4] On the possibility of conflict between the colonies, see David C. Hendrickson, *Peace Pact: The Lost World of the American Founding* (Lawrence, KS: University Press of Kansas, 2003).

[5] Lance Banning, "Republican Ideology and the Triumph of the Constitution, 1789 to 1793," *William and Mary Quarterly*, 3rd ser. 31, no. 2 (April 1974): 168–69. David Waldstreicher has traced similar developments from the 1760s through the early nineteenth century in the United States. His methodology seems particularly well-suited to a nation that eschewed much of the state apparatus associated with nationhood in Europe. Waldstreicher's greatest contribution to the literature on national identity is his insistence that serious political conflict and, eventually, partisan conflict contributed to the formation

As Americans wrestled with the Confederation, many embraced a developmental vision that projected growth westward. This deferred difficult sectional tradeoffs in the hope of increasing the overall size of the economy and wealth of the nation. If there was more for all, battles over how to divide this bounty might be muted, or at least delayed. Thus, associations of merchants called for an end to interstate competition over trade. Men like Thomas Jefferson understood that although economic development was animated by individual initiative, it also required government direction and support. The benefits of trade had to be shared among all citizens. Supporters of a new constitution, like Benjamin Franklin and James Madison, argued that strength to deal with foreign powers and quash interstate rivalries was the surest path to personal liberty: an energetic central government was the key to providing the authority, infrastructure, and security necessary to realize this vision. Great Britain was able to defend the personal liberty of its citizens, one staunch federalist argued, precisely because it had the capacity to exert public force. The Confederation lacked this, with one exception. Even the weak central government under the Articles of Confederation managed to forge a powerful template for orderly territorial expansion, crafting the Northwest Ordinance in 1787. It offered an opportunity to take full advantage of the national bounty that seemed always to stretch just beyond the existing borders.

Under the new Constitution, especially as amended by the Bill of Rights, states would continue to ensure the civil liberties and rights of their citizens. They would continue to fund state-level development, especially through internal improvements. But citizens of the United States would also work in concert through General Government to transcend interstate competition – to develop economic opportunities that deferred sectional rivalries by extending and economically integrating the nation. Many advocates of a strong General Government, like Alexander Hamilton, were wary of popular sovereignty. Yet, the Constitution's

---

of national identity. All too often, scholars have turned the symbolic actions of parades into static icons, "paraded" to demonstrate national consensus, or submerged social conflicts, ignoring the national political advantage sought in such action. Waldstreicher, *In the Midst of Perpetual Fetes: The Making of American Nationalism, 1776–1820* (Chapel Hill, NC: University of North Carolina Press, 1997), 7. For a compelling interpretation of the conflict between supporters of the Constitution and the Anti-Federalists that turns on just how the public sphere should be constructed, see Saul Cornell, *The Other Founders: Anti-Federalism and the Dissenting Tradition in America, 1728–1828* (Chapel Hill, NC: University of North Carolina Press), especially Chap. 9.

drafters grounded national legitimacy in popular sovereignty – "we the people" – hoping that Americans would view the state governments' parochial interests, not national union, as the artificial barrier impeding opportunity. Regardless of one's position on the proposed constitution, the debate that ensued over ratification was a seminal moment in the construction of national identity. The conversation, carried on in taverns and post offices, forced all citizens to consider their relationship to an extended polity.

The authors of the Constitution created the potential for a powerful central government, but one that would tread lightly in domestic policy. For instance, some of its most potent authority resided in the federal judiciary, which required little bureaucracy or revenue. The revenue source that every supporter of the Constitution envisioned was an impost, collected at the nation's ports, rather than imposed on citizens' homes and farms. The new government's access to credit was another important source of authority that, at least in the view of Alexander Hamilton, would sustain liberty through strength. The final document also included more explicit powers. Congress could raise an army, for instance. It could also levy internal taxes, including direct taxes on property, should it have the political will to demand these. Unlike the impost, there was virtually no limitation on how high internal taxes might rise.[6]

The Constitution, however, only provided the platform for national development. The precise powers enumerated by the Constitution and the government's willingness to use them were ultimately determined by political struggle and the public policies that the young nation endorsed in its first thirty years. The second half of this chapter explores some of these policies.

As patterns of policy preference hardened into partisan competition, Federalists like Alexander Hamilton made the case for conspicuous displays of national authority. Initially, this entailed symbolic actions, often embodied in the person of George Washington. But Hamilton's program to finance the state's debts nationally, combined with the creation of the National Bank and a program of internal improvements, soon added substance to symbol. Hamilton created a financial system that melded the authority of the central government with the self-interest of wealthy individuals. It was a hybrid system, with public and private blending,

[6] As Robin Einhorn points out, there was little understanding of what constituted a direct tax, and in any case, few founders expected direct taxes to be employed except in times of emergency. Einhorn, *American Taxation*, 106–10.

sometimes imperceptibly, to finance the developmental vision. As such, it fit squarely with the preference for mixed enterprise displayed at both the state and the national level.

Funding the debt required that another goal of Hamilton's be sacrificed – building the nation's capitol in a highly visible commercial and financial hub. Washington D.C. was closer to being a swamp than a hub. Nevertheless, Federalists extended the scope of the young nation's public policies, reaching too far in the case of the Alien and Sedition Acts and the Direct Tax at the end of the eighteenth century. Jeffersonian Republicans had their own national vision, one that was even imperial in scope. This was Jefferson's "empire for Liberty," that knit Americans together across a vast expanse – not by administrative hierarchy, but rather by bonds of affection reinforced by enduring material interest.

The developmental vision offered a perspective that sustained the second revolution. It bound individual liberty to the prospect of enhanced economic opportunity through nationally enforced public policy. Grounded in self-interest rather than virtue, the institutions and policies its advocates endorsed preserved the possibility of collective action in a society that was self-consciously committed to individual improvement. The compromises that ensued were not always as elegant as those embodied in the Constitution. But they provided durable answers to the vexing question of how liberty could be preserved in a dangerous world. As the rationale for active governance embodied in the ideal of a balanced republic was undermined by empowering autonomous individuals, those same citizens demanded more from their governments – even the General Government – at the same time that they remained ever-vigilant against the tyranny of "consolidation."

"VIRTUE ENOUGH TO SUPPORT A REPUBLIC?" THE CHALLENGE AND OPPORTUNITY OF WAR

Hostility toward a foreign enemy created common bonds among British North Americans from the 1760s through the end of the War for Independence. Symbolic displays disseminated common appeals broadly. During the Stamp Act crisis, for instance, angry colonists conducted a "funeral" for liberty. Upon the Act's repeal, they established holidays to memorialize the first crowd resistance to it. After the British naval schooner *Gaspee* ran aground in 1772, civil disobedience broke out in Rhode Island. The heavy-handed British investigation into the incident inflamed Americans. Opponents of the crown formalized communications through committees of correspondence, expanding the scope of protest along the entire Eastern seaboard and even into the interior. In September 1774, delegates from the colonies met in Philadelphia in the First Continental Congress. They responded to the latest British assault on liberty – the Coercive Acts. After the conflict turned deadly in Lexington and Concord, the Second Continental Congress gathered and authorized the creation of the Continental Army. It issued paper money to fund what it hoped would be more than a paper tiger.[7]

When Americans declared their independence in 1776 demonstrations broke out across the colonies vilifying the king. A statue of George III in New York was hacked to pieces; royal images were ceremoniously burned elsewhere. Benjamin Rush, reported that "the Militia of Pennsylvania seem to be actuated with a spirit more than Roman. Near 2,000 citizens of Philada have lately marched to New-York in order to prevent an incursion being made by our enemies upon the state of New-Jersey." Indeed, there were multiple local resolutions declaring independence from the British. Because the patriot elites couched their grievances in the language of corporate privilege – replete with constitutional protections against royal intrusion – they claimed to speak for all of the "people." For the moment, stark class differences were subsumed in the defense of corporate prerogative.[8]

At the outset of the Revolutionary War, the colonies were gripped by a "passion for arms." Despite the patriotic response, the very idea of a standing army contradicted ideals for which the revolution was being fought. A standing army threatened liberty. It required vast resources that taxed the populace. Indeed, these were some of the same complaints that the revolutionaries lodged against the British. Most Americans, if they fought at all, preferred to enlist in local militias, taking up arms only when the crisis was close to home.[9]

---

[7] Waldstreicher, *Midst of Perpetual Fetes*, 26.

[8] Waldstreicher, *Midst of Perpetual Fetes*, 30; Benjamin Rush to Charles Lee, July 23, 1776, in *Letters of Delegates to Congress, 1774–1789*, ed. Paul H. Smith, vol. 4, May 16–August 15, 1776 (Washington, D.C.: Library of Congress, 1979), cited in David McCullough, *John Adams* (New York, NY: Simon & Schuster, 2001), 139; Peter S. Onuf, "Federalism, Democracy, and Liberty in the New American Nation," (paper presented at the Expansion of English Liberty Overseas Conference, November 2007), 13–14, 23–24, 29. On declarations of independence, see Pauline Maier, *American Scripture: Making the Declaration of Independence* (New York, NY: Random House, 1997).

[9] Extract of a Letter from a Private Gentleman in Philadelphia to a Merchant in London, 6 May 1775," *Lloyd's Evening Post and British Chronicle*, June 28–30, 1775, in Margaret Wheeler Willard, ed., *Letters on the American Revolution, 1774–1776* (Washington,

After the initial burst of enthusiasm, the Continental Congress faced the never-ending problem of meeting its enlistment quotas. It soon abandoned its determination to limit enlistment for soldiers for only one year, seeking instead to sign up men for the duration of the war. Both individual colonies and the Congress offered bounties. Some colonies even resorted to conscription, but to little avail. It was one thing for the Continental Congress to authorize an army of 75,000, as it did in September, 1776. It was another to raise such an army. At no time during the war did the Continental Army reach half that number.[10]

The men responsible for leading the Continental Army learned that preserving liberty required more than effective ideas and symbols. It required disciplined and collective action, a willingness to sacrifice local prerogative and individual liberty in the short run in order permanently to place these freedoms on a more secure footing. Initially, the colonists spent far more time worrying about how to control a standing army than considering ways to maintain one. As the war dragged on, however, the Continental Army came to resemble the professional standing army that the revolutionaries originally feared, although a grossly understaffed and ill-equipped one. Fortunately for the would-be republic, the British had not only to defeat an army. They had to subdue a continent as well.[11]

Trade was another policy that seemed to demand the kind of central direction that many colonists were wary of. The War for Independence probably had as great an impact on the domestic economy as any war in

NY: Kennikat Press, 1925), 101–102, cited in Charles Royster, *A Revolutionary People at War: The Continental Army and American Character, 1775–1783* (Chapel Hill, NC: University of North Carolina Press, 1979), 25. That passion was rewarded when the colonists defeated the British in several New England engagements. Newspaper accounts of parades, toasts, and other localized symbolic actions publicized events nationally. Proliferating accounts gave the reader a sense of belonging. Reports of distant events reinforced readers' belief that theirs indeed was more than a local uprising. Rituals and the use of symbols also reinforced a sense of belonging to something larger, creating consistency across time and space. The most familiar of these symbols during the Revolution, the number thirteen, could be found across the states. Almanacs, previously targeted at specific cities, began to incorporate information about the republic, reminding citizens about national holidays and a chronicling of events leading up to the Revolution. Waldstreicher, *Midst of Perpetual Fetes*, 33–35, 45. See also, Lawrence Delbert Cress, *Citizens in Arms: The Army and Militia in America Society to the War of 1812* (Chapel Hill, NC: University of North Carolina Press, 1982).

[10] Royster, *Revolutionary People at War*, chap. 1; Edling, *Revolution in Favor of Government*, 78.
[11] Edling, *Revolution in Favor of Government*, 79–81; Royster, *Revolutionary People at War*, 38, 97, 116.

American history. With finished goods from Britain cut off by the war-time embargo, Northern manufacturers embraced the prospect of sup-plying their own region and the rapidly developing frontier regions. This experience whetted their appetite for developing the internal market and the high tariff policy that eventually was adopted.[12]

The home market inspired others who sought to liberate trade from the constraint of domestic restrictions. Farmers freed from price controls hoped to sell their surplus crops at more competitive prices. Movements to deregulate prices and abandon customs that fixed the quality of goods were widespread. While the price for every article fluctuated, would-be free traders insisted that "it will ever return of itself, sufficiently near to a proper level, if the banks and dams, or ... injudicious attempts to regu-late it, are not interposed." Land speculators and advocates of internal improvements added their voices to calls for unrestricted markets. The vast potential for internal development and a growing appreciation for the kind of infrastructure it required inspired a new conception of the American political economy. Associations of small producers took their place next to the independent yeoman farmer that republican ideals glori-fied as model citizens.[13]

[12] Jack N. Rakove, review of *A Union of Interests: Political and Economic Thought in Revolutionary America*, by Cathy D. Matson and Peter S. Onuf, *Journal of Economic History*, 50, no. 4 (December 1990): 979; Matson and Onuf, *Union of Interests* (Lawrence, KS: University Press of Kansas, 1990), 46. On the impact of war on the domestic economy, see John Brewer, *The Sinews of Power: War, Money, and the English State, 1688–1783* (Boston, MA: Unwin Hyman, 1989).

[13] As one successful Lancaster farmer bragged in 1777, "the Shops are full of Goods, and every Body busy, so that you would think yourself in a Sea port town whose Trade was open." Letter attributed to Elias Boudinot, cited as "Em B.," (Emmet Collection of Manuscripts Etc. Relating to American History), quoted in Robert A East, *Business Enterprise in the American Revolutionary War Era* (New York, NY: Columbia University Press, 1938), 149–50, as cited in Matson and Onuf, *Union of Interests*, 32–33; Matson and Onuf, *Union of Interests*, 33, 48. Artisans in Philadelphia joined the chorus, pro-claiming that "trade should be as free as air, uninterrupted as the tides." Tanners informed their fellow citizens in Philadelphia, "Having thus stated our ideas of this matter for your consideration, we think ourselves justified before the world in declaring, that we do not consider ourselves bound by the regulated prices of our commodities." Tanners, Curriers, and Cordwainers [James Roney, Chairman], *To The Inhabitants of Philadelphia* (Philadelphia, PA: Thomas Bradford, 1779), Early American Imprints Series I (American Antiquarian Society and NewsBank, 2002 [doc. no. 16547]), 2, http://infoweb.newsbank.com/, cited in Matson and Onuf, *Union of Interests*, 33. On associations and trade, see also, Frederick W. Marks III, *Independence on Trial: Foreign Affairs and the Making of the Constitution* (Baton Rouge, LA: Louisiana State University Press, 1973), 72–82.

By the end of the war, many Americans were asking how the growing thirst for unrestrained trade would generate the collective discipline required to negotiate with foreign powers or restrain self-interested economic parties from turning the political process toward selfish ends. The Confederation was in no position to bargain effectively with foreign powers over trade or to ensure equitable markets at home. It failed to conclude any successful trade agreements with foreign powers. In fact, when Great Britain closed the West Indies trade to American ships in 1783 and placed other restrictions on American trade, Gouverneur Morris, a future senator from New York argued that it would do "us more political good than it could possibly do commercial mischief," by exposing the weakness of the Articles of Confederation. The Confederation's army, which dropped to eighty men at one point in 1783 was hardly intimidating. Nor was the Confederation able to muster the kind of naval power necessary to impress the British. An energetic national government might garner more respect from foreign powers and ensure that self-interest also served public ideals. But could a vigorous, remote polity be trusted? For the time being, most Americans concluded that it could not.[14]

Eliminating the domestic constraints on trade quickly exposed tensions between private interest and the public good. Under these conditions, whatever virtue restrained citizens broke down while demands for more forceful intervention into the economy grew. Overmatched, the Continental Congress threw up its hands and turned to more trusted sources of authority – the state legislatures – which had vast experience in taxing their own citizens, collecting revenue, distributing land, and regulating the flow of goods. State legislatures soon intervened forcefully in the economy. The northern colonies responded to charges of profiteering and wartime shortages by passing legislation that regulated trade, fixed prices and wages, and limited profits.[15]

---

[14] Matson and Onuf, *Union of Interests*, 32; Gouverneur Morris to John Jay, January 10, 1784, in *The Life of Gouverneur Morris, with Selections from His Corrospondence and Miscellaneous Papers*, ed. Jared Sparks (Boston: Gray and Bowen, 1832), 1:267, cited in Marks, *Independence*, 68; Edling, *Revolution in Favor of Government*, 82–83.

[15] Matson and Onuf, *Union of Interests*, 38. As J.R. Pole put it, "The War of Independence was an internal crisis for Americans which placed unprecedented strains on their loyalties, and as time went on without bringing clear improvements, on their self-restraint." J.R. Pole, *American Individualism and the Promise of Progress: an Inaugural Lecture delivered before the University of Oxford on 14 February 1980* (New York, NY: Oxford University Press, 1980), 15. Action on the state level permitted a wide range of laws and practices on the domestic front, even as the colonies joined forces militarily. Harold N.

The ideal of free trade, like that of a standing army composed of citizen-soldiers, proved to be elusive in practice. Both were crippled by the republican fear of distant authority – even though that threat was now American rather than British. Ultimately, Americans were not willing to offer national leaders the discretion to negotiate effective international trade agreements. Americans did not feel the same kind of allegiance to the Continental Army that local militias engendered: citizens would not devote the time or travel the distance that such a national force required. With the end of hostilities, pressure for a more energetic national government quickly dissipated. The brief experiment with freer trade and a standing army did not endure.

Nor did the hand-to-mouth appropriations process that depended on Continental Congress requisitions to the states. The Continental Congress made six requisitions between 1781 and 1787. It received about one third of the funds it requested. By 1787, the Congress was broke. The national government could not pay its own debts. Adding to the problem, British and American creditors renewed their efforts to recoup wartime loans.[16]

Men of substance complained that democracy was out of control. Even in Virginia, no hotbed of radicalism, statesmen like James Madison warned that politicians were paying too much attention to their constituents and insufficient attention to the demands of the Continental Army. Madison may have had fellow Virginian and former Governor Patrick Henry in mind. Henry advocated tax suspension in 1783 and developed a reputation for being the taxpayer's friend.[17]

Part of the problem was that colonists who previously had not shared much in common beyond their mutual animosity toward the British were now forced to work together. They were appalled by the differences they encountered. This was as true in politics as in social and economic relations. Commenting on his dealings with his counterparts from New York in the first session of Congress, Pennsylvania Representative George

Hyman, "Federalism: Legal Fiction and Historical Artifact?" *Brigham Young University Law Review*, 1987, no. 3: 915.

[16] Edling, *Revolution in Favor of Government*, 154–55; Becker, *Revolution, Reform*, 219–20.

[17] John R. Nelson, Jr., *Liberty and Property: Political Economy and Policymaking in the New Nation, 1789–1812* (Baltimore, MD: Johns Hopkins University Press, 1987), 22–29; Becker, *Revolution, Reform*, 201–203. See also Gordon S. Wood, *The Creation of the American Republic 1776–1787* (Chapel Hill, NC: University of North Carolina Press, 1998).

Clymer, who had signed both the Declaration of Independence and the Constitution, acknowledged that "the New Yorkers and I are on an equal footing. ... Mutual civility without a grain of good liking between us." Issues were debated among men who did not know each other – a "Multitude of Strangers," as John Adams put it. Back in the Provincial Assembly, Adams explained, a man's pedigree, profession, and connections were well known. "But here it is quite otherwise. We frequently see Phenomena which puzzle us. It requires Time to enquire and learn the Characters and Connections." Under these conditions, it is not surprising that many doubted the very survival of the republican experiment.[18]

The republican basis for collective action had fallen short of the mark. The war and embargo created ample opportunities for price gouging and shoddy workmanship, which far too many British North Americans had taken advantage of. Sustaining the passion that initially had gripped Americans in their struggle against the British proved to be far more difficult than anticipated. John Adams even wondered if in wartime America "there is public Virtue enough to Support a Republic?" With self-interest driving conscription and desertion rates, and markets setting prices, it was hard for anybody to conceive of a world in which private and material interests did not influence, if not dictate political outcomes. The notion that the polity structured social relations, and that citizenship transcended private interest, was subjected to the harshest test.[19]

[18] John M. Murrin, "A Roof Without Walls: The Dilemma of American National Identity," in *Beyond Confederation: Origins of the Constitution and American National Identity*, ed. Richard Beeman, Stephen Botein, and Edward C. Carter II (Chapel Hill, NC: University of North Carolina Press, 1987), 343; George Clymer to Henry Hill, March 7, 1790, Signers' Collection, New York Society Library, quoted in Joanne B. Freeman, *Affairs of Honor: National Politics in the New Republic* (New Haven, CT: Yale University Press, 2001), 7; "George E. Clymer," *Dictionary of American Biography*, Base Set. American Council of Learned Societies, 1928–1936. Reproduced in History Resource Center. Farmington Hills, MI: Gale, http://galenet.galegroup.com/servlet/HistRC/; John Adams to James Warren, October 24, 1775, in *Papers of John Adams*, ed. Robert J. Taylor, et al., 14 vols. to date (Cambridge, MA: The Belknap Press of Harvard University Press, 1977–), 3:238–39, quoted in Freeman, *Affairs of Honor*, 20, and Andrew S. Trees, *The Founding Fathers and the Politics of Character* (Princeton, NJ: Princeton University Press, 2004), 82; Ellis, *Founding Brothers*, 5.
[19] John Adams to Mercy Otis Warren, January 8, 1776, in *Warren-Adams Letters, Being Chiefly a Correspondence among John Adams, Samuel Adams, and James Warren*. Vol. 2, 1778–1814. Collections of the Massachusetts Historical Society Series, vols. 72 and 73. (Boston, MA: Massachusetts Historical Society, 1925), 72:202, quoted in Matson and Onuf, *Union of Interests*, 37. On the transition to a liberal basis of political economy, see Steven Watts, *The Republic Reborn: War and the Making of Liberal America, 1790–1820* (Baltimore, MD: Johns Hopkins University Press, 1987).

Chastened by this lesson in political economy, and emboldened by their victory over a powerful foe, an influential cross section of Americans embraced a developmental vision of the nation's future that required cooperation between men who hardly knew each other, and sometimes even despised each other. Realizing the developmental vision required more than individual ambition and ample natural resources. It demanded that collective action be overseen and sometimes directed by a government that transcended the well-worn rivalries between states, and increasingly, sections. There was hardly unanimity among those who supported the developmental vision. Future New York Senator and ambassador to Great Britain Rufus King opposed opening the Mississippi, as did Gouverneur Morris and future secretary of state, Timothy Pickering. They worried about the rapid exodus of population from eastern commercial states, and the potential allegiance of this population to Spain. But even George Washington, who originally shared these fears, and Alexander Hamilton came around on this issue. Washington appointed Jefferson secretary of state, rather than Jay, who had been discredited for offering to close trade on the Mississippi in his earlier negotiations with Spain.[20]

The developmental vision provided an interest-based incentive for Americans to support an energetic General Government. It was a government that in some instances, would directly promote, and on other occasions, coordinate, national political and economic development. The developmental vision preserved a republican inclination toward energetic governance, but grounded such collective action in a foundation of liberal self-interest. As public officials embraced elements of the developmental vision, they soon learned that national authority could be extended far more effectively when it was not conspicuous, was exercised at or beyond the borders of the nation, or simply hidden in mechanisms like the impost.

"WE MUST SACRIFICE A LITTLE FOR THE GOOD OF THE WHOLE": THE DEVELOPMENTAL VISION

Victorious in war as a loosely knit confederation, the individual states provided the political backbone of the new nation after the war. It was the Revolution that confirmed the states' stature at the same time that it

---

[20] Arthur Preston Whitaker, *The Spanish-American Frontier, 1783–1795: The Westward Movement and the Spanish Retreat in the Mississippi Valley* (Gloucester, MA: Peter Smith, 1962 [1927]), 74–75, 119–122.

underscored the need for some mechanism that allowed these states to work in concert. Those seeking government assistance turned to states. Improvers were one obvious example. Though wrapped in national-ist rhetoric, the driving force behind internal improvements often was rooted in the possibility of short-term benefits for a particular interest group or local jurisdiction. Because geography did not always accom-modate politically drawn boundaries or man-made economic interests, competition between the states for trade and their inability to act collec-tively left many proponents of internal development searching for a more extensive coordinating agent.[21]

Nor, in these times of foreign intrigue, could the states assume the loyalty of their Western settlers. The situation was particularly volatile in Kentucky. Under the leadership of James Wilkinson, some Kentuckians were prepared to negotiate with Spain for the right to trade on the Mississippi. According to Wilkinson, prominent neighbors supported this mission to alleviate the "inconveniences and distress which they suffer from the restraints on their commerce." They were even willing to con-sider "admission *to her protection as subjects*."[22]

Should America lose the West and, with it, the ability to expand, the country might well be doomed to follow Europe's example. French states-man and essayist Robert Jacques Turgot, who hoped that Americans might avoid Europe's mistakes, worried that they were still "involved in the mists of European illusions." The states would become "a mass of divided powers," Turgot predicted, "quarrelling about territories or the

[21] Robert H. Wiebe, *The Opening of American Society: From the Adoption of the Constitution to the Eve of Disunion* (New York, NY: Knopf, 1984), 3; John Lauritz Larson, *Internal Improvement: National Public Works and the Promise of Popular Government in the Early United States* (Chapel Hill, NC: University of North Carolina Press, 2001), 3–4 and generally; Marks, *Independence*, chap. 2.

[22] Marks, *Independence*, 34–35, 210; James Wilkinson, *Memorial*, quoted in William R. Shepherd, "Wilkinson and the Beginnings of the Spanish Conspiracy," *American Historical Review*, 9 no. 3 (April 1904): 501, cited in Thomas P. Slaughter, *The Whiskey Rebellion: Frontier Epilogue to the American Revolution*, (New York, NY: Oxford University Press, 1986), 55. On Wilkinson, see also Whitaker, *Spanish-American Frontier*, chaps. 7–8. Peter S. Onuf argues that there is no other period in which foreign relations are so important. "Reflections on the Founding: Constitutional Historiography in Bicentennial Perspective," *William and Mary Quarterly*, 3rd ser., 46, no.2 (April 1989): 358. On the threat in North Carolina, see Matson and Onuf, *Union of Interests*, 64. For concerns about alliances with foreign powers that run through the first third of the nineteenth century, see James E. Lewis, *The American Union and the Problem of Neighborhood: The United States and the Collapse of the Spanish Empire, 1783–1829* (Chapel Hill, NC: University of North Carolina Press, 1998).

profits of commerce, and continually cementing the slavery of the people with their own blood." Americans were acutely aware of this possibility. Benjamin Franklin, for instance, alerted his colleagues in September 1787 that the Constitution they were about to sign would "astonish our enemies, who are waiting with confidence to hear, that our councils are confounded like those of the builders of Babel, and that our States are on the point of separation, only to meet hereafter for the purpose of cutting one another's throats."[23]

Those seeking a stronger union had several things going for them. Most Americans readily conceded that the Confederation was a failure – unable to resolve any of the central questions that divided Americans. The states were mired in a postwar economic recession. The threat of foreign intervention in internal affairs, not to mention discrimination in trade, persisted. State governments acted in a self-interested manner as they competed with each other for economic primacy. Caricaturing the situation, the strong proponent of a constitutional convention, Fisher Ames, observed that "the King of New York levied imposts upon Jersey and Connecticut; and the nobles of Virginia bore with impatience their tributary dependence on Baltimore and Philadelphia. Our discontents were fermenting into civil war." Local ties even trumped the emerging factional split that would soon divide Federalists and Republicans. In New York, for instance, Alexander Hamilton worked with his critics to charter a state bank that would enhance local credit.[24]

[23] Anne Robert Jacques Turgot to Richard Price, March 22, 1778, in *Richard Price and the Ethical Foundations of the American Revolution*, ed. Bernard Peach (Durham, NC: Duke University Press, 1979), 220, 222, cited in Matson and Onuf, *Union of Interests*, 66, italics in original; Benjamin Franklin, "Speech in the Convention at the Conclusion of its Deliberations," in *Writings*, J.A. Leo Lemay ed (New York: Library of America, 1987), 1140, quoted in Hendrickson, *Peace Pact*, 4. From the conclusion of the Revolution, Americans worried that the colonies would form two or three regional confederations. Forrest McDonald, *States' Rights and the Union: Imperium in Imperio, 1776–1876* (Lawrence, KS: University Press of Kansas, 2000), 14; Marks, *Independence*, 33.

[24] Edling, *Revolution in Favor of Government*, 84; Thomas K. McCraw, "The Strategic Vision of Alexander Hamilton," *The American Scholar*, 63, no.1 (Winter 1994): 43; Fisher Ames, "The Dangers of American Liberty," in *Works of Fisher Ames*, ed. Seth Ames (Boston, MA: Little Brown, 1854), 2:370, cited in Matson and Onuf, *Union of Interests*, 74, as Fisher Ames, "The Republican No. VI", *Connecticut Courant*, March 19, 1787, reprinted in *New York Journal and Weekly Register*, March 29, 1787, volume 41, issue 13, 2–3, in *Early American Newspapers*, Series I, http://infoweb.newsbank.com/; Brian Phillips Murphy, "Financial Warfare : The Manhattan Company, The Election of 1800, and The Origins of Partisan Banking in New York City, 1791–1805 " (masters thesis, University of Virginia, 2003): 8. On the Continental Congress, see Jack N. Rakove,

James Madison summed up the problems plaguing the Confederation in "Vices of the Political System of the United States." The states simply failed to comply with Constitutional requisitions. The states encroached on Federal authority; when treaties were signed by the Confederation, the states violated these treaties. The states had little more regard for the rights of citizens of other states. Equally troubling to Madison, there was a "want of concert in matters where common interest requires it." For example, "canals and other works of general utility" were easily thwarted. Yet there was no remedy for such transgressions and missed opportunities.[25]

Criticisms of the status quo did not ensure that a majority of Americans would coalesce around a popular alternative. It was the singular contribution of those who supported the Constitution to craft such a compromise. They relied on such crucial mechanisms as federalism and a formula for electing senators that favored less populous states.

Wherever possible, the Constitution also made national authority implicit rather than explicit. It created the legal architecture for a national government that remained out of sight. This was particularly true of the judicial branch of the national government. No wonder that a leading Anti-Federalist warned that "judges and juries, in their interpretations, and in directing the execution of them, have a very extensive influence for preserving or destroying liberty." The actions of legislatures were highly visible and broadly publicized, Federal Farmer continued. A judge's action, on the other hand, might affect "a single individual only, and [be] noticed only by his neighbors and a few spectators in the court." Men like Federal Farmer were prescient in their prediction that the most hidden branch of government established by the Constitution would have a powerful say over Americans.[26]

By 1786, five states were prepared to challenge the status quo directly. Their spokesmen gathered in Annapolis and called for an assembly of representatives from all of the states for the expressed purpose of revising

The Beginning of National Politics: An Interpretive History of the Continental Congress (New York, NY: Knopf, 1979).

[25] James Madison, "Vices of the Political System of the United States," in *Papers of James Madison: Congressional Series*, ed. Robert A. Rutland et. al. (Chicago, IL: University of Chicago Press; Charlottesville: University Press of Virginia, 1959–1991) 9: 350, cited in Hendrickson, *Peace Pact*, 212–19.

[26] Letters from The Federal Farmer, no. 15, January 18, 1788, in *The Complete Anti-Federalist*, ed. Herbert J. Storing (Chicago, IL: University of Chicago Press, 1981), 2:315–16, quoted in Cornell, *Other Founders*, 90–91.

the Articles of Confederation. Congress approved, clearing the path for the gathering that took place in Philadelphia the following year.

The federalist conception of a national republic drew heavily from a perspective that I have labeled the developmental vision. Interests left out of the political maneuvering at the state level, or disenchanted with the outcomes of those machinations, joined coalitions of nationalists who upbraided states for their competitive rivalries. New nationalist-oriented coalitions of merchants, traders, and manufacturers emerged. One such group in Philadelphia thought it "a very *ridiculous idea*, that every State should enjoy a power of regulating its trade; for every State has a *separate* interest to pursue, and their different regulations will always clash." The solution was self-evident: "We must act united; we must sacrifice a little for the good of the whole." The quickest way to achieve this was to vest Congress with more power.[27]

Advocates of the developmental vision argued that an authentically national perspective, embodied in a continental union, could counter centrifugal forces such as interstate rivalries, disorder on the frontiers, and international commercial discrimination. Interest would remain the glue that cemented this union. But rather than pitting local or sectional groups against each other, a common commitment to expansion and development of the West would create truly national relationships capable of binding the states and sections together. Interregional commerce, eased by national internal improvements in transportation and communication, along with international trade, would unify rather than divide Americans.

By projecting trade and commerce westward, the older sections of the nation would be unified. By meshing economic development, the states' political tendencies toward disintegration would be reversed. At its most

---

[27] Marks, *Independence*, 72–80; "Pro Bono Republicae," *Pennsylvania Gazette*, 11 May 1785, in University of Virginia Etext Center, cited in Matson and Onuf, *Union of Interests*, 76–77. Another proto-nationalist from Maryland wrote that if "each state is laying duties on the trade of its neighbours, our commerce cannot be reduced to a system, and our profits must be uncertain." "Messrs. Printers," *Maryland Journal and Baltimore Advertiser*, August 9, 1785, vol. 12, no. 63, 2–3, in Early American Newspapers, Series I, 1690–1876, quoted in Matson and Onuf, *Union of Interests*, 76–77. Hendrickson argues the calling of new Convention was based on "too many vital interests that were not getting vindicated through the federal government, and signal respects on which the Americans believed that their interests met in more points than they differed." *Peace Pact*, 211. For a more class-driven interpretation of the developmental vision, see Charles Sellers, *The Market Revolution: Jacksonian America, 1815–1846* (New York: Oxford University Press, 1991), 31–33. See also Peter S. Onuf, *Jefferson's Empire: The Language of American Nationhood* (Charlottesville: University Press of Virginia, 2000).

abstract level, the developmental vision substituted future integration for past competition and division. In all instances, a national government would play a crucial supporting role for ambitious, entrepreneurial individuals. As two scholars put it recently, Americans would "go it alone more or less together."[28]

Placing this view of political economy at the center of their search for a more energetic government also pushed the nationalists toward the liberal ideal of public gain grounded in individuals' economic success. As the federalists came to grips with the clash of sectional interests, they reconceptualized the political economy. They argued that enterprising citizens could create new value – value that the larger community would ultimately share. Wealth was not just a personal reward for hard work; it produced more wealth in the form of capital. If properly guided, that capital would benefit the entire polity. In this fashion, seemingly opposed economic interests could presumably benefit from their mutual success.[29]

Applying the developmental vision to the West was the key to resolving sectional tensions. As long as interests were aggregated along the lines of North vs South or merchants vs farmers, the potential for national development remained limited. When disparate interests were projected onto the Western landscape, however, Americans would come together as a closer, more "natural" union to exploit the rich natural bounty that they shared in common. This more expansive vision also had the distinct political advantage of appealing to a broad coalition. It certainly transcended elite coastal merchants and staple producers. Ardent nationalist and architect of the strategy that standardized spelling and pronunciation in America, Noah Webster, stated the possibilities boldly: "On an energetic continental government principally depend our tranquility at home and our respectability among foreign nations."[30]

[28] Matson and Onuf, *Union of Interests*, 79; Nicholas Onuf and Peter Onuf, *Nations, Markets, and War: Modern History and the American Civil War* (Charlottesville, VA: University of Virginia Press, 2006), 163. Even when Jefferson began to sharply criticize a too energetic national state in the 1790s, he maintained a commitment to westward expansion as crucial to the union. Onuf, *Jefferson's Empire*. For the roots of American territorial expansion, see Robert Kagan, *Dangerous Nation: America's Place in the World from Its Earliest Days to the Dawn of the Twentieth Century* (New York, NY: Knopf, 2006), chap. 1.
[29] Marks, *Independence*, 201–6; Matson and Onuf, *Union of Interests*, 80.
[30] Noah Webster , *Sketches of American Policy* (Hartford, CT: Hudson and Goodwin, 1785), Early American Imprints Series I [doc. no.19366], 48, quoted in Marks, *Independence*, 121–22; Matson and Onuf, *Union of Interests*, 93.

This vision also appealed to Thomas Jefferson. To be sure, land, and plenty of it, was the starting point for Jefferson. As he wrote John Jay in 1785, with "lands enough to employ an infinite number of people in their cultivation," Jefferson envisioned a republic populated by independent farmers "tied to their country & wedded to its liberty & interests by the most lasting bands." The attachment created by this economic independence and friendly intercourse would do far more than government to ensure the loyalty of Americans. Indeed, Jefferson believed that the egalitarian impact of a land inhabited by independent farmers would create a nation of "one heart and one mind," without the threat of central government regimentation.[31]

Owning their own property, however, hardly ensured that trade connected Americans to each other, or that they could compete internationally. Americans must endeavor, Jefferson wrote Washington in 1784, "to share as large a portion as we can of this modern source of wealth and power." This required government initiative, financing, and organization. The connections between individual opportunity, western expansion, and the national government were forged in what was arguably the Continental Congress's most important act – the Northwest Ordinance of 1787. The Northwest Ordinance spelled out the rules that would apply to territorial expansion in that region and the laws that would apply during the interim territorial phase.[32]

While nature's bounty and willing citizens made such opportunities possible, they could only be realized through properly structured *national* rules that would ensure orderly development, and more importantly, the continued allegiance of an ever-expanding frontier population. This required the exercise of *national* authority to protect land titles, ensure security, forge trading opportunities, and reinforce shared values regarding religion, education, and language. The Northwest Ordinance

[31] Thomas Jefferson to John Jay, August 23, 1785, in *The Papers of Thomas Jefferson*, ed. Julian P. Boyd, 27 vols. to date (Princeton, NJ: Princeton University Press, 1950–), 8:426, quoted in Larson, *Internal Improvement*, 41; Thomas Jefferson, First Inaugural Address, March 4, 1801, in *A Compilation of the Messages and Papers of the Presidents, 1789–1897*, ed. James D. Richardson (Washington, D.C.: GPO, 1896), 1:322, quoted in Onuf, *Empire*, 15.

[32] Jefferson to Washington, March 15, 1784, in Boyd, *Papers of Thomas Jefferson*, 7:27, quoted in Larson, *Internal Improvement*, 41; Peter S. Onuf, *Statehood and Union: A History of the Northwest Ordinance* (Bloomington, IN: Indiana University Press, 1987), cited in Richard R. John, "Governmental Institutions as Agents of Change: Rethinking American Political Development in the Early Republic, 1787–1835," *Studies in American Political Development*, 11, no. 2 (Fall 1997): 370.

perfected this amalgam and underwrote one of the Constitution's central compromises. It endorsed the social and economic impulse that powered American development for the next two centuries – an emphasis on individual initiative that capitalized on abundant opportunity to realize economic benefits central to the pursuit of happiness.

The market would order a great deal of activity through the pursuit of individual opportunity. But the market required a common vision of orderly economic development and the legal wherewithal to impose that vision on a mobile, diverse, and economically opportunistic population. Just as religion and the local commitment to the common good tempered the more aggressive edges of unbridled economic competition, statutes like the Northwest Ordinance, and eventually, the Constitution, provided a template that allowed Americans to envision both an orderly market and an extended polity that transcended state borders.

BETWEEN THE "MARKETPLACE" AND THE "SAVAGE, BARBARIAN WORLD BEYOND": CONSOLIDATING THE VISION

The Anti-Federalists criticized the Constitution on a number of fronts. It would lead to aristocratic control; it did not provide for adequate representation of the people's interests; it did not adequately ensure for the separation of powers; it would lead to judicial tyranny; it did not adequately protect the rights of individuals or the press; it would create oppressive levels of taxation enforced by an army of functionaries. The Anti-Federalists' greatest fear was of "consolidation." Even the states, some Anti-Federalists argued, were too large to protect the liberty of their citizens.[33]

The Anti-Federalist "Lycurgus" spoke for many when he reminded citizens that "all political writers of eminence agree that a republic should not comprehend a large territory." They argued that ceding so much authority to a powerful national government would trade a hypothetical danger – one that the states were particularly well-suited to guard against – for the more tangible threat of tyranny. The government envisioned by the Constitution would not share power with the states, Massachusetts merchant Elbridge Gerry asserted. Gerry, who refused to sign the Constitution, insisted that "the Constitution proposed has few, if any *federal* features." Rather, it was "a system of *national* government."

---

[33] Cornell, *Other Founders*, 30–31.

In the hands of would-be tyrants such consolidation could threaten the liberty of all Americans.[34]

Some Anti-Federalists also insisted that there simply was no need for a stronger central government. Because democratic republics eschewed war, there was little reason to fear that the states would arm and confront each other, James Monroe argued. "The causes of half the wars," Monroe insisted, "are caprice, folly, and ambition: these belong to the higher orders of governments, where the passions of one, or of a few individuals, direct the fate of the rest of the community." Democracies were different, Monroe continued, because "there is an equality among the citizens." With democratically inclined, peace-loving republics occupying the American continent, there was less need for a national union.[35]

The federalists responded that it was the *states* that were artificial. States were impeding the union of natural and national economic interests. The commerce that promised to unite the nation was thwarted by the states' commitment to their existing boundaries and political apparatus. Federalists complained that Americans were unwilling to concede any individual liberties, even though doing so might benefit all in the end. Even the Anti-Federalist "Cato" (most likely George Clinton, Governor of New York) wrote, America's natural advantages were "unoperative, since we refuse to enjoy or direct them to their true and capital purposes" because of "partial and incomplete notions of civil and political liberty." Mature conceptions of liberty required sacrificing absolute liberty.[36]

Federalists who embraced an expansive, dynamic view of the nation insisted that the crucial divide was not one between warring interests but "between the world of the marketplace" – where interests might converge and serve the greater good – and "the savage, barbarian world beyond,"

---

[34] Lycurgus, *New York Daily Advertiser*, April 2, 1787 in *The Documentary History of the Ratification of the Constitution,* ed. Merrill Jensen, John P. Kaminski, Gaspare J. Saladino, et al., 20 vols. to date (Madison: State Historical Society of Wisconsin, 1976–), 13:59; A. Elbridge Gerry to the Massachusetts General Court, November 3, 1787, *Massachusetts Centinal,* in Jensen, et al., *Documentary History of the Ratification* 13:548–50, quoted in Cornell, *Other Founders,* 29.

[35] Jonathan Elliot, ed. *The Debates in the Several State Conventions on the Adoption of the Federal Constitution as Recommended by the General Convention at Philadelphia in 1787 ...,* 2nd edn, 5 vols. (1836; repr. New York: Burt Franklin, 1974), 3:209, quoted in Hendrickson, *Peace Pact,* 12.

[36] Cato, "To the Public," *The New-Haven Gazette, and the Connecticut Magazine,* January 25, 1787, vol. 1, no. 49, in Early American Newspapers, Series I, quoted in Matson and Onuf, *Union of Interests,* 96. On the identity of Cato, see Einhorn, *American Taxation,* 175.

where rival states preyed upon each other for self-interested reasons. It was Great Britain, Fabius noted, that "so perfectly united those distant extremes, *private security* of life, liberty and property, with exertion of *public force*."[37]

Liberty, many federalists argued, was best preserved by powerful, not weak national government. Like it or not, powerful states in Europe had professional armies financed by public debt and reliable revenue streams. Citizens living in any state that did not possess such institutions risked losing their liberty in the interplay of power politics. Sacrificing the illusion of some liberties in the short run, federalists argued, would preserve real independence through strength.[38]

To overcome the prevailing republican rhetoric and established institutional arrangements, federalists needed a political mechanism that would allow them to compromise on issues dear to their opponents without sacrificing national vision. Federalism provided that mechanism. Pushed by recession, increasingly acrimonious interstate commercial rivalries, and the ominous threat of agrarian rebellion foreshadowed in Shays Rebellion, delegates from all of the states save Rhode Island, gathered in Philadelphia. Edmund Randolph had his doubts about stronger national government. But he was certain that the current situation could not endure. "Every day brings forth some new crisis," he wrote George Washington in March 1787. Washington did not need any prodding. "I predict the worst consequences from a half-starved, limping government, always moving upon crutches and tottering at every step," Washington wrote to Virginia governor Benjamin Harrison in 1784.[39]

When Daniel Shays and his fellow debt-ridden supporters marched on the Hampshire County, Massachusetts court, refusing to pay their

---

[37] Matson and Onuf, *Union of Interests,* 97; Fabius, no. 9, "Observations on the Constitution proposed by the Federal Convention," in Jensen, Kaminski, and Saladino, *Documentary History of Ratification,* 17:261, cited in Edling, *Revolution in Favor of Government,* 69.

[38] Edling, *Revolution in Favor of Government,* 220. Peter Onuf argues persuasively that the American provinces were not "terminal polities." They were not autonomous and depended upon the metropolis, both economically and politically. Nor did the Revolution make the states autonomous. Rather, they were now part of a continental union, on which they depended to secure their rights and interests. Onuf, "Federalism, Democracy, and Liberty," 1–3.

[39] Edmund Randolph to George Washington, March 11, 1787, in *The Papers of George Washington Digital Edition,* ed. Theodore J. Crackel (Charlottesville, VA: University of Virginia Press, Rotunda, 2007), http://rotunda.upress.virginia.edu/pgwde/, quoted in Richard B. Morris, "The Confederation Period and the American Historian," *William and Mary Quarterly,* 3rd ser., 13, no. 2 (April 1956): 140; Washington to Benjamin Harrison, January 18, 1784, in Crackel, *Papers of George Washington Digital Edition,* quoted in Morris, "Confederation Period," 139.

taxes, the local militia sat on its hands. Only Virginia responded to the Confederation's request for half a million dollars to raise a fighting force. Federalists found this turn of events particularly disturbing. The delegates who met in Philadelphia were acutely aware of the real possibility of disunion. By grappling with the hard realities of the nation's political dilemma, delegates crafted a remarkable series of compromises that salvaged and significantly strengthened the union.[40]

Surprisingly, the federalists embraced compromises guaranteeing that states would have a powerful say in the national government's affairs. This was a bold move, considering that the colonies had just fought a war over the issues of divided sovereignty within the British empire. Many federalists came to Philadelphia believing that the states' wayward actions lay at the heart of the Confederation's problems. Yet, the fear of disunion, or even worse, the possibility of regional unions drawn along sectional lines, led these men to embrace the "Connecticut Compromise" that preserved an autonomous role for the states through their two votes in Senate. They also relied on the mechanism of federalism which reserved to the states those powers not enumerated for the General Government. Supporters of ratification stressed that the states would remain an important part of governance. They sought to mollify their critics during ratification by insisting that the states were the ultimate assurance against national abuse of citizen's rights. This strategy inadvertently reinforced the strong attachments that many citizens felt for their states.[41]

Like the developmental vision of the West, federalism provided a framework that was vague enough to allow the interested parties to imagine a beneficial outcome in the future, while protecting more proximate interests for the time being. The federal relationship built into the Constitution allowed would-be nation builders to address very real sectional differences without formally writing geographical sections into the constitution, as some had sought to do.[42]

In an ironic twist that rivaled their legitimation of states' authority, supporters of the Constitution also implicitly endorsed the conception of popular sovereignty. Sovereignty, James Wilson of Pennsylvania pronounced, "*resides* in the PEOPLE, as the fountain of government." Determined to

---

[40] E. Wayne Carp, "The Problem of National Defense in the Early American Republic," in *The American Revolution: Its Character and Limits*, ed. Jack P. Greene (New York, NY: New York University Press, 1987), 33; McDonald, *States' Rights*, 14–15.
[41] McDonald, *States' Rights*, 2–5.
[42] Matson and Onuf, *Union of Interests*, 120, 123.

counter local demagogues, federalists justified their position by looking past existing state institutions and embracing the citizens of those states rather than the public officials who represented them. After all, these citizens gave those representatives their political legitimacy. With the proper governing framework, federalists argued, citizens would see past the petty and short-sighted vision of self-interested leadership at the state level.[43]

To create a stronger General Government, federalists like James Wilson appealed to the people directly, hoping that they would reject what nationalizers considered to be their artificial attachment to state government. Popular rejection of leaders, of course, could apply at the national level as well, as Federalists like Hamilton eventually discovered first hand. Nevertheless, grounding the General Government's legitimacy in majoritarian acceptance ultimately paved the way for more energetic national governance. In fact, Jefferson would argue that it was precisely because the national government could rely on the bonds of its citizens' affections that it required no elaborate administrative machinery. While this view clashed sharply with that of Hamilton, it helps us understand how both men, and the disparate group who endorsed the constitution, could agree upon principles as radical as popular sovereignty.[44]

---

[43] James Wilson Speech in the Pennsylvania Ratifying Convention, 4 December 1787, in *Pennsylvania and the Federal Constitution, 1787–1788*, John Bach McMaster and Frederick D. Stone eds. (Philadelphia: Historical Society of Pennsylvania, 1888; New York: Da Capo Press, 1970), 316, quoted in Wood, *Creation*, 530, as cited in Onuf, "Federalism, Democracy, and Liberty," 4; Cornell, *Other Founders*, 73; Matson and Onuf, *Union of Interests*, 143.

[44] Michael Mann would refer to this kind of authority as "infrastructural" authority. Rather than the power to coerce, proponents of the Constitution sought to expand the essential coordinating mechanisms of the state to the territorial expanse that covered the United States (and its territories). While the Federalists required the capacity for unlimited taxation in case of crisis, their national leaders used this authority sparingly. Rather, they sought to use the national government to coordinate and guide key groups in civil society, including some of the powerful states and localities. Mann, "Autonomous Power of the State." For an excellent application of Mann's "infrastructural power," see Brewer, *Sinews of Power*, xx.

Hendrickson's emphasis on unionist thought is also useful. As Hendrickson argues, liberal and republican terms did not apply to the vast expanse of territory that soon became the United States. The order they wanted to constitute would have to take place over a territory of "imperial" dimensions, and that the liberty they wanted to preserve consisted as much of "the liberty of states" as the freedom of individuals. These facts put the problem on an altogether different basis and ensured that the basic categories of liberal and republican thought would be thrown into a state of great perplexity by the problems that lay at the core of the unionist paradigm." *Peace Pact*, 17. See also figure 3, pp. 276, and 266–67.

Whether federalists agreed with Country Party rhetoric or not, they were confronted with a situation in the colonies that was quite different than state builders in Great Britain, as Edling points out. Citizens voted at far higher rates. In other words, they

When it came to slavery, silence accompanied vagueness. Southern supporters of the institution fought unsuccessfully to keep the topic from even being discussed. However, a formula for three-fifths representation derived from earlier discussions of the proper ratio for taxing slaves carried the day. As the correspondence between Adams and Jefferson demonstrates, these two addressed the issue with great caution and trepidation. For the most part, their letters avoided this controversial topic. The one exception occurred in 1819 as the debate over the Missouri Compromise raged. Though Adams made it clear to confidants that he thought that "Negro Slavery is an evil of Colossal magnitude," he maintained his noncommittal position in his correspondence with Jefferson. Adams claimed to be at a loss as to what should be done. For his part, Jefferson clung to the code of silence, reminding Adams that "I have most carefully avoided every public act or manifestation on that subject." Jefferson was content to leave this intractable problem to the next generation.[45]

For many of the men who advocated a more powerful central government, slavery vs independent labor, North vs South, or even state vs national government were not the fundamental divisions that threatened the new nation. Rather, they worried about how a weak and divided union could protect individual liberty at the same time that it underwrote national political and economic development. To protect citizens from the depredations of a savage world, these advocates for an energetic General Government were willing to endorse two positions that on the face of it seemed to undercut their objectives. They endorsed a permanent role for the states by accepting federalism, and the Connecticut Compromise. They also embraced popular sovereignty in the hope that the voters would recognize that their interests were not congruent with the artificial interests of state governments. The first of these compromises would impinge upon national power well into the twentieth century. But it also pushed the central government toward the position it increasingly assumed in the nineteenth century – that of coordinating agent, and developmental field marshall. The second position, embracing popular sovereignty, would

could do something about their antagonism to taxation, forcing the federalists to adapt to this situation. For a succinct summary of these points, see Lance Banning, review of *A Revolution in Favor of Government*, by Max M. Edling, *American Historical Review*, 110, no. 1 (February 2005): 132.

[45] Einhorn, *American Taxation*, 164; Ellis, *Founding Brothers*, 81–88, 239–40; Adams to William Tudor, November 20, 1819, as quoted in Ellis, *Founding Brothers*, 240; Jefferson to George Logan, May 11, 1805, in *The Writings of Thomas Jefferson*, ed. Paul L Ford 10 vols. (New York: Putnam, 1892–99), 9:141, quoted in Ellis, *Founding Brothers*, 240.

empower the federal government by the twentieth century, especially during wartime. But its more proximate impact was to reinforce state governments' constitutional role as guardians of civil rights and to limit the kinds of taxes the central government could politically sustain.

"A REVOLUTION IN FAVOR OF GOVERNMENT":
THE HIDDEN STRENGTH OF THE CONSTITUTION

The debate over ratification proved to be another critical opportunity to forge national identity – even among the Anti-Federalists who bridled at sacrificing local control to a powerful distant government. Because the approval process engaged state conventions, ratification triggered a national debate. The intensity of this debate forced all parties to think about their connection to an extended polity, regardless of their stance on the Constitution. A month after the convention adjourned, one observer in Carlisle, Pennsylvania, commented that "the new Constitution for the United States seems now to engross the attention of all ranks." "The plan of a Government proposed to us by the Convention," one Virginian noted, "affords matter for conversation by every rank of beings from the Governor to the door keeper." Even men and women who were not qualified to vote joined what amounted to a full-fledged national conversation.[46]

Broad, albeit loosely organized coalitions, emerged out of these conversations. They were roughly drawn along the lines of support and opposition. Better able to control the press and adept at putting the written word to work on behalf of their cause, those supporting the Constitution forged a national alliance. But the Anti-Federalists, especially the leaders drawn from society's elite, worked across local and state boundaries as well. Men like Luther Martin, attorney general of Maryland, Elbridge Gerry, a prosperous New England merchant and prominent politician, or Arthur Lee, a delegate to the Continental Congress, were enmeshed in a web of social, business, and political connections that extended well beyond their own states. A host of prominent Virginians – George Mason, James Monroe,

---

[46] Richard Butler to William Irvine, October 11–12, 1787, in Jensen, Kaminski, and Saladino, *Documentary History of Ratification* 2:135, quoted in Cornell, *Other Founders*, 20; George Lee Turberville to Arthur Lee, October 28, 1787, in Jensen, Kaminski, and Saladino, *Documentary History of Ratification,* 8:127, quoted in Cornell, *Other Founders*, 20; Cornell, *Other Founders*, 105. On the debate over the constitution and its interpretation, see Jack N. Rakove, *Original Meanings: Politics and Ideas in the Making of the Constitution* (New York, NY: Vintage Books, 1997).

Richard Henry Lee, to name but a few – joined the chorus. Some of the leadership's national connections dated back to the Revolution in the case of men like Richard Henry Lee and James Warren.[47]

Even though the Constitution legitimized state government, it provided ample tools for building a powerful central government as well. The *Pennsylvania Gazette* pointed out, "The year 1776 is celebrated for a revolution in favor of *Liberty*. The year 1787, it is expected, will be celebrated with equal joy, for a revolution in favor of Government." Federalists sought to build a national government that, like European states, could raise armies, tax its population, and borrow money. Establishing strong credit was a crucial component of effective statecraft, federalists argued.[48]

The unlimited capacity to tax and extend credit was the only means to ensure that financing was available when it was most needed – in times of crisis. "Limiting the powers of government to certain resources, is rendering the fund precarious," Hamilton warned, "and obliging the government to ask, instead of empowering them to command, is to destroy all confidence and credit." The capacity to expand revenues was essential to national security in Hamilton's eyes. "War," Hamilton insisted, "offers but two options – Credit or the devastation of private property. ... Tis the signal merit of a vigorous system of national credit," Hamilton continued, "that it enables a government to support war without violating property, destroying industry, or interfering unreasonably with individual enjoyments." Here was the essence of Hamilton's synthesis of liberty and strength. Only a strong, assertive central government could preserve liberty and personal freedoms.[49]

[47] Cornell, *Other Founders*, 52–53.
[48] *Pennsylvania Gazette*, September 5, 1787, in University of Virginia Etext Center, quoted in Edling, *Revolution in Favor of Government*, vii. Edling, *Revolution in Favor of Government*, 7. Many of these tools were contained in Article 1, Section 8, which provided for Congress "to lay and collect taxes, Duties, Imposts and Excises, to pay the Debts and provide for the common Defence and general Welfare of the United States." For a history of debate over that clause, see Theodore Sky, *To Provide for the General Welfare: A History of the Federal Spending Power* (Newark, NJ: University of Delaware Press, 2003).
[49] Alexander Hamilton, Speech in New York Ratifying Convention, 27 June 1788, in *American Eloquence: A Collection of Speeches and Addresses, by the Most Eminent Orators of America*, ed. Frank Moore (New York: D. Appleton, 1857), 1:202; Hamilton, Defense of the Funding System, in *Papers of Alexander Hamilton*, ed. Harold C. Syrett, et al., 27 vols. (New York: Columbia University Press, 1961–87), 52–53, quoted in Walling, *Republican Empire*, 194. Power to finance times of crisis is the overarching thesis of Walling, *Republican Empire*.

James Madison was no less certain that the national government's fate turned on the unlimited ability to tax. Would not Britain's credit "have been ruined, if it was known that her power to raise money was limited?" Madison asked. "No Government can exist, unless its powers extend to make provisions for every contingency," he proclaimed. Supporters of unlimited powers to tax and extend credit succeeded in writing this authority into the Constitution, but only by adapting to distinctive American attitudes about government.[50]

By granting the General Government the ability to impose an impost and by allowing for the unlimited extension of credit, constitutional proponents crafted a national government that would operate as a "waterfront" state, barely noticed by its citizens. Collecting imposts did not require much of a state bureaucracy. Those customs officials who were required would be confined to the waterfront, while the impost's cost was buried in the price of the goods purchased. Nor was the burden created by debt visible at the time that it was levied. Its full cost stretched into the future, again reducing its visibility. As one scholar recently put it, federalists were able to achieve their fiscal-military ends while mollifying Americans' fears of consolidation by creating a national government "that was both light and inconspicuous."[51]

The Constitution provided that the Congress would have the "Power To lay and collect Taxes, Duties, Imposts, and Excises." States were prohibited from collecting duties on imports or exports. James Madison greeted the First Federal Congress certain that an impost, once a revenue source monopolized by the states, could now be used by the national government to "protect and cherish" manufacturers. The taxing authority granted by Article I of the Constitution was comparable to, and perhaps even greater than, any British revenue program carried out in the previous two decades.[52]

Most shocking to some was the central government's ability to levy internal taxes, like excise taxes on products, or even more provocatively,

[50] James Madison, Convention Debates, June 6, 1787, in Jensen, Kaminski, and Saladino, *Documentary History of Ratification*, 9:997, quoted in Edling, *Revolution in Favor of Government*, 172.
[51] Edling, *Revolution in Favor of Government*, 10, 185–87, 192, 196, 199.
[52] U.S. Const. art. 1, sec. 8, cl. 1–2; McDonald, *States' Rights*, 18; *Annals of Congress*, 1st Cong., 1st sess., 9 April 1789, 116, quoted in Larson, *Internal Improvement*, 45; Slaughter, *Whiskey Rebellion*, 23. This was one of many explicit prohibitions placed upon the states. These corresponded directly to some of the earlier problems faced under the Articles of Confederation.

direct taxes on property (including slaves.) These, opponents feared, were infinitely expandable. The "Federal Farmer" was quick to point out the difference between excise taxes and imposts. "External taxes are import duties, which are laid on imported goods; they may usually be collected in a few seaport towns, and of a few individuals, though ultimately paid by the consumer; a few officers can collect them, and they can be carried no higher than trade will bear." In other words, they were self-limiting. Among eighteenth-century students of political economy this was well understood. "The best taxes are such as are levied upon consumption," David Hume argued, "especially those of luxury; because such taxes are least felt by the people. They seem, in some measure, voluntary; since a man may chuse how far he will use the commodity which is taxed."[53]

Equally important, the mechanism for collecting them was both lightly staffed and invisible to most consumers. As French Enlightenment philosopher Baron de Montesquieu noted, "Duties on commodities are the ones the least felt by the people, because no formal request is made for them." "They can be so wisely managed that the people will be almost unaware that they pay them." The internal administration of imposts required relatively little state machinery. Oliver Ellsworth, a delegate to the Connecticut ratifying convention, emphasized that collecting duties "does not fill the country with revenue officers, but is confined to the sea coast and is chiefly a water operation."[54]

Hamilton had ample experience with direct taxation in his home state of New York. The state lurched from near-rebellion, when tax collectors actually did their job in the early 1780s, to lax tax enforcement. Politicians winked at the latter, eager to do "what will *please*," according to Hamilton, rather than "what will *benefit* the people." State legislators, according to Hamilton, "cabal and intrigue to throw the burthen off their respective constituents," when it came to taxes. As Secretary of

[53] Letter from the Federal Farmer, No.3, October 10, 1787, in *The Antifederalists*, ed. Cecelia M. Kenyon (Indianapolis, IN: Bobbs-Merrill, 1966), 223, quoted in Slaughter, *Whiskey Rebellion*, 24; David Hume, "Essay Twenty: Of Taxes," in *Political Essays*, ed. Knud Haakonssen (Cambridge, UK: Cambridge University Press, 1994), 161–65, quoted in Edling, *Revolution in Favor of Government*, 194.
[54] Charles de Secondat, baron de Montesquieu, *The Spirit of The Laws*. trans. Anne M. Cohler, Basia C. Miller, Harold Stone (New York, NY: Cambridge University Press, 1989), 217, quoted in Edling, *Revolution in Favor of Government*, 194; Edling, *Revolution in Favor of Government*, 185; Oliver Ellsworth, Speech in the Connecticut Convention, January 7, in Jensen, Kaminski, and Saladino, *Documentary History of Ratification*, 15:274, quoted in Edling, *Revolution in Favor of Government*, 196. See also Einhorn, *American Taxation*, 168.

the Treasury, Hamilton presided over a regime that collected almost 95 percent of its tax revenues from the impost.[55]

Internal taxes posed a greater threat. One Anti-Federalist warned that revenues such as poll, land, and excise taxes "may fix themselves on every person and species of property in the community; they may be carried to any lengths, and in proportion as they are extended, numerous officers must be employed to assess them, and to enforce the collection of them." Brutus put the matter more bluntly, writing that "this power, exercised without limitation, will introduce itself into every corner of the city, and country – It will wait upon the ladies at their toilett, and will not leave them in any of their domestic concerns; it will accompany them to the ball, the play, and the assembly; it will go with them when they visit, and will, on all occasions, sit beside them in their carriages, nor will it desert them even at church; it will enter the house of every gentleman, watch over his cellar, wait upon his cook in the kitchen, follow the servants into the parlour, preside over the table, and note down all that he eats or drinks. ... To all these different classes of people, and in all these circumstances, in which it will attend them, the language in which it will address them, will be GIVE! GIVE!" Even those supporting the Constitution were not insensitive to the danger of excise taxes. Hamilton, for instance, argued that their use should be "confined within a narrow compass." "The genius of the people, Hamilton warned, "will ill brook the inquisitive and preemptory spirit of excise laws."[56]

Those opposed to internal taxes envisioned a spiraling cycle of collection, and ultimately military force to back up this authority. These were the same arguments that *all* of the patriots had used recently in

[55] Alexander Hamilton to Robert Morris, August 13, 1782, in Syrett, *Papers of Alexander Hamilton*, 3:135, quoted in Becker, *Revolution, Reform*, 163; Hamilton to Morris, August 13, 1782, in Syrett, *Papers of Alexander Hamilton*, 3:135, quoted in Robin Einhorn, "Institutional Reality in an Age of Slavery: Taxation and Democracy in the States," in *Ruling Passions: Political Economy in Nineteenth-Century America*, ed. Richard R. John (University Park, PA: Pennsylvania State University Press, 2006), 22; Edling, *Revolution in Favor of Government*, 209.
[56] Letter from the Federal Farmer, No.3, October 10, 1787, in Kenyon, *Antifederalists*, 223–24, quoted in Slaughter, *Whiskey Rebellion*, 24; Brutus, no. 6, *New York Journal*, December 27, 1787, in Jensen, Kaminski, and Saladino, *Documentary History of Ratification*, 15:114, quoted in Edling, *Revolution in Favor of Government*, 187; Alexander Hamilton, "The Federalist No. 12," in Jensen, Kaminski, and Saladino, *Documentary History of Ratification*, 14:237, quoted in Edling, *Revolution in Favor of Government*, 196.

overthrowing British rule. Such appeals remained a powerful obstacle to effective central governance. The states and local governments, Anti-Federalists argued, knew best the needs of their citizens, if indeed taxes must be levied. Anti-Federalists feared fighting the American Revolution all over again – this time against their fellow countrymen. Granting the power to levy internal taxes to the General Government also represented a direct threat to the life blood of the states' source of revenue and power. To Hamilton, this meant "concurrent jurisdiction" – both states and central government would need to exercise "prudence and firmness" in sharing this responsibility. To Anti-Federalist Patrick Henry, the power was far more threatening to Virginia's tax base: "I tell you, they shall not have the soul of Virginia," Henry thundered.[57]

If the power of state legislatures to levy taxes was compromised, states would count for little in the political calculus, Anti-Federalists feared. "After this constitution is once established," an opponent warned, "it is too evident that we shall be obliged to fill up the offices of assemblymen and councillors, as we do those of constables, by appointing men to serve whether they will or not, and fining them if they refuse." The states also lost another crucial fiscal resource – the power to issue paper money. Proscriptions on state-issued currency was all the more painful because states had used this mechanism as a way to finance emergencies such as wars and economic recessions, without having to raise property or poll taxes.[58]

By monopolizing the power to tax commerce at the same time that it controlled the ability to issue money, the Constitution eliminated the mechanisms by which the states had funded their debt. Given Hamilton's assumption of state debts, this loss might seem inconsequential. But like

---

[57] Ellis, *Founding Brothers*, 7; Edling, *Revolution in Favor of Government*, 189; Slaughter, *Whiskey Rebellion*, 24–25; Alexander Hamilton, "The Federalist No.31," in *The Federalist*, ed. Jacob E. Cooke (Middletown, CT: Wesleyan University Press, 1961), 198, quoted in Einhorn, *American Taxation*, 174; Patrick Henry, Virginia Convention Debates, June 7, 1788, in Jensen, Kaminski, and Saladino, *Documentary History of Ratification*, 9:1045–46, quoted in Einhorn, *American Taxation*, 174.
[58] "An Old Whig," no. 1, in Jensen, Kaminski, and Saladino, *Documentary History of Ratification*, 13:379, quoted in Edling, *Revolution in Favor of Government*, 183; Richard Sylla, John B. Legler, and John J. Wallis, "Banks and State Public Finance in the New Republic: The United States, 1790–1860," *Journal of Economic History*, 47, no. 2 (June, 1987): 391–403; the practice was so widespread that scholars have referred to it as a system of "currency finance." As Sylla et al. point out, banks soon replaced paper issuance as an important revenue source for the states. See also, E. James Ferguson, "Currency Finance: An Interpretation of Colonial Monetary Practices," *William and Mary Quarterly*, 3rd ser., 10, no. 2 (April 1953): 153–80.

those who advocated for unlimited access to credit for the central government, Anti-Federalists understood that the capacity to incur and fund debt was a crucial source of autonomy.

State and local taxes declined in both the North and the South in the wake of Hamilton's move. What mattered from the vantage points of citizens situated in different states, however, was the revenue's destination. In Massachusetts, which had maintained relatively high state and local taxes, the tradeoff seemed fair in return for the federal assumption of state debts. In Virginia, however, citizens had slashed state and local taxes after the Revolution. They did so, in part, by lowering costs through disestablishment of the Anglican Church. Virginians soon faced a situation in which federal taxes replaced state and local taxes. Not only did the Virginians complain about high taxes, but now those taxes went to a distant, and for many, alien, government. By the mid-90s, the total per capita taxes for free Virginians was $3.22 a year (compared to $3.63 a year in Massachusetts). Of the total per capita tax burden that Virginians paid, however, a whopping 70 percent went to the federal government, compared to 43 percent in the case of Massachusetts.[59]

Proponents of the Constitution also preserved ample military power for the new nation. Armies could be raised directly by the national government. The General Government was granted the authority to organize, arm, and discipline militia, and could use them to suppress insurrections. It could raise and keep armies during peacetime, a grant of power that resembled strong European counterparts and that distinguished it from the Confederation. Like their Anti-Federalist critics, proponents of these clauses understood that America's distance from the centers of European power reduced the need for a large standing army. But they also recognized that the United States was surrounded by potential enemies and that it needed the capacity to respond energetically to potential threats. Nor was war in the modern age a place for amateurs, according to Alexander Hamilton. Rather, it was "a science to be acquired and perfected by diligence, by perseverance, by time, and by practice."[60]

---

[59] James H, Henderson, "Taxation and Political Culture: Massachusetts and Virginia, 1760–1800," *William and Mary Quarterly*, 3rd ser., 47, no. 1 (January 1990): 109–14. For percentages, see Henderson, "Taxation," Table VI, p. 112.

[60] Edling, *Revolution in Favor of Government*, 89, 98–99; Alexander Hamilton, "The Federalist, No. 25," in Jensen, Kaminski, and Saladino, *Documentary History of Ratification*, 15:62, quoted in Edling, *Revolution in Favor of Government*, 98.

Defenders of the Constitution insisted that the alternative to their plan spelled doom. Rather than thirteen independent states, it was likely that a smaller number of confederacies would emerge, each with its own taxing and military power. The situation would soon mirror the European continent, with each confederacy protecting itself and taxing its citizens for this expense. As Publius warned, "The moment of its [American Union] dissolution will be the date of a new order of things. ... Instead of deriving from our situation the precious advantage which Great Britain has derived from hers, the face of America will be but a copy of that of the continent of Europe. It will present liberty everywhere crushed between standing armies and perpetual taxes." Even republican vigilance could not protect warring confederacies from building up the same kind of fiscal/military states that stalked the European continent should union fail.[61]

"SHALL THERE BE A NATIONAL GOVERNMENT OR NOT?": PARTY, PUBLIC POLICY, AND NATION-BUILDING

While the Constitution provided a template for what a national government might become, no issue dominated political discourse in the republic's first thirty years more than the debate over what, in fact, the national government actually was. As Constitutional Convention delegate and Pennsylvania judge Francis Hopkinson noted in his essays and poetry, the Constitution provided a "new roof" for the American "mansion." While Hopkinson satirized those who worried that the walls, constructed of the states, would "moulder away," leaving the roof "suspended in the air, threatening destruction to all who should come under it," he had no doubt that the foundation would hold. The refrain from his poem entitled "The New Roof: A Song For Federal Mechanics" proclaimed, "For our roof we will raise, and our song still shall be, our government firm, and our citizens free."[62]

---

[61] Hendrickson, *Peace Pact*, 8–10; Alexander Hamilton, "The Federalist No. 41," in Cooke, *Federalist*, 272, quoted in Hendrickson, *Peace Pact*, 9.

[62] Francis Hopkinson, *The Miscellaneous Essays and Occasional Writing of Francis Hopkinson, Esq.* (Philadelphia, PA: T. Dobson [etc.], 1792; University of Virginia Library Digital Collections, 1996), 282, 304–5 and refrain, 321. John M. Murrin provided a gloss on this construction, arguing that the Constitution provided a "roof without walls." "Epilogue: 'A Roof Without Walls: The Dilemma of American National identity'," in Beeman, Botein, and Carter, *Beyond Confederation*, 333–348.

Political practices and the very debate over the scope of the General Government helped frame the walls that eventually supported a constitutional "roof." Day-to-day politics ultimately determined which constitutional powers would be exercised and which would remain dormant. This, in turn, influenced perceptions about what was "natural," and what was exceptional. Many of these decisions were crucial to the very life of the fledgling republic. Nor was the survival of this new government assured. There was good reason to label this period the "politics of anxious extremes."[63]

Public policy debates continued the work of self definition begun by the Revolution and carried forward by the constitutional debate. Contests over how to handle the debt, where to locate the nation's capital, whether the General Government had a role to play in developing transportation networks, and debates over territorial expansion addressed some of the questions left unresolved by the Constitution's ratification. Policy outcomes and the debates surrounding them also laid the groundwork for more enduring divisions that transformed national politics from contests between shifting factions to the beginnings of a two-party system. Those who lobbied for interpretations that favored a more energetic General Government did not always prevail – especially after the Jeffersonian "revolution" of 1800. However, it was not uncommon for Jeffersonian opponents of consolidation to strengthen the General Government in order to achieve desired ends. They did so without altering their anti-statist rhetoric.[64]

Threats from powerful European nations impinged on the daily lives of most Americans. By the summer of 1794, the situation was acute. Having recently prepared for war against its old antagonist Great Britain, the Washington administration now shifted gears in response to threats posed by the French Revolution. On the western frontier, the administration could not trust its own citizens. Seeking better opportunities for

---

[63] "Politics of anxious extremes," is the phrase used by Freeman. *Affairs of Honor*, 10. As Michael F. Holt has noted in his sweeping history of the Whig Party, "Events mattered; they, and not just social structures, economic conditions, fixed political contexts, or ideology, often shaped subsequent behavior." *The Rise and Fall of the American Whig Party: Jacksonian Politics and the Onset of the Civil War* (New York, NY: Oxford University Press, 1999), xi. And as Andrew Cayton has reminded us, interests mattered as well. "'Separate Interests' and the Nation-State: The Washington Administration and the Origins of Regionalism in the Trans-Appalachian West," *Journal of American History*, 79, no. 1 (June 1992): 39–67.

[64] On the conflicting strains that constituted the republican "experiment," see Larson, *Internal Improvement*, 1–3.

trade and greater autonomy, these frontiersman viewed foreign governments as potential benefactors.[65]

Whatever one's prescription for governance, it was apparent that the basis of political representation had been shifting ever since the Revolution. Growing numbers of citizens interpreted the Constitution as meaning the "freedom to be left alone." The Bill of Rights provided substantive protections for the individual, not only by specifying his rights, but also by providing the kinds of structural protections for citizens to participate in their own governance through juries and local governments that would guard against the encroachment upon those rights by self-interested government officials. This legal set of protections, however, would have meant little without the social revolution that accompanied it and that changed electoral practices. Rather than deferring to their "betters" through virtual representation, Americans, bound only by localist self-interest, demanded more direct representation by men who shared their immediate interests. Any talk of internal taxes, for instance, like the excise tax on whiskey passed in 1791, was bound to bring the debate over representation to a boil, just as it had in 1765. Writing in 1792, one Westerner spelled out his criticism of distant, virtual representation: "Even the House of Representatives must necessarily be too limited in point of numbers, and in point of information will possess too little knowledge of the citizens, and too feeble a participation in the particular circumstances of the subjects of taxation," to properly levy internal taxes.[66]

---

[65] Meanwhile, British diplomats quietly sought to improve relations with the United States. British diplomats hoped to enlist the Americans as allies in their battle against the dreaded French revolutionary infection. But British *realpolitik* did not stop western settlers from seeking a better deal from Great Britain than the raw deal their own government offered on trade. The British Ambassador to the United States, George Hammond, viewed the tension between western commercial interests and their eastern counterparts as so contradictory that "the adherence of the former to the federal Constitution and the political connection itself between the two divisions of the continent depend on a very precarious sort of tenure." Precarious, in fact, characterized the fledgling nation's very prospects for survival. Hammond is quoted in Slaughter, *Whiskey Rebellion*, 190–91.

[66] Gordon S. Wood, *The Radicalism of the American Revolution* (New York, NY: Knopf, 1992), 336; for the balance between individual protections and structural safeguards in the Bill of Rights, see Akhil Reed Amar, *The Bill of Rights: Creation and Reconstruction* (New Haven, CT: Yale University Press, 1998); for the history of this opposition to decision-making removed from specific local conditions, see Slaughter, *Whiskey Rebellion*, chap. 1; Sidney, "On the Injustice of the Excise Law and the Secretary's Report," *National Gazette*, May 24, 1792, vol. 1, no. 60, p. 1, in Early American Newspapers, Series I, quoted in Slaughter, *Whiskey Rebellion*, 129.

If virtual representation failed adequately to convey direct self-interest, administrative mechanisms threatened to stifle it entirely. Bureaucratic power constituted a particularly ominous threat to individual liberty and republican order. Indeed, legislation that did not conform to a given interest's localistic perspective was often perceived to be the handi-work of executive officers eager to expand their control over a distant populace.[67]

As we have already seen, those men who supported the Constitution in 1787 reluctantly expanded the potential for public participation. In order to create a counterweight grounded in the populace, the Constitution called for a national citizenry – "We the people of the United States." Yet these same men carefully limited access to the deliberations of the constitutional convention. Anti-Federalists complained bitterly about this closed-door policy. How could public opinion be consulted if the debate was hermetically sealed? One Anti-Federalist assailed this rebuke to "public information or opinion." The delegates, according to Centinel, seem "to have been determined to monopolize the exclusive merit of the discovery, or rather as if darkness was essential to its success they precluded all communication with the people, by closing their doors."[68]

Once the document was released, debate over ratification provided an ideal opportunity for Federalists to explain some of the central clauses of the Constitution and to address head-on some of its more unpopular features. The debate also allowed Federalists to spell out some of the benefits of strong central government. A letter from "a Gentleman in Philadelphia," published in July, 1787, explained that any direct taxes contemplated would be used for clearly specified benefits: bounties for shipbuilding and fishing. A standing army supported another tangible benefit: pressuring Spain to open the Mississippi to American trade. The Federalists were after bigger game than a sham ratification; they sought to explain the real need for some of the same powers wielded by European states. They insisted that majority rule distinguished British North America from those European powers, because popular sovereignty protected the new nation from its worst fears about granting such powers.[69]

---

[67] Slaughter, *Whiskey Rebellion*, 130–31.

[68] Waldstreicher, *Midst of Perpetual Fetes*, 86; Centinel, 4, *Philadelphia Independent Gazetteer*, November 30, 1787, Jensen, Kaminski, and Saladino, *Documentary History of Ratification*, 14:323, cited in Edling, *Revolution in Favor of Government*, 24.

[69] Edling, *Revolution in Favor of Government*, 28–29, 75. Edling discounts ideology as the factor that distinguishes the American case from the British. He notes that such fears

As word of ratification from distant parts trickled in, dozens of locales held celebrations that included local craftsmen, clergymen, professionals, and other worthies. Ratification was often linked directly to the Declaration of Independence, which connected supporters to the history of the nation. That these celebrations had an edge to them is amply demonstrated by the exclusion of Anti-Federalists and by the way symbols were manipulated. After the ninth state (New Hampshire) ratified the Constitution, for instance, most celebrations reduced the number of toasts from thirteen, to nine. By 1789, patriotic orators added the constitutional solution to the litany of remarkable achievements accomplished by the nation's founders.[70]

Anti-Federalists responded in kind. But their foes had changed the rules, demanding a greater degree of order and decorum in these street rituals. For instance, the day after Christmas 1787, violence broke out in Carlyle, Pennsylvania, when local Anti-Federalists sought to disrupt a celebration of that state's ratification. Blows were exchanged, a cannon was destroyed, and observers no doubt found it "laughable to see Lawyers, Doctors, Colonels, Captains etc. ... leave the scene of their rejoicing in such haste." The "rioters," however, did not find it funny when they were arrested and jailed. Ultimately, they were freed from the jurisdiction of

existed in both countries. The distinguishing feature was the Americans' ability to *act* on their fears. This was the product of economic and demographic features, particularly the fact that consumer goods were imported in America, the wider distribution of land in America – which meant that direct taxes would be widely distributed as well, and the shorter terms of office held by elected officials [56–57].

The more elite leaders of the Anti-Federalists were concerned about the erosion of deference to virtuous elites. See Wood, *Radicalism*, and Edling, *Revolution in Favor of Government*. Mercy Otis Warren, for instance, chastised the "absurd enthusiasm that often spreads itself over the lower classes of life." American leaders, she hoped, would "find a firmness of mind that renders us independent of popular opinion," restoring disinterestedness and principle to public decisions, and replacing the passions of the mob. Warren to Catherine Macaulay, July 1789, in *Mercy Otis Warren Letter-Book*, Reel 1 of *The Mercy Warren Papers* (Boston: Massachusetts Historical Society; Ann Arbor, MI: University Microfilms International, 1968), 27, quoted in Cornell, *Other Founders*, 71.

[70] Waldstreicher, *Midst of Perpetual Fetes*, 90, 92, 108. For most of the men who would form the Federalist Party in the 1790s, this was their first experience in appealing to a mass electorate. If Federalists were to benefit from the groundswell of democratic participation, they had to perfect this skill. To engage a democratizing polity, Federalists developed a number of stylized public appeals and adapted others from the Revolution. It was no longer easy to identify the virtuous man now that the British had been defeated. Proto-Federalists honed a keenly chiseled set of behaviors best described as a "patriotic sensibility." The patriot had to convert his virtue, formerly a rather abstract sensibility, into the concrete display of feeling for his country. The essence of "patriotic sensibility" entailed the display of a publicly affective bond between citizen and country [67–85].

the state court by the local militia. Hardly consensual, this give and take over the ratification process was an important step toward nationalizing issues about which citizens were passionate.[71]

Partisan competition created national bonds as each political party defined itself through its vision for union. For Hamilton's party, which became known as the Federalists, the Constitution provided a template that promoted organic growth of the General Government. This capacious constitutional interpretation envisioned national institutions that promoted the long-term collective good of the polity. From John Adams's perspective, this revitalized the collective impulse in republican thought. Jefferson and Madison's party, known as the Republicans, looked to the Constitution to protect individual freedom and to guard against government intrusion. The Bill of Rights epitomized this perspective. Republicans stressed individual liberty and the autonomy of local communities best preserved through state, rather than national government (assuming that government was needed at all).[72]

Both perspectives were nationally oriented. Explicit in the Federalist case, Republicans also supported a national vision. In place of visible institutions that mandated respect and allegiance, Jefferson imagined that Americans would rally to national causes when necessary. He believed that they would do so if they shared a common stake in preserving a republic built upon the commitment to equality. While the nation that Jefferson sought to construct was radically opposed to central authority – the amalgam of republican thought and the colonies' experience with the

---

[71] Cornell, *Other Founders*, 110; "One of the People," *Independent Gazetteer*, February 7, 1788, vol. 7, issue 672, p. 3, in *Early American Newspapers*, Series I, quoted in Cornell, *Other Founders*, 110; Cornell, *Other Founders*, 113–14. "To some extent," Waldstreicher concludes, "the Antifederalists were beaten at a game they had played since the Revolution – the game of street theater, the embodiment of the people – by opponents who subtly changed the rules." *Midst of Perpetual Fetes*, 98–99.

[72] Sidney M. Milkis, *Political Parties and Constitutional Government: Remaking American Democracy* (Baltimore, MD: Johns Hopkins University Press, 1999), chap. 1; Michael J. Lacey, "Federalism and National Planning: The Nineteenth-Century Legacy" in *The American Planning Tradition: Culture and Policy*, ed. Robert Fishman (Washington, DC: Woodrow Wilson Center Press, 2000), 93–98. See also Samuel H. Beer, *To Make a Nation: The Rediscovery of American Federalism* (Cambridge, MA: Harvard University Press, 1993), xi–xiii, 4–7; Major L. Wilson, *Space Time and Freedom: The Quest for Nationality and the Irrepressible Conflict, 1815–1861* (Westport, CT: Greenwood Press, 1974), 6. Local autonomy was most forcefully protected in the Ninth and Tenth Amendments. McDonald, *States' Rights*, 22–25. On the Bill of Rights more comprehensively, see Patrick T. Conley and John P. Kaminski, eds., *The Bill of Rights and the States: The Colonial and Revolutionary Origins of American Liberties*(Madison, WI: Madison House Press, 1992), and Amar, *Bill of Rights*.

British metropole – it was aggressively national, even imperial in its ambitions. His was a republic that drew upon affectionate bonds rather than overpowering institutions.[73]

In his first inaugural address in 1801, Jefferson christened this "empire for liberty," asking his fellow citizens to embrace his ideal. "Let us, then, with courage and confidence pursue our own Federal and Republican principles," Jefferson urged, "our attachment to union and representative government." Success did not lie in a powerful military or national administrative capacity. Rather, it depended on the response of citizens to Jefferson's call for them to "unite with one heart and one mind." The nation's strength would reside in citizens' affection for that nation, and their willingness to come to its aid during times of need. The challenge for national leaders was to cultivate this affection, rarely visible except in times of crisis, through a blend of shared commitment to liberty and enduring material interests. Such a nation, even when fully formed, would look stateless to even the keenest observer, and indeed would prove *most* powerful precisely when it appeared to be least visible.[74]

Articulating these two sharply contrasting views of the role of the general government kept questions about national authority and the meaning of national union alive in the minds of Americans. Even those Republicans who supported only the weakest forms of central government inadvertently contributed to a dialogue that prompted Americans to conceive of themselves as citizens of one republic. The debate over just how powerful constitutionally authorized national institutions should be was an essential ingredient in the subtle evolution of national consciousness. It helped turn the house sheltered by a constitutional roof into a home.[75]

---

[73] Onuf, *Jefferson's Empire*, chap. 2. As Onuf notes, "Its strength could not be measured in conventional military terms but rather in the loyalty of the patriotic citizens who would rise up in defense of their own liberties and their country's independence whenever they were threatened" [53]. Kagan argues that the idea of "an empire of sovereign equals," actually takes form in the American struggle against British empire. As Kagan puts it, "The American continental empire would be a federation of equals under a common sovereign, and it is notable that this American federative principle was invented not after the Revolution but in the imperial struggle that preceded it." *Dangerous Nation*, 33.

[74] Jefferson, First Inaugural Address, March 4, 1801, in Richardson, *Messages and Papers*, 1:322–23, quoted in Onuf, *Jefferson's Empire*, 8.

[75] Or as Waldstreicher puts it, "Americans practiced nationalism before they had a fully developed national state – something that may account for the relatively abstract quality of early and subsequent American nationalism." *Midst of Perpetual Fetes*, 112–13.

It also spurred Americans to advocate and organize. Although a number of prominent Anti-Federalists, such as John Taylor and Albert Gallatin, emerged as Republicans in the 1790s, the Republican Party was far more than an extension of Anti-Federalism. It included men like Jefferson and Madison who had supported the Constitution. The Republican genius for press and organization further distinguished it from its Anti-Federalist antecedents. Newspapers like the *National Gazette* projected the Republican message to a national audience, while Republican political societies created networks that circulated opinion to a broad array of citizens. As the Philadelphia Society saw it, "A constant circulation of useful information, and a liberal communication of republican sentiments" were essential to preserving civil liberties. The cultivation and circulation of public opinion laid the groundwork for vigorous national debate.[76]

With the Federalist faction controlling the levers of power in a national government that some opponents viewed as oppressive, Republican societies mobilized public opinion to defend liberties against government encroachment. The organization of the debate along partisan lines was anathema to those who subscribed to classical republican views. President Washington explicitly denounced the societies in 1794 for violating republican principles. Republican partisans responded that the societies were in fact crucial to maintaining responsible governance across a vast national expanse.[77]

The walls of this American home were reinforced by government policies that compromised both parties' philosophies. At times, Republicans looked the other way; they supported energetic, assertive government. Federalists, on the other hand, were willing to compromise on the techniques used to achieve their ends, often embracing local or private means to achieve national goals. Both sides agreed that some national responsibilities were crucial. Defense is the best example of this, but economic development and cultivating an informed citizenry followed closely. Framing programs in market terms helped gain public acceptance, regardless of party. Delivering services through third parties so as to narrow the boundary between the government and civil society often eased public acceptance.

---

[76] Cornell, *Other Founders*, 172–73; Democratic Society of Philadelphia, Circular Letter to the Counties, July 4, 1793, in *The Democratic-Republican Societies, 1790–1800*, ed. Philip S. Foner (Westport, CT: Greenwood Press, 1976), 66, quoted in Cornell, *Other Founders*, 196.

[77] Cornell, *Other Founders*, 198–99.

With the framework for a potentially powerful federal government in hand, it remained for those committed to energetic central government to realize its promise. As Gouverneur Morris commented about the Constitution, "The moment this plan goes forth all other considerations will be laid aside – and the great question will be, shall there be a national Government or not?" Establishing the Constitution was only the first step, in Hamilton's opinion, and hardly the most important one. Looking back in 1802, Hamilton lamented his "odd destiny." Despite sacrificing more for the Constitution than anybody else, Hamilton viewed the results as little more than "frail and worthless fabric" that required constant "laboring to prop."[78]

Nor was Hamilton content with a central government that merely protected liberty, property, and the public safety. Hamilton's government would provide for "the great purposes of commerce, revenue, [and] agriculture"; it would facilitate "domestic tranquility & happiness." For Hamilton, however, such domestic objectives could never be achieved without the "stability and strength" to garner respect abroad. It was precisely by activating the latent powers of the Constitution that the national government would arouse the deep-felt support that such an ambitious program required if it was to succeed politically. At the Constitutional Convention, Hamilton laid bare the sinews that connected citizens to their government: interest, opinion, habit, force, and influence. As Hamilton saw it, the states started with an overwhelming advantage in each of these fields compared to the General Government.[79]

Federalists had to preempt these political resources and direct them toward the national government. For Hamilton, an advocate of elite decision-making who struggled to overcome his own humble origins, war offered the greatest opportunity for citizens to prove their honor and for the central government visibly to demonstrate its worth. Hamilton's earliest surviving letter, written in 1769 while he was a "groveling" clerk, declares: "I wish there was a war." Hamilton got his wish, serving in the

[78] Gouverneur Morris, September 17, 1787, in *Records of the Federal Convention of 1787*, ed. Max Farrand, 4 vols. (New Haven, CT: Yale University Press, 1911), 2:645, http://lccn.loc.gov/11005506, cited in Forrest McDonald, *Alexander Hamilton: A Biography* (New York, NY: Knopf, 1979), 107; Hamilton to Morris, February 27, 1802, cited in McDonald, *Hamilton*, 96.
[79] Hamilton, June 18, 1787, in Farrand, *Records*, 1:287, quoted in McDonald, *Hamilton*, 97; Hamilton, June 29, 1787, in Farrand, *Records*, 1:467, cited in McDonald, *Hamilton*, 97; McDonald, *Hamilton*, 101.

Continental Army. Long after this service, Hamilton was quick to rely on military authority.[80]

Appearances were crucial. Deploying the army commanded respect from citizens, Hamilton believed. The more imposing the force, the more likely it was to achieve this objective. Hamilton put his philosophy into action on the eve of Fries Rebellion in 1799 when he warned Secretary of War McHenry to "Beware ... of magnifying a riot into an insurrection" by employing "inadequate force." It was better to err on "the other side," Hamilton warned. "Whenever the government appears in arms," Hamilton insisted, "it ought to appear like a *Hercules*, and inspire respect by the display of strength." For Hamilton, this spoke to a larger objective: that citizens not lose sight of the government that served them. Visibility commanded respect – except when it came to taxes – the source of Fries complaint.[81]

Nor could the central government afford to appear weak, vis-a-vis the states: appearance was a crucial part of reality for Hamilton. He understood that allegiance to state government threatened the viability of the new national government. That is why he predicted in September 1787 that the federal government would either "triumph altogether over the state governments and reduce them to an entire subordination," or "in the course of a few years ... the contests about the boundaries of power between the particular governments and the general government ... will produce a dissolution of the Union." The nation's first years reinforced Hamilton's conviction. Fisher Ames put the problem succinctly in 1789. "I am inclined to believe that the langour of the old Confederation is transfused into the members of the new Congress," Ames complained. "We lose credit, spirit, every thing. The public will forget the government before it is born."[82]

When it came to making the new government conspicuous, George Washington was the Federalists' man. Washington's personal courage

---

[80] Walling, *Republican Empire*, chap. 6; Trees, *Founding Fathers*, 6; Hamilton to Edward Stevens, November 11, 1769, in Syrett, *Papers of Alexander Hamilton*, 1:5, quoted in Trees, *Founding Fathers*, 6; Walling, *Republican Empire*, 1–2; Trees, *Founding Fathers*, 62.

[81] Trees, *Founding Fathers*, 62–63; Hamilton to McHenry, March 18, 1799, in Syrett, *Papers of Alexander Hamilton*, 22:552. There are two letters addressed to McHenry from March 18, 1799. The one cited is marked "private."

[82] Alexander Hamilton, "Conjectures about the New Constitution," in Syrett, *Papers of Alexander Hamilton*, 4:276–77, cited in Ellis, *Founding Brothers*, 77; Fisher Ames to George Richards Minot, March 25, 1789, in *Works of Fisher Ames*, ed. Seth Ames (Boston, MA: Little, Brown, 1854), 1:31–32, cited in Freeman, *Affairs of Honor*, 3.

was legendary. The fearless general had mounted a parapet at Yorktown in 1781 amidst an artillery attack so that he could survey the field. Ignoring the bullets and shrapnel whizzing by his head, Washington also defied the warnings of his aides, refusing to climb down until he had completed his reconnaissance. Exploits such as these, and the legends surrounding them, helped Washington inspire confidence in the new government.[83]

Unanimously chosen president by the electors who gathered on February 4, 1789, Washington's service during the Revolution embodied balance and mature judgment. Deferential to the legislative branch, skilled from years of negotiations with the Continental Congress, and scrutinized time and again by the public during his service to the Confederation, the first president acquired a symbolic significance that for many was more concrete than the allegiance of citizens to the new nation. Washington's eight-day inauguration procession from Mt. Vernon to New York in the spring of 1789, witnessed by throngs of cheering citizens, confirmed the electors' confidence in the new president.[84]

Washington used his personal prestige to ease acceptance of the new General Government. During Washington's eastern and southern tours at the end of the decade, he mobilized huge crowds of women, young people, and local worthies. Leaving his carriage on the outskirts of a town, Washington mounted his white horse to meet residents. Washington's honeymoon was extended by passage of the Bill of Rights, which neutralized much of the Anti-Federalist criticism of the Constitution. Reflecting on his first year in office, Washington marveled that the first session of Congress had gone so smoothly. The honeymoon, however, was brief.[85]

Washington was an advocate of energetic government. A draft speech written in 1789 challenged Congress to "take measures for promoting

---

[83] Ellis, *Founding Brothers*, 120; Leonard D. White, *The Federalists: A Study in Administrative History* (1948; repr., Westport, CT: Greenwood Press, 1978), 97.

[84] Stanley Elkins and Eric McKitrick, *The Age of Federalism* (New York, NY: Oxford University Press, 1993), 33–46.

[85] Waldstreicher, *Midst of Perpetual Fetes*, 117–22; Cornell, *Other Founders*, 170. "It was indeed next to a Miracle that there should have been so much unanimity, in points of such importance, among such a number of Citizens, so widely scattered, and so different in their habits in many respects as the Americans were," Washington wrote in early 1790. George Washington to Catherine Macaulay Graham, January 9, 1790, in *The Writings of George Washington*, ed. John C. Fitzpatrick, 39 vols. (Washington, D.C.: United States Government Printing Office, 1931–44), 30: 496–97, cited in Elkins and McKitrick, *Age of Federalism*, 75.

the general welfare." "Whenever an opportunity shall be furnished to you as public or private men, I trust you will not fail to use your best endeavors," Washington continued, "to improve the education and manners of a people; to accelerate the progress of arts and Sciences; to patronize works of genius; to confer rewards for inventions of utility; and to cherish institutions favourable to humanity." The speech was never delivered, however. When Washington finally did address Congress in January 1790, he used his powers delicately, no doubt concerned about offending those who feared government consolidation.[86]

Washington restrained his own views about the national government's assertiveness for eight years. It was not until his "farewell" speech that Washington finally spoke from the heart. While the address is best remembered for the President's warning about foreign entanglements, or sectional parties, Washington was at pains to propose a series of steps that would bind the nation together in the absence of war. His program was ambitious. It included federal promotion of domestic manufacturers, subsidies for improvements in agriculture, a national university, a national military academy, and higher compensation for federal employees. Washington's proposals for a national university and a national military academy traded on his own experience in the Continental Army. More than any other institution, the army helped mold citizens loyal to the national government – citizens able to overcome local and regional interests.[87]

Like Jefferson, Washington understood that no political platform or cadre of public officials could rival the bonds of patriotism. However, Washington was less optimistic that patriotism would spring forth spontaneously. The larger purposes of a national university, Washington confided to Hamilton, addressed this pressing issue. In "the general Juvenal period of life, when friendships are formed, & habits established that will stick by one," Washington wrote Hamilton, "the Youth, or young men from different parts of the United States would be assembled together, & would by degrees discover that there was not that cause for those jealousies & prejudices which one part of the Union had imbibed against another part. ... What, but the mixing of

[86] George Washington, "Proposed Address to Congress," in Fitzpatrick, *Writings of George Washington*, 30:307, cited in Larson, *Internal Improvement*, 19; Larson, *Internal Improvement*, 19. Compare this proposed address to the actual first annual message delivered. See Fitzpatrick, *Writings of George Washington*, 30:491–94.

[87] Ellis, *Founding Brothers*, 154–57.

people from different parts of the United States during the War rubbed off these impressions? A century in the ordinary intercourse, would not have accomplished what the Seven years association in Arms did." Washington was searching for a peace-time equivalent of the national bonds forged in war.[88]

Ultimately, the most important message contained in Washington's farewell address was conveyed by the very occasion for which it was drafted: the voluntary abdication of power. Washington was entrusted with power because he could be trusted to give it up. As Americans turned to the prospect of replacing Washington in 1796, the candidates' credentials as revolutionaries trumped other considerations. Memory of the Revolution constituted perhaps the most powerful adhesive in a nation that had few other collective endeavors to hold it together.[89]

"IT WILL BE A POWERFULL CEMENT OF OUR UNION": REALIZING HAMILTON'S VISION

It took more than a propitious start to earn the allegiance of the people. The Federalists, led by Alexander Hamilton, sought to bind Americans to their national government by nurturing an activist national government that promoted balance between agriculture and industry. Forging agreement on the national assumption of the state debt incurred during the Revolutionary War was an important step in this direction. Besides a strong military presence, there was no greater measure of the modern nation-state's power than its ability to finance the obligations it incurred in pursuit of its national interest. But like a standing army, debt raised a host of republican fears – from worries about dependence to concerns that the power of lenders would distort the economy.[90]

Following the European model, Hamilton argued that the federal government should "assume" the states' debts and finance them through a national impost and excise taxes. In Europe, military power and adequate financing were integrally related. Hamilton conceived of power precisely

---

[88] Washington to Hamilton, September 1, 1796, in George Washington, *Writings*, selected by John H. Rhodehamel (New York, NY: Library of America, 1997), 960–61, cited in Ellis, *Founding Brothers*, 154. On the bonds formed during war, see also Theda Skocpol, "Patriotic Partnerships," in *Shaped by War and Trade: International Influences on American Political Development*, ed. Ira Katznelson and Martin Shefter (Princeton, NJ: Princeton University Press, 2002), 142.

[89] Ellis, *Founding Brothers*, 130, 162–63.

[90] On opposition to debt, see McCraw, "Strategic Vision," 49–50.

in these European terms and pursued debt assumption in order to avoid
the hand-to-mouth fiscal existence that had plagued the Confederation
from its start.[91]

Hamilton valued assumption for another reason: the nation's debt was
a highly visible symbol of its creditworthiness. Paying the debt service on
this obligation was a tangible reminder of the nation's honor. That the
debt holders were bound financially to the nation's future and that they
comprised a class of men that transcended section and state was also
appealing. As Hamilton wrote to Robert Morris, "A national debt if not
excessive will be to us a national blessing; it will be a powerfull cement
of our union." Through one political act, Hamilton sought to transmute
state indebtedness into a nation-building opportunity.[92]

Hamilton capitalized on the Constitution's broad power to "borrow
money on the credit of the United States." Retiring the nation's debt on a
scheduled basis through a budgeted sinking fund would solve the nation's
most pressing fiscal problem in a manner that increased the available
pool of capital. Hamilton's plan tapped the taxing power of the United
States government to capitalize the debt that the Confederation and the
individual states had accumulated during the War. This was a policy
explicitly designed to create the kind of attachment to the central government that Hamilton had outlined in "Federalist 27." Hamilton sought to
construct a national fiscal and monetary infrastructure that visibly bound
Americans to each other across region and states.[93]

Hamilton successfully enacted his plan, which required the national
government to pay the interest on $75 million (at face value) in federal
and state debts. By creating long-term, interest-bearing bonds and funding
them largely from impost revenues rather than direct taxes, as the states
had done, Hamilton engineered a fiscal relief program that allowed some
states to cut their taxes by as much as 85 percent. Because the United
States dedicated a stream of revenue to repaying this debt, it was able to

---

[91] For a good overview of Hamilton's approach, see Richard Sylla, "Experimental
Federalism: The Economics of American Government, 1789–1914," in *The Cambridge
Economic History of the United States*, ed. Stanley L. Engerman and Robert E. Gallman,
(Cambridge, UK: Cambridge University Press, 2000), 498–500. For the European influ-
ence on Hamilton, and the relationship between his plans for assumption and a central
bank, see Ron Chernow, *Alexander Hamilton* (New York, NY: Penguin, 2004), 347–53.

[92] Hamilton to Robert Morris, April 30, 1781, in Syrett, *Papers of Alexander Hamilton*,
2:635, quoted in Nelson, *Liberty and Property*, 30. On the British fiscal-military state, see
Brewer, *Sinews of Power*.

[93] Edling, *Revolution in Favor of Government*, 163; McDonald, *Hamilton*, 122. See also
Nelson, *Liberty and Property* 28–36.

lower its interest rate on the loan. When the government of the United States was formed in April 1789, the debt from the former Confederation was worth 15 to 25 percent of its face value, and traded only informally, if at all. After Hamilton's debt assumption plan was passed and Congress met its scheduled obligations, the federal securities soon rose to par or above.[94]

To overcome opposition to this program, Hamilton ultimately sacrificed another powerful symbol of national power – placing the seat of government in a world-class city that would serve as both economic and political capital of the nation. Because the Constitution called only for a "seat of Government" to be carved out of the existing states, wrangling over the site was intense. Many of the men who had supported the Constitution, but who were wary of assumption, were Virginians. They had long hoped for a capital built along the banks of the Potomac River.[95]

James Madison led this faction. The "Big Knife," as Madison was known for the deals he cut on this issue, acknowledged that "The business of the seat of Government is become a labyrinth." While many of the details of these secret negotiations will never be known, it is clear that Virginia and Pennsylvania emerged as the key parties to any compromise. The crucial elements of the deal were the permanent seat of government, the temporary seat of government, and debt assumption. The compromise was confirmed at a private dinner hosted by Thomas Jefferson in June 1790. Madison, who opposed debt assumption, agreed to abstain from organizing opposition to that bill. Hamilton, in return, agreed to support a permanent seat of government on the Potomac. Hamilton would lobby colleagues from Pennsylvania, offering Philadelphia the temporary site of the nation's capital. In July 1790, the House passed, by nearly identical votes, the debt assumption bill and a bill that located the future capital on the Potomac.[96]

---

[94] Richard Sylla, "Shaping the US Financial System, 1690–1913: The Dominant Role of Public Finance," in *The State, The Financial System, and Economic Modernization,* ed. Sylla, Richard Tilly, and Gabriel Tortella (Cambridge, UK: Cambridge University Press, 1999), 256–57; Edling, *Revolution in Favor of Government,* 159. On the size of the debt to be assumed, see McCraw, "Strategic Vision," 52–53.

[95] Ellis, *Founding Brothers,* 69.

[96] James Madison to Edmund Pendleton, June 22, 1790, in Hutchinson, Rachel, and Rutland, *Papers of James Madison,* ed. Robert A. Rutland et al., 26 vols. to date (Charlottesville, VA: University Press of Virginia, 1962-), 13:252, quoted in Ellis, *Founding Brothers,* 70; Chernow, *Hamilton,* 326–331. Writing to Monroe on June 20, 1790, Jefferson reiterated his preference for state rather than federal tax authority. But in the case of debt

Virginians Patrick Henry and Henry Lee were not pleased with Jefferson and Madison's compromise. Lee and Henry crafted a resolution, passed by both houses of the Virginia legislature in December 1790, that labeled assumption "a measure which ... must in the course of human events, produce one or other of two evils, the prostration of agriculture at the feet of commerce, or a change in the present form of federal government, fatal to the existence of American liberty." The whole business again raised fears of dependence and consolidation, resulting in loss of local control, the demise of state governments and the exercise of centralized, arbitrary power.[97]

Those opposed to situating the seat of government on the Potomac did not give up. Some who supported a northeastern location for the capital went along with the compromise under the (quite reasonable) assumption that the seat of government would never actually be built in a desolate swamp. As one journalist (from the Philadelphia press) proclaimed, it was "abhorrent to common sense to suppose they are to have a place dug out of the rocky wilderness, for the use of Congress only four months in the year and all the rest of the time to be inhabited by wild beasts." One representative captured many of his colleagues' feelings: "It will be generally viewed ... [as] a mere political manoeuvre. You might as well induce a belief that you are in earnest by inserting Mississippi, Detroit, or Winnipipiocket Pond."[98]

Hamilton traded more than geography in the deal. He acquired one crucial symbol of national power – the ability to finance the national debt – at the expense of another – a seat of government that symbolized the government's authority in a city that could compete financially and culturally with leading capitals around the world. For decades, the capital was literally out of sight and for even longer, virtually invisible.[99]

---

assumption, which could only be done by the federal government, Jefferson was willing to make an exception. Jefferson saw "the necessity of yielding for this time to the cries of the creditors in certain parts of the union." "Whatever enables us to go to war, secures our peace." Jefferson to Monroe, July 11, 1790, in Boyd, *Papers of Thomas Jefferson*, 17:25, cited in McDonald, *Hamilton*, 184.

[97] Edward Carrington to Madison, December 24, 1790, in Hutchinson, Rachel, and Rutland, *Papers of James Madison*, 13:332, n. 2, quoted in Ellis, *Founding Brothers*, 76–77; Ellis, *Founding Brothers*, 59.

[98] Ellis, *Founding Brothers*, chap. 2, especially 48–51 and 69–80; Philadelphia journalist from *Daily Advertiser*, as quoted in Ellis, *Founding* Brothers, 74; Elbridge Gerry, Debates of July 6, in (NY) *Daily Advertiser*, July 10, 1790.

[99] Ellis, *Founding Brothers*, 79.

Opponents assumed that the seat of government would never leave Philadelphia for the swampy Potomac because they were certain that Congress would revisit the issue before any such move took place. Virginians eager to claim the capital understood that revisiting the issue would likely kill the deal. To head off that possibility, Thomas Jefferson proposed that all of the key decisions be left up to the one man who could be trusted to make decisions unilaterally: George Washington. Based on a report by Jefferson and Madison, Washington designated the capital's location in January 1791. For the next decade, he oversaw every aspect of the capital's development. While this process preserved the compromise hammered out in June 1790, it also established an important precedent on behalf of executive authority. Granting President Washington the discretion to make decisions that affected land, money, and other national treasure meant that at least under certain circumstances, the executive branch could be trusted with a great deal of discretion. This would not be the last time that those concerned about undue executive authority would sacrifice principles for other objectives.[100]

Alexander Hamilton had no qualms about executive discretion. He was both an advocate for energetic central government and a skilled "national economic strategist," as one historian of business put it. Hamilton pushed the limits of executive power as Secretary of the Treasury, turning it into the young government's largest and most assertive department. As Hamilton remarked in 1792, "Most of the important measures of every government are connected with the Treasury." His department touched the lives of many Americans through customs and excise officers and through land agents.[101]

After absorbing the states' debt, Hamilton founded the Bank of the United States. A national bank, Hamilton argued, would provide a reliable currency for the nation and would manage the Treasury's financial transactions. It would also provide loans and support the nation's credit. Like his plan to fund the national debt, a national bank linked "the interest of the state," as Hamilton put it, "in an intimate connexion with those of the rich individuals belonging to it [so] that it turns wealth

---

[100] Ibid., 74–76.
[101] McCraw, "Strategic Vision," 47–48; Hamilton to Edward Carrington, May 26, 1792, in Syrett, *Papers of Alexander Hamilton*, 11:442, cited in White, *Federalists*, 117. By 1801, the Treasury employed over one half of the total civilian government personnel. White, *Federalists*, 123.

and influence of both into a commercial channel for mutual benefit." This intimate connection between wealthy citizens and the government assured political loyalty internally and provided a conduit to the commercial world beyond the borders of the United States.[102]

It also created the kind of hybrid institution that leveraged national authority to get the most out of private capital. As Hamilton wrote as early as 1780, "The Bank of England unites public authority and faith with private credit." The same was true of the bank of Amsterdam. "And why cannot we have an American bank?" Hamilton asked. Hamilton feared that the sensitive nature of monetary policy was too easily abused by politicians – so he sought to insulate his bank from politics. But he was determined to turn private purpose to public ends, insisting that the government retain a minority share, thus establishing a public hand in the direction of the bank. Toward that end, Hamilton accepted the securities that Treasury had just issued as payment for private subscriptions to the bank, enhancing the value of the securities, and further yoking the public and private elements of the bank.[103]

To Hamilton, "consolidation" and "nationalization" were not concepts to fear. Rather, they were the political prerequisites for creating a dynamic economy that would undergird the nation's development. Economic integration, in turn, would further strengthen the political and emotional bonds that citizens from different sections of the nation held in common. Creating hybrid institutions that tapped public authority and private wealth held the key to achieving these ends.[104]

After successfully funding the debt and establishing a national bank, Hamilton promoted mixed enterprise by proposing bounties for manufacturing. This too was to be a hybrid system, blending public and private elements to stimulate manufacturing at the same time it supported the nation's public credit. The Society for Establishing Useful Manufacturers (SEUM) was chartered (in New Jersey) in 1791. Its private subscribers pledged government bonds or national bank stock, further combining public and private financing. This capital would be enlarged by using it as security for foreign bank loans. The Society would then be in a position

---

[102] Elkins and McKitrick, *Age of Federalism*, 225–27; Nelson, *Liberty and Property*, 30; Hamilton to?, December 1779–March 1780, in Syrett, *Papers of Alexander Hamilton*, 2:248, cited in Nelson, *Liberty and Property*, 30.

[103] Hamilton to James Duane, September 3, 1780, in Syrett, *Papers of Alexander Hamilton*, 2:414, quoted in Chernow, *Hamilton*, 347; Chernow, *Hamilton*, 347–49; Elkins and McKitrick, *Age of Federalism*, 123.

[104] Ellis, *Founding Brothers*, 62–64.

to underwrite domestic manufacturing, which could compete with goods imported from abroad.[105]

Hamilton's Report on the Subject of Manufacturers, submitted to Congress on December 5, 1791, called for a combination of tariffs, bounties, and other incentives to provide active government support for the manufacturing sector. Congress rejected Hamilton's vision. Buffeted by charges of speculation and criticism of Hamilton's plan leveled by manufacturers – the very group it was supposed to help – SEUM also died an ignominious death.[106]

Hamilton hoped to extend the appeal of the national government beyond elites. Through institutions like the United States Mint, Hamilton encouraged small denomination coins, making it routine for Americans to handle money. He favored small denominations in order to appeal to the poor, "by enabling them to purchase in small portions and at a more reasonable rate the necessaries of which they stand in need." Tilting toward commercial and manufacturing interests, Congress also passed an excise tax and a mildly protective tariff to fund the debt. Both proved to be valuable sources of revenue. In the case of the excise tax, Hamilton wanted to be sure that this stream of revenue was dedicated exclusively to federal endeavors, writing " it [is] well to lay hold of so valuable a resource of revenue before it was generally preoccupied by the State governments."[107]

For some Federalists, the long-term survival of the national government depended on establishing its autonomy from the states. As the retiring Robert Goodloe Harper wrote his constituents in 1801, "the federalists considered it as a principle of the utmost importance for the preservation of the federal government, to render it as independent as possible of state influence; to give it a movement of its own, and complete power to

[105] Nelson, *Liberty and Property*, 38–39, 41–43. The more proximate impact of the SEUM, however, was to support the price of government securities.
[106] Elkins and McKitrick, *Age of Federalism*, 258–63, 271, 276–77; Nelson, *Liberty and Property*, 44–49.
[107] Chernow, *Hamilton*, 355–57; Hamilton, *Report on the Mint*, January 27, 1791, in Syrett, *Papers of Alexander Hamilton*, 7:601, quoted in Chernow, *Hamilton*, 356; McDonald, *Hamilton*, 198; Elkins and McKitrick, *Age of Federalism*, 66–67; Alexander Hamilton, "Objections and Answers Respecting the Administration of the Government," in *The Works of Alexander Hamilton*, ed. John C. Hamilton, 7 vols. (New York, NY: Charles S. Francis, 1851), 4: 256, quoted in White, *Federalists*, 404. See also Kermit L. Hall, *The Magic Mirror: Law in American History* (New York, NY: Oxford University Press, 1989), 89. On Federalist tax policies see also White, *Federalists*, ch. 27.

enforce its own laws; to resist state encroachments; and to restrain the state governments within their just and proper bounds." The Federalists hardly achieved all of these objectives, even with Washington, Adams, and Hamilton in power. The Bill of Rights limited the central government's expansion into the realm of civil liberties, and Congress placed limits on Hamilton's penchant for manufacturing subsidies. Hamilton's preference for highly visible institutions that would command respect, loyalty, or in the case of the military, inspire fear, triggered reactions, most famously in the case of the Bank, that challenged the very existence of the Federalist system.[108]

Nevertheless, the power to tax, to raise armies, to extend credit, and to shape the nation's financial system prevailed. So too did the more fundamental tendency to create hybrid institutions that tapped private initiative and structured markets. As we will see in subsequent chapters, Hamilton's opponents often relied on the very mechanisms they had opposed to finance their own version of the developmental vision. And Hamilton's program hardly exhausted the range of federal powers that contributed to the political and economic development of the nation.

Perhaps it was because Hamilton was an immigrant, with no allegiance to any particular state in the union, that he could maintain such a single-mindedly national perspective. Or perhaps it was his voracious appetite for European financial models that sustained this perspective. Whatever the reason, Hamilton's commitment to energetic central direction of the economy shaped not only the public face of finance for the future; it influenced the course of private financial development as well. In the case of the Bank of the United States and debt assumption, Hamilton's determination to blend public and private capital and commitment undoubtedly enhanced the public credit. But it also spawned a "Federalist financial system," largely populated by private banks and financiers, who eventually fueled a capital market with access to international lenders. Private credit, in turn, stimulated private manufacturing and transportation networks. It also enabled dramatic public initiatives. The French gladly accepted federal securities for their claims in Louisiana in 1803, doubling the size of the United States. As Hamilton originally envisioned, that system enabled the United States to finance its military operations, from the War of 1812, to the Mexican War of

---

[108] Robert Goodloe Harper, *Select Works of Robert Goodloe* (Baltimore, MD: OH Neilson, 1814), 332, quoted in White, *Federalists*, 509.

1846. Detested by Jefferson, Madison, and many other Republican opponents, the Federalist system financed the developmental vision that they forged.[109]

THE LIMITS OF NATIONAL INTERVENTION:
SPEAKING AND TAXING DIRECTLY

Americans consistently resisted assertive, distant government when it threatened basic protections embodied in the Bill of Rights or extracted revenues too visibly. Republicans capitalized on this sentiment in the wake of the Alien and Sedition Acts. This legislation responded to Federalist fears that the contagion of the French Revolution would spread to the United States. Against this ideological backdrop, tensions mounted as the French preyed upon American shipping, while the Directorate issued one belligerent statement after another. Committed to diplomacy, President John Adams showed remarkable patience, even after learning of a French attempt to extract a bribe from the American delegation. With Republicans blaming Federalist leadership rather than the French for the deteriorating international situation, a Federalist-dominated Congress was not as patient as their president. They crafted a series of acts that sought to limit foreign contagion and to reign in domestic criticism.[110]

Passed by one vote in both the House and the Senate in June 1798, the Naturalization Act was aimed at the large influx of emigrants who, once citizens, disproportionately voted Republican. The legislation extended the naturalization period from five to fifteen years. Another law aimed at aliens empowered the President to deport foreigners whom he deemed dangerous to the nation. The Sedition Act, passed in July 1798, targeted the severe criticism that Republicans had leveled at the Federalist regime. It stipulated that any effort to impede government policy or falsely defame the President or Congress was subject to steep fines or imprisonment.[111]

[109] Sylla, "Shaping the U.S. Financial System," 250–51, 259–261; Max M. Edling, "So Immense a Power in the Affairs of War: Alexander Hamilton and the Restoration of Public Credit," *William and Mary Quarterly*, 3rd Ser., 64, no. 2 (April 2007): 287–326.
[110] McCullough, *John Adams*, 497–504.
[111] Elkins and McKitrick, *Age of Federalism*, 590–93. For the influence of the emergence of libertarian thought on the meaning of freedom of speech, see Leonard W. Levy, "Liberty and the First Amendment: 1790–1800," *American Historical Review*, 68, no. 1 (October 1962): 22–37.

The Sedition Act, which required that malicious intent be proven, was no greater threat to civil liberties than the prevailing common law interpretations of seditious libel in the states. Federalizing this crime, however, enflamed Republicans, already wary of the central government's reach. Anti-Federalists had framed the issue as one of states rights in their opposition to the Constitution and support for the First Amendment. This was an amendment designed to ensure that the states, not the central government, regulated free speech. Republicans voiced these concerns in the House debate over the Sedition Act. "The States have complete power on the subject," Nathaniel Macon insisted. He spoke for a host of Republican colleagues, including Albert Gallatin and Edward Livingston.[112]

The Sedition Act pushed Republicans toward a defense of civil liberties that had been embraced by federalist defenders of the Constitution. Federalism had served as the compromise mechanism that assuaged fears of distant government. Defenders of the Constitution had gestured toward state-based protections in an effort to secure ratification. It was supporters of the Constitution who, in 1788, cited state vigilance to "descry the first symptoms of usurpation." The states "would sound the alarm to the public."[113]

Who better to remind Federalists than James Madison? He defended these rights through the Virginia Resolution, introduced by John Taylor in December 1798. Revised, a year later Madison's "Report of 1800" became one of the central pillars in the antistatist pantheon. Madison's colleague Thomas Jefferson went farther in the Kentucky Resolution introduced at roughly the same time. Jefferson argued for the right of individual states to nullify unconstitutional federal legislation – a right based in the state's participation in the original constitutional compact that ratified the Constitution.[114]

In opposing federal legislation to regulate the freedom of speech, Republicans also drew upon powerful libertarian ideas that had not informed their thinking when they fought for the Bill of Rights several years earlier. Nothing in the First Amendment had changed the common law – and more importantly – common understanding that freedom of

[112] McDonald, *States' Rights*, 41; Levy, "Liberty," 30–31; *Annals of Congress*, July 10, 1798, 5th Cong. 2nd sess., 2152, quoted in Levy, "Liberty,"30.

[113] Cornell, *Other Founders*, 239, 242–43; Madison, "Report of 1800," in Hutchinson, Rachel, and Rutland, *Papers of James Madison*, 17:350, quoted in Cornell, *Other Founders*, 242.

[114] Cornell, *Other Founders*, 14, 240–41; Levy, "Liberty," 30. For Madison's and Jefferson's position on these resolutions, see also Onuf, *Jefferson's Empire*, 96–98.

the press protected only the right to publish without being subjected to prior restraint by the government. What the government did *after* publication, was ultimately subject to the determination of a jury. James Wilson spoke for the broadly accepted meaning of first amendment rights when he stated in the Pennsylvania ratifying convention that "what is meant by the liberty of the press is that there should be no antecedent restraint upon it; but that every author is responsible when he attacks the security or welfare of the government."[115]

This understanding changed dramatically over the course of the decade, from rejecting prior constraints to a blanket protection of speech aimed at the government, prior to and *after* its publication. Epitomized by the writings of Tunis Wortman of New York, advocates of unfettered speech argued that limitations against prior constraint were a frail protection. As Madison put it, "It would seem a mockery to say, that no laws shall be passed, preventing publications from being made, but that laws may be passed for punishing them in case they should be made."[116]

The basis for these assertions was as important as its practical implications for the meaning of free speech. Republicans argued that because the government was now elected and its authority was based on the consent of the people, – the "principles of the social state" – as Wortman put it, free and open discussion among that constituency was essential to the very life of the state. The Sedition Act threatened the government's life blood, the free speech that ensured informed governance.

The battle over the Sedition Act resuscitated two of the fundamental compromises Federalists embraced in order to secure the Constitution: the right of states to protect civil liberties, and the admission that the central government's very legitimacy was grounded in the direct consent of the people (as opposed to the consensus of the states). Much to the dismay of Federalists, Republicans popularized both elements of this compromise, making explicit the restraints built into the Constitution against unilateral national authority and underscoring the limits of representative, as opposed to direct, democracy.[117]

---

[115] Levy, "Liberty," 23–24; James Wilson, Speech in the Pennsylvania Ratifying Convention, 1 December 1787, in McMaster and Stone, *Pennsylvania and the Federal Constitution,* 308–9, as quoted in Levy, "Liberty," 25.

[116] Levy, "Liberty," 28, 31–37; Madison, Report of 1800, in Hutchinson, Rachel, and Rutland, *Papers of James Madison,* 17:336, in Levy, "Liberty," 33.

[117] Wortman, *A Treatise, Concerning Political Enquiry, and the Liberty of the Press,* (New York: George Forman, 1800: repr. New York: Di Capo Press, 1970), 29, quoted in Levy, "Liberty," 36.

The powerful reaction to the Sedition Act actually helped to create the very network of partisan press that Federalists so feared. In total, seventeen men were indicted under the Sedition Act. Many of the key figures indicted were opposition printers who criticized the administration. Thomas Cooper, a recent immigrant who founded the *Northumberland Gazette* in 1799, was a good example. After lashing out at the Adams administration he was tried for sedition. Cooper used the trial to comment on the growing partisan divide. "[T]he one," Cooper proclaimed, "thinks the liberties of our country endangered by the licentiousness, the other, by the restrictions of the press." The controversy over the Alien and Sedition Acts exacerbated partisan divisions and forced printers to choose sides in this battle.[118]

Republicans did not always adhere to the principles that they fought so hard to articulate and disseminate. Republicans prosecuted Federalist editor Harry Croswell in 1803, charging him with seditious libel against President Thomas Jefferson. Jefferson himself wrote to the governor of Pennsylvania the same year, suggesting that a "few prosecutions" against a newspaper critical of the Jefferson administration "would have a wholesome effect in restoring the integrity of the presses." And Jefferson's opponents complained of the president's "reign of terror" in 1806 when six men were indicted on charges of seditious libel of the President. Nonetheless, Jefferson's party was instrumental in articulating principles for free speech that were grounded in democratic consent and the role of the states as the first line of protection for the civil liberties codified in the Bill of Rights. In this interpretation, the "revolution in favor of Government" was not about expanding the authority of the General Government, or ensuring that it was sufficiently energetic. Rather, the revolution began by insisting that citizens had as much discretion to criticize the government as did their elected officials. That "social state," or the contract state, as Lockean liberals would

---

[118] Cornell, *Other Founders*, 233–36; while partisan papers like Matthew Lyon's *Farmer's Library* in Vermont, or *The Herald of Liberty* in western Pennsylvania, gained a foothold in the mid-90s, these were the exceptions. Jeffrey L. Pasley, *"The Tyranny of Printers": Newspaper Politics in the Early American Republic* (Charlottesville, VA: University Press of Virginia, 2001), 109–16; "Trial of Thomas Cooper, for a Seditious Libel, in the Circuit Court of the United States for the Pennsylvania District, Philadelphia, 1800," in *State Trials of the United States During the Administrations of Washington and Adams,* ed. Francis Wharton (1849; repr., New York, NY: Burt Franklin, 1970), 664, quoted in Cornell, *Other Founders*, 234. As Hendrickson points out, as early as 1779, French minister Gerard referred to the English party and the French party. *Peace Pact*, 177.

eventually call it, relied on the ongoing consent of its citizens to govern properly.[119]

If the flap over free speech popularized a political perspective that imposed severe restraints upon the central government's capacity to enforce consent, the battle over direct taxes exposed the limits of the General Government's capacity to extract resources – at least in a highly visible fashion. The question of revenue beyond the tariff and the few excise taxes that helped fund Hamilton's debt assumption plan was broached in 1798, as trade was threatened due to French attacks on American shipping and costs rose as Americans prepared for war against France. The Federalists won the initial battle, passing a direct tax in 1798. Because the Constitution required that direct taxes be apportioned according to the population of each state (including the three-fifths formula), Federalists, who controlled Congress, sought a program that prevented Republicans from making inroads into vulnerable segments of the Federalist constituency – in this case, New England farmers. The 1798 direct tax levied a flat rate tax on all slaves (50 cents), a tax on all houses worth more than $100 at a rate that escalated progressively, and a tax on land at a rate necessary to make up the balance of each state's quota. Samuel Sewall, a Federalist from Massachusetts, was pleased with his handiwork. The tax "would principally fall on houses in the cities." They "would be taxed much higher than houses in the country."[120]

While Federalists might have won the distributive battle, Republicans won the war. Thomas Jefferson grasped an enduring truth about Americans and taxes. As a leading scholar of nineteenth-century tax policy put it, "promises of tax equity are less effective than promises of tax cuts." Jefferson promised these tax cuts as part of his "revolution" of 1800. The Direct Tax of 1798, Jefferson asserted, would soon be in remission. "[T]he Doctor is now on his way to cure it, in the guise of a tax gatherer." For some time, Republicans had sought to make taxes more visible as a means of rallying voters to their cause. Republican representative from Pennsylvania, John Smilie, spelled out this rationale in 1794.

[119] Jefferson to Governor Thomas McKean, February 19, 1803, in Ford, *Writings of Thomas Jefferson*, 8:218–19, quoted in Levy, "Liberty," 31; "Hampden," *A Letter to the President of the United States, Touching the Prosecutions, Under His Patronage, Before the Circuit Court in the District of Connecticut* (New Haven, CT: Oliver Steele, 1808), Early American Imprints Series II (American Antiquarian Society and NewsBank, 2004 [doc. no. 15422]), 28, quoted in Levy, "Liberty," 31.
[120] Einhorn, *American Taxation*, 191–94; *Annals of Congress*, 5th Cong., 2nd sess., May 30, 1798, 1854, quoted in Einhorn, *American Taxation*, 193.

Taxes, he suggested, "ought to be raised in such a way, that the public might not only pay them, but at the same time, *feel* them. This would teach them to think a little better in what way their money goes," causing "an abridgement of the expenses of the Federal Government." The Republicans delivered on some of their promise, eliminating all internal taxes in 1801. Once in office themselves, however, they relied even more heavily on the tariff, the clear favorite of any administration charged with running a government, precisely because it was not felt as palpably by citizens as direct taxes.[121]

***

In the heat of political battle, British North Americans first forged, and then customized, a set of ideas that fused republican and liberal materials. Free trade was appealing, but in a world of European mercantilist powers, it required a central government with more authority than the Confederation to bind citizens with few common interests and even less good feeling for each other. War with one of those great powers united the colonies but challenged the virtue of even the most patriotic citizens. Harnessing the energy and imagination of individual citizens while guarding against excess and promoting the collective welfare of the republic was no easy task. For the time being, a developmental vision that pushed some of these difficult choices westward and into the future enabled a young nation to craft the compromises embodied in its federal constitution.

That constitution contained formidable powers. But they were latent powers that could only be unleashed through political sparring. Ironically, it was just such battles, fought between two emerging parties with contrasting views about the power of the General Government, that nationalized debate. How best to preserve a union that existed largely in theory was the question that united both Federalists and Republicans, even though each party offered different answers. Led by Alexander Hamilton, the Federalists sought to unchain the potential embedded in the Constitution, placing their faith in powerful institutions like the U.S. Treasury, a standing army, or the Bank of the United States.

---

[121] Einhorn, *American Taxation*, 194; Jefferson to John Taylor, November 26, 1798, in Ford, *Writings of Thomas Jefferson*, 7:310, quoted in Einhorn, *American Taxation*, 195, as cited in Elkins and McKitrick, *Age of Federalism*, 724–25; *Annals of Congress*, 3rd Cong., 1st sess., May 2, 1794, 625. For a good example of the Federalist loss of a key constituency, see Manning J. Dauer, *The Adams Federalists* (Baltimore, MD: Johns Hopkins University Press, 1953), 207.

Citizens, Hamilton believed, would only respect a government they could see and had reason to fear. Even before the "revolution" of 1800, Republicans challenged this approach. They expanded dramatically the meaning of freedom of speech and exposed one part of the Federalist program that nobody was eager to shed light on – direct taxes. Although Jefferson eliminated these direct taxes (keeping the less visible tariff) the Federalist financial system endured. And as Jefferson would soon learn, energetic governance had its uses. Employing it in ways that were less obvious held the key to success for Jefferson and a long line of public officials who followed.

4

"To Strengthen and Perpetuate that Union": Republican Political Economy

To judge by the size of the nation's capital, President Thomas Jefferson would have little trouble delivering on his promise to keep the federal government "rigorously frugal & simple." The grand plans for Washington, D.C., stood unfinished, federal buildings dilapidated. Even in the heart of the capital, government remained relatively invisible. Including the President, only 153 federal employees worked in Washington when Jefferson assumed office. Over the next thirty years, the number barely doubled, despite a 150 percent increase in the nation's population.[1]

---

[1] Thomas Jefferson to Elbridge Gerry, January 26, 1799, in *The Works of Thomas Jefferson*, ed. Paul Leicester Ford, 12 vols. (New York, NY, 1898), 9:17, as discussed in John L. Larson, *Internal Improvement: National Public Works and the Promise of Popular Government in the Early United States* (Chapel Hill, NC: University of North Carolina Press, 2001), 51; Charles Sellers, *The Market Revolution: Jacksonian America, 1815–1846* (New York, NY: Oxford University Press, 1991), 36–37; United States Census Bureau, *Measuring America: The Decennial Census From 1790 to 2000*, Appendix A, http://www.census.gov/prod/2002pubs/pol02marv-pt1.pdf.

The story of Thomas Jefferson's opposition to the Federalist regime in the waning years of the eighteenth century is well known. Interpreting the Tenth Amendment in a manner that favored states at the expense of national power, Vice President Jefferson drafted the Kentucky Resolutions in 1798. This inflammatory defense of state's rights even raised nullification as a means of checking federal encroachment. Running for President in 1800, Jefferson promised to lower taxes, reduce the size of government, and rely on local militias for the nation's defense. Larson, *Internal Improvement*, 51.

As Dan Carpenter has noted, the antagonism towards a visible administrative apparatus continued throughout the nineteenth century. "Before 1900," Carpenter writes, "most Americans simply did not believe in the capacity of most government agencies to ameliorate national economic and social dilemmas." Daniel P. Carpenter, *The Forging of Bureaucratic Autonomy: Reputations, Networks, and Policy Innovation in the Executive Agencies, 1862–1928* (Princeton, NJ: Princeton University Press, 2001), 30.

Illustrating just why advocates of the Constitution had fought for the exclusive right to levy imposts, Jefferson asked rhetorically, "What farmer, what mechanic, what laborer ever sees a taxgatherer of the United States?" Under Jefferson, Congress eliminated the direct tax and slashed most excise taxes, collecting 90 percent of federal revenues through customs duties. Now that they were in office, and especially because they presided over a surplus, Republicans were less eager to make taxpayers "feel" the pain of financing the General Government. Republicans refused to recharter the Bank of the United States when its twenty year charter expired in 1811. Federally funded internal improvements also came in for their share of opposition; critics charged that such projects threatened to empower the government, burden the taxpayer, redistribute wealth from one locale to another, and become self-perpetuating instruments of distant control over independent citizens.[2]

Given the localistic nature of American society and the growing importance of individual choice at the end of the eighteenth century, what would bind the nation together? Because Jefferson embraced both localism and individual rights, it is worth examining his views on these matters. Jefferson, Madison, and many other founders shared a vision of union that was grounded in three bonds: territory – especially the potential for continental expanse, affection resulting from a common past, and political views about representation in a democratic republic. Jefferson's perspective linked local autonomous governance to concentric bands of allegiance, ultimately extending across the continent.[3]

It would take more than affective bonds to cement the union, however. Jeffersonians' naturalized self-interest, forging it into a powerful tool. For National Republicans like Henry Clay, internal improvements, carefully calibrated land policy, and nationally imposed restrictions on imports would provide the material basis for a close-knit union. He embraced a variety of solutions that yoked individual interest to government-assisted

---

[2] Jefferson, Second Inaugural Address, March 4, 1805, in *A Compilation of the Messages and Papers of the Presidents, 1789–1897*, ed. James D. Richardson 10 vols. (Washington, D.C.: GPO, 1896), 1:379, available online at www.heinonline.org, quoted in Theodore Sky, *To Provide for the General Welfare: A History of the Federal Spending Power* (Newark, DE: University of Delaware Press, 2003), 114; Forrest McDonald, *States' Rights and the Union: Imperium in Imperio, 1776–1876* (Lawrence, KS: University Press of Kansas, 2000), 51–52; Larson, *Internal Improvement*, 50.

[3] Rogan Kersh, *Dream of a More Perfect Union* (Ithaca, NY: Cornell University Press, 2001), 5–6, 23–103. On Jefferson specifically, see Peter S. Onuf, *Jefferson's Empire: The Language of American Nationhood* (Charlottesville, VA: University Press of Virginia, 2000).

means in order to achieve developmental ends. President James Monroe, who vetoed a bill that would have erected tolls on the Cumberland Road, subscribed to an expanded interpretation of the Constitution's "general welfare" clause, opening the door for the General Government to finance – but not construct – a variety of internal improvements. Republican claims on the authority of the General Government culminated in John Quincy Adams's sweeping call for "the progressive improvement of the condition of the governed," accompanied by an ambitious program that triggered a strong counterattack, even within his own party. Those public officials who pushed for the "American System" and other ambitious national policies insisted that these programs would stimulate the very affective bonds that Jefferson hoped would spring forth naturally.[4]

This chapter charts Jefferson's conception of union, discusses the evolving role of self-interest in political discourse, and then turns to the more materially based political battles that were waged over the "the American System." Treated as a whole, these elements of Republican political economy laid the foundation for a political philosophy that questioned the need for an energetic General Government at the very time that it created a variety of nationally financed initiatives.

BINDING THE REPUBLIC TOGETHER WITH LOVE

Jefferson's vision was surprisingly national in scope. To many contemporaries, and no shortage of latter-day observers, Jefferson was either naïve, or simply posturing, when he discussed his conception of an "empire for liberty." While Jefferson's ideal was radically opposed to central authority – the amalgam of republican thought and his experience with the British metropole – it was aggressively national, even imperial in its ambitions. As one leading Jefferson scholar put it, "Its strength could not be measured in conventional military terms but rather in the loyalty of the patriotic citizens who would rise up in defense of their own liberties and their country's independence whenever they were threatened." This was to be a nation that was bound by more than its fear of visible central authority (whether external or internal). Rather, it was to be united by its citizens' shared affection for liberty and self-government.[5]

---

[4] John Quincy Adams, First Annual Message, 6 December 1825, in Richardson, *Messages and Papers*, 2:311.
[5] Onuf, *Jefferson's Empire*, 1–2, 53, 55. See also chap. 2, generally.

Thomas Jefferson was no less a nationalist than Hamilton. In contrast to Hamilton, however, Jefferson envisioned a nation linked through the affective bonds of citizenship, rather than a conspicuous and powerful central government. For Jefferson, union was a matter of the heart, not the stuff of administrative apparatus and coercion. In his inaugural address of 1801, Jefferson equated his supporters to the "sons of liberty" who had cast off the rule of a corrupt ministry and Parliament a quarter of a century earlier.

National identity would be sustained through a hierarchy of interlocking authorities. Popular sovereignty legitimized each, in Jefferson's view – from village through state and state through federal union. Equality at each level was crucial to this vision. Citizens had to be equal to each other within their states and states had to be equal within the union. Whatever affinity Americans shared would be cultivated through their common commitment to this egalitarian framework. Protecting citizens' civil liberties was essential to this scheme. It ensured that each citizen was equal to the next. This did not mean that each was equally talented, wealthy, or wise. Nor did it do much for women, slaves, and those other Americans denied the rights of citizenship. It did mean, however, that the status of citizens – as citizen – was equal. Equality guaranteed that each citizen within his state, or each state within the union, would retain their independence.[6]

Only a union that ensured equality could guarantee uncoerced consent by its members. The British empire had failed precisely because its parts had been unequal, allowing the metropole to dominate the provinces, threatening the liberties of individual citizens. Interlocking authority that *constituted* central government would allow for expansion while preserving citizens' independence.[7]

Patriotism, from Jefferson's perspective, was not cerebral; it was visceral and affective. In the emotional victory of 1800, popular sovereignty, not the Constitution, provided the connection back to America's revolutionary fathers. Senator Nathaniel Macon of North Carolina shared Jefferson's views on this. "Artificial regulations," enforced by a distant government, Macon feared, would destroy any chance of extending the reach of a true republic. Mutual affection and warm feelings was the

---

[6] Ibid., 8, 10–11, 14.
[7] Robert Kagan, *Dangerous Nation* (New York, NY: Knopf, 2006), 32–33; Onuf, *Jefferson's Empire*, 95–96.

bond that would hold the states of the union together. "They must be bound together by love," Macon preached.[8]

Like Hamilton, Jefferson worried that Americans would forget what united them. Unlike Hamilton, however, Jefferson did not believe that a conspicuous government – especially at the national level – was the solution to the problem. As one legal scholar put it, "Republicans hoped that the federal government could carry on its limited affairs and conduct its administration so softly and invisibly that citizens would hardly know that it existed." Rather, protecting the libertarian legacy of the Revolution – as ultimately embodied in the Bill of Rights – would solidify the nation. These principles would remind Americans of their common identity and would propel citizens collectively to defend them. Without these commonly shared beliefs, reinforced through a commitment to self-government at the local level, it might indeed take an oppressive national apparatus to preserve the union – a prospect that Jefferson viewed as even more frightening than disunion. This is why Jefferson considered the Federalist Alien and Sedition Acts to be a direct attack on the liberties shared by all citizens.[9]

Constant vigilance was required if the bonds of affection, and the equality that activated them, were to prevail. Citizens had to remain vigilant in order to preserve the liberties shared by all. This was no easy task because civil liberties required protection just when it was politically unpopular to do so. Only states could assure these protections, Jefferson believed.[10]

Jefferson's party ultimately came to see the Federalists as threatening the affective bonds that preserved the American nation. Federalists

---

[8] Onuf, *Jefferson's Empire*, 13–14; *Register of Debates in Congress*, 20th Cong., 1st sess., 20 May 1828, 794, http://memory.loc.gov/ammem/amlaw/, quoted in Major L. Wilson, *Space, Time, and Freedom: The Quest for Nationality and the Irrepressible Conflict, 1815–1861* (Westport, CT: Greenwood Press, 1974), 68. As Onuf concludes, "The nation Jefferson imagined was united in principle, harmonious in its interdependent interests, homogenous in character: an expansive family of families, cherishing the legacy of the revolutionary fathers while looking forward to the spread of successive generations across an empty continent." Onuf, *Jefferson's Empire*, 78. Summing up the views of Macon, Randolph, and Tyler, Major Wilson concludes that "The Union in this sense was not a 'thickening' institutional or coercive presence, but rather a fellowship of freemen faithful to the simple charter made by the fathers." Wilson, *Space, time, and Freedom*, 68.

[9] Jerry L. Mashaw, "Reluctant Nationalists: Federal Administrative Law in the Republican Era, 1801–1829," *Yale Law Journal*, 116, no. 8 (June 2007): 1640; Onuf, *Jefferson's Empire*, 81–82.

[10] Onuf, *Jefferson's Empire*, 13, 78, 85.

were too quick to embrace statist coercion. This shortcut to national solidarity undermined the true basis for union, as Republicans envisioned it.
Republican mobilization in defense of civil liberties became virtually synonymous with national security – more powerful than standing armies or
national banks.[11]

Ultimately, Jefferson equated national solidarity with the Republican
Party itself. The passions aroused by political parties served his purposes
well. In a remarkable letter written in 1811 to Republican editor William
Duane, Jefferson claimed that the "union of all [this country's] friends"
(by which he meant Republicans) was essential in order "to resist its enemies within and without." "If we do not act in phalanx, as when we rescued it from the satellites of monarchism [in the election of 1800], I will
not say our *party*, [for] the term is false and degrading, but our *nation*
will be undone. For the republicans are the *nation*." This, of course,
placed the Federalists outside the nation. As Jefferson saw it, Republicans
had rebuffed the Federalist counter-revolution of the 1790s with their
own "revolution" of 1800. It was only then that Americans secured their
future by demonstrating that their love of liberty and equality could support national ambitions.[12]

"TRUE VIRTUE CANNOT REQUIRE THAT MEN SHOULD BECOME TOTALLY DETACHED FROM THEMSELVES": UPDATING VIRTUE

In spite of appearances, governing Republicans were more than willing
to use the latent authority of the General Government once they moved
from minority to majority status. Though Jefferson's victory was hailed
as a "revolution," Republicans eventually embraced a large part of
Hamilton's economic policy. The expansion-oriented Jefferson ordered
plans drawn up for a national road – the nation's first interstate internal
improvement. Madison approved the Tariff of 1816, which was the first
impost designed explicitly to protect manufacturing. Addressing Congress
in 1816, President Madison cited "flourishing conditions" as the catalyst
for pressing forward with "undertakings conducive to the wealth and

[11] Onuf, *Jefferson's Empire*, 190–91, 131.
[12] Jefferson to William Duane, March 28, 1811, in *The Writings of Thomas Jefferson*,
ed. Andrew A. Lipscomb and Albert Ellery Bergh, 20 vols. (Washington, D.C.: Thomas
Jefferson Memorial Foundation, 1903–4), 13:28–29, quoted in Onuf, *Jefferson's Empire*, 131.

individual comfort of our citizens." These included a national university
and an enlarged military. Congress rechartered the Bank of the United
States in 1816 with Madison's support. Monroe and John Quincy Adams
further committed the national government to internal improvements by
backing a series of regional canals.[13]

It was Jefferson's party that recalibrated the balance between the
commonweal and private interests to justify nineteenth-century national
internal improvements. Conceived as public investment that promoted
individual liberty, as opposed to wise governance administered by enlightened elites, publicly funded internal improvements at the state and local
level remained a staple of American governance, despite their colossal
financial failure in the 1790s. Naturalizing interest and acknowledging
that it was an inevitable part of the political process paved the way for
even more internal improvements, including many funded by the General
Government. Despite the public's concern about corruption, the demand
for publicly funded internal improvements only increased over the next
forty years.[14]

The notion that politics could be organized around virtue was put to
the test by easy access to land, economic development, and war. In each
instance, the give and take of politics broke down many of the theoretical
distinctions between republican ideals of virtuous independence and liberal conceptions of markets forged by self-interested parties. Influential
leaders in the political economy that emerged acknowledged that politics was driven by self-interest, but drew upon the potential to advance
both self-interest and collective interests through government-guided
endeavors.[15]

[13] Saul Cornell, *The Other Founders: Anti-Federalism and the Dissenting Tradition in America, 1728–1828* (Chapel Hill, NC: University of North Carolina Press, 1999), 274–75; Sellers, *Market Revolution,* 34, 74–75; Madison, First Annual Message, December 5, 1815, in *A Compilation of the Messages and Papers of the Presidents, 1789–1897,* ed. James D. Richardson, 10 vols. (Washington, D.C.: GPO, 1896), 1:56, quoted in Sellers, *Market Revolution,* 71; Kermit L. Hall, *The Magic Mirror: Law in American History* (New York, NY: Oxford University Press, 1989), 89. As Forrest McDonald put it, "the rule of thumb seemed to be, when one's rivals or enemies were in control of the central government, one was prone to savor states' rights, but when one's own faction was in control, the doctrine lost its zest." *States' Rights,* 48.
[14] Larson, *Internal Improvement,* 37; Daniel Feller, *The Public Lands in Jacksonian Politics* (Madison, WI: University of Wisconsin Press, 1984), 82.
[15] Daniel Walker Howe explores the relationship between self-interest and virtue in Benjamin Franklin's thought, arguing that Franklin urged virtuous behavior out of enlightened self-interest. Hard work, and thrift, for instance, were the logical consequences of self-interest, rightly understood, as they would lead both to individual happiness and the happiness of

Interest replaced public virtue as the glue that connected citizens to their government. This evolution, which allowed strangers to cooperate toward mutual ends, was part of a larger shift in the definition of citizenship as it expanded dramatically to include most adult white males. Both the expansion of citizenship and the extensive nature of the union were important American adaptations to republican ideals. Virtue was still revered, but in the public sphere it was increasingly associated with republican vigilance, which placed far fewer demands on the citizen. With the growing acceptance of men's self-interest, honesty in commercial dealings remained a valued trait. But virtue also was associated with the domestic sphere, especially, middle-class white women. Acknowledging the crucial role of self-interest, both Republicans and even some Democrats perceived the public good to be inextricably linked to personal gain and individual improvement. Effective public policy would stimulate private action that redounded to the benefit of all citizens.[16]

Politically successful public policy, however, remained hidden in plain sight. It avoided, at all costs, the traditional trappings of state power. Any semblance of an administrative state took a back seat to increasingly ubiquitous market mechanisms. Americans naturalized the market even as they turned to federal fiscal and legal policy to promote it.

A different conception of virtue replaced older understandings as the franchise expanded, and citizens discarded past patterns of deference. One Anti-Federalist wrote that "the several orders of men in society

the greatest number. Jonathan Edwards, on the other hand, demanded that individuals transcend self-interest, if they were to be granted divine grace. *Making the American Self: Jonathan Edwards to Abraham Lincoln* (Cambridge, MA: Harvard University Press, 1997), 27–29, 38–39.

[16] I would like to thank Michael Holt for making the points about vigilance and honesty in commercial transactions. For a summary of these points, see Holt, *The Rise and Fall of the American Whig Party: Jacksonian Politics and the Onset of the Civil War* (New York, NY: Oxford University Press, 1999), 3–5. On the domestic sphere, and links between it and public sphere, see Mary P. Ryan, *Cradle of the Middle Class: The Family in Oneida County, New York, 1790–1865* (New York, NY: Cambridge University Press, 1981). On the emergence of self-interest, see Sellers, *Market Revolution*. In contrast to Sellers, besides linking the conception of self-interest to virtue – at least among thinkers like Benjamin Franklin, Howe provides a valuable discussion of a related cultural concept – improvement – which, as he points out, was applied by leaders like John Quincy Adams to both public affairs (internal improvements) and individuals. See *Making the American Self*, 122–28, and *What Hath God Wrought: The Transformation of America, 1815–1848* (New York, NY: Oxford University Press, 2007), 243–45. On the topic of self-improvement over two hundred and fifty years, see Joseph Kett, *The Pursuit of Knowledge Under Difficulties: From Self-Improvement to Adult Education in America, 1750–1990* (Palo Alto, CA: Stanford University Press, 1994).

which we call aristocratical, democratic, merchantile, mechanic, & c."
represented distinct interests that could only be checked by opposing
interests. The solution? "Each order must have a share in the business of
legislation actually and efficiently." As interest replaced virtue as the basis
for political participation, virtue became a personal rather than a public
trait. Virtue became a quality associated with one's private life, especially
the white women who epitomized the domestic sphere.[17]

Advocates for greater democratic participation questioned the classical
link between property, independence, and virtue. The Republican operative and lawyer Tunis Wortman was a good example. Wortman wondered
whether independence was even desirable. "True virtue cannot require that
men should become totally detached from themselves," Wortman wrote in
1800. Understanding one's true interests, not rising above such interests,
was the prerequisite that Wortman and an increasing number of middle-
class Americans considered essential to proper political behavior. Property,
Wortman argued, did not automatically produce independence. Americans
without property had vital rights and deserved access to the polity in order
to defend their rights. In any case, property in America was too fluid,
Wortman argued, to make it the sole prerequisite for virtuous behavior.[18]

Republican leader Albert Gallatin also fused liberal and republican
ideals. A manufacturer himself, Gallatin endorsed commercial growth
and sought to expand the American market in ways that would promote
a variety of individual interests. Gallatin did not neglect the collective
elements of republicanism, even as he warned of the dangers of national
consolidation. Gallatin believed that economic development could and
should be directed by the government for the common benefit of the
public. He preferred to use state government to achieve these ends, but
as Jefferson's Secretary of the Treasury, Gallatin did not balk at crafting ambitious plans for national promotion of both transportation and
manufacturing.[19]

---

[17] Letters from the Federal Farmer, no. 7, in *The Complete Anti-Federalist*, ed. Herbert J.
Storing (Chicago, IL: University of Chicago Press, 1981), 2: 266–68, cited in Cornell,
Other Founders, 98; Trees, *Founding Fathers*, 2. On the dichotomy between male and
female virtue, and the implications for the rights of citizenship, see Linda K. Kerber,
Women of the Republic: Intellect and Ideology in Revolutionary America (Chapel Hill,
NC: University of North Carolina Press, 1980).

[18] Tunis Wortman, *A Treatise, Concerning Political Enquiry, and the Liberty of the Press*,
(New York, NY, 1800: repr. New York, NY: Di Capo Press, 1970), 104, quoted in Cornell,
Other Founders, 256; Cornell, *Other Founders*, 256–58.

[19] Cornell, *Other* Founders, 180. While I do not subscribe to all aspects of Charles Sellers's
interpretation of the Jacksonian era, I do agree with his assertion that "Commercial

As Republicans consolidated their majority, and especially in the wake of the 1812 War, the party attracted an increasing number of men wedded to entrepreneurial enterprise. They clamored for state aid to private enterprise. Public officials responded in the commercial states. As the preamble to an act granting a state loan to Pennsylvania steel workers proclaimed, "Works of public importance deserve public encouragement." While the vast majority of legal and fiscal aid to commercial development took place on the state and local level, the General Government was hardly immune to appeals from determined constituencies.[20]

Some public officials who warned of consolidation made exceptions when government promoted private economic development. And those who leaned toward stronger general government justified their position by citing the private benefits that government stimulated. Surrounded and enmeshed in interest, Americans naturalized it. They placed interest at the heart of politics and public policy. Americans perceived interest and the public good to be inextricably linked, especially in the service of economic development. In a number of instances, both Federalists and Republicans concluded that the nation was best served by purposeful public action that promoted private interest. Successful development, in turn, promoted discourse, trade, and shared values that knit the nation together. Considered from another angle, sustained public commitment to energetic government was justified in part by the opportunities for the private gain and self-improvement that it created.[21]

Self-interest eclipsed virtue as the life blood of governance by the early nineteenth century. Explaining the relationship between self-interest and collective benefits was still crucial to the success of any political program. But the growing belief that the market would "naturally" sort out these competing interests easily overshadowed the significant role that the General Government played in guiding this process.

---

boom made government promotion of economic growth the central dynamic of American politics." *Market Revolution: Jacksonian America, 1815–1846* (New York, NY: Oxford University Press, 1991), 32.

[20] Sellers, *Market Revolution*, 40;; Theodore Sky, *To Provide for the General Welfare: A History of the Federal Spending Power* (Newark, DE: University of Delaware Press, 2003), 132–38; Robert Alan Rutland, *The Presidency of James Madison* (Lawrence, KS: University Press of Kansas, 1990), 195.

[21] On the growing competition between interests to capture the regulatory and administrative capacity of the state in an earlier period, see John Brewer, *The Sinews of Power: War, Money and the English State, 1688–1783* (Boston, MA: Unwin Hyman, 1989), 248–51.

"THEIR INTERESTS WILL BE IDENTIFIED,
AND THEIR UNION CEMENTED":
THE POLITICAL CONSTRAINTS ON PLANNING

Republicans supported internal improvements because roads and canals remained a crucial way to link the nation together. In 1796, Congress provided subsidies to Zane's Trace, a trail running from western Virginia to Ohio. In the public land states that subsequently joined the Union, as well as Ohio, 5 percent of the net proceeds for public land sales were set aside for road construction. Two-fifths of this portion was reserved for the General Government to improve interregional transport after states were carved out of this territory.[22]

In the final analysis, Jeffersonians were committed to a developmental vision that required access to and control over resources that lay west of the existing line of settlement. Although Congressional Republicans during the 1790s applied "strict construction" interpretations of the constitution to block some internal improvements, Jefferson and his Republican successors were too wedded to the vision of expansion to scuttle internal improvements completely. Beneath the internal improvements advocates' appeal to the common welfare of the nation lay a variety of conflicting motivations. Some backers were driven solely by the possibility of private gain. Others cited national advantages but were grounded in local or regional competition.[23]

---

[22] Mary W.M. Hargreaves, *The Presidency of John Quincy Adams* (Lawrence: University Press of Kansas, 1985), 6; Feller, *Public Lands*, 8–9.

[23] There was, however, no lack of interest in internal improvements during the 1790s. Larson, *Internal Improvement*, 18–19, 39–41.

   Even Washington was afraid to propose federal projects, for fear of stirring up anti-consolidation feeling. Though a strong advocate of nationally supported internal improvements, Washington left them out of his initial address to Congress. He feared that such a proposal might be too controversial. On Washington's "Western" perspective, see Ellis, *Founding Brothers*, 133–35.

   On the role that rivers played in Jefferson's vision of the West, see James P. Ronda, "A Promise of Rivers: Thomas Jefferson and the Exploration of Western Waterways," in *Frontier and Region: Essays in Honor of Martin Ridge*, ed. Robert C. Ritchie and Paul Andrew Hutton (Albuquerque, NM: University of New Mexico Press, 1997), 27–42. On competition with other states, see p. 31.

   In the case of Washington's beloved Potomac project, Henry Lee was attracted by the potential for spectacular gain. While Lee went to jail firmly believing that his speculation provided a public service, others remembered him merely as "the swindling Harry Lee." By contrast, James Madison did not expect to gain personally from the project. Rather, he saw it as a way to propel Virginia's development at the expense of its rivals. In opposition to Washington's Atlantic Coast-based vision for trade, Madison felt it was impossible folly

Motivation mattered little when it came to results. All of these ventures failed. Dividends were rare, expenses hefty. By December 1804, New York canal projects had gobbled over $350,000. The Potomac Canal had swallowed $450,000 in capital by 1808, while yielding annual earnings that barely averaged $6,500. Expertise was in short supply, but even the projects attended by nationally recognized experts failed financially. All promoters vastly overestimated traffic and underestimated costs.[24]

To be sure, private investors bore many of these losses. Yet most Americans interpreted failure as evidence that corruption had prevailed over virtue. Public expenditures were committed first and recovered last. To make matters worse, pressure for quick returns on the first public dollar, and the quest for local advantage, often forced short-sighted design changes that virtually ensured long-term failure.[25]

Corruption plagued some projects. There was enough outright fraud and mismanagement to justify the public's disgust. Internal improvements were large, visible, and permanent. Whether measured as benefits promised or taxes levied, few other publicly funded services or ventures affected as many lives. Failed internal improvements during the 1790s undermined the Federalist conceit that a natural harmony of interests would coalesce given proper national leadership. Not even George Washington's steady hand could calm the cauldron of interests and parochial loyalties that seethed just below the surface of republican rhetoric.[26]

Public expenditures undertaken by the states were one thing. Given Jefferson's fear of consolidation, federally managed internal improvements were another matter. In 1796 Jefferson bridled at his friend James Madison's legislation that proposed federal funding for a survey of a national post road that ran from Georgia to Maine. Jefferson warned his friend that the bill would prove a "source of boundless patronage to the executive, jobbing to members of Congress & their friends, and a bottomless abyss of public money." The appropriations might come from the

to bottle up the natural flow of settlers and trade. These would inevitably flow through the Mississippi. Larson, *Internal Improvement*, 21, 23.
[24] Larson, *Internal Improvement*, I 28–29; on engineering expertise at the time, and for a good comparison to the far more centralized French approach, see Todd Shallat, *Structures in the Stream: Water, Science, and the Rise of the U.S. Army Corps of Engineers* (Austin, TX: University of Texas Press, 1994), 15–36.
[25] Larson, *Internal Improvement*, 30.
[26] Ibid., 31–32, 37.

post office surplus initially, Jefferson hectored, but other revenues would soon be encumbered. This would set off a "scramble" in Congress to see who "can get the most money wasted in their State."[27]

As president, however, Jefferson supported national projects whenever a constitutionally feasible rationale could be crafted. While Jefferson preferred to keep government close to the people, he understood that internal improvements financed by the states faced the kind of obstacles that had led groups in Pennsylvania, Maryland, North Carolina, and his own Virginia right back to the General Government.[28]

Republican principles were no match for partisan advantage in the face of continued pressure for internal improvements. Jefferson signed the Cumberland Road Act without hesitation. This legislation provided for the construction of a road from Cumberland, Maryland to the Ohio border. Because the original compact was signed with a territory, constitutional authority for this construction was not disputed. Between 1806 and 1820 the federal government appropriated more than $1.5 million for the Cumberland Road – which became known as the National Highway – despite charges of corruption and sectional advantage. Politically, support for this national road certainly made sense to Republicans. Republicans responded to the growing constituent demand for nationally funded internal improvements, targeting the Federalist establishment in the old Ohio territory. It was now the Federalists who worried about strict construction, fearing that the majority of projects would benefit Republican districts.[29]

Jefferson was overwhelmed by the demands for projects. Recoiling at the interest-based squabbling, often between factions within the

---

[27] Madison's proposal passed in the house but died in the Senate. Larson, *Internal Improvement*, 22, 41, 48; Jefferson to Madison, March 6, 1796, in *The Works of Thomas Jefferson*, Federal Edition, ed. Paul Leicester Ford, 12 vols. (London: GP Putnam's; New York, Knickerbocker Press, 1904), 8:226, online at Library of Congress, *The Thomas Jefferson Papers*, http://memory.loc.gov/ammem/collections/jefferson_papers/index.html, quoted in Larson, *Internal Improvement*, 48.

[28] Larson *Internal Improvement*, 73.

[29] W. Stull Holt, *The Office of the Chief of Engineers of the Army: Its Non-Military History, Activities, and Organization*, Institute for Government Research: Service Monographs of the United States Government No. 27 (Baltimore, MD: Johns Hopkins University Press, 1923), 4; Pamela L. Baker, "The Washington National Road Bill and the Struggle to Adopt a Federal System of Internal Improvement," *Journal of the Early Republic*, 22, no. 3 (Autumn 2002): 440; Larson, *Internal Improvement*, 54–55. Bartholomew H. Sparrow, "U.S. Territorial Policy: Subsidy and Settlement, 1783–1898," (Paper presented to Journal of Policy History Conference, 1999), 25.

Republican Party, Jefferson called for a constitutional amendment. At the same time, he endorsed the public advantages that internal improvements might yield, in spite of the self-interested motivations that drove many of the demands. "New channels of communication will be opened between the States; the lines of separation will disappear, their interests will be identified, and their union cemented by new and indissoluble ties," Jefferson wrote in 1806. Jefferson struggled to craft a policy that articulated his vision for the nation's development while satisfying his interpretation of the Constitution and his constituents.[30]

Republican support for a road that provided access to a territory, rather than one that connected two or more existing states, suggests that there was a substantive basis behind the states rights argument – one based on experience. The states had already established well-worn patterns of influence and allegiance among their citizens. They had a track record. This was precisely the kind of attachment that Hamilton so desperately hoped to cultivate between citizens and the national government. It epitomized the affective bonds that Jefferson idealized. But this experience and attachment did not extend to the national government in most instances.[31]

Established state loyalties proved to be a formidable obstacle to national planning. Many Americans clamored for internal improvements. But they worried about distant government dictating routes and larding improvements with political patronage and "jobbing." It was not simply that Americans wanted government that was small and close to home, although that was certainly important. They also wanted services delivered by a unit of government that they were experienced with and that itself had experience.

It was Thomas Jefferson's Secretary of the Treasury, Albert Gallatin, who crafted the most ambitious plan for internal improvements in the first half of the nineteenth century. Gallatin owned a glassworks that also contracted with the state militia to produce munitions. He was elected to

---

[30] Sky, *To Provide for the General Welfare*, 114–16; Jefferson, Sixth Annual Message to Congress, December 2, 1806, in Richardson, *Messages and Papers*, 1:409.

Where Jefferson determined that he did have clear authority, he was unyielding to local demands. When Gallatin informed the President in 1807 that the Pennsylvania legislature had approved the Cumberland Road, but preferred an alternative route that satisfied more constituents, Jefferson flatly refused to compromise (despite Gallatin's endorsement of the change). Jefferson would not brook "a single example of yielding to the State the direction of a road made at the national expense and for national purposes." Jefferson to Gallatin, April 22, 1808, in Lipscomb and Bergh, *Writings of Thomas Jefferson*, 12:31–32, quoted in Sky, *To Provide for the General Welfare*, 127.

[31] Sparrow, "U.S. Territorial Policy," 25.

the Senate in 1793, soon unseated, and then returned to Congress from western Pennsylvania in 1795. Gallatin backed efforts to charter a state bank in Pennsylvania because he opposed creating more national debt. While a strong advocate of Republican "economy," Gallatin did not balk at government intervention in the economy if it served public ends.[32]

With the "revolution" of 1800, Gallatin was finally in a position to act upon his convictions: economic ties held the union together, and it was the General Government's obligation to promote commercial interaction within its borders. His Report on Manufactures, issued in 1810, called for increased tariff protection and direct federal loans to key manufacturing sectors. Although Congress never passed this proposal, the cumulative payout that Gallatin proposed – $20 million – demonstrated that there was substantial support for direct aid to business even within the Republican Party. Like Adam Smith, Gallatin believed that internal improvements that helped to integrate the market and a nation were a legitimate public responsibility. "Good roads, canals, and navigable rivers," Smith wrote, "by diminishing the expense of carriage, put remote parts of the country more nearly upon a level with those in the neighborhood of the town. They are upon that account the greatest of all improvements."[33]

Gallatin used similar language in 1802 when he proposed that 10 percent of the revenues from land sales be dedicated to the construction of turnpikes linking navigable waterways and remote areas of the country. This would "contribute toward cementing the bonds of the Union between those parts of the United States whose local interests have been considered as most dissimilar," Gallatin argued. In 1807 the Senate passed a resolution calling for the Secretary of the Treasury to prepare a plan for national internal improvements, specifying the means to finance such a plan. A year later, Albert Gallatin submitted his *Report on the Subject of Roads and Canals*. The *Report* included an inventory of all road and canal projects underway or planned in the states. It also

---

[32] John R. Nelson, *Liberty and Property: Political Economy and Policymaking in the New Nation, 1789–1812* (Baltimore, MD: Johns Hopkins University Press, 1987), 154; Cornell, *Other Founders*, 179; Robin L. Einhorn, *American Taxation, American Slavery* (Chicago, IL: University of Chicago Press, 2006), 189.

[33] Nelson, *Liberty and Property*, 116, 156–57; Adam Smith, *An Inquiry into the Nature and Causes of the Wealth of Nations*, ed. R.H. Campbell and A.S. Skinner (Oxford, UK: Clarendon Press, New York, NY: Oxford University Press, 1981), 1:147, 681–82, cited in Nelson, *Liberty and Property* 119. On John Quincy Adams's fascination with Smith regarding internal improvements, see Howe, *What Hath God Wrought*, 252.

contained recommendations for ways to fuse and supplement these projects in order to form a national system of transportation.[34]

The plan bound together each state east of the Mississippi through waterways that radiated from an axis in the Ohio River. Where natural waterways failed, man-made roads and canals were envisioned. Gallatin advocated funding this $20 million proposal out of future federal surpluses. Only the General Government, Gallatin argued, was in a position to support internal improvements in such a comprehensive and coordinated fashion. "With these resources and embracing the whole Union," Gallatin promised, "it will compete on any given line all the improvements, however distant, which may be necessary to render the whole productive, and eminently beneficial."[35]

Like Hamilton, Gallatin argued that the plan integrated more than commerce. Good roads and transportation would "unite by a still more intimate community of interests, the most remote quarters of the United States. No other single operation within the power of the government can more effectually tend to strengthen and perpetuate that union, which secures external independence, domestic peace and internal liberty." By shortening the travel time between sections and promoting communications and intercourse, internal improvements would also strengthen the affection that Americans felt for each other and their union.[36]

The rhetoric of national integration was hard to resist. Even advocates of state projects, like Governor Clinton, who soon promoted the Erie Canal, considered it a means to benefit "the whole republic ... bound together by the golden ties of commerce and the adamantine chains of interest." States consistently (and unsuccessfully) sought federal funding

---

[34] Nelson, *Liberty and Property*, 124; Albert Gallatin to William B. Giles, in *The Writings of Albert Gallatin*, ed. Henry Adams, 3 vols. (Philadelphia, PA: JB Lippincot, 1879; repr. New York: Antiquarian Press, 1960), 1:79, cited in Nelson, *Liberty and Property*, 124; Michael J. Lacey, "Federalism and National Planning: The Nineteenth-Century Legacy," in *The American Planning Tradition: Culture and Policy*, ed. Robert Fishman (Washington, D.C.: Woodrow Wilson Center Press, 2000), 101–4; Shallat, *Structures in the Stream*, 118–21.

[35] Lacey, "Federalism and National Planning," 102; Albert Gallatin, *Report of the Secretary of the Treasury on the Subject of Roads and Canals*, Reprints of Economic Classics (New York: Augustus M. Kelley, 1968), 7–8, quoted in Lacey, "Federalism and National Planning," 103–4.

[36] Gallatin, *Report 8*, quoted in Lacey, "Federalism and National Planning," 104. See also Drew Evan VandeCreek, "Make It National!": Economic Expertise and the Development of the Progressive Economic Policymaking System, 1890–1933" (PhD diss., University of Virginia, 1996), 54.

for local projects. However, once they had poured their own funds into these large-scale projects, they were loath to support federal funding for projects that might compete with their own investments.[37]

Gallatin's plan was never enacted. It was opposed by the Old Republicans on the grounds that it dangerously expanded the power of the federal government. Even nationally oriented Republicans, from Jefferson to Monroe, expressed misgivings on constitutional grounds. Although Gallatin believed that the plan could be enacted through a series of agreements between federal and state government, all three presidents demanded a constitutional amendment before undertaking such an ambitious project.[38]

Gallatin was also a strong supporter of the Bank of the United States – a position that initially distinguished him from many of his Republican colleagues. Gallatin successfully lobbied for a branch bank in the nation's capital and pressed for another in New Orleans. Like good transportation, Gallatin argued, these banks would strengthen the bonds of Union through improved commercial ties between distant partners. He suggested sweeping revisions that actually would have expanded the Bank of the United States. When these failed, Gallatin advocated rechartering the Bank.[39]

In the wake of the the financial disruptions caused by the War of 1812, Republicans reconsidered their position on the Bank. Congress, with the support of James Madison, chartered the Second Bank of the United States in 1816. It more than tripled the capitalization of Hamilton's original bank. Starved for cash during the War and eager to regularize currency discrepancies exacerbated by the proliferation of state banks, Madison swept aside constitutional concerns and embraced the idea of a national bank. Within the Republican Party, support came from National Republicans such as Henry Clay and John C. Calhoun, along with representatives of commercial enterprise such as Gallatin and Treasury Secretary Alexander Dallas. The General Government appointed one-fifth of the new Bank's directors, agreed to deposit the Treasury's funds in

---

[37] DeWitt Clinton, Message to the Legislature, 1819, in *Jacksonian America, 1815–1840: New Society, Changing Politics*, ed. Frank Otto Gatell and John M. McFaul (Englewood Cliffs, NJ: Prentice-Hall, 1970), 11, quoted in Steven Siry, *DeWitt Clinton and the American Political Economy: Sectionalism, Politics, and Republican Ideology, 1787–1828* (New York, NY: Peter Lang, 1990), 8; Feller, *Public Lands*, 55–57; McDonald, *States' Rights*, 75.

[38] Hargreaves, *Presidency of John Quincy Adams*, 4.

[39] Nelson, *Liberty and Property*, 129.

this bank, and agreed to accept notes from Bank of the United States for payment of obligations to the federal government. The Bank also paid the U.S. government a bonus of $1.5 million. In return, the Bank received the exclusive right to operate nationally and establish branch banks.[40]

Madison also supported tariffs for textiles and iron, subsidizing the manufacture of these products more generously than Hamilton's failed bounties would have. Adding a few cents to the cost of imports was far less intrusive than Hamilton's plan. All this was too much for some Federalists, who had endured nonstop Republican complaints about similar programs when in the minority. "The Party now in Power seems disposed to do all that federal men ever wished," Gouverneur Morris exclaimed. It would "do more than is good to strengthen and consolidate the federal government," he complained.[41]

An assertive interpretation of national authority did not die with the Federalist Party. Variants of this perspective were extended through the nationalist wing of the Republicans. In the daily give and take of politics, on matters like internal improvements, National Republicans acknowledged the powerful role of self-interest. Indeed, the very purpose of government was to unleash and promote the energy that was often fueled by self-interest. Properly harnessed by the General Government, that energy could be directed toward improving individuals and society alike. Federally financed internal improvements might strengthen the affective bonds of union without stifling the individual initiative that was an essential ingredient in the developmental vision.

"LET US CONQUER SPACE": DEVELOPING THE "AMERICAN SYSTEM"

The American System built upon a nationalist spirit that emerged in the years following Jackson's victory at New Orleans and the protectionist practices that resulted from that war's disruption of foreign trade. Most

---

[40] Ibid., 131; McDonald, *States' Rights*, 74. For perspective on why even Republican local bankers might support rechartering the Bank of the United States in the wake of the 1812 war, see Andrew R.L. Cayton, *The Frontier Republic, Ideology and Politics in the Ohio Country, 1780–1825* (Kent, OH: Kent State University Press, 1986), 117–19; see also, Sellers, *Market Revolution*, 59–72.

[41] McDonald, *States' Rights*, 74; Gouverneur Morris to Rufus King, 26 January 1816, in *The Life of Gouverneur Morris, with Selections from His Corrospondence and Miscellaneous Papers*, ed. Jared Sparks (Boston: Gray and Bowen, 1832), 3:345, quoted in McDonald, *States' Rights*, 74.

directly associated with Henry Clay of Kentucky, the American System
called for the national government to act as a catalyst and coordinator in nurturing an American market for agricultural products by creating demand for them in developing industrial centers. The sectors of
the economy and the regions characterized by these diverse economic
activities would be integrated through internal improvements in transportation and communications. John C. Calhoun, an ardent supporter
of the American System in his brief nationalist phase, pleaded in 1817,
"Let us then ... bind the Republic together with a perfect system of roads
and canals. Let us conquer space. It is thus the most distant parts of the
Republic will be brought within a few days travel of the centre; it is
thus that a citizen of the West will read the news of Boston still moist
from the press." These men believed that geographical isolation presented
the greatest threat to citizens, the states they lived in, and the successful
union of those states.[42]

An energetic General Government animated this system. Foreign policy measures like the Louisiana Purchase, which provided rich opportunities for expansion, and the Monroe Doctrine, which sought to blunt
European penetration into the Americas, were one crucial component.
The tariff was another. Besides protecting fledgling American industry, the
tariff (along with the sale of public lands) also funded internal improvements like roads and canals. A national banking system provided the
basis for credit and a reliable currency. Differences between the advocates
of the American System were most pronounced in foreign policy, where
the emotional and enthusiastic Henry Clay was far more eager to project
American democracy abroad than the more cautious and introspective
New Englander, John Quincy Adams.[43]

Although designed to bind sections to each other, proponents of the
American System never transcended fully their own sectional loyalties,
as evidenced by John C. Calhoun's change of heart, and the intensity
with which Clay and Adams were willing to promote the tariff. The
middle Atlantic states and the western states were the most enthusiastic

---

[42] Hargreaves, *Presidency of John Quincy Adams*, 12, 33; *Annals of Congress*, 14th Cong.
2nd sess., 854, 4 February 1817, http://memory.loc.gov/ammem/amlaw/, quoted in Wayne
E. Fuller, *The American Mail: Enlarger of the Common Life* (Chicago, IL: University of
Chicago Press, 1972), 87; Larson, *Internal Improvement*, 3. Sellers, *Market Revolution*,
places particular emphasis on the war in his interpretation.

[43] Lacey, "Federalism and National Planning," 100; Hargreaves, *Presidency of John Quincy
Adams*, 34, 113.

supporters of the American System. Not coincidentally, these states also stood to benefit most directly from the system.[44]

Advocates of the American System sought to employ the public sector to create a whole that was greater than the sum of its programmatic parts. Advocates of the American System believed that the General Government could identify and promote the general interest. They believed as well that this general interest represented more than the mere aggregation of special interests. Thus, promoting the common good of the nation some- times "may apparently be opposed to the interest of particular sections," John Calhoun argued. This vision of the public good shaped the way that elected officials carried out their duties. "We are, then, each one of us the representative of every interest," Henry C. Martindale of New York lectured his colleagues in the House, "and, of course, of the whole. "Let us be Americans sir, and feel and act Americans." Martindale urged his colleagues to "feel that we have a country, and let those feelings embrace the whole of it." Did the country not stretch from Florida to Yellowstone? From Maine to Oregon? "A warm and expanded patriotism can embrace this wild region," Martindale insisted, "and entertain a common feeling for their remote and distant inhabitants."[45]

By forging bonds of mutual dependence, whether through the national bank, the tariff, or internal improvements, American System advocates sought to build not only roads and a sound credit, but a national char- acter and identity as well. They hoped to enrich the common life of the nation, which would strengthen political support for their more positive view of the General Government. They leaned toward a more capacious interpretation of the constitutional powers of General Government. In their view, there was far greater danger in the government's failure to act than in the potential for abuse of these powers.[46]

At its roots, the American System envisioned a new basis for patriotism and national identity. Proponents of the American System cared deeply

[44] McDonald, *States' Rights*, 72; Wilson, *Space, Time, and Freedom*, 54–55.
[45] *Annals of Congress*, 14th Cong., 2nd sess., February 4, 1817, 854, quoted in Wilson, *Space, Time, and Freedom*, 55; *Annals of Congress*, 18th Cong., 1st sess., February 24, 1824, 1631–32, quoted in Wilson, *Space, Time, and Freedom*, 57.
[46] Wilson, *Space, Time, and Freedom*, 4. There were of course differences of emphasis among the proponents of the American System. Adams was wary of the tariff, but a strong proponent of internal improvements; for Henry Clay, on the other hand, both the tariff and internal improvements were essential., [49–50] On the connection between the American system and Henry Clay's own life experience, see Howe, *What Hath God Wrought*, 270–71.

about the nonmaterial, affective implications of their design. Boosters sought to modulate federal land sales in ways that would limit the flow of population to the West. They hoped to deepen the loyalty that grew from the multigenerational attachment to place. Commercial ties created by the tariff and internal improvements, advocates argued, would create "a close community of interests" that yielded "a daily recollection of their consanguinity." Or as Henry Clay put it, the advocates of the American System hoped to fill out the "merely political" entity created by the Constitution with a thick economic and social network of daily intercourse. "Encourage fabrication at home," Clay urged his colleagues, "and there would instantly arise animation and a healthful circulation throughout all parts of the Republic." Advocates of the American System believed that the constitutional roof not only required sturdy walls; it required all of the amenities of home, including the cozy familiarity inspired by good communications, social interchange, and common economic interests.[47]

In 1816 Henry Clay's nationalist wing of the Republican Party, strengthened by the influx of Federalists after their party collapsed, pushed two bills through Congress that were designed to bind the nation together economically. Besides chartering the Second Bank of the United States for twenty-one years, Congress also passed a mildly protective tariff. Embarrassed by the humiliation that the United States suffered at the hands of Great Britain during its second war with that nation, Madison strengthened peace time defenses.[48]

Henry Clay and John Calhoun also attempted to seize the moment to advance another crucial component of the American System: nationally funded roads and canals. The legislative vehicle for this plan was the Bonus Bill of 1817. It committed a "bonus" of $1.5 million and future dividends that the new Bank of the United States owed the federal government to a restricted fund dedicated to building roads and canals. In its national scope and forthright claims about federal responsibility, the

---

[47] Wilson, *Space, Time, and Freedom*, 63; "The Erie Canal: Meeting of the Waters," from New York *Commercial Advertiser*, October 11, 1823, reprinted in *Niles' Weekly Register*, vol. 25, October 18, 1823, 1, in American Periodicals Series Online, 1740–1900 (Proquest, [doc. no. 811843842]), http://www.proquest.com/, quoted in Wilson, *Space, Time, and Freedom*, 63; *Annals of Congress*, 16th Cong., 1st sess., April 26, 1820, 2044, cited in Wilson, *Space, Time, and Freedom*, 63.

[48] Holt, *American Whig Party*, 3–4; Wilson, *Space, Time, and Freedom*, 58. In 1824, when the presidential election was thrown into the House, Clay threw the support of the Kentucky delegation to John Quincy Adams, largely due to their shared vision for high tariffs and an assertive national role in the transportation project. Paul C. Nagel, *John Quincy Adams: A Public Life, A Private Life* (New York, NY: Knopf, 1997), 293.

legislation revived many of Gallatin's objectives. Seeking to establish this principle without running afoul of local interests, the bill's backers left the knotty problem of specifying projects to future legislators. Calhoun sought to avoid a tangle of parochial squabbles by putting Congress on record that federal funds should be appropriated. The specifics could be debated later. The Bonus Bill did not select any specific routes. In the meantime, Calhoun sought to tap a national constituency for federal largesse.[49]

That the bill addressed funding and constitutional questions rather than specific routes speaks volumes about Calhoun's and Clay's agenda: they sought to establish an important precedent through the legislation in 1817. Politically, it might have been easier to concentrate on constituencies back home. But for Calhoun, both the economic and political future of the union required that the General Government solve problems that distance presented. What, Calhoun asked, "can add more to the wealth, the strength and the political prosperity of our country?"[50]

The bill ran into a buzz saw of opposition. Thomas Bolling Robertson of Louisiana insisted that "The States are better judges of their wants and interests; they know best whether they most require roads or canals, or schools, or dykes, or embankments." The bill would create "one grand, magnificent, consolidated empire" according to Robertson – and he did not mean these words as praise. This Old Republican fear of centralized power forced a series of amendments that stripped the bill's potential to plan nationwide projects and to set priorities among the many claims that were bound to pour in from all of the states. The amendments required that funds be appropriated in proportion to state population and that states consent to any project built in their jurisdiction. Despite the compromises, the bill passed by only two votes.[51]

Jefferson, Madison, and Monroe also wanted to overcome the problems of distance, but they were less eager to compromise the rights of states in doing so. Only days before leaving office, Madison shocked the bill's supporters by vetoing it. Both Madison and Jefferson had supported, or at least tolerated, all of the components of the American System in the past. Madison balked at the kind of pork barrel politics that Congress

[49] Larson, *Internal Improvement*, 64, 66; Baker, "Washington National Road," 442.

[50] Larson, *Internal Improvement*, 65; *Annals of Congress*, 14th Cong., 2nd sess., February 4, 1817, 851, cited in Larson, *Internal Improvement*, 65.

[51] *Annals of Congress*, 14th Cong., 2nd sess., February 4, 1817, 865, cited in Larson, *Internal Improvement*, 66; Larson, *Internal Improvement*, 67.

might pursue if the Bonus Bill passed. Even worse, he feared that, should the bill pass, constitutional safeguards would become mere tokens of the founders' past sentiments, easily overridden by popular will.

To interpret the common defense and general welfare clause of the Constitution as permitting the national government to construct roads and canals would render "the special and careful enumeration of powers, which follow the clause, nugatory and improper." Madison insisted on strict construction that preserved the "definite partition of powers between the General and State Governments." The kind of national initiative proposed in the Bonus Bill could only proceed if the Constitution were amended. And on this issue, Madison had the final word.[52]

That is not to say that advocates of the American System gave up. Senator James Barbour introduced a constitutional amendment that provided explicit Congressional authority to appropriate funds for roads, canals, and improved navigation. Barbour's intent was economic and political integration, not consolidation. He stated clearly that "whatever could be as well done by the States as the General Government ... should be retained exclusively to the States. But "establishing military roads from one end to the other of this extensive empire, or an internal navigation on the same scale, required the resources and the superintending power of the General Government." In Barbour's opinion, "that which is national should belong to the General Government." Despite President Monroe's support, the amendment did not make it out of the Senate. In the House, Henry St. George Tucker issued a committee report that summed up the relationship between internal improvement and national power. As the Confederation had proven, *inadequate* authority to act on behalf of the nation, and *not* too much power, was the real threat to the union.[53]

Henry Clay found nothing to fear in an ambitious national program. He lashed out against those who would impose upon the Constitution a "water-gruel regimen" or construe it as a "dead letter," reducing it "to an inanimate skeleton." "Who should deny to the Constitution," Clay asked, "the sheet-anchor of the national safety – the vigor which is necessary, in the exercise of its powers, to fulfill the purposes of its institution, and to carry this country to the high destination which it is one day to reach?" While those merely listening to the Congressional debate might be

---

[52] *Annals of Congress*, 14th Cong., 2nd sess., March 3, 1817, 12, cited in Larson, *Internal Improvement*, 68–69. See also Sky, *To Provide for the General Welfare*.

[53] Larson, *Internal Improvement*, 111; *Annals of Congress*, 15th Cong., 1st sess., December 9, 1817, 24, cited in Larson, *Internal Improvement*, 112.

tempted to believe "that Congress were about to introduce some plague or pestilence – some gorgon dire – which was to destroy the liberties of the country," in fact, the advocates of internal improvements merely sought to "promote social intercourse; to facilitate commerce between the States; to strengthen the bonds of our Union; to make us really and truly one family – one community in interest and in feeling." If preserving the Union was the most important objective of the federal government, internal improvements were one of the most important means toward realizing that end. Contrasting his views with those of the strict constructionist Philip Pendleton Barbour, Clay elaborated the difference: "he considers everything gained to the States from the General Government as something snatched from a foreign Power. I consider it as a Government coordinate with them, and the true construction, I think, is to give it all that vigor and vitality which rightfully belong to it."[54]

Legislators wedded to states rights or local privilege responded with vigor of their own. James Johnson of Virginia sarcastically admitted that he "never aspired to attain the sublime height, from which the Speaker ... views in prospect the destinies of this great nation." Johnson was content to follow at "a humble distance," taking aim at Clay's "new system of political economy." "Commerce is to be diverted from its wonted channel; agriculture to assume a new character; human skill and industry to be placed under the tutelage of the Government; the condition of the people, in the different sections of the country, to be rendered precisely equal, by an artificial system of legislation." Allowing the General Government to construct projects without the consent of the States, Lemuel Sawyer of North Carolina responded, sounded like Nero, not the American Constitution. "Those who may come with their axes, spades, and shovels, to tear the virgin bosom of our country, in defiance of us," Sawyer warned, "may find themselves forced to intrench themselves behind the first bank they throw up – for the very first hole they dig may prove the grave of some or others of us." Sawyer, for one, would fight "till the flesh were hacked from my bones" before he submitted "to such despotism."[55]

[54] *Annals of Congress*, 15th Cong., 1st sess., March 7, 1818, 1165, 1167, 1179–80, cited in Larson, *Internal Improvement*, 113–14.
[55] *Annals of Congress*, 15th Cong., 1st sess., March 10, 1818, 1233, cited in Larson, *Internal Improvement*, 116; *Annals of Congress*, 15th Cong., 1st sess., March 11, 1818, 1270, cited in Larson, *Internal Improvement*, 116.

Strict constructionists won most of the battles. But the improvers captured the occasional victory. After days of debate, the House voted on several measures designed to gauge the members' attitudes toward federally funded internal improvements. Clay and his backers won the most narrowly construed proposition: by an 89–75 majority, the House agreed that Congress might appropriate funds for national roads and canals, though it could not construct them directly.[56]

As was the case with Gallatin's plan, highly visible grand designs were a formula for defeat. In other roll calls, Clay's colleagues rejected the assertion that national roads and canals were justified by national defense or postal needs; they voted down the proposition that national roads and canals should be built to promote commercial development. The votes confirmed that the nation would not likely fund the expansive American System envisioned by men like Clay and Calhoun. Any strategy that featured planning by the General Government drew staunch opposition from those most wary of national consolidation – first the Old Republicans, and later the Democrats. Yet, a vast majority of elected officials were pressured by their constituents for internal improvements. That is why Congress authorized federal spending for narrowly tailored projects when the right combination of local, partisan, and national interests came together.[57]

Vetoing a bill that would have erected tolls on the Cumberland Road in 1822, James Monroe specified the problem: direct, and highly visible contact with the General Government. Monroe understood that the nation's first national transportation project lay in disrepair because states refused to maintain the portions that ran through their jurisdictions, and he was not pleased by this. Yet plans like Gallatin's, or even Clay's threatened to project the federal bureaucracy directly into the lives of tens of thousands of Americans. This was not politically feasible, Monroe explained. As Monroe described it, federal supervision would "cause our Union to be examined by men of science, with a view to such improvements; to authorize commissioners to lay off the roads and canals in all proper directions; to take the land at a valuation if necessary, and to construct the works; to pass laws with suitable penalties for their protection; and to raise revenue from them, to keep them in repair, and make further improvements by the establishment of turnpikes and tolls." This, Monroe

---

[56] Baker, "Washington National Road," 443, n4; Larson, *Internal Improvement*, 117.
[57] Ibid., 117.

argued, would propel the General Government directly into the lives of its citizens in ways that simply could not be ignored.[58]

Appropriating Federal dollars to fund state-administered projects that achieved a national purpose was a different matter. Here, the federal presence was ameliorated through a branch of government that was closer to its citizens. Like Jefferson and Madison, Monroe initially interpreted the grant of power to Congress contained in Article I, Section 8 of the Constitution – "to pay the debts and provide for the common defense and general welfare of the United States," as a limited right. It meant that Congress could do little more than appropriate: it could not construct, maintain, or regulate. But in his veto message, Monroe acknowledged that "my mind has undergone a change." Sounding like Hamilton in the *Report on Manufactures,* Monroe argued that, "More comprehensive terms than to 'pay the debts and provide for the common defense and general welfare' could not have been used."[59]

Monroe concluded from this construction that the founders had intended these powers to be general and unqualified. "Had it been intended that Congress should be restricted in the appropriation of the public money to such expenditures as were authorized by a rigid construction of the other specific grants," Monroe conjured, "how easy it would have been to have provided for it, by a declaration to that effect." This interpretation went well beyond Jefferson's and Madison's insistence that federal dollars be spent only on projects explicitly enumerated by the constitution.[60]

The critical threshold for Monroe was that the projects be national in scope, not that they be explicitly enumerated in the Constitution. If they met that test, and if the General Government's role was simply fiscal, they were constitutional. To prove his case, Monroe cited a long list of appropriations approved during the Jefferson and Madison administrations. "My idea is," Monroe concluded, "that Congress have

[58] Baker, "Washington National Road," 443; Feller, *Public Lands*, 56–58; James Monroe, "Views of the President of the United States on the Subject of Internal Improvements," May 4, 1822, in Richardson, *Messages and Papers* 2:175, cited in Larson, *Internal Improvement*, 139–40. After John W. Taylor's proposal that the national road be returned to the states failed in the House by a two-to-one margin, the toll-gate idea, which passed narrowly, had been a last ditch effort to save the national road. Larson, *Internal Improvement*, 139.
[59] Sky, *To Provide for the General Welfare*, 151, 158; *Annals of Congress*, 17th Cong., 1st sess., May 4, 1822, 1838–39, quoted in Sky, *To Provide for the General Welfare*, 154–55.
[60] Sky, *To Provide for the General Welfare*, 155; *Annals of Congress*, 17th Cong., 1st sess., May 4, 1822, 1839, quoted in Sky, *To Provide for the General Welfare*, 155.

an unlimited power to raise money, and that, in its appropriation, they have a discretionary power, restricted only by the duty to appropriate it to purposes of common defense, and of general, not local, national, not State, benefit." Monroe distinguished between Congressional power to construct roads and canals – which he opposed – and the obligation to finance projects that were national in scope but carried out by the states. Financing, rather than planning or administering, was the key to solving this enigma.[61]

Monroe deployed this more capacious interpretation of the "general welfare" clause to endorse Congressional authorization of Army Corps of Engineers surveys for national projects. The General Survey Bill, introduced in 1824, provided funding to conduct surveys and studies of national transportation routes. The Board of Engineers for Internal Improvements, formed by the Army Corps of Engineers, planned ambitiously, at the outset. But this nationwide planning soon deteriorated into a piecemeal approach – one that was far more conducive to Congressional appropriations. As the Institute for Government Research concluded in 1923, "This was the only attempt ever made by the Corps of Engineers to view the country as a whole." On his last day in office, Monroe signed legislation that extended the Cumberland Road from Wheeling, in western Virginia, to Zanesville, Ohio.[62]

The debate over internal improvement legislation rehearsed familiar arguments on both sides. Improvers cited national defense, better postal service and, most of all, commercial benefits. They cited the "general welfare" and "necessary and proper" clauses in the Constitution. Opponents questioned whether any of the contemplated projects were really national in scope, whether they would not be better executed by the states, and whether federal largesse would be distributed equitably. They raised questions of corruption and pointed to the growing sectional divide over federal powers that might one day threaten slavery. The legislation passed both houses with solid majorities. Regardless of who won the specific battles, the number of precedents continued to grow, bolstering Monroe's interpretation of the general welfare clause. Favoring an active national

---

[61] Sky, *To Provide for the General* Welfare, 144, 158–59; *Annals of Congress*, 17th Cong., 1st sess., May 4, 1822, 1849, cited in Sky, *To Provide for the General Welfare*, 159; Baker, "Washington National Road," 443. See also Sky, *To Provide for the General Welfare*, chap. 7.

[62] Baker, "Washington National Road," 443–46; Holt, *Office of the Chief*, 6–7; Sky, *To Provide for the General Welfare*, 161; Shallat, *Structures in the Stream*, 126–34.

role in a broad range of policies, John Quincy Adams regularly cited Monroe's extension of the Cumberland Road and the survey legislation to justify federal appropriations for Adams's own ambitious initiatives.[63]

"ALL THE IMPOTENCE OF GOVERNMENT ... THUS BECOMES THE IMPOTENCE OF THE PEOPLE": THE NATIONALIST VISION OF JOHN QUINCY ADAMS

President John Quincy Adams used the July 4, 1828, groundbreaking ceremonies for the Chesapeake and Ohio Canal as the opportunity to lay out his quasi-religious vision for the nation's development. The General Government had purchased stock valued at $1 million and this investment underscored the President's larger message. Adams delineated the two stages through which the nation had already passed: the Declaration of Independence and the union achieved under the Constitution. The third, in which it was currently engaged, required the national improvement of "its moral and political condition, by wise and liberal institutions – by the cultivation of the understanding and the heart – by academies, schools, and learned institutes – by the pursuit and patronage of learning and the arts; of its physical condition, by associated labor to improve the bounties, and to supply the deficiencies of nature." Adams's speech reflected his broader concern with "improvement" – the individual and social obligation to cultivate God-given talents and resources. Adams advocated federal funding for international exploration, claiming that "one hundred expeditions of circumnavigation like those of Cook and La Perouse would not burden the exchequer of the nation ... so much as the ways and means of defraying a single campaign in war." Adams viewed the nation's obligations in spiritual terms: the national government had the power to carry out the Lord's will that man "replenish the Earth, *and subdue it.*"[64]

---

[63] Baker, "Washington National Road," 446–47; Sky, *To Provide for the General Welfare,* 169. On the impact of slavery, see Einhorn, *American Taxation,* and Howe, *What Hath God Wrought.*

[64] John Quincy Adams, Speech delivered July 4, 1828, in *Memoirs of John Quincy Adams, Comprising Portions of His Diary from 1795–1848,* ed. Charles Francis Adams, 12 vols. (Philadelphia, PA: J.B. Lippincott, 1874–77), 8:48–49, quoted in Hargreaves, *Presidency of John Quincy Adams,* 178; Howe, *What Hath God Wrought,* 244; Adams, First Annual Message, 6 December 1825, in Richardson, *Messages and Papers,* 2:312, quoted in William H. Goetzmann, *New Lands, New Men: America and the Second Great Age of Discovery* (New York, NY: Viking, Penguin, 1986), 266.

Pushing proposals for an activist General Government even farther, John Quincy Adams advocated an unprecedented expansion of the federal government's authority. It proposed a federal Department of Interior, a national university, a national observatory, a national naval academy, a national system of weights and measures, a national militia law, a national bankruptcy law, and a national system of transportation improvements.[65]

Adams, who began his political career as a Federalist and crowned it as the fourth consecutive Republican president (1825–1829), proved to be that party's strongest advocate for internal improvements. His administration was unabashedly nationalist. Unlike his presidential predecessors, Adams had few qualms about the federal government's constitutional authority to act. "The organization of this Constitution is not of a confederacy," Adams wrote in the early 1820s, "but of a national government complicated with a federation." Writing to a friend in Massachusetts in 1822, Adams insisted that "the first *duty* of a nation" was to better "its own condition by internal improvement." To underscore his commitment to internal improvements, Adams offered Albert Gallatin his old position as Secretary of Treasury (and Gallatin declined).[66]

As president, Adams continued to ignore the constitutional restrictions cited by his predecessors. He pointed to the internal improvements that previous presidents approved as grounds for even greater activity. Adams cited Jefferson's and Madison's financial assistance to the Cumberland

---

Adams used this phrase, which comes from the Bible, more than once, including in a Congressional debate over the annexation of Oregon, when he had the clerk read Genesis 1:28 into the record, "And God blessed them, and God said unto them, Be fruitful, and multiply, and replenish the earth, and subdue it: and have dominion over the fish of the sea, and over the fowl of the air, and over every living thing that moveth upon the earth." See Gary V. Wood, *Heir to the Fathers: John Quincy Adams and the Spirit of Constitutional Government* (Lanham, MD: Lexington Books, 2004), 249.

[65] Hargreaves, *Presidency of John Quincy Adams*, 166. Little came of these proposals. See Adams's First Annual Message, December 6, 1825, in Richardson, *Messages and Papers*, 299–317. In the words of Stephen Skowronek, "The Adams administration projected a political departure more definitive than anything since 1801." Skowronek, *The Politics Presidents Make: Leadership from John Adams to Bill Clinton* (Cambridge, MA: Belknap Press of Harvard University Press, 1997), 118. See also Skowronek, "Order and Change," *Polity*, 28, no. 1 (Fall 1995): 91–96.

[66] Skowronek, *Politics Presidents Make*, 117; Hargreaves, *Presidency of John Quincy Adams*, 29; John Adams, "Parties in the United States," in Koch and Peden, *Selected Writings*, 325, quoted in Lacey, "Federalism and National Planning," 108; Adams to James Lloyd, October 1, 1822, in Koch and Peden, *Selected Writings*, 342, quoted in Hargreaves, *Presidency of John Quincy Adams*, 29.

Road, and Monroe's support for extending that road, as well as the General Survey legislation he signed.[67]

Adams's expansive view of government went well beyond internal improvements. As he made clear in his first annual message to Congress, "The great object of the institution of civil government is the improvement of the condition of those who are parties to the social compact, and no government, in whatever form constituted, can accomplish the lawful ends of its institution but in proportion as it improves the conditions of those over whom it is established." Adams argued that improvement was required to advance the nation's condition, and that the Constitution encouraged such improvement. To refrain from such actions constituted "treachery to the most sacred of trusts." Adams defined broadly the conditions for which government was responsible: the list included roads and canals, which by "multiplying and facilitating the communications and intercourse between distant regions and multitudes of men, are among the most important means of improvement." But, Adams continued, "moral, political, intellectual improvement are duties assigned by the Author of our existence to social no less than to individual man. For the fulfillment of those duties governments are invested with power, and to the attainment of the end – the progressive improvement of the condition of the governed – the exercise of delegated powers is a duty as sacred and indispensable as the usurpation of powers not granted is criminal and odious."[68]

The government should be as committed to the improvement of the collective conditions of its citizens as it was to the protection of their individual rights and liberties, Adams insisted. Particularly when placed in the international context, a nation's failure actively to pursue the common good of its citizens left it at a distinct disadvantage. For Adams, "All the impotence of government ... thus becomes the impotence of the people who formed it; and in its results places the nation itself on a footing of inferiority compared with others in the community of independent nations." Adams forcefully addressed the question of constitutional restrictions in this comparative context, arguing that they should

---

[67] Sky, *To Provide for the General Welfare*, 169.

[68] J Adams, "First Annual Message," December 6, 1825, in Koch and Peden, *Selected Writings*, 360–61, quoted in Lacey, "Federalism and National Planning," 109; Larson, *Internal Improvement*, 159; Adams, "First Annual Message," in Koch and Peden, *Selected Writings*, 361, 366, cited in Larson, *Internal Improvement*, 159; Lacey, "Federalism and National Planning," 109.

not impede the nation's progress. His first annual message to Congress warned that "While foreign nations less blessed with that freedom ... than ourselves are advancing with gigantic strides in the career of public improvement, were we to slumber in indolence or fold up our arms and proclaim to the world that we are palsied by the will of our constituents, would it not be to cast away the bounties of Providence and doom ourselves to perpetual inferiority?"[69]

Adams concluded with a more piercing comparison – a rehearsal of some of the ambitious undertakings completed by the states. States had begun to build universities. The state of New York had sponsored the nation's most ambitious civil engineering project, the Erie Canal. "If undertakings like these have been accomplished in the compass of a few years by the authority of single members of our Confederation," Adams asked Congress, "can we, the representative authorities of the whole Union, fall behind our fellow-servants in the exercise of the trust committed to us for the benefit of our common sovereign by the accomplishment of works important to the whole and which neither the authority nor the resources of any one State can be adequate?"[70]

If Adams was ready to ignore constitutional objections where previous Republican presidents had drawn the line, the Congress was not. In fact, Adams's staunchly statist position became a lightning rod around which the emerging Democratic opposition organized. A few senators introduced a resolution indicting Adams for usurpation of power. Even some of the president's own cabinet members balked when Adams subjected them to his ninety minute draft message to Congress. It included the proposal for a national observatory where an astronmer would be "in constant attendance of observation upon the phenomena of the heavens."[71]

Adams vision may have been quasi-religious, but the portions of his program that succeeded maintained a lower profile. He made use of the General Survey Act to begin planning for some federal internal improvements. Over the course of Adams's administration, Congress authorized over 100 surveys, including those of two national roads. Eight brigades eventually crisscrossed the country, examining possible internal improvements. Each stop raised the hopes of the local population that they, too, might benefit from federal largesse, further fanning the demand for internal

---

[69] Adams, "First Annual Message," in Koch and Peden, *Selected Writings*, 367.
[70] Ibid.
[71] Nagel, *John Quincy Adams*, 303; Adams, "First Annual Message," in Koch and Peden, *Selected Writings*, 363, quoted in Nagel, *John Quincy Adams*, 301.

improvements. Congress used land grants to encourage state transportation development in the West and to subsidize work on rivers and harbors in 1826. Congress also funded, although it exercised little control over, four small canal projects during the Adams administration.[72]

Nevertheless, the vision crafted by Gallatin and embraced by Clay remained largely unfulfilled twenty years after it was proposed. The Congress that authorized surveys during John Quincy Adams's administration had long since given up pretensions of speaking for the national interest. Perhaps Gallatin believed, in 1808, that Congress could discern a common interest. But by 1825 few elected officials hoped to accomplish more than staking a claim for their district or faction. John Calhoun succumbed to sectional interest, and politicians like Martin Van Buren disparaged the notion that a distinct national interest could exist beyond more immediate benefits to be delivered to constituents in the home district. Congress used the General Survey Act to craft localistic responses to constituents. Sometimes this resulted in the use of federal funds to survey obscure creeks and paths. Parochial politics dominated a process that Adams (and Gallatin before him) had hoped would nurture national planning. This experience further undermined the case presented by national improvers, making it all the more difficult to overcome local or economic interests threatened by an energetic national program.[73]

The advocates of the American System won a partial victory in the first third of the nineteenth century. They successfully defended the Bank of the United States. They imposed a tariff that accounted for an increasing portion of national revenues. Public land sales were an important source of revenue. In fact, John Quincy Adams looked forward to the day when "the swelling tide of wealth with which they replenish the common Treasury" could "be made to reflow in unfailing streams," toward internal improvement. There was some progress on internal improvements as well. Small-scale projects with clear practical objectives – programs like harbor development and stream-bed clearance – met with substantial support. The General Government also provided financial aid to states

---

[72] Hargreaves, *Presidency of John Quincy Adams*, 6; Baker, "Washington National Road," 448; Sellers, *Market Revolution*, 152; Lacey, "Federalism and National Planning," 110; Feller, *Public Lands*, 82–83, 96–98. Overall, four million acres of land grants were assigned to the states to build canals and the government purchased $3 million in canal stock. Bruce Seely, "A Republic Bound Together," *Wilson Quarterly*, 17, no. 1 (Winter 1993): 24.

[73] Larson, *Internal Improvement*, 149–50, 173. Congress rejected the vast majority of the program that Adams outlined in his message. Nagel, *John Quincy Adams*, 303.

through public land for right of way in the West, and subscriptions to private corporations like the Delaware Canal Corporation and the Dismal Swamp Canal Company in the East. Secretary of the Treasury Richard Rush could report in 1828 that the Adams administration alone had committed $14 million over the past four years to internal works. By 1861, Congress had poured $43 million – roughly six times the cost of the Erie Canal – into waterway projects.[74]

There were mitigating factors, particularly the sectional conflict and the debate over slavery, which by the 1820s, began to temper all discussion of federal-state relations. Any extension of national authority was viewed warily by those who feared that this foreshadowed the kind of national government that might interfere with the slave economy.[75]

The fear that activating unspecified constitutional powers might set a precedent that would make it easier for the General Government to flex its muscles over the issue of slavery was never far from Southerners' minds. Both the national bank and internal improvements triggered such alarms. John Randolph addressed the problem explicitly. "If Congress possesses the power to do what is proposed by this [internal improvements] bill," Randolph warned in 1824, "they may not only enact a sedition law – for there is precedent – but they may emancipate every slave in the United States – and with stronger color of reason than they can exercise the power now contended for." Toward the end of his life, John Quincy Adams, who had consistently advocated a broad interpretation of the general welfare clause, spelled out the challenge posed by Southern opponents: "Slavery stands aghast at the prospective promotion of the general welfare," he warned in 1842. Most Americans had realized the connection long before this. The Federalists' threat to take New England out of the Union at the Hartford Convention in 1814 and the Missouri debates in the early 1820s left no doubt in the minds of most Americans that nation building remained a tenuous project at best.[76]

[74] John Quincy Adams, in Richardson, *Messages and Papers* 2:305, quoted in Hargreaves, *Presidency of John Quincy Adams*, 197; Hargreaves, *Presidency of John Quincy Adams*, 173–76; Holt, *Office of the Chief*, 7–8; Shallat, *Structures in the Stream*, 118. Shallat notes that this spending peaked during Jackson's presidency (and again in 1852). [118]

[75] Lacey, "Federalism and National Planning," 111. The year 1820, with the heightened tensions that led to the Missouri Compromise, appears to be an important turning point. Proposals by Ohio, and by Illinois one year later, for federal aid to state projects created sharp divisions along sectional lines in Congress. Feller, *Public Lands*, 53–55.

[76] Wilson, *Space, Time, and Freedom*, 23; *Annals of Congress*, 18th Cong., 1st sess., January 30, 1824, 1308, cited in Wilson, *Space, Time, and Freedom*, 52. John Quincy Adams,

So great was the concern that extending federal power might establish a precedent for national intervention in the slavery question that one of the nation's longest-running, and arguably most uncontested, uses of the general welfare clause was stifled between 1840 and 1860: federal disaster relief. Before that, Congress regularly awarded aid to victims of disasters. Congress acted more like the judiciary than a legislative body in sorting out the deserving from undeserving disaster victims: it doled out aid based on precedent. What seemed to link federal relief for disasters, ranging from damage related to the Whiskey rebellion to slave insurrections (not to mention fires and floods), was the victims' inability to foresee or predict these sudden events, and the recipients' innocence of any responsibility for them. By the mid-1820s, general relief bills were directed at entire classes of victims.[77]

Where the federal government did not preempt existing state claims, the interpretation of the Constitution's general welfare clause could be quite forgiving, especially because aid was administered through a temporary relief apparatus. The constitutional legitimacy of such practices was rarely challenged. In fact, many of the disaster relief bills passed without debate.[78]

Another program that passed constitutional muster was the Federal Marine Hospital system. The General Government funded hospitals located throughout the union to treat seamen who fell ill or were injured on the job. The program was financed, in part, by monthly deductions from sailors' wages, and administered by the Treasury Department. The number of mariners treated grew from 4,000 in 1823 to 13,000 by 1858.[79]

The Marine Hospital system sustained broad political support because it was vital to the developmental vision shared by most Americans. Maintaining the health of a work force that literally made commerce move, in what all recognized was an interstate, if not international activity, drew national supervision from the start. Even as states' rights arguments gained momentum, Kentuckians in 1832 demanded a "NATIONAL HOSPITAL," with national funds, and administered by national agents."[80]

Address to His Constituents, 17 September 1842, in Koch and Peden, *Selected Writings*, 392, quoted in Sky, *To Provide for the General Welfare*, 197.

[77] Michelle Landis Dauber, "The Sympathetic State," *Law and History Review*, 23, no. 2, (Summer 2005): 394–95.

[78] Ibid., 384.

[79] Gautham Rao, "Sailor's Health and National Wealth: The Political Economy of the Federal Marine Hospitals, 1799–1860 (Paper presented to the University of Chicago Social History Workshop, October 2005): 7.

[80] Ibid, 37.

The Marine Hospital system, even with its bureaucracy, wage with-holding, and federal subsidies, provided a crucial safety net for a vital part of the nation's workforce. Supreme Court justice Joseph Story rec-ognized the special peril that mariners faced and sought to preserve their "commercial service." In *Harden v. Gordon* (1823), Story defended the federal system because, as he opined, it "encourages seamen to engage in perilous voyages with more promptitude, and at lower wages."[81]

Perhaps the best example of the potential domestic capacity of the General Government, and the coordinate methods that often worked best can be glimpsed through the history of the American Colonization Society (ACS). Originally founded in 1817 as a mechanism for returning freed slaves to Africa, the ACS picked up momentum in the second decade of the nineteenth century, as several Border States and six northern states pro-vided support, along with the endorsement of a host of national religious organizations. In 1819, Virginia Congressman Charles Fenton Mercer pre-vailed upon the Monroe administration to fund the effort as well. Like a number of nationally subsidized internal improvement ventures and the Bank of the United States, the American Colonization Society was a hybrid organization that defied any clear boundaries between public and private control. The General Government added support in kind when the U.S. Navy intervened to purchase land adjacent to Sierra Leone, which was used to found the nation of Liberia. President Monroe was duly honored when the Society chose "Monrovia" as the new capital's name.[82]

Henry Clay was an enthusiastic supporter of the ACS effort, and con-tinued federal funding to the society during the Adams administration. As the idea of colonization became increasingly linked with emancipa-tion (rather than individual manumission) political leaders from the deep South – who were not keen on the idea in the first place – dug in their heels. Many advocates of colonization from the Border South also lost interest as the demand for slaves from newly opened territory in the Southwest made it clear that the fear of being overrun by freed slaves might be solved more profitably than by manumission and transport to a distant continent.[83]

---

[81] *Harden v. Gordon*, 11 F. Cas. 480, 483 (1823), available online at http://www.lexisnexis.com/universe, cited in Rao, "Sailor's Health," 49.

[82] William W. Freehling, *The Reintegration of American History: Slavery and the Civil War* (New York, NY: Oxford University Press, 1994), 25; Howe, *What Hath God Wrought*, 261–62.

[83] Howe, *What Hath God Wrought*, 264–65, 402.

Like so many other initiatives carried out by an energetic General Government, federal support for the ACS was ultimately killed by linking it to the possibility that this power could be used to override state prerogatives when it came to slavery. Henry Clay included funding for the ACS in his "distribution bill" passed in 1833. The legislation also would have included federal aid to the states for internal improvements and education. It died in the White House, where Andrew Jackson refused to sign it, and the possibility of colonization dwindled away. Yet despite its ignominious end, the example of the American Colonization Society demonstrates the degree to which a broad cross section of Americans, in this case, from all regions, were willing to turn to the General Government to solve problems that were stubbornly national in scope. As we will see in the next chapter, both constitutional authority and political will were even more readily tapped when the issue broached was one at, or beyond, the boundaries of the nation.[84]

Episodic disaster relief, a health care system for workers vital to the union's economic development, and a nationally funded effort to transport freed slaves that resettled roughly ten thousand beneficiaries over forty-five years were not mere exceptions in the 1820s. Combined with elements of the American System and the remnants of the Federalist financial system, it was clear that many Americans could and would turn to the General Government, especially when economic development was concerned. Far more expected the General Government to play an active role in foreign policy. Fifty years after declaring their independence from Great Britain, Americans were feeling more secure about their place in the world. Burgeoning population, expansion, economic diversity, and the formation of new states convinced Americans that the union would survive if it could overcome sectional differences. With external threats at bay, Americans were far more sensitive to internal dangers – consolidation among them. The differences that inhered in each section's relationship to the political economy and conflicting conceptions of the political safeguards that protected these relationships, however, further exacerbated the problem of national development.[85]

The mixed success of those who advocated the American system suggests that a sizeable portion, if not a majority, of the American electorate

[84] Howe, *What Hath God Wrought*, 402.
[85] James E. Lewis, Jr., *The American Union and the Problem of Neighborhood: The United States and the Collapse of the Spanish Empire, 1783–1829* (Chapel Hill, NC: The University of North Carolina Press, 1998), 205–7; Freehling, *Reintegrating*, 25.

was open to more energetic central government in spite of fears about consolidation. It also confirms that those opposed to government consolidation were not tilting at windmills. By the 1830s, the Whig Party would embody some of the core principles that animated the American System. The Whigs articulated more explicitly the collective impulse that bound citizens to each other, if only for reasons of self-interest and self-improvement. Daniel Webster captured this transition neatly when he declared that "there are many objects of great value to man, which cannot be attained by unconnected individuals, but must be attained by association." For Webster and the Whigs, internal improvements epitomized the kind of public projects that required collective, public action, in order to promote the welfare of private citizens and in order that those citizens exercise proper stewardship, both individually and collectively. Funding internal improvements, as the biographer of the "Father of American Manufactures," put it, was like "putting into operation a moral machine which ... tends most effectually to perfect the civilisation, and elevate the moral character, of the people." This desire to free the potential of individuals and at the same time improve society through the actions of energetic government is a theme that Americans returned to, time and again.[86]

While it is impossible to tally a won-lost record on the question of energetic national government, it is clear that neither side in this debate was able to deliver a knockout punch. There was an ever-present threat, or opportunity – depending on one's point of view – that the General Government would be part of the solution. The debate helped shape the very way in which Americans forged partisan identities. Those political parties, in turn, were among the few institutions that laid claim to national allegiance.[87]

John Quincy Adams sought to recombine the two strands of republican thought that had coalesced under the threat of external domination

---

[86] Lacey, "Federalism and National Planning", 6; Holt, *American Whig Party*, 3–9; VandeCreek, "Make it National," 75; Daniel Webster, "Address Delivered to the Citizens of Pittsburgh," July 8, 1833, *The Writings and Speeches of Daniel Webster*, National Edition, ed., 18 vols. (Boston, MA: Little Brown, 1903), 2:154, cited from Lawrence Frederick Kohl, *The Politics of Individualism: Parties and the American Character in the Jacksonian Era* (New York, NY: Oxford University Press, 1989), 119; George S. White, *Memoir of Samuel Slater: The Father of American Manufactures*, 2nd edn (Philadelphia, PA, 1836), 121.

[87] Wilson, *Space, Time, and Freedom*, 53. As Major Wilson noted, "Had no adversary to freedom existed, it is tempting to say, there would have been the need to invent one." [53]

and through the unifying symbols of revolutionary times. These strands were the collective impulse in the commonwealth tradition and the fierce distrust of distant authority that required constant vigilance. Particularly in the wake of Jefferson's "revolution," the two strands had come undone, undermined, in part, by explicitly self-interested claims. What good was such liberty, Adams asked, if it thwarted government's ability to better individuals?[88]

For John Quincy Adams, "improvement" was the equivalent of Jefferson's "happiness." Both terms were integrally linked to conceptions of an "upward moral trajectory." Adams sought to recapture what he conceived to be the original and complete view of the founders. Doing so required reenergizing the national government. Sadly, from Adams's perspective, he labored at the very time that the powerful thrust of democratization – at least for white men – strengthened the hand of those who claimed that the market, not the national government, would best achieve republican ideals. Indeed those republican ideals, by this time, had been narrowed to little more than vigilant distrust of public power.[89]

Politics itself had become more market-like. As universal white male suffrage became the norm, self-interest, rather than civic virtue or public spiritedness, became the common currency of politics. Projects requiring collective sacrifice were still possible, and indeed, still popular. But the rationale increasingly was the self-interested payoff that such public undertakings would deliver. Jefferson's idealized conception of affective bonds, forged in egalitarian status among citizens, might have been sufficient to rally many Americans during times of crisis, but it carried little weight in the day-to-day struggle to translate parochial interest into enduring national bonds. When they existed at all, bonds of affection operated best along local and state lines. In public policy much of the action was in the field of internal improvements and, especially with the demise of the Second Bank of the United States, in banking as well. "States rights" loomed larger as a legitimate challenge to national authority.[90]

This is the most familiar part of our narrative. Though significant for illuminating the possibilities and limitations on national authority in the contested terrain where the General Government shared power with the states, it neglects those policy areas in which the national government did have a clear constitutional mandate to act. We turn to a discussion

[88] Larson, *Internal Improvement*, 160.
[89] Ibid., 160. The phrase "upward moral trajectory" is Larson's.
[90] Ibid., 178; McDonald, *States' Rights*, chap. 5

of the national domain and foreign policy next, to get a more rounded perception of the way American lives were influenced by the federal government in the first third of the nineteenth century. Although we will cover some of the same ground chronologically, we will encounter an even more assertive General Government, less encumbered by both constitutional restrictions and the perennial fear that consolidation would lead to emancipation.

5

Outside the Boundaries:
"Powers and Energies in the Extreme Parts"

In 1796 a Frenchman who had fought with Lafayette during the American Revolution paid a call on Secretary of War James McHenry. The visitor was surprised to find that there was no sentinel at the door. The building was virtually empty. Indeed, he could only encounter two clerks. The visitor was informed that the Secretary was at a neighbor's house getting a shave. This was surprising, as it was 11:00 in the morning. The observer was even more surprised to learn that the two clerks and one servant he met *were* the entire War Department, with the exception of the well-coiffed Secretary.[1]

No wonder scholars have referred to central government in the early national period as a "midget institution in a giant land." According to the standard accounts, the national government went from little to nothing after the Jeffersonian "revolution" of 1800. The small chance to create a large state rested on the vision of men like Alexander Hamilton and a few other Federalists. The hopes of these men were "smothered," the story goes, by the Jeffersonian Republicans, who read conspiracy into any attempt to strengthen the General Government. Symbolic of this trajectory was the fate of the capital city itself. Washington, D.C. performed "visual therapy" for citizens concerned about consolidation. There were no grand buildings, courts, or imposing corridors. In fact, baffled citizens

---

[1] United States War Department, *The Work of the War Department of the United States* (Washington, D.C.: GPO, 1924), 10, cited in Leonard D. White, *The Federalists: A Study in Administrative History* (1948; repr., Westport, CT: Greenwood Press, 1978), 147.

who asked where the capital could be found were often surprised to learn that they were standing in its center.[2]

Measured by traditional standards such as staff size, the presidency was virtually invisible. As late as 1825, John Quincy Adams could count on only one staff member – his son, who had just been expelled from Harvard. Combined with Adams's open door policy, this made for minutiae-filled days. As Adams recounted after a string of meetings with constituents and members of Congress, "I was from ten this morning till ten at night never five minutes without one or more of these marginal notes. And I can scarcely conceive a more harassing, wearying, teasing condition of existence. It literally renders life burdensome."[3]

With so few visible trappings of a national government, it is logical to conclude that federal activities had little impact on the lives of Americans. American political culture, combined with the checks and balances built into the Constitution, hobbled state building in the nineteenth century. Without a significant administrative apparatus, most scholars have concluded that the national government was marginal.[4]

---

[2] John M. Murrin, "The Great Inversion, or Court versus Country: A Comparison of the Revolution Settlements in England (1688–1721) and America (1776–1816)," in *Three British Revolutions: 1641, 1689, 1776*, ed. J.G.A. Pocock, (Princeton, NJ: Princeton University Press, 1980) 368–453 at 425; Charles Sellers, *The Market Revolution: Jacksonian America, 1815–1846* (New York, NY: Oxford University Press, 1991), 36–37; Stanley Elkins and Eric McKitrick, *The Age of Federalism* (New York, NY: Oxford University Press, 1993), 21, 177; Joseph J. Ellis, *Founding Brothers: The Revolutionary Generation* (New York, NY: Knopf, 2000), 79. See also Richard R. John, "Governmental Institutions as Agents of Change: Rethinking American Political Development in the Early Republic, 1787–1835," *Studies in American Political Development* 11, no. 2 (Fall 1997): 360.

[3] Mary W.M. Hargreaves, *The Presidency of John Quincy Adams* (Lawrence, KS: University Press of Kansas, 1985), 210; John Quincy Adams, *Memoirs of John Quincy Adams, Comprising Portions of His Diary from 1795 to 1848*, ed. Charles Francis Adams, 12 vols. (Philadelphia, PA: J.B. Lippincott, 1874–77), 7:235, cited in Hargreaves, *Presidency of John Quincy Adams*, 210.

[4] Michael Kammen, "The Problem of American Exceptionalism: A Reconsideration," *American Quarterly*, 45, no. 1 (March 1993): 22–23. On the cultural and constitutional restraints to state-building, see Daniel P. Carpenter, *The Forging of Bureaucratic Autonomy: Reputations, Networks, and Policy Innovation in Executive Agencies, 1862–1928* (Princeton, NJ: Princeton University Press, 2001). James Sterling Young described the scene in Washington in the early nineteenth century this way: "Almost all the things that republican governments do which affect the everyday lives and fortunes of their citizens, and therefore engage their interest, were in Jeffersonian times *not* done by the national government." *The Washington Community, 1800–1828* (New York, NY: Columbia University Press, 1966), 31–32, quoted in R. Shep Melnick, "Governing More but Enjoying it Less," in *Taking Stock: American Government in the Twentieth Century*, ed. Melnick and Morton Keller (New York, NY: Cambridge University Press, 1999), 289.

Yet, as we have already seen in some of the arenas that were most hotly contested during the emerging partisan divide, the national government intervened in the lives of Americans in ways that were crucial. It did operate out of sight, whenever possible, financing rather than constructing or managing internal improvements, taxing through imposts collected at the nation's ports rather than by an army of functionaries. Instead of expropriating land from existing states, the federal government invited debt, which it financed abroad, and paid off in the distant future. These invisible and indirect mechanisms created the basis for a national union of interests while the partisan rancor between Federalists and Republicans funneled debate into national channels.

That so few Americans could *see* the national government has been interpreted by generations of scholars as confirming the "stateless" nature of nineteenth-century America. Those odds and ends that the central government undertook in its haphazard way, they reasoned, could hardly be crucial. As one legal historian put it, "few prewar Americans ever saw federal officials except for village postmasters and equally familiar land sales personnel." The same scholar added one more caveat: "Except against pirates, Indians, Mormons, and those who aided runaway slaves, the military expedient was largely theoretical." The nation, another scholar noted, did not do much by the time of Jefferson, "except at the borders."[5]

This view of the federal government's role has hardly been confined to scholars. As Senator Thomas Hart Benton famously stated in 1843, American expansion "was not an act of government leading the people and protecting them, but like all the other great emigrations and settlements of that race on our continent, it was the act of the people going forward without government aid or countenance, establishing their possession and compelling the Government to follow with its shield and spread it over them." Popular perception and subsequent historical interpretation blended easily in the consensus that the federal government did little during the nineteenth century.[6]

---

[5] Harold N. Hyman, "Federalism: Legal Fiction and Historical Artifact?" *Brigham Young University Law Review*, 1987, no. 3: 920.

[6] Thomas Hart Benton, *Thirty Years View; or, A History of the Working of the American Government for Thirty Years, from 1820 to 1850*, 2 vols. (New York, NY: D. Appleton, 1883), 2:468–69, quoted in Richard White, *"It's Your Misfortune and None of My Own": A New History of the American West* (Norman, OK: University of Oklahoma Press, 1991), 57. For an alternative interpretation, see Forrest McDonald, *States' Rights and the Union: Imperium in Imperio, 1776–1876* (Lawrence, KS: University Press of Kansas,

Yet, the federal government ruled most effectively precisely when it was least visible. If this was the case, what better place to deploy its substantial powers than at the borders of the nation, beyond those borders in the territories, and through international relations? Early nineteenth-century governance inverted the traditional locus of power. The territories, not the capital, were the repository of national authority.

It was outside the boundaries of conventional domestic politics that the General Government acted most powerfully. It was here that the General Government enjoyed plenary power. It did not have to share its authority with state and local government. It was here that citizens came into direct contact with the General Government, unmediated by federalism. In foreign policy, the General Government operated unilaterally, acquiring the Louisiana Territory or summarily clearing Indians from eastern lands. Even the most cursory examination of some of the supposedly marginal chores performed by the General Government at the edges of the nation suggests that what seems inconsequential to modern-day scholars was indeed vital to early nineteenth-century Americans.[7]

This chapter examines some of the federal activities that played out at the "margins," of America's territory, but at the center of many Americans' lives. Acquiring, exploring, surveying, and ultimately selling land was crucial to the nation's future and essential to most Americans. Pacifying Indians, whether through treaty or brute force, was a life or death matter for some Americans and affected the economic well-being of hundreds of thousands more. Protecting existing borders, extending those borders, and guaranteeing trade routes beyond the existing borders touched virtually every Americans' life. The military, even during times of peace, stimulated innovation through its armory system and subsidized a nascent arms industry. It also cultivated expertise, especially in the armory and the Corps of Engineers. While many of these activities took place out of sight of most Americans, their impact was hardly remote. Security,

---

2000). McDonald argues that "when the nation was swept into the maelstrom of international affairs, Republicans came by degrees to exert national authority on a scale that dwarfed the measures employed earlier by the Federalists." [48]

[7] For instance, the government guided settlers when it did not lead them outright. At a minimum, it cleared obstacles and facilitated trade for those who moved west. White, *It's Your Misfortune*, 58. Indeed, David C. Hendrickson has argued that the colonies themselves posed a basic security threat to each other and that the "peace pact" represented by the Constitution served as a surrogate for any real sense of common national bonds. David C. Hendrickson, *Peace Pact: The Lost World of the American Founding* (Lawrence, KS: University Press of Kansas, 2003).

land, trade, and communications were never far from most Americans' thoughts and the national government took the lead on these matters.[8]

Accepting the premise that those activities conducted by the national government *did* matter prompts us to ask how the United States met these challenges without creating a centralized, hierarchical state. What other forms of governance, at the national level, satisfied the demands of citizens for security, land, and trade? What novel forms did American state builders use to craft a "flexible and effective" alternative to European models of governance? How did the very shape of the territory that constituted the national government – its expansion, its consolidation – alter some of the central social, economic, and political relations of the young republic? These questions place the role of the central government in historical perspective, and measure its impact by the tasks it undertook and the results it achieved rather than by the size of its bureaucracy or budget.[9]

Featuring activities that occurred at and beyond the borders requires that we retrace our steps chronologically. I have teased out these policies not because they occurred in isolation, but rather, to ensure that they are not pushed to the margins yet again, overshadowed by the American System, the Bank, war, or other more traditional chapters in the narrative of American political development. I have "isolated" policies that played out at the margins of the union for another reason as well: that is, to consider explicitly how readily these "foreign policy" matters blended with domestic affairs.

MERGING FOREIGN AND DOMESTIC POLICY

Taking seriously the problems that early nineteenth-century national government addressed erases the bright line scholars traditionally draw

[8] Bartholomew H. Sparrow, "U.S. Territorial Policy: Subsidy and Settlement, 1783–1898" (paper presented to the Journal of Policy History Conference, St. Louis, MO, May 27–31, 1999), 33.
[9] Ira Katznelson, "Flexible Capacity: The Military and Early American State building," in *Shaped By War and Trade: International Influences on American Political Development*, ed. Ira Katznelson and Martin Shefter, (Princeton, NJ: Princeton University Press, 2002), 89. Katznelson notes that the federal government was able to secure its major goals without creating a sizeable central state, because it invented novel forms of action. See also Michael Mann, "The Autonomous Power of the State: Its Origins, Mechanisms and Results," *European Journal of Sociology*, 26, no. 2 (1985): 208. Along these lines, Richard John has noted that the national government was the most geographically extensive organization in the country. "Affairs of Office," 56.

between "domestic" politics and foreign policy. With borders shifting daily and trade subjected to the whims of powerful nations that dominated sea lanes, the distinction between domestic and foreign policy was meaningless. Land, security, and trade required the intervention of the national government. That, in turn, affected virtually all public policy, from internal improvements to debt financing.[10]

Given Americans' appetite for development, the demands for security, and the precarious position the United States occupied in the international system at the turn of the nineteenth century, foreign and domestic policy were virtually indistinguishable. As Madison wrote in "Federalist 14," "WE HAVE seen the necessity of the Union, as our bulwark against foreign danger, as the conservator of peace among ourselves, as the guardian of our commerce and other common interests." These concerns contributed to the distinctive shape of American political development. Americans crafted the kind of state that would tread lightly in matters traditionally associated with domestic affairs, yet mobilize substantial resources and wield impressive sovereignty when facing outward.[11]

Writing from Paris as the Constitutional Convention took shape in 1786–7, Thomas Jefferson tried to disaggregate foreign and domestic policy. Jefferson was in the midst of what amounted to trade negotiations with France, deeply immersed in the details of rice, turpentine, and tobacco regulations. He sought to keep foreign and domestic politics separate. "To make us one nation as to foreign concerns," Jefferson wrote Madison, "and keep us distinct in Domestic ones, gives the outline of the proper division of powers between the general and particular governments."[12]

---

[10] Peter S. Onuf has argued that in the early republic, even relations between the states should be viewed through the lens of international relations. Introduction to *Maryland and the Empire, 1773: The Antilon-First Citizen Letters*, ed. Peter S. Onuf and Charles Carroll (Baltimore, MD: Johns Hopkins University Press, 1974). See also Hendrickson, *Peace Pact*. For shifting historiography see Katznelson and Shefter, *Shaped by War and Trade*, and Sparrow, "U.S. Territorial Policy."

[11] James Madison, "Federalist 14: Objections to the Proposed Constitution From Extent of Territory Answered," in *The Federalist: A Commentary on the Constitution of the United States*, ed. Paul Leicester Ford (New York, NY: Henry Holt, 1898; Avalon Project, 1996), http://www.yale.edu/lawweb/avalon/federal/fed14.htm; Katznelson, "Flexible Capacity," 104–5. See also Peter J. Kastor, *The Nation's Crucible: The Louisiana Purchase and the Creation of America* (New Haven, CT: Yale University Press, 2004), 112–13. It is only modern-day scholarship, with its emphasis on specialization, that has categorized these policies into "domestic" and "foreign policy" domains.

[12] Thomas Jefferson to James Madison, December 16, 1786, in *The Papers of Thomas Jefferson*, ed. Julian P. Boyd, 34 vols. To date (Princeton, NJ: Princeton University Press, 1950–), 7:51, cited in John Lauritz Larson, *Internal Improvement: National Public*

Madison wrote back, explaining that this was easier said than done. Sectional distrust, threats of secession, and domestic strife were integrally linked to foreign intrigue and Indian wars, Madison explained. The malleable boundary between domestic and foreign policy exacerbated an already difficult relationship between Jefferson and Alexander Hamilton during Washington's first administration. Although Jefferson was Secretary of State and Hamilton Secretary of Treasury, it was Hamilton, Jefferson charged, who was driving American policy in regard to France and England. "Which of us has ... stepped farthest into the controul of the department of the other?" Jefferson asked Washington in the fall of 1792.[13]

For Hamilton, credit played a crucial role in determining the nation's future. Sound credit required effective relations with European nations. Ultimately Jefferson agreed, supporting debt assumption as part of the deal to locate the capital on the Potomac. In addition, the Treasury Secretary well understood that foreign relations also determined whether there would be sufficient revenue to pay debt service and eventually retire the bonds. Tariffs were the source of that revenue, and trade with Europe ultimately determined how much the tariff would yield.[14]

This chapter examines the ways in which international and domestic policy converged in the face of perceived foreign threats and fears of internal subversion. Contributing to this convergence were the General Government's prodigious responsibilities as landlord and real estate

Works and the Promise of Popular Government in the Early United States (Chapel Hill, NC: University of North Carolina Press, 2001), 43.

[13] Madison to Jefferson, March 19, 1787, in Boyd, *Papers of Thomas Jefferson*, 11:219–25, cited in Larson, *Internal Improvement*, 43. Jefferson to George Washington, September 9, 1792, in *The Writings of Thomas Jefferson*, ed. Paul L. Ford, 10 vols. (New York, NY: G.P. Putnam, 1892–1899), 10: 281, quoted in White, *Federalists*, 233. See also, Madison to Jefferson, 23 April 1787, in *Papers of James Madison: Congressional Series*, ed. William T. Hutchinson, William M.E. Rachel, et al., 17 vols. (Chicago: University of Chicago Press; Charlottesville: University Press of Virginia, 1959–1991), 9:398–401.

[14] Forrest McDonald, *Alexander Hamilton: A Biography* (New York: Knopf, 1979), 264; Jefferson to James Monroe, 20 June 1790, in Boyd, *Papers of Thomas Jefferson*, 16:537, cited in McDonald, *Hamilton*, 184. It was "for the sake of union, and to save us from the greatest of all calamities, the total extinction of our credit in Europe" that Jefferson was willing to support debt assumption and the federal taxes that went along with it. [537] Strong credit, which could only be obtained in Europe, was the key to keeping the peace. "Our business is to have great credit and to use it little," Jefferson wrote to Monroe. July 11, 1790, in Boyd, *Papers of Thomas Jefferson*, 17:25, quoted in McDonald, *Hamilton*, 184. See also Lawrence S. Kaplan, *Entangling Alliances With None: American Foreign Policy in the Age of Jefferson* (Kent, OH: Kent State University Press, 1987), 14–15.

developer. The chapter then analyzes the federal government's Indian clearance programs – another set of policies that could not easily be categorized as domestic or foreign policy. The military did far more than fight Indians, as our review of exploration, the armory system, and the Corps of Engineers suggest. The chapter concludes with a summary of one of the most famous moments in the state-building Pantheon – President Andrew Jackson's opposition to nullification. I contrast this well-known story with one of those "marginal" tasks, again carried out at the nation's margins – lighthouses. The latter, though hardly dramatic, was far more representative of the ways in which national authority was extended on a day-to-day basis in nineteenth-century America.

Land, trade, and security were the essential components of the developmental vision, and the General Government was the key to obtaining all three. It acquired vast tracts of land through treaties and devices like the Louisiana Purchase. The General Government also secured that land by integrating territories into the union, by establishing law in previously lawless tracts and through Indian clearance and military deployment. Secure land was valuable land. Secure land that could be sold to settlers was also a crucial source of revenue for the national government. Thus America's Indian policy, which often treated tribes as foreign powers, and certainly considered Indians to be controlled by foreign powers, was driven by matters traditionally categorized as domestic – such as tax revenues. Even secure land did not ensure economic prosperity. Ultimately, this required trade. In the fifty years following the constitutional convention, the General Government led the way in acquiring and distributing land, securing that land, linking the various parts of that land by lighting the seas, and ensuring access to trade for citizens and settlers alike.[15]

The prospect of expansion, more than any other single theme, crossed the boundaries that otherwise separated domestic and foreign

---

[15] John R. Nelson, Jr., *Liberty and Property: Political Economy and Policymaking in the New Nation, 1789–1812* (Baltimore, MD: Johns Hopkins University Press, 1987), 81; Katznelson, "Flexible Capacity," 98–100; Reginald Horsman, *Expansion and American Indian Policy, 1783–1812* (East Lansing, MI: Michigan State University Press, 1967), 5; Gregory H. Nobles, *American Frontiers: Cultural Encounters and Continental Conquest* (New York, NY: Hill and Wang, 1997), 130–31; James P. Ronda, "A Promise of Rivers: Thomas Jefferson and the Exploration of Western Waterways," in *Frontier and Region: Essays in Honor of Martin Ridge*, ed. Robert C. Ritchie and Paul Andrew Hutton, 27–42 at 32 (San Marino, CA: Huntington Library Press, and Albuquerque, NM: University of New Mexico Press, 1997), 32.

affairs. Just as federalism proved to be the constitutional compromise that allowed Americans to resolve their differences by projecting them into the future, the developmental vision promised to reconcile conflicting interests in a manner acceptable to most. Expansion also illuminated for thousands of Americans the bonds they shared in common. The General Government's dominion was far from seamless, its ability to enforce its will spotty and sporadic. Nevertheless, in acquiring and distributing land, securing newly acquired or settled territory, and protecting access to trade, it operated in an arena relatively unencumbered by competition with the states. The explosion of movement across borders, as one scholar has called it, required the active assistance of the national government.[16]

The General Government was most energetic where states did not exist, or where they willingly relinquished their jurisdiction, and where the Constitution granted the national government undisputed authority. Decisions by hundreds of thousands of individuals powered the expansion westward. Yet if these individual actions were to redound to the benefit of an entire nation, direction and purposeful action by the central government was essential. The General Government used the full range of diplomacy, a variety of land distribution and financing mechanisms, and its repertoire of military options to develop land that was secure and that provided its residents with access to trade. Until 1815, the novelty of union itself and the real external threats this fledgling union faced reinforced the founders inclination to blend domestic and foreign policy considerations.[17]

A PASSION FOR TREATIES

Diplomacy touched the lives of all Americans in the early national period. To be sure, the national government's inability to enforce some of the

---

[16] Katznelson, "Flexible Capacity," 101; Nelson, *Liberty and Property*, 81; Sparrow, "U.S. Territorial Policy," 33–35; William W. Freehling, *The Reintegration of American History: Slavery and the Civil War* (New York, NY: Oxford University Press, 1994), 152–53, cited in John, "Governmental Institutions," 378. See also Peter S. Onuf, *Jefferson's Empire: The Language of American Nationhood* (Charlottesville, VA: University Press of Virginia, 2000). Major L. Wilson, *Space, Time, and Freedom: The Quest for Nationality and the Irrepressible Conflict, 1815–1861* (Westport, CT: Greenwood Press, 1974).
[17] Nobles, *American Frontiers*, 103; James E. Lewis, Jr., *The American Union and The Problem of Neighborhood: The United States and the Collapse of the Spanish Empire, 1783–1829* (Chapel Hill, NC: University of North Carolina Press, 1998), 216.

treaties it signed remained a constant source of frustration. The Treaty of Paris, which ended the American Revolution, was a case in point. The British remained in their Northwestern posts long after the treaty and discriminated at will against American trade. British diplomats treated their American counterparts with contempt. Indeed, the British did not even send a minister to the United States until 1791. The Americans had trouble imposing concessions on their fellow citizens. A weak confederation could only "earnestly recommend" that states force the repayment of debts to British merchants as required by the Treaty. It was not until 1796, after the Supreme Court ruled in *Ware v. Hylton* that this problem was remedied. The United States had no better luck with friends. In spite of Secretary of State Thomas Jefferson's personal warmth toward France and his explicit warnings to emissary "Citizen Genet," France flagrantly violated American sovereignty by outfitting privateers and raising troops on American soil.[18]

Yet, diplomacy was essential to growth and security, and Americans demanded both. Some advocates of the Constitution had supported the national government's enumerated diplomatic and commercial powers precisely because they hoped that a strong General Government would provide the kind of collective security that the social contract was supposed to deliver to individuals. Benjamin Rush was effusive upon the adoption of the Constitution: "we are no longer the scoff of our enemies, he bragged." British consul Sir John Temple confirmed "a vast alteration in the minds and sentiments of the people in general."[19]

[18] Robert O. Keohane, "International Commitments and American Political Institutions in the Nineteenth Century," in Katznelson and Shefter, *Shaped By War and Trade*, 58, 61–64; E. Wayne Carp, "The Problem of National Defense in the Early American Republic," in *The American Revolution: Its Character and Limits*, ed. Jack P. Greene, (New York, NY: New York University Press, 1987), 32; Kaplan, *Entangling Alliances With None*, 55; William H. Goetzmann, *New Lands, New Men: America and The Second Great Age of Discovery* (New York, NY: Viking Penguin, 1986), 111. Injured American pride threatened to plunge the two countries into war again. Even Federalists inclined to side with England in its war with France recognized the seriousness of the situation. They embarked on preparations for war. After the President submitted to Congress an official account of British seizure of over 250 ships in the West Indies and ruthless treatment of American sailors, a thirty-day embargo was passed by both houses. Elkins and McKitrick, *Age of Federalism*, 390–92.

[19] Hendrickson, *Peace Pact*, 7; Benjamin Rush, "Observations on the Federal Procession in Philadelphia," July 9, 1788, in *Letters of Benjamin Rush*, ed. Butterfield, 1:475, quoted in Frederick W. Marks III, *Independence on Trial: Foreign Affairs and the Making of the Constitution* (Baton Rouge, LA: Louisiana State University Press, 1973), 207; Sir John Temple quoted in Marks, *Independence on Trial*, 207.

As new land came into production Americans supported an aggressive foreign policy that would open markets and secure their holdings. Market expansion affected virtually every American. Farmers benefited from this expansion in two ways. They were able to sell surplus crops for extra income. This, in turn, increased the value of the land they farmed. The Treaty of Paris doubled the size of the republic. Support for the new Constitution was strongest in these newly opened Western regions.[20]

With protected markets formerly secured by Great Britain no longer an option, Americans turned to the General Government to regulate commerce with foreign countries and provide access to trade routes. The vast new territory was of little value if settlers could not secure markets for their crops. Westerners and most Southerners also needed outlets to these markets. They supported diplomatic efforts to ensure that the Mississippi River remained open to American trade. Those who feared that vested Eastern interests might have different ideas were galvanized when John Jay proposed surrendering these rights for other commercial considerations by the Spanish government in 1786.[21]

The treaty that John Jay ultimately negotiated a decade later with the British demonstrated just how passionately Americans felt about diplomacy. It invoked strong feelings among a broad cross section of citizens. In May 1794, President Washington sent the Chief Justice of the Supreme Court, John Jay, to negotiate a solution to a series of insults stemming from Britain's blatant disregard for neutral shipping. Jay's instructions from Alexander Hamilton were to secure compensation for damage done to American shipping and to negotiate an agreement to protect neutral

---

[20] Nelson, *Liberty and Property*, 16, 94–96; Sparrow, "U.S. Territorial Policy," 5. For a summary of the recent literature that grounds market expansion in the eighteenth century, see Daniel Walker Howe, *What Hath God Wrought: The Transformation of America, 1815–1848* (New York, NY: Oxford University Press, 2007), esp. chap. 5.

[21] Max M. Edling, *A Revolution in Favor of Government: Origins of the U.S. Constitution and the Making of the American State* (New York, NY: Oxford University Press, 2003), 85; Reginald Horsman, "The Dimensions of an 'Empire for Liberty': Expansion and Republicanism, 1775–1825," *Journal of the Early Republic*, 9, no. 1 (Spring 1989): 4; Arthur Preston Whitaker, *The Spanish-American Frontier:1783–1795: The Westward Movement and the Spanish Retreat in the Mississippi Valley* (Gloucester, MA: Peter Smith, 1962), 9. After the War for Independence, British trade was restricted to those items considered strategically important to the former mother country. Hendrickson, *Peace Pact*, 201. American fishing rights in the Gulf of St. Lawrence and along the coast of Nova Scotia, which had been protected before the war, were now subject to diplomatic negotiation. A.L. Burt, *The United States and Great Britain and British North America: From Revolution to the Establishment of Peace After the War of 1812* (New Haven, CT: Yale University Press, 1940), 42–44.

shipping by defining contraband goods as narrowly as possible. Jay was also instructed that Great Britain must remove its troops from posts that should have been vacated ten years earlier.[22]

As with his proposal to finance the nation's debt, Hamilton sought to *project* a plan that promised benefits so great that all parties would be willing to make short-term concessions to realize them. Hamilton's agenda for Jay was not confined to settling old scores. Rather, it was about trade. Both Hamilton and Jay hoped to clear the obstacles that thwarted a mutually beneficial commercial partnership between the United States and Great Britain. Trade might bring both nations together in the future, Hamilton believed. After months of negotiations with a distracted Lord Grenville, John Jay achieved most of the objectives he realistically could hope to obtain.[23]

That Jay got much of what he sought did little to mollify critics of the deal. The very idea of negotiating with Great Britain, which had flagrantly ignored diplomatic appeals in the past, inflamed many Republicans even before Jay set sail. Washington had chosen Jay over Hamilton in the hope that the Chief Justice would prove to be less of a lightening rod for criticism. The President miscalculated. Even before the details of the treaty were known, Jay was attacked for being a servant to British interests.[24]

Jay's treaty galvanized partisans on both sides. The controversy also reflected the strong anti-British and pro-French stance of Republicans. Even though Jay had made his case forcefully regarding British compensation for damages to shipping, when Jay's brief was published, Republicans poked fun at the diplomatic language it employed. Euphemisms for what

[22] Elkins and McKitrick, *Age of Federalism*, 397–98. Great Britain justified the presence of these troops by the Americans' failure to compensate British creditors for assets lost in the Revolution.

[23] Ibid., 407. The conception of projection is their thesis.

[24] Elkins and McKitrick, *Age of Federalism*, 395. Although Jay made little progress in his efforts to compel the British to grant American shipping full rights of neutrality, he did come away with compensation for past seizures, a commitment by the British to vacate all posts in American territory, and limited access to the British West Indian Trade. In return, he agreed to limitations on goods that could be reshipped in American bottoms from the West Indies (a provision that ultimately was eliminated by the Senate) and to the right of British settlers to trade with Indians south of the Canadian border. [412] Even if Jay convinced Great Britain to indemnify American shipping interests, he would merely be recovering "mercantile wealth" on behalf of a pro-British faction that was essential to Federalist political success. See *Philadelphia General Advertiser*, April 28, 1794, no. 672, p. 2, in Early American Newspapers, Series I, 1690–1876 (Newsbank and American Antiquarian Society, 2004), http://infoweb.newsbank.com/, cited in Elkins and McKitrick, *Age of Federalism*, 395.

many Americans considered to be piracy, like "irregularly captured" ships, struck critics as "pusillanimous," or "courtier-like." One blast perfectly summed up the strong feeling against Great Britain and the tilt toward France: "There is not a nation upon earth so truly and justly abhorred by *the People* of the United States as Great Britain; and if *their* temper and sensibility were consulted, no Treaty whatever with her would have been formed, especially at the expence of the *French Republic*."[25]

The Senate approved the treaty along strict party lines in June 1795. Public debate raged between early July and mid-August, when President Washington signed the Treaty. Across the country, large meetings criticized the treaty. Alexander Hamilton was slammed by a stone while speaking to a crowd. Jay was burned in effigy in all the leading cities. Rioting broke out in Philadelphia, where windows at the British counsel and minister's homes were smashed. Citizens memorialized and petitioned the President from every state in the Union.[26]

The passion was not entirely one-sided. Hamilton penned a series of essays that sought to inform and persuade. To reject the treaty would return the United States to the brink of war with Great Britain, Hamilton warned. While Hamilton's opponents grudgingly acknowledged his effectiveness, even supporters of the treaty worried about overkill. As Fisher Ames remarked after reading Hamilton's case for the Treaty's constitutionality, "so much answer to so little weight of objection is [at] odds. ... Jove's eagle holds his bolts in his talons, and hurls them, not at the Titans, but at sparrows and mice."[27]

Conditions on the ground ultimately shifted the trajectory of public opinion. Benefiting from war in Europe, the American economy steadily improved. General Wayne's 1795 victory over the Northwest Indians also helped. The Treaty of Greenville ceded a chunk of territory consisting of the majority of present-day Ohio and a portion of southeastern Indiana. With the nation prospering economically, few Americans wanted to risk war with Great Britain. Western citizens and prospective

---

[25] Elkins and McKitrick, *Age of Federalism*, 415–449; "Franklin," *Letters of Franklin on the Conduct of the Executive, and the Treaty Negociated, by the Late Chief Justice of the United States, with the Court of Great Britain* (Philadelphia, PA, 1795), Early American Imprints, Series I (American Antiquarian Society and NewsBank, 2002, [doc. no. 29256]), http://infoweb.newsbank.com/, quoted in Elkins and McKitrick, *Age of Federalism*, 416.
[26] Elkins and McKitrick, *Age of Federalism*, 419–21.
[27] Ibid., 436; Fisher Ames to Jeremiah Smith, January 18, 1796, in *Works of Fisher Ames*, ed. Seth Ames, 2 vols. (Boston, MA: Little, Brown, 1854), 1:183, quoted in Elkins and McKitrick, *Age of Federalism*, 436.

settlers understood from the hard experience of four previous treaties that peace with the Northwest Indians meant little as long as British, rather than American troops, continued to occupy posts in the Northwest territory.[28]

Public opinion mattered, despite the fact that both Washington and the Senate had long since approved the Treaty. That is because Republicans in the House sought to block funding to implement the treaty in the spring of 1796. This proved politically costly. Many Republicans reevaluated their position. They recognized that they had a great deal to gain from the American-British rapprochement. Jonathan Dayton of New Jersey, who disliked the treaty, nonetheless explained to his colleagues in the House that "the effects of a rejection would operate like a subtle poison, which, though immediately applied to only one part, would quickly insinuate itself into the system, and affect the whole mass." Perhaps the report from home that Dayton had just received influenced his thinking. It warned that citizens "would tear any of their representatives to pieces who should vote against the treaty." Small wonder that the appropriation for the Treaty passed in April 1796.[29]

The public passion expressed over Jay's Treaty demonstrates the degree to which Americans believed that foreign policy affected their lives. Certainly, the initial reaction to the treaty was fueled by visceral feelings toward Great Britain and, to a lesser degree, the desire to protect a past friend and fellow republic, France. Nonetheless, these outbursts were episodic. This was not the case in the sober assessment of the Treaty's likely economic impact upon a broad range of interests and classes. It was this

---

[28] Elkins and McKitrick, *Age of Federalism*, 431–49.

[29] Elkins and McKitrick, *Age of Federalism*, 445–49; *Annals of Congress*, 4th Cong., 1st sess., April 29, 1796, 1276, http://memory.loc.gov/ammem/amlaw/, cited in Elkins and McKitrick, *Age of Federalism*, 448; Theodore Sedgwick to Loring Andrews, April 5, 1796, quoted in Jerald A. Combs, *The Jay Treaty: Political Battleground of the Founding Fathers* (Berkeley, CA: University of California Press, 1970), 185, in Elkins and McKitrick, *Age of Federalism*, 448. A number of Republican leaders, who had initially opposed the Treaty, reversed their position after hearing from home. Samuel Smith of Maryland was one of the defectors. Although he had many objections, he "believed it to be the opinion of the great majority of the people of Maryland ... that, although their dislike to the Treaty continues, yet that less evils will grow out of its adoption than may be apprehended from its rejection." *Annals of Congress*, 4th Cong., 1st sess., April 22, 1796, 1157, cited in Elkins and McKitrick, *Age of Federalism*, 447. On the widespread nature of the debate, see Saul Cornell, *The Other Founders: Anti-Federalism and the Dissenting Tradition in America, 1728–1828* (Chapel Hill, NC: University of North Carolina Press), 228–30.

dispassionate response that carried the day after the patriotic rhetoric had cooled. Ultimately, these assessments turned on calculations about land, security, and trade, and the crucial role that diplomacy played in enhancing all three.[30]

Although the early republic is often portrayed as a polity rooted in local politics, the debate over Jay's Treaty proved to be a national policy so important that even state and local elections were swayed by the debate. Jay's Treaty affected sparsely populated territories. With the exception of military occupation of the Northwest posts, implementing the treaty required little in the way of visible state apparatus. Nevertheless, as the reaction to the House Republican's efforts to throttle the treaty demonstrated, a vast majority of voters from both emerging parties recognized that access to land meant little without the promise of security and trade.

The negotiation and ratification process that led to Jay's Treaty also established crucial precedents that shaped federal executive-legislative relations in the young republic. Washington himself was initially unsure about the president's role in initiating and overseeing treaty negotiations. With the support of key Federalist senators, Washington took that initiative. He was careful to seek Senate approval for Jay, nominating him as "envoy extraordinary." Washington's actions established a pattern of executive leadership for diplomatic initiatives.[31]

Secrecy was another legacy of the diplomatic process. When the House voted on March 25, 1796 to request all of the papers related to Jay's negotiations, Washington denied the request. To "admit, then, a right in the House of Representatives to demand, and to have, as a matter of course, all the papers respecting a negotiation with a foreign Power, would be to establish a dangerous precedent," Washington, informed the House. Washington's decision struck an important blow for executive privilege.[32]

The debate over the treaty provided yet another opportunity for Americans to discuss and further refine their interpretations of the nation's founding. A Massachusetts tavern keeper, William Manning from Billerica, for instance, offered his own constitutional history in response

---

[30] Elkins and McKitrick, *Age of Federalism*, 376, 432. See also, Ellis, *Founding Brothers*, 136.
[31] Elkins and McKitrick, *Age of Federalism*, 388–89, 395. For ways in which public policy debates rekindled antifederalists arguments, see Cornell, *Other Founders*, 222.
[32] "Report of President to the House of Representatives," *Annals of Congress*, 4th Cong., 1st sess., March 30, 1796, 760, cited in Elkins and McKitrick, *Age of Federalism*, 445.

to the uproar over Jay's Treaty. The Treaty underscored his Antifederalist suspicion that the Constitution had been designed to deceive. It seemed, "too much like A Fiddle, with but few Strings." It put those in power at a distinct advantage, as it allowed them to "play any tune upon it they pleased." Jay's Treaty provided opportunities to test and clarify the true meaning of the Constitution, and through this debate, define the kind of nation the United States would be.[33]

Another treaty, concluded roughly at the same time as Jay's Treaty, was far less controversial but equally beneficial to Americans. In October 1795, Thomas Pinckney signed the Treaty of San Lorenzo with Spain. Fearing the tidal wave of American settlers that approached 240,000 in Kentucky and Tennessee, and wary of its tortured alliance with Great Britain (particularly after hearing that Great Britain was negotiating with the Americans), Spain gave Pinckney virtually everything that he asked for. The Treaty stipulated free navigation along the Mississippi, and the opportunity for Americans to store goods, duty-free, in New Orleans before transferring them to ocean-going ships. Americans had sought unfettered access to the Mississippi and its key port since the Revolution. The Treaty of San Lorenzo also conveyed large parts of what today is Alabama and Mississippi to the United States (excepting the Gulf Coast). The negotiation was so successful that Albert Gallatin, seeking to block Jay's Treaty, argued that Westerners supported Jay's Treaty only because they believed it provided a stepping stone to Pinckney's deal.[34]

Westerners, and many other Americans, hoped that the constitutional powers forged in 1787 would be used to bring order on the frontier. As we saw in the case of Kentucky and North Carolina, some settlers did not hesitate to pledge allegiance to foreign countries if the Confederation failed to secure access to trade. When the self-proclaimed "Regulators" of Shay's Rebellion launched armed assaults in the fall of 1786, many New Englanders feared that the rebellion might soon be supported by Canada. Farther south, George Washington was worried as well. "There are combustibles in every State," the General wrote to Henry Knox, "which a spark might set fire to." Great Britain, in Washington's opinion, was

---

[33] Cornell, *Other Founders*, 221–29; William Manning, "The Key of Liberty," in *The Key of Liberty: the Life and Democratic writings of William Manning, 'a laborer,' 1747–1814*, ed. Michael Merrill and Sean Wilentz, 148 (Cambridge, MA: Harvard University Press, 1993), cited in Cornell, *Other Founders*, 229.

[34] Whitaker, *The Spanish-American Frontier*, 222; Kastor, *Nation's Crucible*, 37; Elkins and McKitrick, *Age of Federalism*, 438–40, 447.

never far removed from these disturbances. "That she is at this moment sowing the Seeds of jealousy and discontent among the various tribes of Indians on our frontier," Washington continued, "admits of no doubt, in my mind. And that she will improve every opportunity to foment the spirit of turbulence within the bowels of the United States, with a view of distracting our governments, and promoting divisions, is, with me, not less certain."[35]

Procuring, securing, and increasing the value of land through trade were core elements of the developmental vision that bound Americans to each other. Diplomacy was essential to realizing these three objectives. In the process of negotiating and ratifying diplomatic outcomes, Americans clarified the relationship between executive and legislative representation, and between public access and executive privilege. Besides treaties like Jay's and Pinckney's, Americans used a variety of techniques to push adversaries farther from rapidly expanding settlement. No mechanism was simpler than outright purchase, especially at discounted prices.

"TO STRAIN SOME OF THE ENUMERATED POWERS": THE LOUISIANA PURCHASE

The Louisiana Purchase, although an exceptional act of diplomacy, distilled many of the central trends in a developing nation at pains to expand and integrate simultaneously. As long as Westerners could trade on the Mississippi, as guaranteed by the Treaty of San Lorenzo, tensions at the Southwestern border remained manageable. But when Americans received word in 1801 that Spain had transferred control of the Louisiana Territory to France, there was good reason to worry. Westerners' worst fears were soon realized. In the fall of 1802, Spain summarily suspended Americans' rights to deposit goods in New Orleans, crippling trade and plunging the nation into crisis.[36]

While Federalists advocated a military response, Jefferson hoped to solve the problem diplomatically. He dispatched James Monroe to France,

---

[35] Thomas P. Slaughter, *The Whiskey Rebellion: Frontier Epilogue to the American Revolution* (New York, NY: Oxford University Press, 1986), 30; Horsman, "Dimensions of an 'Empire for Liberty,'" 3; Ronda, "A Promise of Rivers," 33; Edling, *Revolution in Favor of Government*, 47–48, 86; George Washington to Henry Knox, December 26, 1786, in *The Papers of George Washington Digital Edition,* ed. Theodore J. Crackel (Charlottesville, VA: University of Virginia Press, Rotunda, 2007), 484 http://rotunda.upress.virginia.edu/pgwde/, quoted in Nobles, *American Frontiers,* 101.

[36] Kastor, *Nation's Crucible,* 37–38.

where he joined Robert Livingston, the American ambassador in Paris. Jefferson had long viewed control of rivers, especially the Mississippi, as crucial to both economic and political integration. "I will venture to say," Jefferson wrote Madison after Spain shut down navigation on the Mississippi in 1784, "that the act which abandons the navigation of the Mississippi is an act of separation between the Eastern and Western country. It is a relinquishment of five parts of eight of the territory of the United States, an abandonment of the fairest subject for the paiment of our public debts, and the chaining those debts on our necks in perpetuum." Jefferson feared that without access to trade, Westerners might well declare themselves a "separate people." Should they do so, Jefferson warned Madison, "we are incapable of a single effort to retain them."[37]

Jefferson and Madison sent detailed instructions, authorizing American negotiators to spend up to $10 million to purchase the territory around the mouth of the Mississippi and Western Florida. The objective was not the vast territorial expansion that Monroe ultimately procured. Rather, it was to ensure that American trade along the Mississippi would never again be controlled by a foreign power, to stabilize diplomatic relations, and to further consolidate the political loyalties of settlers living east of the Mississippi for the United States.[38]

With war once again engulfing Europe and chastened by its defeat in Saint Domingue, France had other plans. It sought to unload entirely its American holdings. The deal that Livingston and Monroe struck secured New Orleans and the Mississippi. But it also procured the vast territory owned by France west of the Mississippi. For $11.5 million and an assurance that $3.5 million in French debts would be annulled, the Louisiana Purchase doubled the size of the United States. The Purchase included millions of acres that encompassed land west of the Mississippi from the Gulf of Mexico to Canada. It ranged as far as the Rockies. Monroe and Livingston signed the agreement in April 1803.[39]

When news reached American shores two months later it was received with great enthusiasm, but some trepidation as well. What would the incorporation of such a vast territory do to republican government? Even

---

[37] Ibid., 39; Ronda, "A Promise of Rivers," 33; Jefferson to Madison, January, 30, 1787, in Boyd, *Papers of Thomas Jefferson*, 11:93, quoted in Ronda, "A Promise of Rivers," 33. Gallatin also understood the potential of the Louisiana Purchase, with proper transportation facilities, to extend market opportunities. Nelson, *Liberty and Property*, 125.

[38] Kastor, *Nation's Crucible*, 39.

[39] Ibid., 41–42. The agreement did not, however, resolve American designs on Spanish-controlled Western Florida.

without Louisiana, New Hampshire Senator William Plumer worried that settlements were "too sparse, for the security of our government." Republican government, as Plumer put it, required frequent town meetings and county assemblies. "An extension of the body politic will enfeeble the circulation of its powers & energies in the extreme parts."[40]

Political advantage was at stake as well. Plumer worried that the Northeast would be overwhelmed politically by a slaveholding South. "Admit this western world into the union," Plumer warned, "& you destroy with a single operation the whole weight & importance of the eastern states in the *scale* of politics." Other Federalists grumbled that while both the South and the Republicans would benefit most from the acquisition, the North would end up footing most of the bill.[41]

For the moment, however, the President and Congress focused on the land itself, rather than its governance. Although the definition of the ceded territory was vague, Congressional approval was relatively quick and uncontested. There was little debate about the constitutionality of Jefferson's actions, although some opponents complained that the president had exceeded his authority by acquiring so much land with so little Congressional consultation. Jefferson insisted that both houses of Congress approve the agreement, since the House of Representatives would need to appropriate funds to conclude the treaty. The treaty was ratified by the Senate, and both houses approved the territorial exchange in October 1803.[42]

Theoretically, doubling the size of the republic through one executive action should have raised howls of protest from those who feared government consolidation. Indeed, Madison exceeded even President Jefferson's instructions. Furthermore, the acquisition would be financed by issuing more national debt – a policy that Jefferson and many of his supporters had often railed against. But acquiring land lay at the heart of the developmental vision, and Americans of all political persuasions rarely worried about consolidation when that government promoted development. That the Louisiana Purchase would also enhance the value and productivity of existing western lands sealed the deal. Questions of naturalization,

---

[40] *William Plumer's Memorandum of Proceedings in The United States Senate, 1803–1807,* ed. Everett Somerville Brown (New York, NY: Macmillan, 1923), 6, cited in Kastor, *Nation's Crucible,* 46.

[41] Kastor, *Nation's Crucible,* 41–46; Plumer, *Memorandum of Proceedings,* 9, quoted in Horsman, "Dimensions of an 'Empire for Liberty,'" 7–8.

[42] Kastor, *Nation's Crucible,* 46; Nobles, *American Frontiers,* 118.

slavery, loyalty to republican principles, and many others aside, the Louisiana Purchase seemed to satisfy the demands of Mississippi Valley settlers for trade and security.[43]

Louisiana's purchase did not resolve the challenge faced by the national government at its borders. It simply created a new set of border issues to be negotiated through the intermediary of a new territory and the federal representatives to that territory. As Secretary of State, James Madison understood better than any other public official that the attachment of Louisiana's citizens to the United States remained tenuous. Plots like the one contemplated by Aaron Burr in 1806 prompted Madison to write Jefferson that "Sundry persons, citizens of the U.S. or residents within the same, are conspiring and confederating together," in preparation for an expedition aimed at Spain.[44]

Day-to-day dealings in other parts of the territory offered little more assurance of loyalty. A large swath of land that sprawled across territory that would become Texas, Louisiana, and Arkansas, for instance, was known as the "Neutral Ground." While the three parties who created the "Neutral Ground" could agree that European troops should not enter this territory, that was about all that the Caddo Indians, the Spanish, and the Americans could agree on.[45]

This style of diplomacy, which in the case of the Neutral Zone stabilized relations for decades, was further distinguished by the federal officials who carried it out. They were not high-level presidential emissaries like Jay and Pinckney. Nor did they seek Congressional approval. Rather, local governors and military officers were the prime movers in this borderland diplomacy. Their objective was regional stability, regardless of the twists and turns in foreign negotiations between elites. They sought local advantage through transatlantic negotiation, often mediated by mid-level federal officials. Such pragmatic diplomacy was all the more significant because high-level negotiations between Spain and the United States had collapsed.[46]

The United States Department of State was indeed a small and sleepy backwater. Yet federal officials, both civilian and military, conducted vital

---

[43] Kastor, *Nation's Crucible*, 40, 42.

[44] Madison to Jefferson, November 27, 1806, in *The Republic of Letters: The Correspondence between Thomas Jefferson and James Madison 1776–1826*, 3 vols, ed. James Morton Smith (New York, NY: Norton, 1995), 1460–61, cited in Kastor, *Nation's Crucible*, 2.

[45] Ibid., 1–2, 120.

[46] Ibid., 120–23.

diplomatic tasks at the borders. They extended the federal policymaking structure well beyond the confines of Washington, D.C., and in the process added to the extensive federal role that remained beyond the view of most U.S. citizens.[47]

American-style governance inverted the geographic locus of national authority: it projected national power toward the periphery, where mid-level officials treated domestic and foreign issues as complementary. This was hardly the model of hierarchical command that students of European state-building equated with national authority. It defied even Senator Plumer's assumption that extending the nation would "enfeeble the circulation of its powers" in the "extreme parts." No wonder that Washington, D.C. paled in comparison to Paris or London.[48]

Those seeking national authority in the United States fared better when they looked for it in New Orleans rather than the nation's capital. There, they might find men like the territorial governor of Louisiana, William C.C. Claiborne. The Governor was not one to distinguish between domestic and foreign policy. He embodied both, as well as the federal presence on this border. Claiborne reported to the Secretary of State. So did the rest of the territorial civil structure – even the coroner. A more prosaic factor reinforced the tendency to view territorial governance through a foreign policy lens: it took almost as long (one month) to send a letter from New Orleans to Washington, D.C. as it took to send a letter to Europe. Territorial officials were often left to their own devices and made crucial decisions affecting domestic and international matters with little advice from Washington.[49]

"Local diplomacy" meant that the United States could maintain its official position of neutrality yet bow to local pressure in a region where national loyalty was still a work in progress. This "local diplomacy" was sometimes at odds with stated national policy, as was the case with enforcement of America's neutrality policy. Naval officials in New Orleans interpreted neutrality strictly, stopping any European vessel violating federal law, which prohibited these ships from operating out of American ports. But naval officers spent as much time arguing with territorial officials sympathetic to French vessels as they invested in monitoring European ships. In 1810, the commander of the New Orleans naval station, David Porter, charged civil officers in New Orleans with collusion, making the

[47] Ibid., 112.
[48] Ibid., 114.
[49] Ibid., 113–14.

enforcement of neutrality impossible. President James Madison was well aware of this situation. That he chose to remain silent suggests that the decentralized and, at times, bifurcated nature of American foreign policy actually served national objectives quite nicely.[50]

Jefferson understood that the purchase violated his strict construction of constitutional sanction to purchase land or carve new states out of that land. Both required a constitutional amendment, in Jefferson's opinion. But such action, even if politically feasible, threatened the whole deal. Ultimately, Jefferson was not willing to risk losing this opportunity. He accepted the Senate's broad interpretation of the Constitution's treaty-making authority and the general welfare clause.[51]

Jefferson's decision to follow the expedient rather than constitutionally cautious path established an important precedent that was cited by advocates for energetic government for decades. Defending his "bonus bill" in 1817, John C. Calhoun pointed to Jefferson's actions in Louisiana. "If we are restricted in the use of our money to the enumerated powers," Calhoun asked, "on what principle can the purchase of Louisiana be justified?" If it cannot be justified, Calhoun continued, "then we are compelled either to deny that we had the power to purchase, or to strain some of the enumerated powers to prove our right?" Each time Republican critics called for constitutional amendments in order to block John Quincy Adams's internal improvements program, Adams recalled his own failed efforts to obtain an amendment before approving the Louisiana purchase. As late as 1832, Adams cited Louisiana as crucial precedent for a capacious interpretation of the general welfare clause of the Constitution. Advocating greater trade protection for manufacturers, Adams wrote to the Speaker of the House lambasting the nation's strict construction of the general welfare clause. How could the House leadership maintain this position in light of the precedent established by the Louisiana Purchase, Adams asked.[52]

The General Government, even under a Republican president, exercised impressive authority when it came to acquiring land, securing that

[50] Ibid., 117–19. "Local Diplomacy" is the term coined by Kastor in *Nation's Crucible*. See also, Lewis, *American Union*, 78–82, 116–119.

[51] Theodore Sky, *To Provide for the General Welfare: A History of the Federal Spending Power* (Newark, DE: University of Delaware Press, 2003), 117–18, 193.

[52] *Annals of Congress*, 14th Cong., 2nd sess., February 4, 1817, 856–57; Adams to Andrew Stevenson, 11 July 1832, in *John Quincy Adams and Speaker Andrew Stevenson of Virginia: An Episode of the Twenty-Second Congress (1832), from the Proceedings of the Massachusetts Historical Society,* ed. Charles Francis Adams (Cambridge, MA: John Wilson and Son, 1906), 535–553.

land, and ensuring access to trade. The Louisiana Purchase projected federal power to the borders of the nation, where it remained invisible to most citizens. Those who did live near the borders were well aware of the balancing act performed by mid-level federal officials. These men negotiated the tensions between local and national interests and served as pragmatic ambassadors in the republic's day-to-day interactions with foreign powers. Federal authority was more readily found on the periphery of the nation than at its core. Precedents like the Louisiana Purchase, however, ultimately influenced the ways that the federal government exercised power closer to home. Political leaders, ranging from John Calhoun to John Quincy Adams cited the Louisiana Purchase as proof that the constitution permitted an energetic federal government to pursue a broad range of initiatives in order to enhance the prospects of its citizens.

"THE SPOILT DAUGHTER OF THIS GOVERNMENT": TRADE

Only the General Government could represent American interests in an international trading system that was dominated by mercantilist nation-states. The Government's trade policy directly influenced the lives of most citizens, as farmers sold an increasing share of their crop in the expanding market and virtually all Americans consumed products from abroad. The American impulse toward free trade suggested a minimal role for the state. "I have seen so much Embarrassment and so little Advantage in all the restraining & Compulsive Systems" Benjamin Franklin noted in 1783, "that I feel myself strongly inclined to believe that a State which leaves all her Ports open to all the World upon equal Terms, will by that means have foreign Commodities cheaper, sell its own Productions dearer, and be on the whole the most prosperous." Yet Americans could not reshape the international trading system by themselves. Indeed, they could not even hope to engage it until other trading nations took American power seriously.[53]

The nation's first nationally oriented interest groups formed around questions of trade. Initially, these groups coalesced in the small manufacturing sector. The shipbuilding sector had the most direct stake in

---

[53] Edling, *Revolution in Favor of Government*, 220; Nelson, *Liberty and Property*, 94–96; Franklin to Robert R. Livingston, July 22, 1783, in *The Emerging Nation: A Documentary History of the Foreign Relations of the United States under the Articles of Confederation, 1780–1789*, ed. Mary A. Giunta, vol. 1, *Recognition of Independence, 1780–1784* (Washington, DC: National Historical Records Publications and Records Commission, 1996), 895–96, cited in Hendrickson, *Peace Pact*, 170.

national trade laws. Its objectives were straightforward: navigation laws that granted reciprocity for American shipping in foreign nations and tariff advantages for ships built in the United States. Manufacturers of consumer goods, though smaller in number, also demanded protection, largely in the form of high tariffs on imported goods. Tanners, hatters, glass manufacturers, and manufacturers of cloth all clamored for protection against foreign imports. Even with such protection, they faced competition from better capitalized British agents.[54]

Interrupting trade had a dramatic impact on the American economy, as we have already seen during the Revolutionary War. In December 1807, in response to growing British harassment of American shipping, President Jefferson imposed an embargo on American trade that lasted until March 1809. Republican leaders needed no reminder that "this country must have commerce to preserve the union," as one constituent wrote Madison in 1812. "Consider how many people have their all in ships and the greater proportion of the Eastern people supported by them." Nothing less than American independence and long-term commercial prospects were at stake.[55]

The United States could not hope to impose its will on European nations through military force, Republicans reasoned. Asking citizens to sacrifice economically in order to achieve greater independence and long-term commercial stability seemed like a reasonable alternative. As Jefferson wrote to Benjamin Smith in May 1808, despite some opposition to the embargo, it would be enforced because in America "every man feels a vital interest in maintaining the authority of the laws, and instantly engages in it as in his own personal cause." "The spontaneous aid of our good citizens in the neighborhoods" would see the United States through these difficult times, Jefferson assured Smith. The embargo was a way to punish Europe by drawing on Americans' virtue and determination, in Jefferson's eyes.[56]

[54] Nelson, "*Liberty and Property*, 83–86. This is not to say that these groups transcended regional interest. In fact, they would not do so for at least a century. But they did seek to create coalitions that would influence *national* trade policy. The British could offer merchants extended credit for goods received on consignment. For the most part, manufacturers turned to state governments, not the federal government, for loans that might allow them to compete with British competition.

[55] Kaplan, *Entangling Alliances With None*, 114; William Montgomery to James Madison, August 25, 1812, in *The Papers of James Madison*, Presidential Series, ed. J.C.A. Stagg, 5 vols. (Charlottesville, VA: University of Virginia Press, 2004), 5:199, cited in Lewis, *American Union*, 42; Ibid., 42–43.

[56] Jefferson to Benjamin Smith, May 20, 1808, in *The Works of Thomas Jefferson*, Federal Edition, ed. Paul Leicester Ford, 12 vols. (London: GP Putnam's; New York,

The policy failed on both fronts. France and Great Britain hardly noticed. Americans did. Even Jefferson soon despaired. In August 1808, he wrote to Secretary of the Treasury Albert Gallatin that "this embargo law is certainly the most embarrassing one we have ever had to execute. I did not expect a crop of so sudden & rank growth of fraud & open opposition by force could have grown up in the U.S." Flagrant disregard for the law was not limited to Federalist strongholds. It was pervasive in Republican regions as well. The Embargo and subsequent Enforcement Act of January 1809, which shifted some of the administrative and military burdens to state government, also demonstrated the limits of national authority when it came to enforcing unpopular legislation, Jefferson's musings about vital interest in maintaining the law notwithstanding.[57]

The embargo produced visceral reactions such as the man who wrote Jefferson that "I have agreed to pay four of my friends $400 to shoat you if you dont take off the embargo by the 10th of Oct 1808 which I shall pay them, if I have to work on my hands & nees for it." Another correspondent threatened: "Mr. President if you know what is good for your future welfare you will take off the embargo that is not such a check upon the American commerce and lay it upon something else or if you could lay it upon the hot weather it would add more to your credit." Wherever the embargo was enforced it was despised. The Jefferson administration wilted under this steady barrage of criticism.[58]

Like the Louisiana Purchase, the Embargo Act of 1807 demonstrated that Jefferson was willing to sacrifice his call for limited government in order to achieve a longer-term purpose. Once again, Republicans acted in ways that belied their ideological commitment to small and local government. Although Gallatin found an embargo "for a limited time" preferable to war, he noted his objections to such a measure. "Governmental prohibitions," Gallatin warned, "do always more mischief than had been calculated; and it is not without much hesitation that a statesman should

Knickerbocker Press, 1904), 8:226, online at Library of Congress, *The Thomas Jefferson Papers*, http://memory.loc.gov/ammem/collections/jefferson_papers/index.html, cited in Lewis, *American Union*, 44; Ibid., 43.

[57] Jefferson to Gallatin, August 11, 1808, in Ford, *Works of Jefferson*, online at Library of Congress, *The Thomas Jefferson Papers*, cited in Lewis, *American Union*, 44; Lewis, *American Union*, 43–45.

[58] Anon. to Jefferson, September 19, 1808, in *To His Excellency Thomas Jefferson: Letters to a President*, ed. Jack McLaughlin (New York, NY: W.W. Norton, 1991), 27, cited in Lewis, *American Union*, 44; "A lover of his Country" to Jefferson, July 4, 1808, in McLaughlin, *To His Excellency*, 19, quoted in Lewis, *American Union*, 44; Lewis, *American* Union, 45.

hazard to regulate the concerns of individuals as if he could do it better than themselves." Notwithstanding, Gallatin supported what one scholar has called the "greatest invasion of property rights before the Civil War."[59]

As John C. Calhoun lectured his colleagues in March 1818, foreign commerce "is the spoilt daughter of this Government. We deck her out in the most precious and costly jewels ...; we send agents abroad to every clime and every sovereign; from the Emperor of Hayti to the Czar of Moscow, to prosecute her interests. But when the old respectable matron Agriculture asks us for something for her accommodation, gentlemen will not give her a gown even of Virginia cloth." Thomas Cooper, editor of *The Emporium of Arts and Sciences* and a Jeffersonian Republican, also questioned the nation's commercial policies. He chastised merchants who clamored for "prohibitions and bounties." Their designs led to "protection by engaging in wars on account of it, or manning navies for its defence." Cooper advocated treating trade like any other activity: "it ought like every other losing scheme to be left to its own fate, without taxing the rest of the community and their posterity for its support."[60]

The General Government's trade and tariff policies, which were far more than a mere source of revenue, were forged into a powerful political tool that favored certain economic interests and regions over others. The embargo and the interruption of trade caused by the War of 1812 underscored the ways in which national policy was crucial to economic well-being. While the embargo was the most dramatic demonstration of the impact of trade, it was hardly the only one. By the 1820s, Northeastern manufacturers, their employees, and some suppliers aligned to form the most reliable backbone for the National Republican and eventually, the Whig parties. They endorsed the American System, especially its call for high tariff protection. On the other side of the partisan divide, New York City traders and their cotton growing allies in the South combined to form what became the Democratic Party over the next century. Supplying Great Britain with the raw materials for its voracious textile mills and happy to purchase British consumer goods with the profits from these

[59] Gallatin to Jefferson, December 18, 1807, in *The Writings of Albert Gallatin*, ed. Henry Adams, 3 vols. (New York, NY: Antiquarian Press, 1960), 1:368, cited in Nelson, *Liberty and Property*, 117; Nelson, *Liberty and Property*, 117.

[60] *Annals of Congress*, 15th Cong., 1st sess., March 7, 1818, 1175; Thomas Cooper, *Emporium of Arts and Sciences*, 1:165, quoted in Steven Watts, *The Republic Reborn: War and the Making of Liberal America, 1790–1820* (Baltimore, MD: Johns Hopkins University Press, 1987), 227–28.

sales, the New York/Southern axis lobbied for low tariffs and free trade. From the Democrats' perspective, the tariff was no more than a hidden subsidy – making the products they bought more expensive and subsidizing northern economic growth.[61]

Because the General Government's major source of revenue was derived from trade, attitudes toward the tariff inevitably reflected the parties' appetite for federal expenditures. By the 1830s, Whigs advocated greater investment in national improvements to be funded from the tariff; Democrats lobbied for lower federal expenditures, which undergirded their low tariff position. But because the interests who stood to benefit were so highly contested, political leaders walked a thin line when it came to this issue. Although he was elected as a Democrat in 1828, Andrew Jackson offset his opponents' appeal in the Mid-Atlantic and Western states by going along with the National Republican position on protective tariffs before Congressional elections in 1830. Vice President John C. Calhoun, on the other hand, precipitously ended his "nationalist" commitments, railing against the protective tariff – a position that prevented an alliance between Calhoun and National Republicans eager to capitalize on the rift between Jackson and his Vice President. A few years later Calhoun led the charge for South Carolina's right to "nullify" the Tariff of 1828 and 1832.[62]

Federal trade policy was not confined to the boundaries of the nation. It affected every American and was the subject of some of the nation's most contested political battles. When Jefferson's embargo drew national attention, it quickly provoked opposition – even within the President's own political party. The bonds of affection that Jefferson had imagined were no match for this highly visible use of one of the General Government's most powerful tools. Yet, the tariff, which was also a highly controversial issue and the subject of much Congressional debate, not to mention near secession, remained a remarkably nonintrusive mechanism for funding the General Government. Buried in the price of imported goods, the

---

[61] Martin Shefter, "War, Trade, and U.S. Party Politics," in Katznelson and Shefter, *Shaped by War and Trade*, 115–16; Sellers, *Market Revolution*, 277. For the precursors of this policy, see Kaplan, *Entangling Alliances With None*, 9. See also, Sidney M. Milkis, *Political Parties and Constitutional Government: Remaking American Democracy* (Baltimore, MD: Johns Hopkins University Press, 1999).

[62] Michael F. Holt, *The Rise and Fall of the American Whig Party: Jacksonian Politics and the Onset of the Civil War* (New York, NY: Oxford University Press, 1999), 11–12, 20. Hamilton put in place a system of debt funding that relied on the tariff and that proved to be a remarkably durable source of revenue, in part because it raised fewer concerns about internal revenue collectors.

tax itself (as opposed to the public policy debate that swirled around it) remained hidden in plain sight.

A "RESOURCE OF GREAT EXTENT AND DURATION": DISTRIBUTING AND ADMINISTERING THE LAND

Expanding the size of the republic was one proposition that most American could agree upon by the end of the eighteenth century. While acknowledging that republics had been small in the past, Americans drew on theories promulgated by James Harrington to advocate a "commonwealth for increase." Wrestling land from foreign powers and Indians was only the first step toward realizing this vision, however. The General Government had to decide how to distribute the land to individual settlers and how best to govern that vast territory until its inhabitants were ready for citizenship in the United States. Settlement and loyalty were not simply the product of a series of individual choices. They required difficult public policy decisions, some of which engaged Americans' most fundamental beliefs.[63]

The General Government oversaw this development. Whether through charting and exploring newly acquired lands, determining the price and quantities of land to be sold, financing the sale of land directly, distributing land to individual settlers through third parties, or deciding how settlers would be represented in territories and when these territories were ready for statehood, national public policy shaped development. Experience with these difficult issues on the periphery of United States, in turn, helped to define just what it meant to be a citizen of the United States, how the General Government would administer far-flung territories, and how newly admitted states would interact with the rest of the union.

When it came to land and how the public domain should be distributed, a General Government that enjoyed a great deal of latent constitutional authority once again defied the prevailing political culture. That culture questioned central direction and insisted on limited government. It was

---

[63] James Harrington, *The Oceana and Other Works of James Harrington, with an Account of His Life by John Toland* (London: printed for T. Becket and T. Cadell; and T. Evans, 1771), in Eighteenth Century Collections Online, Gale Group, 2003, [doc. no. CW103440112]), 34 http://galenet.galegroup.com/servlet/ECCO, cited in Horsman, "Dimensions of an 'Empire for Liberty,' " 2. As Harrington put it, "If your liberty be not a root that grows," Harrington argued in *Oceana*, "it will be a branch that withers." [182]

no match, however, for developmental pressure. Unlike internal improvements or a host of other public policies, the Constitution provided unencumbered federal authority in this sphere. Congress was authorized to "make all needful Rules and Regulations respecting the Territory or other Property belonging to the United States."[64]

Nor were there any restrictions on the use of revenue procured from the sale of the public domain. "The vast amount of vacant lands, the value of which daily augments," James Monroe proclaimed in his First Inaugural Address, "forms an additional resource of great extent and duration." Like most Americans, Monroe believed that these lands served as capital to be improved, further enhancing its value. By 1821, the General Government, despite land sales and largesse, still owned 90 percent of the acreage in the new Western states. The General Government did not share political or administrative authority for distributing land with the states, although it did at times compete with states over the price of land. Instead of fitting into a preexisting pattern of state governance, the national government was in the business of *creating* states, rather than sharing authority with them in this crucial policy domain.[65]

Due to the presence of both the British and Indians, and surplus land sold at lower prices by individual states, settlement remained relatively restricted in Western territories before 1815. National initiatives to keep trade flowing on the Mississippi and the Louisiana Purchase managed expansionist pressures. After the War of 1812, a torrent of settlers poured into the Western territories. Over the course of six years, five new states were created in the trans-Appalachian West.[66]

National policy was a major factor in the pace of development, the tenor of citizenship, and perhaps most importantly, the orientation of these newly minted citizens. A series of debates, often grounded in sectional differences, determined whether land would be handed out at low prices, speeding the pace of migration west, or whether it would only

[64] Daniel Feller, *The Public Lands in Jacksonian Politics* (Madison, WI: The University of Wisconsin Press, 1984), 5; U.S. Constitution, art. 4, sec. 3, cl. 2, quoted in Feller, *Public Lands*, xiii. Even the hapless Confederation Congress enjoyed disproportionate powers when it came to the public domain. Unable to collect even minimal taxes from existing states, the Confederation enjoyed virtually plenary power and commanded ample resources in the public domain.

[65] James Monroe, First Inaugural Address, March 4, 1817, in *A Compilation of Messages and Papers of the Presidents, 1789–1897*, ed. James D. Richardson, 10 vols. (Washington, D.C.: GPO, 1896), 2:9, available online at http://www.heinonline.org/, cited in Feller, *Public Lands*.

[66] Ibid., xi, 10.

be distributed at a pace that would satisfy demands by the population already living in these regions. Decisions about the distribution of land also affected funds available to improve the land, since land sales were a crucial source of revenue. The General Government also faced a series of difficult choices about how the inhabitants of the new territories would be governed. To what extent would they be represented in the important decisions that influenced their affairs? Could they be trusted to make the right decisions? And if they could not be trusted, how would republican values be inculcated in men who many Americans viewed with suspicion, if not disdain?[67]

THE "EXCITING THEME":
THE PRICE OF LAND AND THE PACE OF SETTLEMENT

The methods for selling and pricing land were grounded in legislation passed by the Confederation Congress in May 1785. The key provisions that endured after 1787 were surveys that established six-mile-square townships. These townships were then subdivided into 640 acre lots (later labeled "sections"). Townships and sections were sold at auctions; land was to be priced at a minimum of $1 per acre. A series of land laws between 1796 and 1804 incorporated these key provisions of the 1785 Act and made three important changes. In 1796, Congress doubled the minimum price of land to $2 per acre. However, this steep price hike was offset by offering credit. By 1800, a purchaser could secure land by putting 5 percent down and promising to pay an additional 20 percent in the next forty days. The balance could be paid over the next four years. The legislation passed in 1800 also decreased the minimum size of an allowable purchase to 320 acres. This minimum was halved again in 1804. Overseeing these policies, the General Land Office struggled to keep pace with burgeoning demand.[68]

Federal land sales ran at a relatively steady pace, averaging 350,000 acres a year from 1801 to 1813. In 1805 Congress faced a difficult decision when the legislatively authorized deadline for credit extension (five

---

[67] Karl Hess, Jr., *Visions Upon The Land: Man and Nature on the Western Range* (Washington, D.C.: Island Press, 1992), 66.

[68] Feller, *Public Lands*, 6–8; Patrick Griffin, *American Leviathan: Empire, Nation, and Revolutionary Frontier* (New York, NY: Hill and Wang, 2007), 258.; See also Malcolm J. Rohrbough, *The Land Office Business: The Settlement and Administration of American Public Lands, 1789–1837* (New York, NY: Oxford University Press, 1968).

years) ran out for thousands of settlers who had deferred payment for as long as possible. By this time, settlers owed more than $2 million – a sizeable portion of the total purchase price. Yet Congress, rejecting the advice of Albert Gallatin who advocated scrapping the credit system and lowering the price of land, chose the easiest way out of the bind. It extended deadlines and deferred foreclosures. For the moment, it appeared that Congress chose wisely. Even though debt extension legislation became an annual ritual, the national land debt stabilized. It remained around $2 million in 1813. In the mean time, the Treasury had collected more than $7.3 million. The price per acre worked out to $1.62 in actual cash paid – higher than the price Gallatin recommended.[69]

Gallatin had the last word, however. The War of 1812 changed settlement patterns dramatically. Settlers streamed into the Ohio Valley and the territory ceded by Georgia in what would become the Southeastern United States. Population in the Old Northwest territory tripled between 1810 and 1820. Population in Indiana increased sixfold; the increase was twelvefold in Alabama. With trade on the Mississippi assured, and Indian tribes in Georgia and Alabama vanquished by Jackson and William Henry Harrison, millions of acres looked attractive. Spurred by rising commodity prices, the rush of settlers overwhelmed the General Land Office's capacity to handle claims.[70]

Land sales topped 1 million acres annually for the first time in 1815 and rose to 1.5 million acres the following year. Sales peaked in 1818, reaching 2.5 million acres. Prices on the open market were rising rapidly as well. Commercial farming could not possibly support some of the prices that would-be farmers paid. But many felt that they could not afford to miss out on land that seemed to increase in value daily. Settlers funded this speculative boom on credit offered by the United States government. Land debt doubled between 1813 and 1815. It doubled again by 1818. Much of the debt was concentrated in Alabama and Mississippi.[71]

Thousands of settlers, not to mention the Bank of the United States and the General Land Office, were overextended when the worst panic in the country's history struck in 1819. The panic was precipitated by the collapse of cotton prices, which plummeted to half their previous value. Steep declines in other commodities followed. Land sales came to a screeching halt, but not before settlers had purchased 4 million acres

[69] Feller, *Public Lands*, 9–13.
[70] Ibid., 14–16.
[71] Ibid., 16, 20.

over the course of the year, running up a staggering debt of $22 million. This sum exceeded the annual budget of the federal government (excluding debt service). In Alabama, a population of 128,000 was saddled with a land debt of over $10 million. The massive debt acquired during times when values were rising would now have to be paid back in deflated dollars. To make matters worse, Westerners had grown accustomed to Congressional leniency regarding debt extension. They now faced the prospect of massive foreclosures.[72]

The General Government aided and abetted the speculative bubble through its policies. The Louisiana Purchase opened millions of acres to settlement. Even the otherwise ignominious performance of the federal military redounded to the benefit of land speculators as patriotic sentiment inspired by victory in New Orleans stimulated expansion, fueled by confidence in the future of a continental empire. Indian clearance made that land more secure. And extended public credit kept the party going. Once again, Americans turned to the General Government to ameliorate the credit crisis.

The Sixteenth Congress debated land policy in December 1819. It had already faced a dispute that threatened to shatter the nation over Missouri's admission as a state. Some Americans were as passionate about the land issue as the question of state rights and slavery. The *Albany Register,* for instance, warned that mass forfeiture could lead to "a civil war, if not an ultimate dissolution of the federal compact." More dispassionately, a federal land surveyor cautioned "I much fear a Spirit of disaffection & & & towards the general government is arising in the West sufficient to alarm its fast friends and certainly requires vigilance." Regardless of one's attitude toward the credit system, it was not easy to hold the line for the first time in twenty years when debtors had little prospect of paying off their loans.[73]

Congress responded by affirming Gallatin's approach. The cash-for-land concept had been updated in a bill drafted by the reigning land expert in Congress, Jeremiah Morrow. However, Morrow's bill, which called for an end to the credit system by pricing land at $1.25, was narrowly defeated

---

[72] Whitaker, *The Spanish-American Frontier,* 129–31; Lewis, *American Union,* 129–31; Feller, *Public Lands,* 22, 27.

[73] Feller, *Public Lands,* 26–27; *Albany Register,* reprinted in *National Intelligencer,* August 11, 1819, quoted in Feller, *Public Lands,* 22; Tiffin to Meigs, October 31, 1819, General Land Office Letters Received (The National Archives, Washington D.C.) quoted in Rohrbough, *Land Office Business,* 142.

in the final session of the Fifteenth Congress. Revived by Senator Rufus King in the Sixteenth Congress, the legislation passed both the Senate and the House by large margins and was signed into law by President Monroe in April 1820. Besides lowering the price of land and ending the credit system, the legislation also reduced the minimum size of land parcels to eighty acres.[74]

Eliminating federal credit lowered the value of land in all the regions where a massive influx had maintained prices at artificially high levels. Having lost the credit battle, these Westerners turned their attention to securing federal relief. Relief advocates argued that the federal government had changed the rules in the middle of the game. The *Cincinnati Gazette* considered the change in policy akin to swindling: it was an "unequivocal violation of public faith." Arguments like these garnered a broad consensus for relief, supported by President Monroe and delivered in the form of the Relief Act of 1821. The legislation allowed land holders to keep sections of their property proportionate to amounts already paid for the entire tract. The remainder was traded back to the government and the debt cancelled. The legislation also formally extended by ten years the time that debtors had to pay off the General Government should they choose to hold on to the portion of the land that had not yet been paid off. The Act had an immediate impact, cutting land debt in half in just one year.[75]

Policies regarding the distribution of land linked the most local perspective – the settler on his tract of eighty acres on the frontier – to national public policy and its enforcement. While the market and individual initiative played important roles in the geographic expansion of the United States, national public policy determined prices and prospects for settlers. It is not surprising that citizens in a rapidly growing nation contiguous to a large land mass were constantly thinking about, arguing over, and acquiring land. What is surprising, given the rhetoric of local governance, is the degree to which the federal government's resources – from the land itself to its lending capacity – shaped life chances for hundreds of thousands of Americans.[76]

Debate over federal land policy was national in scope and passionate. The *New York Evening Post* captured the intensity when it reported

---

[74] Feller, *Public Lands*, 21, 27.
[75] "The Public Lands,: from the *Cincinnati Gazette*, reprinted in *Illinois Intelligencer*, December 23, 1820, 4, in Early American Newspapers, Series III, quoted in Feller, *Public Lands*, 35; Feller, *public Lands*, 35–37.
[76] Wilson, *Space, Time, and Freedom*, 51.

in 1830 that "The public lands – the public lands – this is the exciting theme, which brings every man to his seat, and every other question – tariff, roads, revenue, education – all slide insensibly into this."[77]

Millions of Americans made life-altering decisions based on the outcome of the national debate over land distribution. They counted on the annual extensions of credit, calculated that future settlers would also benefit from federal largess, and came to view subsidies as a birthright earned by the challenging work of nation building out on the frontier. That national public policy on these matters was a central variable in the developmental vision shared by most Americans explains the persistent attention lavished on this topic through much of the nation's early history. National policy regarding the price and availability of land was also inextricably linked to broader concerns about how best to bind settlers far removed from existing population centers to national purposes and political practices.

"THE NERVES AND SINEWS OF THE UNION": GOVERNING NEW TERRITORIES

As states ceded western territory to the national government, and settlers pushed West, the General Government faced increasing pressure to provide a system of territorial administration. The national government was the only governing body with jurisdiction over citizens living in the territories. It faced predictable practical problems – ranging from security to transportation. Creating a governing structure that would eventually turn settlers into citizens offered an opportunity to spell out ideas about citizenship and to put these ideas into action. This debate and the actions it inspired offers a window into the ideals Americans held dear. In many instances, national policy in the territories established important precedents that influenced the nature of citizenship throughout the country.

The practical problems of settling and governing vast territories forced compromises. The Northwest Ordinance of 1787, which was styled as a "compact" between the existing states and states yet to be formed, established the basic ground rules of incorporation. It laid out the process by which territories could become states. It confirmed earlier legislation that ensured national control over the public domain, even after new states had been formed, and prohibited states from taxing this federal land. It also guaranteed that, when a territory reached a population of 60,000,

---

[77] *New York Evening Post*, January 26, 1830, quoted in Feller, *Public Lands*, 111.

it would be admitted as a state and would enjoy "equal footing" with all of the other states. The measures prescribing statehood embodied in the Northwest Ordinance guided state incorporation well into the nineteenth century.[78]

With its set-asides for churches and schools, its plan for orderly development, its reliance on the judiciary, and the dearth of local participation, the 1787 Ordinance came close to providing a Federalist template for settlement. Settlers were "in danger of losing all their habits of government, and allegiance to the United States," Ohio Company Associate Manasseh Cutler warned. But provisions in the Northwest Ordinance, especially its support for education, would "revive the ideas of order, citizenship, and the useful sciences." More importantly, the Constitution, which incorporated the approach to settlement laid out in the Northwest Ordinance, would convince settlers that "the Government of the United States was not a mere shadow: – their progeny would grow up in habits of Obedience and Respect – they would learn to reverence the Government; and the Countless multitudes which will be produced in that vast Region would become the nerves and Sinews of the Union," Northwest Territory Governor Arthur St. Clair wrote President Washington in 1789.[79]

While territorial leaders like St. Clair and the men of the Ohio Company embraced these prospects, the vast majority of settlers found such prescriptions impractical at best, and in many instances, insulting. The primitive conditions and naked self-interest that seemed to dominate frontier regions challenged the Federalist approach to citizenship. The persistent struggle over how to handle squatters demonstrated the wide gap that separated Eastern and Western views about settlement. Squatters occupied land on the frontier without purchasing it. Periodic efforts by the General Government to clear out squatters or force them to purchase the land they lived on failed adequately to address the problem. Even Republican leaders grew frustrated at what appeared to them to be a

[78] Thomas Donaldson, *The Public Domain: Its History, with Statistics* (Washington D.C.: GPO, 1884), 153–56, cited in Feller, *Public Lands*, 6; Andrew R.L. Cayton, *The Frontier Republic: Ideology and Politics in The Ohio Country, 1780–1825* (Kent, OH: Kent state University Press, 1986), 3. On the sectional implications of the Northwest Ordinance, see Hendrickson, *Peace Pact*, 5.
[79] Manasseh Cutler, "An Explanation of the Map Which Delineates ... the Federal Lands" (Salem, MA: Dabney and Cushing, 1787), 21, in Eighteenth Century Collections Online, Gale Doc. NO. CW100515769, cited in Cayton, *Frontier Republic*, 31; St. Clair to Washington, August 1789, in *The Territorial Papers of the United States*, ed. Clarence Edwin Carter, vol. 2, *The Territory Northwest of the River Ohio, 1787–1803* (Washington, D.C.: GPO, 1934), 212, cited in Cayton, *Frontier Republic*, 35.

flagrant violation of the law. President James Madison, for instance, issued a statement in December 1815 that warned "uninformed or evil-disposed persons ... who have unlawfully taken possession of or made any settlement on the public lands" to clear out or face the consequences.[80]

As usual, these consequences ultimately amounted to nothing. Madison's statement, however, inflamed some Westerners. From their vantage point, many of the so-called squatters could not file claims legally, even if they wanted to. The General Land Office was too backed up and the government's surveys too far behind to allow everybody who wanted legally to file a claim to do so. Most squatters, Westerners argued, were already good citizens. They improved the land, fought Indians, and helped extend the land available for settlement. Western newspapers labeled Madison's proclamation an "injustice," and bridled at this "ingratitude."[81]

In Ohio, the General Government's failure to quell hostilities between settlers and Indians was a constant source of tension. Officially, Congress pursued a policy of conciliation and negotiation. Referring to settlers and the Indians in 1787, Secretary of War Henry Knox concluded that "Either one or the other party must remove to a greater distance, or Government must keep them both in awe by a strong hand, and compel them to be moderate and just." The problem was that the government did not have the resources to back up this statement. A year after Knox's pronouncement, the government deployed only 350 troops on the frontier. Nor were its efforts at negotiation fruitful. Persistent raids by settlers enflamed Indians and provoked counterstrikes.[82]

By 1790, the situation had deteriorated to the point that federal officials decided that war was the only option. Mobilizing militias from Virginia and Pennsylvania, but also relying disproportionately on the very men in Kentucky who had exacerbated relations with Indians, Governor St. Clair led the charge. Both this campaign and a subsequent one ended in disaster. Peaceful relations with Indians in the Ohio Territory were not secured until Wayne's successful campaign in 1794. As one settler concluded after Wayne's victory, "the prospect of migration to the westward exceeds any thing ever known before."[83]

[80] Feller, *Public Lands*, 16–18; Madison Proclamation, December 12, 1815, in Richardson, *Messages and Papers*, 1:572, quoted in Feller, *Public Lands*, 17.

[81] *Vincennes Indiana Western Sun*, January 20, 1816, quoted in Feller, *Public Lands*, 17.

[82] Cayton, *Frontier Republic*, 35–38; Report of the Secretary of War to Congress, July 10, 1787, in Carter, *Territorial Papers*, 2:31, cited in Cayton, *Frontier Republic*, 37.

[83] Cayton, *Frontier Republic*, 38–39; John Brown to Innes, May 15, 1795, Harry Innes Papers, General Correspondence, LC, quoted in Griffin, *American Leviathan*, 252.

Once established, peace did not reproduce the conditions that Federalists would have preferred. Settlers crowded into the Ohio Country after 1795. The Miami Valley near Cincinnati was home to 15,000 by 1801. These settlers seemed more interested in amassing wealth and less attached to any form of government than the Federalists imagined. When these settlers did turn to politics, they favored the kind of self-interested parochial politics that had begun to undermine deference to traditional leadership back in the East and that fueled a groundswell of resentment in the territories.[84]

Ohio's Jeffersonian Republicans considered their territorial leadership to be "an old train of Sycophants." With all appointments flowing from the territorial governor, the system was compared to British patronage. Instead of men of inherited wealth appointed from on high, Republican leadership demanded a greater voice for a broader range of men. Republicans also demanded elections and local representation. Michael Baldwin, a young Republican lawyer, insisted in 1802 that power flow "from the people." They "were the only proper judges of their own interests and their own concerns." Ohio Republicans lobbied for statehood and sought a state constitution that would embody this more egalitarian, localist, interest-based approach to governance. The crux of the conflict was whether government would come from above or below, from outside or inside the territory.[85]

In 1802, beating back St. Clair's attempt to divide the Ohio country and slow the march toward statehood, Republican leaders prevailed upon Jefferson to begin the statehood process. That fall, Ohioans elected Republicans as the vast majority of a constitutional convention. The delegates produced a constitution for the proposed state that authorized a powerful legislature and weak governor. The constitution also placed judicial appointments under strict legislative control. As one advocate put it, the delegates created a government that would guard the natural rights of constituents "with such republican strength, that all the inveterate rage and subtle craft of arbitrary power and aristocratic despotism, will never be able to invade."[86]

---

[84] Cayton, *Frontier Republic*, 35, 52.

[85] Thomas Worthington to Nathaniel Massie, March 5, 1802, Massie Papers, quoted in Cayton, *Frontier Republic*, 68; Michael Baldwin "To the Electors of the County of Ross," *Scioto Gazette*, 28 August, 1802 in *Nineteenth Century U.S. Newspapers*, (GaleGroup, 2008), http://infotrac.galegroup.com/; quoted in Cayton, *Frontier Republic*, 69; Cayton, *Frontier Republic*, 68–72.

[86] Cayton, *Frontier Republic*, 77–78; "An Address," *Western Spy*, July 17, 1802, quoted in Cayton, *Frontier Republic*, 77.

Ironically, Ohio Republicans succeeded only because of the national power yielded by their Jeffersonian sponsors. "In the end, it was an act of the United States Congress," one scholar noted, "not an election, that enabled Ohio to become a state in 1803; the procedures established by the Northwest Ordinance of 1787 had been observed." The very same powers of patronage, and the authority derived from U.S. army outposts and troops, were also crucial to Republican rule in Ohio as they had been for the Federalists. The case for the enduring impact of the General Government was even more pronounced in Louisiana, where the young republic sought to integrate thousands of new residents who had formerly lived under foreign regimes.[87]

"AN APPRENTICESHIP TO LIBERTY":
GOVERNING ORLEANS

While Americans had ample experience with geographic expansion by 1804, there was little precedent for suddenly incorporating new populations as was the case in Louisiana. Could a mere treaty that proclaimed the inhabitants of the Louisiana Territory to be American citizens actually make them that? Could it replace the naturalization process designed to convert foreigners to Americans? Timothy Pickering, for instance, argued that the formerly French and Spanish citizens were "incapable of performing the duties or enjoying the blessing of a free government – They are too ignorant to elect suitable men." Incorporation advocate Samuel Mitchell, Congressman from New York, asked one opponent "What would the gentleman propose that we shall do with them? Send them away to the Spanish provinces, or turn them loose in the wilderness? Mitchell argued that making citizens out of Louisiana natives was a process. He suggested that they "serve an apprenticeship to liberty; they are to be taught the lessons of freedom; and by degrees they are to be raised to the enjoyment and practice of independence." Mitchell's reasoning formed the basis of a governance bill that began the naturalization and statehood process.[88]

Orleanians, like citizens in other territories, initially were governed by executive fiat rather than legislative statute. They had no voice in either branch of government. Passed in March 1804, the Governance

---

[87] Cayton, *Frontier Republic*, 80.

[88] Kastor, *Nation's Crucible*, 47, 50; Plumer, *Memorandum of Proceedings*, 111; *Annals of Congress*, 8th Cong., 1st sess., 25 October 1803, 480, quoted in Kastor, *Nation's Crucible*, 50.

Act provided a political structure for the vast territory that would oversee this population until its attachment to the United States could be demonstrated. It divided the territory into two parts, labeling the upper portion the "District of Louisiana," and the remainder, "Orleans." As with the provisions of the Northwest Ordinance, all of the officials in both districts were appointed by the General Government. There were no elected officials in either district. Congress passed a second Governance Act a year later, which for the first time gave Orleans an elected House of Representatives. It placed the Territory of Orleans on an equal footing with other territories by applying the Northwest Ordinance's standard of 60,000 free inhabitants as the criteria for admission to statehood.[89]

If the liberating influence of frontier life was at play in Louisiana, it certainly was not reflected in the procedural rights of its citizens. Even as Congress hashed out the details of the initial Governance Act, the United States was governing. While legislators debated, C.C. Claiborne, the former governor of the neighboring Mississippi territory, arrived. He was accompanied by what would soon be the largest concentrated deployment of federal troops during peacetime. Although the troops suggested a willingness to coerce if necessary, Claiborne was more eager to win the affection of his charges than to bully them into submission. As was the case in other Western territories, the line between civil and military authority was hazy at best.[90]

The military proved instrumental in assuring white Louisianians that their slave property was secure in the territory of Orleans. It was an important tool for both co-opting white residents and protecting against unruly citizens. For their part, white residents of Orleans were eager to meet representatives of national authority half way. They craved the rule of law, security, services, and ties to national assets that the Governor represented. They understood that his authority counted for little without the power of military force to back it up. While the large presence of military force was partially a response to potential Spanish, British, and French threats, in practice federal troops and the territorial militia were a crucial bulwark against the more immediate "foreign" presence of slaves and Indians.[91]

[89] Kastor, *Nation's Crucible*, 51, 80.
[90] Ibid., 52, 55.
[91] Ibid., 77–81, 90. On military policy for upper Louisiana and Orleans, see Francis Paul Prucha, *The Sword of the Republic: The United States Army on the Frontier, 1783–1846* (New York, NY: MacMillan, 1968), 63–76.

Because the vast majority of the men who governed the Western territories were appointed by the federal government, no mechanism was more crucial to the march toward statehood than the appointment process. Nor was there any room for public participation in this process. Kinship was the key criterion employed in appointing men to the Orleans Territory. This sometimes meant blood relations; more often than not, the kinship was figurative. It encompassed men who shared political views, social milieu, and similar educations. Most importantly, it entailed personal loyalty. While these qualities guided appointments across the West, they were particularly important in a territory that sought to assimilate a foreign population like Orleans.[92]

The appointment of Claiborne himself illustrates the reasoning that went into key appointments. Jefferson initially sought men of greater stature than Claiborne. He wanted men whose commitment to republican ideals, partisan loyalties, and personal attachment to Jefferson himself were beyond a shadow of a doubt. When he could not procure their services, he turned to Claiborne, even though "there were characters superior to him whom I wished to appoint, but they refused the office," as Jefferson informed John Dickinson.[93]

Loyalty to the executive kinship network, not democratic representation, was the key to success. Claiborne's lineage was an important credential. He was born in Virginia. Jefferson and Madison turned to a disproportionate number of Virginians to govern the territories. When they ran out of Virginians, they chose men from Kentucky. These men were one step removed from safe Virginian attitudes toward governance and had the added advantage of frontier experience. Claiborne was reappointed time and again, despite questions about his competence, because he proved to be a loyal friend of the administration, who could be trusted to represent its interest in a foreign place with a population whose loyalty was often doubted by the administration.[94]

Appointing the right governor was important because of the governor's own considerable powers of appointment. Claiborne appointed a number of relatives. But beyond blood kinship he deployed criteria

---

[92] Peter Kastor put it more succinctly: "The West was ruled by appointees." *Nation's Crucible*, 92.

[93] Ibid., 94; Jefferson to Dickinson, January 13, 1807, in Ford, *Works of Thomas Jefferson*, online at Library of Congress, *The Thomas Jefferson Papers*, cited in Kastor, *Nation's Crucible*, 95.

[94] Kastor, *Nation's Crucible*, 95.

similar to those used by the Jefferson administration. While Jefferson's initial appointments excluded natives from Orleans, Claiborne soon added men of "foreign" background to the appointed legislative council, and to both the territorial militia and the army. It was through this intricate network of kinship that federal appointees reached out to the local citizens of Orleans and that white citizens of Orleans pressed their claims for incorporation. It was also how they demonstrated their loyalty. This administrative framework, held together through kinship (broadly defined), was perhaps the most important reason that Orleans was more closely linked to the United States by 1810. Although the object was republican citizenship, the means to that end was through the executive branch of government.[95]

Dramatic displays of loyalty did not hurt the quest for full citizenship. The Aaron Burr conspiracy was the most visible of a number of incidents that provided an opportunity for the white citizens of Orleans to show their mettle. In 1806, former vice president Aaron Burr set off down the Mississippi, ostensibly to meet up with the territorial military commander, James Wilkinson, toward highly suspicious ends. Burr had been a busy man. After failing to foment disunion among New England Federalists, Burr killed Alexander Hamilton in a duel and was indicted for his murder. Jefferson, apprised of the conspiracy, later concluded that Burr had planned to "extend his empire to the Alleghany, [by] seizing on New Orleans as the instrument of compulsion for our Western States." Not since "the days of Don Quixote," Jefferson wrote one confidant, had such an extraordinary enterprise been attempted.[96]

For Jefferson, the botched coup confirmed that his own idealistic conception of national patriotism was correct. Jefferson responded by mobilizing sentiment, not arms. And the results were gratifying. The conspiracy collapsed as Westerners confirmed their allegiance to the union. This, according to Jefferson, offered "the most remarkable ... proof [of the] innate strength of government." When "[a]pprised ... that there were traitors among them," Jefferson wrote, the citizens "crushed by their own strength what would have produced the march of armies and civil war in any other country." As Jefferson told one territorial governor, "On the whole, this squall, by showing with what ease our govern-

[95] Ibid., 101–8.

[96] Ibid., 74; Jefferson to Charles Clay, January 11, 1807, in Ford, *Works of Thomas Jefferson*, online at Library of Congress, *The Thomas Jefferson Papers*, cited in Lewis, *American Union*, 32.

ment suppresses movements which in other countries requires armies, has greatly increased its strength by increasing the public confidence in it." In this case, Jefferson's bet on the affective bond that linked Americans was confirmed.[97]

Visible displays of loyalty worked hand in hand with less visible networks of administrative governance to bind white Orleanians to the nation and to counter strongly held convictions that foreigners could not be incorporated en masse into the American polity. The citizens of Orleans used the occasion to underscore their abiding loyalty and American qualities. The failure of Orleanians to embrace the Burr conspiracy and their ceaseless proclamations of loyalty caught the attention of a number of important observers. John Dickinson, for instance, wrote to Jefferson early in 1807 to dismiss reports that "the people settled in the Country ceded by France to the United States, are universally dissatisfied with our Government." If anything, these citizens were upset "from their not partaking as fully as they hoped, of Benefits from the Cession, and from the expected Difficulty of procuring slaves." In other words, they wanted to be treated *more* like other Americans, not less.[98]

The incorporation of Louisiana required Republicans to embrace a kind of national governance that appeared to be at odds with statements expressed while they were in the minority. Republican presidents sought reliable mechanisms for executing public policy. Territorial governance, whether in the hands of a Federalist or Republican administration, was

---

[97] Jefferson to Isaac Weaver, Jr., June 7, 1807, in *The Writings of Thomas Jefferson*, ed. Andrew A. Lipscomb and Albert Ellery Bergh 20 vols. (Washington, D.C., 1903–4), 11:220–21, quoted in Onuf, *Jefferson's Empire*, 134; Jefferson to Gov. William C.C. Claiborne, February 3, 1807, in Lipscomb and Bergh, *Writings of Jefferson*, 11: 151, quoted in Onuf, *Jefferson's Empire*, 134.

New Orleanians were at pains to demonstrate those affective bonds. While Wilkinson backtracked to New Orleans, most Americans who learned of the conspiracy worried that Burr would be greeted by citizens in Orleans eager to embrace the conspiracy. Burr was captured and tried (though not convicted) for treason. In the meantime Wilkinson made a conspicuous display of tracking down Burr's co-conspirators. Wilkinson also wrote to the New Orleans City Council that "an evil of greater magnitude & more dangerous tendency is the influx of Strangers," emphasizing the outside agitators responsible for this plot. The Council responded by granting unprecedented power to local patrols in order to guard against such "strangers." Kastor, *Nation's Crucible*, 137; Prucha, *Sword of the Republic*, 95–97; Wilkinson to Council, January 1, 1807, in Letters, Petitions, and Reports Received by the Conseil de Ville, New Orleans public Library, 1:545, quoted in Kastor, *Nation's Crucible*, 137–38.

[98] John Dickinson to Jefferson, January 1, 1807, *The Thomas Jefferson Papers* Series 1. General Correspondence. 1651–1827, online at Library of Congress, *The Thomas Jefferson Papers*, cited in Kastor, *Nation's Crucible*, 138.

heavily skewed toward executive authority, especially military authority. Jefferson and Madison proved just as eager as their Federalist counterparts to extend control over the territories through executive control. This left little more than a token role for Congress (or for that matter, territorial elected representatives).[99]

Despite executive dominance, the path to formal statehood ultimately traveled through Congress. Congress debated statehood for Orleans in 1811. The key test was whether residents, both individually and collectively, were sufficiently attached to the United States. Was Louisiana attached to the other states in the Union? Was it sufficiently *de*tached from foreign powers to admit as a state. The Burr conspiracy provided valuable evidence that Orleaneans indeed were ready. "When some citizens of the old States forgot the love every honest heart owes to his country," Representative Macon preached, Louisianians "showed their attachment to the Union by the readiness with which they lent their aid to repel them. To make them a State would make the attachment still greater." While some Federalists, who understood that the new state would add two Senators and a representative to the Republican majority, questioned the degree of detachment from France, Orleans followed the path of other territories and was admitted to statehood without much controversy. On April 8, 1812, Congress accepted the Orleans constitution and admitted the new state of Louisiana to the Union, effective exactly nine years after the Louisiana Purchase. While the date of statehood provided a nice symmetry, the confirmation that Louisiana truly understood the benefits of statehood came several years later. That is when Mayor MaCarty petitioned Congressman Thomas Bolling Robertson, his Congressman, for federal money to fund a new quay for the Port of New Orleans.[100]

The saga of Louisiana's statehood is not one of overwhelming national power, hierarchical chains of command extending outward from a strong central administration, or a professionally skilled civil service advancing the national flag across a vast expanse of territory. Rather, it is a story of reciprocity and mutual advantage organized on behalf of the General Government in order to attach a foreign population to the union and to incorporate the political mechanisms that linked local to national interest in a permanent embrace. Many of the bonds were administrative, rather than legislative. It was the day-to-day interactions among

---

[99] Kastor, *Nation's Crucible*, chap. 4.
[100] Ibid., 144, 148, 201; *Annals of Congress*, 11th Cong., 3rd sess., January 2, 1811, 485, quoted in Kastor, *Nation's Crucible*, 145.

national officials, local officials, and the citizens of Orleans that cemented attachments. The problems that these interactions sought to address were not easily categorized into foreign or domestic issues. Nor did the civil and military authorities who wrestled with these problems necessarily hold fancy job titles. Yet the federal government was able to establish a system of governance sufficiently stable to turn the white inhabitants of Orleans, and even a few of the free blacks who lived there, into American citizens over the course of a decade. In the process they helped an entire nation settle just what was foreign and what was not.[101]

PROMOTING "PEACE AND PLENTY AND BRIGHT PROSPECTS OF WEALTH": FIGHTING INDIANS

Of the many institutions caricatured by accounts of America's stateless stature in the nineteenth century, the military was perhaps the one most frequently parodied. And for good reason. The army was never big enough for the task at hand. In spite of its victory over the British, the American army was demoralized and poor. The troops at Newburgh refused to demobilize until Congress paid them. General Washington's appeal to virtue and the extra ration of whiskey he ordered, however, were enough to stave off the threat of mutiny. By June 1784, Congress discharged the soldiers who remained, leaving only twenty-five men at Fort Pitt and fifty-five at West Point to guard military stores. The highest ranking officer was a captain. No wonder that Secretary of the Army Knox hectored his generals about cutting costs. He even went so far as to suggest that troops use beef cattle to carry flour and other supplies so as to "eat" the cost of transportation. On the eve of the Civil War, fewer than 20,000 men protected a nation that stretched across a continent.[102]

Nor was this a finely honed fighting force. Poorly disciplined, short even of the numbers authorized by Congress, and quick to desert, the army was a lightning rod for foreign observers' scorn. The "worthless characters" who populated it were a "mélange of English deserters,

---

[101] Kastor, *Nation's Crucible*, 9–10, 228.

[102] Prucha, *Sword of the Republic*, 3–4, 6, 33, 319; Lawrence Delbert Cress, *Citizens in Arms: The Army and the Militia in American Society to the War of 1812* (Chapel Hill, NC: University of North Carolina Press, 1982), 90–91; Carp, "Problem of National Defense," 28; Theda Skocpol et al., "Patriotic Partnerships: Why Great Wars Nourished American Civic Voluntarism," in Katznelson and Shefter, *Shaped by War and Trade*, 143.

Dutch, French and Americans," Englishman James E. Alexander observed in 1833. Indeed, the army relied on a steady stream of recent immigrants who could not speak English. Desertion throughout the army ran at 10 to 20 percent. Economy, remote assignments, and understaffing turned soldiers into farmers and day laborers. "The ax, pick, saw & trowel, has become more the implement of the American soldier," Zachary Taylor worried in 1820, "than the cannon, musket, or sword." Given the cost and distance of supplying rations, it was not uncommon for soldiers to grow their own vegetables and engage in other activities that left little time for soldiering.[103]

Fears of standing armies, however, should not be confused with antimilitarism. As the need for a national fighting force became apparent during and following the Revolution, many Americans embraced a conception of military power that accepted standing armies so long as Congress tightly controlled the military's fiscal appetite. This is why there were so few soldiers in the early nineteenth-century American army and why they grew their own vegetables. Nevertheless, the Constitution did provide for, in principle, an army capable of serving the needs of the entire nation, transcending (again in theory) the powerful constraint of localism.[104]

While the possibilities for standing armies were limited, the need for one was urgent. Turmoil in Europe, an aggressive mercantilist world system, domestic strife, and conflict with Indians, exacerbated by Americans' seemingly insatiable quest for territory, challenged national security. One student of American foreign policy identified such threats as the "major preoccupations of Americans in the 1790s." During that decade, the army was called upon to fight Indians, quell two domestic rebellions, and intimidate Algerian pirates. The United States drew close to the brink of war with England three times and almost went to war with France in 1798. When Europe was plunged back into war in 1803, American security was threatened again. Those threats were realized in the War of 1812.[105]

---

[103] James E. Alexander, *Transatlantic Sketches, Comprising Visits to the Most Interesting Scenes in North and South America and the West Indies, with Notes on Negro Slavery and Canadian Emigration*, 2 vols. (London, 1833) 2:281, quoted in Prucha, *Sword of the Republic*, 323; Prucha, *Sword of the Republic*, 324–27; Taylor to Thomas S. Jesup, September 18, 1820, in *Zachary Taylor Papers* (Washington, D.C.: Library of Congress, 1958), quoted in Prucha, *Sword of the Republic*, 169; Prucha, *Sword of the Republic*, 169–181.

[104] Cress, *Citizens in Arms*, xiii, 11–14.

[105] Ira Katznelson, "Rewriting the Epic of America," in Katznelson and Shefter, *Shaped By War and Trade*, 9; Carp, "Problem of National Defense," 35; Nelson, *Liberty and Property*, 143.

An important argument mounted in defense of the Constitution by Federalists was that united colonies would make collective defense easier than separate states. "Leave America divided into thirteen or, if you please, into three or four independent governments," John Jay asked in *Federalist Number 4* and "what armies could they raise and pay – what fleets could they ever hope to have? If one was attacked," Jay continued, "would the others fly to its succor, and spend their blood and money in its defense?" The obvious solution to these foreign threats lay in a General Government that could speak with one voice.[106]

A standing army would have great diplomatic value. Whatever Americans' views on a professional army might be, the reigning international system recognized armies as indicative of a nation's strength. Federalists associated a strong army and navy with commercial advantage. The British agreed. They did not mince words in rebuffing American efforts to secure a commercial treaty after the American Revolution, informing the former colonists that Britain "derived greater profits from the present situation of our commerce than we could expect under a treaty: and you have not kind of power that can compel us to surrender any advantage to you." The impasse with Spain over access to the Mississippi placed Americans in a similar position.[107]

Some supported a stronger constitution to remedy this situation. Because the government would be "more powerful and respectable, it will be more feared," George Nicholas argued. And "as they will have more power to injure Spain, Spain will be more inclined to do them justice, by yielding it, or by giving them an adequate compensation." The same logic applied to negotiations with Indians. In the wake of the War for Independence, American envoys threatened swift retribution if tribes failed to negotiate agreements. Effective in the short run, Indians soon recognized that the United States could not back up these threats and revised their tactics accordingly.[108]

---

[106] Aristide R. Zolberg, "International Engagement and American Democracy: A Comparative Perspective," in Katznelson and Shefter, *Shaped by War and Trade*, 31–32; John Jay, "Federalist 4: Concerning Dangers from Foreign Force and Influence," in Ford, *The Federalist*, http://www.yale.edu/lawweb/avalon/federal/fedo4.htm.

[107] Carp, "Problem of National Defense," 24; William Richardson Davie, Speech at North Carolina ratifying convention, in *The Debates in the Several State Conventions on the Adoption of the Federal Constitution*, ed. Jonathan Elliot, 5 vols. (Washington, D.C., 1836), 4:18, http://memory.loc.gov/ammem/amlaw/, quoted, in Edling, *Revolution in Favor of Government*, 87.

[108] George Nicholas, Speech in Virginia Ratifying Convention, June 10, 1788, in *The Documentary History of the Ratification of the Constitution*, ed. Merrill Jensen, John

Relations with Indians for much of the nineteenth century demonstrated the integral connection between the federal government, national security, territorial expansion, and the economy. Decisions about the allocation of scarce military resources shaped the prospects for entire regions. After the Treaty of Greenville (1795) secured a truce that brought the "joy of an uninterrupted peace with the Indians" to the Ohio Valley, the prospects for settlement and economic prosperity changed dramatically. A settler named John Gano noted the changes that followed on the heels of the Treaty of Greenville. "Hostilities ceased, and the settlements began to increase rapidly every thing relating to them put on a new aspect." "The change was great," Gano bragged, "from alarm, Danger, and Death which the inhabitants was exposed to, peace plenty and bright prospects of wealth and happiness began to open to view."[109]

The "peace" and "plenty" that Gano and tens of thousands of other settlers enjoyed was in fact the product of national policy that placed, what one scholar has labeled, the power of an "American Leviathan" at the disposal of settlers in the Ohio Valley. By embracing the Western settler's perspective and increasing the military resources it was willing to devote to the problem, the General Government accomplished something that even the British had failed to achieve: it ended the state of war.[110]

In Secretary of War Henry Knox's account of these developments, the state was an "invisible hand" that quietly responded to the demands of Western settlers. It did so in order to retain the allegiance of that same population. "Although the present government of the United States can-

---

P. Kaminski, Gaspare J. Saladino, et al., 20 vols. to date (Madison: State Historical Society of Wisconsin, 1976–), 9:1129–30, quoted in Edling, *Revolution in Favor of Government*, 87; Horsman, *Expansion and American Indian Policy*, 22.

[109] William Preston to John Preston, 10 October 1795, Preston Family Papers, 1940, as quoted in Griffin, *American Leviathan*, 249; Ganno quoted in Griffin, *American Leviathan*, 265. Securing these lands, in turn, was crucial to the fiscal health of the government itself, since its lands, particularly in the Northwest territory, would be worth a fortune if made secure. Cayton, "'Separate Interests' and the Nation-State: The Washington Administration and the Origins of Regionalism in the Trans-Appalachian West," *Journal of American History*, 79, no.1 (June 1992): 47.

"The Settlmt. Of the Western Country and making a Peace with the Indians are so analogous," George Washington noted in 1783," that there can be no definition of the one without involving considerations of the other." Washington to James Duane, 7 September 1783, in *The Writings of George Washington*, ed. John C. Fitzpatrick, 39 vols. (Washington, DC: United States Government Printing Office, 1931–44), 27:139–40, quoted in Francis Paul Prucha, *American Indian Policy in the Formative Years: The Indian Trade and Intercourse Acts, 1790–1834* (Cambridge, MA: Harvard University Press, 1962), 28.

[110] Gano quoted in Griffin, *American Leviathan*, 265.

not with propriety be involved in the opprobrium," Knox asserted, "yet it seems necessary ... that some powerful attempts should be made to tranquilize the frontiers, particularly those south of the Ohio." The General Government had to act because the people "loudly demand the interference and protection of government."[111]

That Knox could describe the Federal government's role as "hidden" holds one of the keys to the mystery of national authority in early America. Federal presence was soon forgotten by the very people who benefited from the bargain Knox described. Subsequent histories reinforced that vanishing act.

Those who suffered at the hands of the U.S. Army had a different perspective. At the peace negotiations, a Shawnee captain reacted to the eagle at the center of the United States Coat of Arms. He questioned this choice of bird. Why not a dove? It "would not do harm to the smallest creature." The eagle, on the other hand, was "the largest of all birds and the enemy of all birds. He is proud, because he is conscious of his size and strength." The eagle "looks down disparagingly upon all birds," the captain noted. The Shawnees had felt the power of the American eagle, and would not soon forget it. For settlers, however, the powerful myths of self-sufficiency soon merged with the cultural appeal of American exceptionalism to erase the memory of the federal government's role. Whether Leviathan or eagle best captured that role, those who had been on the receiving end of its wrath remembered its power far better than its beneficiaries did.[112]

The decision to deploy federal troops in the 1790s to fight Indians north of the Ohio River created strong bonds between the settlers in the Ohio Valley and the fledgling Union. That Northern territories were the beneficiary of these military resources, at the expense of Southern territories facing similar problems, helped to define the very attitudes each region developed toward the General Government. Congress and the administration decided to concentrate its military resources in the Northwest Territory for a variety of reasons, ranging from geographic proximity to protecting the government's financial stake in the land it held. The Northern territories returned the favor through greater fealty to the General Government.[113]

---

[111] *Pittsburgh Gazette,* January 24, 1795, quoted in Griffin, *American Leviathan,* 265.

[112] "Narrative of John Heckewelder's Journey to the Wabash in 1792," *Pennsylvania Magazine of History and Biography* 12, no. 1, (January 1888): 49–50, quoted in Griffin, *American Leviathan,* 269.

[113] Cayton, "'Separate Interests' and the Nation-State," 41–42, 47–48. The behavior of the tribes that they were negotiating with played an important role as well. See also Edling, *Revolution in Favor of Government,* 122.

The best indication that troop allocation was vital to those living beyond the borders of the United States is the reaction from settlers denied federal protection. Many of those who supported the Constitution in the South had expected help from the newly empowered government. George Nicholas, for instance, wrote to James Madison from Kentucky in 1789, warning that the nation's Indian policy was dominated by men "living on, and interested in the welfare of, the other side of the Ohio." William Blount, Governor of the Southwest Territory, had cast his lot with those who backed a stronger constitution so that the federal government would offer more protection to settlers living in the Southern border areas. His pleas for assistance went unheeded, as did the requests of his constituents. "My situation," Blount wrote Knox, "is that of daily hearing their complaints without the power of redress." That these military resources were the object of such fierce competition suggests the decisive impact that they had on regional security and economic development.[114]

The American military expanded and contracted in fits and starts in response to Indian wars, domestic unrest, and threats from other nation-states. The First American Regiment stood at 1,216 men in 1790. After several embarrassing defeats, the army swelled to 5,800 in 1794, eventually stabilizing at 3,000 after the Treaty of Greenville in 1795. This was puny compared to the size of the continental European armies, but it established an important principle for those who advocated a standing army.[115]

---

[114] Prucha, *Indian Policy*, 41; Nicholas to Madison, November 2, 1789, in *Papers of James Madison: Congressional Series*, ed. William T. Hutchinson, William M.E. Rachel, et al., 17 vols. (Chicago: University of Chicago Press; Charlottesville: University Press of Virginia, 1959–1991), 12:444–45, quoted in Cayton, "'Separate Interests' and the Nation-State," 49; Whitaker, *The Spanish-American Frontier*, 20; Blount to Knox, May 28, 1793, in Carter, *Territorial Papers*, 4:264; Cayton, "'Separate Interests' and the Nation-State," 61. On the importance of the military, see also Nelson, *Liberty and Property*, 16–17.

To make matters worse, resources that poured into the Northwest Territory were administered by men who stood to gain personally by carrying out American Indian policy. President Washington appointed former Continental Army officers to govern the Northwest Territory, many of whom were members of the Society of Cincinnati. From Washington's perspective, this reinforced the bonds of loyalty to the United States (the same reasons that Jefferson appointed Virginians to the Orleans Territory). To those denied federal resources, however, it appeared that regional economic development traveled hand-in-hand with privilege. Cayton, "'Separate Interests' and the Nation-State," 50.

[115] Edling, *Revolution in Favor of Government*, 138–39. After the War of 1812, the peacetime army fluctuated between 5,000 and 12,000 men. See also, Prucha, *Sword of the Republic*, 20–27.

Dramatic expansions, when necessary, were funded by the Constitution's hard-fought fiscal authority. The government borrowed $1 million from the First Bank of the United States to fund the expedition that stifled the Whiskey Rebellion. The United States also borrowed heavily to pay the costs associated with the War of 1812.[116]

When in office, Jeffersonian Republicans once again expanded the reach of the federal government, reversing their position on the military and debt. Although most Federalists opposed increased troop strength to fight Indian wars, nascent Republicans from the nation's mid-section and South supported such measures. Adams and Jefferson maintained troop levels in equal numbers. Republicans proved just as willing as Federalists to increase the size of the army. In response to growing international tension, Jefferson raised troop levels to 9,300 in 1809. To preserve free trade and protect neutrality, the Republicans sent those troops into battle in the War of 1812.[117]

"DANGERS WHICH ARE POSSIBLE WILL OCCUR": THE WAR OF 1812

The United States was not prepared for war when it came. Republican policy makers imagined an offensive war to subdue Canada and force Great Britain to recognize America's commercial claims. Jefferson infamously predicted that conquering Canada would "be a mere matter of marching." Yet two years into the war, the United States had not come close to achieving this objective. The Americans had not anticipated any need to defend their homeland. Before the war, Secretary of State Monroe did not fear "invasion, the desolation of our coast, the battering [of] our towns, or even any greater injury to our commerce than [had] existed since 1807." He was wrong on all counts and, like most Americans, could not have imagined that the capital's public buildings would be burned by a British expeditionary force. To Monroe's credit, he acknowledged this miscalculation. It was "safest to act on the presumption that dangers which are possible will occur," Monroe conceded.[118]

---

[116] Edling, *Revolution in Favor of Government*, 138; Carp, "Problem of National Defense," 38.

[117] Carp, "Problem of National Defense," 37–38; Edling, *Revolution in Favor of Government*, 138.

[118] Lewis, *American Union*, 48–49; Jefferson to William Duane, August 4, 1812, in Lipscomb and Bergh, *Writings of Thomas Jefferson*, 13:180, quoted in Lewis, *American Union*, 48; Monroe to Taylor, June 13, 1812, in *The Writings of James Monroe*, ed. Stanislaus

Some of the same factors that had undermined Jefferson's embargo and the Non-Intercourse Act handicapped the war effort. Until Washington, D.C. was sacked, there was little popular support for the war. In fact, the problem of trading with the enemy continued unabated from the days of the embargo. Americans were even less willing to pay for the war. Rather than levy steeper taxes, the Republican leadership turned to deficit spending to finance the war. They issued Treasury certificates and relied on massive loans – the very kinds of federal fiscal mechanisms that Republicans earlier opposed.[119]

Federalist opposition and obstruction undermined the war effort. An undersized and poorly trained military, one reason the embargo was needed in the first place, also crippled the American effort. The wartime Congress passed a dozen measures authorizing troop increases in the first six months of the war. Congress authorized an army of 58,000, but only a third of this target had been met nine months into the war.[120]

An object lesson in the limits of national authority for the first two years, the War of 1812 ironically proved to be a turning point in the trajectory of that power. Several developments at the very end of the war were instrumental to this shift. Perhaps the most important event was Napoleon's defeat and subsequent abdication in April 1814. Although this freed up British troops to raid American cities, it ended war in Europe – one of the underlying causes of the British-American conflict. The Treaty of Ghent, negotiated by John Quincy Adams and Henry Clay, once again demonstrated the power of diplomacy. American negotiators succeeded where the military and the American populace had failed. Although the treaty merely restored the pre-war status quo, the British dropped their territorial claims. Diplomatically, at least, the Americans held their own against a long-standing, powerful foe.[121]

Andrew Jackson's victory in New Orleans also became a great source of national pride. Unaware that a peace treaty had already been signed, Jackson's men held off the British assault on New Orleans in December 1814. When the smoke cleared, roughly 300 British troops lay dead, another 1500 were wounded. The Americans lost only 13 men, with

Murray Hamilton, 7 vols. (1898; repr. New York: AMS Press, 1969), 5:211–2, quoted in Lewis, *American Union*, 49; Monroe to Unknown Recipient, July 3, 1814, in Hamilton, *Writings of James Monroe*, 5:286, quoted in Lewis, *American Union*, 50.
[119] Lewis, *American Union*, 50–51; Watts, *Republic Reborn*, 278–79.
[120] Lewis, *American Union*, 51; Cress, *Citizens in Arms*, 173–74.
[121] Don Edward Fehrenbacher, *The Era of Expansion, 1800–1848* (New York, NY: Wiley, 1968), 23.

39 wounded. This victory over British veterans, battle hardened in the Napoleonic Wars, was a tremendous symbolic triumph for the young nation. It had fought the mighty British to a standstill. Citizens across the United States celebrated the end of the war and Jackson's symbolic victory. The receding British threat, a treaty that ratified this retreat, and the stunning military victory in New Orleans fueled a growing sense of nationalism among Americans.[122]

For many Americans, this newfound sentiment for the nation that united them did not translate into support for stronger General Government. "Old Republicans," like John Taylor and John Randolph, had opposed the war in the first place, fearing that it would consolidate government and increase taxes. For them, the War merely confirmed such fears and stiffened their resolve to check centralized power. In the mean time, many New England Federalists, opposed to the War, championed local prerogatives and obstructed national initiatives.[123]

The outcome of the War, however, alerted Republican leaders like Jefferson and Madison to the need for organization and infrastructure that could only be provided by a more assertive General Government. In the aftermath of the War, they advocated a far-reaching program of military preparedness that included annual funding for coastal and frontier defense, a peacetime army, an expanded navy, and greater control over state militias. While Jefferson advocated a diplomatic course that would ensure a lasting peace, he believed that preparing for war was essential to securing that peace. "Our whole business ... ought to be a sedulous preparation for it [war] fortifying our seaports, filling our magazines, classing and disciplining our militias, [and] forming officers." Jefferson's, Madison's, and Monroe's support for wider-ranging federal measures, including the Second Bank and internal improvements, was partially the result of their experience with the problems the United States encountered during the War of 1812.[124]

A more expansive view of government's potential gripped a number of national Republicans. Young men like Henry Clay and John Calhoun imagined that republican government would absorb and reflect the dyna-

---

[122] Sean Wilentz, *Andrew Jackson* (New York: Times Books, 2005), 31–33; David Waldstreicher, *In the Midst of Perpetual Fetes: The Making of American Nationalism, 1776–1820* (Chapel Hill, NC: University of North Carolina Press, 1997), 296.

[123] Lewis, *American Union*, 57, 59; Watts, *Republic Reborn*, 280–83.

[124] Lewis, *American Union*, 58, 61; Jefferson to DuPont De Nemours, February 28, 1815, in Lipscomb and Bergh, *Writings of Thomas Jefferson*, 14:256, quoted in Lewis, *American Union*, 60.

mism evident in each section of the nation and their growing economies. That dynamism was not supported by revenues, which were limited by the traditional Republican commitment to low taxes. "With a country consisting of the best materials in the world," James Monroe wrote Jefferson in frustration, "whose people are patriotic & virtuous, & willing to support the war; whose resources are greater than those of any other country; & whose means have scarcely yet been touched, we have neither money in the treasury or credit."[125]

Just as the Revolutionary War had opened Alexander Hamilton's eyes to the power of self-interest, the War of 1812 stripped away the remaining vestiges of older republican ideas for many public officials. Mocking quaint notions of war loans offered from virtuous sentiments, the Republican chair of the House Ways and Means Committee Ezekial Bacon argued that "the truth is, if we can make it for the interest of capitalists to lend us this money, we shall undoubtedly obtain it, even from our enemies; and on no other consideration should we flatter ourselves from obtaining a single cent from those whom we call our friends."[126]

James Monroe still had the War of 1812 in mind when he delivered his inaugural address in 1817. Monroe backed a stronger military force (both army and navy), increased spending on fortifications, internal improvements, and tariff protection. Monroe's Secretary of War, John Calhoun, insisted that he would continue his predecessor's efforts to strengthen the nation's defenses. "None felt more deeply than myself," Calhoun promised, "that total want of preparation which preceded the last war; and which had nearly been succeeded by the most disastrous consequence."

The juxtaposition of nationalist sentiment that emerged out of Jackson's victory in New Orleans and the successful conclusion (if not prosecution) of the War on the one hand, and the exposure of gaping holes in the General Government's capacity on the other, encouraged young Republicans like Matthew Carey to seek a new kind of politics. In his pamphlet, *The Olive Branch*, the Philadelphian argued that the presence of conflicting economic interests such as agriculture and manufactures should be acknowledged – even embraced. Rather than playing one

[125] Pamela L. Baker, "The Washington National Road Bill and the Struggle to Adopt a Federal System of Internal Improvement," *Journal of the Early Republic*, 22, no. 3 (Autumn 2002): 440; Sellers, *Market Revolution*, 70; Watts, *Republic Reborn*, 86–87, 269; Monroe to Jefferson, December 21, 1814, in Hamilton, *Writings of James Monroe*, 5:305, quoted in Watts, *Republic Reborn*, 278.

[126] *Annals of Congress*, 12th Cong., 1st sess., February 25, 1812, 1097, quoted in Watts, *Republic Reborn*, 305.

off the other, Carey argued, their interdependence should be celebrated. Internal development held the key to success in this approach.[127]

The War of 1812 provided a powerful rationale for the kind of cooperation, assisted by the General Government, that advocates of the American System sought. National Republicans pointed to models of state-assisted internal development that they hoped to extend to the national stage. Pennsylvania, for instance, had taken bold measures to integrate its economy by authorizing a canal to connect the Delaware River and the Chesapeake Bay. In explaining its support, the legislature expressed a desire to "establish a perfectly safe and rapid transportation of our armies and the munitions of war through the interior of the country," in conjunction with the desire to serve as the economic means "to operate as a cement to the union between the states." By 1814, the Pennsylvania legislature was lobbying Congress for a "great national road" that would connect Maine to the Mississippi." This project would not only aid the military, it would promote economic growth, and make "the manufacturers of the northern, the growers of the southern, and the raisers of consumable produce in the middle states, mutually dependent upon, and serviceable to each other."[128]

John Quincy Adams, Henry Clay, and John Calhoun sought to address national problems that, in their view, extended well beyond military preparedness or even fiscal infrastructure. They welcomed the increased economic activity evident throughout the land, but feared the spatial segregation of that activity. For Clay, the "different scenes to which commercial pursuits lead the citizens of different districts of the Union" was the source of dangerous sectional conflicts. The Constitution provided all the tools necessary for enlightened leaders to increase national authority – a key step toward integrating these "scenes." But Republican leadership had not vigorously deployed all of the powers available under the Constitution. Instead, according to Clay, an emphasis on states' rights

---

[127] Lewis, *American Union*, 99; John C. Calhoun to Charles Jared Ingersoll, December 14, 1817, in *The Papers of John C. Calhoun*, ed. Robert L. Meriwether, 28 vols. (Columbia, SC: University of South Carolina Press, 1959–), 2:17, quoted in Lewis, *American Union*, 99; Watts, *Republic Reborn*, 304. See also, Mathew Carey, *The Olive Branch ...,* 7th edn (Philadelphia, PA, 1815).

[128] "Law of Pennsylvania," *Niles' Weekly Register*, April 3, 1813, American Periodicals Series Online, 1740–1900 (Proquest, doc. no. 811784702), http://proquest.umi.com/pqdweb, cited in Watts, *Republic Reborn*, 309; Watts, *Republic Reborn*, 309–10; "Legislature of Pennsylvania," *Niles' Weekly Register*, February 5, 1814, APS Online, (Proquest, doc. no. 811789672), cited in Watts, *Republic Reborn*, 310.

had promoted "if not disunion itself, such a state of disorder and confusion as must inevitably lead to it."[129]

In one corollary to Hamilton's dictum about government "out of sight," Clay insisted that only the General Government could provide the wherewithal for Americans to realize their full potential. Once citizens realized this, they would direct their own energy "to the support and strength of the Union." Energizing the national government would "afford to every man in the union an obvious, palpable evidence of the benefits afforded to him by the government under which he lives," Clay preached. Failure to prepare for war against Great Britain had already cost Americans dearly. Jefferson and Madison's naïve reliance on the bonds of affection to support the embargo had only made matters worse. Luckily, Jackson's symbolic victory, federal diplomacy, and peace in Europe offered Americans a second chance to be a great nation. Once Americans experienced the tangible benefits that institutions like the Second Bank of the United States delivered, or the improvement in commerce and communications offered by internal improvements, citizens would see for themselves just what an energetic national government could do. Only then, Clay believed, might citizens develop those bonds of affection that stretched the length of the union.[130]

With the Northwest Indians subdued, the Mississippi secured, and even the British neutralized, the United States entered the first period in its history during which it enjoyed relative security. Not only were fears about foreign threats dampened, Americans were less concerned that Westerners would break from the Union. In fact, Americans began to assume that the Union would endure, providing that the growing threat of sectional division over the issue of slavery, could be resolved.[131]

"THIS SORT OF MACHINERY CAN MOVE THE WORLD": REMOVING INDIANS

Continued territorial expansion constantly produced new challenges. The most immediate threat to union, besides the ever-present danger of sectional division over the expansion of slavery, was the festering

---

[129] Lewis, *American Union*, 64; Henry Clay, Speech of March 13, 1818, in *The Papers of Henry Clay*, ed. James F. Hopkins, 11 vols. (Lexington, KY: University of Kentucky Press, 1959–1992), 2:472, quoted in Lewis, *American Union*, 65.
[130] Ibid., 65.
[131] Ibid., 217.

relationship with Indians. While military action was always a possibility, and one that was employed often, treaties and regulated trade were the preferred instruments for Indian relations. The Constitution, many believed, would allow colonists to speak with one voice when it came to these "diplomatic" relations. The United States sought treaties to establish clear boundaries that would restrict whites from Indian country, control the disposition of Indian lands, and regulate trade with the Indians. A string of federal laws, beginning with the "Trade and Intercourse" Act of 1790, reinforced this policy.[132]

Yet American Indian policy never wavered from the fundamental premise that advancing the frontier was the first order of business. Treaties and statutes sought to mitigate some of the more egregious consequences of informal action. The government hoped to reign in whites who sought to exploit the Indian trade. Federal policy sought to protect the interests of white settlers without tarnishing the nation's honor. While the army intervened on occasion to enforce the law, these actions were largely ineffective. They would have required far more resources than Americans were willing to provide. At the state and local level, there was rarely even any pretense that the laws were being enforced.[133]

Disputes over Indian land in Georgia proved particularly contentious and eventually embroiled the entire nation in a Constitutional crisis. At the time of the Revolution, only one-eighth of Georgia was occupied by white colonists. The remainder was held by Indians. Georgians signed three treaties in defiance of the Confederation's principles of preemption. Georgia continued to insist upon these claims even after the United States government signed a treaty with the Creeks. Periodically, Georgians took military matters into their own hands. They also persistently petitioned the federal government for assistance, but received little. By 1824, Georgia had pressed its Indians into a corner of the state. The governor was angling for that land, too, through a series of forced cessions. John Quincy Adams suspended these cessions upon learning the details of their circumstances, but soon backed down when Governor Troup ordered the Georgia militia "to repel any hostile invasion of the territory of this State."[134]

[132] Horsman, *Expansion and American Indian Policy*, 56–57; Prucha, *Indian Policy*, 1–3, 45–46.

[133] Ibid., 3; Ronald N. Satz, *American Indian Policy in the Jacksonian Era* (Lincoln, NE: University of Nebraska Press, 1975), 1–2; Keohane, "International Commitments," 66–7. See also Horsman, *Expansion and American Indian Policy*, 54–56.

[134] Prucha, *Sword of the Republic*, 49–562; Troup to James Barbour, 17 February 1827, as printed in *Niles' Weekly Register* 32, no. 807, (March 3, 1827): 16, in APS Online,

Andrew Jackson, campaigning for president and seeking to consolidate his Southern base, added fuel to the fire. While American presidents had paid lip service to Indian removal from Southern states, Andrew Jackson actively encouraged such actions in his presidential campaign. He followed up his words with action. Jackson had had extensive experience with Indians, as the territorial governor of Florida and as a general. He had extracted massive concessions from the Creeks and other Indian tribes in the Southwestern Territory after the 1812 War. He had little faith that the Indians who remained within the states would voluntarily leave their lands in the South and viewed the General Government's policy as deeply flawed. Jackson's political victories in the South in 1828 were attributable in part to his heated rhetoric on the subject of removal. Animated by the discovery of gold in the western part of the state, and encouraged by Jackson, Georgia enacted laws that distributed Cherokee holdings to county governments. Rather than Indian customs (protected by federal treaty), state law would prevail. Alabama and Mississippi soon passed similar legislation.[135]

The Georgia laws intentionally delayed implementation until June 1830, in the hope that the General Government would force, persuade, or entice Indians to leave voluntarily. Having encouraged the states to assert their claims to Indian land, Jackson now faced a crisis that, in part, he had helped to create. State law and public passion challenged constitutional authority, which had clearly resided with the federal government since its inception.[136]

Already facing rising demands for nullification over the tariff, Jackson used executive power to salvage his claim to national authority – in the name of states' rights. Jackson deployed his chief deputy for Indian affairs, who organized a grassroots campaign to secure legislation that would grant presidents discretionary power to remove Indians. Jackson showed his hand in the early days of his administration when he appointed John H. Eaton, an advocate of Indian removal, as Secretary of War.[137]

At the same time, Jackson claimed that Indian affairs should be left to the individual states. Generally a fierce defender of national authority,

Proquest doc. no. 811857602, cited in Sellers, *Market Revolution*, 279.
[135] Satz, *American Indian Policy*, 6–11; Nobles, *American Frontiers*, 127–29; Sellers, *Market Revolution*, 90; Joseph C. Burke, "The Cherokee Cases: A Study in Law, Politics, and Morality," *Stanford Law Review*, 21, no. 3 (February 1969): 503.
[136] Burke, "Cherokee Cases," 503; Satz, *American Indian Policy*, 11.
[137] Satz, *American Indian Policy*, 12.

Jackson now claimed that he could not intervene in the affairs of states. The General Government's hands were tied, he informed both Indians and constituents. Shortly after his inauguration, Jackson sent an agent to inform "my red Choctaw children, and my Chickasaw children" that "their father cannot prevent them from being subject to the laws of the state of Mississippi."[138]

After offering the Cherokees and Creeks a deal that Jackson considered generous, and after being flatly rebuffed, the President entered the political fray directly. He needed to counter the impassioned opposition of the American Board of Commissioners for Foreign Missions, a society comprised of Presbyterians and Congregationalists. The Board insisted that Indians retained the right to their lands in the Southern states. Appealing to Americans in religious and humanitarian terms, the Board for Foreign Missions was a formidable foe.[139]

Jackson tapped Thomas L. McKenney, a leading Indian affairs expert, to galvanize removal sentiment. McKenney, who headed the Bureau of Indian Affairs under Adams, put the power of the presidency and the resources of the executive branch to work in this fight. The American Board of Commissioners was a leading recipient of federal funds to civilize the Indians. Believing that removal was a key step toward this objective, McKenney put federal funds to more efficient political use by creating the New York Board for the Emigration, Preservation, and Improvement of the Aborigines of America. The Board was initiated with the *"understood invitation of the Executive."* Even though the federal funds that subsidized it had been appropriated for the purpose of civilizing Indians, the Board pressed on with its political agenda. McKenney also garnered the support of Stephen Van Rensseler, a prominent New Yorker and president of the Missionary Society of the Dutch Reformed Church.[140]

Pleased with his work, McKenney reported to the Secretary of War that these actions would be "wide & deep – & will be a *shield & buckler* in the future." McKenney stayed on top of these activities, diverting funds intended for Indian education to the publication of two thousand copies of a tract advocating removal. "I think the blow is struck that will silence all opposers upon this branch of the clamors of the day," McKenney

---

[138] Jackson to Creeks, 22 March 1829, as quoted in Michael P. Rogin, *Fathers and Children: Andrew Jackson and the Subjugation of the American Indian* (New York, NY: Knopf, 1975), 216–17, quoted in Sellers, *Market Revolution*, 310.

[139] Satz, *American Indian Policy*, 13.

[140] Ibid., 14–15.

wrote Eaton. "This sort of machinery can move the world." The Jackson administration also reached out to other religious groups, especially the Baptists, to build support for his removal agenda.[141]

The administration moved quickly to secure legislation. The Removal Act of 1830 authorized the president to exchange public domain territory west of the Mississippi for Indian-held land in the Southern states. Congress appropriated $500,000 to carry out this plan. The debate was intense, and the vote was both partisan and close. But in the end, Jackson got the legislation he sought and signed the bill on May 28, 1830. From Jackson's perspective, the legislation and his larger campaign to ensure that Indians did not form a "nation within a nation" were critical to preserving the Union.[142]

The irony that Jackson had championed the rights of states like Georgia in order to preserve the union was not lost on his opponents. Nor did those who opposed Indian removal ignore the fact that proponents of limited, frugal government were prepared to spend large amounts of federal funds on this project and intervene directly in the lives of tens of thousands who had been previously offered the protection of the federal government. Apparently government "consolidation" rested in the eye of the beholder. For Jackson and his supporters, the General Government was simply removing an impediment that would allow the natural process of territorial expansion to continue its course.[143]

The Cherokees had already lobbied Congress in an effort to stop the state laws that threatened to remove them from their ancestral lands. Outmaneuvered by Jacksonian Democrats in 1830, the tribe turned to the Supreme Court. Former Attorney General William Wirt argued the case and launched his own publicity campaign. In March 1831, Wirt brought a case directly to the Supreme Court. He sought an injunction prohibiting the state of Georgia from carrying out its Indian laws. Standing, Wirt argued, was based on the tribe's status as a foreign nation. The Court declined the case, but Chief Justice Marshall hinted that, based on the merits of the case, he agreed with the Indians, and went so far as

[141] McKenney to Eaton, undated, in Records of the Office of Indian Affairs, Letters Received Cherokee Agency East, (Record Group 75, National Archives, Washington, D.C.), quoted in Satz, *American Indian Policy*, 16; McKenney to Eaton, 14 August 1829, in Records of Office of Indian Affairs, RG75, quoted in Satz, *American Indian Policy*, 16; Satz, *American Indian Policy*, 17–19.

[142] Sellers, *Market Revolution*, 311; Satz, *American Indian Policy*, 31.

[143] Ibid., 10, 30.

to suggest ways to place the substantive questions contained in the case before his colleagues.[144]

Worcester, decided by the Supreme Court in 1832, followed Marshall's advice. The Court overturned the state law regarding the rights of missionaries to live in Cherokee Territory without a license. Marshall's decision ruled that state law conflicted with both treaties and federal law. In both cases, the state was subordinated to federal authority, the Court concluded. But when Georgia defied the Court's ruling and refused to comply, Jackson claimed that this was not his problem. "John Marshall has made his decision," a Congressman recalled Jackson muttering, "*now let him enforce it!*"[145]

For thousands of Indians, however, the process of removal had already begun under the 1830 legislation. The Choctaws of Mississippi were the first to be relocated under the provisions of the Act. Although the Jackson administration was at pains to make this early test a success, the premium placed on speed and economy ultimately undermined the effort. The five to six thousand Choctaws who negotiated the Treaty of Dancing Rabbit Creek in the fall of 1830 were subjected to bureaucratic inefficiency at best, and in many cases, great hardship and death.[146]

During the "Trail of Tears," one out of eight Cherokees died on the trek, or soon after they crossed the Mississippi. While the Jackson administration sought to learn from this experience, the multiple waves of Indian removal that followed over the course of the decade ended tragically. The undertaking's size exposed the limited administrative capacity of the General Government. To cope with the challenge, tasks were increasingly shifted from the civilian sector to the military. By the time Jackson retired, the U.S. government had signed approximately seventy treaties like the one with the Choctaw. It had freed up one hundred million acres of Indian land.[147]

A process that had begun in the name of states' rights embroiled the General Government in a massive and costly undertaking that, for many, could not have been more intrusive. The Government had long been engaged in the Indian question as a fundamental element of its foreign policy. Although Jackson did all he could to support claims for states'

---

[144] Burke, "Cherokee Cases," 505, 508–9, 513, 515.

[145] Ibid., 525; Keohane, "International Commitments," 67–68; Jackson is quoted in Sellers, *Market Revolution,* 311.

[146] Satz, *American Indian Policy,* 64–70, 73.

[147] White, *It's Your Misfortune,* 87; Satz, *American Indian Policy,* 77–79, 106–8.

rights, he was overruled by the Supreme Court and outmaneuvered by those who believed that the General Government's commitments superseded the claims of states, especially when the matter was construed as foreign policy.[148]

When the states' rights approach to Indian clearance failed, Jackson did not hesitate to use military force to remove Indians. There was little talk about states' rights in this endeavor, and even less concern about the civil or political rights of the Indians themselves. This costly and prodigious federal effort eventually spawned the Bureau of Indian Affairs, which over time would become one of the more visible – and visibly corrupt – manifestations of the federal presence in the West. Tasked with civilizing the Indians, its responsibilities soon ranged from regulating alcohol, to education and economic development.[149]

"AN IMMEDIATE AND DECISIVE EFFECT": FUSING MILITARY AND CIVILIAN RESPONSIBILITIES

Jackson was able to call upon a trained officer corps and extensive network of logistics and procurement personnel in his military endeavors due to the twenty-five year history of the United States Military Academy at West Point. The Academy, which was modeled after European counterparts that viewed a professional army as one of the core responsibilities of powerful states, had an unlikely founder: Thomas Jefferson. But Jefferson had opposed the idea of an academy when his Federalist opponents first proposed it. Jefferson, however, squared his constitutional misgivings with his policy agenda once he was in office, concluding that neither the states nor the private sector were up to the task of organizing and "disciplining the militia." Thus, it was the General Government's responsibility to carry out this constitutionally authorized task. If vigilant citizens were to "fly to the standard of the law, and ... meet invasions of the public order as [their] own personal concern," they would need to be directed by men who would "republicanize" the officer corps, better reflecting the larger society that it was designed to protect.[150]

---

[148] Sean Wilentz contends that Jackson himself ultimately supported removal for reasons of foreign policy. Jackson was concerned that granting tribal sovereignty would not only violate the Constitution's restriction upon creating a state within an existing state, but would offer opportunities to foreign powers to meddle in American affairs. *Jackson*, 69.

[149] White, *It's Your Misfortune*, 89; Prucha, *Indian Policy*, 58–60.

[150] Todd Shallat, *Structures in the Stream: Water, Science, and the Rise of the U.S. Army Corps of Engineers* (Austin, TX: University of Texas Press, 1994), 80–81; David N.

As with the Louisiana Purchase, and the Embargo that would follow, Jefferson was simply giving the bonds of affection an institutional jump start. West Point would also provide officers with some common ground beyond their own memories of the Revolution, which was just the kind of experience that fanned Jefferson's fears of separate civilian and military perspectives. Professional training and a strong background in science and technology, many advocates of West Point hoped, would close the gap between an elite officer corps and the citizen-soldier.[151]

West Point's knowledge base turned out to be an important bridge between military and civilian affairs. In fact, it was often difficult to distinguish military from civilian activities. West Point's Army Corps of Engineers produced civil engineers for the entire nation trained in engineering techniques modeled on the French École Polytechnique. The Corps was a major force behind many internal improvements. It supervised civilian contractors in the construction of military roads. These roads were the subject of intense lobbying from civilian agencies, ranging from the post office to state houses. Michigan Territorial Governor Lewis Cass argued in 1826 that his territory was not equipped to construct roads – only the General Government could perform this task. The job logically fell to the military, Cass argued, because they would "produce an immediate and decisive effect upon the migration to the territory. They would be lined with hardy and vigorous farmers, interested in the preservation of the country, and be able and willing to defend it. The physical strength of the frontier would be increased, and the supplies required for the subsistence of the troops, produced where they are to

Mayer, "'Necessary and Proper:' West Point and Jefferson's Constitutionalism," in *Thomas Jefferson's Military Academy: Founding West Point*, ed. Robert M.S. McDonald (Charlottesville, VA: University Press of Virginia , 2004) 56, 65–66; Jefferson, First Inaugural Address, 4 March 1801, in Richardson, *Messages and Papers*, 1:322, quoted in Peter S. Onuf, "Introduction," in McDonald, *Jefferson's Military Academy*, 4.

[151] Theodore J. Crackel, "The Military Academy in the Context of Jeffersonian Reform," in McDonald, *Jefferson's Military Academy*, 112; Elizabeth D. Samet, "Great Men and Embryo-Caesars: John Adams, Thomas Jefferson, and the Figure in Arms," in McDonald, *Jefferson's Military Academy*, 84–85; Wayne Hsieh, *The Old Army in War and Peace: West Pointers and the Civil War Era, 1814–1865* (Ph.D. Diss., University of Virginia, August 2004), 54; Jennings L. Wagoner, Jr., and Christine Coalwell McDonald, "Mr. Jefferson's Academy: An Educational Interpretation," in McDonald, *Jefferson's Military Academy*, 131.

For a detailed history of the Army Corps of Engineers, see W. Stull Holt, *The Office of the Chief of Engineers of the Army: Its Non-Military History, Activities, and Organization*, Institute for Government Research: Service Monographs of the United States Government No. 27 (Baltimore, MD: Johns Hopkins University Press, 1923).

be consumed." Military and civilian tasks were intermingled because the army, in a self-conscious fashion, defined its mission to include national development.[152]

The army's scientific missions and exploration expeditions were conceived in a similar vein. The Lewis and Clark expedition was the most famous of these. The army also conducted missions to explore Pike's Peak and the Yellowstone River. A letter from President Monroe to his Secretary of War John C. Calhoun captures the range of purposes that such missions sought to fulfill: "The people of the whole Western country take a deep interest in the success of the contemplated establishment at the mouth of the Yellow Stone River," Monroe wrote in 1819. "They look upon it as a measure better calculated to preserve the peace of the frontier, to secure to us the fur trade, and to break up the intercourse between the British traders and the Indians, than any other which has been taken by the government."[153]

The Army also stimulated the development and dissemination of technology through its armory system. The National Armory at Harper's Ferry, Virginia, and its sister institution in Springfield, Massachusetts, served as hubs for what became known as the "American System" of manufacturing. Characterized by strict standards for uniformity and interchangeable parts, the rifles produced at Harper's Ferry and Springfield served as models for the production of a host of other mass-produced, machine-tooled goods. New England inventor John H. Hall, who moved to Harper's Ferry where he worked for twenty years, summed up his innovation when he pitched it to the Secretary of War in 1815: "if a thousand guns were taken apart & the limbs thrown promiscuously together in one heap they may be taken promiscuously from the heap & will all come right." Although Hall operated out of the national armory, he was in fact a contract employee.[154]

---

[152] Shallat, *Structures in the Stream*, 23–26; Sellers, *Market Revolution*, 81; Prucha, *Sword of the Republic*, 191–92; "Memoir of Governor Cass," House Report No. 42, 19th Cong., 1st sess., serial 141, January 11, 1826, 6–18, quoted in Prucha, *Sword of the Republic*, 190.

[153] Monroe to Calhoun, July 5, 1819, *American State Papers: Military Affairs*, 7 vols. (Washington D.C., Gales & Seaton, 1832–1861), 2:69, quoted in Prucha, *Sword of the Republic*, 141.

[154] Merritt Roe Smith, *Harpers Ferry Armory and the New Technology: The Challenge of Change* (Ithaca, NY: Cornell University Press, 1977), Introduction and chaps. 7–8; Hall to Crawford, 28 October 1816, in Letters Received, Records of the Office of the Secretary of War, (Record Group 107, National Archives, Washington D.C.), quoted in Smith, *Harper's Ferry*, 191.

This was indicative of the ways in which the General Government parceled out its authority, even in the military sphere. Like some of the larger arms makers, such as Eli Whitney, Hall was only able to complete his prototype with the aid of a government subsidy. But the integral relationship between private and public sectors did not end with development and production. Knowledge about machine tooling and uniform production was spread by the open dissemination of plans and techniques, and by the migration of Hall's skilled workmen throughout the arms industry. The private mass production of arms was also stimulated by the General Government. Few arms manufacturers would have mechanized without the promise of government contracts to cover the considerable cost of investment that this entailed.[155]

The near-disastrous experience during the War of 1812 galvanized a series of reforms at West Point and throughout the army. None were more influential than the changes that occurred within the Office of the Quartermaster. Under the guidance of Thomas S. Jesup from 1818–1860, the office attracted a cadre of men trained at West Point and loyal to their professional colleagues – even in the face of relentless partisan pressure. The Mexican War gave them experience in the logistics of extended supply lines – experience they put to use on a continental scale as they covered the territory newly acquired in that conflict. The Quartermaster's office cut a broad swath through local communities due to the sheer size of its operations, even during peace time. Annual spending in 1844 (before the Mexican War) was a little under $900,000 annually. By 1850, even though the nation was at peace, spending sky-rocketed to $4.3 million annually. As in the Ordinance division, this spending was largely mediated through private contractors, who spawned hundreds of businesses, especially in the field of transportation.[156]

Whether crafting models for the "American System" of interchangeable mass-produced parts at its Harper's Ferry Armory, or spurring economic development through the construction of military roads and troop deployment, or seeding new businesses through contracts and subsidies, the military left an impressive imprint on the nation long before the rise of the military-industrial complex. As important as the specific tasks carried out by the army was the rationale that advocates of energetic

[155] Smith, *Harper's Ferry*, 325–26.
[156] Mark R. Wilson, *The Business of Civil War: Military Mobilization and the State, 1861–1865* (Baltimore, MD: Johns Hopkins University Press, 2006), 44–56; Hsieh, *Old Army*, 8–9, 53–57, 65, 111, 138.

government crafted over the first half of the nineteenth century: national security turned on effective communications and transportation, which in turn, reduced both distance and sectional difference. Of equal significance, West Point, the armory system, and departments like that of the quartermaster, demonstrated the capacity for professional training and administrative control that allowed for the development of systematic public policy. The army boasted a number of institutions that served as catalysts for innovation. Government policy did not simply follow social trends, or partisan whims – at times, it was capable of directing these disparate forces. Except amid scandal, or crises and war, the daily influence of the military was not noticed by most citizens. The relatively decentralized nature of contracting conspired with the remote location of many army facilities to obscure the army's role. Those officers located in urban areas, where many in the Quartermaster's Department were stationed, blended in with the local business scene that they, in fact, helped cultivate. For the most part, however, military personnel were literally out of sight, whether exploring territory or fighting Indians.[157]

***

The most explicit and impassioned defense of national prerogative was delivered by Andrew Jackson in the controversy over nullification at the end of his first administration. Jackson's hand was forced by a South Carolina nullification convention assembled shortly after Jackson's reelection in 1832. It asserted the right of any state to nullify legislation passed by an oppressive majority in Congress. The right of nullification, in turn, was based on the assertion that the union was formed from a compact between states. The government created by that compact could never contravene state sovereignty. The nullification furor began in reaction to the "tariff of abominations," passed during the summer of 1828. Even though Jackson subsequently pushed through a tariff that was only

[157] Smith, *Harpers Ferry*; Crackel, "Military Academy," in McDonald, *Jefferson's Military Academy*, 110; Sellers, *Market Revolution*, 78–84; Larson, *Internal Improvement*, 112, 127–28; Richard R. John, "Taking Sabbatarianism Seriously: The Postal System, the Sabbath, and the Transformation of American Political Culture," *Journal of the Early Republic*, 10, no. 4 (Winter 1990): 532–33. The phrase "catalyst for innovation," is from Richard R. John, "Ruling Passions: Political Economy in Nineteenth-Century America," in *Ruling Passions: Political Economy in Nineteenth-Century America*, ed. Richard R. John, (University Park, PA: Pennsylvania State University Press, 2006), 13. This edited volume provides excellent examples of the broad range of such institutions.

mildly protective, the damage had been done and, at least in minds of a majority of South Carolina voters, nullification was still necessary.[158]

Jackson was willing to compromise on the tariff issue but he was not prepared to bend his interpretation of constitutional principles. He issued a special proclamation in December 1832 that rejected the notion that the constitution was formed by a compact of sovereign states. "The Constitution of the United States ... forms a *government*, not a league," Jackson insisted. No state had the power to repudiate laws passed by Congress. To grant such a power would ultimately lead to disunion. Jackson had already backed up his interpretation of the Constitution by ordering federal facilities in Charleston to brace for attacks and by sending revenue cutters farther off shore, where they were to continue collecting duties.[159]

The real test came in other Southern states where feelings about the tariff and the nature of federal union also ran strong. One by one, these states backed away from outright support for nullification. A compromise was reached on the new tariff rates that adjusted them downward gradually until 1842, when they were to drop precipitously. Politically isolated, South Carolina eventually pulled back from the brink. "[N] ullification is dead; and its actors and exciters will only be remembered by the people to be execrated for their wicked designs," Jackson wrote shortly after the crisis was defused. This was an accurate enough assessment for the time being. More prescient, however, were the words of a South Carolinian who had opposed the actions of many of his fellow citizens. "Nullification has done its work," James Petigru warned. "It has prepared the minds of men for a separation of the States – and when the question is mooted again it will be distinctly union or disunion."[160]

The crisis over nullification sharpened the divide between those who sought to circumscribe the authority of General Government and

---

[158] Wilentz, *Jackson*, 63–64, 93–94; J. Burke, "Cherokee Cases," 530. Jackson changed his tune as he muted his states' rights rhetoric to stem the Southern rush toward nullification.

[159] Andrew Jackson, Proclamation, December 10, 1832, in Richardson, *Messages and Papers*, 2:648, quoted in Wilentz, *Jackson*, 94–97.

[160] Ibid., 97–100; Jackson to Andrew Crawford, 1 May 1833, in *Correspondence of Andrew Jackson*, ed. John Spencer Bassett, 7 vols. (Washington, D.C.: The Carnegie Institution, 1926–1935), 5:72, quoted in Wilentz, *Jackson*, 101; Petigru to Hugh Swinton Legare, 15 July 1833, in *Life, Letters, and Speeches of James Louis Petigru: The Union Man of South Carolina*, ed. James Petigru Carson (Washington, DC: W.H. Lowdermilk, 1920), 125, cited in Manisha Sinha, *The Counterrevolution of Slavery: Politics and Ideology in Antebellum South Carolina* (Chapel Hill, NC: University of North Carolina Press, 2000), 60.

those who embraced it. That Jackson, energetic government's staunchest defender, previously had been one of its severest critics reinforced a familiar pattern. Just as Jefferson could not resist the opportunity to double the size of the nation or to impose economic regulation through the embargo in order to prevent war, Jackson, who in the course of his first administration had derailed the Second Bank of the United States and championed the cause of states' rights in the quest of states to remove Indians, boldly asserted national prerogatives when challenged by a more radical restatement of Jefferson's own compact theory of the union.

Such dramatic confrontations, which paled by comparison to the ultimate crucible of civil war, occurred when the unmitigated authority of the General Government was unmasked. But such occasions, though the stuff of history text books, were also the exception when it came to extending national authority. They were necessary but not sufficient. It is indeed ironic that a revenue source that had been designed to operate with little notice grew to proportions that garnered the moniker "abomination," triggering a constitutional crisis of memorable proportions. This was precisely the kind of naked and highly visible clash of perspectives on the power of General Government that effective American state builders scrupulously avoided. Instead, national authority was enhanced when advocates worked in conjunction with, not against, state and local government – as a coordinate power. Successful state building also blurred the line between public and private, and operated at the boundaries of the nation, far from sight.

Although this chapter has emphasized the Western boundaries of the nation, a relatively uncontested national program that was initially aimed at the eastern seaboard serves as a quiet rejoinder to the bluster and prominence of Jackson's defense of national prerogatives. Lighthouses in other nations often served as highly visible reminders of the power and grandeur of the national government. France, for instance, built elaborate baroque style lighthouses in the Sixteenth Century to match the splendor of the Court. This was, no doubt, just the kind of national symbol that Hamilton had in mind when he warned Americans that a government "out of sight can hardly be expected to interest the sensations of the people." Yet, Hamilton's approach to state building in the United States ultimately failed.[161]

---

[161] Allen S. Miller, "The Lighthouse Top I see: Lighthouses as Instruments and Manifestations of State Building in the Early Republic," (draft article Revision #1, August 31, 2007): 10. Hamilton's "out of sight" quotation is, of course, from *Federalist 27*.

The General Government's adaptation to the local and private land-scape ultimately rendered lighthouses politically invisible, their shining beacons notwithstanding. Because the General Government absorbed existing state lighthouses and, more importantly, their personnel, the nationalization of this program was never viewed as a power grab. Rather, it was a matter of one coordinate power asserting incremental control with the welcome embrace of states, eager to be relieved of the cost and responsibility. The General Government also contracted out to private designers for the new lighthouses it constructed, further diminishing the Government's visibility. The result was a prodigious program that operated 331 lighthouses by 1852. Long before this, lighthouses had formed a national system that promoted commerce and intercourse throughout the nation. This adaptive process, especially when carried out at the nation's borders in the service of a developmental vision, proved far more effective than Hamilton's approach to governance, or for that matter, Jackson's bombast. Though less spectacular than either, American state building would not have occurred without it.[162]

[162] Miller, "Lighthouse," 3–4, 7, 48.

6

The Uncontested State: Letters, Law, Localities

Standard accounts of American political development in the first half of the nineteenth century are constructed around the triumph of the private over the public. The expanding franchise, which ushered in Jacksonian democracy, coupled with market expansion, empowered mobile individuals who embraced *laissez-faire*. Yet, we have already seen that the federal government carried out crucial activities beyond its boundaries. It conducted relations with foreign nations, sovereign tribes, and settlers, who, aided by federal land policy and military support, were constantly redrawing the nation's boundaries. Without these public actions, the shape of both polity and market would have been quite different.

This chapter examines three vibrant extensions of the state in the first half of the nineteenth century that were not confined to the margins of the nation, or engaged in foreign policy. At the federal level, the Post Office Department dwarfed foreign counterparts in its reach and its ambition. It also overshadowed domestic counterparts in the private sector. Viewed as a nationally subsidized information infrastructure, the Post Office was instrumental in promoting political debate. The second critical element was the law. Lodged at the federal, state, and local levels, the law was a crucial ingredient in a society that eschewed visible trappings of public authority. It constructed a framework that made private economic and social decisions both feasible and predictable. Finally, Americans trusted expansion at the local level more than through the General Government. Americans were far more willing to use local public authority and financing than to go through their national counterparts. Citizens turned to state and local means to realize developmental ends when markets failed. Local government affirmed social norms that markets cared little for.

Still, the General Government was the only game in town in a number of policy venues. Most prominently, this was the case in foreign policy. Even inside the United States, however, the General Government retained exclusive control in many venues. Its responsibilities ranged from delivering the mail to conducting the census to administering the public domain. Where economic development was at stake, the public sector served as both catalyst and ongoing instrument of development – usually at the state and local levels. Whenever possible, governments sought to harness private initiative to achieve public ends. This was crucial to the success of both the post office and publicly financed economic development in the form of roads, canals, and eventually railroads.

Americans preferred that public authority be deployed in self-executing ways that avoided bureaucracy. The law, at both the federal and state levels, was crucial to establishing self-executing mechanisms, from contracts to charters. These vehicles were imbued with a public purpose that placed sharp limits on rights that today would be defined as private.

"AN ASTONISHING CIRCULATION OF LETTERS AND NEWSPAPERS AMONG THESE SAVAGE WOODS": THE CNN OF ITS DAY

By 1831, the American Post Office Department employed over 8,700 postmasters and accounted for over three-quarters of the civilian federal work force. The thousands of postal employees even dwarfed the army. Reflecting the broad expanse of territory that the post office served, but also its commitment to cover the entire country, the American postal system maintained seventy-four post offices for every 100,000 inhabitants. By comparison, Great Britain provided seventeen post offices for every 100,000 inhabitants, and France, four. The scale and scope of this responsibility went well beyond the capacity of private enterprise at the time. In fact, it was not until the Gilded Age that America's largest enterprise, the Pennsylvania Railroad, employed more people than the post office. As one leading communications scholar put it, "for the vast majority of Americans the postal system *was* the central government." It extended throughout the land and penetrated the daily lives of most Americans.[1]

---

[1] Richard R. John, *Spreading the News: The American Postal System from Franklin to Morse* (Cambridge, MA: Harvard University Press, 1995), 3–6.

As with other energetic federal policies, the Post Office filled a gap that the private sector and the states could not bridge. The cornerstone of its authority rested on the bedrock of an explicit constitutional authorization. Congress, the Constitution enumerated, shall have the power "to establish post offices and post roads." This language distinguished postal policy from constitutionally contested tasks performed by the central government, like internal improvements. Some states did attempt to establish their own postal services, but the obvious need to transcend state, not to mention national boundaries, limited these efforts.[2]

Despite explicit constitutional authority and the dearth of potential competitors, a vigorous postal system was hardly preordained. Bold legislation and administrators committed to the developmental ethos shared by national Republicans turned the possibility for an assertive presence into fact. Before the Post Office Act of 1792, the American postal system looked much like its British counterpart: it was confined to the major port towns and was expected to generate revenue for the central government. The 1792 Act sparked three major changes. It subsidized the circulation of newspapers, it provided safeguards against surveillance by public officials, and it transferred responsibility for authorizing new postal routes from the executive branch to Congress, virtually ensuring that the system would expand from the existing network that hugged the Atlantic seaboard to cover the trans-Appalachian West and South. The legislation also established fiscal policies that would guide the post office throughout its history. The Post Office Department would be self-supporting and Congress would use profits from the post office to extend service.[3]

By subsidizing newspaper circulation, the legislation produced a diversified and highly decentralized press. The 1792 legislation stipulated that newspapers mailed up to 100 miles would pay one cent postage; those mailed greater distances were charged one and a half cents. This was an extremely modest charge compared to rates charged for letters. For instance, a four-sheet letter – the weight comparable to many newspapers – cost twenty-four cents to travel thirty miles. Under the guidance of Postmaster General John McLean (who served from 1823

[2] U.S. Constitution, art. 1, sec. 8; John, *Spreading*, 45.

[3] John, *Spreading*, 25, 31; Wayne E. Fuller, *The American Mail: Enlarger of the Common Life* (Chicago, IL: University of Chicago Press, 1972), 43. In 1788, the national postal service supported about seventy-five post offices and continued many of the policies developed under its colonial predecessor. Richard B. Kielbowicz, *News in the Mail: The Press, the Post Office, and Public Information, 1700–1860s* (New York, NY: Greenwood Press, 1989), 32.

until 1829), the postal system underwrote a new national transportation system by subsidizing stagecoaches to carry the mail. Andrew Jackson recognized the significance of postal operations, elevating the postmaster generalship to a cabinet-level position in 1829. But Jackson and his successors, caught in the competition spawned by the emergence of mass-based political parties, also politicized the appointments process and short-circuited the developmental thrust of McLean's policies.[4]

The Post Office knit Americans together in a variety of ways and contributed to the creation of a shared culture that transcended state and regional political and economic boundaries. A reliable post had always been essential for commercial transactions and this remained one of the primary responsibilities of the expanded American Post Office. The decision to subsidize newspaper circulation combined with the franking privileges provided to public officials, and hundreds of postmasters pushed the Post Office Department far beyond a narrow business base. As one Congregationalist minister put it, "[T]his is a machinery which, in a sense, extends your presence over the whole country, even to the edge of the wilderness, where the last traces of government and of civilized life disappear." That news flowed so readily across topographic and political barriers stunned Alexis de Tocqueville. "There is an astonishing circulation of letters and newspapers among these savage woods," Tocqueville recorded as he traveled through Kentucky and Tennessee. "I do not think that in the most enlightened rural districts of France there is intellectual movement either so rapid or on such a scale as in this wilderness," Tocqueville continued.[5]

Postal policy, at least in the eyes of some advocates, was a conscious effort to knit together a sprawling nation. Those who argued for subsidized delivery of newspapers emphasized the crucial role of information

---

[4] Kielbowicz, *News in the Mail*, 34; John, *Spreading*, 64, 67. By the 1860s the American postal system had fallen behind its European counterparts, eschewing postal telegraphy and moving slowly into railway mail and city delivery. John, *Spreading*, chap. 6

[5] Leonard Bacon, "The Post-Office System as an Element of Modern Civilization," *New Englander* 1 (1843): 14, quoted in John, *Spreading*, 10; Alexis de Tocqueville, *Journey to America*, ed. J.P. Mayer, trans. George Lawrence ([1835;1840]; Garden City, NY: Doubleday/Anchor Books, 1971), 283, quoted in John, *Spreading*, 1. For a concise summary of this point, see Richard R. John, "Governmental Institutions as Agents of Change: Rethinking American Political Development in the Early Republic, 1787–1835," *Studies in American Political Development* 11, no. 2 (Fall 1997), 347–380. See also, Kielbowicz, *News in the Mail*, 46–47. Both Kielbowicz, *News in the Mail*, and Fuller, *American Mail*, emphasize the importance of newspaper circulation and franking privileges to Post Office expansion throughout their work.

for sustaining the far-flung republic. Benjamin Franklin Bache, son of a former postmaster, and grandson of yet another – Benjamin Franklin – argued for postage-free newspaper distribution because such information was "the necessary ground of enlightened confidence." Postage-free status would "permit the rays from this focus to reach every part of the empire." After John C. Calhoun exhorted Congress to "bind the Republic together with a perfect system of roads and canals," he went on to argue that "the mail and the press ... are the nerves of the body politic. By them, the slightest impression made on the most remote parts, is communicated to the whole system." Whether they envisioned the subsidized press as a means for extending the central government's authority, as was the case with the Federalists, or whether they viewed low-cost news as an essential check on the power of that government as was the case with the National Republicans, a broad cross section of Americans supported the active role that the post office played in encouraging the free flow of information through the mail.[6]

The Post Office was an essential public service that further stimulated expansion of the public sphere. By the early nineteenth century, the vast majority of post offices largely handled newspapers. While only a small percentage of any given post office's customers actually subscribed to newspapers, periodicals were treated as public property. As one commentator put it in 1822, "There is scarcely a village or country post office in the United States, particularly if it be kept in a tavern or store ... in which the newspapers are not as free to all comers, as to the persons to whom they rightfully belong." Post offices, like saloons or court houses, were bastions of white male solidarity where men, particularly men of affairs, gathered to receive and mull over the news. While restricted by gender and race, they were a crucial site for integrating local and national perspectives. Partisan competition reinforced the integration of local and national perspectives. With the emergence of national political parties,

---

[6] Fuller, *American Mail*, 3–7; Kielbowicz, *News in the Mail*, 31, 36–38; *General Advertiser*, December 1, 1791, no. 366, in Early American Newspapers, Series I, 1690–1876 (Newsbank and American Antiquarian Society, 2004), http://infoweb.newsbank.com/, cited in John, *Spreading*, 36; John C. Calhoun, "Speech on Internal Improvements," February 4, 1817, in *The Papers of John C. Calhoun*, ed. Robert L. Meriwether, 16 vols. (Columbia, SC: University of South Carolina Press, 1959–1985), 1:401, quoted in Kielbowicz, *News in the Mail*, 3; John, *Spreading*, 59. See also, Richard D. Brown, "Early American Origins of the Information Age," in *A Nation Transformed by Information: How Information Has Shaped the United States from Colonial Times to the Present*, ed. Alfred D. Chandler, Jr. and James W. Cortada (New York: Oxford University Press, 2000), 39–53.

editors increasingly selected materials along partisan lines, reinforcing the reach of political parties. Easily accessible newspapers forced communities to consider where they fit into the larger polity. They also encouraged partisans to conceive of their allegiance as part of a network that transcended local and even state jurisdictions. Given Congressional commitment to fund postal coverage, Americans sometimes knew their out-of-state compatriots better than those just down the road. The reach of the postal system and the content it transported seemed to defy the standard political and social calculus. "There is no French province," Toqueville concluded, "in which the inhabitants knew each other as well as did the thirteen million men spread over the extent of the United States." That is because many editors, until the 1850s, ran national and international stories at the expense of local news. These decisions, in turn, were the product of postal policies that provided a cornucopia of material to be printed from distant locations at no cost to the local editor.[7]

The ability of newspaper editors to exchange papers with their colleagues for free amounted to a *de facto* wire service. Most newspapers were compendiums of news that the editor received free of charge from other papers around the country. One seasoned editor described the result of this exchange policy succinctly: "Who could edit a paper ten minutes without scissors!" The role that these exchanges played in connecting the periphery to cultural and political centers is illustrated best by an analysis of newspapers processed by urban post offices. During one week in 1850, New York City's post office received 40,000 newspapers: 88 percent of these papers were postage-free exchanges.[8]

The Post Office also played a critical role in disseminating knowledge about the vast expanse of territory that constituted the nation. Abraham Bradley, Jr., a topographer and first assistant postmaster, authored an innovative set of maps that displayed every single postal route in the country. These maps could be found in the larger post offices throughout the

[7] Kielbowicz, *News in the Mail*, 20, 149; John, *Spreading*, 41, 154, 162; *National Intelligencer*, March 18, 1822, quoted in John, *Spreading*, 154–55; Alexis de Tocqueville, *Democracy in America*, ed. J.P. Mayer, trans. George Lawrence (New York, NY: Harper/ Perennial Library, 1988) 385, quoted in John, *Spreading*, 1. Newspapers and the postal service were integrally related. The first regularly published newspaper, the *Boston News-Letter*, was launched by Boston postmaster John Campbell in 1704. It was handwritten by Campbell's brother, and sent to several correspondents connected by the weekly coastal mail service. Kielbowicz, *News in the Mail*, 14.
[8] Alonzo F. Hill, *Secrets of the Sanctum: An Inside View of an Editor's Life* (Philadelphia, PA: Claxton, Remsen & Haffelfinger, 1875), 69, quoted in Kielbowicz, *News in the Mail*, 147; Kielbowicz, *News in the Mail*, 151. See also, Kielbowicz, *News in the Mail*, chap. 8.

land and received wide distribution when they were included in Jedediah Morse's *Geography* of the United States. Thousands of Americans were able to visualize for the first time the vast extent of the United States through the medium of Bradley's maps. What had been hazy notions of distant territories were clarified into a more coherent canvas with clearly demarcated boundaries. If newspapers filled out the political coordinates of the United States, Bradley's maps fused the geographic and affective contours of the union.[9]

Postal policy literally stimulated political discourse by encouraging politicians to create more of it. Franking privileges were hard to resist. By the 1820s, Congressmen were regularly delivering speeches for "Bunkum." These were entries into the Congressional Record intended for few colleagues in the room but were published and sent free of charge to constituents back home. Petitions to Congress flowed in the opposite direction. More often than not the folks back home wrote to request a new postal route. The thousands of petitions generated in the first three decades of the nineteenth century contributed to the rise of mass-based parties. The parties, in turn, were designed specifically to enhance this more participatory style of politics.[10]

The bottom-up approach to postal expansion, funneled through Congress, demonstrated that the General Government could provide valuable resources for social and economic development and that it could promote prosperity. In almost all instances Americans concluded that these benefits were not necessarily accompanied by assaults upon local rights or the market economy. The Post Office Department conformed to the geographic boundaries of a growing nation – as opposed to being confined to regions or states within that vast expanse. It penetrated the daily lives of most Americans, cutting against the other strong political tendencies that were decidedly local in the first half of the nineteenth century. A current rather than a tidal wave, the post office countered the persistent undertow of region, race, and republican preference for small units of government.[11]

---

[9] John, *Spreading*, 69–70.

[10] Ibid., 50, 57, 63; Fuller, *American Mail*, 46.

[11] Fuller, *American Mail*, 83–84. On the influence of the territorial scope of the unit of government, see also Michael Mann, "The Autonomous Power of the State: Its Origins, Mechanisms and Results," *European Journal of Sociology* 26, no. 2 (1985): 185–213. In *Spreading the News*, Richard John convincingly argues that the reliable flow of information across the United States introduced Americans to two ideas. The first was "that the boundaries of the community in which they lived extended well beyond the confines of

Subsidizing the news and supporting an extensive postal system appeared to be another important corollary to Hamilton's dictum about visible government. Measured solely by its size, the Post Office was prodigious. It more than fulfilled Hamilton's plea for visibility. Its authority was also apparent, as it was explicitly designated a federal responsibility in the Constitution. But that is where the parallel to Hamilton's approach ended.

Rarely considered an intrusion, often taken for granted, the Post Office provided information vital to citizenship and deep-seated attachment to the polity. The cut-and-paste nature of newspapers conveyed news from distant parts of the nation. It did not appear triumphant. Rather, its services blended with local custom, its subsidies seemed to be a very part of the fabric that constituted the market for both goods and information. Unlike the strong reaction to Hamilton's military suppression of the Whiskey Rebellion, or Jefferson's imposition of an embargo, local citizens clamored for more, not less, government when it came to delivering the news.

"A COINCIDENCE OF PRIVATE WITH PUBLIC
CONSIDERATIONS":
NATURALIZING LEVIATHAN

How, in a society cautious about grants of power to the central government, could that very government come to play such a major role in domestic politics? Why did even South Carolina, which led the fight for nullification, clamor for more federal government when delivered by the Post Office? While the dearth of competitors for the job provides a partial answer, the essential economic development role served by the Post Office, its self-financing nature, and the manner in which this service was structured and delivered explain more.[12]

The rapid and reliable flow of information was a prerequisite to the corresponding traffic in goods. By using the revenues from letters to subsidize the low-cost transmission of newspapers, the General Government cobbled together a national market for information half a century before a comparable market for goods was established. Only the General

---

their individual locality, state or region and coincided more or less with the territorial limits of the United Sates." Second, "that the central government might come to shape the pattern of everyday life." [7].
[12] Fuller, *American Mail*, 83.

Government had the financial wherewithal to provide such an extensive network, and only the federal government had the capacity to administer such a network at the time. Americans, including merchants who paid a disproportionate share of the cost because the news subsidy came primarily at the expense of letter writers, chose to support such a system because they viewed it as crucial to the economic infrastructure of the country. Richard Rush, Secretary of the Treasury during the John Quincy Adams presidency, captured this rationale when he argued that the Post Office promoted national prosperity – "the highest purposes of revenue" – by investing a portion of its revenues in improvements that contributed to "the intercourse, the trade, and the prosperity of the country."[13]

Expanding postal service was an easy decision because it not only paid for itself, it also returned revenue to the General Government. Although Americans were willing to forego potential revenue in return for low-cost news, the Post Office regularly returned a surplus, even as it expanded service. In the nearly thirty years before the McLean administration, the postal service transferred more than $1 million to the general treasury.[14]

The manner in which the Post Office delivered its services smoothed its political acceptance. The "transportation" circuit of the postal service, which was responsible for carrying the mail to distribution centers and individual post offices (as opposed to sorting the mail) was contracted out to private entrepreneurs. Although the post office experimented with fleets of coastal mail packets and direct operation of a Government-owned stagecoach line, by 1828 an army of over 700 mail contractors handled this business.[15]

The Post Office Department also promoted a symbiotic relationship between local and central government. One factor that guided Post Office decisions about routes was the quality of local roads. A primary incentive for improving those roads, in turn, was the possibility of improved

[13] John, *Spreading*, 37, 53; Kielbowicz, *News in the Mail*, 6–7, 43–44; Richard Rush, "Report ... of the Public Revenue and Expenditure of the Years 1824 and 1825," December 2, 1825, in *American State Papers*, 3, *Finance*, 5:240, http://memory.loc.gov/ammem/amlaw/, quoted in John, *Spreading*, 107–8.
    As the post office began to run deficits by the 1830s, the regional nature of the subsidy played a greater role. Densely settled portions of the East were clearly subsidizing the South and the West, and began to complain more vociferously about it. Fuller, *American Mail*, 62–64.
[14] John, *Spreading*, 107.
[15] Ibid., 90–91; Kielbowicz, *News in the Mail*, 48; Leonard D. White, *The Federalists: A Study in Administrative History* (1948; repr., Westport, CT: Greenwood Press, 1978), 184.

228

8228

A Government Out of Sight

postal service. Thus local government was stimulated by the possibility of obtaining a federal postal route.[16]

Federal decisions also had a dramatic impact on the transportation sector of the economy – shaping market decisions. The Post Office had to choose between post riders and stagecoach service. Where there were sufficient potential passengers it opted for the latter. Especially after some of the reforms pushed through by Postmaster McLean in 1824, stagecoach service became a heavily subsidized form of carrying the mail. It also provided the backbone of a national transportation system. For routes in more thinly populated areas, getting the federal mail contract could make the difference between success and failure for these "private" entrepreneurs. Overall, postal subsidies made up almost one-third of the total revenues that the stagecoach industry received. The stagecoach subsidies continued until Congress changed the rules in 1845, although routes were subsidized in the West long after this.[17]

Tocqueville missed the important role that the General Government played in sustaining the close relationship between the stagecoach industry and the mail. Perhaps he should be forgiven, however, since millions of Americans also missed this relationship. True, residents of towns understood that the "Mail Stage" was likely to be the quickest way to get somewhere, and proprietors emblazoned "U.S. Mail" on the sides of their coaches. But the industry was associated in most people's minds with private, not government, enterprise, despite the significant financial stake that the postal service held in its destiny. The Overland Mail, a stagecoach line that stretched between Ohio and California, established by veteran contractor John Butterfield in 1858, is a good example. Remembered for the enterprising spirit of this private entrepreneur, Butterfield was sustained by a mail subsidy: 30 percent of the stage's revenue came from his contract with the U.S. Government.[18]

The Pony Express, established by William Russell in 1860 as a horse relay from Missouri to California, was, by contrast, a purely private operation. However, the whole short-lived project was little more than a "put-up" job designed to garner publicity and win for Russell the lucrative Overland Mail contract. The "workhorses" of the postal system, though

---

[16] Fuller, *American Mail*, 86.

[17] John, *Spreading*, 91–99.

[18] Ibid., 90, 98–99. For a more extended analysis of what Tocqueville missed, see Rogan Kersh, *Dreams of a More Perfect Union* (Ithaca, NY: Cornell University Press, 2001). Thanks to Richard John for steering me to this discussion.

feeding at the public trough (at least one-third of the time) appeared to fit squarely with the ascendant model of the entrepreneurial capitalism of the day.[19]

Blending into the fabric of the local community and integrally connected to the local economy, postmasters helped to naturalize and minimize the central government's presence in the community, rather than boldly proclaiming national prerogatives. Undoubtedly, in an age of patronage, a good number of the 8,000 or so postmasters were also feeding at the public trough. Nevertheless, they were hardly the regime's placemen. In fact, postmasters were not even salaried employees: they worked on a commission that paid up to a maximum of $2,000 annually. Only 3 percent of the nation's postmasters in 1829 earned more than $300 annually, the equivalent of an unskilled artisan's annual earnings. As late as 1845, 85 percent of the post offices in the United States netted their postmasters less than $100 a year. Most held down second jobs or supplemented their income through some other means.[20]

These postmasters were selected based on their standing in the local community and for their contributions in the private as well as public sectors. Perhaps the best example of this occurred high up in the postal administration. Abraham Bradley, Jr., the postal service's chief financial officer, also served as the president of the Union Bank of Georgetown. This arrangement not only supplemented Bradley's income, it also allowed him to sign the bank notes that disbursed postal funds across the country.

Because a broad range of federal employees, from counsels to surveyors, were paid on a fee for service basis, it was the standard practice for most of these officials to supplement their federal fees with income from the private sector, thus breaking down the distinction between private and public employees and often merging local and federal employment. Particularly in the territories, the assumption was that federal officials would supplement their low salaries with opportunities to capitalize on their knowledge and position in order to profit from land purchases. Secretary of State Timothy Pickering was explicit about these incentives. Writing to a candidate for a federal position in the Northwest Territory, Pickering confessed that the salary "presents no allurement: but knowing that you were interested in the lands reserved or ceded to Connecticut,

---

[19] John, *Spreading*, 99–100; Kielbowicz, *News in the Mail*, 173.
[20] John, *Spreading*, 121–23.

within that territory; and thinking it possible that a coincidence of private with public considerations might persuade you to go to that country, I ask (with the privity of the President) whether the office of judge in the Territory will be agreeable to you?" Disbursing officers, such as military paymasters, often held other federal positions and were paid a percentage of the funds disbursed.[21]

The men who collected revenues derived from excise taxes faced a particularly difficult set of problems as the agents were often perceived as federal intruders. Yet these federal employees were also contractors. They were paid a percentage of their collections or half the penalties collected in suits against whiskey distillers. In Kentucky, the despised excise tax made collection difficult at best, and law suits impossible, since the territorial attorney refused to initiate them in the 1790s. On the other hand, agents often refused to turn over the revenue they did collect. By the early 1800s, as a new district attorney imposed a more orderly collection regime, the number of suits against revenue agents threatened to surpass the number of charges brought against distillers.[22]

The fluid boundaries between public and private were perhaps best reflected in the actual space that post offices occupied. Rarely were post offices located in free-standing buildings. Instead, they often occupied a room in a building housing other commercial interests. Baltimore's post office in the first decades of the nineteenth century was located in the basement of a popular hotel; in Philadelphia, the corner of the mercantile exchange served postal customers. In rural areas, many post offices were housed in stores. It was impossible to tell where the store stopped and the post office began. As one contemporary reminisced, "Kegs and barrels – nail boxes and soap boxes – customers and letter-writers – men and boys – women and dogs – the box stove and the Department letter boxes ... are all mingled at the post office establishment with picturesque incongruity."[23]

Ambitious in its commitment to bring the news to all Americans, the Post Office sought to blend into the local scenery and use resources available through the market and local folkways rather than clear a path for national aggrandizement. The Post Office fulfilled an essential economic

[21] White, *Federalists*, 296–98, 340–41; Pickering to Zepheniah Swift, 8 December 1797, in *The Timothy Pickering Papers*, ed. Frederick S. Allis, Jr. (Boston, MA: Massachusetts Historical Society, 1966), 7:525, quoted in White, *Federalists*, 296.
[22] Mary K. Bonsteel Tachau, *Federal Courts in the Early Republic: Kentucky, 1789–1816* (Princeton, NJ: Princeton University Press, 1978), 99–100, 121.
[23] John, *Spreading*, 112–13; "The Country Postmaster," *United States Mail and Post-Office Assistant*, 7 (1867): 1, quoted in John, *Spreading*, 114–15.

task. The phalanx of postal workers blended into the landscape through payments that were contracted and commissioned (rather than salaried) and through subsidies – which were buried in the cost of transportation. The entire service was self-financing, another quality that diminished political visibility. Although directed by federal agents, the Post Office accommodated its operations to local preferences and provided incentives to improve local roads. It was precisely the postal system's blend of the local with the national, combined with its encouragement of entrepreneurial capital, that allowed it to expand. Unlike federally funded internal improvements, where the debate often pitted the local versus the national, and public versus private, the early republic's postal system managed to accommodate enough of the local and the private to keep the mail moving.[24]

SPREADING GOD'S WORD

A large postal operation that swayed the nation's economic and public communications did not charm every patriot wary of an expanding central government. The issue was first broached systematically by Americans eager to protect the sanctity of the Sabbath. Between 1810 and 1817, and then again with even more passion between 1826 and 1831, Americans railed against sending mail and opening post offices on Sundays. No less a figure than Presbyterian minister Lyman Beecher proclaimed in 1829 that the debate over the central government's practice requiring "its eight thousand Post-Masters, and several thousand other agents to violate the Lord's Day, is perhaps the most important that ever was, or ever will be submitted for national consideration."[25]

Fueled by the Second Great Awakening, coalitions of clergy and their religious followers argued that requiring postmasters and those

---

[24] Kielbowicz, *News in the Mail*, 5, 32. "Links in the postal network," Kielbowicz concludes, "were added largely in response to local demands for improved communication. Local residents received appointment as postmasters, local or regional transport companies usually won contracts to carry the mail, and the resulting traffic prompted improvements in local roads. At least initially, local autonomy did not seem compromised by augmenting the national network." [5]

[25] Richard R. John, "Taking Sabbatarianism Seriously: The Postal System, the Sabbath, and the Transformation of American Political Culture," *Journal of the Early Republic,* 10, no. 4 (Winter 1990): 517–567; John, *Spreading*, chap. 5; Lyman Beecher, "Pre-Eminent Importance of the Christian Sabbath," *National Preacher,* 3 (1829): 156, American Periodicals Series Online, 1740–1900 (Proquest, [doc. no. 567662012]), http://proquest. umi.com/pqdweb, quoted in John, *Spreading*, 169.

transporting the mails to work on Sunday forced workers to violate their most deeply held beliefs. The General Government's policy also violated a web of local and state statutes restricting the kind of activities that could be pursued on the Lord's Day. Though local authorities might wink at violations, the fact remained that the Post Office was the only institution in many communities that remained impervious to these laws and social norms.[26]

Intensifying concern on the part of those who would uphold the sacred status of the Sabbath was the overwhelming popularity of the mail. Clergy in New Hampshire, for instance, complained that even the passage of a mail coach could divert citizens from the "sacred design and employments of that holy Day." Even worse, when mail actually arrived, citizens would bolt "in multitudes" to collect letters, read newspapers, and catch up on the latest news.[27]

The Sabbatarians took advantage of the very target of their rage – the Post Office – to spread the news and organize a national movement that sustained their social protest. The dispute underscored the degree to which the General Government penetrated civil society and demonstrated just how important mail delivery was to those who sought to challenge the government. Without the extensive use of the mails, this would have been impossible. Bowing to religious pressure, Postmaster General McLean was forced temporarily to suspend delivery of the mail on one major route and instruct some postmasters to ban access by the public at large on Sundays. Nevertheless, the Government fought back both waves of Sabbatarian protest, continuing to deliver the mail and open post offices on Sundays in most regions.[28]

Fears about local prerogatives and concerns that a distant General Government might overwhelm civil society were not figments of paranoid citizens' imaginations: their worries were motivated by the very real expansion of the General Government in some realms. The Sabbatarian

---

[26] John, "Taking Sabbatarianism Seriously," 517–529.
[27] Printed Petition signed by the inhabitants of Hollis, New Hampshire, opposing Sabbath mails [1815], Petitions Received, Senate Committee on the Post Office and Post Roads, Records of the U.S. Senate, 46 (Record Troub 46, National Archives, Washington, D.C.), quoted in John, "Taking Sabbatarianism Seriously," 529.
[28] John, *Spreading*, 200. These techniques would be deployed, toward very different ends, by the abolitionists several decades later. As John notes, "It was hardly coincidental that several leading Sabbatarians – including William Lloyd Garrison, Lewis Tappan, and William Jay – would soon expand their perceptual horizons to implicate the central government in the perpetuation of the institution of slavery. Now that the central government had invaded civil society, it had also become morally accountable to God." [204–5]

skirmishes illustrate how quickly the palpable sense that the central government threatened to overwhelm local decision making could explode into social protest. When the Post Office's central function – delivering the mail in a swift and predictable manner to the extensive network of post offices throughout the nation – was exposed by Sabbatarian criticism, the danger appeared to be legitimate to many. Jacksonian Democrats capitalized on the tension created by the penetration of an energetic central government into local social practices by honing their antistatist rhetoric even as Jackson himself fueled the very expansion that many of his supporters feared.[29]

LAW

The Federal courts were another arena in which the government shaped the lives of Americans in the first half of the nineteenth century, although it did not start out that way. While the "Marshall Court" raised the Supreme Court to coequal status with Congress and the executive branch, before that the federal judiciary was an abstraction to most Americans. The concept of judicial review of legislation and the authority to rule such legislation unconstitutional was fiercely contested in the late eighteenth century. Many Americans felt more comfortable leaving the ultimate decision on such matters to popularly elected legislatures. Some judges who advocated judicial review were even threatened with removal.[30]

At the national level, the Supreme Court exuded little supremacy before John Marshall was elevated to Chief Justice in 1801. Former Chief Justice John Jay left the Court in 1795 to become governor of New York. When President Adams asked him to return (before Adams invited Marshall) Jay rejected the offer, noting that the judicial system could never "obtain the energy, weight, and dignity which are essential to its affording due support to the national government, nor acquire the public confidence and respect which, as the last resort of the justice of the nation, it should possess." It was an accurate assessment.[31]

---

[29] John makes this important historiographic point in Ibid., 20, 208.

[30] Stanley Elkins and Eric McKitrick, *The Age of Federalism* (New York, NY: Oxford University Press, 1993), 64; Richard E. Ellis, *The Jeffersonian Crisis: Courts and Politics in the Young Republic* (New York, NY: Oxford University Press, 1971), 9.

[31] Michael J. Klarman, "How Great were the 'Great' Marshall Court Decisions?" *Virginia Law Review*, 87, no. 6 (October 2001): 1153; John Jay to John Adams, January 2, 1801, in *The Correspondence and Public Papers of John Jay*, ed. Henry P. Johnston, 4 vols.

While all branches required the constant scrutiny and vigilance of citizens, this was particularly important in the case of the judiciary because so much of what it did was invisible to most citizens. Unlike legislative action, a judge's decision might initially affect only "a single individual," which would be "noticed only by his neighbors, and a few spectators in the court," Federal Farmer warned. Calls resonated throughout the early nineteenth century for elective judges on the state level.[32]

Republicans feared that a national judiciary would erode democratic access. The distance entailed in federal proceedings made the threat of a powerful judiciary doubly dangerous. With travel difficult under the best of circumstances, citizens worried that an extensive federal judiciary might require expensive journeys simply to defend basic rights. As one Anti-Federalist tract warned, "an inhabitant of Pittsburgh, on a charge of crime committed on the banks of the Ohio, may be obliged to defend himself at the side of the Delaware, and so *vice versa*." Americans also worried that the right to be judged by a jury of their peers would be eroded as the national judiciary assumed a more prominent role.[33]

While the Constitution encouraged a capacious interpretation of federal authority among some, the political opposition that any effort to create a powerful national judiciary engendered stopped even the most ardent Federalists from seeking such powers. The Judiciary Act of 1789 retained a strong role for state courts, limited federal jurisdiction, and provided few federal district courts. State courts, which had existed for some time and had developed a dense network of interests and support, continued to play a vital role in the nation's legal framework.[34]

Yet a national legal system emerged by the middle third of the nineteenth century, and some argued that it was too powerful. Rarely imposed top down by the Supreme Court, touching the lives of most Americans

---

(1890–93; repr., New York, NY: Burt Franklin, 1970), 4:284–285, quoted in Klarman, "Marshall Court Decisions," 1154.

[32] Letters from the Federal Farmer, no. 15, 18, January 1788, in *The Complete Anti-Federalist*, ed. Herbert J. Storing (Chicago, IL: University of Chicago Press, 1981), 2:315–16, quoted in Saul Cornell, *The Other Founders: Anti-Federalism and the Dissenting Tradition in America, 1728–1828* (Chapel Hill, NC: University of North Carolina Press, 1999), 91; Charles Sellers, *The Market Revolution: Jacksonian America, 1815–1846* (New York, NY: Oxford University Press, 1991), 61.

[33] "The Address and Reason of Dissent of the Minority of the Convention of the State of Pennsylvania to their Constituents," in *Pennsylvania and the Federal Constitution, 1787–1788*, ed. John Bach McMaster and Frederick D. Stone (Lancaster, PA, 1888; New York, NY: DaCapo Press, 1970), 2:475, quoted in Ellis, *Jeffersonian Crisis*, 11.

[34] Elkins and McKitrick, *Age of Federalism*, 62–64; Ellis, *Jeffersonian Crisis*, 12.

through state and local courts and on occasion federal district courts, this system began with a legal discourse that grew increasingly national in scope over the course of the century.

The law became a common denominator across state lines and even regions – one of the ways that Americans spoke to each other across the vast expanse that they occupied. Federal district courts played an important mediating role in this process, adapting a national conversation to local dialects where necessary, bringing stability and security to land transactions, for instance. But the conversation would have fallen on deaf ears were it not for the assertively nationalist perspective that the Marshall Court took in critical debates, ranging from the scope of the commerce, contract, and general welfare clauses of the constitution, to the even more fundamental right of the Court to mediate disputes between the states and the branches of the federal government itself.

A NATIONAL DISCOURSE

Whether operating on the state or national levels, the law provided a compelling way to think about and describe issues that might otherwise have been left to legislative or executive political action. Legal "discourse" emerged as a powerful source of national cohesion in nineteenth-century America, even though the principles that contributed to it were often articulated by state courts. This is not to argue that the law was homogenized across all states. Local and regional variance persisted. Rather, it is to underscore that a common approach to resolving some key issues, ranging from the public interest in private property to the nature of contract obligations, was forged in the first half of the nineteenth century and that with the guidance of an increasingly assertive national judiciary, any consensus reached was extended to a nation that valued rapid economic development and the kind of predictable legal environment required to promote it.

Law bound the nation together. Law became one way that Americans explained their relationships to each other. That way of thinking and reasoning, in turn, shaped both public and private transactions, and it determined which assets mattered most in those interchanges. As one legal historian has described it, the law consolidated what had been a series of "discrete and loosely connected discourses [in]to one holistic, 'scientific,' Anglocentric discourse"; it moved from a concentration on parochial debt and property issues to the law of contract; its geographical and institutional gaze shifted from the local to the trans-local. Tethered to local preference through justices of the peace, legal discourse extended outward to a national conversation on the meaning of contracts, the freedom to contract, the dynamic nature of property, the freedom of commerce, and the obligations of publicly chartered corporations.[35]

By creating an independent Supreme Court and judiciary department, the Constitution empowered this branch of government to rule on the relations between the constituent parts of the union – states and federal government – and to rule on the relationship of public and private rights – two of the most hotly contested political questions of the day. Although it took fifty years to articulate these powers, by the eve of the Civil War, the law knit a resilient connective web, though one insufficiently powerful in and of itself, to preserve the Union.[36]

Law made by judges often challenged the collective rights and obligations of republican citizenship. Tradition and the local administration of the law, however, tempered the antidemocratic thrust of the law. At the state level, the law extended its domain by embracing common law precedents. The newly liberated states enacted "reception statutes" that formally incorporated those portions of English common law that were not at odds with colonial practice.[37]

Thus, at the height of anti-British sentiment and during the very era that Americans debated constitutional protections against replicating the abuses of British rule, the nation embedded a legal system with distinctly British roots deep within the judiciary. Preserving this core of judge-made law in the midst of elected legislatures and written constitutions was akin to sanctioning a "state within a state." Nevertheless, the common law's disproportionate concern with property rights and suspicion of power resonated with many Americans. That this embedded "state" often operated at the local level made it all the more effective, given the republican fear of distant government.[38]

The common law required a set of personnel who produced and popularized legal ways of thinking. Due to its arcane nature, judge-made law required a degree of expertise not readily acquired by citizens. Lawyers

[35] Christopher L. Tomlins, *Law, Labor, and Ideology in the Early American Republic* (New York, NY: Cambridge University Press, 1993), 21–22.

[36] Ibid., 39, 70.

[37] Kermit L. Hall, *The Magic Mirror: Law in American History* (New York, NY: Oxford University Press, 1989), 50; See also, William E. Nelson, *Americanization of the Common Law: The Impact of Legal Change on Massachusetts Society, 1760–1830* (1975; repr., Athens, GA: University of Georgia Press, 1994).

[38] Tomlins, *Law, Labor, and Ideology*, 33–34, 92; Sellers, *Market Revolution*, 49.

soon developed the professional self-consciousness and skills to provide these services. With no class of elite administrators to compete with, judges and lawyers acted as the *de facto* day-to-day rule makers with only occasional interruptions by statutory law. The British, in fact, had introduced the common law into America as a means of imposing some kind of uniformity on a hodgepodge of local practices.[39]

Lawyers increasingly dominated court rooms as both litigants and judges, and narrowed the terrain available to juries by expanding judicial instructions to these juries, hemming in jury-driven interpretations of the law and overturning decisions on appeal because juries failed to abide by the judge's instructions. A premium on predictability began to eclipse the crucial local connection that juries had guaranteed. With lawyers and judges dominating the process, the arguments used to reach judicial decisions acquired new significance.[40]

The formalization of the decision-making process, combined with increased, albeit informal, training of lawyers, contributed to a legal discourse that transcended local and state boundaries. By 1815 a number of the larger commercial states required written opinions at the appeals court level. Court reporters were not uncommon in these venues. Treatises contributed to this nationalization of the law. They purported to systematize the entire body of judge-made law. The two lawyers most influential on this front were Joseph Story, a federal Supreme Court Justice who commuted to his job at Harvard Law School for much of his treatise-writing time, and James Kent, chancellor of New York. As judges in lower courts turned to published opinions and treatises, the legal conversation, though never standardized, grew more uniform.[41]

Courts rationalized and systematized some of the most highly contested political questions of the day. Labor relations is a good example. In a series of rulings about labor's right to organize, the relationship of workers to their employers, and the obligations of employers to employees injured in accidents, the courts established minimal rights for employ-

[39] Tomlins, *Law, Labor, and Ideology*, 21–22; Sellers, *Market Revolution*, 49–50; Hall, *Magic Mirror*, 17. William E. Forbath discusses the rise of the court-centered American state and also discusses the roles of federalism, parties, and the lack of an administrative elite (or alternatively suggested by Forbath as the judiciary's role *as* the administrative elite) in creating an environment where courts could work as they did to limit the collective action available to American workers. *Law and the Shaping of the American Labor Movement* (Cambridge, MA: Harvard University Press, 1991), 26–36.
[40] Sellers, *Market Revolution*, 49; Nelson, *Americanization of the Common Law*, 3–9.
[41] Sellers, *Market Revolution*, 50.

ees. These included the right to contract for their labor and the right to associate. The general influence of this discourse was conservative, however, favoring the security of property and the sanctity of the contract system over the collective rights of workers, or for that matter, the safety and well-being of workers.[42]

The courts consistently pushed issues that had been part of a vigorous political discourse into a realm that the judiciary defined as private – subject to the courts' mediation between two parties to a contract. Establishing its exclusive domain over a broad spectrum of "private" relationships, the "rule of law" was one of the few institutions in the early nineteenth century that could legitimately claim to be truly national in scope. In this regard, it was perhaps the most effective part of the Federalist initiative to foster greater national unity in the union. Federal and state actions "Americanized the common law" in the first half of the nineteenth century, adapting it to dictates of a burgeoning capitalist economy.[43]

Like the Post Office, federal district courts mediated national and local concerns. District courts were the workhorses of the federal judiciary and the institutions that most litigants encountered at this level. The career of Harry Innes, who presided over Kentucky's federal district court, illustrates the ways in which a federal judge could negotiate between national and local concerns. Innes was a judge for the United States Court for the District of Kentucky from 1789 through 1816. A Virginian by birth, Innes moved to the Kentucky District of Virginia in 1783 where he speculated in land, farmed, and served as a state-level judge. He was also active in the movement to secure statehood for Kentucky. No fan of the Constitution, Innes accepted it, once it was ratified. Shortly after the Judicial Act of 1789 was passed, Innes was named as the District Court judge for Kentucky at a salary of $1,000. A follower of Jefferson, Innes made little secret of his partisan leanings.[44]

Innes reconciled citizens of Kentucky to a federal government that, for the most part, remained "out of sight." Over his twenty-five year tenure, Innes's "private" caseload grew significantly because the judge assured

---

[42] Tomlins, *Law, Labor, and Ideology*, Parts 2–4.

[43] Ibid., 105–6; Hall, *Magic Mirror*, 109. The courts were all the more effective because of their transparency. As Tomlins points out, they rendered the system of power that lay behind them invisible. *Law, Labor, and Ideology*, 297.

[44] Tachau, *Federal Courts*, 12, 31, 33, 36–37. Innes was educated at the College of William and Mary, tutored in the law under Jefferson's mentor, George Wythe, and was admitted to the bar in 1773.

litigants a predictable, professional venue that promised due process. He was sensitive to local law and practice and went out of his way to assure trials by jury when appropriate. Innes's court became one of the most visible links between the citizens of Kentucky and the national government. The decisions that his court issued transformed the chaos that surrounded legal settlement and sale of land into a process that most Kentuckians could trust.[45]

Federal district court judges served as brokers between national and local concerns because, in spite of their rhetoric, National Republicans did little to alter the trajectory of the Federalists judicial policies: they remained energetic, and from the perspective of many republican patriots, intrusive. To be sure, Jefferson responded to a last-minute Federalist attempt to stack the deck in their favor after the election in 1800. This lame duck Congress passed the Judiciary Act of 1801, which would have created six new circuit courts and sixteen new judges (presumably Federalist judges), reduced the Supreme Court from six justices to five (upon the first retirement, thereby precluding Jefferson from appointing his own man), and further expanded the standing of federal circuit courts into issues previously delegated to state courts. Jefferson could not ignore this blatant effort to lock in what was already a strong tilt toward the Federalist perspective in the judiciary. He led a successful effort in Congress to repeal the Judiciary Act of 1801.[46]

Jefferson, however, would not go as far as many of the radical anti-judiciary proponents in his party urged him to go. They questioned the whole premise of lifetime appointments for federal judges, for instance. In the final analysis, Jefferson's actions and those of his Republican supporters merely restored the status quo that had existed since 1789. The size of the Supreme Court remained the same, Federal judges enjoyed tenure for life, and the partisan makeup of the judiciary remained distinctly Federalist. Jefferson probably described the situation best, writing to a friend that Congress had restored "our judiciary to what it was while justice & not federalism was its object."[47]

---

[45] Tachau, *Federal Courts*, 17, 30–33, 53. Although a federal judge, it was Innes's responsibility to master both the common law that had been incorporated into the district he presided over and Kentucky's constitution and statutes. Because Innes's jurisdiction paralleled that of the state courts for most issues, little business other than revenue cases brought by the federal government was anticipated. [191, 193]

[46] Ellis, *Jeffersonian Crisis*, 15, 45–51.

[47] Ibid., 51, 235; Cornell, *Other Founders*, 275; Thomas Jefferson to Count de-. Volney, April 20, 1802, in The Thomas Jefferson Papers, Series 1, General Correspondence, 1651–1827,

The legal system anchored the young republic in ancient British common law tradition at the same time that it forged one of the few truly national discourses. A specialized group of practitioners disseminated this language, housed in one of the few institutions that connected federal constitutional prerogatives to the most local matters. Operating at the interstices of this loose network, district court judges like Harry Innes severed as brokers who slowly systematized local practice, at the same time that they brought predictability and stability to decisions that resolved issues fundamental to the property and livelihoods of citizens.

THE "INTERESTS AND WELFARE OF THE COMMUNITY AT LARGE": DISCERNING THE PUBLIC STAKE IN PRIVATE PROPERTY

While some elements of the common law eroded the collective impulse that had been part of the republican compound, the commonwealth tradition endured, and even thrived at the state and local level in antebellum America. *Salus populi suprema lex est* ("the welfare of the people is the supreme law"), an influential common law maxim, was applied broadly. Commonwealth interpretations embedded individual rights in an elaborate web of social relations and obligations: one's rights were derived from society and hence always subject to the consent of that community.[48]

The government was obliged to use its regulatory power to act for the common public good. Judge Lemuel Shaw's decision upholding the legislative authority to regulate the construction of wharves in Boston Harbor in *Commonwealth v. Alger* (1851) was representative of this kind of reasoning and served as a model for subsequent decisions. Shaw synthesized some of the basic principles that had been operative in Massachusetts and other states for some time: "every holder of property, however abso-

---

online at Library of Congress, *The Thomas Jefferson Papers*, http://memory.loc.gov/ammem/collections/jefferson_papers/index.html, cited in Ellis, *Jeffersonian Crisis*, 52.

[48] William J. Novak, *The People's Welfare: Law and Regulation in Nineteenth-Century America* (Chapel Hill, NC: University of North Carolina Press, 1996), 9, 38–39. Harry N. Scheiber argues that ideas about public rights have real life importance: "state governments, operating in a decentralized federal system that largely conformed to the theoretical model of 'dual federalism,' had enormous influence in shaping the rules of the economic marketplace and of the social order" "Public Rights and the Rule of Law in American Legal History," *California Law Review* 72, no. 2 (March 1984): 226. See also Novak, *The People's Welfare*, chap. 1.

lute and unqualified may be his title, holds it under the implied liability that his use of it may be so regulated, that it shall not be injurious to the equal enjoyment of others having an equal right to the enjoyment of their property, nor injurious to the rights of the community. All property in this commonwealth ... is derived directly or indirectly from the government, and held subject to those general regulations, which are necessary to the common good and general welfare."[49]

Shaw sought to delineate a set of positive public rights – obligations owed the public by their government. Shaw's court spelled out these principles as they related to private property. Five years before *Alger*, Shaw's court pronounced that "All property is acquired and held under the tacit condition that it shall not be so used as to injure the equal rights of others, or to destroy or greatly impair the public rights and interests of the community." It was not just the rights of individual citizens that Shaw was at pains to protect. Rather, it was the "interests of the community" that had to be balanced against the rights of the individual property owner.[50]

State courts played a major role in speeding development through their interpretation of property rights. States articulated doctrines of "public purpose" and "public use" that supported energetic interpretations of eminent domain. In 1848 the Supreme Court confirmed over twenty years of state rulings: every state had "the right and duty of guarding its own existence, and of protecting and promoting the interests and welfare of the community at large" by taking private property. By defining just compensation in terms that encouraged the developer, and by supporting the wholesale transfer of the right of eminent domain to the private sector, states encouraged rapid development and extraction of resources. As one state court ruled, takings were authorized "not only where the safety, but also where the interest or even the expediency of the state is concerned." By mid-century, one Massachusetts court pronounced that "Everything which tends to enlarge the resources, increase the industrial energies, and promote the productive power of any considerable number of the inhabitants of a section of the State, or which leads to the growth of towns and the creation of new sources for the employment of private

[49] Scheiber, "Public Rights and the Rule of Law," 221; *Commonwealth v. Alger*, 61 Mass. 53, 84–5, (1851), online at http://www.lexisnexis.com/universe, quoted in Novak, *The People's Welfare*, 19–20.

[50] Scheiber, "Public Rights and the Rule of Law," 220; *Commonwealth v. Tewksbury*, 52 Mass. 55, 57 (1846), available online at http://www.lexisnexis.com/universe, quoted in Scheiber, "Public Rights and the Rule of Law," 224.

capital and labor, indirectly contributes to the general welfare and to the prosperity of the whole community." It would have been difficult to define public purpose more broadly.[51]

The national legal discourse that emerged in the first half of the nine-teenth century at the state level laid the foundation for "self-executing" and "self-supporting" forms of governance. Rather than protecting the community by ensuring fair exchange in each negotiation, the courts embraced the right of individuals to decide this for themselves and focused judicial scrutiny instead on policing the impact of these negotiations on the community. Courts moved away from pre-Revolutionary conceptions that focused on the fairness of the exchange of property between two individuals, toward legal doctrines that normalized competition.[52]

Ironically, as the courts allowed individuals to sell their property as they saw fit – even if the exchange did not appear to be fair – the litmus test for measuring exchange shifted to one that considered the transac-tion's impact on the entire community. The welfare of the community meant something quite different in a democratic republic than it did in a monarchy. When the threat was from an all-powerful (and some-times land hungry) Crown, absolute control of one's own property was a deeply held community value. When the government was increasingly one's own neighbors, individual transactions sometimes proved to be the most dangerous threat to community values. An 1823 Massachusetts case illustrates the point nicely. When a citizen brought suit complain-ing that the highway surveyor had damaged his property by lowering

---

[51] Harry N. Scheiber, "Federalism and the American Economic Order, 1789–1910," *Law & Society Review*, 10, no. 1 (Fall 1975): 57–118; *West River Bridge Company v. Dix*, 47 U.S. 507, 531 (1848), available online at http://www.lexisnexis.com/universe, quoted in Scheiber, "Public Rights and the Rule of Law," 225; *Beekman v. Saratoga & Schenectady Railroad Co.* 3 Paige 45, 73 (NY Chanc. 1831), quoted in Scheiber, "Federalism and the American Economic Order," 96; *Talbot v. Hudson*, 82 Mass. 417, 425 (1860), avail-able online at http://www.lexisnexis.com/universe, cited in Harry N. Scheiber, "Property Law, Expropriation, and Resource Allocation by Government, 1789–1910," *Journal of Economic History*, 33, no. 1 (March 1973): 244; James Willard Hurst, *Law and the Conditions of Freedom in the Nineteenth-century United States* (Madison, WI: University of Wisconsin Press, 1956), 63; Gerald D. Nash, *State Government and Economic Development: A History of Administrative Policies in California, 1849–1933* (Berkeley, CA: University of California Press, 1964), 350.
[52] Lawrence M. Friedman, *Contract Law in America: A Social and Economic Case Study* (Madison, WI: University of Wisconsin Press, 1965), 150, quoted in Harry N. Scheiber, "Government and the Economy: Studies of the 'Commonwealth' Policy in Nineteenth-Century America," *Journal of Interdisciplinary History*, 3, no. 1 (Summer 1972): 141; Nelson, *Americanization of the Common Law*, 7.

the grade of road that ran in front of it, the court ruled in favor of the surveyor. Comparing the situation to that of school placement, the court opined that even though schools created noise and drew crowds, starting one did not require "the public ... to consult the convenience of the individual so far as to abstain from erecting the schoolhouse, or to pay the owner of the dwellinghouse for its diminished value." In other words, the rights of the community came first, despite the damage to individual property holders.[53]

Whether merely reacting to concentrated interests – like the railroads, which were capable of overpowering the political process in particular states, or actively organizing and articulating the commonwealth ideal of aiding private ventures and sacrificing the rights of individuals for the good of the whole, as was the case with early canal ventures, states mobilized the dynamic use of property. The states provided a legal framework that governed the incorporation of businesses, the sanctity of contracts, the rules for bankruptcy, the workings of the monetary system, and the enforcement of tax law. They protected "ventures," not "holdings." They ensured that the market for land was "open and mobile." They favored the efficient use of property, as measured by return to the entire community, over inefficient use when it came to riparian rights or the use of new technology.[54]

The judge-made underpinnings for such policies, which proliferated among the commercially oriented states after 1815, were the least visible component of the high profile capital accumulation and public works projects initiated at the state level. Nonetheless, this legal framework was a crucial prerequisite for active state policy. Collectively, it constituted a national commitment to the dynamic use of property. Although they

---

[53] Nelson, *Americanization of the Common Law*, 133; *Callender v. Marsh*, 18 Mass. 418, 432 (1823), available online at http://www.lexisnexis.com/universe, cited in Nelson, *Americanization of the Common Law*, 132.

[54] Sellers, *Market Revolution*, 50–55; Hurst, *Law and the Conditions of Freedom*, 24; Oscar Handlin and Mary Flug Handlin, *Commonwealth: A Study of the Role of Government in the American Economy, Massachusetts, 1774–1861* (New York, NY: New York University Press, 1947); Oscar Handlin and Mary Flug Handlin, *The Dimensions of Liberty* (Cambridge, MA: Harvard University Press, Belknap Press, 1961), 70–72; Harry N. Scheiber, *Ohio Canal Era: A Case Study of Government and the Economy, 1820–1861* (Athens, OH: Ohio University Press, 1969); Scheiber, "Federalism and the American Economic Order," 59, 66–7; Lawrence M. Friedman, *A History of American Law*, 2nd edn (New York, NY: Simon and Schuster, 1985), 240, quoted in Charles W. McCurdy, *The Anti-Rent Era in New York Law and Politics, 1839–1865* (Chapel Hill, NC: University of North Carolina Press, 2001), 39; Nelson, *Americanization of the Common Law*, 8.

were often crafted at the state level, legal decisions established a national framework for guiding social and economic development. States intervened in order to nurture and protect predictable economic and social exchange. In a surprising number of instances, the courts sacrificed private rights for the public welfare.[55]

Nowhere was the tension between protecting the vested rights that inhered in land ownership on the one hand, and the community's interest in the productive use of such land, on the other, greater than in New York's system of "lease in fee" land tenancy. This antiquated system survived among the state's great Eastern manors well into the nineteenth century. By the 1840s, both Whigs and Democrats sought to empower "tenants" in this system to reap the benefits of the improvements that their families had made over generations. Yet the sanctity of contract law, as consistently interpreted by the courts, precluded any easy solution to the problem. The arguments made by public officials who sought to treat the land in more dynamic fashion are illustrative of the way in which the commonwealth ideal penetrated one of the most fundamental questions of state-level governance.[56]

Because the lease in fee system stifled productive use, retarding economic opportunity and contributing to economic stagnation, the Whigs argued that the New York legislature was legally justified in using its powers of eminent domain to revise these long-standing contracts (providing that just compensation was provided). Dynamic use of the land and the community's broader interest required abrogation of the long-standing contracts. One of the clearest statements of these principles was articulated by William A Duer, Jr., a talented thirty-six-year-old lawyer. In 1840, the New York Whig party turned to this assemblyman to chair a Select Committee. It was charged with reforming land law affecting the sprawling Rensselaerwyck Manor.[57]

Duer's report argued that the state had a stake in land use: "that the land within her limits should be made as productive as possible, all her natural resources developed, and her territory and all its parts occupied

---

[55] Sellers, *Market Revolution*, 4

[56] McCurdy, *Anti-Rent Era*, xiv-xv.

[57] Ibid., 45, 50. Duer's challenge was to "assimilate the tenures in question to those ... more accordant with the principles of republican government, ... without the violation of contracts." Governor Seward's Second Message, January 1840, quoted in "William H. Seward," *The American Whig Review*, 11, no. 30 (June 1850): 630, available online at Cornell University Library, Making of America Digital Archive, http://cdl.library.cornell. edu/moa/, quoted in McCurdy, *Anti-Rent Era*, 39.

by an independent, industrious, and intelligent population." Because tenants could not benefit from their improvements, there was no incentive for them to make the land more productive. While the contracts that the ancestors of these tenants had entered into should not be dismissed lightly, Duer argued, the legislature had a compelling reason to revise these contracts.[58]

For Whig Governor William Seward, policy trumped contractual obligation. "When contracts embrace something contrary to the policy of the state, something though lawful when entered into, which is found upon experience to tend to immorality, or be in any way detrimental to the public interest, may not the state interpose for the public good, and drawing to itself, *upon just compensation*, the property of the creditor in the contract, release the debtor from its obligation?" Public policy should prevail, Seward contended, precisely because it embodied the entire community's interest, in contrast to individual contractual rights.[59]

New York law was clear on the power of eminent domain, Duer argued. He cited an opinion handed down in 1831, italicizing key portions for emphasis: "*[I]f the public interest can be in any way promoted* by the taking of private property, it must rest *in the wisdom of the legislature* to determine whether the benefit to the public will be of sufficient importance to render it expedient for them to exercise the right of eminent domain." In this instance, the state had delegated its power of eminent domain to a private corporation in order to promote the public welfare. If the state could delegate such authority to a private corporation, Duer argued, surely it could act directly to remedy a set of contracts that impaired the public welfare.[60]

The arguments mounted by both parties illustrate the capacious legal authority that states retained, even in the era during which the sanctity of contract was forged. New York Democrats also advocated assertive state action, supporting direct intervention even if it meant abrogating existing contracts. Democrats, of course, framed the issue differently than the Whigs. They invoked the Declaration of Independence and emphasized

---

[58] "Report of the Committee on so much of the Governor's Message as relates to the difficulties between the landlord and tenants of the Manor of Rensselaerwyck," [Duer Report] New York Assembly Document 271, 63 sess. (1840), 4–5, quoted in McCurdy, *Anti-Rent Era*, 45.

[59] Duer Report, 14, quoted in McCurdy, *Anti-Rent Era*, 49–50.

[60] Ibid., quoted in McCurdy, *Anti-Rent Era*, 51. The emphasis is Duer's, who quoted Chancellor Reuben Walworth writing in *Beekman v. Saratoga and Schenectady Railroad Co.* (1831).

individual rights-based arguments. An 1841 manifesto proclaimed that "the holding of so large a territory of land by one man, as claimed by the patroon of the colony of Rensselaerwyck, is in direct violation of that sacred declaration upon which American independence has been so long proudly maintained." Individual rights-based appeals acquired traction in an era particularly sensitive to the Jacksonian antipathy toward any legislation that favored a particular class or any special segment of the community.[61]

In the case of the archaic lease in fee tenancy system, the power of existing law defeated the rhetoric and programmatic agendas of both Democrats and Whigs. Neither party could untangle this legal conundrum. Nor were private property rights easily ignored, even when a clear public benefit might be achieved. This was amply demonstrated by another New York case decided in 1843. *Taylor v. Porter* was about access to a public highway even though that access required crossing a neighbor's land. When Mr. Taylor would not provide an easement for the landlocked Porter to reach the public road, Porter used a long-existing statute to prevail upon the highway commissioners to construct such a road. Taylor sued, arguing that the statute was not constitutional.[62]

The Private Road Act, which was at the heart of *Taylor v. Porter*, embodied all of the public justifications enumerated in Duer's Report. How could one fulfill his obligations as a good citizen – ranging from voting to serving in the militia – if he did not have access to the public highways without trespassing on his neighbor's land? The implications for a developmental perspective were even more profound. Economic development and the most productive use of land obviously turned on reasonable access to the public road. Yet these arguments were rejected by a majority of the Court's justices. Justice Bronson, a Democrat, summed up the majority's reasoning when he wrote, "When one man wants the property of another, I mean to say that the legislature cannot aid him in making the acquisition." Narrow interpretations of one individual's right

---

[61] *Albany Argus*, May 6, 1841, quoted in McCurdy, *Anti-Rent Era*, 69; Howard Gillman, *The Constitution Besieged: The Rise and Demise of Lochner Era Police Powers Jurisprudence* (Durham, NC: Duke University Press, 1993), 128, cited in Scheiber, "Private Rights and Public Power: American Law, Capitalism, and the Republican Polity in Nineteenth-Century America," review of *The People's Welfare: Law and Regulation in Nineteenth Century America*, by William J. Novak, *Yale Law Journal* 107, no. 3 (December 1997): 846.

[62] McCurdy, *Anti-Rent Era*, 110–11.

to control, absolutely, his property found plenty of support in this era, the welfare of the community at large notwithstanding.[63]

The tug of war between the sanctity of private property and the states' interest in ensuring the general welfare of the community affected by that property was a source of vigorous debate throughout the nineteenth century. As the failure to resolve the impasse between contractual rights on the one hand, and the most productive use of land on the other, illustrate in the lease in fee tenancy issue, two opposing principles were fiercely contested during the Age of Jackson. The commonwealth tradition pushed Americans to regard property rights as subject to community interest first. This perspective treated the security of land and its productive potential as benefits derived, in part, from the state's legal protection. This perspective vied with a more narrowly defined individual rights-based perspective, articulated by the court in *Taylor v. Porter*. Advocates of the latter perspective were far quicker to label property private, and limit the community's stake in the use of that property. While the Democratic Party leaned toward narrower interpretations of community interest, its partisans were not immune to the commonwealth appeal, especially when it enhanced the dynamic use of property. States retained the right to articulate and carry out the public's interest in property, even when that property was considered by some to be private.

The battle over how much interest the broader community would retain in "private" holdings extended beyond contract and real property to publicly chartered corporations. As corporations began to assume tasks that were considered to be private and extended their reach into regional markets, states were instrumental in crafting a *de facto* national policy that determined just how much influence the public would retain in these corporations. Corporations had been chartered by the people but increasingly served the private interests of their investors. The resolution to this dilemma ultimately shaped the lives of millions of Americans and the political economy they built.

Historically, corporate rights were the product of political contest and subject to public regulation: no distinction between public and private was drawn in the first American corporations. They were all "bodies-politic." Corporations in the early republic were exceptions in a legal system built upon the individual's natural rights. Virtually all corporations

---

[63] Ibid., 111; *Taylor v. Porter*, 4 Hill 140, 147 (NY Sup. Ct. 1843), available online at http://www.lexisnexis.com/universe, quoted in McCurdy, *Anti-Rent Era*, 112.

before the Revolution entailed governance of some sort, such as towns or parishes. They were created to pool individual preferences in order better to serve the community. Chartered by the states, they all carried out a specific public purpose: they built and operated roads and bridges, then railroads.[64]

The judiciary treated these public utilities as "creatures of the state." Corporations, unlike people, were the product of law, the courts argued – artificial constructions delegated certain privileges by the state in return for their potential to improve the commonweal. As Chief Justice Marshall opined in 1804 in *Head v. Providence Insurance Co.*, corporations were "mere creature[s]" of legislation, their charters enumerated "all the power they possess." The powers that these fictitious persons possessed included legal standing, property rights, the right to exist in perpetuity, and eventually limited liability for their shareholders regarding corporate debts.[65]

The public's control over corporations was blunted by two developments in the 1830s. The first was the proliferation of "private" corporations and the state courts' ratification of this distinction. With the rise of profit-seeking corporations like manufacturing and mining firms, state courts began to distinguish between two corporate forms. One, the governmental or "public" corporation, had the power to tax its members. The "private" corporation, on the other hand, could not compel contributions from its members, nor could it require participation. The inability to compel contributions and membership soon became the legal basis for limiting the liability of private corporate shareholders. Because the corporation itself could not mandate contributions from all of its members,

[64] Morton J. Horwitz, *The Transformation of American Law, 1870–1960: The Crisis of Legal Orthodoxy* (New York, NY: Oxford University Press, 1992), 75; Robert W. Gordon, "Legal Thought and Legal Practice in the Age of American Enterprise, 1870–1920," in *Professions and Professional Ideologies in America*, ed. Gerald L. Geison (Chapel Hill, NC: University of North Carolina Press, 1983), 100; Oscar Handlin and Mary Flug Handlin, "Origins of the American Business Corporation," *Journal of Economic History*, 5, no. 1 (May 1945):19–22; Nelson, *Americanization of the Common Law*, 6.
[65] Gerald Berk, "Constituting Corporations and Markets: Railroads in Gilded Age Politics," *Studies in American Political Development*, 4, no. 1 (1990), 141; Scott R. Bowman, *The Modern Corporation and American Political Thought: Law, Power, and Ideology* (University Park, PA: Pennsylvania State University Press, 1996), 38, 46–47; James Willard Hurst, *The Legitimacy of the Business Corporation in the Law of the United States, 1780–1970* (Charlottesville, VA: University Press of Virginia, 1970), 7, 8, 11, 43; *Head v. Providence Insurance Co.*, 6 U.S. 127, 167, 169 (1804), available online at http://www.lexisnexis.com/universe, cited in Charles W. McCurdy, "The *Knight* Sugar Decision of 1895 and the Modernization of American Corporation Law, 1869–1903," *Business History Review*, 53, no. 3 (Autumn 1979): 318.

it would be unjust, state courts ruled, to allow creditors to collect from any individual shareholder, since he might shoulder an unequal portion of the debt.[66]

The second development that drove a wedge between the community interest in corporations and their private, profit-seeking capacity was animated by Jacksonian fears about legislation that favored special classes, especially corporate privileges. These egalitarian concerns fueled the movement to make incorporation more accessible. Beginning with Connecticut in 1837, several states began to craft general incorporation laws.[67]

Though access to a corporate charter no longer required specific authorization by the legislature in these states, the general incorporation legislation continued to require that corporations provide a public service. Even those few states that passed general incorporation laws before the Civil War continued to specify the structure of industrial corporations. Although it was now easier to incorporate, the general incorporation laws levied a dense web of restrictions on the corporations they chartered, imposing regulations at the very time that the nation ostensibly embraced *laissez-faire*.[68]

As corporations increasingly became associated with entrepreneurial activity (as opposed to special privilege), many Americans began to view them as individuals endowed with legal rights rather than artificial creations of the legal system. By the time of the Civil War, the United States Supreme Court had ratified some of the core legal rights of corporations, ensuring the survival of this form of business. The Court made it clear that corporations were not citizens protected under the Constitution. Nevertheless, they benefited from constitutional protections for their property, and had standing to sue in federal court.[69]

---

[66] Bowman, *Modern Corporation*, 42; Nelson, *Americanization of the Common Law*, 7, 135–36.

[67] Hurst, *Legitimacy of the Business Corporation*, 120, 132; Nelson, *Americanization of the Common Law*, 133; Bowman, *Modern Corporation*, 51; Alan Dawley, *Struggles for Justice: Social Responsibility and the Liberal State* (Cambridge, MA: Belknap Press of Harvard University Press, 1991), 22.

[68] Gordon, "Legal Thought", 100; Berk, "Constituting Corporations and Markets," 141; Hurst, *Legitimacy of the Business Corporation*, 56; Donald J. Pisani, "Promotion and Regulation: Constitutionalism and the American Economy," *Journal of American History*, 74, no. 3 (December 1987): 750–55. On the history of corporations in America, see Pauline Maier, "The Revolutionary Origins of the American Corporation," *The William and Mary Quarterly*, 3rd ser., 50, no. 1 (January 1993): 51–84.

[69] Bowman, *Modern Corporation*, 50, 52–53.

Americans in the middle third of the nineteenth century struggled to reconcile two competing perspectives that were particularly powerful at the state and local levels. The battles occurred over issues that ranged from the use of private property to the meaning of contractual obligations, to the degree to which the public retained a voice in the oversight of corporations. The commonwealth perspective considered property to be derived "directly or indirectly from the government," as Judge Lemuel Shaw had put it. All private use of that property was therefore subject to tests of the broader community's interest in that property. A competing perspective grounded the protection of property in each individual's natural rights. Advocates of this perspective, like Justice Bronson, placed the protection of that individual's rights ahead of any other interest, even when the competing claim might serve the broader public purpose.

INTERPRETING THE "SPIRIT OF THE CONSTITUTION": THE SUPREME COURT

Legal discourse, a growing network of legal specialists, and a national pattern of judge-made law at the state level would have carried little weight nationally had the *federal* judiciary remained the subordinate branch of government it started out as being. A series of landmark decisions delivered during the thirty-four year reign of Chief Justice John Marshall (1801–1835) established the Supreme Court as an influential branch of government. More importantly for our story, these decisions consolidated, and in some instances advanced, the legal infrastructure for developmental capitalism that state courts were crafting. That these patterns were endorsed by the federal judiciary made the subsequent development of a national market possible, if not certain.[70]

Among many other achievements, the Marshall Court established the Supreme Court's right as the final arbiter and interpreter of the

[70] Klarman, "Marshall Court Decisions," 1113; Scheiber, "Government and the Economy," 147; Pisani, "Promotion and Regulation," 755.

    Pisani cites the conflict between state law and federal law that is inherent in the Constitution itself as one of the roots of the promotional Court. For instance, he notes that even as the nineteenth-century Supreme Court disallowed punitive state measures against corporations that did business in rival states, it encouraged states to enact tax breaks and other incentives to lure businesses away from rivals, thus stimulating the economy. Supreme Court decisions therefore reflected the Constitutional "attempt to order essentially inconsistent values ... to balance differences rather than to eliminate them entirely." "Promotion and Regulation," 741.

Constitution. Only the Supreme Court, among the three federal branches of government, could declare legislation to be unconstitutional. The Marshall Court defined commerce broadly and, in support of that position, endorsed extensive Congressional power to regulate commerce. Under Marshall, the Supreme Court limited the power of states by precluding them from taxing agencies of the federal government and by rejecting a popular conception that the Constitution was a compact between the states. On this matter and any other disputes between a state and the federal government, the Court would have the last word. The Marshall Court staunchly defended the sanctity of contracts and in general, sided with propertied interests. It was wary of unbridled democracy even as it presided over a period of unparalleled democratization.[71]

The Court was comprised of a disproportionate number of men who were unabashed advocates for enhancing the authority of the General Government. While the Marshall Court began with a preponderance of Federalists, its tenure witnessed the appointment of numerous Republicans and, ultimately, of Democrats. For instance, five Republicans were appointed between 1806 and 1811. Yet the proclivities of men appointed to the Supreme Court were national. A frustrated Thomas Jefferson was the first of many presidents to bemoan the ideological transformation that seemed to overcome justices, once appointed: "the leaven of the old mass seems to assimilate to itself the new, and after twenty years' confirmation of the federal system by the voice of the nation, declared through the medium of elections, we find the Judiciary on every occasion still driving us into consolidation."[72]

The man who led this foray into "consolidation" was John Marshall. By all accounts a humble but ambitious man, Marshall was born in 1755 and grew up in Fauquier County, Virginia – a northwestern frontier outpost of the Commonwealth. Marshall's father, Thomas, brought a degree

---

[71] Klarman, "Marshall Court Decisions," 1153–55; Scheiber, "Government and the Economy," 147. See also, R. Kent Newmyer, *John Marshall and the Heroic Age of the Supreme Court* (Baton Rouge, LA: Louisiana State University Press, 2001).

[72] Klarman, "Marshall Court Decisions," 1172; David Robarge, *A Chief Justice's Progress: John Marshall from Revolutionary Virginia to the Supreme Court* (Westport, CT: Greenwood Press, 2000), 256; Jefferson to Spencer Roane, September 6, 1819, in *The Writings of Thomas Jefferson*, ed. Paul L. Ford, 10 vols. (New York, NY: G.P. Putnam, 1892–1899), 10:140, cited in Robarge, *Chief Justice's Progress*, 256.

For the role of federal courts in shoring up the federalist version of national citizenship through the "diversity clause" of the Constitution, see Rogers Smith, *Civic Ideals: Conflicting Visions of Citizenship in U.S. History* (New Haven, CT: Yale University Press, 1997), 149–50.

of civilization to the region as he acquired significant land holdings. The American Revolution was a formative event in John Marshall's life. Marshall served his country in the militia and then in Washington's Army for six years. Like Hamilton, his military service taught him the limits of man's "virtue," and opened his eyes to the hazards of decentralized governance during wartime.[73]

John Marshall was an unequivocal supporter of the new constitution. His ties to General Washington, and his own stature as a rising Virginian who strongly endorsed the new constitution, garnered him an appointment as a special commissioner to France in 1797. After serving one term in Congress, Marshall was appointed Secretary of State by President Adams in 1800. Shortly after this, he was nominated to be Chief Justice. Taking the oath of office in January, 1801, Marshall served as both Secretary of State and Chief Justice until Thomas Jefferson was inaugurated in March.[74]

A Federalist from a region that was staunchly Republican, a nationalist who began his tenure during the Jefferson Revolution of 1800, Marshall defended national prerogatives. Marshall was not the aggressive aggrandizer that some have posited. Rather, he was a "beleaguered champion" of a union that was fragile at best, as one biographer put it. Besides his intellectual contributions to some of the key decisions the Court rendered, Marshall was an institution builder. He went to great pains to ensure that the Court spoke with one voice, insisting that the justices live together at a Washington boardinghouse. Marshall also initiated the practice of issuing one "opinion of the Court," replacing the multiple readings of opinions by many of the justices.[75]

If the Supreme Court were to play a significant role in the nation's political future, it had to establish its autonomy vis-a-vis the other branches of the federal government, and assert the prerogatives of the federal government vis-a-vis the states. The federal judiciary asserted the latter power during the 1790s by ruling several state laws unconstitutional. The Marshall Court established the former by claiming its right to decide

---

[73] Newmyer, *John Marshall*, 12–14, 20–27; Robarge, *Chief Justice's Progress*, chap. 2.

[74] Newmyer, *John Marshall*, 36–37, 49–51. Marshall studied briefly at the College of William and Mary, where he also read law. He practiced law and, like his father, speculated in land early in his career. Elected to the Virginia House of Delegates in 1782, Marshall later served as delegate to Virginia's convention to ratify the U.S. Constitution in 1788.

[75] Newmyer, *John Marshall*, xvi; Klarman, "Marshall Court Decisions," 1157–58; Robarge, *Chief Justice's Progress*, 254.

upon the constitutionality of a federal statute in *Marbury v. Madison* (1803). The case entailed a plea by William Marbury (and others) in December 1801 for the court to issue a writ of mandamus requiring that Secretary of State James Madison deliver Marbury's commission as a justice of the peace in the District of Columbia. Marbury, along with dozens of others, had been appointed by the outgoing Adams administration to fill one of the new positions hastily created by the lame duck Congress in the Judiciary Act of 1801. Approved by the Senate, these appointments were never delivered. Incoming President Thomas Jefferson instructed his new Secretary of State James Madison not to deliver these appointments, leading to Marbury's legal action.[76]

The Supreme Court ruled unanimously that "it is emphatically the province and duty of the judicial department to say what the law is," establishing the principle of judicial review in unequivocal terms. The opinion continued, "if then the courts are to regard the constitution; and the constitution is superior to any ordinary act of the legislature; the constitution, and not such ordinary act, must govern the case to which they both apply." The opinion concluded that Congress, in drafting the Judiciary Act of 1789, had overstepped its bounds in granting the Supreme Court the power to issue writs of mandamus – the relief that Marbury requested. Because the 1789 statute transgressed powers enumerated in Article III of the Constitution, the legislation was unconstitutional, the Court ruled.[77]

Marbury established the principle of judicial review of federal statutes with little resistance (although the Court used that principle sparingly over the next fifty years), because Marshall carefully avoided a constitutional confrontation with Jefferson. What if the Court ordered the President to deliver the appointments and the President simply ignored the Court? Such a humiliation might have ended any hope for judicial parity for decades. Instead, Marshall elided the issue by interpreting the Constitution as restricting his own court's power to issue writs of mandamus. In spite of the legally nonbinding tongue lashing that Marshall delivered to the President for his failure to carry out his administrative obligations, Marbury was out of luck and a constitutional crisis was averted.[78]

---

[76] Klarman, "Marshall Court Decisions," 1114–16; *Marbury v. Madison,* 5 U.S. 137 (1803), available online at http://www.lexisnexis.com/universe.

[77] *Marbury v. Madison,* 177–78.

[78] Ellis, *Jeffersonian Crisis,* 66–67; Klarman, "Marshall Court Decisions," 1123. Ironically, this powerful declaration of judicial review did not provoke a reaction from Republicans

If the reaction to *Marbury* was muted, this was certainly not the case when the Supreme Court rendered its decision in *McCulloch v. Maryland*. The Court took on two volatile issues in this case – the question of state sovereignty as embodied in the compact theory of the Constitution, and the constitutionality of the Bank of the United States. It did so at a time of rising sectional tension and economic instability. The Court's opinion in *McCulloch v. Maryland* (1819) provided strong constitutional support for a national government that was far more than its component parts. The decision also confirmed that the federal government had the authority to create powerful institutions like the Bank of the United States.

Few federally supported institutions were more visible than the Bank of the United States. When former bank critic James Madison was forced to charter the Second Bank of the United States in order to stabilize currency and restore economic stability, he did not change the minds of many other Republicans. Advocates of state banks and local control attacked the Bank as a bastion of privilege and national consolidation. In 1818 the state of Maryland sought to cripple the Second Bank of the United States when it placed a tax on the issuance of its bank notes. After the Bank's cashier, James W. McCulloch, refused to pay the tax, Maryland sued. It argued that the legislation creating the Second Bank of the United States was unconstitutional because the Constitution did not explicitly give Congress the power to create banks. Even if the bank were constitutional, the plaintiff argued, state sovereignty ensured that Maryland had the authority to tax it.

The Court's unanimous opinion, delivered by Chief Justice Marshall, did not equivocate: Congress had the legislative authority to create a national bank (and any other corporation that achieved the ends spelled out in the Constitution) and states did *not* have the authority to tax federal entities. That the bank was ruled constitutional was hardly shocking, since it and the first Bank of the United States had operated for decades without constitutional challenge. But Marshall defended the national government's legislative discretion in the broadest terms. The heart of his defense turned on the Court's interpretation of the "necessary and proper" clause found in Article I, Section 8 of the Constitution. This clause added to enumerated powers the power to make "all laws which

wary of government consolidation, especially at the hands of its least representative branch. Perhaps this was because the substantive matter on which the Court ruled *limited* its own power to issue writs of mandamus.

shall be necessary and proper, for carrying into execution the foregoing power."[79]

The founders, the Court argued, intended this language to be expansive, not restrictive. The clause was added in order to ensure that the national government had the *means* to carry out the ends spelled out in the Constitution. In this case, these ends included the power to lay and collect taxes, to borrow money, and to regulate commerce. "Let the end be legitimate," the Court opined, "let it be within the scope of the constitution, and all means which are appropriate, which are plainly adapted to that end, which are not prohibited, but consist with the letter and spirit of the constitution, are constitutional." The Court also reminded its audience that it had not forgotten its responsibility to exercise judicial review: it would not hesitate to rule legislation unconstitutional if there were a proper basis to do so.[80]

Having confirmed the Bank's constitutionality, the Court turned to the question that went to the very heart of sovereignty in the federal system – Maryland's bank tax. Marshall addressed head-on the argument mounted by the counsel for Maryland that the "construction of the constitution" did not emanate from the people, but rather, was "the act of sovereign and independent states." True, Marshall conceded, as a practical matter, the Constitution was approved state by state. But that did not mean that the measure they adopted was the instrument of a league of states. In order to turn a confederation into "a more perfect union," one "possessing great and sovereign powers," ratification was referred to all the people, not to the states. "The government of the Union ... is, emphatically and truly," Marshall pronounced, "a government of the people. In form, and in substance, it emanates from them. Its powers are granted by them, and are to be exercised directly on them, and for their benefit."[81]

The power to tax, the court concluded, was the power to destroy. Allowing states to tax the federal government would destroy this national sovereignty and could not be allowed under the constitution, Marshall argued. If states could tax the Bank, why would they stop there? Why not tax the mail or any other instrument of the national government? This would make the General Government dependent on the states. The Court was certain that the American people "did not design to make their

---

[79] *McCulloch v State of Maryland*, 17 U.S. 316, 412 (1819), available online at http://www.lexisnexis.com/universe.
[80] Ibid., 403, 408, 421.
[81] Ibid., 402–5.

government dependent upon the states." Quite the opposite. "The question is, in truth, a question of supremacy; and if the right of the states to tax the means employed by the general government be conceded, the declaration that the constitution, and the laws made in pursuance thereof, shall be the supreme law of the land, is empty and unmeaning declaration." The Court declared the Maryland law unconstitutional and void.[82]

Marshall's decision confirmed the very consolidation that many Republicans feared. *McCulloch* stimulated a powerful reaction in the press and a great deal of debate over the meaning of the Constitution. In response, advocates of the compact theory redoubled their efforts. John Taylor spelled out some of these concerns in *Construction Construed*. The notion of a national popular will was fantasy, Taylor explained. To the extent that the popular will could be expressed, it was through corporate identities. This, in turn, could only take place through the political agencies of the states. It was at the state level that the people's rights were best guarded, Taylor insisted. The editor of the *Richmond Enquirer*, Thomas Ritchie, wrote that the decision was "fraught with alarming consequences."[83]

While Taylor and Ritchie spoke for the old Virginian aristocracy, more populist criticisms were mounted by men like Stephen Simpson, writing in Philadelphia's *Aurora*. Assuming the name "Brutus," this democrat proclaimed the decision to be "the most stupendous and mortal usurpation" of power since the Revolution. In Ohio, *The Western Herald* announced "The United States Bank, Everything! The Sovereignty of the State, Nothing!!" The debate over the admission of Missouri and the more immediate financial exigencies brought on by the panic of 1819 soon eclipsed *McCulloch*. However, they did not erase the powerful principles laid down by the Court in *McCulloch*, which interpreted the constitution's powers to be broad and, its foundation in will of the people across the union, deep.[84]

---

[82] Ibid., 427, 432–33.

[83] *Richmond Enquirer*, 11 June 1819, quoted in Klarman, "Marshall Court Decisions," 1143. Cornell, *Other Founders*, 278–87. That Republicans had triumphed at the ballot box only heightened concerns that the Supreme Court was a rear-guard bastion of Federalist thought. [281]

[84] Cornell, *Other Founders*, 285; "Brutus" [Stephen Simpson], *Aurora* (Philadelphia), March 16, 18, 21, 26, 1819, quoted in Cornell, *Other Founders*, 286; *Western Herald and Steubenville Gazette*, March 20, 1819, quoted in Andrew R.L. Cayton, *The Frontier Republic: Ideology and Politics in the Ohio Country, 1780–1825* (Kent, OH: Kent State University Press, 1986), 132.

The Marshall Court carved out national prerogatives in another contested sphere – the federal government's regulation of commerce. *Gibbons v. Ogden* (1824) defined the commerce clause of the Constitution broadly. The case resulted from a New York State law that limited steamboat traffic on New York waters to two operators. When Thomas Gibbons sought to operate a ferry from New Jersey to New York City, he was enjoined by Aaron Ogden, a former U.S. Senator and Governor from New Jersey. Ogden cited his exclusive right to provide service between these two points (the result of his license with Robert Livingston and Robert Fulton, who had been granted the original monopoly rights). Gibbons claimed rights of his own under a 1793 Act of Congress regulating the coastal trade. The Court found in favor of Gibbons and declared the New York statute void. Defining commerce broadly, the Court ruled that Congressional authority to regulate navigation between states was supported by the Commerce Clause of the Constitution.[85]

In *Trustees of Dartmouth College v. Woodward* (1819), the Marshall Court helped to create a stable legal environment for private corporations by protecting the sanctity of their charters under the contract clause of the Constitution. The case arose when New Hampshire sought to alter the terms by which the college had originally been chartered in 1769. Dartmouth had expanded the number of trustees and created a board of overseers. Claiming protection under the clause of the federal constitution that prohibited states from passing any law that impaired contracts, the majority of the trustees refused to accept the altered charter. They argued that the New Hampshire legislature had no right to alter the original charter.[86]

In a five-to-one decision, the Supreme Court agreed. Chief Justice Marshall, again, drafted the opinion. The charter was indeed a contract that would be impaired by the New Hampshire legislation. In discerning whether the charter constituted a contract, Marshall drew an important distinction among corporations. Dartmouth College had been founded as a charity school for the instruction of Indians. It was a private "eleemosynary" institution, and thus a private corporation, the Court ruled. It was Dartmouth's private status – "endowed with a capacity to take

---

[85] *Gibbons v. Ogden*, 22 U.S. 1, 240 (1824), available online at http://laws.findlaw.com/us/22/1.html. Klarman, "Marshall Court Decisions," 1127–31. See also Sellers, *Market Revolution*, 146–8.

[86] *Trustees of Dartmouth College v. Woodward*, 17 U.S. 518, 626 (1819), available online at http://laws.findlaw.com/us/17/518.html; Hall, *Magic Mirror*, 110.

property, for objects unconnected with government" that entitled it to protection of its property. Marshall also enumerated some of the characteristics that corporations possessed. "Among the most important," Marshall proclaimed, "are immortality, and, if the expression may be allowed, individuality; properties by which a perpetual succession of many persons are considered as the same, and may act as a single individual."[87]

The decision gave a green light to those businessmen who had previously questioned the legal stability of the corporate form. The Court's ruling in *Dartmouth* and the language it used to distinguish private from public corporations, in conjunction with some of the state-level rulings about corporations discussed in the previous section, served as a catalyst that propelled corporations from an "artificial being, invisible, intangible, and existing only in contemplation of the law" toward the status of individuals entitled to constitutional protection of their property. Although Dartmouth's charter was indeed created to perpetuate what today we would call a voluntary organization, the Court signaled that its ruling applied to all private corporations.[88]

It was not easy to parse corporate charters into private and public realms when in fact corporations had traditionally straddled both worlds. But Story, more than any other jurist, embraced the challenge. His reasoning cleared a constitutionally protected sphere of private conduct, free from public interference and national in scope. Justice Story began this process four years before *Dartmouth* in *Terrett v. Taylor*. Here the corporation was a Virginia church that sought protection from legislation authorizing the confiscation of lands owned by the church. Although Story did not ground the decision in specific constitutional protections, as *Dartmouth* did, he did pave the way for the public/private distinction that Marshall relied on in *Dartmouth*. Story conceded that if the corporation existed "only for public purposes, such as counties, towns, cities, &c. [,] the legislature may, under proper limitations, have a right to change, modify, enlarge or restrain them."[89]

---

[87] Bowman, *Modern Corporation*, 44; *Dartmouth v. Woodward*, 630, 636.

[88] Hall, *Magic Mirror*, 111; *Dartmouth v. Woodward*, 636; Bowman, *Modern Corporation*, 44–45.

[89] Bowman, *Modern Corporation*, 42–44; *Terrett v. Taylor*, 13 U.S. 43, 52 (1815), available online at http://laws.findlaw.com/us/13/43.html; Hendrik Hartog, *Public Property and Private Power: The Corporation of the City of New York in American Law, 1730–1870* (Chapel Hill, NC: University of North Carolina Press, 1983; Ithaca, NY: Cornell University Press, 1989), 193. Citations are to the Cornell Paperbacks edition.

Story drew a bright line, however, between public purpose corporations and corporations that he deemed "private." "We are not prepared
to admit," Story opined, "that the legislature can repeal statutes creating
private corporations, or confirming to them property already acquired
under the faith of previous laws, and by such repeal can vest the property
of such corporations exclusively in the state, or dispose of the same to
such purposes as they may please, without the consent or default of the
corporators." In his concurring *Dartmouth* opinion, Story again drew the
distinction between "private" and "public" corporations, with the latter
entailing towns and cities – corporations that existed for "public political
purposes only."[90]

Joseph Story pushed the Marshall Court toward a powerful legal
framework that envisioned national support for burgeoning private enterprises and markets. Story served on the Supreme Court from 1811 until
his death in 1845. Andrew Jackson, however, refused to appoint him as
Chief Justice upon Marshall's death, turning to Roger B. Taney instead.
Even though Story was a member of Jefferson's National Republican
party, he advocated a capacious interpretation of federal authority. "Let
us extend the National authority over the whole extent of power given
by the Constitution," Story wrote shortly after the peace was concluded
in the 1812 War.[91]

Hartog describes a 1791 waterlot grant and how the terms differed from pre-revolution
grants. The newer grants did not require the same improvements, but only obligated future
improvements when the council decided they were necessary for the public good. It also
allowed the council to take back land to install streets and gave no compensation for such
a reclamation. "Before this," writes Hartog, "a covenanted grant had embodied a public
obligation expressed in the private terms of a real estate deed. Now, in the new world of
the new republic, a private deed would serve the private interests of the corporation and its
grantees, and public action would await public expression by the Common Council. The
terms of these grants tell us that city leaders were learning to distinguish the public from
the private self of the corporation." *Public Property,* 114.

[90] *Dartmouth v. Woodward,* 636, 668; Hall, *Magic Mirror,* 111; Bowman, *Modern
Corporation,* 44–45. On the history of "public" corporations, see Hartog, *Public
Property.*

[91] Theodore Sky, *To Provide for the General Welfare: A History of the Federal Spending
Power* (Newark, DE: University of Delaware Press, 2003), 220–21; Story to Nathaniel
Williams, February 22, 1815, in *The Life and Letters of Joseph Story,* William W. Story,
ed. (Boston, MA: Little, Brown, 1851), 1:254, cited in Charles Warren, *The Supreme
Court in United States History,* 2 vols. (Boston, MA: 1926), 1:452, available online at
http://www.heinonline.org/, as quoted in Sellers, *Market Revolution,* 58.
Story was a talented jurist and politician from Massachusetts. He served in the
Massachusetts legislature and as a U. S. representative in 1808–1809. Story broke with
Jefferson over the embargo. Although Jefferson warned Madison against appointing Story,

It took an assertively nationalist perspective to carve out protection for the private sphere. Both elements – energetic national legal authority, and the unrestrained zone of private activity carved out from publicly chartered corporations – were highly contested. Whether directly enforcing the contract clause, defining franchises and corporations as contracts to be strictly upheld, or prohibiting the retroactive relief of debt through bankruptcy laws, the Court gave businessmen and those who sought to perpetuate their charitable endeavors every reason to believe that contractual obligations would be strictly enforced. Story argued for the inviolable stature of contractual obligations, such as the one that Dartmouth College's charter bestowed upon its trustees. As Story concluded in his concurring opinion in that case, "any act of a legislature which takes away any powers or franchises vested by its charter in a private corporation ... or which restrains or controls the legitimate exercise of them, or transfers them to other persons, without its assent, is a violation of the obligations of that charter."[92]

Story's *Commentaries on the Constitution of the United States,* published in 1833, became a central repository for nationalist thought. Story's legal scholarship, as distinct from his role on the Court, proved particularly influential in the ongoing debate over the meaning of the "General Welfare Clause" of Article I, Section 8 of the Constitution. That no Supreme Court case resolved this debate definitively made Story's views all the more consequential. Story refuted what was purported to be a Federalist interpretation of the General Welfare Clause that expanded the national government's enumerated powers to provide for the general welfare. Restating the clause as he understood it, and adding his own italics for emphasis, Story wrote: "The Congress shall have power to lay and collect taxes, duties, imposts, and excises, *in order* to pay the debts, and to provide for the common defence and general welfare of the United States." The clause did not provide general authority to legislate beyond the enumerated powers: its object was the Congressional power to tax and appropriate only. As Story interpreted the Constitution, Congress could tax in a broad range of spheres in

---

Madison turned to the young lawyer after being turned down by three other candidates. Story preferred to apply the common law when possible. Sellers, *Market Revolution,* 57–59.

[92] Sellers, *Market Revolution,* 87–89; Klarman, "Marshall Court Decisions," 1144; McCurdy, *Anti-Rent Era,* 107; *Dartmouth v. Woodward,* 712.

The Supreme Court championed an interstate economy that fostered economic growth. For an excellent account of how it was able to balance this objective while retaining a clear sphere for state action, see Pisani, "Promotion and Regulation."

order to provide for the defense and general welfare of the nation, but it could only regulate or otherwise legislate in the spheres explicitly enumerated in the Constitution.[93]

This interpretation, however, went farther toward national consolidation than some of Story's Jeffersonian and Jacksonian colleagues were prepared to travel. Madison, for instance, insisted that the clause simply had no meaning, since the ability to tax would destroy the Constitution's enumerated powers. Story adamantly rejected this interpretation as "an attempt to obliterate from the Constitution the whole clause 'to pay the debts, and provide for the common defence and general welfare of the United States' as entirely senseless, or inexpressive of any intention whatsoever." Story refused to believe that the founders would have added a clause that had no meaning. Instead, he argued that the power to tax was indeed an independent authority vested in the national government, and one that was not confined to the enumerated powers.[94]

In the *Charles River Bridge* (1837), Chief Justice Taney, a Jacksonian Democrat, embraced the key commonwealth principle of dynamic capital serving the public interest. Though most of the legal action regarding corporations and contracts occurred at the state level, the federal judiciary clearly endorsed and contributed to the economically dynamic spirit of the times. In *Charles River,* the contract clause of the federal Constitution was again at issue. This time, it was the Massachusetts legislature that chartered a new bridge, technologically superior to the preexisting Charles River Bridge, which had received its charter from the legislature in 1785. The Taney Court held that contrary to *Dartmouth College,* there was no monopoly right implied in granting a charter. Furthermore, Taney, wrote, "the community also have rights," and the "happiness and well-being of every citizen depends on their faithful preservation."[95]

Finding a legal basis that allowed a competitively superior bridge to be built across the Charles was no easy task. As we have already seen, English common law of property turned on the concept of "absolute domain," which vested complete control of private property in its owner.

---

[93] Sellers, *Market Revolution,* 85; Sky, *To Provide for the General Welfare,* 212, 219–32; Joseph Story, *Commentaries on the Constitution of the United States,* 3rd edn (Boston, MA: Little, Brown, 1858), 1:630, (emphasis is Story's), cited in Sky, *To Provide for the General Welfare,* 223.

[94] Sky, *To provide for the General Welfard,* 228; Story, *Commentaries,* 1:637, cited in Sky, *To Provide for the General Welfare,* 228.

[95] *Charles River Bridge v. Warren Bridge,* 36 U.S. 420, 548 (1837), online at http://supreme. justia.com/us/36/420/case.html; Ibid., 548, cited in Hall, *Magic Mirror,* 118.

Through federal decisions like *Charles River Bridge,* and state rulings that required that the public interest be considered in matters of eminent domain and riparian water rights, the courts developed a more instrumental approach to property. It stressed competition as the best way to ensure efficient use of resources, which, in turn, would serve the public best. With *Charles River,* the Taney Court virtually enshrined competitive free enterprise as a constitutionally protected principle. Though Story's dissent worried about the prospect of corporate investment, given what he perceived to be weakened protection for contracts, the majority of the Court sided with Taney's vision of social progress through technological and entrepreneurial competition.[96]

The Taney Court, however, soon signaled that it had no intention of gutting contractual obligations. Its 7–1 decision in *Bronson v. Kinzie* overruled state legislation that interfered retrospectively with the rights of creditors to foreclose upon and keep the property of debtors. Delivering the Court's opinion, Taney confirmed that the Illinois legislature had every right to alter the statutory remedy for regulating the way contracts were enforced, such as shortening the statute of limitations for enforcement, or exempting work-related property from foreclosure. But the legislature had gone too far, acting not "merely on the remedy, but directly upon the contract itself." The result was "to engraft upon it new conditions injurious and unjust to the mortgage" – a consequence that the Court found impermissible because it violated the contract clause of the Constitution. While Western states erupted in protest over *Bronson,* the decision reassured those concerned about the sanctity of property and contracts rights in a democratic age.[97]

The General Government was freest to promote the dynamic use of property where it had explicit Constitutional authority to do so, as was the case with patent law. Article I, Section 8 stipulated that Congress shall have the power "to promote the Progress of Science and useful Arts, by securing for limited Times to Authors and Inventors the exclusive Right to their respective Writings and Discoveries." The federal government sought to fulfill this mission by balancing the property rights of inventors against the social benefits of their inventions.[98]

---

[96] Hall, *Magic Mirror,* 114; Sellers, *Market Revolution,* 353; Pisani, "Promotion and Regulation," 750; Bowman, *Modern Corporation,* 48.

[97] *Bronson v. Kinzie,* 42 U.S. 311, 316, 319 (1843), available online at http://www.lexisnexis.com/universe; McCurdy, *Anti-Rent Era,* 108–9.

[98] U.S. Constitution, Art. 1, Sec. 8, Cl. 8.

Americans approached this problem by providing access to a broad range of would-be inventors. Joseph Story was a key legal architect of this process. He summed up his philosophy best when he addressed a gathering of mechanics in 1829: "Ask yourselves, what would be the result of one hundred thousand minds ... urged on by the daily motives of interest, to acquire new skill, or invent new improvements." In practice, Americans faced lower barriers to patenting their inventions and secured patents for smaller, but more practical contributions than was the case in Great Britain. Even citizens normally excluded from the public sphere were eligible for patents. Women's patents, for instance, were protected by federal law. Overall, the legal system assumed that there was a happy coincidence between private invention and public policies protecting such inventions in the first half of the nineteenth century.[99]

Until 1836, the validity of patents was largely determined by the federal courts. Administratively, it fell to the Secretary of State to review patents, a job that Thomas Jefferson took seriously, but few of his successors did. In 1836, Congress revised patent legislation, establishing the Commissioner of Patents. The newly empowered Office of Patents beefed up the requirements for patent review and undertook careful analysis of each application. This, in turn, enhanced the value of patents granted by the U.S. Government. This exclusive grant of authority (states were not involved) and the expertise that the Office of Patents developed in consultation with Congress, made it a "bastion of administrative autonomy deep within the federal bureaucracy," as two scholars recently put it.[100]

* * *

With foreign threats diminished and its mobile population participating in the political process as never before, the strong preference for local government and parochial interest threatened to overwhelm national

[99] B. Zorina Khan, *The Democratization of Invention: Patents and Copyrights in American Economic Development, 1790–1920* (New York, NY: Cambridge University Press, 2005), 8–12; Story speech reported in *American Jurist and Law Magazine*, vol. 1 (1829), as cited in Khan, *Democratization of Invention*, 3. Note that state law did not always protect patents for women. For a later period, see Steven W. Usselman, *Regulating Railroad Innovation: Business, Technology, and Politics in America, 1840–1920* (New York, NY: Cambridge University Press, 2002), 97–139.
[100] Steven W. Usselman and Richard R. John, "Patent Politics: Intellectual Property, the Railroad Industry, and the Problem of Monopoly," in *Ruling Passions: Political Economy in Nineteenth-Century America*, ed. Richard R. John, (University Park, PA: Pennsylvania State University Press, 2006), 100, 121.

perspectives, not to mention authority. The weakest branch of government at the nation's founding, the judiciary, emerged as the most visible champion of national interest. Because it operated with little personnel and an even smaller budget, however, it was easy to overlook its influence. Reinforcing a legal discourse that operated even more vigorously on the state and local levels, however, that influence was significant. This powerful nationalist perspective proved especially important in carving private protections out of publicly chartered corporations and guaranteeing that federal law would back the integrity of contracts for private and voluntary entities.

The first order of business for the Supreme Court was to establish its standing among the three branches of the federal government. It did so through opinions that determined the Court's supreme position regarding the constitutionality of Congressional statutes, at the same time that it avoided head-on confrontations with the executive branch. The Court also dismissed interpretations of the Constitution that imagined the union to be the result of a compact between the states. Having achieved its goal, as final interpreter of the rules that both the General Government and the states would operate under, the Supreme Court embraced a vigorous interpretation of national authority in those spheres, like commerce, that were enumerated in the Constitution. Its rulings on cases that involved the contract clause of the Constitution both established firm expectations that contracts would be enforced, and carved out exceptions to this rule when monopoly control threatened to impede the dynamic use of property. The public interest would be served best through the competitive process – whether this occurred by deploying new bridge technology or encouraging invention through democratic patent policy.

"A STRONGER BIAS TOWARDS THEIR LOCAL GOVERNMENT": STATES AND LOCALITIES

Hamilton warned about a government out of sight because he understood that "the people of each State would be apt to feel a stronger bias towards their local government than towards the government of the Union." Throughout the nineteenth century, Americans displayed a strong preference for local government: the closer to home the better. Although I have focused on the capacity of the General Government to influence the lives of its citizens, Americans did not think of Washington, D.C. first when they turned to politics and governance. Local government had one "transcendent" advantage, according to Hamilton. It was the "immediate and visible guardian of life and property, having its benefits and its terrors in constant activity before the public eye, regulating all those personal interests and familiar concerns to which the sensibility of individuals is more immediately awake." The remainder of this chapter surveys some of the ways in which Americans engaged local and state government.[101]

Local governance accommodated the growing respect for individual autonomy – the emerging belief that individuals could manage their own affairs in both the private and public spheres that an expanding civil society created. Individual liberty was often pitted against strong government that threatened individual autonomy. Localizing governance allowed suspicious citizens to monitor their government and scrutinize carefully the money it spent. The antipathy toward taxation was rigorously enforced at the local level. Nineteenth-century Americans limited taxes to less than 4 percent of national income.[102]

Nationalizing programs conjured up fears of dependent citizens and runaway expenditures. President Franklin Pierce cited just such fears when he vetoed legislation that would have funded mental hospitals in 1854: "should this bill become a law ... the fountains of charity will be dried up at home, and the several States, instead of bestowing their own means on the social wants of their own people, may themselves, through

---

[101] Alexander Hamilton, "Federalist 17," in *The Federalist: A Commentary on the Constitution of the United States,* ed. Paul Leicester Ford (New York, Henry Holt, 1898; Avalon Project, 1996), http://www.yale.edu/lawweb/avalon/federal/fed17.htmCarter Goodrich, *Government Promotion of American Canals and Railroads, 1800–1890* (New York, NY: Columbia University Press, 1960), 288.

[102] White, *Federalists,* 390–91, 470; Novak, *People's Welfare,* 14; Scheiber, "Private Rights and Public Power," 852. The push for individual autonomy was accompanied by a "profound attachment to private property" and a strong "suspicion of government." This is one reason that the public sector remained small. On the eve of the Revolution, for instance, only about 2 percent of the adult male working population were employed in the public sector. J.R. Pole, *American Individualism and the Promise of Progress: An Inaugural Lecture delivered before the University of Oxford on 14 February 1980* (Oxford: Clarendon Press, 1980), 12–14, quoted in Jack P. Greene, *Pursuits of Happiness: The Social Development of Early Modern British Colonies and the Formation of American Culture* (Chapel Hill, NC: University of North Carolina Press, 1988), 195; Greene, *Pursuits of Happiness,* 185.

Taxation rates varied widely among states and localities. See John Lauritz Larson, *Internal Improvement: National Public Works and the Promise of Popular Government in the Early United States* (Chapel Hill, NC: University of North Carolina Press, 2001), 99–100. See also Harold N. Hyman, "Federalism: Legal Fiction and Historical Artifact?" *Brigham Young University Law Review,* no. 3 (1987): 914. Hyman argues that tenacious localism of states and parties is the real connective tissue of the United States. See also, White, *Federalists,* 390–7, 470.

the strong temptation, which appeals to States as to individuals, become humble supplicants for the bounty of the Federal Government, reversing their true relation to this Union."[103]

The states themselves had little supervisory capacity, leaving towns a great deal of discretion. This meant that laws on the books were often not enforced, or enforced only through the consensual compliance of the community. Education is a good example. All states claimed to supervise education, which was delivered on the local level. As late as 1890, however, the median size of state departments of education across the United States was two people, *counting* the superintendent of education. Americans got their first taste of federalism in the relationship between state and town. It was a federalism that was "tenaciously localistic."[104]

THE PRIVATIZED CITY

As cities developed, however, maintaining careful control over spending and services was impossible – even at the local level. Some cities responded by delegating control to neighborhoods and special tax assessment districts and by relying even more heavily on market mechanisms. Nowhere was a regime of private, localistic control more highly developed than in Chicago between 1845 and 1865.[105]

---

[103] Barry D. Karl and Stanley N. Katz, "The American Private Philanthropic Foundations and the Public Sphere, 1890–1930," *Minerva*, 19, no. 2 (June 1981): 240. Pierce anticipated the emergence of a powerful state and local government lobbying axis, a phenomenon labeled by one political scientist as "technocratic federalism." See Samuel H. Beer, "The Modernization of American Federalism," *Publius*, 3, no. 2 (1973): 45–95.

[104] Pauline Maier, "The Origins and Influence of Early American Local Self-Government," in *Dilemmas of Scale in America's Federal Democracy*, ed. Martha Derthick (New York, NY: Cambridge University Press, 1999), 77; Derthick, "How Many Communities? The Evolution of American Federalism," in Derthick, *Dilemmas of Scale*, 131; Hyman, "Federalism," 914.

As with taxation, services provided and the basis for them varied broadly between localities. For a good summary of the debate in the literature between Hartog – and the rise of police power on the one hand, and Novak – and the persistence of the commonwealth ideal on the other hand, see John, "Governmental Institutions," 374.

[105] Robin L. Einhorn, *Property Rules: Political Economy in Chicago, 1833–1872* (Chicago, IL: University of Chicago Press, 1991), 16. The phenomenon of "privatization" has been studied most thoroughly in Chicago. For examples of a similar process in New York City, see Eugene P. Moehring, *Urbanism and Empire in the Far West, 1840–1890* (Reno, NV: University of Nevada Press, 2004), and Stephen Diamond, in *Journal of Legal Studies*, 12, no. 2 (June 1983): 201–40. For an example of the way privatization is put to use in a more recent setting toward racialized ends, see Carl V. Harris, *Political Power in Birmingham, 1871–1921* (Knoxville, TN: University of Tennessee Press, 1977).

"Privatism" replaced conceptions of public good with a framework that more closely resembled shareholders voting their interest in a corporation. The city was divided into a series of districts defined by the special assessments each was prepared to fund. At its height, the reigning principle was that public improvements should be measured by their impact on property values and that those who stood to benefit directly should finance the improvements. The value of a citizen's votes was measured by the number of shares he controlled. Property ownership determined the citizen's equity stake. Fairness, as measured by the return that property owners received for their special assessment dollar, displaced democracy as the reigning principle. Property owners were treated as investors who deserved to get what they were willing to pay for in the way of municipal services.[106]

There was little room for independent or discretionary action by municipal officials – what some might call politics. Independent action by elected officials was virtually synonymous with corruption in this scheme. This privatized system minimized the redistribution of resources by avoiding general taxation and held those providing the services accountable by yoking the delivery of a service to its purchasers in transparent fashion.[107]

Chicago's "bridge wars" during the 1840s illustrate the shift from city-wide collective decision making, with its attendant redistributive impact, to more privatized methods. In 1837, Chicago had only one bridge over the river that divided the city into northern and southern halves. While northern residents lobbied for much-needed repairs and additional bridges, those on the south side of Chicago wanted to destroy the one existing bridge. Remarkably, the southerners persuaded the City Council to do just that in 1839. Fearing that the Council would reverse its decision, a crowd gathered before daylight the next morning and took matters into their own hands – chopping the bridge to pieces.[108]

This passion was fueled by profit, not engineering. Because the bridge was replaced by a ferry that could only carry one wagon at a time, it was now prohibitive for Indiana farmers to ship their grain to distributors located across the river. Rather, they began to patronize the middlemen, who increasingly frequented the southern portion of Chicago. Financing was not the issue, as northern business men pledged sufficient funds to build multiple crossings. Rather, the redistribution of economic

---

[106] Einhorn, *Property Rules*, 6–14, 76–77. On privatism generally, see ibid., chap. 3.
[107] Ibid., 15, 84, 125.
[108] Ibid., 58.

advantage, facilitated by the citywide decision making, was the real object of this debate.[109]

By 1849, that decision-making process had changed. Special assessments ensured that if property owners ponied up, bridges, or other public works, would be built. South Siders could no longer use their votes to obstruct North Side economic development under the guise of protecting the City's general welfare. Special assessments promoted a privatized city comprised of districts that paid for what they got.[110]

Even this highly privatized, localized system retained a role for public officials, albeit a supporting one. Aldermen became facilitators. They cut through the required paperwork and were often central to achieving consensus among neighborhood property holders. Public officials also facilitated financing, going so far as to offer private citizens loans in order to complete projects. Most significantly, municipal law and the criminal justice system sought to spread the cost of improvements equitably among all who benefited. Under the reign of special assessments, the City estimated the value of all improvements. Costs were distributed based on these calculations. The city also enforced assessments, which was essential to the success of the whole system. This method of matching individual benefits to costs financed miles of paved roads, sidewalks, and bridges during the 1840s and 1850s.[111]

In Chicago's privatized system, the costs of decision making became more apparent as Chicago grew and the same street was dug up time and again, first for water pipes, next for the gas company, despite the fact that the street had just been paved. Demands for greater coordination, a Supreme Court ruling that ordered the City to mix general revenues with special assessments in many cases, and the rise of wealthy landowners who had only marginal ties to the City, brought an end to this phase of Chicago's development by the Civil War. Nor could the special assessment method be adapted to all of Chicago's services. Water was handled by both private corporations and independent commissions. Fire service, which was promoted by insurance companies, was handled on a citywide basis. But even when decisions were made on a citywide basis, there was a broad consensus that economic development and business promotion was good for the city and its citizens.[112]

[109] Ibid., 58–59.
[110] Ibid., 60.
[111] Ibid., 91, 106–110.
[112] Ibid., 44–49, 134–35, 151, 170, and Chap. 6 generally; Moehring, *Urbanism and Empire*, 360, 367.

Chicago in the 1840s was emblematic of the fiercely localistic political culture that quickly turned to private solutions whenever possible. It reacted to prodigious growth by subdividing the burgeoning city into neighborhoods and special assessment districts. Property holding became a proxy for citizenship in many instances – and citizenship, in turn, resembled investment in a joint business venture. Even at the local level, Americans did not turn to government because they liked it. Americans turned to government because their vision of private, local, and individual autonomy could not operate without it – especially if they hoped to turn a profit. Americans also turned to government because the commonwealth tradition continued to animate appeals to collective action.

THE PERSISTENCE OF "RECIPROCAL GOOD FEELING": ADAPTING THE COMMONWEALTH IDEAL

Even at the peak of Chicago's privatized regime, the commonwealth conception retained its grasp – especially when it was applied to external funding from the federal government. Reacting to President Polk's 1846 veto of omnibus legislation that contained funding for Western internal improvements, Chicago hosted the River and Harbor Convention of 1847. Polk questioned whether commonwealth principles could be applied on a national scale. Democrats had long opposed national internal improvements. Strict construction of the Constitution, Polk insisted, was essential to combat the inevitable tendency in large, complex societies for the government "to embrace objects for the expenditure of the public money which are local in their character, benefiting but few at the expense of the common Treasury of the whole." Logrolling, Democrats argued, was the result of commonwealth principles applied to communities too large to truly share anything in common.[113]

Chicagoans may have worried about South Side subsidies to the North Siders, but they had no problems embracing Eastern subsidies to the Western development in the United States. The 10,000 delegates from nineteen different states who assembled in Chicago for the River and Harbor Convention in 1847 agreed. The thousands of citizens from

---

[113] Einhorn, *Property Rules*, 61–67; Polk, "Veto Message," August 3, 1846, in, *A Compilation of Messages and Papers of the Presidents, 1789–1987*, ed. James D. Richardson, 10 vols. (Washington, D.C., GPO) 4:460–66, available online at http://www.heinonline.org/, quoted in Einhorn, *Property Rules*, 69.

Chicago who joined them well understood that the explosive growth of their city depended on federal assistance. Federal funds had dredged the harbor that now served as a gateway to Lake Michigan and beyond. The Illinois and Michigan Canal owed its existence to a federal land grant. Westerners viewed these and the projects that Polk vetoed in the River and Harbor bill as the very kinds of stimulus to *national* economic development that would knit the nation together. Nor did partisan divisions deter this consensus. Democratic congressmen from northern Illinois, Stephen Douglas and John Wentworth, broke with their fellow Democrat, Polk, on the veto. Whigs heartily welcomed their support.[114]

Sixteen years later, in the midst of the Civil War, Westerners gathered again in Chicago for the National Ship Canal Convention. This time, Democrats did not have to anguish about choosing between their party and their sectional interests. They demanded their fair share of federal largesse. Not surprisingly, their brief for a canal that would connect the Mississippi and the Great Lakes rested on military defense. But the broader rationale that delegates articulated turned on national economic development. As the bipartisan "committee on statistics" put it, Westerners had voted for appropriations to protect Eastern ocean-going commerce. "[N]ow they have a right to demand, as a matter of justice and reciprocal good feeling, that appropriations shall be made for *Lake* commerce." Harkening back to the earliest arguments for a postal service, a broad constitutional interpretation of commerce, and every national internal improvement project, the committee insisted that such a ship canal "would establish, between the East and the West, closer commercial and political affiliations, and forge a chain which no convulsion could sever."[115]

In dozens of states and hundreds of localities, Americans displayed few qualms about government intervention into the economy or social relations at the local level. Legal historians have demonstrated the disparity between America's ideological commitment to *laissez-faire* and the pragmatic uses Americans found for states and localities, especially when they promoted economic development. The expanding franchise

---

[114] Einhorn, *Property Rules*, 61, 69, 71–75.

[115] Ibid., 188; Committee on Statistics for the City of Chicago, *The Necessity of a Ship-Canal between the East and the West* (Chicago, IL: Tribune Co., 1863; Ann Arbor, MI: University of Michigan Library, 2005), 41, 45 available online at http://name. umdl.umich.edu/ajq1175.0001.001, quoted in Einhorn, *Property Rules*, 189. For a good discussion of sectional interest in Western internal improvements, see Goodrich, *Government Promotion*, 45–46.

pushed the American polity toward liberal *laissez-faire* understandings of the political economy. That economy, however, especially on
the state and local levels, was still penetrated by frequent government
intervention.[116]

Entrepreneurial interests focused their attention on local and state
government precisely because resistance to government initiatives was far
lower at these levels. Political opportunities were often greater at the local
level. Ambitious politicians like DeWitt Clinton, for instance, resigned
from the U.S. Senate to become mayor of New York City. Politics was
built from the local level up. It was designed to preserve flexible options
for politicians to cater to local needs.[117]

Expensive high profile projects like the Erie Canal inspired other public projects and demonstrated that the General Government was not
needed to achieve grand results. States and municipalities, however, were.
They were the most likely source of capital in a rapidly expanding nation.
As William H. Seward told his colleagues on the Senate floor, states had
acted to hasten internal improvements because "a great and extensive
country like this has need of roads and canals earlier than there is an
accumulation of private capital within the state to construct them." States
also dwarfed corporations in size and borrowing capacity. And states and
localities were far more willing to wait for returns on their investment – a

---

[116] See for example, Nash, *State Government and Economic Development*; Paul W. Gates,
History of Public Land Law Development (Washington, D.C.: Public Land Law Review
Commission/ Government Printing Office, 1968); and Colleen A. Dunlavy, *Politics
and Industrialization: Early Railroads in the United States and Prussia* (Princeton, NJ:
Princeton University Press, 1994), as summarized by John, "Governmental Institutions,"
376.
   Forrest McDonald has noted that the vigorous defense of states' rights did not mean
that states and localities were passive when it came to promoting their own economic
development. Forrest McDonald, *States' Rights and the Union: Imperium in Imperio,
1777–1876* (Lawrence, KS: University Press of Kansas, 2000), 122. Sidney Fine has
argued that although there was no coherent philosophical rationale that justified government intervention into the economy, there was certainly plenty of ad hoc intervention.
*Laissez Faire and the General-Welfare State: A Study of Conflict in American Thought,
1865–1901* (Ann Arbor, MI: University of Michigan Press, 1956). Richard McCormick
confirms this and notes that Democrats, though more wary of state intervention, were
eager to participate in distributive policies as well. Richard L. McCormick, "The Party
Period and Public Policy: An Exploratory Hypothesis," *Journal of American History*, 66,
no. 2 (September 1979): 287. "The idea of mixed economic activity," Kermit Hall notes,
"in which government intervenes in the private marketplace to serve the public good, better captures the law's impact on the antebellum economy than does strict laissez-faire."
Magic Mirror, 88.
[117] Sellers, *Market Revolution*, 37–40.

crucial prerequisite in an economy where competitive financial gains were
easily extracted by exploiting natural resources quickly.[118]

Even though the "commonwealth" idea animated public intervention
into the economy most frequently at the state and local levels, entrepreneurs and politicians tested the General Government regularly. Clinton and
Gouverneur Morris sought funding for a canal connecting New York to the
West as early as 1811. But the Erie Canal, like many of the other major internal improvements, was ultimately funded by sources closer to home.[119]

"One did not mobilize and discipline scattered resources merely by
exhorting government to keep its hands off." Nor did states and localities
have the fiscal resources, administrative structure, skills, or discipline to
plunge into development directly. Local government lacked the expertise,
administrative structure, and discipline to build and staff huge projects
directly. But they could and did serve as a fiscal and legal catalyst in meeting community needs. Underpinning the whole system was a widespread
popular faith in the power of enhanced economic development to serve
community needs. Although states had little capacity to administer programs directly, they could and did harness the law to assign functions to
the market.[120]

They used their substantial fiscal capacity as well. States made direct
capital investments in the construction and maintenance of transportation facilities. Following the lead of New York, several states constructed
canals in the 20s and 30s, hoping to emulate the Erie Canal's fabulous
success. Of the $59 million spent on canals before 1834, the vast major-
ity of the funds came from state governments. They paid for an even
higher percentage of the $72 million in canal construction over the next
ten years. Overall, state and local governments financed $425 million
of internal improvements before the Civil War. By comparison, the federal government's cash contribution was paltry, although it did provide
important technical assistance and all-important land grants to the states.
By the 1850s, states were pursuing similar strategies, with a newer technology – the railroad. Between 1866 and 1873, states approved over 800

[118] Goodrich, *Government Promotion*, 7–8, 10, 45; *Congressional Globe*, Senate, 31st
Cong., 1st sess., 851, available online at http://memory.loc.gov/ammem/amlaw/, quoted
in Goodrich, *Government Promotion*, 9.
[119] Hall, *Magic Mirror*, 94; Goodrich, *Government Promotion*, 36.
[120] Hurst, *Law and the Conditions of Freedom*, 17; Scheiber, "At the Borderland," 746,
748–49. Scheiber has emphasized the direct involvement of states in transportation funding, planning, and administration, a series of interventions that had more direct redistributive effects than Hurst suggests. Scheiber has also emphasized the egalitarian values
that accompanied many of these capital projects.

proposals that granted local aid to railroad companies, and state courts upheld this use of government authority. Between 1840 and 1880, largely as the result of transportation subsidies and stock subscriptions, local indebtedness increased from $25 million to $840 million.[121]

Beyond internal improvements, states performed a dizzying array of functions that supported economic development, including regulating waterways for both fishing and navigation, developing harbors, overseeing labor relations, and enforcing the phalanx of laws related to slavery. States distributed tangible largesse to favored groups and localities including land, water, and mineral resources, in addition to subsidies and tax credits. State governments also distributed a vast array of fiscal and legal benefits that included tax exemptions for corporations and limited liability privileges. Between 1812 and 1830, for instance, Vermont granted manufacturers tax exemptions in order to promote that sector of the economy. While most of these reforms favored business – like the establishment of limited liability for shareholders in corporations – pressure from Democratic legislators resulted in bankruptcy laws that eased the plight of debtors.[122]

States also played an active role in banking and insurance. Besides providing access to credit and currency, banks were a crucial source of revenue for the states. Fiscal benefits were derived in two ways. States taxed banks; but they also invested in banks, a policy that yielded significant returns in some cases. By the 1830s, banks provided more than half of state revenue. Besides these direct mechanisms for enhancing balance sheets, states used banks as a crucial source of public credit. This was an effective means of carrying out public obligations while avoiding government taxing and spending.[123]

[121] Scheiber, "Federalism and the American Economic Order," 90–91; Cayton, *Frontier Republic*, 132–153; Sellers, *Market Revolution*, 44; Goodrich, *Government Promotion*, 268; Morton Keller, *Affairs of State: Public Life in Late 19th Century America* (Cambridge, MA: Belknap Press of Harvard University Press, 1977), 165; Charles W. McCurdy, "Justice Field and the Jurisprudence of Government-Business Relations: Some Parameters of Laissez-Faire Constitutionalism, 1863–1897," *Journal of American History*, 61, no. 4 (March 1975): 981.

[122] Scheiber, "Public Rights and the Rule of Law," 226; Scheiber, "Federalism and the American Economic Order," 88, 90; Hall, *Magic Mirror*, 96, 101. For a good review of this literature, see Robert A. Lively, "The American System: A Review Article," *Business History Review*, 29, no. 1 (March 1955), 81–96. See also, Fine, *Laissez Faire*, 20–23, and Handlin and Handlin, *Commonwealth*.

[123] Hall, *Magic Mirror*, 97; Richard Sylla, John B. Legler, and John J. Wallis, "Banks and State Public Finance in the New Republic," *Journal of Economic History*, 47, no. 2 (June 1987): 393–99, 402.

Antebellum politicians had few qualms about using state and local resources to achieve the broadly popular developmental goals of society. They were eager to seek the public good through private mechanisms. What's more, because of the competitive framework in which they operated, states often had little choice: if they sought more restrictive policies, private corporations were happy to take their business elsewhere. One scholar has aptly labeled this interventionist, decentralized, economic policy making system, one of "rivalistic state mercantilism." Though the national government's prerogatives in the field of contract law were boldly asserted by the Marshall Court early in the century, the antebellum Supreme Court left the states largely in control on matters of economic significance. This left ample opportunity for national legislative intervention, but Congress preferred to let dormant powers rest.[124]

The constraints that states faced were ultimately self-imposed. Many of the projects pursued by the states were risky at best. As public officials cut deals necessary to garner political support, projects became unwieldy. Too many projects competed for too little business. Added to the inevitable corruption of such fast-paced development, the very conception of publicly funded public works was tarnished. By the 1850s, a number of Western states passed constitutional prohibitions against state-funded internal improvements. In Indiana, even Whigs, such as Schuyler Colfax, soured on state-financed internal improvements. "When we look back upon the scenes of excitement through which our State has passed," Colfax reflected, "when we remember that so enthusiastic were the people in favor of the mammoth system ... it does seem as if now in our cooler moments, with the results of that infatuation in full view before us, we should so act as to prevent, if possible, their repetition." In this context, chartering private railroad corporations seemed to be a far better alternative.[125]

It was in the quest to protect the community's morals that local government seemed most willing to sacrifice individual liberty for the sake of the public welfare. We have already encountered the intensity of this moral fervor in the Sabbatarian effort to halt mail delivery. Localities did

---

[124] McCurdy, "Justice Field," 970; Scheiber, "Federalism and the American Economic Order," 71–86.

[125] Larson, *Internal Improvement*, 196–221; Goodrich, *Government Promotion*, 138–149; *Debates and Proceedings of the Convention for the Revision of the Constitution of the State of Indiana*, 2 vols. (Indianapolis, IN: A.H. Brown, Printer, 1850; Ann Arbor, MI: University of Michigan Library, 2005), 1:653, available online at http://name.umdl.umich.edu/aew7738.0001.001, quoted in Larson, *Internal Improvement*, 216.

not devote all of their energy to internal improvements in the first half of
the nineteenth century. They were equally active in policing community
standards. Local government actively intervened to promote the health
and safety of their citizens, using regulation and judicial interpretation to
fight fire and disease.[126]

Public morality was a central objective of criminal, municipal, and police
regulation in the first half of the nineteenth century. It was deeply rooted in
Anglo-American common law and broader conceptions of ordered governance. Common law and statutory offenses included "adultery, fornication,
solicitation, incest, bigamy, polygamy, bestiality and sodomy ... keeping
bawdy houses, publishing obscene prints and writings, obscene speech,
indecent exposure and all acts of 'gross and open lewdness' ... Sabbath-
breaking, profane swearing, blasphemy, and corpse stealing and dissec-
tion ... common gaming houses, disorderly alehouses or inns, mountebank
stages, cockfighting, and 'every public show and exhibition which outrages
decency, shocks humanity or is contrary to good morals.' " Connecticut
statutes included provisions for dealing with " 'lascivious carriage and
behavior,' drunkenness, unauthorized and foreign lotteries, horse racing
and wagering, billiard tables, playing cards (or selling them) for money,
circuses, horse and animal shows, theatrical exhibitions, and other indecent displays: 'games, tricks, plays, shows, tumbling, rope dancing, puppet
shows, or feats of uncommon dexterity or agility of body.' "[127]

In a small world of face-to-face dealings, the presumption was that
this "well-regulated society" matched its laws to community standards.
By the beginning of the nineteenth century, most states had passed laws
to deal with the vaguely defined categories of "rogues, vagabonds, common beggars, and other idle, disorderly and lewd persons." It was up to
judges, magistrates, and the police to define these categories. The proper
use of liquor was policed carefully as well. State licensing provided the
first line of defense here, with local ordinances, criminal codes, and the
common law filling in the gaps.[128]

[126] Novak, *The People's Welfare*, chaps. 2, 6.
[127] Ibid., 151–52; Joel Prentiss Bishop, *Commentaries on the Criminal Law*, 4th edn (Boston, MA: Little, Brown, 1868), 1:545–50, cited in Novak, *The People's Welfare*, 155; Public Statute Laws of the State and Connecticut (1830), c. 1, 268–76, quoted in Novak, *The People's Welfare*, 155.
[128] Novak, *The People's Welfare*, 170, 173; "An Act for suppressing and punishing Rogues, Vagabonds, common Beggars, and other idle, disorderly and lewd persons," *The General Laws of Massachusetts, 1780–1822*, ed. Asahel Stearns and Lemuel Shaw, 2 vols. (Boston, MA, 1823), 1 (1787), c. 54, 322, quoted in Novak, *The People's Welfare*, 167.

Cities and towns were far more cautious when it came to providing welfare. Nevertheless, during times of severe crisis, such as the Panic of 1819, larger cities offered aid. Cincinnati, for instance, established soup kitchens for the poor. By 1823, it had spent so much on poor relief that road repairs had to be postponed. The State of Ohio created a system of poorhouses in response to the crisis and its critically depleted resources.[129]

* * *

One did not have to travel beyond the boundaries of the United States to encounter a strong public presence at the national level. The Post Office played a crucial role in stimulating communications. That network, in turn, helped to create a national polity. At the national and state levels, the legal system established boundaries within which markets could operate in predictable fashion, often sacrificing individual rights for developmental objectives. The legal system stimulated a national language that could encompass local dialects. States and localities actively intervened in the market to promote economic development and enforce community social norms. In all of these venues, public action reinforced private activity that promoted the general welfare but limited central administration. An informed citizenry would protect against metropolitan domination and state building. A legal system that promoted self-executing contracts between individuals minimized the need for bureaucratic decision making. Public subsidies to stimulate private enterprise – especially at the local level – ensured that the market served all Americans. And public statutes that enforced social norms embraced by local communities ensured that the need for enforcement remained minimal. The easy merger of public and private, however, would not have been possible had Americans failed to embrace a conception of their own history as exceptional. Endowed by nature, God, and the market, it appeared to many that the kind of social turmoil and war that so often had engulfed European nation states, could easily be avoided with the proper intermixture of public and private endeavor.

[129] Cayton, *Frontier Republic*, 126–27, 142.

7

Restoring "Spontaneous Action and Self-Regulation": Civil War and Civil Society

For most Americans living in the mid-nineteenth century it was not government, but rather civil society, that forged the nation. The market, religion, and America's unique history (which kept government at bay, they believed) created national unity. The Civil War severely tested those assumptions, at the same time that it propelled the consolidation of both the Union and Confederate states. Yet the dream of a nation united through economic, social, and religious ties died hard. Many of the public institutions created during the war were quickly swept aside.

This was not the case, however, in the voluntary and private sectors, where the Civil War proved to be a catalyst for national consolidation. A nationalizing economy quickly outgrew the locally oriented political structures that Americans fiercely reconstructed in the wake of the Civil War. Ultimately, the changes wrought by the market proved to be insurmountable. Class conflict and capitalist consolidation forced the hand of those who had hoped the nation was exempt from these historical forces. As we will see in Chapter 8, however, the very nature of the national market that emerged in the last third of the nineteenth century was, in no small part, the result of actions taken by a national legal infrastructure that even today remains largely out of sight.

"A DIVINE HARMONY BETWEEN PRIVATE ADVANTAGE AND THE PUBLIC GOOD": BRINGING ORDER, NATURALLY

One reason that Americans eschewed the visible trappings of government was their abiding faith in a liberal system of exchange. Many believed that this was the real source of national social cohesion. Although they viewed the market as a natural phenomenon, most Americans were also convinced that their form of governance was exceptionally poised to maintain the delicate balance between market and polity. For all the chaos it produced, some saw in the market a remarkable capacity to bring order to a society without restricting the rights of individuals. Nature had endowed human beings with the ability to reason and to pursue their own self-interest, advocates of classical liberalism insisted.[1]

That citizens would act in their self-interest was a fundamental principle that society could count on – a predictable social phenomenon in an otherwise unknowable range of human behavior. Moving from observations about economic activity in the late seventeenth century to more systematic generalizations, students of classical liberalism characterized society as a "natural and spontaneously ordered system." Work integrated society and did so without government or religious coercion. Drawing upon Adam Smith and other students of the economy, claims for the power of market exchange in early America transcended economics.[2]

Nevertheless, a well-ordered market depended on a relatively unqualified conception of private property; this, in turn, required that government define and enforce this right (often at the expense of the rights of the community). The relative strength of the "rule of law" compared to other aspects of state capacity, its growing embrace of market relations during the first half of the nineteenth century, and its self-conscious insistence that judicial decisions were based on the natural order of things, provided just the kind of protection for liberal exchange that Smith envisioned. Although it did not do so "naturally,"

---

[1] These views were grounded in the work of Scottish moral philosophers such as Thomas Reid and John Locke. See Daniel Walker Howe, *Making the American Self: Jonathan Edwards to Abraham Lincoln* (Cambridge, MA: Harvard University Press, 1997), 21–22, and Herbert Hovenkamp, *Enterprise and American Law, 1836–1937* (Cambridge, MA: Harvard University Press, 1991), 74–77.

[2] Thomas Jefferson, for instance, was more interested in the economy's capacity to order society without imposing the visible trappings of government than the market's potential to produce wealth. Joyce Appleby, *Liberalism and Republicanism in the Historical Imagination* (Cambridge, MA: Harvard University Press, 1992), 1, 288, 337. On claims for market exchange, see for example, the writings of Thomas Cooper, editor of *The Emporium of Arts and Sciences*, cited in Steven Watts, *The Republic Reborn: War and the Making of Liberal America, 1790–1820* (Baltimore, MD: Johns Hopkins University Press, 1987), 226–28. On Adam Smith, see Jerry Z. Muller, *Adam Smith in his Time and Ours: Designing the Decent Society* (New York, NY: Free Press, 1993).

the law secured property rights and bolstered the productive power of the economy.[3]

Classical prescriptions for the political economy emerged full-blown during the Jacksonian period. They influenced economic, political, and legal thought for the rest of the century. As one scholar put it, classicism "offered a complete view of human nature, an ethical defense of self-interest, a theory of political economy that seemed to work – and all of this in a package that complemented American moral and religious beliefs about independence and individual freedom." Those who subscribed to these views generally opposed state intervention, but not because they feared that the government would be captured by the masses. Rather, they insisted on exposing the many ways in which government intervention had privileged the wealthy – through corporate charters that granted monopoly privileges to special interests, for instance. Political leaders like Andrew Jackson, and advocates of substantive due process like Thomas Cooley, sought to make the machinations of government more transparent in order to ensure that no group was privileged over another. These men had never lost sight of the many ways in which government intervened in the market, and they were determined to forge equal access, which often meant eliminating state-subsidized privilege, like the Bank of the United States. Underlying the notion that the government should not play favorites was an abiding faith that the market, left untrammeled, worked pretty well.[4]

Economic exchange would serve as the predominant unifying force in America's classical political economy. Writing in 1926, John Maynard Keynes characterized this perspective best, pointing to the idea "of a divine harmony between private advantage and the public good." It was political economists like Adam Smith, Keynes argued, who supposed that "by the working of natural laws individuals pursuing their own interests with enlightenment in [a] condition of freedom always tend to promote the general interest at the same time!" Through the alchemy of the market, society could be unified through the individual actions of its members without any intrusive state mechanisms.[5]

---

[3] Christopher L. Tomlins, *Law, Labor, and Ideology in the Early American Republic* (New York, NY: Cambridge University Press, 1993), 78; Harry N. Scheiber, "At the Borderland of Law and Economic History: The Contributions of Willard Hurst," *American Historical Review*, 75, no. 3 (February 1970): 747.

[4] Hovenkamp, *Enterprise and American Law*, 1–5, quotation on 2.

[5] John Maynard Keynes, "The End of Laissez-Faire" (Dubuque, IA: Wm. Brown Reprint Library, 1927 [1926]), 10–11.

Most nineteenth-century citizens did not need Keynes or Smith to discover this phenomenon. Democrats embraced *laissez-faire* most heartily. They subscribed to a rich tradition of classical liberal thought that enshrined exchange epitomized by the market. The very commerce and the entrepreneurial spirit that threatened to overrun the ideal republic with self-interest in the late eighteenth century was now glorified as natural, God-given, and a sure path to progress. Whigs were not opposed to using market means to promote acquisition. They, however, were more concerned about the political and social ramifications of an increasingly acquisitive populace.[6]

At stake here was nothing less than the shift from a polity-centered view of social interaction to a "sociocentric" view – the recognition of civil society as the dominant force in people's lives, rather than their obligations as citizens. Behavior that had once been considered selfish was now shown to produce not only private, but public benefits. Because it supposedly operated outside of the polity and was considered to be a natural phenomenon, the market could invoke voluntary action where government coercion would surely fail. Social order was the "natural" byproduct of these myriad uncoordinated exchanges. The best way to serve the public good was through the pursuit of private interest in the market place – *laissez-faire*. Natural laws were at play in the market, and they were best left "untrammeled," as Democratic partisans liked to put it. This was the case in mid-century Chicago, where services like bridges and roads were subjected to market tests rather than political deliberation. Politicians ostensibly facilitated these market decisions, but they did so only when they steered clear of "natural" market mechanisms.[7]

There was precious little role for government in this view of man, nature, and the public good. As Walt Whitman wrote, "the wealth and happiness of the citizens can hardly be touched by the government. ... Men must be masters into themselves and not look to Presidents and legislative bodies for aid. In this wide and naturally rich country the best government is

[6] Baker, *Affairs of party*, 144.
[7] Michael J. Lacey and Mary O. Furner, "Social Investigation, Social Knowledge, and the State: an Introduction," in *The State and Social Investigation in Britain and The United States*, ed. Michael J. Lacey and Mary O. Furner (New York, NY: Cambridge University Press, 1993): 20; Appleby, *Liberalism and Republicanism*, 336; Jean H. Baker, *Affairs of Party: The Political Culture of Northern Democrats in the Mid-Nineteenth Century* (Ithaca, NY: Cornell University Press, 1983), 144; Robin L. Einhorn, *Property Rules: Political Economy in Chicago, 1833–1872* (Chicago, IL: University of Chicago Press, 1991).

indeed that which governs the least." The reign of natural law, however, was distinctly grounded in local practice for many Democrats. They started with the postulates of Edmund Burke, who emphasized the sanctity of established institutions, existing arrangements, and the power of local custom. God's law may have been universal, but it had to be adapted to each particular environment, just as the common law had accrued wisdom through experience and use over the years.[8]

CHRISTIANITY:
"THE GREATEST BOND OF CIVIL SOCIETY"

The exchange nexus that lay at the heart of classical liberalism never existed in isolation. Its history was embedded in a powerful moral and religious context that tempered market exchange in nineteenth-century America. For John Locke, individual liberty was bounded by divinely established natural law. It placed the obligation of duty in the path of unfettered freedom. The American Enlightenment was also influenced by Scottish common sense philosophy. Men like Adam Smith assumed that individuals were part of broader communities that held them morally accountable for their actions.[9]

An ethically alert liberalism was eventually subsumed in its less sensitive and far hardier *laissez-faire* evil twin. Nevertheless, belief that the economy might act as a neutral and natural arbiter proved powerful. As Americans transformed the land, creating farms and expanding the transportation infrastructure, it was easy to believe that "enterprise built character."[10]

---

[8] *Brooklyn Eagle*, July 26, 1847, http://www.brooklynpubliclibrary.org/eagle/, cited in Baker, *Affairs of Party*, 144; Baker, *Affairs of Party*, 181, 195.

[9] James T. Kloppenberg, "The Virtues of Liberalism: Christianity, Republicanism, and Ethics in Early American Political Discourse," *Journal of American History*, 74, no. 1 (June 1987): 16–18. On the fit between natural rights, individualism, and nineteenth-century Protestantism, see also Muller, *Adam Smith and his Time*, and Sidney Fine, *Laissez Faire and the General-Welfare State: A Study of Conflict in American Thought, 1865–1901* (Ann Arbor, MI: University of Michigan Press, 1956), chap. 1.

[10] Kloppenberg, "Virtues of Liberalism," 29; Appleby, *Liberalism and Republicanism*, 4. But for a brief moment at the end of the eighteenth century, the tradition of liberalism "based on responsibility rather than cupidity" had survived, and according to Kloppenberg, "its memory has lingered into the present." "Virtues of Liberalism," 27. For a far less sanguine view of the fit between religion and capitalism in the early nineteenth century, see Charles Sellers, *The Market Revolution: Jacksonian America, 1815–1846* (New York, NY: Oxford University Press, 1991), 29, and Paul E. Johnson, *A Shopkeeper's Millennium: Society and Revivals in Rochester, New York, 1813–1837* (New York, NY: Hill and Wang, 1978).

Religion remained a powerful bond for nineteenth-century Americans. To be sure, with the demise of established churches, denominations competed for members, ultimately stooping to commercial techniques and commodification to "sell" their brand of God. Battles over religion also stimulated their share of divisions in the American social fabric. At work, at home, in politics, and even in business, however, Protestantism remained the central faith that bound the nation together. Christianity, Leveret Saltonstall of Massachusetts pronounced in 1820, "is the greatest bond of civil society, and we ought to take great care not to lessen its influence." The Second Great Awakening, afoot as Saltonstall spoke, democratized American churches and made each member the judge of his or her own relationship to God.[11]

Only self-restraint and individual morality reined in self-interest. Little wonder that the clergy were preoccupied with morality. Lyman Beecher captured the tension between enterprise and morality in a sermon from 1812 entitled "A Reformation of Morals Practicable and Indispensable." Dark forces, from "avarice" and "cupidity," to drunkenness threatened "productive labor," according to Beecher. The profit motive, too often, was all that mattered: "If their fields bring forth abundantly, if their professions be lucrative, if they can buy and sell and net gain, it is enough." Only integrity, "industry, and temperance, and righteousness" could counter this force. Fortunately, in Beecher's opinion, the growing evangelical movement promised to remedy the situation. The nation was "beginning to learn righteousness," as the Great Awakening spread.[12]

Fledgling social scientists took pride in their rational and objective empiricism. Yet here too, religious beliefs prevailed. Henry Carey is a good example. Carey mobilized mountains of facts to support his pro-tariff

[11] R. Laurence Moore, *Selling God: American Religion in the Marketplace of Culture* (New York, NY: Oxford University Press, 1994); *Journal of Debates and Proceedings in the Convention of Delegates, Chosen to Revise the Constitution of Massachusetts, Begun and Holden at Boston, November 15, 1820, and Continued by Adjournment to January 9, 1821* (Boston, MA: *Daily Advertiser*, 1853), 207, cited in Gordon S. Wood, The *Radicalism of the American Revolution* (New York: Knopf, 1992), 331. On the variety of religions experience in this period, and its influence on political and social thought, see Daniel Walker Howe, *What Hath God Wrought: The Transformation of America, 1815–1848* (New York, NY: Oxford University Press, 2007).

[12] Wood, *Radicalism*, 333; Lyman Beecher, *A Reformation of Morals Practicable and Indispensable: A Sermon Delivered at New-Haven on the Evening of October 27, 1812*, 2nd edn, (Andover, MA: Flagg and Gould Printers, 1814), in Early American Imprints, 2nd Ser. II (American Antiquarian Society and NewsBank, 2004, [doc. no. 30834]), http://infoweb.newsbank.com/, 4–5, 9, 23, 29, cited in Watts, *Republic Reborn*, 120.

position. One critic begrudgingly acknowledged that Carey "made protection convincing by bringing to its support a vast armament of facts and figures, more exhaustive than anything previously assembled." To support protectionism, he "evolved a system of economic thought which seemed to glorify the coldly materialistic appeal of the industrialist with the triumphant idealism of the philosopher."[13]

Yet Carey considered the Whig Party's blend of ideas and interests to be part of a divine plan. Positive science would articulate and carry out that plan. Evidence was useful insofar as it confirmed God's harmonious design. Brown University president Francis Wayland popularized the connection between God's will and English classical economics. A minister, Wayland published *Elements of Political Economy* in 1837. It went through eighteen editions by 1860. Wayland argued that government had no right to interfere with the way individuals chose to use their property, challenging even the state's right to construct internal improvements.[14]

By the 1830s, many Americans shared common cultural predispositions toward relatively unbridled enterprise, Protestant moralism, and a belief in the power of the individual. Classical economic thought placed a special emphasis on removing barriers from entry into the marketplace and leveling any government-stimulated privilege that might advantage special (and specially connected) interests. These features were fused in the cult of the "self-made man." It celebrated a domestic ideal that protected Americans from some of the excesses of the public world of markets and political parties. As sectional tension mounted, and as powerful regimes continued to repress slaves, Indians, and women, the United States was hardly free from conflict. Yet the belief that religion, the market, and the pursuit of individual self-interest would lead to social harmony was palpable.[15]

---

[13] Carey turned from ardent supporter of *laissez-faire* to the tariff's most prolific promoter a decade before the Civil War. Malcolm Rogers Eiselen, *The Rise of Pennsylvania Protectionism* (PhD diss., University of Pennsylvania, 1931; repr., Philadelphia, PA: Porcupine Press, 1974), 272–73, 277, cited in Drew Evan VandeCreek, *"Make It National!": Economic Expertise and the Development of the Progressive Economic Policymaking System, 1890–1933* (Ph.D. diss., University of Virginia, 1996), 82. See also, Martin J. Burke, *The Conundrum of Class: Public Discourse on the Social Order in America* (Chicago, IL: University of Chicago Press, 1995), 115, and Dorothy Ross, *The Origins of American Social Science* (New York, NY: Cambridge University Press, 1991), 44–47.

[14] VandeCreek, *"Make it National!"* 81; Hovenkamp, *Enterprise and American Law*, 74–77; Fine, *Laissez Faire*, 11, 52–53.

[15] Watts, *Republic Reborn*, 11. For a view that pits democratization against the spread of capitalist enterprise, see Sellers, *Market Revolution*, 29–32.

Americans subscribed to a belief in social harmony that so dominated public discourse as to virtually constitute a national bond in and of itself. The market filled out God's divine plan. Many believed that the natural laws that produced individual wealth also best served public purposes. Writing in 1837, *Democratic Review* editor John O'Sullivan stated that "the natural laws which will establish themselves and find their own level are the best laws. The same hand was the Author of the moral, as of the physical world; and we feel clear and strong in the assurance that we cannot err in trusting, in the former, to the same fundamental principles of spontaneous action and self-regulation which produce the beautiful order of the latter." Government was notably absent from this harmonious mix.[16]

The impact of *laissez-faire*, the association of natural law with God's divine plan, the presumption that both this plan and natural law led to social harmony, and faith in America's progress and its exceptional place in history, eroded what perhaps had stood as the most fundamental republican premise: that citizenship defined men and that virtuous men placed the public good ahead of private interest. Whereas America's revolutionary elite had imbibed the classical assumption that social divisions were the product of government abuses, their successors attributed these divisions to society itself – and the many opportunities for private gain that a dynamic economy created. It was society, without government interference, that ultimately would harmonize these divisions. If the merchant as citizen had no role in classical republican thought, classical liberalism "returned the favor." It downplayed the relative importance of citizenship in social relations.[17]

---

[16] John O'Sullivan, "Introduction," *The United States Magazine, and Democratic Review* 1, no. 1 (October 1, 1837): 7, in American Periodicals Series Online, 1740–1900 (Proquest, [doc. no. 331683851]), http://proquest.umi.com/pqdweb, cited in Baker, *Affairs of Party*, 144.
   Frederic Bastiat and Henry Carey made much of the natural harmony of economic laws. See for instance, Fine, *Laissez Faire*, 8, and Eiselen, *Rise of Pennsylvania Protectionism*, 277. Eiselen writes, "He made protection respectable by substituting for the taint of self-interest the picture of it as an instrument of a beneficent Providence working in accord with the universal harmonies of natural law." But the belief in such harmony was hardly confined to narrow intellectual circles in the first half of the nineteenth century in America.

[17] Wood, *Radicalism*, 5; Appleby, *Liberalism and Republicanism*, 288–89. See also Daniel Walker Howe, *The Political Culture of American Whigs* (Chicago, IL: University of Chicago Press, 1979), 82. Howe discusses how the Whig view of the origin of government is based on an organic view of society. Behind every government there is a society, and government owes its existence to this society. Society entails much more than just people. It is hierarchy, property, and various traditions.

WARTIME CONSOLIDATION

The Civil War, the quickened pace of industrialization that followed, and open class conflict severely tested the enduring myth of America's exceptionalist status and social harmony. Producers and intellectuals alike challenged the exceptionalist myth. Perhaps because America's progress no longer seemed self-evident, those who defended the natural laws shored up these barricades. Safeguarding a political economy that allowed these natural laws to prevail was the last line of defense against the ravages of historical change. If the founders had achieved the perfect balance with natural law, the emergence in the United States of the kinds of conflict that Europe had grappled with for centuries surely portended decline.[18]

The Civil War shredded the political and social fabric of the nation, severely challenging America's perceived exemption from the stream of history. For both Northerners and Southerners, the Civil War was the central event in their lives. The exigencies of war produced two armed camps that dwarfed the old Republic in power and scope. The Confederacy developed into an even more powerful government than the Union, eventually crafting all-encompassing economic and social controls. Because the Confederacy could not rely on well-developed private industrial and transportation sectors like the North's, it depended far more heavily on state mandates, planning, and coordination. The Confederacy not only regulated manpower, it also assumed direct control over some private factories. It impressed their products as well as those of Southern farmers, and even went so far as to construct state-owned plants when the private sector fell short.[19]

The Confederate States of America passed a remarkably sweeping law granting the government the power to confiscate a broad range of property owned by citizens who were deemed to be disloyal. And unlike the

---

Morton J. Horwitz notes "the conviction that only a decentralized political and economic system could increase wealth, while maintaining freedom and avoiding the tyranny of European statism was a central tenet of American exceptionalism. *The Transformation of American Law, 1870–1960: The Crisis of Legal Orthodoxy* (New York, NY: Oxford University Press, 1992), 66.

[18] Ross, *Origins of American Social Science*, 53.

[19] Foner, *Reconstruction*, 34; Richard Franklin Bensel, *Yankee Leviathan: The Origins of Central State Authority in America, 1859–1877* (New York, NY: Cambridge University Press, 1990), 95–98, 233. On the relationship between popular will, national sentiment, and military strategy, see Gary W. Gallagher, *The Confederate War* (Cambridge, MA: Harvard University Press, 1997).

Union, the Confederate government enforced its law. The Sequestration Act required that families turn over property of members living in the North. Bankers and businesses had to open their books in order to reveal property of Northern business partners or clients. The Act also declared that debts owed to a Northerner had now to be paid to the Confederate government.[20]

The Union also bulked up. Conscription swelled the army from 16,000 to millions. Public officials found during the war that they could assert themselves and national power as never before. Elected officials used the political opportunity provided by one-party rule to push through a series of internal improvements. The Homestead Act, passed in 1862, offered settlers free land in return for the guarantee that they farm it. In his 1863 annual message, President Lincoln proudly reported that 1.4 million acres (of 3.8 million allocated) had been settled. The Land Grant College Act provided the foundation of the state higher education system. Massive land grants for the nation's first transcontinental railroad, completed in 1869, propelled the federal government into the race to build (and, eventually, overbuild) a national rail network.[21]

The Union actively intervened in the economy, taking advantage of Southern secession to erect a political economy that swept aside barriers to a national economy. It built the financial and physical infrastructure to support that nationalizing economy. The Union created a national banking system by levying a prohibitive tax on state-chartered bank notes, quickly driving the latter out of the money supply and forcing state banks into the national system. The Union also suspended the gold standard in

---

[20] Daniel W. Hamilton, *The Limits of Sovereignty: Property Confiscation in the Union and the Confederacy during the Civil War* (Chicago, IL: University of Chicago Press, 2007), 5–7.

[21] Foner, *Reconstruction*, 21; Morton Keller, *Affairs of State: Public Life in Late 19th Century America* (Cambridge, MA: Belknap Press of Harvard University Press, 1977), 17; Theodore Sky, *To Provide for the General Welfare: A History of the Federal Spending Power* (Newark, NJ: University of Delaware Press, 2003), 264–66. Heather Cox Richardson, *The Greatest Nation of the Earth: Republican Economic Policies during the Civil War* (Cambridge, MA: Harvard University Press, 1997) elaborates on above legislation as does Williamjames Hull Hoffer, *To Enlarge the Machinery of Government: Congressional Debates and the Growth of the American State, 1858–1891*(Baltimore: Johns Hopkins University Press, 2007), 1–88. On the preexisting military capacity that facilitated in some ways, and hampered in others, the ability to fight such a bloody war, see Mark R. Wilson, *The Business of Civil War: Military Mobilization and the State, 1861–1865* (Baltimore, MD: Johns Hopkins University Press, 2006), and Wayne Hsieh, *The Old Army in War and Peace: West Pointers and the Civil War Era, 1814–1865* (Ph.D. Diss., University of Virginia, August 2004).

the winter of 1861–2 and toyed with foreign exchange controls. When suspension of the gold standard undermined credibility in the Treasury Department's notes, the Union legislated that irredeemable paper currency (the greenback) be accepted as legal tender.[22]

This monetary policy affected the value of every contractual agreement in the Union, touching the lives of all Americans. Representative Samuel Cox of Ohio summed up the impact when he observed that "the party in power ... have established a paper-money banking system, under the control of the General Government, which concentrates power in the Administration ... and gives it control over the property and pecuniary interests of the people." Through its monetary policy and by financing debt through bond sales, the Union created powerful sets of client groups.[23]

Congress consolidated other sets of interests as it employed public policy to fulfill the Republican vision of capitalist westward expansion. The Homestead Act, the Land Grants College Act, and subsidies to the railroads created powerful groups with vested interests in national public policy. Thomas Scott, vice president of the Pennsylvania Railroad, was a good example of such an interested party. Scott helped organize military transport in his role as Assistant Secretary of War. His wartime experience sensitized him to the value of federal charters and subsidies. Aid to railroads was the most visible link between the central government and a powerful interest group. Congress approved massive land grants and public debt devoted to the construction of a transcontinental railroad. Starting with the Union Pacific in 1862, the General Government eventually assisted twelve lines. The railroads quickly turned this land into capital. Undergirded by a higher tariff, these policies raised government support for economic development from the local to the national level.[24]

The railroad boom began in the 1830s, as public frustration with corruption tempered the demand for government-funded internal improvements. The railroads, like stage coaches, were viewed as private, not public,

---

[22] Bensel, *Yankee Leviathan*, 10–11, 124, 152, 162.

[23] *Congressional Globe*, 38th Cong., 1st Sess., June 2, 1864, 2683, in Library of Congress, *A Century of Lawmaking for a New Nation: U.S. Congressional Documents and Debates, 1774–1875*, http://memory.loc.gov/ammem/amlaw/, quoted in Bensel, *Yankee Leviathan*, 162.

[24] Keller, *Affairs of State*, 11; Samuel P. Hays, *The Response to Industrialism, 1885–1914*, (Chicago: University of Chicago Press, 1957), 18–19. See also, Samuel R. Kamm, *The Civil War Career of Thomas A. Scott* (Ph.D. diss., University of Pennsylvania, 1939).

services. Yet few roads could legitimately be deemed purely "private." Government subsidies ranged from county and municipal financing, to tax exemptions, and federal tariff breaks on the cost of iron. It was not until the mid-1840s that private investors began to claim that railroads were profitable private investments. By then, the constitutional prohibitions against state financing for internal improvements were in full force. Ironically, at the very time that Northern states denounced public financing, Southern states took up the call.[25]

The Civil War revived the demand for federal subsidies to transcontinental lines. But it did little to change the image of railroads as the prototypical private enterprises. In fact, the transcontinental lines were built with the presumption that the General Government could not be trusted with the railroads. This did not prevent the General Government from passing legislation that granted millions of acres and rights of way through the public domain to dozens of railroad projects between 1850 and 1857. While advocates of a transcontinental line could not agree upon the route, few believed that any could be built without substantial federal aid.[26]

In 1862, and then again in 1864, Congress legislated subsidies for the Union Pacific in two forms. Over the course of construction, the federal government provided loans of approximately $60 million. It also granted 24 million acres of land to the Union Pacific. Although loans were eventually phased out, the land grants increased for subsequent transcontinental lines. Before the land grants were terminated, roughly 130 million acres of public land had been transferred to the roads.[27]

Because so much of the subsidized mileage ran through the territories rather than existing states, aid was provided directly to the railroads. This, combined with the sparse population in these territories and the physical barriers that had to be surmounted, muted traditional states' rights arguments against such a large-scale national commitment. Charles Francis Adams was correct when he pointed out that "in any other country"

---

[25] John Lauritz Larson, *Internal Improvement: National Public Works and the Promise of Popular Government in the Early United States* (Chapel Hill, NC: University of North Carolina Press, 2001), 226, 229–33, 236–39; Carter Goodrich, *Government Promotion of American Canals and Railroads, 1800–1890* (New York: Columbia University Press, 1960), 169–70. See also Steven W. Usselman, *Regulating Railroad Innovation: Business, Technology, and Politics in America, 1840–1920* (New York, NY: Cambridge University Press, 2002), 9–13.

[26] Goodrich, *Government Promotion*, 172–73, 176–79, 204.

[27] Ibid., 183–85, 197.

the first transcontinental line "would have been built by the Government as a military road." In the United States, with its tradition of "mixed enterprise," the boundary between public and private remained murky, obscuring the significant investment made by the General Government in a national transportation infrastructure.[28]

Interest groups did not wait for the government to come calling. Where it did not create client groups outright, the federal government established strong incentives for groups to organize and seek government support. The exigencies of war stimulated a variety of economic groups to organize along national lines. It was during the Civil War that the first national trade associations emerged, including the American Bureau of Shipping, the National Association of Wool Manufacturers, and the National Paper Manufacturers Association.[29]

Whether seeking support, or looking to avoid the pain of taxes and tariffs, Americans recognized a host of shared interests because of the General Government's more active role in the Civil War economy. Even if they were untouched by subsidies or contracts, most Americans had a stake in the Union's fiscal policies. Congress raised tariffs annually, reaching 1864 levels that were almost half the value of the goods subject to duty. While a high tariff policy funded the General Government well into the twentieth century, the income tax, which ultimately supplanted the tariff as the Government's key source of revenue, was also introduced during the Civil War. By the end of the War, 10 percent of all Union households were paying an income tax.[30]

The loosely connected patchwork of charitable and service organizations that we call the voluntary sector today was the focus of a great deal of energy during the Civil War. Voluntary agencies turned to the federal government at an unprecedented rate. Calling upon Lincoln to ask Congress to create a Bureau of Emancipation, Henry W. Bellows pressed the claims of the National Freedmen's Relief Association of New York. "It is the magnitude, not the nature of the work, that appalls us, and drives us to government for aid and support," Bellows explained. Although the

[28] Ibid., 199, 201; U.S. Congress, *Report of the Commission and of the Minority Commissioner of the United States Pacific Railway.* Bound with 50th Cong., 1st sess., (Sen. Ex.Doc.51/3. Serial Set 2505), in Serial Set Digital Collection, available from LexisNexis Congressional, http://web.lexis-nexis.com/congcomp/, quoted in Goodrich, *Government Promotion,* 201.

[29] Keller, *Affairs of State,* 11.

[30] W. Elliot Brownlee, *Federal Taxation in America: A Short History* (New York, NY: Cambridge University Press, 1996), 24, 27; Foner, *Reconstruction,* 469.

War hardly ended the great tension between central and local power in America, the Union did manage momentarily to narrow this divide. One student of Reconstruction has suggested that the expansion of federal power during the war "might be called the birth of the modern American state." The American Freedmen's Aid Societies of New York, Boston, and Philadelphia, for instance, served as the model for the federal Freedmen's Bureau. And the Grand Army of the Republic, which originated as a fraternal organization, emerged as a powerful advocate of veterans' pensions following the War.[31]

The crucible of war also helped consolidate and nationalize several voluntary organizations that served as models for those seeking to improve society without federal intervention. The United States Sanitary Commission was the foremost example of these. It was established in 1861 by Boston, New York, and Philadelphia elites in order to care for Union troops wounded in battle. It soon assumed a far larger role in the war, acting "not merely as a Board of Military Health, but as a kind of Cabinet & Council of War – boldly seizing anomalous power, advising the Government, & seeking to influence the men, military and otherwise who command the position," bragged Bellows, who along with Frederick Law Olmstead guided the Commission. Efforts to convert some of the Commission's momentum into a permanent public body failed, culminating in the brief and unhappy life of the National Board of Health, established in 1879.[32]

While program expansion at the national level represented the most striking departure from precedent, a number of the states also moved forcefully to expand programs during the Civil War decade. State expenditures in the North increased from three to six times their earlier rate

---

[31] *Senate Executive Documents*, 38th Cong., 1st sess., no. 1 (1863) (serial 1176) in Serial Set Digital Collection, quoted in Robert H. Bremner, *The Public Good: Philanthropy and Welfare in the Civil War Era* (New York, NY: Knopf, 1980), 113; Foner, *Reconstruction*, 23; Keller, *Affairs of State*, 12; Theda Skocpol, *Protecting Soldiers and Mothers: The Political Origins of Social Policy in the United States* (Cambridge, MA: Belknap Press of Harvard University Press, 1992), 17.
    Bremner reveals that Bellows claims authorship of the letter in correspondence with Jonathan Sturges on December 12, 1863. *Public Good*, 114n2.
[32] Henry W. Bellows to C.A. Bristol, September 13, 1861, Bellows Papers, Mass. Historical Society, quoted in George M. Fredrickson, *The Inner Civil War: Northern Intellectuals and the Crisis of the Union*, Illini Books edition (Urbana, IL: University of Illinois Press, 1993; New York: Harper & Row, 1965), 108 also cited in Keller, *Affairs of State*, 10; Barry D. Karl and Stanley N. Katz, "The American Private Philanthropic Foundations and the Public Sphere, 1890–1930," *Minerva*, 19, no. 2 (June 1981): 241.

in many states. The volume of legislation increased as well. Led by New York, Pennsylvania, and Wisconsin, states raised their spending on schools and consolidated urban school districts. Public expenditure on education tripled between 1860 and 1870.[33]

The War reconstituted the very basis on which the Republic had been founded. The three Civil War amendments to the Constitution nationalized the concept of citizenship. By ending slavery, the Thirteenth Amendment placed the responsibility for defining citizenship squarely in national hands. The due process clause of the Fourteenth Amendment enshrined the principle of equality before the law for all citizens of the United States. Again, the final arbiter of the law would be the General Government. The Fifteenth Amendment, seeking to shore up the privileges of national citizenship, ensured the right to vote, regardless of race and place. These bold legal claims to national authority followed a war that had already vastly expanded the authority of the executive branch, from the President's capacious war powers to the assertive use of the general welfare clause of the Constitution.[34]

The amendments were pushed through by ideologically charged Radical Republicans who were willing to harness the enhanced wartime power of the Union to seek equality for the nation's newly enfranchised citizens. The "one body of men about Washington who had any positive affirmative ideas," one Senator-elect discovered when he arrived in Washington, "... were the vanguard of the radical party. They knew exactly what they wanted to do, and were determined to do it." And why not? These men had seen positions that were chastised as extreme when introduced – opposition to slavery's expansion, emancipation, and arming black troops – move to the center of the Republican Party on their watch.[35]

While proposals for large-scale land redistribution failed to gain broad political support, Radical Republicans pushed through the Civil Rights Act in 1866. It spelled out the rights that all citizens were to enjoy without regard to race. The Freedmen's Bureau, established a year

[33] Keller, *Affairs of State*, 110–11, 134. See also John Teaford, *The Unheralded Triumph: City Government in America, 1870–1900* (Baltimore, MD: Johns Hopkins University Press, 1984).

[34] On the general welfare clause, see Sky, *To Provide for the General Welfare*, chap. 11.

[35] Foner, *Reconstruction*, 238–39; O.M. Roberts, "The Experience of an Unrecognized Senator," *Texas State Historical Association Quarterly*, 12, no. 2 (October 1908): 132, http://www.tshaonline.org/shqonline/, quoted in Foner, *Reconstruction*, 238. This journal is now known as *Southwestern Historical Quarterly*.

earlier, sought to protect freed slaves in their dealings with hostile local authorities, to ensure that they were educated, and to introduce a workable system of free labor. These measures represented a monumental shift in the degree to which the General Government was permitted and, in the case of the Bureau, encouraged, to intervene directly in the lives of citizens.[36]

There is no better measure of the radical nature of these programs than the reaction of Andrew Johnson who vetoed both (the case of the Civil Rights Bill veto was overridden by Congress). Johnson labeled the Freedmen's Bureau an "immense patronage" that the nation could simply not afford. There was no precedent for Congress's providing schools, economic relief, or purchasing land for "our own people," Johnson continued. The aid threatened the "character" and "prospects" of freedmen by implying that they did not have to work for a living. Johnson's message vetoing the Civil Rights Bill warned that it constituted "another step, or rather stride, toward centralization, and the concentration of all legislative powers in the National Government."[37]

The Civil War also illuminated two conflicting views of property within the Union government itself. Whereas the Confederacy pursued confiscation wholeheartedly, this issue was hotly contested within the Union, and the final legislation, combined with lackluster enforcement, suggests that the debate ended in a draw. Advocates of energetic confiscation, like Charles Sumner and Benjamin Wade, grounded the authority to confiscate in the long-standing power of the state to define property rights and alter them in the public interest. This view had prevailed through the first third of the nineteenth century and, as we have seen, shaped legal decisions right up to the Civil War. Opponents of broad powers to confiscate cited Joseph Story, James Kent, and John Marshall, to warn against the dangers of legislative confiscation. They successfully capped the growing tendency on the part of the state and federal courts to defend the liberal premise that property entailed an individual right to be protected, regardless of the public costs. This "individualized, rights-oriented conception of property," as one scholar put it, gained increasing traction.[38]

---

[36] Foner, *Reconstruction*, 142, 244; Bensel, *Yankee Leviathan*, 122–23.

[37] Andrew Johnson, "Veto Message," February 19, 1866, in *A Compilation of Messages and Papers of the Presidents, 1789–1897*, ed. James D. Richardson, 10 vols. (Washington, D.C.: GPO, 1896), 8:3599, 3611, available online at http://www.heinonline.org/, cited in Foner, *Reconstruction*, 247.

[38] Hamilton, *The Limits of Sovereignty*, 7–9, quoted on 9.

"SOMETHING AKIN TO PATRIOTISM AND PUBLIC SUPPORT": FORGING THE SENTIMENTAL STATE

Radical reform after the Civil War was tightly circumscribed. While all Republicans could agree that deploying national power to put down a rebellion was a legitimate use of the state, and while most Republicans agreed that the state should promote economic development – through the tariff and internal development – a hard boundary was drawn between these functions and social or humanitarian reform. The collapse of Reconstruction efforts to promote the rights of African Americans underscored just how firm that boundary could be. The principles of *laissez-faire*, violated repeatedly in matters of political economy, proved more formidable when it came to social reform. Liberal Republicans opposed even those development-oriented exceptions to *laissez-faire*, arguing for free trade and against government aid to commercial enterprises.[39]

To better accommodate this diversity of views, the Republican Party moved away from its ideologically charged moorings. It adapted an "organizational" mode of politics that emphasized distribution of tangible benefits and patronage. In New York, the power of radical Republicans was usurped by "Stalwart" political operator Roscoe Conkling. The wartime governor of Pennsylvania and his radical supporters were supplanted by Senator Simon Cameron's machine. It, in turn, relied on the support of the Pennsylvania Railroad and urban machines for political clout. While portions of the financial mechanisms used to finance the war remained (not to mention the debt it created), virtually all of the military, and much of the domestic, policy-making apparatus was quickly dismantled. Eventually, the Fourteenth Amendment became a powerful weapon used by corporations to protect their right to due process. But the Supreme Court did little else to capitalize on the three constitutional Amendments that came out of the war.[40]

The Civil War created a powerful set of emotional attachments that outlived its institutional legacy. Veterans' pensions were the best example of the divergence between sentiment and state capacity. Ultimately, the

---

[39] Fredrickson, *Inner Civil War*, 193–4.
[40] Foner, *Reconstruction*, 484–85; Morton Keller, "The Politicos Reconsidered," review of *Politics and Power: The United States Senate, 1869–1901*, by David J. Rothman, *Perspectives in American History* 1, (1967): 406–7; See also, Richard L. McCormick, "The Party Period and Public Policy: An Exploratory Hypothesis," *Journal of American History*, 66, no. 2 (September 1979): 279–298.

federal government lavished huge sums on its Civil War veterans, creating a "precocious social spending regime." However, the basis for this spending was the sacrifice that veterans had made to preserve the Union. The small size of the federal bureaucracy, and the decentralized nature of the partisan support that drove the expansion of Civil War pensions, did not lead to a centralized bureaucracy, as had been the case with the French Revolution. Rather, in the United States, the democratic mass mobilization was one "without centralized bureaucratic controls."[41]

For all its expense, Civil War pensions never achieved the redistributive coherence of some European programs. Many poor people were excluded. Despite the strong sentimental base of support for veterans, by the 1890s benefits had little to do with brave service to country. Administrative discretion was built into the system, and partisan social networks determined the outcome of many of these decisions. Consequently, money flowed to the politically advantaged, rather than to those with the greatest need or those who had sacrificed the most during the war. The pension system reflected the localized nature of late nineteenth-century distributive politics. It also reflected the tension between popular support for a vaguely defined sense of obligation to the nation's veterans and the limited administrative apparatus Americans were willing to construct in order to fulfill that obligation.[42]

Despite the "precocious" nature of the national financial commitment, two mitigating factors distinguished the entire program. First, pension spending was inextricably bound to the Republican policy of tariff protection. Continuing the tariff after debts were paid produced large surpluses. Politically, the pension system was designed to channel those surpluses directly to the Republican Party's mass base. Second, pensions did not represent an open-ended commitment. Despite the ingenious schemes devised to broaden eligibility, the necessity of establishing some link to the Civil War meant that pensions would eventually end as the Civil War generation died off.

Rampant corruption and partisan advantage associated with the system tainted the prospects for subsequent social reform. Progressive Era efforts to create old-age pensions were consistently attacked on the grounds that they would sustain patronage politics. Like the Civil War itself, veterans' pensions created deep-rooted social attachments that left a powerful legacy. But they did so without enhancing the administrative

---

[41] Skocpol, *Protecting Soldiers and Mothers*, 163, 103, 105.
[42] Ibid., 135.

or redistributive capacity of the federal government, despite the strong emotions attached to the war.[43]

Sacrifice and commitment did trigger a surge of nationalism. "The issue of the war marks an epoch by the consolidation of nationality under democratic forms," announced the newly founded *Nation* magazine. "This territorial, political, and historical oneness of the nation is now ratified by the blood of thousands of her sons. The prime issue in the war was between nationality one and indivisible, and the loose and changeable federation of independent States." Calling itself the "National Union" party after the war, Republicans placed both words at the center of their party's platform for decades to come. In 1876, they reminded voters that "the United States of America is a nation, not a league." In 1884, the platform read, "The people of the United States, in their organized capacity, constitute a Nation and not a mere confederacy of States."[44]

Calls for unity abounded at the abstract level of political theory. There was a pervasive desire to restore order, particularly among the nation's eastern elites. They were willing to sacrifice individual liberty in order to do so. Even Ralph Waldo Emerson, one of the nation's leading exemplars of romantic individualism before the war, trimmed his sails in response to the national crisis. In 1837, Emerson discouraged aspiring politicians, urging that they "quit the false good and leap to the true, and leave governments to clerks and desks." By 1862, Emerson had reversed field, claiming that "government must not be a parish clerk, a justice of the peace. It has, of necessity, in any crisis of the state, the absolute powers of a dictator." Emerson and other staunch defenders of the individual came to endorse a far larger role for institutions during the war. That support endured beyond 1865.[45]

---

[43] Ibid., 59.

[44] Democratic Nationality, *The Nation*, 1, no. 2 (July 13, 1865): 38, online at The Nation Archive, accession number 14197233, http://search.ebscohost.com/, cited in Foner, *Reconstruction*, 24–5; Eldon J. Eisenach, *The Lost Promise of Progressivism* (Lawrence, KS: University Press of Kansas, 1994), 50; Donald Bruce Johnson and Kirk H. Porter, eds., *National Party Platforms, 1840–1972* (Urbana, IL: University of Illinois Press, 1973), 53, 74, cited in Eisenach, *Lost Promise of Progressivism*, 50.

[45] Fredrickson, *Inner Civil War*, vii–xiii, 177–86; Ralph Waldo Emerson, "The American Scholar: An Oration Delivered Before the Phi Beta Kappa Society, at Cambridge, August 31, 1837," in *The Complete Works of Ralph Waldo Emerson*, vol. 1, *Nature, Addresses, and Lectures* (Boston, MA and New York, NY: Houghton Mifflin, 1904; Ann Arbor, MI: University of Michigan Library, 2006): 107, http://www.hti.umich.edu/e/ emerson/, quoted in Fredrickson, *Inner Civil War*, 176–77.

Still, most intellectuals refused to give up on more "natural" mechanisms for restoring and ensuring social order. In place of a crumbling religious hierarchy, men like Charles Francis Adams, Jr., turned to science. He discovered Comte while recuperating from the War. "I emerged from the theological stage, in which I had been nurtured, and passed into the scientific," Adams wrote. Adams applied the science of economics to an analysis of the railroad situation in the United States, eventually chairing the Massachusetts Board of Railroad Commissioners. Another strain of science, Herbert Spencer's brand of Social Darwinism, guided Adams's attitude about government intervention. He believed that the evolutionary process should not be hurried by coercive regulation. For others, charitable organizations filled the gap. The voluntary sector, which raised its stature during the War, benefited from the continued support of the thousands who had pitched in during the crisis.[46]

Americans also hoped that Northern capital could heal a divided nation. Reunion, by the 1880s and 1890s, was increasingly romanticized. A close reading of popular plays and novels in this period reveals a pattern quite different than the Southern "lost cause" cult or Grand Army of the Republic attitudes. In these sentimentalized versions of reunion, Southern belles, though properly dedicated to the cause of their Confederate brothers and fathers, ultimately succumbed to the romantic appeal of Northern gentlemen. Gendering the capitulation served the dual purpose of depoliticizing the reunion and reinforcing the Victorian ideal of separate spheres. Suffering the indignity of poverty, Southern aristocracy was often rescued by Northern capital. Nor was the romanticized appeal of reunion play-going and novel-reading confined to the Northern upper classes. Reform groups grounded in the middle and lower classes claimed the moral high ground, and with it, the promise of sectional reconciliation.[47]

The strong sectional differences that drove Americans to war were replaced by wonder at former enemies uniting. Dedicating the first Northern memorial to Confederate soldiers who died during the war, former Confederate politician Wade Hampton told the crowd gathered in Chicago in 1895 that "the scene presented here to-day is one that could

---

[46] Charles Francis Adams, *An Autobiography, 1835–1915, with a Memorial Address delivered November 17, 1915, by Henry Cabot Lodge* (Boston, MA and New York, NY: Houghton Mifflin, 1916), 179, quoted in Fredrickson, *Inner Civil War,* 206; Fredrickson, *Inner Civil War,* 206; Bremner, *Public Good,* 207.

[47] Nina Silber, *Romance of Reunion: Northerners and the South, 1865–1900* (Chapel Hill, NC: University of North Carolina Press, 1993), 94, 121, 171, and chap. 4 generally.

not be witnessed in any country but our own." By that time, Memorial Day was being celebrated in both the South as well as the North. Blue-Gray reunions were held on a regular basis, starting in the early 1880s. As one Northern vet put it in 1894, "There was no personal feeling between the men of the south and the men of the north. ... They were always pleasant to each other when they met." These men never reconciled the larger principles for which they fought. Those principles were muted, however, by the emphasis placed upon valor.[48]

Americans could agree that the War had been a heroic struggle for both sides. While the reality of sectional strife was not eradicated by such wishful thinking, romantic rhetoric did offer a template from which many Americans began to construct, for the first time, an emotional attachment to nation, as opposed to section or state. Ultimately, such attachments were forged in the crucible of wars against foreign enemies. Until the Spanish-American War and World War I, however, the West and the wilderness would have to suffice as subjects of national conquest and the incubator of national identity.[49]

In the meantime, men could sharpen their skills on the athletic field, particularly football fields. Coliseums like Harvard's Soldiers Field, donated by Henry Lee Higginson in honor of his comrades slain during the War, became the battleground for a new generation of elites. "The time given to athletic contests and the injuries incurred on the playing-field are part of the price which the English-speaking race has paid for being world-conquerors," boomed Henry Cabot Lodge. As Francis A. Walker argued in his Phi Beta Kappa address to Harvard in 1893, it was on the playing fields that "something akin to patriotism and public spirit is developed." He concluded that it was "a good thing that the body of students should now and then be stirred to the very depths of their souls; that they should have something outside themselves to care for; that they

---

[48] Wade Hampton, "Dedicatory Oration," in *Report of Proceedings Incidental to the Erection and Dedication of the Confederate Monument*, ed. John Cox Underwood (Chicago, IL: Wm. Johnston, 1896), 117, cited in Silber, *Romance of Reunion*, 1–2; Lecture by John Jenkins, Comerford Post Minutes, February 21, 1894, James Comerford Post 68 Records Collection, (Madison, WI), quoted in Stuart McConnell, *Glorious Contentment: The Grand Army of the Republic, 1865–1900* (Chapel Hill, NC: University of North Carolina Press, 1992), 190.

[49] John Pettegrew, "'The Soldier's Faith': Turn-of-the-century Memory of the Civil War and the Emergence of Modern American Nationalism," *Journal of Contemporary History*, 31, no. 1 (January 1996): 54; Fredrickson, *Inner Civil War*, 222. As Fredrickson notes, Theodore Roosevelt became the "living exemplar" of using a frontier experience as "one way to live 'the strenuous life' without actually going to war."

should learn to love passionately, even if a little animosity toward rivals must mingle with their patriotic fervor." Football would deliver some of the benefits of war with fewer casualties, but equal passion.[50]

At the root of this new source of loyalty was a manliness that could be shared across section and class. And while it might manifest itself most often on playing fields, this "cult of strenuosity" formed the basis of a new kind of national patriotism. It was Civil War veterans, both Northern and Southern, who best exemplified this ideal. "The great fatherhood of our country," orator Theodore Bean pronounced in 1888, "left a progeny North and South, whose loyalty to leaders, whose bravery in battle, whose industry and indurance, demonstrates the glory of our enheritance, and in the grand battles fought between ourselves, however unfortunate in some respects, reveals a manhood of the Republic, as now reunited, capable and willing to protect and defend the Union against the political powers of the earth." Within fifteen years, the Civil War had been transformed into an intra-squad game: costly due to the number of key injuries, but essential to forging a squad sufficiently united and strenuous to take on the real rivals.[51]

At all levels of government, both the ideological fervor and the willingness to abandon private and voluntary means to solve problems that accompanied it receded during the 1870s. The Civil War altered the terms of public discourse and provided highly visible examples of what an active General Government could accomplish. But these bold visions that expanded the government's reach were often dashed by social realities. In their wake, an abstract and sentimental commitment to reunion and strenuous calls for patriotism filled a gap that other nations had

---

[50] Henry Cabot Lodge, "Commencement Alumni Dinner Remarks," *The Harvard Graduates Magazine*, 5, no. 17 (September 1896): 67, quoted in Kim Townsend, *Manhood at Harvard: William James and Others* (New York, NY: W.W. Norton, 1996), 103; the Lodge remarks are also cited in Mark C. Carnes, "And to Think That it Happened on Mt. Auburn Street: Dr. James, Harvard, and the Making of Manhood," Review of *Manhood at Harvard: William James and Others*, by Kim Townsend, *Reviews in American History*, 25, no. 4 (December 1997): 594; Francis A. Walker, "College Athletics: An Address before the Phi Beta Kappa Society, Alpha, of Massachusetts at Cambridge, June 29, 1893," reprinted from *Technology Quarterly*, 6 (July 1893): 2–3, 6, 13, quoted in Fredrickson, *Inner Civil War*, 224; Fredrickson, *Inner Civil War*, 224.

[51] Kristin Hoganson, *Fighting for American Manhood: How Gender Politics Provoked the Spanish-American and Philippine-American Wars* (New Haven, CT: Yale University Press, 1998), 15–41; *Address of Theodore W. Bean of Norristown, Pennsylvania, Delivered at Seven Pines National Cemetery on Memorial Day, May 30, 1888, Under the Auspices of Phil Kearny Post No. 10, GAR of Richmond, Virginia* (Richmond, VA: 1888), quoted in Silber, *Romance of Reunion*, 169. See also Townsend, *Manhood at Harvard*.

addressed through administrative centralization. America's political institutions absorbed the lessons of the War slowly, if at all. This was not the case in the private sector and civil society.[52]

GETTING OUT OF THE "IMPROVEMENT" AND "DEVELOPMENT" BUSINESS: THE LEGACY OF LOCALISM AND VOLUNTEERISM

In spite of the wartime constitutional amendments, federalism provided a political device that allowed a diverse nation to settle its ethnic, religious, racial, and industrial differences without tearing itself apart. Confining these kinds of disputes to thousands of state and local venues helped the nation avoid the kind of gruesome experience it had just witnessed. The Civil War did not shatter a commitment to government that began at home. Community leaders still regarded property taxes as their own money. They watched its expenditure just as carefully as the funds they contributed to their church or local charity. Confining social provision to localities eased the distinction between public and private spheres.[53]

The Democratic Party challenged the enhanced power of the union. At the grass roots, Democratic voters in New York rioted in July 1863. They bridled at the Union's most blatant expansion of power – conscription. More formally, Democrats hammered away at themes that challenged high protective tariffs, aid to business, and any other efforts by the government to intervene in the economy. When Massachusetts Representative George Hoar proposed a federal labor commission it met opposition by both Democrats and Republicans. "Where shall we stop?" asked one Senator. "What is there in private life that shall be sacred from the intrusion of this Government?[54]

Democratic Party platforms after the War conceded little to the Republican theme of union. In 1880, the platform warned of "that dangerous spirit of encroachment, which tends to consolidate the powers of all the departments in one, and thus to create whatever be the form of government, a real despotism." In 1888 the Democratic Party's platform

[52] Keller, *Affairs of State*, 35. Richard Bensel argues that the Republican project, powerful as it was, was also self-limiting because of the ideological constraints that business elites placed upon use of the state. They were unwilling to go beyond its expanded role in finance and infrastructure., *Yankee Leviathan*, 14.
[53] Karl and Katz, "Foundation and the Public Sphere," 237, 241–42.
[54] Foner, *Reconstruction*, 32; *Congressional Globe*, 42nd Congress, 2nd Session, May 29, 1872, 4016, quoted in Foner, *Reconstruction*, 483.

called for "a plan of government regulated by a written Constitution, strictly specifying every granted power and expressly reserving to the States or people the entire ungranted residue of power."[55]

Integrally linked to the belief that central government threatened to extend too far into the civil sphere was the widespread perception that politics was corrupt. Not only did government fail to keep pace with an increasingly complex society, argued E.L. Godkin, it was run by men that most people did not trust. Expanding the scale and scope of government inevitably extended the possibilities for corrupt behavior. The political era that Mark Twain dubbed "the Gilded Age" for its worship of the material and rampant corruption certainly lived up to its reputation. Scholars have offered convincing structural explanations for the explosion of visible graft. Chief among them was the cozy relationship that emerged between interests and government during the Civil War and Reconstruction, and the rapid pace of development. Americans were willing to accept, indeed they demanded, state aid for ventures that ostensibly served the public good. But to many contemporaries, corruption appeared to be caused by the steep moral decline among public officials and businessmen alike.[56]

Particularly alarming was the blatant nature of some of this corruption. One California candidate promised in 1873 that: "If I am elected to the Legislature I shall serve as well as I can ... and if I should unfortunately steal anything, I will bring it down here to San Joaquin and divide it with you." Nor should his constituents worry that he was a novice. "I know how to steal; I can steal as well as any man, and I think that is the kind of man to send to Sacramento." Machine politics produced outrageous instances of corruption. Boss Tweed of New York was perhaps the most notorious. The "Tweed" Court House was a perfect example of the kind of padded expenses, sweetheart contracts, and outright embezzlement that party bosses thrived on. Estimated to cost $250,000, the final bill came in at over $13 million. The entire state of Pennsylvania was known for its corrupt ways. When Kansas earned a reputation for similar practices, it was dubbed the "Western Pennsylvania." In the South, where Reconstruction governments sought to rebuild, partisan wrangling and animus toward any measures that might improve the condition of African Americans

---

[55] Johnson and Porter, *National Party Platforms*, 56, 77, cited in Eisenach, *Lost Promise of Progressivism*, 51.
[56] Fine, *Laissez Faire*, 55.

combined with actual corrupt practices to tarnish efforts at state intervention for generations.[57]

The General Government was subject to the same pressures. In the Whiskey Ring scandals, Republican Party officials, internal revenue agents, and distillers conspired to rob the national government of millions of dollars in revenues. The Credit Mobilier scandal distributed shares of stock to influential public officials through a dummy corporation. It funneled excessive profits from the construction of the Union Pacific transcontinental line to shareholders. Among the office holders tainted by this scheme were House Speaker Blaine and Grant's Vice Presidents, Schuyler Colfax and Henry Wilson.[58]

The high visibility of corruption and its seemingly all-pervasive nature led a good number of Republicans to question the role of active government. Even the call for a merit-based civil service system may have owed more to the attempt to staff the government with men sufficiently trained in social science to leave well enough alone. Educated civil servants would know better than to meddle with the natural laws that strictly circumscribed the role of government. Liberal Republicans concluded that the best way to guard against corruption was strictly to limit the role of the state. This fit neatly with the precepts of Social Darwinism and *laissez-faire* to which many of them subscribed. One leading liberal, E.L. Godkin, stated the philosophy clearly: "The Government must get out of the 'protective' business and the 'subsidy' business and the 'improvement' and 'development' business. ... It cannot touch them without breeding corruption."[59]

---

[57] *Cincinnati Enquirer,* Oct 2, 1873, quoted in Mark Wahlgren Summers, *The Era of Good Stealings* (New York, NY: Oxford University Press, 1993), 3; Summers, *Era of Good Stealings,* 4; F. Munson to Benjamin H. Bristow, April 1876, in B.H. Bristow Papers, Library of Congress, quoted in Summers, *Era of Good Stealings,* 5.

    I experienced this legacy directly when I worked for the New York City Council President in the late 1970s. My office was housed in the "Tweed" Court House. It was a lovely setting, except that I had to cover my desk with plastic whenever it rained. I thought it odd that the banister was made out of iron until I learned that this was supposed to be marble. Tweed's contractors had at least painted the original white.

[58] Foner, *Reconstruction,* 468, 486.

[59] Edward Chase Kirkland, *Dream and Thought in the Business Community, 1860–1900* (Ithaca, NY: Cornell University Press, 1956; Chicago, IL: Quadrangle Books, 1964), 139–40, cited in Fredrickson, *Inner Civil War,* 209. Citations are to the Quadrangle Books edition; Fredrickson, *Inner Civil War,* 194; "The Moral of the Credit Mobilier Scandal," *Nation,* 16, issue 396 (January 30, 1873): 68, online at The Nation Archive, accession number 14107805, cited in John G. Sproat, *"The Best Men": Liberal Reformers in the Gilded Age* (New York, NY: Oxford University Press, 1968), 172–73, also cited in Foner, *Reconstruction,* 489.

Liberals pulled back from the experiment of the Civil War and Reconstruction. They agreed with Radical Republicans on the principle of state guarantees of civil and political equality but felt that state authority should stop there. Public authority was "by nature wasteful, corrupt, and dangerous." Ultimately, the California politician who ran on his ability to steal inspired a reaction like the bill proposed at the California constitutional convention of 1879. There, a Workingman's Party delegate introduced an article stipulating that: "There shall be no legislature convened from and after the adoption of this Constitution, ... and any person who shall be guilty of suggesting that a Legislature be held, shall be punished as a felon without benefit of clergy."[60]

The desire to improve society, the faith that professional techniques could apply science to society, and the need to insulate effective management from popular democracy continued to resonate with citizens. The Sanitary Commission provided a powerful model after the War for those who sought social reform without violating the natural law of the market. A good example was Louisa Lee Schuyler, who had gathered supplies for the Sanitary Commission in the New York area during the War. After the War, Schuyler organized the New York State Charities Aid Association. Like the Sanitary Commission, it was a semipublic group of local elites who inspected public institutions such as poorhouses and recommended reform based on "scientific" principles. This "charity organization society" model dominated work in social welfare well into the 1890s. It – rather than direct public provision – was the predominant legacy of Civil War mobilization in the field of social welfare. This ensured that the government did not penetrate a sphere preserved for civil society or introduce corrupt politics into decisions best left to those who were supposedly protected morally from such possibilities.[61]

---

[60] Harold M. Hyman, *A More Perfect Union: The Impact of the Civil War and Reconstruction on the Constitution* (New York, NY: Knopf, 1973), 533; Foner, *Reconstruction*, 492; Noel Sargent, "The California Constitutional Convention of 1878–9," California Law Review 6, no. 1, (November 1917): 12, http://www.heinonline.org/, quoted in Keller, *Affairs of State*, 114.

The Democratic Party quickly regained its national strength. This provided elite sanction for open and vigorous attack on the Republican vision of public policy. Martin Shefter, "Trade Unions and Political Machines: The Organization and Disorganization of American Working Class in the Late Nineteenth Century," in *Working-Class Formation: Nineteenth-Century Patterns in Western Europe and the United States*, ed. Ira Katznelson and Aristide R. Zolberg (Princeton, NJ: Princeton University Press, 1986): 248.

[61] Bremner, *Public Good*, 156–8; Fredrickson, *Inner Civil War*, 211–16.

If the Civil War shattered the myth that America was exempt from history, it is fair to say that Americans who were dedicated to the preservation of that myth did a remarkable job of gluing it back together in the aftermath of the War. The social upheaval caused by the War, although never entirely forgotten, was soon embalmed in the romance of reunion. The redistribution of income, wealth, and skills that might have resulted from active enforcement of the Civil War amendments to the Constitution was aborted by the quick return to local control in the South. The emotional attachment to the Union, as epitomized by the ever-increasing size of veterans' pensions, was realized through traditional patronage politics, not the creation of a more sophisticated administrative capacity. While some of the fervor for social reform remained, it was funneled into the voluntary sector where it did not threaten to drag the state into the cesspool of politics.

Though the memory of active government and social strife could not be entirely dismissed, the nation emerged from the Civil War with a far more diversified and impressive set of private and voluntary institutions through which to pursue its destiny. Thus, what might have been an unmistakable wake-up call from history could soon be dismissed by those anxious to preserve the myth of American exceptionalism as a political aberration in a world of natural law where politics played an exceedingly minor role. Because the War itself was a powerful economic stimulus to the Northern economy, some argued that once freed from political obstacles, social harmony bolstered by a booming economy would restore America's "natural" march toward progress. What could not be as easily dismissed was the unwelcome results that the market was beginning to yield in virtually every segment of society.

AMERICAN EXCEPTIONALISM: IT'S THE ECONOMY, STUPID

With Union expenditures soaring from 2 percent of GNP to a wartime average of 15 percent, those sectors of the economy most closely related to the mobilization expanded rapidly. Railroads profited the most, carrying troops and supplies at the same time that the roads were freed from competition. Meat packing thrived, as did New England's woolen mills. Wartime profits permanently altered the scale of industrial enterprises and the way in which they were financed. As one contemporary observer noted, "the sudden rise of great fortunes; the necessary concentration of vast capitals, public and private; the elevation of speculators and adventurers of every sort to the command of millions of money … all these brought new men and new dangers to the front."[62]

Phillip Armour was a good example. A grocer who moved into meat packing, Armour speculated heavily at the end of the Civil War. Betting that the price of pork would plummet, he sold futures at the going rate of $30 a barrel. With the Union victory, prices did dive, and Armour snapped up pork at $18 a barrel. He then delivered it at the contractual price for a hefty profit. This netted him $2 million – the capital he used to launch his systematic consolidation of the meat packing business in the 1870s.[63]

One factor that distinguished the United States from its industrial-ized counterparts was that its most dynamic period of private-sector expansion coincided with a relatively low point in its politics and state-initiated development. America's market economy now stood at the heart of the nation's exceptional promise. With politics mired in self-interest at best, and corruption at worst, the public sphere was sharply distin-guished from the private. The economy grew at an unusually high rate from the late 1860s through 1893. While immigration and population expansion accounted for some of this growth, the high per capita rate of growth suggests that large-scale increases in productivity were behind much of the economic boom. Despite economic stagnation in the South, the nation's industrial production rose 75 percent in less than a decade following the Civil War.[64]

Railroads led the way. More track was laid from 1865 to 1873 than had existed when the War began. By 1890, America had approximately 165,000 miles of railroad track in operation. Railroads also pioneered many of the techniques that came to characterize national corporations, including the public sale of stocks and bonds to raise huge pools of capital,

[62] Brownlee, *Federal Taxation*, 23; Foner, *Reconstruction*, 18; Simeon E. Baldwin, "Recent Changes in Our State Constitutions," *Journal of Social Science*, 10, (December 1879): 136, http://pao.chadwyck.com/home.do, cited in Foner, *Reconstruction*, 20.
[63] Daniel J. Boorstin, *The Americans: The Democratic Experience* (New York, NY: Random House, 1973), 320
[64] Louis Galambos, "State-Owned Enterprises in a Hostile Environment: The U.S. Experience," in *The Rise and Fall of State-Owned Enterprise in the Western World*, ed. Pier Angelo Toninelli (New York, NY: Cambridge University Press, 2000), 296; Louis Galambos and Joseph Pratt, *The Rise of the Corporate Commonwealth: U.S. Business and Public Policy in the Twentieth Century* (New York, NY: Basic Books, 1988), 26–27; Foner, *Reconstruction*, 461. On the private/public sector ratio and its implications for the political economy, see Colleen Dunlavy, *Politics and Industrialization: Early Railroads in the United States and Prussia* (Princeton, NJ: Princeton University Press, 1994).

a hierarchical managerial structure, the development of specialized tasks, division of labor in the workforce, and integrated systems for communicating and reporting information from far-flung operations.[65]

Railroads provided an important model for the growth of big business at the same time that they helped consolidate a national market. The economies of scale that manufacturers began to reap in the late nineteenth century meant little if the market could not absorb the vast quantity of goods that poured from shop floors. The transportation revolution lowered the cost of delivery and opened new markets for these goods. At the same time, the nation built a national communications network, crucial to the efficient management of far-flung operations and intercourse with distant markets. Between 1846 and 1866 the telegraph industry consolidated its operations in a virtual monopoly – Western Union – and expanded its operations across the entire nation. The telephone soon replaced messengers in urban areas; technical innovations reduced the cost and increased the circulation of newspapers; and advertisers began systematically to use magazines and newspapers to market consumer goods.[66]

After the Civil War, it was primarily individual entrepreneurs like Philip Armour who took advantage of these opportunities. By the 70s and 80s, a number of industries had begun to construct business empires that were national in scope. Armour, for instance, used the capital acquired at the end of the Civil War to move his operations to Chicago. He introduced an assembly-line approach to slaughtering and butchering livestock. He found a use for every part of the carcass. Perfecting and capitalizing on the introduction of refrigerated railroad cars, he soon bought and sold in a national market. Another industry that began to take advantage of a national market and the tremendous demand created by the completion of the nation's rail grid was steel. Creating a giant, Andrew Carnegie invested heavily in new technology and wrestled control of raw material away from suppliers. He even maintained his own fleet of steamships and company railroad.[67]

---

[65] Foner, *Reconstruction*, 461; Glenn Porter, *The Rise of Big Business, 1860–1910* (New York, NY: Crowell, 1973), 41; Alfred D. Chandler, *The Visible Hand: The Managerial Revolution in American Business* (Cambridge, MA: Belknap Press of Harvard University Press, 1977), 266–67

[66] Hays, *Response to Industrialism*, 7–8; Menachem Blondheim, *News over the Wires: The Telegraph and the Flow of Public Information in America, 1844–1897* (Cambridge, MA: Harvard University Press, 1994), 190–94. On the importance of communications and transportation generally, see also Howe, *What Hath God Wrought*.

[67] Boorstin, *The Americans*, 320; Porter, *Rise of Big Business*, 53–54.

John D. Rockefeller pioneered the use of the trust to combine a number of producers into a single firm in the oil industry and by 1880 had created Standard Oil, which controlled approximately 90 percent of the nation's refining capacity. Similar developments swept the sugar and tobacco manufacturing industries. Just as national manufacturing firms began to replace the local blacksmith, national – even international networks – of transportation and communications allowed farmers to sell to (and made them subject to) a far broader market. Relying more heavily upon technology produced by entrepreneurs like John Deere and Cyrus McCormick, the farmer also became a specialist, concentrating on the one or two crops that the soil and climate produced most efficiently. He purchased rather than produced his other staples.[68]

Creating a national economy entailed a significant degree of geographic specialization. Influenced by the location of raw materials, transportation hubs, and concentrations of capital, industry centered north of the Ohio River and east of the Mississippi. The South and the West produced raw materials and served as markets for finished goods. Specialization also delineated urban and rural sectors within regions. Cities were the nerve centers of the system. Cities also attracted the majority of immigrants and rural Americans unable to carve out a niche in the rapidly commercializing and specialized world of agriculture.[69]

While the nation's economic success was punctured periodically by recessions in the three decades after the Civil War, the emergence of a national market, economies of scale, technological advances, and a reliable work force contributed to a steady decline in prices, increased wages, and a rising standard of living. The post-War boom and declining prices pushed average real wages up 40 percent between 1865 and 1873.[70]

Participation in this economic surfeit, while hardly universal, was sufficiently widespread to encourage its broad appeal. Material success became the measure of achievement and successful businessmen garnered a new degree of prestige. The economic miracle seemed to be self-replicating, spreading across the continent as new states were integrated into the nation. Though unable to live up to the fevered predictions made on behalf of the New South, even the ex-slave states ultimately were touched, if not transformed, by the emerging national economy. It produced delights that transcended material gain and enhanced consumer choice.

---

[68] Porter, *Rise of Big Business*, 63; Hays, *Response to Industrialism*, 13–14.
[69] Ibid., 15–17.
[70] Foner, *Reconstruction*, 475.

National corporations like the railroads offered middle-class Americans opportunities for mastery previously undreamed of. A middle-level manager like Thomas Doane, chief engineer of the Burlington and Missouri River Railroad Company in Nebraska, literally created the towns that would line the road. He named them and laid out their grid-like streets around the Burlington line.[71]

* * *

The sweeping changes that brought these benefits to some, however, sowed fear and resentment among virtually every American, at one point or another. At the heart of many of these concerns was the conviction that the national economy threatened to destroy the very tenets of America's exceptional history. As industry incorporated on a national scale, it threatened to destroy the delicate relationship between state and society by overpowering local governance. Americans were more than willing to protect the market against excessive state intervention. As the mass revulsion with corrupt relations between business and politicians revealed, however, they were not willing to trust business alone to dictate politics. Nor were Americans comfortable with a handful of businesses dictating the market.

The emergence of monopolies like Standard Oil and oligopolies like U.S. Steel challenged the nation's commitment to free market competition every bit as much as did government consolidation. The unintended consequence of America's system of free exchange seemed to be the emergence of giant firms that, by their very existence, threatened competition. While managers might experience the delight of town planning, would-be residents of such towns, while savoring the potential economic benefits of the railroad line, readily came to resent the power wielded by distant corporate headquarters. Skilled workers, though enticed by rising standards of living, suffered the greatest loss of autonomy, as the wage system replaced the ideal of free labor. Farmers, who squeezed out marginal gains in their standard of living, felt whipsawed by higher fixed costs for requisite technology and fluctuating railroad rates. They bridled at their lack of control over the railroads – now the lifeblood of commercial

---

[71] Hays, *Response to Industrialism*, 22; Edward L. Ayers, *The Promise of the New South: Life after Reconstruction* (New York, NY: Oxford University Press, 1992); Olivier Zunz, *Making America Corporate, 1870–1920* (Chicago, IL: University of Chicago Press, 1990), 54–55.

agriculture. In the nation's teeming cities, problems ranging form vice to poor sanitation abounded.[72]

What troubled apologists for America's political economy the most was the unmistakable signs that class lines were being drawn. The juxtaposition of huge personal fortunes and the evolution of industry toward permanent wage labor violated the ideal of a socially mobile, classless society. The hedonistic displays of upper class wealth exposed the gap that yawned between rich and poor. This division was captured graphically in Matthew Smith's best-seller, *Sunshine and Shadow in New York* (1868). It opened with an engraving that contrasted department store magnate Alexander T. Stewart's mansion, built at a cost of $2 million, with a row of tenements.[73]

Efforts on the part of workers to organize in order to retain control over the conditions in which they worked threatened social strife that could not be dismissed as a mere political aberration: it threatened precisely the kind of class conflict that Americans felt that they had been exempted from. In the face of such challenges, Americans turned to the General Government. But because Americans did not embrace European models that featured a more powerful administrative state, many historians have missed this development. Rather than the administrative state, Americans endorsed judicial activism at the highest level. What made such activism acceptable, however, was the Court's insistence that it was doing little more than systematizing the law to better serve a "night watchman" state.

[72] Hays, *Response to Industrialism*, 28.
[73] Alan Dawley, *Struggles for Justice: Social Responsibility and the Liberal State* (Cambridge, MA: Belknap Press of Harvard University Press, 1991), 31–38; Foner, *Reconstruction*, 477.

8

Judicial Exceptions to Gilded Age *Laissez-Faire*

The turmoil that punctuated the Gilded Age occurred during the period of American history that scholars and informed citizens alike equate with anemic governance. Historian Sidney Fine concluded that in the "period between Appomattox and the accession of Theodore Roosevelt to the presidency in 1901, *laissez-faire* was championed in America as it never was before and has never been since." The influence of Charles Darwin, interpreted through men like Herbert Spencer and William Graham Sumner, pervaded American thought. Spencer coined the phrase "the survival of the fittest," and popularized it in England. Sumner was even more pessimistic than Spencer about the implications of Social Darwinism. Sumner called for vigilance against those who would employ state power to ameliorate the inevitable pain that the Darwinian struggle caused.[1]

Darwin's work demonstrated on a cosmic scale the principle of unintended consequences. Until the rise of social evolutionary thought, men explained events by referencing tangible, proximate influences, like the conscious will of other men, or one very remote agent – divine will. An influential exception to this was classical economics, which showed how irrelevant an individual's intention might be to the public consequences of his actions. Individual profit-seeking

---

[1] Sidney Fine, *Laissez Faire and the General-Welfare State: A Study of Conflict in American Thought, 1865–1901* (Ann Arbor, MI: University of Michigan Press, 1956), 29; Mike Hawkins, *Social Darwinism in European and American Thought, 1860–1945: Nature as Model and Nature as Threat* (Cambridge, MA: Cambridge University Press, 1997), 82, 108–13.

activities were often the surest path to broad social benefits, proponents argued.[2]

Like classical economics, those who applied Darwin's theories to society did not attribute causality to the conscious intentions of individuals or to divine guidance. But this Darwinian perspective was not confined to one aspect of human life, as was the case with economics. Darwin's evolutionary biology soon served as the basis for theories that explained a broad spectrum of human interaction and even the rise and fall of civilizations. Darwin captured public attention at a time when rapid industrialization and urbanization bombarded Americans with unintended consequences: wage labor and growing class conflict.[3]

In the midst of this turmoil and calls to ameliorate it, Sumner worried that Americans might forget the only law that mattered, in his opinion – the struggle to survive. It was this American dedication to individual competition that had distinguished the United States from other societies. In the wake of the railroad strikes of 1877, Sumner feared that America was developing the same collectivist tendencies inspired by class divisions as those of the "old country." The nation's ability to avoid class struggle, Sumner believed, depended on America's unique capacity to ensure individual competition. He saw that "the peculiar circumstances have been

---

[2] Thomas L. Haskell, *The Emergence of Professional Social Science: The American Social Science Association and the Nineteenth-Century Crisis of Authority* (Urbana, IL: University of Illinois Press, 1977), 41–42, 243. As James T. Kloppenberg has put it, "Not only did the geology of Lyell and the biology of Lamarck challenge literal readings of the Bible, Darwin's theory of natural selection indicated that the world was neither well ordered nor harmonious." *Uncertain Victory: Social Democracy and Progressivism in European and American Thought, 1870–1920* (New York, NY: Oxford University Press, 1986), 23.

[3] Haskell, *Emergence of Professional Social Science,* 244. Even the intellectuals who embraced positivism saw the importance of understanding unintended consequences. Donald Winch has traced the origins of the perception of unintended consequences to Scottish Enlightenment thought. "More important than any particular finding it might produce," Lacey and Furner observed of the Scottish Enlightenment, "it suggested a method of connecting individual behavior with social outcomes, revealing the mechanisms, but also the limitations, of an invisible hand." Citing the work of Donald Winch, Lacey and Furner note that the recognition of limitations of the invisible hand, which could be recognized and disclosed through a methodological program, gave birth to the modern social sciences [to be discussed later in this chapter]. See Donald Winch, "The Science of the Legislator: The Enlightenment Heritage," 63–91, and Michael J. Lacey and Mary O. Furner, "Social Investigation, Social Knowledge, and the State: an Introduction," in *The State and Social Investigation in Britain and The United States,* ed. Michael J. Lacey and Mary O. Furner, 3–62 (New York, NY: Cambridge University Press, 1993): 20.

steadily, if not rapidly, passing away, and that they must surely pass away with time, until we come into the same position, and have the same problems to deal with, as other old and fully developed nations." Americans might be tempted to ameliorate the short-term pain of evolutionary competitions, sacrificing the long-term benefits that such competition had showered on the nation for the past century.[4]

Bolstered by evolutionary theory, Sumner applied the tenets of classical liberal economic theory to the polity. This meant that government existed solely to protect contract rights – particularly property. Any extension of the authority of government beyond that threatened to destroy the independence of its citizenry and the competition crucial to long-term survival. "The value of *laissez-faire* and free competition," Sumner wrote in 1886, "is not that that system gives any guaranties of ideal result ... but that it throws out arbitrary action, and leaves rights and interests to be adjusted by their own collision and struggle, until they find their true resultant in the facts and conditions of the case."[5]

Having achieved a reprieve from class conflict in the past, America could only stave off this scourge by strict adherence to the principles that had historically protected it from such ravages. Sumner acknowledged that the United States was subject to some of the same historical forces as European nations. As Sumner put it, "We are on trial ... as to whether we can appreciate and deserve our inheritance of institutions, rights, powers, and opportunities. The great test problem of our time is whether we can now, after overthrowing all the old privileges, hold steadily the balance of truth and justice." Only by guarding against "extravagant governments, abuses of public credit, wasteful taxation, legislative monopolies and special privileges, juggling with currency, restrictions on trade, wasteful armaments on land and sea, and other follies in economy and statecraft" could Americans preserve "the gains of civilization."[6]

---

[4] Kloppenberg, *Uncertain Victory,* 23; William Graham Sumner, "The Strikes," (1878) unpublished essay quoted in Dorothy Ross, *The Origins of American Social Science* (New York, NY: Cambridge University Press, 1991), 86.

[5] Ross, *Origins of American Social Science,* 88; William Graham Sumner, "How Far Have Modern Improvements in Production and Transportation Changed the Principle That Men Should Be Left Free to Make Their Own Bargains? II," *Science,* 7, no. 161 (March 5, 1886): 228.

[6] Sumner, "How Far Have Modern Improvements," 226; William Graham Sumner, "Sociology," *Princeton Review,* 57 (November 1881): 321, in American Periodicals Series Online, 1740–1900 (Proquest, [doc. no. 343326131]), http://proquest.umi.com/pqdweb, quoted in Ross, *Origins of American Social Science,* 87. The leading gentry social scientists who did embrace naturalism and historicist thought insisted that change, though

Given this determination to preserve what they perceived to be America's distinctive political tradition in the face of historical change, it is not surprising that men like Sumner advocated a political program that consisted primarily of civil service reform and the establishment of state investigatory commissions. The commissions provided a way to ensure that men familiar with the central principles of republican government would be in a position to execute those principles; civil service reform simply applied that concept to a broad spectrum of offices. At the national level, the Pendleton Act, passed in 1883, established the basis for merit-based, as opposed to patronage-based, hiring in the federal civil service. But expansion of the civil service was slow and highly contested.[7]

That the battle was framed as *preserving* America's *laissez-faire* tradition was in and of itself a strategic victory for those who eschewed government intervention. This interpretation of America's past ignored the tradition of public authority that Americans consistently embraced – especially at the local level. In this intellectual climate, the local commonwealths, constructed on tradition and experience as embodied in the common law, faced a formidable challenge by the second half of the nineteenth century.

inevitable, need not revise America's most vaunted social and political institutions. As Ross has argued, "At the outset their overriding concern was to show that the social sciences could reconfirm the traditional principles of American governance and economy and replace religion as a sure guide to the exceptionalist future." [64]

Burgess, Adams, Sumner, and many others among America's first generation of social scientists admitted that America could not remain immune from history: they dismantled portions of the exceptionalist myth – divine and materialist – that had distinguished America from Europe and acknowledged that American history was linked to universal natural law. On the other hand, as Ross has eloquently argued, they "turned natural law and historical principle into unchanging bases for the established course of American history. So far as possible, change was contained and history rendered harmless." [60–61]

Howard Gillman demonstrates how constitutionalism, built around a belief in original intent, reinforced this process. That few institutional changes disrupted America's political development in the nineteenth century solidified the belief that the Constitution's original intent continued to suffice, thus inhibiting greater delegation of responsibility to the federal government. *The Constitution Besieged: The Rise and Demise of Lochner Era Police Powers Jurisprudence* (Durham, NC: Duke University Press, 1993). On the political and social backgrounds of these men, see also, Lacey and Furner, "Social Investigation, Social Knowledge, and the State," 24.

[7] Haskell, *Emergence of Professional Social Science*, 91, 120; See also Ballard C. Campbell, *The Growth of American Government: Governance from the Cleveland Era to the Present* (Bloomington, IN: Indiana University Press, 1995); Stephen Skowronek, *Building a New American State: The Expansion of National Administrative Capacities, 1877–1920* (New York, NY: Cambridge University Press, 1982).

The barriers were not exclusively ideological. The very feature that made state-funded economic privileges and subsidies to business attractive politically – the capacity to disaggregate and distribute these benefits broadly – undercut their economic effectiveness because these privileges tended to ramify. Granting a special charter to one constituent only created greater demand for these privileges from other constituents. State-chartered incorporation suffered a similar fate. Jacksonian Democrats had routinized these privileges. Corporate privileges were not the same, however, when anybody could get one. By 1880, almost every state had replaced customized corporate charters with general incorporation acts.[8]

The demand for state aid to private railroad companies also increased geometrically. In parts of the nation that suffered from overbuilding, localities staggered under the burden of massive debt. The immediate result was hundreds of law suits repudiating local debts. Taxpayer dollars proved to be scarcer and drew greater public scrutiny than public land or corporate charters.

With private capital now more readily available, and the railroads distressingly overbuilt, many of the early public subsidies looked more like boondoggles than bold efforts to promote the public welfare. Instances in which the public welfare had so clearly been damaged by government support for private initiatives directly challenged the commonwealth assumptions upon which such funding had been secured. Legislators responded by limiting or prohibiting local subsidies.[9]

Consensus on the centrality of free market exchange, the conviction that work was in fact a great integrating and moralizing force, and the scientific authority of Social Darwinism overwhelmed, at least in the short term, even the Civil War's powerful statist legacy. Gone, the

---

[8] Harry N. Scheiber, "Government and the Economy: Studies of the 'Commonwealth' Policy in Nineteenth-Century America," *Journal of Interdisciplinary History,* 3, no. 1 (Summer 1972): 143; Charles W. McCurdy, "Justice Field and the Jurisprudence of Government-Business Relations: Some Parameters of Laissez-Faire Constitutionalism, 1863–1897," *Journal of American History,* 61, no. 4, (March 1975): 970; Oscar Handlin and Mary Flug Handlin, *The Dimensions of Liberty* (Cambridge, MA: Belknap Press of Harvard University Press, 1961), 74–75; Morton Keller, *Affairs of State: Public Life in Late Nineteenth Century America* (Cambridge, MA: Belknap Press of Harvard University Press, 1977), 184. See also Harry N. Scheiber, "Federalism and the American Economic Order, 1789–1910," *Law & Society Review,* 10, no. 1 (Fall 1975): 57–118; James Willard Hurst, *Law and the Conditions of Freedom in the Nineteenth-Century United States* (Madison, WI: University of Wisconsin Press, 1974).

[9] Keller, *Affairs of State,* 187; Fine, *Laissez Faire,* 23.

standard accounts report, was the republican world of civic virtue; gone was the commonwealth local order of mixed economic enterprise and community standards; gone, too, was the common law that supported it. In their place stood the dictates of *laissez-faire* and the rules dictated by the natural order.[10]

Yet *laissez-faire* did not triumph – even at the height of its ideological appeal. Intense and persistent pressure from producers yielded some results: heightened stature for the Department of Agriculture, creation of the Interstate Commerce Commission, and the origins of merit-based hiring. As we will discuss in Chapter 9, the tariff provoked charges of ideological inconsistency leveled at those who otherwise advocated a "hands-off" stance for the federal government. American citizens in the West experienced the direct authority of the national government's administrative apparatus firsthand.

It was the judiciary, however, that proved to be most assertive, on the one hand, and least visible, on the other. Preempting both legislation and collective action by labor, the courts established boundaries that were soon internalized by the labor movement itself. Less commonly understood is the crucial assistance that the national government provided to corporations and the national market. The federal judiciary and, to a lesser degree, the executive branch of the federal government were the key instruments of this assistance.

Often invisible, rarely noted, even by contemporary observers, the judiciary radically reshaped the legal standing of corporations between Reconstruction and the first decade of the twentieth century. Corporations were transformed from publicly crafted organizations – whose special privileges were government-granted, and that operated under state-fashioned restrictions and public service requirements – into natural outcroppings of the economy. By the 1890s, the Constitution protected their fundamental rights from state interference.

Capitalizing on the protections embodied in the Fourteenth Amendment – an amendment enacted to protect Southern blacks after the War – corporations emerged as "rights bearing individuals." The notion that corporations were divorced from the public service obligations mandated by their state charters would have seemed preposterous, not to mention illegal, to most Americans for the first seventy-five years

[10] McCurdy, "Justice Field," 1004. See also William J. Novak, *The People's Welfare: Law and Regulation in Nineteenth-Century America* (Chapel Hill, NC: University of North Carolina Press, 1996).

of the nation's history. By the dawn of the twentieth century, however, corporations were the prototypical private organization in the eyes of many.[11]

During the Gilded Age, the federal government fashioned and protected a national market that ensured the predictable, stable environment essential to interregional, and eventually international, corporations. The federal judiciary also carved out a new role in the Gilded Age – determining the boundaries between public and private activities and ensuring that the two did not intermingle. Justice Stephen Field led this effort and insisted that restraining government action in spheres that were best left to the market would ensure the integrity of both public and private spheres. Ironically, the very effort to parse private and public was in itself an historic intervention into social relations by the court, and a groundbreaking expansion of the national judiciary's penetration into matters previously left to state and local government.

"THE RAGGED EDGE OF ANARCHY": THE COLLECTIVIST RESPONSE TO INEQUALITY

Faced with what appeared to be insurmountable evidence that America could no longer rely on natural law to assure its progress, a number of Americans began to entertain the possibility of more explicitly statist methods to guide the change sweeping the nation. Having entered the stream of history, it was up to Americans to mobilize politically to navigate it. Many workers, farmers, and others who felt that rapid change was working against their interest and the welfare of the nation, pushed for a government ready to intervene on behalf of producers. This position was reinforced by a number of intellectual currents and examples from Europe. If America indeed was faced with the same kinds of social problems that gripped Europe, socialism, or some variant of it, might

---

[11] Robert W. Gordon, "Legal Thought and Legal Practice in the Age of American Enterprise, 1870–1920," in *Professions and Professional Ideologies in America, 1730–1940,* ed. Gerald L. Geison (Chapel Hill, NC: University of North Carolina Press, 1983), 100–101; Gerald Berk, "Constituting Corporations and Markets: Railroads in Gilded Age Politics," *Studies in American Political Development,* 4, no. 1 (1990): 135; Scott R. Bowman, *The Modern Corporation and American Political Thought: Law, Power, and Ideology* (University Park, PA: Pennsylvania State University Press, 1996), 54–55. See also, Charles W. McCurdy, "The Knight Sugar Decision of 1895 and the Modernization of American Corporation Law, 1869–1903," *Business History Review,* 53, no. 3 (Autumn 1979): 304–42.

well provide the solution. These were precisely the kinds of policies that advocates of *laissez-faire* most feared.[12]

Advocates of *laissez-faire* had few qualms about turning to the courts and the military to stifle labor unrest, however. State and federal troops were required to quell the most contentious strikes, including the Great Railroad Strike of 1877, the Haymarket Incident in 1886 and the Pullman Strike of 1894. Each of these conflagrations was started by a railroad strike but soon pulled in other workers, many of whom had never engaged in protest before. In April 1886, Nicholas Murray Butler acknowledged that," No thoughtful man can have watched the development of labor troubles during the last few years with any feeling short of anxiety. The increase in the number and frequency of strikes, the growing percentage of them that are successful, the hostility and ill feeling too often shown by employers and employed, have all forced themselves upon our notice, but society seems helpless before them." As the prominence of "the labor question" during the Gilded Age suggests, the fit between America's working class and the newly industrialized political economy was far from settled.[13]

In 1886, the number of workers who struck topped 407,000, compared to an average of 124,000 for the five previous years. At the low point of the economic depression that wracked America in 1894, over 505,000 workers participated in strikes. Remembering the Great Railroad Strike of 1877, historian James Ford Rhodes wrote years later that "We had hugged the delusion that such social uprisings belonged to Europe and had no reason of being in a free republic where there was plenty of room and an equal chance for all." Class conflict could no longer be ignored, though some might still deny its true cause. America's exceptional reprieve from the historical forces that had created conflict elsewhere seemed to have run its course.[14]

[12] Daniel T. Rodgers, *Atlantic Crossings: Social Politics in a Progressive Age* (Cambridge, MA: Belknap Press of Harvard University Press, 1998).
[13] Samuel P. Hays, *Response to Industrialism, 1885–1914,* (Chicago, IL: University of Chicago Press, 1957), 40; Nicholas Murray Butler, "Settlement of Labor Differences," *Science,* 7, no. 167 (April 16, 1886): 340. For an excellent review of the range of tactics available to workers, see Martin Shefter, "Trade Unions and Political Machines: The Organization and Disorganization of American Working Class in the Late Nineteenth Century," in *Working-Class Formation: Nineteenth-Century Patterns in Western Europe and the United States,* ed. Ira Katznelson and Aristide R. Zolberg (Princeton, NJ: Princeton University Press, 1986), 197–276.
[14] Shefter, "Trade Unions and Political Machines," 236; James Ford Rhodes, *History of the United States from the Compromise of 1850,* vol. 8, *From Hayes to McKinley, 1877*

Workers responded to the new economic and political conditions in a variety of ways. Besides strikes and boycotts, they organized both producer and consumer cooperatives. Although socialism played a relatively minor role in the labor movement after the Civil War, socialists did control a number of individual unions in the 1890s, such as the bakers and confectioners, and the United Brewery Workers. Even the American Federation of Labor (AFL), which led the charge to narrow worker demands – focusing strictly on wages by the twentieth century – was influenced by socialist ideals. The vicissitudes of unemployment drove many producers to organize cooperatives. In Massachusetts, workers organized thirty such producer cooperatives between 1867 and 1885. But these cooperatives did not last long. Nor did most union leaders – or the rank and file, for that matter – seek solutions that challenged the fundamental organization of the capitalist political economy.[15]

Indigenous appeals to solidarity, collective action, and republican ideology overlapped with elements of the socialist program. During this amorphous stage of the labor movement, socialists and other labor reformers could work together because they shared a common vocabulary and similar analysis of the institutions that dominated the Gilded Age. They all questioned some of the techniques of industrial capitalism, especially its competitive nature. Each, in turn, envisioned a set of worker/employer relations far more cooperative than the existing system allowed. This critique and prescription were embodied in the largest labor organization of late-nineteenth-century America, the Knights of Labor. Founded as a fraternal society in 1869 by Philadelphia garment workers, the loose organization and goals of the national chapter allowed for explosive growth. In 1886 alone, the Knights grew from 100,000 members to over 700,000. The Knights used a broad spectrum of techniques, ranging from boycotts and strikes to drafting political

to 1896 (New York, 1919), 46, quoted in Hays, *Response to Industrialism*, 38; Ross, *Origins of American Social Science*, 58.

[15] Shefter, "Trade Unions and Political Machines," 213–21; Martin J. Burke, *The Conundrum of Class: Public Discourse on the Social Order in America* (Chicago, IL: University of Chicago Press, 1995), 133–58; Alexander Keyssar, *Out of Work: The First Century of Unemployment in Massachusetts* (New York, NY: Cambridge University Press, 1986), 184–85. William E. Forbath notes that an 1894 plebiscite poll of the AFL's member unions endorsed a socialist platform that included the appeal for "independent labor politics." *Law and the Shaping of the American Labor Movement* (Cambridge, MA: Harvard University Press, 1991), 14. See also Katznelson and Zolberg, *Working Class Formation*.

candidates and even creating third parties. They asserted that economic equality was instrumental to political equality: in their view, the survival of the republic depended on it.[16]

Because white males were fully integrated into the system of electoral politics, labor grievances were just one of a number of concerns expressed through the two-party system. However, as organized labor faced increased opposition, the Knights of Labor and other organizations representing workers crafted a strategy of broad political reform. In 1888, for instance, the Knights of Labor promoted a national political program of currency reform and public control of natural monopolies like the railroads and the telegraph. Labor had long advocated state intervention to restrict work to an eight-hour day.[17]

In spite of rhetorical allegiance to the doctrine of *laissez-faire*, industrial capital turned to the government for assistance, ranging from military intervention to the tactical use of injunctions. One legal historian has estimated that judicial review thwarted pro-labor legislation on more than sixty occasions in the final two decades of the nineteenth century. Judicial intervention also violated another hallowed principle, that of local control. The federal judiciary erected a powerful defense against the vagaries of local law by allowing interstate employers to litigate liability cases in federal courts. The federal courts not only provided uniformity, they offered a venue hospitable to large employers.[18]

Those students of state-building who measure governance by the size of administrative structures have been quick to dismiss the contributions of the judiciary because the American courts possessed little in the way of visible bureaucracy. Nor did they make a dent in the national budget. At a time when social strife demanded assertive leadership the courts appeared to be the most passive branch of government. Judges could not initiate cases. But corporate lawyers did. As the bar became professional and as prestigious positions were increasingly aligned with law firms that specialized in corporate work, there was no dearth of litigation to protect

[16] Shefter, "Trade Unions and Political Machines," 223–25; Forbath, *Law and the Shaping*, 12–13. See also Leon Fink, "The New Labor History and the Powers of Historical Pessimism: Consensus, Hegemony, and the Case of the Knights of Labor," *Journal of American History*, 75, no. 1 (June 1988): 115–36.

[17] Burke, *Conundrum of Class*, 143; Forbath, *Law and the Shaping*, 13.

[18] Forbath, *Law and the Shaping*, 26, 38; Tony A. Freyer, "The Federal Courts, Localism, and the National Economy, 1865–1900," *Business History Review*, 53, no. 3 (Autumn 1979): 351.

the interests of large employers and to create and stabilize a predictable national market.[19]

The federal courts also used judicial injunctions to intervene forcefully in both rate- making cases and labor disputes. Employers fought back against strikes and boycotts by obtaining injunctions from the courts. The most impressive example of federal judicial mobilization came during the second Cleveland administration in response to the Pullman Strike near Chicago in 1894. With train traffic disrupted from Chicago to the Pacific coast, Attorney General Richard Olney obtained an injunction from a federal district court. He also prevailed upon the President to send troops to quell the mob violence that had accompanied the strike, even though Illinois Governor John P. Altgeld, a labor sympathizer, opposed this action. Ultimately, the federal government sent in 14,000 troops as Olney warned reporters that America faced "the ragged edge of anarchy."[20]

Greater than the impact of any single action, the persistent failure of pro-labor legislation in the courts and the naked use of injunctions to stop one of labor's most effective organizing tools, was the impact of these actions on labor leaders' expectations. Labor narrowed its demands and techniques. Experience taught labor leaders both to distrust the state and to demand very little from it.[21]

Farmers, like most Americans, were also wary of creating a centralized bureaucracy. They feared that they might be the last to benefit from such a mechanism. Following the Civil War, however, deflationary pressure led farmers to support a series of movements that promised to use the power of the federal government to loosen the money supply. Because the major parties avoided the issue of monetary reform, no fewer than

[19] Edward A. Purcell, Jr., *Brandeis and the Progressive Constitution: Erie, the Judicial Power, and the Politics of the Federal Courts in Twentieth-Century America* (New Haven, CT: Yale University Press, 2000); Daniel R. Ernst, "Law and American Political Development, 1877–1938," *Reviews in American History*, 26, no. 1 (March 1998): 211–12.

[20] "Talk of Civil War," *Washington Post*, July 5, 1894, 5, cited in Robert Higgs, *Crisis and Leviathan: Critical Episodes in the Growth of American Government* (New York, NY: Oxford University Press, 1987), 94–95. Injunctions were used in a broad range of policy areas. As Daniel Ernst has noted, they were seen by some as enhancing the administrative capacity of the state. "Law and American Political Development," 210.

[21] Forbath, *Law and the Shaping*, 169–71. The narrowed demands were epitomized by the AFL. See also Gretchen Ritter, *Goldbugs and Greenbacks: The Antimonopoly Tradition and the Politics of Finance in America* (New York, NY: Cambridge University Press, 1997).

five independent parties addressed the issue between 1872 and 1896, when the Democratic Party claimed the issue as its own.[22]

The farmer's panacea of an inflated currency fit quite nicely with their nation's long-standing preference for governance hidden from sight. Although it required federal intervention, inflating the currency appealed to farmers because it required very little in the way of administrative apparatus. In that regard, it was the farmer's version of the tariff. Both currency inflation and tariff policy manipulated the free market in the name of economic development – albeit with distinctly different benefi- ciaries – without augmenting the General Government's visible adminis- trative apparatus. To a much greater degree than workers, farmers also pursued producer and consumer cooperatives, as the Farmer's Alliances sought to reduce competition and gain control over prices.

By the early 90s, Populism combined both the call for an inflated currency and more explicit federal intervention into the economy. The Populists proposed a sub-treasury system that would use the General Government to sponsor low-interest loans secured by crops, public own- ership of the railroads and telegraph, national regulatory power to break up the monopolies that (in their opinion) controlled prices and interest rates, a progressive income tax, and, by the time of William Jennings Bryan's first run as the Democratic presidential nominee in 1896, the free coinage of silver in order to inflate the currency. Fusing an evangelical political impulse to demands for active state intervention on behalf of producers, the Populists offered the broadest vision of federal interven- tion articulated since Reconstruction. Like prohibitionists, Populists jus- tified their call for state intervention by claiming that nothing less than the survival of American families was at stake.[23]

[22] Richard Franklin Bensel, *Sectionalism and American Political Development, 1880–1980* (Madison, WI: University of Wisconsin Press, 1984), 56; Ritter, *Goldbugs and Greenbacks,* 7–47.

[23] Rebecca Edwards, *New Spirits: Americans in the Gilded Age, 1865–1905* (New York: Oxford University Press, 2006), 235–240; Richard Franklin Bensel, *The Political Economy of American Industrialization, 1877–1900* (New York, NY: Cambridge University Press, 2000), 238–39; Mary O. Furner, "The Republican Tradition and the New Liberalism: Social Investigation, State Building, and Social Learning in the Gilded Age," in Lacey and Furner, *State and Social Investigation,* 172; John F. Witte, *The Politics and Development of the Federal Income Tax* (Madison, WI: University of Wisconsin Press, 1985), 72; Ajay K. Mehrotra, "Sharing the Burden: Law, Politics, and the Making of the Modern American Fiscal State, 1880–1930" (Cambridge University Press, forthcoming).

But Populists no longer viewed intemperance as the root of the problem. They replaced moral waywardness with economic causation. "[T]he Populist theory is: Better to go

Middle-class reformers added their voices to those calling for greater planning and control at the national level. Some, like Henry George, felt that government held the key to crafting technical solutions to America's struggle against inequality. The unearned increment that rising land values provided to the rich was the source of this inequality, George argued. His single tax movement sought to redistribute this wealth to all the members of society. It was producers' economic activity that pushed up land values: they justly deserved the unearned increment that resulted from their labor.[24]

While George merely sought to equate social progress with Spencer's natural laws of evolution, other influential reformers challenged the competitive basis of social evolution head-on. Edward Bellamy's *Looking Backward* (1888), for instance, took aim at the central tenet of Social Darwinism – the efficacious results of competition. Bellamy's critique of Spencer is best summed up by one of the characters of the utopian novel, who recalls the misguided energy of nineteenth-century society. "Selfishness was their only science, and in industrial production selfishness is suicide," the dreamer pronounced. "Competition, which is the instinct of selfishness, is another word for dissipation of energy, while combination is the secret of efficient production." Bellamy called for the nationalization of industry in order to harness the full potential of man's cooperative capacity. Bellamy's nationalist state would be a vast one, directed by functionaries. But unlike the real Gilded Age state, the futuristic one would eliminate waste and inequality. It would be "so logical in its principles and direct and simple in its workings that it all but runs itself."[25]

---

home drunk, than to have no home to go to either drunk or sober," claimed Sarah Van De Vort Emery, author of the tract, "Seven Financial Conspiracies Which Have Enslaved the American People (1887)," *The Corner Stone 1*, no. 1 (January 1893): 3, as quoted in Pauline Adams and Emma S. Thornton, *A Populist Assault: Sarah E. Van De Vort Emery on American Democracy, 1862–1895* (Bowling Green, OH: Bowling Green State University Popular Press, 1982), 63. See also, Rebecca Edwards, *Angels in the Machinery: Gender in American Party Politics from the Civil War to the Progressive Era* (New York: Oxford University Press, 1997). For an excellent overview of the political impact of populism see M. Elizabeth Sanders, *Roots of Reform: Farmers, Workers and the State, 1877–1917* (Chicago, IL: University of Chicago Press, 1999).

[24] Robert H. Wiebe, *The Search for Order, 1877–1920* (New York, NY: Hill and Wang, 1967), 137.

[25] Edward Bellamy, *Looking Backward* (1888; repr., New York, NY: Dover Publications, 1996), 244, quoted in Hofstadter, *Social Darwinism in American Thought*, rev. ed. (Boston, MA: Beacon Press, 1955; Philadelphia, PA: University of Pennsylvania

Measured by federal employees added or administrative structures enhanced, a good case can be made that *laissez-faire* did indeed prevail at the national level. With the exception of the Pendleton Act (civil service), the elevation of Agriculture to cabinet status in 1889, and the creation of a relatively ineffectual Interstate Commerce Commission in 1887, there was little administrative growth beyond the veterans' pensions programs already discussed. When the familiar story of government through injunction is added, and the dampening effect this had on expectations considered, the power of *laissez-faire* ideology appeared to be more tenuous.[26]

Acknowledging the powerful role that the courts played during this period, as they used their authority to draw a hard and fast boundary between public and private activities, endowed national corporations with a full set of constitutionally protected rights, and created the legal infrastructure for a national economy, however, changes the calculus. National authority in the Gilded Age should be gauged by the dramatic changes that Americans experienced in the ways that they worked, the items that they produced and consumed, and the degree to which they sought to disaggregate private affairs from those considered to be public. The federal government, primarily through the national judiciary, shaped each of these relationships.

"A DANGEROUS INTERFERENCE WITH PRIVATE RIGHTS": PARSING PUBLIC AND PRIVATE

The national judiciary sought more explicit boundaries between the public and the private. The example of Supreme Court Justice Stephen J. Field is instructive. Field could be a staunch defender of public authority. In *Illinois Central R.R. Co. v. Illinois* (1892), a case in which the state sought to repossess a portion of the harbor of Chicago granted to the railroad in 1869, Field sided with the State of Illinois. It was preposterous, opined Field, that a railroad might get "converted into a corporation to manage and practically control the harbor of the City of Chicago, not simply for its own purposes as a railroad corporation, but for its own profit generally." Despite his determination to protect the private sphere

---

Press, 1944), 113; Bellamy, *Looking Backward*, 181 quoted in Wiebe, *Search for Order*, 138.
[26] For an excellent summary and details on expansion of other of services, see Campbell, *Growth of American Government*, 74–78.

from public intrusion, Field saw no reason to abdicate fundamental public powers.[27]

Field was determined, however, to draw a bright line between the public and the private sectors so as to avoid situations – all too common in his opinion – in which the public arena became "a harbor where refuge can be found" for the demands of competing interest groups. Thus Field's interpretation of "public use" sharply proscribed government support for a broad range of businesses. In *the Slaughterhouse Cases* (1873), Field's dissent took aim at Louisiana's authority to grant a monopoly to one group of New Orleans meat cutters. By 1886, Field's campaign to make the federal judiciary the ultimate arbiter of public and private interest won over the majority of his colleagues on the bench.[28]

Field had no qualms about projecting the national judiciary into intricate public policy questions that previously had been decided at the local and state levels. He was determined to use this power to distinguish public from private. Though it took some time, Field ultimately prevailed, triggering a "constitutional revolution" that restricted government grants of privilege and subsidies to business, and imposed limits on government's power to regulate prices.[29]

Newly defined constitutional rights restricted the scope of local common law decisions that had favored informal over formal protections. The heightened concern for individual rights growing out of abolitionism and radical Republicanism spawned a renewed interest in the natural rights tradition and absolute rights for individuals. As it worked its way through the court system, constitutionalism constricted the informal, traditional understandings implicit in common law. In *People v. Turner* (1870), for instance, the Illinois court declared unconstitutional an act establishing the Chicago Reform School for vagrant children because it violated the right of habeas corpus. These children had committed no crime and had not been convicted of any offense, Justice Thornton

[27] *Illinois Central Rail Road Co. v. Illinois,* 146 U.S. 387, 451 (1892), available online at http://www.lexisnexis.com/universe, quoted in McCurdy, "Justice Field," 994.
[28] McCurdy, "Justice Field," 976–79; *Yick Wo v. Hopkins,* Sheriff, 118 U.S. 356 (1886), available online at http://www.lexisnexis.com/universe.
[29] McCurdy, "Justice Field," 971; William Forbath, "The Ambiguities of Free Labor and the Law in the Gilded Age," *Wisconsin Law Review* (July/August 1985): 782, 795–800.
 "Field believed that the proper solution to the nation's policy conflicts lay in uncompromising judicial application … of 'public purpose,'" McCurdy has written. Like many other Americans seeking to make sense out of the socioeconomic dislocation in the wake of the Civil War, Field "was obsessed with formulating rules that separated the public and private sectors as far as practicable." "Justice Field," 1004–5.

argued. Due process was now required before the state could act in such a paternalistic fashion, the court insisted. In similar fashion, the Maine Supreme Court struck down a Portland pauper law: it violated the due process clause of the new Fourteenth Amendment. This abridgment of citizens' rights, Justice Walton made clear, could not be tolerated in the aftermath of the Civil War. "If white men and women may be thus summarily disposed of at the north, of course black ones may be disposed of in the same way at the south; and thus the very evil which it was particularly the object of the fourteenth amendment to eradicate will still exist."[30]

Constitutional law formally divided public from private interest in communities and commercial endeavors that had formerly mixed the two. Intellectual currents that emphasized a classical political economy, protecting individual rights and preserving social harmony through market exchange, certainly explain some of this movement. The growing size and complexity of many communities explains a great deal as well. The commonwealth's will was no longer so easily determined. Even if public purpose could be discerned, enforcing it was often the job of a functionary, removed from the people themselves. Legislation and administration were disentangled from each other.[31]

The leap from local to state enforcement of prohibition, for instance, changed the way courts viewed due process rights even before the Civil War. In 1852, shortly after Massachusetts passed its first statewide prohibition law, Barnstable County Justice of the Peace Lothrop Davis ordered Sandwich constable Patrick McGirr to forcibly enter Theodore Fisher's house and make a careful search for liquor. McGirr was instructed to seize all the liquor he found. When the constable did indeed find liquor, Davis ordered him to destroy it and fined Fisher twenty dollars and costs.

---

[30] Novak, *People's Welfare*, 170–71, 244; *City of Portland v. City of Bangor*, 65 Me. 120, 121 (1876), available online at http://www.lexisnexis.com/universe, quoted in Novak, *People's Welfare*, 170.

[31] Skowronek, *Building a New American State*, 41–42. In some states, these changes could be glimpsed even before the Civil War. The Handlins stated the problem most simply when they noted that, "The business of police, no matter how defined, involved compulsion which in the seventeenth and eighteenth centuries had been administered by elected officials guided by commonly agreed upon standards. Compulsion took on quite another aspect in the complex, changing communities of the nineteenth century. ... The city of 1850 needed more effective means of apprehending murderers and thieves than the village of 1750; yet the enforcement of Sabbath-observance laws by professional police officers seemed tyrannical at the later date as it did not at the earlier." Handlin and Handlin, *Dimensions of Liberty*, 76–77.

Fisher filed suit, and in 1854, Massachusetts Supreme Judicial Court Justice Lemuel Shaw overturned the law.[32]

As the government penetrated (literally, in Fisher's case) deeper into citizen's homes, these new powers, Shaw opined, had to be balanced with more formal protections of citizens' rights, starting with greater care for due process. Shaw acknowledged a broad police power, but took aim at the process used to enforce that police power. In the law, Shaw raged, "No provision is made by the statute for a trial, for a determination by judicial proofs of the facts, upon the truth of which alone the property can be justly confiscated and destroyed." Shaw, who in the past had not hesitated to use common law to protect public welfare at the expense of procedural niceties, offered a constitutional remedy to the Massachusetts legislators. "In a law directing a series of measures, which in their operation are in danger of encroaching upon private rights ... it is highly important that the powers conferred, and the practical directions given, be so clear and well defined, that they may serve as safe guides to all such officers and magistrates ... the statute itself must, on its face, be conformable to the constitution." Procedural protections, Shaw believed, would offset the political distance created by legislation emanating at the state level but carried out on the local level.[33]

Throughout the second half of the nineteenth century the object of public policy moved vertically from local to state, and in rare instances, national jurisdiction. Particularly in the sphere of economic policy making, the scope of activities to be aided, subsidized, regulated, or policed grew dramatically. The reach of local jurisdictions, not to mention their capacity, was dwarfed by comparison. The regulation of provisions stipulated in corporate charters might have been possible when corporations remained primarily local enterprises. But as industrialization pushed the scale of corporate operations toward national scope, even state regulation was hopelessly overmatched by the size, and often complexity, of tasks to be regulated.[34]

---

[32] Novak, *People's Welfare*, 181.

[33] *Theodore Fisher v. Patrick McGirr & others*, 67 Mass. 1, 36 (1854), available online at http://www.lexisnexis.com/universe, quoted in Novak, *People's Welfare*, 182; *Fisher v. McGirr*, 40. As Novak sums up, "Prohibition was not analogous to local fire or market regulations. It was a comprehensive statutory revocation of preexisting liberties, properties, and rights. It replaced local, discretionary liquor licensing, with a formal, centralized, and uniform system of rules guiding the administrative and judicial conduct of law enforcement officials throughout the state. Such newly delineated "public" powers were met by careful defenses of more closely designated "private" rights."

[34] Scheiber has labeled this the "problem of areal-functional congruity." "Federalism and the American Economic Order," 70.

Just as states had superseded localities in the control and regulation of alcohol, critics of railroad policy demanded and got (in limited fashion with the Interstate Commerce Commission) more systematic, and not coincidentally, more politically distant regulation. That localities within each state were spending millions of dollars to attract more lines made the likelihood of tough sanctions that could lead to the loss of business highly unlikely. Even where a state was prepared to play hardball, the spatial reach of its jurisdiction thwarted such efforts.[35]

The courts responded to the shift upward in the locus of decision making by subjecting legislative fiats to closer constitutional scrutiny in order to ensure due process and to insist on drawing a line between public and private endeavors that had for decades defied such simple distinction. Simultaneously, the courts moved to protect the rights of individuals from increasingly distant mechanisms of enforcement. The commonwealth conviction that public support for and intervention into the private sphere could promote the welfare of all was subjected to withering attack.

By hardening the boundary between public and private after the Civil War, the judiciary wrote into the law prevailing attitudes about the exceptional nature of America's national development and the central role that individual competition played in ensuring the harmony of all interests in a society guided by free market exchange. "Classical Legal Thought," as this body of case law and treatises was labeled by scholars, insisted that the judiciary was neutral and apolitical. Courts merely ensured that the fundamental elements of America's compact – embodied in the constitution – were adhered to. This was the supposed "night watchman" state, that with the occasional intervention of the courts, would leave substantive decisions to the "natural" market.[36]

Jurists sought uniformity of the law as they systematized it and generalized from its particulars. The hand of the state in this case was to remain steady and predictable, but hidden. Not surprisingly, many late-nineteenth-century jurists viewed private law – contract, property, and commercial law – as the ideal vehicle for executing this vision. This body of law was seen as the preserve for "natural" transactions, protected from state intervention. Influenced by trends in the social sciences, the courts

---

[35] Novak, *People's Welfare*, 188; Scheiber, "Federalism and the American Economic Order," 100.

[36] Morton J. Horwitz, *The Transformation of American Law, 1870–1960: The Crisis of Legal Orthodoxy* (New York, NY: Oxford University Press, 1992), 4, 11, 20.

embraced objectivity as their holy grail. Increasingly, judges searched for the "customary" or average meaning in cases rather than seeking the subjective or actual intent of the parties in a case. What mattered was not what the parties to a contract may have actually meant. Rather, the ability to predict the legal consequences of transactions, based on generally accepted understandings of the language used, legal precedent, and public policy in place, eclipsed the particularistic nature of the adversarial process.[37]

The rise of private law and the quest to systematize that law bolstered the illusion of judicial neutrality. The starting premise, for instance, for contract enforcement was the "will theory." This assumed that the original contract resulted from a "meeting of the minds" of the contracting parties and that it was the court's job to discern the true meaning, neutrally. Even though the court undoubtedly imported numerous external considerations, will theory was premised on the principle that the judge merely held both parties to the agreement that they had ratified originally, and privately.[38]

The best example of the courts' determination to keep its hands hidden was in the field of labor relations. The courts were anything but neutral in this field. Yet the prevailing doctrine – "liberty of contract" – was premised upon a conception of the judiciary as neutral arbiter.

Liberty of contract was far more than a judicial artifact. Its power derived from deeply held views about free labor and the rights of all Americans. In the words of its staunchest legal defender, David Dudley Field, it was "the right to labor when, where, and for such reward as the laborer and his employer may agree to between themselves." This perceived freedom to sell one's own labor was exceptional. For Field, it was "purely American, without precedent in the past and ready for development in the future."[39]

---

[37] Horwitz, *Transformation*, 15, 35, 48–49. As Horwitz put it, "the perfect analogue to an increasingly dominant conception of a self-regulating market." [11]

For an illuminating discussion of the way that numbers were used to help overcome the uncertainty created by larger, less personal communities of professionals and to enhance the authority of these professions, see Theodore M. Porter, *Trust in Numbers: The Pursuit of Objectivity in Science and Public Life* (Princeton, NJ: Princeton University Press, 1995).

[38] Horwitz, *Transformation*, 35.

[39] David Dudley Field, "American Progress in Jurisprudence," *American Law Review* 27 (1893): 643, http://www.heinonline.org/, quoted in Charles W. McCurdy, "The 'Liberty of Contract' Regime in American Law," in *The State and Freedom of Contract*, ed. Harry N. Scheiber (Stanford, CA: Stanford University Press, 1998), 161, http://www.netlibrary.com/.

The language that supported judicial rulings ultimately shaped the very terms of the debate in which labor leaders engaged. The passion for free labor was shared by many labor leaders after the Civil War. They too imbibed the language of free labor, and sought to preserve their independence in workplaces that increasingly were dominated by industrial giants seeking wage labor. Labor waged war within a universe defined by the judiciary. Liberty of contract, as interpreted by the courts, was pervasive in these rulings.[40]

The courts stridently rejected the premise that workers and large-scale capital might not be equal parties when it came to bargaining power. Even as state legislatures began to formulate policies that proscribed the terms of contracts based on the rationale that labor and concentrated capital were bargaining from positions of unequal strength, courts refused to intervene in what they viewed to be a private matter between employee and employer. In one of the earliest cases, *Western & Atlantic R.R. CO. v. Bishop* (1873), the Georgia court did not mince words about the right of employees to voluntarily contract away state-legislated liability protections that governed the railroads. "It would be a dangerous interference with private rights to undertake to fix by law the terms upon which the employer and employee shall contract," the judge wrote. "For myself, I do not hesitate to say that I know of no right more precious, and one which laboring men ought to guard with more vigilance, than the right to fix by contract the terms upon which their labor shall be engaged."[41]

Even as the Court began to insist on liability between businesses contracting with each other, it continued to exempt labor contracts as the exclusive province of private exchange. In the nation's most famous freedom of contract case – *Lochner* (1905) – eight out of nine Supreme Court justices rejected the argument that unequal bargaining strength justified state interference with the sacred freedom of contract principle. Justice Oliver Wendell Holmes, Jr. did dissent, but as one eminent legal historian tersely noted: "He had only one vote."[42]

[40] Forbath, *Law and the Shaping*, xii, 7; Eric Foner, *Reconstruction: America's Unfinished Revolution, 1863–1877* (New York, NY: Harper, 1988), 481; Christopher L. Tomlins has documented the resistance to the myth that labor was free before Field. *Law, Labor, and Ideology in the Early American Republic* (New York, NY: Cambridge University Press, 1993), 9. See also, Forbath, "Ambiguities of Free Labor."
[41] McCurdy, "Liberty of Contract," 173; *Western & Atlantic R.R. CO. v. Bishop*, 50 Georgia, 465, cited in McCurdy, "Liberty of Contract," 174.
[42] Ibid., 176–77, 180.

By the late nineteenth century, liberty of contract had been elevated to "a sacred constitutional principle," representing some of the most basic themes in Classical Legal Thought. It embodied the logic of *laissez-faire* and the belief in market exchange. Its corollary was that government should serve as a passive bystander and neutral arbiter when necessary. It assumed that the market naturally and equitably distributed benefits through the contract mechanism that balanced the wills of two equally positioned parties.[43]

Wherever possible, a hard line had been drawn between public and private, relegating the former to a distinctly subordinate position. By the end of the nineteenth century, the courts had endowed even corporations with many of the same rights as individuals, employing the due process clause of the Fourteenth Amendment in order to protect these constitutional rights. Modern corporations were in form, if not substance, the creation of Classical Legal Thought. Yet apologists claimed that the laws of man merely followed the laws of nature. Corporations were natural entities, they argued, arising out of the inexorable flux of the free market: the law protected them as such, but had little to do with their creation. The corporation was now seen as existing prior to the state.[44]

"CORPORATIONS ARE PERSONS WITHIN THE MEANING OF THE FOURTEENTH AMENDMENT": PROTECTING THE RIGHTS OF CORPORATIONS

Although the first American corporations were "bodies-politic," by 1875 it was common for state incorporation statutes to grant corporate charters "for any lawful purpose." Nevertheless, states restricted the duration of the franchise, regulated governance, and restricted indebtedness. After all, it was Jacksonian fears about corporate privilege that fueled the movement to make incorporation more accessible. The purpose was to guard against special privilege, not enable it. The same spirit ensured that the general incorporation legislation spelled out public service obligations. Although it was now easier to incorporate, the general incorporation laws levied a dense web of restrictions

---

[43] Horwitz, *Transformation*, 33.
[44] Keller, *Affairs of State*, 112–115; Daniel Walker Howe, *The Political Culture of the American Whigs* (Chicago, University of Chicago Press, 1979), 302; Horwitz, *Transformation*, 20, 77, 102–4. As James Kloppenberg succinctly put it, "the ideal of the virtuous republic was sacrificed in exchange for the 'main chance. ...' Only the distrust of state authority survived from the legacy of civic humanism." *Uncertain Victory*, 173.

on corporations, imposing regulations at the very time that the nation ostensibly embraced *laissez-faire*.[45]

By granting corporations the right to hold stock in other corporations in 1889, New Jersey began a "race to the bottom" between the states. Although a pamphlet issued by Maine bragged about "the comparatively low organization fees and annual taxes," and highlighted "the absence upon restrictions upon capital stock or corporate indebtedness," and even though New York repeatedly revised its statutes in an effort to outbid New Jersey for corporate headquarters, by 1904, the seven largest trusts in the country, capitalized at over $2.5 billion collectively, were all organized under New Jersey law.[46]

Long before New Jersey sparked a race to the regulatory bottom, the Supreme Court broadened the constitutionally guaranteed rights protecting *all* American corporations. As general incorporation laws became the norm the federal judiciary reconceptualized just what corporations really were. Federal judges began to perceive corporations as bundles of contracts between private investors rather than as entities granted public authority to carry out special public purposes. The courts' revised perceptions, however, did not curtail investors' limited liability privileges.[47]

Nobody grasped this historical shift better than Supreme Court Justice Louis Brandeis. Brandeis had devoted a career to battling corporate encroachment on the rights of small businesses and individuals. As Brandeis reminded his brethren in 1933, "The prevalence of the corporation in America has led men of this generation to act, at times, as if the privilege of doing business in corporate form were inherent in the citizen; and has led them to accept the evils attendant upon the free and unrestricted use of the corporate mechanism as if these evils were the inescapable price of civilized life, and hence, to be borne with

---

[45] *Louis K. Liggett Co. v. Lee*, 288 U.S. 517, 555 (1933), available online at http://www. lexisnexis.com/universe; Gordon, "Legal Thought," 100; James Willard Hurst, *The Legitimacy of the Business Corporation in the Law of the United States, 1780–1970* (Charlottesville, VA: University Press of Virginia, 1970), 56. Hurst notes that by the 1840s, an increasing number of charters were for manufacturing and mining, and not for public utilities such as transportation and bridges. [18] See also, Bowman, *Modern Corporation.*

[46] Horwitz, *Transformation,* 83; Hurst, *Legitimacy of the Business Corporation,* 69; Gordon, "Legal Thought," 100; Corporation Trust Company pamphlet, "Business Corporations Under the Laws of Maine," (1903) cited in *Liggett v. Lee,* 558, n. 35; *Liggett v. Lee,* 562–63.

[47] Berk, "Constituting Corporations," 141.

resignation. Throughout the greater part of our history a different view prevailed."[48]

Of all the steps Brandeis took to mitigate the impact of "free and unrestricted use of the corporate mechanism" during his long legal career, his majority Supreme Court opinion in *Erie Railroad Co. v. Tompkins* (1938) was probably the most significant. *Erie* overturned *Swift v. Tyson* (1842). Post-Reconstruction federal courts had used *Swift* to broaden the federal common law at the expense of the states. By the first decade of the twentieth-century, the federal judiciary had deployed federal common law decisions to establish control over tort law, the law of common carriers, such as Western Union, and insurance law. Justice Oliver Wendell Holmes criticized the ever-expanding use of the federal common law because it assumed "a transcendental body of law outside of any particular State but obligatory within it unless and until changed by statute." In these and many other areas of judge-made law, the federal judiciary both nationalized the law and strengthened the judiciary's standing vis-a-vis the legislative branch of government.[49]

Santa Clara v. Southern Pacific Rail Road (1886) and its companion cases placed the nation's highest court squarely behind the principle that corporations were protected by the Fourteenth Amendment. Asked as to determine whether "corporations are persons within the meaning of the Fourteenth Amendment," Chief Justice Waite issued a definitive, albeit verbal, opinion on the matter. It was brief. The entire opinion consisted of the following: "The court does not wish to hear argument on the question whether the provision in the Fourteenth Amendment to the Constitution, which forbids a State to deny to any person within its jurisdiction the equal protection of the laws, applies to these corporations. We are all of opinion that it does."[50]

How did the Court arrive at this opinion, given that the Fourteenth Amendment was intended to protect freed slaves? In part, the Court's

[48] *Liggett v. Lee,* 548. Brandeis's dissent in a 1933 Supreme Court case, *Liggett v. Lee,* restricting the rights of a chain store in Florida is still one of the best concise histories of the nineteenth-century transformation of corporate standing in the law.

[49] Purcell, *Brandeis and the Progressive Constitution,* 51–56; *Erie Railroad Co. v. Tompkins,* 304 U.S. 64 (1938), available online at http://www.lexisnexis.com/universe; *Black and White Taxicab and Transfer Company v. Brown and Yellow Taxicab and Transfer Company,* 276 U.S. 518, 532–36 (1928), available online at http://www.lexisnexis.com/universe, cited in *Erie v. Tompkins,* 79, n23.

[50] Horwitz, *Transformation,* 66–71; Hurst, *Legitimacy of the Business Corporation,* 65; *Santa Clara County v. Southern Pacific Railroad Company,* 118 U.S. 394 (1886), available online at http://www.lexisnexis.com/universe.

radical departure in its interpretation of the Fourteenth Amendment reflected the growing success of Justice Field's relentless campaign to interpret the amendment broadly. Through this capacious reading, the Court eventually ratified the Union's victory in the Civil War and its dominance over the several states.[51]

With the rise of restriction-free incorporation, the courts also sought to regularize their treatment of corporations, turning to the law of partnership as their model. In other words, the decision also represented a shift in the federal judiciary's understanding of the basis for incorporation. Interpreted through the partnership framework, corporate control resided in the owners – the shareholders. This is precisely what Justice Field argued in his circuit opinion in *San Mateo*, the companion case to *Santa Clara*. Why, Field asked, would the Fourteenth Amendment apply to every person *except* those who owned shares in a corporation? The assumption that "corporation" was merely the "name of the artificial being" that stood in for constitutionally protected shareholders was most likely at the root of the Supreme Court's decision to treat corporations as persons.[52]

The larger dilemma that the Court pondered when grappling with the legal rights of corporations was how best to treat an association – a group – in a legal system built around the rights of individuals. The *Santa Clara* solution sought to extend the rights of corporations by treating them as bundles of individuals. As for those who spoke for the organizations themselves, such as the directors of corporations, they were regarded as mere agents of the shareholders. In veering toward an interpretation that narrowed the distinction between a partnership and a corporation, the Gilded Age court came perilously close to creating the very situation that Justice Taney had hoped to avoid almost fifty years earlier.[53]

---

[51] Especially because the Slaughterhouse decision in 1873 confirmed that the equal protection clause reached no further than determining the status of recently freed slaves. See Hurst, *Legitimacy of the Business Corporation*, 68; Horwitz, *Transformation*, 69. In the second half of the 1880s, the U.S. Supreme Court quietly imbued the corporation with the rights of a person, including the right to due process. A few years later, the Court ruled that corporations were entitled to protect their "liberty" against the unreasonable discrimination of state laws. As Willard Hurst noted long ago, extending these rights to corporations "was as much an exercise of judicial lawmaking as it had been to bring a corporation charter within the contract clause." *Legitimacy of the Business Corporation*, 66.

[52] Horwitz, *Transformation*, 70, 73; *County of San Mateo v. Southern Pacific Railroad Co.*, 13 F. 722, 744 (Circuit Court, D. California, 1882), available online at http://www.lexisnexis.com/universe, quoted in Horwitz, *Transformation*, 70.

[53] Horwitz, *Transformation*, 74.

To consider corporations as no more than aggregations of shareholders might erode the limited liability of shareholders that the "entity" interpretation reinforced. Taney posited a tension between those who viewed corporations as distinct entities and those who regarded them as mere aggregations of shareholders. Taney leaned toward the former. The latter interpretation would expose shareholders to liability, he believed. As Taney wrote in 1839, "the result of this would be to make a corporation a mere partnership in business, in which each stockholder would be liable to the whole extent of his property for the debts of the corporation; and he might be sued for them in any state in which he might happen to be found." *Santa Clara* imbued corporate entities with a powerful set of rights at the same time that it protected the individual rights of shareholders.[54]

"AUTONOMOUS, SELF-SUFFICIENT AND SELF-RENEWING": THE TRIUMPH OF "PRIVATE" CORPORATIONS

More than just the sum of their parts, corporations were the first organizations to be certified as legitimate nongovernmental actors in an emerging national pluralist political economy where individuals increasingly exercised their political and economic preferences through groups. In this world inhabited by associations rather than individuals, the federal courts weighed in directly to shore up the legal status of corporations as integrated, unified systems. The private corporation, endowed with a full set of constitutionally protected rights, sat front and center in this pluralist theater. It was standing room only for labor.

To most Americans in the 1880s there was little that seemed "natural" about gigantic trusts that sought to control prices for products that ranged from oil to sugar, tobacco to whiskey. By the end of the century, however, most Americans had accepted these behemoths as necessary, the price the country paid to sustain economic progress and expand its standard of living. Although the *Santa Clara* decision relied on a conception of corporations that likened them to loosely organized partnerships, it was the hierarchically organized, centrally directed management structure of corporations that made them distinctive. The ability to monitor and control

---

[54] Ibid., 76; *Bank of Augusta v. Joseph B. Earle*, 38 U.S. 519, 586 (1839), available online at http://www.lexisnexis.com/universe, quoted in Horwitz, *Transformation*, 76; Hurst, *Legitimacy of the Business Corporation*, 66.

distant activities allowed the largest railroads, and corporations like the Singer Manufacturing Corporation, to reshape the American economic and social landscape. Whether accepted as natural entities, or endured as artificially constructed organizations that were the most efficient units in a rapidly nationalizing economy, corporations were seen as more than the sum of their parts and far more than the sum of their shareholders' investments.[55]

Federal courts normalized the once radical conception of corporations as rights-bearing economic and social actors in a national market. They embedded this concept in the law. The law, in turn, influenced cultural conceptions of corporations. *Santa Clara* regarded corporations as persons for purposes of Fourteenth Amendment litigation, but arrived at that conclusion only because corporate shareholders were persons protected by the Amendment. Subsequent Supreme Court decisions moved far beyond this tangential corporate status. The Court soon treated corporations as integrated wholes, readily distinguishable from those individuals who happened to own shares. Corporations were to be regarded as persons in their own right, indeed persons with big personalities and a capacious set of rights, not mere shadows of their shareholder's personalities and protections.[56]

The issue that forced the Courts to choose between treating corporations as extensions of their shareholders or autonomous entities fully endowed with legal protections was management-controlled receivership by railroads. In the *Wabash* decision, the court came down squarely on the side of corporate autonomy. In 1884 notorious robber baron, Jay Gould, convinced a Federal District Court judge to place Gould's still-solvent, but financially crippled, Wabash, St. Louis, and Pacific Railway in receivership. In St. Louis, Judge David Brewer granted control to the railroad's management, upending clear legal precedent that traditionally viewed a company's bondholders as the rightful owners should corporate management default. Even Brewer's fellow circuit Judge, Samuel Treat, acknowledged that the proceeding had a "peculiar" aspect: "that the application was made by the corporation itself, instead of being made by the mortgagee on default of payment of interest."[57]

---

[55] Horwitz, *Transformation*, 73–75.
[56] Ibid., 65–90.
[57] *Central Trust Co. of N.Y. v. Wabash, St. L. & P.RY. Co.*, 29 F. 618 (Circuit Court, E.D. Missouri, 1886), available online at http://www.lexisnexis.com/universe, cited in Berk, "Constituting Corporations," 144–45; Gordon, "Legal Thought," 102; Berk, "Constituting Corporations," 141; *Wabash, St. L. & P.RY. Co. v. Central Trust Co.*

Granting control under receivership to the very management that had driven the corporation into default added insult to injury by the legal logic of the early 1880s. Yet Judge Brewer was persuaded by Gould's managers that the corporation was more than the sum of its parts. Brewer accepted the railroad's managers' argument that "here was a vast property, running through several states, burdened with a variety of local encumbrances and obligations, whose value consisted largely in its being preserved in its entirety and with all its connections. Split up into a hundred fragments, the aggregate value of the varied fragments ... would be as nothing compared with the value of the single, intact property." Judge Treat, who concurred with Brewer, noted that the Court must maintain the road as a "going concern," or else "you have nothing but a streak of iron-rust on the prairie."[58]

This was not the conclusion that Illinois Circuit Court Judge Walter Gresham drew when a group of disgruntled bondholders challenged Brewer's decision. Gresham concluded, correctly, that portions of the line operated quite successfully, drawing local traffic that more than paid back fixed costs. They might well go it alone, or find willing buyers. What they could *not* continue to do and remain financially viable, however, was subsidize the remaining portions of Gould's sprawling system. So Judge Gresham created a separate receivership, this one managed by the bondholders, for the Eastern division of the line, temporarily thwarting Gould's system-saving gambit.[59]

Gould had the last word, however. By preemptively securing receivership, yet retaining his control over management (at least in the Western division), Gould destroyed the value of Wabash securities in the open market. He then used the prospect for restoring some value to these now worthless assets to wring concessions from creditors who slashed both principle and interest payments. With his operating costs significantly reduced, the line emerged from receivership in 1889. Gould was still in control, and the original system remained intact.[60]

Though Gould was a one-of-a-kind operator, the tactics he used were soon replicated by system builders across the nation. Corporate

of N.Y., 22 F. 272, 273 (Circuit Court, E.D. Missouri, 1884), available online at http://www.lexisnexis.com/universe.

[58] *Wabash v. Central Trust and Central Trust v. Wabash,* 23 F. 513, 514–15 (Circuit Court, E.D. Missouri, 1885), available online at http://www.lexisnexis.com/universe; for Treat, see *Central Trust v. Wabash* (1886), 626.

[59] Berk, "Constituting Corporations," 144.

[60] Ibid.

reorganizations became the largest practice of eminent New York law firms by the 1880s. By 1895, a dozen railroads (or significant portions of them) had moved preemptively, as Gould had in 1884, to continue the existing management under the protection of court-ordered receivership. These "consent receiverships," as they were called, left management in a better position to renegotiate with creditors and squeeze costs out of the system.[61]

System builders required essential federal support in order to ensure that their organizations operated efficiently. By preempting receivership and keeping management intact, the courts retroactively embraced the value that inhered in systems *if those systems could be sustained*. It was judicial protection, not market forces, however, that ultimately sustained these systems. The federal judiciary shaped the emerging corporate economy in the Gilded Age through these often arcane legal battles. Courts provided the tools through which national system builders were able to reduce costs that the market had imposed on their risky ventures without sacrificing management's longer-term ambitions. The government helped to wring the risk out of system building – or at least lower its costs.

Such "efficiencies" often accrued *after* the federal judiciary intervened forcefully, though hardly visibly. No civil service here, no uniformed officers of the state – save a few more black robes. No higher taxes either.

This sequence diverged dramatically from the rationale for management's legal prerogatives – the presumed administrative advantages and economies of scale of larger systems – that soon was offered as the reason for corporate consolidation in the first place. By the end of the century, the scope and power of the legal ground rules that emerged from the Gilded Age federal judiciary touched the lives of all Americans, whether they worked for corporations, consumed their products, or simply sought to participate in a polity that remained solidly grounded in state and local politics, but that also increasingly played by rules hammered out in distant, inaccessible, and virtually invisible venues.[62]

Preemptive receiverships required a broader reconceptualization of corporations on the part of the judiciary. Embracing corporations as natural entities served this purpose neatly. Slowly, courts moved beyond the partnership paradigm that construed corporations as bundles of contracts with their shareholders. Instead, the courts began to embrace the concept that corporate integrity existed prior to, and endured beyond, the

---

[61] Gordon, "Legal Thought," 101–2; Berk, "Constituting Corporations," 142.
[62] Berk, "Constituting Corporations," 150.

capital invested by shareholders. The courts also concluded that the value of corporations comprised more than the sum of its material assets. State legislatures, especially that of New Jersey, aided the cause of corporate "liberation" by freeing them from limitations placed upon capitalization and internal organization. For practical purposes, the private corporation emerged with the "legal personality" of a fully entitled citizen.[63]

The interpretation that prevailed by the turn of the twentieth century required a double erasure on the part of its proponents. The memory that corporations had been spawned and overseen by the states vanished in a wave of general incorporation laws which were soon upstaged by New Jersey's capacious legislation. While legal doctrine treated corporate management during this phase as mere agents of the bondholders, the most important distinction between partnerships and corporations prevailed: the corporation, not its owners, was legally liable. By the mid 1880s, however, decisions like *Wabash* began to limit more than liability when it came to the shareholders. Increasingly, courts ruled that management best represented the longer-term interests of corporations, and that it "spoke" for a sum that transcended its discrete parts. Corporations were now viewed as integrated systems that transcended their tangible assets. Limited shareholder liability fit more comfortably with this modern interpretation, which presaged an age of relatively autonomous management. Deeply buried, however, and soon forgotten, was the crucial role that the federal judiciary had played in this double erasure.

Soon the debate over just what kind of autonomous *private* entity the corporation was crowded out memories of the corporation's public history. Although advocates of "natural entity" theory fiercely disputed the premise that corporations were simply bundles of contracts held by bondholders, they shared crucial common ground with those "contractualists." Both schools believed that corporations were private entities – prior to and separate from the state.[64]

By the 1890s, the conception that corporations were "natural entities" prevailed. For the "natural entity" advocates like Gierke and Maitland, corporations were "autonomous, self-sufficient and self-renewing bodies," and "neither the group nor its functions is created by the state." Subscribers to the "natural entity" perspective viewed concentration as the natural result of market economies – a fortuitous development. As William W. Cook declared in 1891, concentration was "a law of

---

[63] Gordon, "Legal Thought," 101.
[64] Horwitz, *Transformation*, 101.

nature." "These great concerns," Cook continued, "arise because by doing business on a large scale they can do it more cheaply." Some of the strongest supporters for this perspective were historically inclined economists. From their vantage point, the movement toward concentration was simply part of the organic development of capitalism. "The laws of trade are stronger than the laws of men," Cook confidently pronounced at the beginning of the fifth edition of his corporate law treatise.[65]

Like the national market it helped to create, the Court came to regard the corporation as a natural entity, which it sought to protect. The Court was influenced on this matter, as were many Americans, by the popularity of evolutionary thought which insisted that the laws of nature – in this case the inexorable economies of scale embodied in the corporate form of organizing – should inform manmade law. By inscribing this social theory into the nation's law, the Supreme Court contributed to a self-fulfilling prophecy. It endowed corporations with the same due process rights enjoyed by individuals, hastening the consolidation it belatedly asked the states to control. Sailing under the protection of the Court's due process interpretation, corporations were shielded from regulatory actions that might be construed as depriving the corporation of its property in numerous efforts to regulate rates. By 1906, the Supreme Court could pronounce that "corporations are a necessary feature of modern business activity," adding that "their aggregated capital has become the source of nearly all great enterprises."[66]

Eclipsed between the 1880s and the first decade of the twentieth century, the state-derived origins of corporate development were soon revived by Progressives. They, like the natural entity crowd, accepted the corporation as a real and powerful actor in the political economy. As such, it should be treated as an organic whole. But Progressives insisted that ultimately the corporation was the artificial creation of the state through the laws of that state. Like individuals, corporations merited rights, Progressive legal theorist Gerard Henderson argued. However,

[65] Ibid., 75; John P. Davis, "The Nature of Corporations," *Political Science Quarterly*, 12, no. 2 (June 1897): 273, 278, quoted in Horwitz, *Transformation*, 101; William W. Cook, *The Corporation Problem*, (New York: Knickerbocker Press, 1893 [1891]), 226, http://books.google.com/, quoted in Horwitz, *Transformation*, 84–85; Cook, *Treatise on the Law of Corporations Having a Capital Stock*, 5th edn (Callaghan 1903), vii, quoted in Horwitz, *Transformation*, 85.

[66] Horwitz, *Transformation*, 68–75; Bensel, *Political Economy*, 334–36; *Hale v. Henkel*, 201 U.S. 43, 76 (1906), quoted in Purcell, *Brandeis and the Progressive Constitution*, 39.

both corporations *and* individuals derived those rights from manmade law, not from nature.[67]

As with so many of the Gilded Age attempts to establish clear boundaries between public and private spheres, the contest petered out in the early twentieth century with the grudging acceptance that the two were hopelessly intermingled. Like so many other fierce battles over the boundaries between state and society during the Gilded Age, the stakes heightened as the outcomes increasingly governed national, rather than merely state and local behavior.

"TO INSURE UNIFORMITY AGAINST DISCRIMINATING STATE LEGISLATION": CREATING THE LEGAL INFRASTRUCTURE FOR A NATIONAL MARKET

The national market that emerging corporate giants hoped to tap was hardly a foregone conclusion. States sought to protect local producers and distributors from "foreign" competition. Although naked imposition of tariffs on other states was clearly proscribed by the constitution, by the last quarter of the nineteenth century, states deployed more subtle devices to protect hometown producers. Much of this legislation relied on long-standing prerogatives like licensing and inspection that were unquestionably state, not federal, powers. Strategically directed, these tools could offer significant protection from out-of-state competition. Nobody questioned the constitutional authority of Congress to clear local barriers to interstate trade. However, the parochial orientation of Congress – where even U.S. senators were elected by state legislatures – precluded Congressional action.[68]

Federal courts harbored no such reservations when it came to ensuring an unencumbered market. Between 1875 and the late 1890s, the Supreme Court walked a fine line between preserving government control over the structure of corporations chartered by the states and ensuring a national market in which corporations could sell their goods and services. Despite the growing tendency of federal courts to imbue corporations with a full set of rights and ensure due process, states continued to oversee corporate regulation. The states used this power to favor local interests whenever possible.

---

[67] Horwitz, *Transformation*, 104–5.

[68] Charles W. McCurdy, "American Law and the Marketing Structure of the Large Corporation, 1875–1890," *Journal of Economic History*, 38, no. 3 (September 1978): 631–32.

Erecting barriers to the distribution of goods manufactured out of state
was a common practice in some states. In *Welton v. Missouri* (1875), the
Supreme Court ruled that the state of Missouri could not license peddlers
just because the merchandise they sold had been manufactured outside of
the state. The merchandise in question were sewing machines. I.M. Singer
& Company, which mass produced these machines, began to retail them
directly to consumers by the 1870s. Singer employed a network of company stores and traveling salesmen. Because Congress had not weighed in
on this highly fraught field of interstate commerce, several states filled the
vacuum. They claimed a settled right to tax, including licensing articles
produced outside the state. When Singer agent M.M. Welton violated an
1845 Missouri statute, he was convicted and jailed. With its entire distribution at stake, Singer challenged the constitutionality of the law.[69]

As the Supreme Court knew well, the Constitution had vested the right
to regulate interstate commerce in the legislative branch, yet Congress had
remained silent on this matter and was likely to remain so for some time.
Undeterred, Justice Stephen Field delivered the Supreme Court's opinion,
overturning Welton's conviction on constitutional grounds. Determined
to head off interstate tariff wars, Field noted that, "It will not be denied
that that portion of commerce with foreign countries and between the
States which consists in the transportation and exchange of commodities
is of national importance, and admits and requires uniformity of regulation. The very object of investing this power in the General Government
was to insure this uniformity against discriminating State legislation."
Field was not troubled by Congressional silence on the issue. Coupled
with its legislation imposing a national tariff on foreign goods, Field
insisted, Congressional inaction was "equivalent to a declaration that
inter-State commerce shall be free and untrammeled." Field was clearly
more confident in his ability to interpret Congressional sign language
than his predecessors had been.[70]

Perhaps that is because the signals coming from the nascent national
market were more urgent, given the rise of corporations like Singer and
McCormick. They and many other corporations were eager to market their
wares nationally and even internationally. Prior federal decisions, while
confirming Congressional prerogative in this field, had deferred to state
and local legislative preference in the absence of Congressional guidance.

[69] *Welton v. Missouri*, 91 U.S. 275 (1875), available online at http://www.lexisnexis.com/
universe; McCurdy, "Marketing Structure," 637, 639, 640.
[70] *Welton v. Missouri*, 280, 282.

The Marshall Court refused to pick sides in the tug-of-war between the states and the national government that Congress had failed to address through legislation. This left ample room for the states to restrict markets in ways that advantaged hometown producers. Subsequent Supreme Court decisions claimed a judicial prerogative where Congress refused to intervene, but failed to articulate any overriding principle for deciding the limits of the state's power to deflect trade in advantageous directions.[71]

The states' legal proscription of markets proved every bit as influential in shaping trade as so-called natural barriers, whether the Appalachians or the Mississippi River. If the history of British North America and the early American Republic taught anything, it was that political jurisdiction played a crucial role in defining markets. By the mid-nineteenth century, the increased pace of interstate commerce pressured states to protect key constituencies who could not compete with lower-priced goods and services produced beyond their borders. The transportation and communications revolutions, engineered by the phenomenal growth of rail transportation, rapid industrialization, the continued migration West of millions of Americans, and the economic specialization that followed from concentrated production, created the *potential* for an integrated national market. But that potential, much like the potential value that inhered in portions of railroad systems, could not be realized without imposing interstate stability from above.[72]

After the Civil War, state legislatures crafted a variety of measures to protect their "home" markets. Out-of-state insurance companies were one target. Often the assets of these companies were beyond the reach of courts in their clients' state. Out-of-state companies also took away local business (while energizing local political action). States were creative in their efforts to protect local business and control out-of-state operators. In 1879, for instance, North Carolina required a hefty deposit in U.S. bonds before an out-of-state company could conduct business. States also sought to protect liquor by exempting local production from taxation. Southern states kept a lid on local labor costs by taxing out-of-state agents who recruited sharecroppers.[73]

Those who sought to take advantage of what might become an integrated national market required national legal protection if that market was to become a reality. State-level regulation and even financing,

---

[71] McCurdy, "Marketing Structure," 635.
[72] Bensel, *Political Economy*, 290.
[73] Ibid., 322–23.

of course, were nothing new. The parochial interests that turned to state government for protection knew their way around legislative hallways and governor's mansions. Advocates of national action had few options. They were wary of Congress – with its political roots buried deeply in the local soil of state-based political parties. Nor did the White House seem any more likely to surmount local, partisan ties in this era of weak presidents. Relatively insulated from public opinion, nationalist in perspective, the federal judiciary appeared to be the last best hope.

It did not disappoint. Companies like Singer crafted sophisticated, long-term strategies to engineer what in retrospect was portrayed as a natural phenomenon – an integrated national market free from the interference of states and localities. Why nature should stop at the Mexican or Canadian border was a question that international corporations would defer for another century. In the meantime, the national judiciary ensured that states would not impede the flow of goods across the United States.

The national market trumped local restraint, even when long-standing responsibility for health and safety, not to mention scientific evidence, favored local prerogative. The question of a state's authority to conduct inspections was broached in *Minnesota v. Barber* (1890). It pitted two of the nation's most powerful associations against each other. One was a classic trust. The other epitomized the kind of trade associations that increasingly yoked together smaller producers and merchants. The combination of refrigeration, favorable railroad rates, economies of scale, and cooperation on pricing among the "Big Four" meatpackers challenged butchers in what previously had been local markets across the country.

The Butchers Protective Association fought back. It was created explicitly to seek relief in familiar places – state legislatures. It persuaded three states to enact legislation requiring that beef, mutton, and pork be inspected by state inspectors before it was slaughtered. This effectively neutralized all of the advantages held by the Big Four. The meatpackers disregarded the legislation, inviting a Supreme Court Challenge.[74]

Led by Justice Field, the Supreme Court ruled in 1890. Brushing aside the explicit language in the Constitution granting states the power to inspect, deflecting Supreme Court precedent in earlier cases that upheld state inspection laws "despite the fact that they 'm[ight] have … a considerable influence on commerce,'" and disputing the scientific evidence that the Minnesota brief deployed to justify inspection on the hoof, a

---

[74] McCurdy, "Marketing Structure," 644.

unanimous Court cited the precedent of *Welton* to overturn the Minnesota law. That law, the Court argued, would in effect prohibit *interstate* sale of meat. The state legislature would have to find another means to protect the health of its citizens – one that did not restrict the right of meatpackers to sell their goods to Minnesotans and for that matter, the right of Minnesotans to a choice of products including those shipped from other states.[75]

Justice Harlan, writing for the Court, spelled out the relationship between federal and state authority: "It is one thing for a state to exclude from its limits cattle, sheep, or swine actually diseased." It was another matter, Harlan warned, for Minnesota to legislate "that fresh beef, veal, mutton, lamb, or pork-articles that are used in every part of this country to support human life – shall not be sold at all for human food within its limits unless the animal from which such meats are taken is inspected in that state, or, as is practically said, unless the animal is slaughtered in that state."[76]

That the Court, by 1890, regularly sacrificed time-honored state prerogatives when they interfered with interstate commerce, despite, or even *because* of Congressional silence on the matter, marked a crucial turning point in the assertion of national judicial authority. As Chief Justice Fuller put it in *U.S. v. E.C. Knight* (1895), "the failure of congress to exercise this exclusive power [regulating commerce among the several states] ... is an expression of its will that the subject shall be free from restriction or impositions upon it." Given Congress's local perspective, it was also an essential intervention that secured a "natural" national market.[77]

The federal judiciary's influence is best measured in the local response to national legal intervention. One Iowa representative summed up a widely shared view in his state and in much of the West and the South: "The tendency of the wealth of the country is toward associate capital. Colossal insurance companies, gigantic railroad enterprises, and other multifarious corporate organizations exist in every locality." The agents of these corporate giants throughout the land were federal courts. They "have grown," his colleague from Michigan insisted, "to be largely corporation mills, in which the tolls are largely taken from the individual

[75] Ibid., 646–47; *Minnesota v. Barber*, 136 U.S. 313 (1890), available online at http://www.lexisnexis.com/universe.
[76] *Minnesota v. Barber*, 328.
[77] *United States v. E.C. Knight Company*, 156 U.S. 1, 11 (1895), available online at http://www.lexisnexis.com/universe.

citizen[;] … it has become the fact that … the old feudal system has sought refuge behind the judicial system." Although the cost of the federal judiciary increased from \$500,000 in 1850 to \$3.3 million by 1875, such costs were barely visible compared to the corporate value created, or the size and scope of the market these corporations operated in.[78]

The Gilded Age Court ambitiously undertook the nearly impossible task of distinguishing public from private transactions, especially in its commitment to "freedom of contract." With cases like *Welton* and *Barber,* it tried to distinguish local and national functions in an approach that came to be known as "dual sovereignty." It divided commerce between local and interstate components. In both instances, the Court marched boldly into territory that Congress scrupulously avoided. A crucial shot in the arm for organizations and associations that already looked across state borders for members and customers, legal opinion exacerbated the tension between local and national political jurisdiction by removing legal barriers and vesting a new set of national actors – corporations – with a powerful set of rights and privileges. Like the legal construction of a national market, this was done in the name of protecting the "natural" order.[79]

Once again, a "government out of sight" proved far more effective and far more powerful than the ubiquitous administrative apparatus that we associate with national public authority today. Powerful governments, of course, had created both markets and corporations in the past, but they had demanded, in highly visible fashion, reciprocal obligations from the corporations they chartered; and deference, if not tribute, from those favored by the markets they protected. What distinguished the Court's role in the creation of a national market in the United States, and the privileges it bestowed on that markets' premier beneficiaries, was the minimal weight it attached to its own role in this remarkable achievement.

"A SINGLE GOLD STANDARD IS THE ONLY BASIS FOR SOUND MONEY": CREATING A NATIONAL MONETARY POLICY

Access to foreign capital and confidence in the nation's currency were also crucial elements in the creation of a national market. For members

---

[78] Congressional Record, 10, pt. 1, 5 February 1880 (Washington, D.C.; GPO, 1880), 724–25, available online at www.heinonline.org, quoted in Freyer, "Federal Courts" 359; Freyer, "Federal Courts," 353.

[79] Bensel, *Political Economy,* 327.

of the Eastern financial establishment, these objectives would never be achieved without rigid adherence to the gold standard. Cyclical recessions, especially the severe economic downturn in the early 1890s, also created demands from a number of sectors of the economy for greater monetary control. The federal government played a crucial role in returning the nation to the gold standard after the Civil War, working closely with a largely private banking system. Once again, Congress played a relatively minor role in what was perceived by most interests to be a public policy that clearly favored Easterners over Southerners and Westerners, tilting toward creditors over debtors.

The challenge for those who sought adequate capital and the monetary tools to manage a national market was similar to the conundrum that the Court faced in balancing local and national claims to commerce. Advocates presumed that the advantages of a national market would benefit the entire nation, once such a market was established. Yet the very act of creating such a national market inevitably favored some interests over others. Deploying the authority of the national government merely cleared obstacles to a nascent national (and in the case of gold – an international) market that lay waiting to deliver its bounty to all Americans, proponents argued.

Farmers and small business men disagreed, sometimes violently. Federal policies that promoted large corporations and maintained a rigid gold standard exposed agriculture and small business to competition from afar, overruling long-standing state prerogatives. It preserved a deflationary policy that favored large creditors. And it appeared to be anything but "natural."[80]

The United States government maintained the gold standard against all odds. Shortly before Reconstruction ended, Congress passed the Resumption Act of 1875. It required the Treasury to sell bonds that restored the value of greenbacks (issued during the Civil War) to parity with dollars backed by gold by January 1, 1879. Because the executive branch remained committed to this goal, and indeed stayed the course for the remainder of the century, the United States did not waiver from its commitment to the gold standard.[81]

Powerful social movements called for monetary policy that would inflate the currency to serve a growing population and economy. Twice,

[80] Ibid., 356; James Livingston, *Origins of the Federal Reserve System: Money, Class, and Corporate Capitalism, 1890–1913* (Ithaca, NY: Cornell University Press, 1986), 67, 80.
[81] Bensel, *Political Economy,* 376.

Congress passed legislation that called for the coinage of silver – measures that many hoped would force the nation off the gold standard. Under the Bland-Allison Act, passed over President Hays' veto in 1878, the treasury was ordered to purchase and coin $2 million in silver a month. It did so dutifully for more than a decade. However, because the coins were redeemable for gold, and because the government was committed to demonstrating its will to back up its word with gold, most of these coins were quickly redeemed for gold or dollars backed by gold. This meant that they wound up right back where they started: in Treasury vaults. Even before the Sherman Purchase Act (1890), which more than doubled the government's annual silver coinage requirement, the Treasury had run out of room to store its silver. In Philadelphia, the mint was forced to haul 20 million newly minted coins to the post office – the only place left to store the growing surplus of silver.[82]

Through its daily intervention into the gold market, the Treasury was able to continue redeeming dollars for gold despite the mounting drag of silver purchases. By the early 1890s, the fear that political pressure would force the United States off the gold standard, combined with a severe economic downturn, led to a run on gold. In 1893, gold reserves dropped perilously below the level deemed essential by Treasury officials. With his own political party on record favoring soft money, Grover Cleveland strong-armed Congress into repealing the Sherman Silver Purchase Act.

Further action, however, was required if the United States was to remain committed to the gold standard. When Congress ignored the President's request for authorization to issue additional bonds, Cleveland was forced to appeal to the private sector to preserve the gold standard. Two of the nation's leading bankers, J.P. Morgan and August Belmont agreed to transfer $60 million in gold in return for government bonds that returned 4 percent for thirty years. Cleveland's actions, in conjunction with an upturn in the economy, saved the gold standard. But not without Herculean efforts by the Treasury. It issued in excess of $250 million in long-term debt between 1894 and 1896 in order to defend the gold standard.[83]

Leading investment bankers worked closely with the Cleveland administration to protect a "hard" American dollar. For financial conservatives, backing dollars with gold meant that the market, not government functionaries, would dictate the value of money. Morgan made the

---

[82] Ritter, *Goldbugs and Greenbacks*, esp. chap. 5; Bensel, *Political Economy*, 377, 392.
[83] Bensel, *Political Economy*, 411–17, 422–23.

connection clear upon his return from London in March 1896. He urged the Republican Party to come out solidly for sound money. "European investors are watching the situation here closely," Morgan warned. "They will not invest in American securities until they know in what kind of money we propose to pay our debts," the banker instructed. "A single gold standard is the only basis for sound money."[84]

This time it was the executive branch, rather than the judiciary, that intervened behind the scenes. As those silver coins piled up at the post office, the Treasury articulated a national monetary policy built on the gold standard. Whether a policy that inflated the currency to match the growth of the American economy and population would have been more or less "natural" than the Treasury Departments' fiscal gymnastics is an open question.

What we can be sure of is that without the executive branch's often unpopular and costly defense of gold, the national market that emerged in the twentieth century would have operated quite differently. The election of 1896 put the currency issue to rest once and for all. While Americans voted for the Republican McKinley over Democratic silverite Bryan for many reasons, the gulf between the two candidates was widest on the currency issue. The election of 1896 swept a solid Republican majority into Congress and began a reign of Republican presidents broken only by Republican factionalism, the Great Depression, and Franklin D. Roosevelt.

"TO DEAL WITH MONOPOLY DIRECTLY AS SUCH":
THE RACE TO THE BOTTOM

Although the Supreme Court insisted that long-standing state prerogatives, like inspection, give way to the national market, the Court found states best suited to charter and supervise corporations. States worked overtime to restrict the merger of corporations chartered in their jurisdiction during the 1880s. Goaded into action by the popular outcry against gigantic trusts that threatened to monopolize industries like oil, sugar – even whiskey, attorneys general in six states drew upon their power to charter. The attorneys general sued in order to prevent corporate restructuring that led to trusts. In each instance, they demanded dissolution of the trust or holding company. In Louisiana it was the Cottonseed-Oil

---

[84] Ritter, *Goldbugs and Greenbacks*, 85; "The Financial Situation," *Commercial and Financial Chronicle* 62, June 13, 1896, 1060, quoted in Bensel, *Political Economy*, 424.

Trust; public utilities in Illinois; the Sugar Trust in California and New York; and whiskey in Nebraska and Illinois. Every case was successful, including Ohio's action against Standard Oil.[85]

The Supreme Court's interpretation of the Sherman Anti-Trust Act of 1890 has often been cited as the catalyst for the flood of mergers that swept the nation in the late 1890s. It is certainly true that, in rejecting the U.S. government's claim against a horizontal combination like the American Sugar Refining Company, the Court defended its long-standing distinction between commerce and manufacturing. In *United States v. Knight* (1895), the Court ruled that the sugar trust engaged in the latter, and as such, was subject to state, not federal control. Chief Justice Fuller could not have stated the distinction more clearly: "the contracts and acts of the defendants related exclusively to the acquisition of the Philadelphia refineries and the business of sugar refining in Pennsylvania, and bore no direct relation to commerce between the states or with foreign nations." As the majority concluded, "the subject-matter of the sale was shares of manufacturing stock ... yet the act of Congress only authorized the circuit courts to proceed by way of preventing and restraining violations of the act in respect of contracts, combinations, or conspiracies in restraint of interstate or international trade."[86]

The Court's decision, however, was also guided by the presumption that the states remained the most effective jurisdiction for regulating corporate excess because states, not the federal government, chartered corporations in the first place. As the successful defense of that authority in the 1880s demonstrated, states could *un*charter corporations for violating that grant of public authority. By distinguishing between commerce and manufacture, the Supreme Court preserved the states' power to regulate corporate activity, including the power to tax or even prohibit manufacturing by corporations chartered beyond state borders. Upholding this right to regulate "foreign" corporations, the court ruled in *Paul v. Virginia* (1869) that Virginia's foreign corporation law was constitutional. To rule otherwise would deny a state's citizens the meaningful right to charter *any* corporations. As Justice Field, speaking for a unanimous Court, put it, "if, when composed of citizens of one State, their corporate powers and franchises could be exercised in other States without restriction, it is easy to see that, with the advantages thus possessed, the most important business of those States would soon pass into their hands. The principal

---

[85] McCurdy, "Knight Sugar," 321–22.
[86] *U.S. v. Knight*, 17.

business of every State would, in fact, be controlled by corporations created by other States." This portended political disaster, potentially freeing footloose corporations from the very jurisdictions that were both legally and politically best poised to hold these artificial entities to their public obligations.[87]

The *Knight* decision *preserved* the rights of states to regulate or even exclude foreign corporations. Writing for the court, Fuller insisted that "it is vital that the independence of the commercial power and of the police power, and the delimitation between them, however sometimes perplexing, should always be recognized and observed, for while the one furnishes the strongest bond of union, the other is essential to the preservation of the autonomy of the states as required by our dual form of government." The states had the right to regulate corporations: the Supreme Court assumed that they would act on that right. As Chief Justice Fuller concluded, the states had all the tools they needed "to deal with monopoly directly as such."[88]

Several developments eventually undercut this logic. The most obvious was engineered by a traitor among the states: New Jersey. Happy for the business, New Jersey crafted an incorporation statute in 1889 that allowed corporations chartered in New Jersey to acquire the stock or assets of corporations chartered in other states. In effect, it invited them to merge with foreign corporations. States, of course, still had the legal authority to block the manufacture of goods or provision of services, like insurance, offered by foreign corporations. This was precisely the legal remedy that the Supreme Court struggled to preserve in the *Knight* decision.[89]

Legal rights, however, did not always match political mandates. Faced with the choice of fighting or switching – or to put it another way, taking collective action against one "traitor" state or following New Jersey's lead and abdicating control over corporations – a growing number of states opted to gut their incorporation statutes in the hope of tapping new sources of revenue from the corporations that would flock to the latest haven for would-be trusts. By the turn of the century, states abandoned

---

[87] *Paul v. Virginia*, 75 U.S. 168, 182 (1869), available online at *http://www.lexisnexis.com/universe/*, quoted in McCurdy, "Knight Sugar," 315.

[88] *U.S. v. Knight*, 13, 16. The only justice to dispute this was Harlan, who, in his dissent, blasted the notion that the national government could not do what the states clearly were empowered to do – prevent consolidation that might lead to monopoly power over pricing. [18]

[89] McCurdy, "Knight Sugar," 322; Hurst, *Legitimacy of the Business Corporation*, 69–70.

their campaign to adopt a model incorporation statute that would inhibit consolidation. The legal tools remained available; the political will, however, had either dissipated or been redirected toward the race to the bottom.[90]

Having breathed life into the legal conception of "private" corporations, outfitted them with a formidable array of rights, and issued visas to conduct commerce in any state, the federal courts handed the task of regulating these rambunctious adolescents back to the states. The federal courts contributed materially to the radical shift in perception that occurred in the thirty years following the Civil War. By the end of the century, corporations were viewed by many as the product of market forces that required political protection only from those who dared to interfere with natural law. It is this intellectual transformation, aided and abetted by the Supreme Court's unwavering endorsement of corporate personhood, that explains why many states chose to jump on the bandwagon started by New Jersey's relaxation of corporate regulation. States still had the legal right to regulate corporations. But to many, the task seemed hopeless, if not unnatural.

* * *

By making the market more predictable – more uniform – across states, and friendlier to large employers, the courts were a powerful national force during the Gilded Age. They tried mightily to sort between national and local issues, private and public matters. Through injunctions, they sought to preempt certain behaviors, taking on an administrative cast in a government with little capacity in that field.

Progressive Era activists took pride in exposing the ways in which elites corrupted the courts. They railed against the elite power politics, exercised through the courts, that crushed workers and farmers alike. Elites did have the upper hand in the law schools, the law firms, and the national business-oriented interest groups that were emerging in the late nineteenth century. These key actors did have a disproportionate advantage in steering the national judiciary in a direction that favored interstate corporate business. Seeking to systematize the law, to make it more predictable and more amenable to administered remedies, the courts responded favorably to litigants who shared these values. That

[90] McCurdy, "Knight Sugar," 338–40.

the national judiciary added its own administrative hierarchy in 1891, establishing the Circuit Court of Appeals, symbolized both the increased workload and the growing articulation of the law.[91]

Progressive muckrakers, however, missed a far more important insight. That three decades of judicial expansion and intervention into the civil sphere and local prerogatives was perceived by many to be a neutral response to the kind of "statist" programs advocated by some workers, farmers, and progressive intellectuals is a testimonial to the power of governance that is hidden in plain sight. The courts sought to carry out a vision of national integration that was shared by millions of Americans, including a good number of producers. It was a vision that imagined society progressing harmoniously, if only the national government could carve out sufficient space for natural law, which now worked side-by-side with divine guidance. Once restored, the federal government could withdraw – just as the federal courts did when it came to overseeing the actual regulation of corporate consolidation – leaving the task to the states. That this conception ignored the aggressive intervention by the courts into local and state matters, or their remarkable conversion of corporate standing from public to private, speaks more to the power that Americans historically had been willing to grant to a federal government that did not increase taxes or build bureaucratic strongholds, than to elite collusion.

Ultimately, the national judiciary was unable to sustain the very balancing act it sought to institutionalize. It choked on the increasingly tenuous distinctions it drew between public and private during an era in which Progressives questioned the very distinction between an individual and his surrounding environment. The Court's ability to administer and specialize also proved limited compared to the administrative mechanisms of "continuous management" that Progressives favored. Eventually the courts withdrew and claimed that the market would sort things out. Having set an integrated national market in motion, this retreat contributed to the perception that the market was a "natural" phenomenon. Increasingly, the courts called it that. Of course, these were the corporations, and this was the market, that the courts had helped to construct. In economics, it might be called a free market economy. In politics, it looked a lot like interest group pluralism, with the corporate sector leading a well-organized, and amply supported, charge.[92]

---

[91] Ernst, "Law and American Political Development," 210.
[92] Gilman, *Constitution Besieged*, 14; Hurst, *Legitimacy of the Business Corporation*, 162.

9

"A Special Form of Associative Action": New Liberalism and the National Integration of Public and Private

In the spring of 1885, a group of economists representing the "new school" of economics issued a statement that founded the American Economic Association (AEA). The AEA, in turn, was a key contributor to the "new liberalism" that emerged in the late nineteenth century and forged the intellectual foundation for the Progressive Era. Among the leaders of the American Economic Association were such prominent economists as Henry C. Adams, John Bates Clark, Richard Ely, and Edwin R.A. Seligman. Their platform was endorsed by prominent clergymen engaged in social reform, including the Rev. Dr. Lyman Abbot and the Rev. Dr. Washington Gladden. Carroll D. Wright, Commissioner of the U.S. Bureau of Labor, also lent his support. Several aspects of the AEA's platform raised eyebrows among Americans schooled in the political economy of *laissez-faire*. But no statement drew as much attention as the first sentence of the platform, which proclaimed, "We regard the state as an educational and ethical agency whose positive aid is an indispensable condition of human progress."[1]

Seeking to disseminate the core principles of this new approach to its readers, *Science* provided a platform for economists from the new school of economics in a series of essays sprinkled through its 1886 volumes. Critics of the new approach, most prominently William Graham Sumner, were also invited to contribute. Those looking for a knockdown, drag-out fight must have been disappointed. Despite essays by Ely, Seligman, and E.J. James, one critic complained that the new

---

[1] Richard Ely, "Report of the Organization of the American Economic Association," *Publications of the American Economic Association,* 1, no. 1 (March 1886): 6–8.

school had pulled its punches. There had been little discussion of the main point of difference between the "old school," and the new: "that it looks with more favor upon government intervention in the process of industry and trade."[2]

For the new school, the state was simply one of many associative and cooperative techniques available. Or as E.J. James put it, "Perhaps the most general formulation of the essential characteristic of state action … is that it is preeminently a co-ordinating power. It is a special form of associative action." It is true that one can find some pretty direct statements of the need for state intervention in these essays. Yet the critic was correct in his overall assessment of the new school's failure to emphasize state intervention.[3]

New liberals embraced a wide range of options regarding the relationship between state and society in the late nineteenth century. Some of these options did indeed contribute to national statist solutions. As such, they neatly confirm a host of standard interpretations of the rise of the twentieth-century national administrative state. Far more often, however, new liberals stressed other forms of cooperative action: state and local intervention rather than intervention by the national government; action by voluntary and private organizations compelled by the force of public opinion to do the right thing; and most significantly, delegating national authority to private and voluntary groups so that they, rather than the national government directly, could compel individuals to comply with policies that served the greater good of the country. Thus the national government, acting alone, was indeed a "special" form of associative action – not only because it wielded the club of compulsion, but more significantly, because that form of associative action was rarely sought, and even less frequently granted, at the end of the nineteenth century. Other forms of associative action, however, including those that relied on the delegation of federal authority, flourished.

---

[2] Simon Newcomb, "Aspects of the Economic Discussion," *Science,* 7, no. 176 (June 18, 1886): 538.

[3] E.J. James, "The State as an Economic Factor," *Science,* 7, no. 173 (May 28, 1886): 486. James summed up the new school's position by declaring that "in order to secure a healthy economic progress, large quantities of capital and labor must be expended along lines where a few individuals, by their ignorance or obstinacy, may prevent that collective action without which such investment cannot be made. It is necessary for the state to interfere in such cases; and its action is as truly economic action as that which removes by a tunnel the obstruction presented to trade by a hill, or which renders commerce across a river easy by the construction of a bridge." [487]

New liberals favored associative action for four reasons. First, they were sensitive, and willing to adapt, to practical politics. Second, they had great faith in the power of public opinion: they believed that it could compel socially beneficial action. Third, their theory of knowledge was self-consciously social in its construction and democratic in its orientation. They rewarded experience over fixed, timeless truths. They factored public misgivings about socialism into their program because truth for them lay in experience and that experience had to take account of the will of the people. Fourth, new liberals placed a great deal of faith in the historical evolution of society.

Looking back to history, new liberals found that state action had been a staple of economic, social, and political development. But they also found that a commitment to protecting the rights of individuals had endured. Indeed, the surest bond between new liberalism and the older "classical" liberalism was the commitment to the rights of individuals. Historically, merging state and private action on the local level had been essential to resolving this tension between collective and individual action. But increasingly, a national regime that promised to divide private from public action threatened older political traditions. New liberals agreed that given the expansion of the market and civil society, national intervention was indeed required. But they sought to restore the more cooperative approach that had characterized much of American political development. On the eve of the twentieth century, new liberals hoped to overturn what they viewed as the exceptional regime of *laissez-faire* and replace it with a more enduring, and historically consistent, associative vision that could serve the entire nation.

New liberalism is widely credited with providing the intellectual underpinning for an active national government that for the first time admitted national statist solutions to social problems. Yet, many of the intellectuals who forged this intellectual movement went to great lengths to demonstrate that their interpretation of contemporary events resonated with long-standing patterns in the relationship between state and society, and that their programs for social reform were consistent with much of that history. They were at pains to show that *laissez-faire* was an historical phase in the evolution of the American polity, not a constant.

While a necessary precondition to the growth of central government, new liberalism did not lead automatically to a national administrative state. Rather, it reopened the door to the intermingling of state and private means of extending public authority, breaking down the bulwarks constructed during the exceptional period of *laissez-faire*. New liberals applied what they considered to be historically proven methods to new conditions.

There was an important difference, however. What distinguished state-society relations in the last third of the nineteenth century from the commonwealth and republican period before it was that interaction increasingly was national in scope. The General Government served as an eligible, though hardly autonomous, actor. The range of national voluntary and private associations that were now available for the federal government to work with also distinguished this period. And work with them it did, parceling out state authority to interest groups, professional societies, the voluntary sector, corporations, and eventually even to labor unions.[4]

New liberals' historicist rejection of the tyranny of changeless natural law, their embrace of the collective, and their insistence that man was the product of his environment and social relations, cleared away many Gilded Age barriers to the construction of a more active General Government by the turn of the century. It helped create a General Government that could take autonomous action in policy areas such as pure food and drugs, or conservation. But to fully grasp the trajectory of governance in the twentieth century, we must reexamine new liberal thought with an eye toward understanding the way in which it supported

---

[4] For an influential account of the ways in which corporate liberals mobilized to regulate and restrict competition, thereby delegating the authority to regulate the market to corporations, see Martin J. Sklar, *The Corporate Reconstruction of American Capitalism, 1890–1916: The Market, The Law, and Politics* (New York, NY: Cambridge University Press, 1988).

Labor waited far longer to receive equal protection, in both the figurative and legal sense of the phrase. Nevertheless, new liberals pressed for such protections and won grudging victories by the end of the Progressive Era. Daniel R. Ernst demonstrates this in rich detail in *Against Labor: From Individual Rights to Corporate Liberalism* (Urbana, IL: University of Illinois Press, 1995). Ernst follows the campaign of a reactionary association of employers, The American Anti-Boycott Association, (ABBA) founded in 1902. The ABBA, rallying behind the doctrine of liberty of contract, sought to deny organized labor the very kind of legal legitimation that corporations had gained far earlier. Even the leadership of the ABBA grudgingly acknowledged the status of organized labor by the 1920s. Ernst sums up the transition: "For Daniel Davenport [the ABBA's first lawyer/lobbyist] law was an a priori system, a manufacturing firm was the private property of its proprietor, unions were voluntary associations of independent workers, and labor relations were a private matter into which the state had no business intruding. By 1917, Meritt, [the new lawyer/lobbyist of the ABBA] the product of a quite different education, publicly parted company with his senior colleague on each of these points," committing the organization to a "progressive" approach to labor relations that embraced a pluralist view of labor's place at the bargaining table." [8]

the range of other associative actions embraced by new liberals – actions that were not so "special." These state-society relations drew on a more enduring political tradition in America – the partnership between public and private authority – more often than not cemented by the law.

"IT COSTS MORE TO BE A VERTEBRATE THAN A JELLYFISH": STATUTORY AND ADMINISTRATIVE EXCEPTIONS TO *Laissez-Faire*

Not all of the federal government's expanded clout was mediated through the judiciary. Besides the Treasury Department's creative efforts to shore up gold, there were two major exceptions to governance through the hidden hand of judicial activism after 1870. The most visible was the Republican position on protection. By the 1880s, the pro-tariff position had evolved from support for a crucial revenue-raising device, particularly useful in times of crisis like the Civil War, to a full-blown defense of the tariff as a powerful tool for economic development. Such a rationale fit neatly with the recurring surpluses produced by a high tariff. Protectionists argued that the tariff was a unifying force in American politics. Industries were "pillar[s] in a structure," "interrelated with and dependent upon every other," one protectionist claimed: "Let some free trade Samson pull down one of these pillars ... and the whole temple of American industry must fall."[5]

Protection often was defended as merely an evolutionary adaptation to the natural laws discerned by Adam Smith. Robert Ellis Thompson, one of the first political economists at the Wharton School, argued that the tariff would actually stimulate competition. It "maximizes ... the initiative of the individual," and "minimizes ... interference by the state." The ex-governor of Pennsylvania, Henry Hoyt, used Darwinian metaphor to hammer home his point. Because "it *costs* more to be a vertebrate than a jelly-fish. The nation must submit to the *tax*." If Americans were to survive the deadly competitive struggle, they had to use acquired advantages as well as their natural advantages. The state should be employed to keep at bay "destructive forces from without," unleashing "productive forces" from within. We should apply "laissez faire to ourselves and

---

[5] Joanne R. Reitano, *The Tariff Question in the Gilded Age: The Great Debate of 1888* (University Park, PA: Pennsylvania State University Press, 1994), 47, 50; *Congressional Record*, 50th Cong., 1st sess., 14 May 1888, 19:4107, online at heinonline.org, quoted in Reitano, *Tariff Question*, 47.

hands off to all other nations." Protection, Hoyt argued, was merely a way to ensure that competition within the United States remained free of foreign interference.[6]

While the debate over the tariff was one of the most visible lines of demarcation between the Democratic and Republican parties, the mechanism for collecting this revenue remained relatively hidden from the consumers who paid it. University of Chicago Professor of Economics Van Buren Denslow stressed the advantages of the tariff as a nonintrusive taxing mechanism: The "most convenient time and manner in which to pay a tax is when we pay it without knowing it." Denslow understood one of the tariff's key advantages: the tax itself was melded into the cost of virtually every imported item. It was collected at the nation's ports through a relatively small cadre of officials. It did not require the kind of intrusion into the private affairs of individuals that an excise or income tax did.[7]

Less controversial, but arguably far more statist, was the General Government's role in Western expansion. Even more than Republican protectionist policy, Western expansion was an incubator for direct national intervention into the lives of individuals. Yet the role played by the central government in developing the West was denied even as it unfolded. Indeed, Westerners forged a powerful myth of rugged individualism, even as they lobbied the General Government for hundreds of millions of dollars in irrigation projects. In reality, the General Government paved the way for settlement, guiding its pace and direction. The pattern established in the first half of the century continued apace. The military was instrumental in Indian clearance and securing the land. Agencies like the Geological Survey, founded in 1879, explored and mapped the land and its resources. The Department of the Interior parceled out land to settlers and regulated resource extraction in what one scholar has labeled the "single largest SOE [state owned enterprise] in any of the capitalist countries of the West."[8]

[6] Robert Ellis Thompson, *Protection to Home Industry: Four Lectures Delivered in Harvard University, January, 1885* (New York: D. Appleton, 1886), 13, quoted in Reitano, *Tariff Question,* 52; Henry M. Hoyt, *Protection Versus Free Trade: The Scientific Validity and Economic Operation of Defensive Duties in the United States* (New York: D. Appleton, 1886), 113, 217, 263 quoted in Reitano, *Tariff Question,* 53.
[7] Van Buren Denslow, *Principles of the Economic Philosophy of Society, Government and Industry* (New York: Cassell, 1888), 461, quoted in Reitano, *Tariff Question,* 54.
[8] Richard White, *"It's Your Misfortune and None of My Own": A New History of the American West* (Norman, OK: University of Oklahoma Press, 1991), 58, 204 402–6; Louis Galambos, "State-Owned Enterprises in a Hostile Environment: The U.S. Experience," in *The Rise and Fall of State-Owned Enterprise in the Western World,* ed. Pier Angelo Toninelli (New York, NY: Cambridge University Press, 2000), 284.

It was in the West that the General Government dealt directly with citizens, performing functions that would have been handled by state and local government in the East. Eastern state militias were common: in the West, settlers came face to face with the U.S. Army. America's most elaborate bureaucracy – the Department of the Interior – dealt primarily with Westerners, and it dealt with many of them directly. As was the case with the Forest Service, bureaucracies like the Geological Survey were among the nation's first national institutions to professionalize and to consider local resources from a national perspective. The Geological Survey was the focal point for earth sciences well into the twentieth century. John Wesley Powell, also the director of the Bureau of American Ethnology, directed the federal government's first coordinated efforts into the study of man.[9]

The dearth of local institutions juxtaposed against these federal bureaucracies exaggerated the political distance between public policy and citizens in the West. The West served as testing ground for the direct expansion of the federal administrative state. Those Westerners who encountered its palpable presence constantly complained about it. But Westerners also made inroads into these bureaucracies. Savvy Eastern administrators soon learned how to adapt to locals when they could not coopt them. As was the case with Indian removal and many other federal activities at the boundaries of the nation before the Civil War, the high visibility of the General Government in the West was obscured because it generally operated in sparsely populated areas and at the margins of the nation.[10]

White's book is an excellent review of the New Western history, including the distance between myth and reality of Western independence. On that topic, see also Patricia Nelson Limerick, *The Legacy of Conquest: The Unbroken Past of the American West* (New York, NY: Norton, 1987).

[9] Morton Keller, *Affairs of State: Public Life in Late Nineteenth Century America* (Cambridge, MA: Belknap Press of Harvard University Press, 1977), 103–4; Brian H. Balogh, "Scientific Forestry and the Roots of the Modern American State: Gifford Pinchot's Path to Progressive Reform," *Environmental History*, 7, no. 2 (April 2002): 198–225; William H. Goetzmann, *New Lands, New Men: America and The Second Great Age of Discovery* (New York, NY: Viking Penguin, 1986), 400, 407. On Powell, see Donald Worster, *A River Running West: The Life of John Wesley Powell* (Oxford: Oxford University Press, 2001). On another towering scientific figure and founder of the U.S. Geologic Survey, see Thurman Wilkins, *Clarence King: A Biography* (Albuquerque, N.M.: University of New Mexico Press, 1988).

[10] Brian H. Balogh, *Gifford Pinchot and the Tangled Roots of Progressivism* (forthcoming). As Richard White concludes, "The West provided an arena for the expansion of federal powers that was initially available nowhere else in the country. By exercising power, the government increased its power." *It's Your Misfortune*, 59.

Because of its controversial nature, tariff supporters argued that their program protected free exchange and competition, even though it required active national intervention. America's exceptional position in history, they insisted, could be assured with a little help from the protective tariff. Western expansion seemed to flow so inevitably from America's manifest destiny, from the quest of individuals to improve their lives, from the natural resources – abundant land, for instance – which had encouraged the developmental vision in the first place, that the national government's muscular role in this development was barely noticed by most Easterners. Many of the men who sought to deploy the technology to develop the continent also subscribed to a romantic vision of the West. If technological change and class conflict threatened to derail the American experiment, the vast expanse of Western land, exploited with Eastern expertise, would restore the social harmony that America had effortlessly enjoyed in the past. That the administrative structure and direct contact between federal bureaucrats and American citizens occurred far from population centers only reinforced the sense that this development was an "act of the people going forward without government aid or countenance."[11]

NEW LIBERALISM

In sharp contrast to those who denied the national government's role, or flatly opposed it, new liberals embraced greater public efforts to guide the political economy. Included in the panoply of methods they endorsed was a far more active national government. Lester Ward was among the first to challenge prevailing *laissez-faire* ideology head on. While working at the Bureau of Statistics in Washington, Ward called for the instrumental use of statistics, arguing that this should be the basis of legislation.

Ward believed that politics, like the physical world, was subject to scientific control and that the state was a proper vehicle for exercising that control. His commitment to social reform required that such controls be pursued. In America, the third stage proved to be extraordinarily difficult.

[11] Edward G. White, *The Eastern Establishment and the Western Experience: The West of Frederic Remington, Theodore Roosevelt, and Owen Wister* (New Haven, CT: Yale University Press, 1968), 172, 181; Thomas Hart Benton, *Thirty Years View; or, A History of The Working of the American Government for Thirty Years, from 1820 to 1850* (New York, NY: D. Appleton and Co., 1883), 2:468–69, quoted in White, *It's Your Misfortune*, 57.

But Lester Ward was instrumental in crafting the intellectual rationale for such actions. He was hardly alone.[12]

Ward pointed to events in Europe that confirmed the trend toward an activist state. "The Cobden Club and other 'Free Trade' societies are scattering tracts with a liberal hand," he wrote in 1881. "What is the result? Germany answers by purchasing private railroads and enacting a high protective tariff. France answers by decreeing the construction of eleven thousand miles of Government railroad, and offering a bounty to French ship-owners. England answers by a compulsory education act, by Government purchase of the telegraph, and by a judicial decision laying claim to the telephone." Citing legislation to regulate railroads in America, Ward insisted that "the whole world has caught the contagion, and all nations are adopting measures of positive legislation."[13]

Social democrats like Richard Ely and Walter Rauschenbusch endorsed programs that called for the expansion of the welfare state and public ownership. Starting with the quest for an eight-hour workday, these demands were broadened by the end of the century to include state protection of the right to unionize, public assistance in employment, health and safety regulations in the workplace, protection for child labor, and minimum wage legislation. Both Ely and Rauschenbusch endorsed the public ownership of natural monopolies. At points in his career, Ely's statism knew few bounds. In one text, Ely endorsed the concept of the state as a divine institution, granting it sovereignty over both national

---

[12] Michael J. Lacey and Mary O. Furner, "Social Investigation, Social Knowledge, and the State: an Introduction," Lacey and Furner, eds., *The State and Social Investigation in Britain and the United States* (New York: Cambridge University Press, 1993), 29.

"[T]he operations of a state constitute a department of natural phenomena," Ward suggested, "which, like other natural phenomena, take place according to uniform laws. The pure science, then, consists in the discovery of these laws. The intermediate, or inventive, stage embraces the devising of methods for controlling the phenomena so as to cause them to follow advantageous channels, just as water, wind, and electricity are controlled. The third stage is simply the carrying-out of the methods thus devised." Ward, "The Claims of Political Science," in *Glimpses of the Cosmos*, 3:334, quoted in Dorothy Ross, *The Origins of American Social Science* (New York, NY: Cambridge University Press, 1991), 92.

[13] Lester F. Ward, "Politico-Social Functions," in *Glimpses of the Cosmos*, 6 vols. (New York: G.P. Putnam, 1913–18), 2:336–37, quoted in Richard Hofstadter, *Social Darwinism in American Thought* (Boston: Beacon Press, 1955 [1944]), 72. For a penetrating interpretation of international influences on new liberal thought and Progressive programs, see Daniel T. Rodgers, *Atlantic Crossings: Social Politics in a Progressive Age* (Cambridge, MA: Belknap Press of Harvard University Press, 1998).

economy and the "welfare of the people." As founder of the American Economic Association in 1885 and effective popularizer of complex economic thought, Ely's views reached a broad spectrum of informed opinion in the late nineteenth century. While many of Ely's colleagues pulled back from proposals that smacked of socialism, most acknowledged a crucial role for the state.[14]

Mountains of data contributed to a shift during the Gilded Age away from individualist categories of social interpretation toward a more environmental and interdependent interpretation of social interaction. These data often were wedged into inflexible molds cast by theory or religious belief. Nonetheless, the accumulated evidence did serve to overturn what had previously been presented as inviolable truths. The data exposed underlying weakness in market processes, for instance, ultimately contributing to a reorientation of the political discourse. Urban surveys exposed the hazards of modern industrial life, documenting and publicizing problems.[15]

Just as legal scholars sought more objective ways to categorize and judge human intent in a society that was growing more impersonal, research communities reacted to the increased scope of problems and the distended boundaries they crossed by embracing numbers and statistics as objective measures that could be universally understood by strangers. Quantification provided "a technology of distance" that the social sciences used to gain public trust and internal coherence. Quantification was ideally suited for associations that transcended local and traditional community boundaries. Knowledge alone did not reshape policy in the last third of the nineteenth century. But research did leave a public legacy expressed by the expansion of the national government's capacity to collect more data. In the United States, this was embodied in an improved census bureau and a new bureau of labor statistics.[16]

A new conception of the basis for the state's authority and an economically based conception of liberty lay behind the new liberals' demands for

---

[14] James T. Kloppenberg, *Uncertain Victory: Social Democracy and Progressivism in European and American Thought, 1870–1920* (New York, NY: Oxford University Press, 1986), 254; Richard T. Ely, *An Introduction to Political Economy* (New York, NY: Chautauqua Press, 1889), 30, quoted in Ross, *Origins*, 109.

[15] Lacey and Furner, "Social Investigation," 36.

[16] Theodore M. Porter, *Trust in Numbers: The Pursuit of Objectivity in Science and Public Life* (Princeton, NJ: Princeton University Press, 1995), ix. "If the laboratory, like the old-regime village, is the site of personal knowledge," Ted Porter suggests, "the discipline, like the centralized state, depends on a more public form of knowing and communicating." See also Lacey and Furner, "Social Investigation," 30–31.

enhanced public authority. Rauschenbusch, for instance, acknowledged that when the state had represented only elite interest, opposition was warranted. But he was convinced that the state was becoming more democratic. "Under true democracy state action comes to mean action of the People for their own common good, and why should we fear that?"[17]

By the late nineteenth century, social democrats contended that the greatest threat to liberty came in the guise of economic, not political, inequality. Industrialization was the most significant reason for this. Industrialization piqued the interest of social reformers for two reasons. First, it brought with it a new kind of dependence that was not addressed by the old classical liberal formula. Second, economists like Simon Patten argued that under the proper guidance, industrial productivity offered the way out of poverty and provided unrivaled opportunities for raising the living standards of all. Rauschenbusch argued that fundamental changes in the economy required equivalent adaptations in conceptions of property. The sanctity of property rights embodied in classical liberalism was fine for the world that Adam Smith had lived in, but hardly appropriate for an urban-industrial society.[18]

Though Rauschenbusch did not call for an end to private property, he and others who were influenced by the social gospel invoked the idea of "stewardship" in ways reminiscent of the commonwealth era. They insisted that communal obligations were inseparable from property rights. Individuals "owned" property only in trust for society. If that property was not put to socially constructive use, society had the right to revoke the privilege of individual ownership for the sake of the whole.

Stewardship required that government act decisively to ensure that the impediments to improvement and independence created by industrial society were removed. It entailed the active obligation to improve not only one's own condition, but the condition of all members of the community as well. "True liberty," Ely wrote, could no longer be defined in the negative terms of protecting against government intrusion. Rather, it meant "the expression of positive powers of the individual." Industrialization, Rauschenbusch argued, had created a world in which "the extremes of wealth and poverty are much farther apart than formerly." At a minimum, society had the obligation to keep "from perpetuating and increasing the

[17] Walter Rauschenbusch, *Christianizing the Social Order* (New York: Macmillan, 1917 [1912]), 430, quoted in Kloppenberg, *Uncertain Victory*, 255; Kloppenberg, *Uncertain Victory*, 278–80.
[18] Kloppenberg, *Uncertain Victory*, 282; Ross, *Origins*, 91.

handicap of the feebler by such enormous inequalities of property as we now have."[19]

Effective stewardship required that natural resources be used in the most productive manner possible, that education be provided to those who otherwise would not have the means to receive it and that government services be funded by a progressive tax system that returned the benefits derived by those who profited from the community's property to those who had not. Because economic equality was so crucial to the individual's freedom, new liberalism placed egalitarian claims ahead of unrestricted property rights. Individuals were the product of the environment that shaped them, not simply irreducible products of their character or God's will. Remaking that environment in ways that allowed individuals a fighting chance was central to the new liberal agenda. Within the capitalist framework, that meant support for policies like workers compensation, compulsory education laws, and the embrace of state-supported pensions, welfare, and health insurance programs. New liberalism revised classical liberalism by demonstrating a greater willingness to use the power of associations – including the state – to ensure that individuals had the ability to compete on a level playing field.

TAKING DEMOCRACY SERIOUSLY: THE PROGRESSIVE CASE AGAINST FEDERAL INTERVENTION

The implications for state-society relations of this sea change seem straight forward enough: state intervention at the national level. Not surprisingly, the scholarly movement "to bring the state back in" is grounded in Progressive Era accounts of federal state-building at the turn of the century. Long before this recent scholarly trend, the standard account of this period had been fixed in America's collective historical memory. The nation's first truly modern president, Teddy Roosevelt, rode (literally) to the rescue because he heard the voice of the people and translated popular concerns into action. The national government forcefully intervened in the economy, not to mention other parts of the globe. Deploying the

---

[19] Richard T. Ely, *Studies in the Evolution of Industrial Society* (New York: Chautauqua Press, 1903), 402, cited in Kloppenberg, *Uncertain Victory*, 280; Walter Rauschenbusch, *Christianity and the Social Crisis* (New York: George H. Doran, 1911), 249, quoted in Kloppenberg, *Uncertain Victory*, 284; Rauschenbusch, *Christianizing*, 364, quoted in Kloppenberg, *Uncertain Victory*, 284.

"bully pulpit" on behalf of a newly refurbished agenda surely injected the federal government into the lives of Americans in the most visible way imaginable. Powerful statist forces made inroads into the American psyche. The rest is history.[20]

Like the town that chartered a private corporation to build a road in early nineteenth-century America, or the U.S. Postal Service, which subsidized passenger travel on "private" stage coaches that also carried the mail, however, the line between public and private was not clear cut on the eve of the Progressive Era. That is because Progressives often relied on voluntary and private institutions to extend the authority of the national government. New liberals viewed unilateral intervention into the economy by the General Government as just one of many forms of associative actions. It was rarely their first choice for such action.[21]

---

[20] Alan Brinkley has deftly summed up the intellectual basis of what he calls "reform" liberalism, noting liberals' "belief in the interconnectedness of society, and thus in the need to protect individuals, communities, and the government itself from excessive corporate power, the need to ensure the citizenry a basic level of subsistence and dignity, *usually through some form of state intervention* [emphasis added]." Mary Furner, on the other hand, has complicated our understanding of new liberalism, pointing to a split within its ranks. Both camps embraced collectivist solutions to economic and social problems, according to Furner, and both were united in their rejection of classical and neoclassical individualism as the solution. But one form of the new liberalism leaned toward more statist and democratic solutions, while the other, "corporate liberalism," "left economic and social ordering largely to cooperative arrangements between organized private parties, agreeing voluntarily among themselves." *The End of Reform: New Deal Liberalism in Recession and War* (New York, NY: Knopf, 1995), 9; Mary O. Furner, "The Republican Tradition and the New Liberalism: Social Investigation, State Building, and Social Learning in the Gilded Age," in Lacey and Furner, *The State and Social Investigation*, 175.
  On strong presidents, see John Morton Blum, *Progressive Presidents: Roosevelt, Wilson, Roosevelt, Johnson* (New York, NY: Norton, 1980). On bringing the state back in, see Theda Skocpol, "Bringing the State Back In: Strategies of Analysis in Current Research," in *Bringing the State Back In*, ed. Peter B. Evans, Dietrich Rueschemeyer, Theda Skocpol, 3–44 (New York, NY: Cambridge University Press, 1985); Theda Skocpol, *Protecting Soldiers and Mothers: The Political Origins of Social Policy in the United States* (Cambridge, MA: Belknap Press of Harvard University Press, 1992); Stephen Skowronek, *Building a New American State: The Expansion of National Administrative Capacities, 1877–1920* (New York, NY: Cambridge University Press, 1982); Daniel P. Carpenter, *The Forging of Bureaucratic Autonomy: Reputations, Networks, and Policy Innovation in Executive Agencies, 1862–1928* (Princeton, NJ: Princeton University Press, 2001).
[21] "Although it would be difficult *not* to find in their writings discussions of state and national systems of health and unemployment insurance and public employment schemes, old age pensions, worker's compensation, and even child allowances," Eldon J. Eisenach notes of the Progressives, "one also discovers a systematic skepticism regarding their feasibility and even desirability in America *by the national government presently constituted* [his emphasis]." *The Lost Promise of Progressivism* (Lawrence, KS: University Press of Kansas, 1994), 150; see also Chap. 5 generally.

New liberals balked at national statist solutions for four reasons, all related to the central role that democracy and its history in America played in their thought. The most straightforward reason for the willingness to compromise on the role of the national government was political. "Whereas in Europe social democrats worried about maintaining their legitimacy as radicals in order to preserve their power base in the working class," one scholar noted, "in the United States excessive radicalism guaranteed powerlessness." Forced to work within the two-party system, new liberals faced a choice of coalition-building or oblivion. Explaining his willingness to work with mainstream politicians like Teddy Roosevelt, Rauschenbush contended in 1901 that "the current of socialist thought and sentiment does not run in the channel of socialist parties, but is leavening the ideas of the people and will transform our social organization in the direction of socialism quietly and gradually. If dogmatic socialists choose to sit on the fence and criticize the men who do this work, that is their look-out. The work will be done, almost as fast anyway."[22]

Intellectuals inclined to endorse statist methods understood the depth of the opposition. Both Ely and Rauschenbusch were critical of independent regulatory agencies, in part because they viewed these steps as only half measures, but also because they felt that such mechanisms would only confirm the American public's low esteem for public intervention. Advocates of the social gospel grounded their popular support in an interclass religious base that allowed them a far more charitable view of class conflict. They envisioned social cooperation across classes: social democracy consisted of melding individual, group, and class interests into the larger interests of the nation. "The true aim of the best socialism," Ely argued, "is that general social amelioration which proposes to sacrifice no class, but to improve and elevate all classes." Labor leaders able to overcome their abiding distrust of the state also understood the need to build popular coalitions. Shared religious convictions, not class antagonism, was often the foundation. Take the special session of the Church Congress called in 1886 where the former president of the Amalgamated Association of Iron and Steel Workers and Henry George "testified to the power of Jesus Christ," and a Baptist minister spoke of "the duty of flushing the cold law of supply and demand with the warm colors of Christ's

---

[22] Kloppenberg, *Uncertain Victory,* 264; Walter Rauschenbusch, "Dogmatic and Practical Socialism," Address delivered at Rochester Labor Lyceum, February 24, 1901, Rauschenbusch Papers. American Baptist Historical Society, Colgate-Rochester Divinity School, Rochester, N.Y., cited in Kloppenberg, *Uncertain Victory,* 210.

truth of brotherhood." An Episcopal minister concluded, "I don't know whether the Knights of Labor have captured us or we the knights; but thank God we are beside them."[23]

Intellectuals were drawn toward the "social question" by the industrial and agrarian strife that erupted in the last third of the nineteenth century. In the wake of the bloody Haymarket Riot of 1886, some intellectuals, particularly among the academic social scientists, beat a retreat from the front lines of radical reform. John Bates Clark, for instance, who had embraced historicism and challenged the laws of classical economics, forged in marginalist theory a set of laws that reconstituted, on a more scientific basis, a "static" theory of the market. Individuals interacting with each other through market choice might not always make the correct decisions for themselves, but when viewed cumulatively from the proper intellectual distance, their choices would tend toward that normative ideal. Clark was a member of an emerging profession within the social sciences that sought to establish its public authority by building a body of esoteric knowledge founded on science.[24]

Whether the venue was electoral or professional, advocates of the "new liberalism" consistently compromised with opponents of statist solutions out of practical political considerations. Strident public debate between prominent members at either end of the political spectrum – in the case of economics, Sumner and Ely – damaged the prestige of the entire would-be profession. Leading lights in the *laissez-faire* camp forged a compromise with those who insisted on public advocacy and the integral role of ethics in the field of economics. They steered the American Economics Association toward an academic ideal of internal debate over

---

[23] Kloppenberg, *Uncertain Victory*, 256; Richard T. Ely, *Socialism and Social Reform* (New York, NY: Thomas Y. Crowell, 1894), 7, quoted in Kloppenberg, *Uncertain Victory*, 286; "The Cleveland Convention" in *Labor: Its Rights and Wrongs: Statements and Comments by the Leading Men of our Nation on the Labor Question of To-day: With Platforms of the Various Labor Organizations* (Washington, D.C.: Labor Publishing Company, 1896: repr. Westport, CT: Hyperion, 1975), 245, 268–69, cited in Leon Fink, "The New Labor History and the Powers of Historical Pessimism: Consensus, Hegemony, and the Case of the Knights of Labor," *Journal of American History* 75, no. 1 (June 1988): 129.

[24] Ross, *Origins*, 121–22. See also, Mary O. Furner, *Advocacy and Objectivity: A Crisis in the Professionalization of American Social Science, 1865–1905* (Lexington, KY: University Press of Kentucky, 1975), chap. 5; Thomas L. Haskell, *The Emergence of Professional Social Science: the American Social Science Association and the Nineteenth-Century Crisis of Authority* (Urbana, IL: University of Illinois Press, 1977); Kloppenberg, *Uncertain Victory*.

technique as opposed to public pronouncements about the most pressing political and social issues of the day.[25]

New liberal intellectuals and progressive politicians avoided national statist solutions for another practical political reason: they worried about partisan capture. New liberalism came of age at the same time that partisan domination of the political system reached its peak. Even those most inclined to advocate federal intervention worried that any administrative capacity developed by the national government would become the preserve of party-dominated patronage politics. The two largest federal administrative structures operating at the time – the Post Office and the Pension Bureau – served as cautionary tales.

A second reason that new liberals eschewed central government was their faith in the power of social cooperation and informed public opinion. Municipal ownership of utilities – a program endorsed by many social democrats – was valued as much for its ability to engage citizens in active governance as for its redistributive potential. Public ownership would instruct citizens and teach them that they were, in fact, the government. Both labor and agrarian reformers envisioned a cooperative commonwealth in which public opinion would substitute for bureaucratic state mechanisms of enforcement. While calling for government ownership of monopolies, the Knights of Labor viewed such a step as merely a means of moving closer to such a cooperative commonwealth. Theirs was an associative vision that deployed the state to shore up civil society and key economic institutions, but was wary of replacing these institutions.[26]

Labor leaders imagined "an invisible government of public opinion that would accomplish tangible results" in lieu of bureaucracies. Like many other elites, they regarded public opinion as the unitary product of educated discussion. Labor leaders, at times, invested public opinion with the independent authority to serve as a powerful coercive agent – restraining employers in its own right or, at a minimum, serving to enforce the results of plebiscitary democracy.[27]

---

[25] Furner, *Advocacy*, Chap. 5.

[26] Eisenach, *Lost Promise*, 163; Richard Schneirov, "Political Cultures and the Role of the State in Labor's Republic: the View from Chicago, 1848–1877," *Labor History* 32, no. 3 (Summer 1991): 400.

[27] Alexander Yard, "Coercive Government Within a Minimal State: The Idea of Public Opinion in Gilded Age Labor Reform Culture," *Labor History* 34, no. 4 (Fall 1993): 445. For a good summary of Progressive attitudes toward public opinion, see Adam Sheingate,

Advocates envisioned a state that would administer the "people's money," the "people's tax system," and a "people's antimonopoly law" without granting new authority to a new administrative class of experts. These visions shared an egalitarian thrust and recognition of the interdependent status of producers, at the same time that they remained wary of centralized state control and hierarchical administrative structures. More broadly, they assumed that public opinion was a rationally constructed process of winnowing out ideas and "propaganda," a technically efficient dissemination of information.[28]

In their quest to discover "Truth," social scientists increasingly turned to experience rather than abstract deduction. This was the third factor that predisposed reformers toward employing a wide range of mechanisms toward associative action. The radical theory of knowledge that underlay this move was self-consciously social in its construction and democratic in its orientation. The philosophers who informed new liberal thought charted a course between extreme volunteerism on the one hand, and extreme positivism, on the other. They sought to understand a world in which individuals could still choose and act, yet they recognized that in many instances individual action would be circumscribed by general laws that might one day be discerned. This was one of the central insights articulated in William James' philosophy, fully worked out in *Pragmatism* in 1907. Long before that, John Dewey also embraced experience as the ultimate test of "Truth."[29]

The new liberalism differed from classical liberalism because it focused on the community, associations, and society. These were the "environmental" influences that formed the individual. Experience was a social phenomenon, not a solitary one. Older conceptions idealized the individual, abstracting him from the very connections that had formed him. Unlike older notions of the truth as fixed, a truth that was subject to experience and environmental influences was subject to historical change, reshaping individuals along the way.

"Progressive Publicity and the Origins of Political Consulting," (paper presented to the Miller Center of Public Affairs Colloquia Series, Charlottesville, VA., October 2007.)
[28] Ellis W. Hawley, "The New Deal State and the Anti-Bureaucratic Tradition," in *The New Deal and its Legacy*, ed. Robert Eden (New York, Greenwood Press, 1989) 77–92; Michael J. Sproule, *Propaganda and Democracy: The American Experience of Media and Mass Persuasion* (New York, NY: Cambridge University Press, 1997), 27. See also Sheingate, "Progressive Publicity."
[29] Kloppenberg, *Uncertain Victory*, 41, 242; Haskell, *Emergence*, 249.

Rejecting the notion of *a priori* truths, Dewey argued as early as 1892 that "Truth" is created by man's thought, reason, and activity. This is revealed in his "social relationships, the way in which he connects with his fellows." Because democracy "enables us to get truths in a natural everyday and practical sense," Dewey continued, the methods of social science and democratic interaction are integrally connected. Immediate experience contains a social dimension; verification of truth is not a personal project – it is a social project. Individuals do have the freedom to choose and act; but they do so as conscious members of communities that constantly tested the validity of ideas and actions.[30]

The approach to knowledge that propelled the Progressive political agenda embraced an interdependent world in which social interaction was the ultimate determinant of the truth. It was for these reasons that new liberals embraced historicism: they turned to history as a way of placing man in his social context, in a web of past experience. But history was not complete; thus the discovery of truth was an ongoing process. Given the unstable, pluralist, and restless universe in which men lived, testing, experimentation, and adaptation were the only solution. Many of these ideas became the basis of an approach to social interaction that Robert Wiebe labeled "bureaucratic." As Wiebe brilliantly summed up,

They pictured a society of ceaselessly interacting members and concentrated upon adjustments within it. Although they included rules and principles of human behavior, these necessarily had an indeterminate quality because perpetual interaction was itself indeterminate. No matter how clear the evidence of the present, a society in flux always contained that irreducible element of contingency, and predictability really meant probability. Thus the rules, resembling orientations much more than laws, stressed techniques of constant watchfulness and mechanisms of continuous management.

Abandoning their quest for certainty, what all of these thinkers shared was a willingness to experiment and a distaste for established truths. There were good methods, progressive approaches, but the truth that these might reveal was in flux and, at best, elusive."[31]

[30] Lacey and Furner, "Social Investigation," 34; John Dewey, "Democracy and Christianity," in *John Dewey: The Early Works, 1882–1898*, ed. Fredson Bowers, 5 vols. (Carbondale, IL: Southern Illinois University Press, 1971), 4:7–8, quoted in Kloppenberg, *Uncertain Victory*, 43; Ibid., 1 Kloppenberg, *Uncertain Victory*, 13, 150. See also Eisenach, *Lost Promise*, Chap. 6.
[31] Kloppenberg, *Uncertain Victory*, 82, 94–95, 114; Robert Wiebe, *The Search for Order, 1877–1920* (New York: Hill and Wang, 1967), 145.

To say the least, a pragmatic conception of truth as elusive undermined a dogmatic statist approach. Embracing uncertainty and experimentation undercut in fundamental ways any commitment to a specific approach to resolving social problems. The deeply held belief that truth emerged from social interaction, from testing ideas and action in a democratic community, eroded an exclusive commitment to statist techniques in a democratic community that was strongly anti-statist. The social dimension of the pragmatic theory of truth ensured that regardless of the compelling arguments made on behalf of state action, like any other experiment, the validity of this test ultimately would be determined by its reception in the community.

Committed to a methodology, dedicated to a process of inquiry, the intellectual foundation of progressive social reform – because it relied on the unforeseeable outcome of democratic interchange – easily embraced a broad range of mechanisms that garnered support precisely because they were seen as alternatives to expanding the administrative capacity of the administrative state. Testing all ideas against the bar of social experience undercut from the start what in the American context would have been an uphill struggle, even for an army of true believers.[32]

For Albion Small, sociology would formulate a path less "visionary" and radical than socialism toward realizing the "equalization of social relations." Small was the recipient of the nation's first chair in sociology, created in 1892 by the University of Chicago. A Baptist minister who embraced the social gospel, Small studied in Germany and continued his work at The Johns Hopkins University with Herbert Baxter Adams and Richard Ely. The "dynamic sociology" that Small crafted was intended to change "the actual into the ideal." Like Ely's historical economics, religious fervor and integration of ethics into social science were a fundamental part of Small's approach. Although he found in socialism a valid critique of industrial capitalism, he could not embrace its proposed remedies. "In the Hegelian idiom," Small wrote, "conventionality is the thesis, Socialism is the antithesis, Sociology is the synthesis." Despite Small's social concern, the alternative to statist solutions lay in the kind of research and investigation that the professional social sciences promised.[33]

---

[32] Ibid.
[33] Albion W. Small and George E. Vincent, *An Introduction to the Study of Society* (New York, NY: American Book Co., 1894), 41, 70, 79, quoted in Ross, *Origins*, 125–26; Ross, *Origins*, 123–26.

The two were not mutually exclusive. However, Small's conception of a method grounded in social relations blunted the likelihood that this would-be Christian socialist would endorse statist techniques. For scientific discoveries to be "real," Small argued by the late 90s, a majority needed to embrace it – a precondition that made centralized bureaucratic action highly improbable. Most Americans, Small continued, disagreed with the solutions proffered by Bellamy and the socialists. Thus their solution was not "real," and it was "insane" to lobby on its behalf. Ethical ideals could only be reached through individuals' "practical judgments of conduct," which "are the raw material of the only ethics that promises to gain general assent." Ethical ends, no matter how noble, were of little value if they were not amenable to "conduct" likely to achieve them. In fact, those ends had to be determined, in part, by practical parameters of conduct.[34]

EMBRACING AMERICA'S HISTORICAL RELATIONSHIP TO THE STATE

A double-edged appreciation for the ways in which the laws of market behavior were historically contingent, and for the manner in which state action had consistently structured civil society in the past, provided a fourth foundation for the new liberals as they embraced associative action. The integral and diversified role that the American state had played historically in structuring the political economy illuminated ways in which contemporary law might reinforce voluntary action while preserving a role for the individual. Because new liberals turned to history for much of the evidence that they mounted against the supposed "natural laws" of economics, they could not ignore America's recent love affair with *laissez-faire*. It was the most recent iteration of their nation'shistory. But their historical understanding reached past that. Ultimately, a full century of history provided a rich source of evidence for the case they made for associative action.

New Liberals embraced history as a means of demonstrating the recent pedigree and tenuous grip of universal laws, such as classical

[34] Albion W. Small, "Sanity in Social Agitation," *American Journal of Sociology*, 4, no. 3 (November 1898): 338–42, quoted in Ross, *Origins*, 136; Albion W. Small, "The Significance of Sociology for Ethics," in *Investigations Representing the Departments: Political Economy, Political Science, History, Sociology, and Anthropology: Decennial Publications of the University of Chicago*, 1st ser., 4 (Chicago, IL: University of Chicago Press, 1903), 115, quoted in Ross, *Origins*, 137.

economics. This was a methodological bond that was thicker than political prescription. E.R.A. Seligman stated the case most forcefully in an article entitled "Change in the Tenets of Political Economy with Time." For Seligman, the "very marrow" of the new school of economics was historicist. It was "the essential interrelation between economic theories and the changing external conditions of industrial life." The "historical and critical school," as he called the new economics, believed that any generation's economic theories were a product of its time and that no particular set of beliefs could lay claim to "immutable truth, or the assumption of universal applicability" to all times. What might have been valuable at one time could be "positively erroneous and misleading" in a later historical period.[35]

Seligman cited as examples the various relationships between state and society that had prevailed over time: the Hellenic epoch, during which the state reigned supreme and the individual was swallowed up; the Middle Ages – a period of customary pricing that eschewed market competition. Adam Smith, viewed through Seligman's historicist lens, was simply adapting the laws of economics to his own times – "pulling down the rotten fences which obstructed the path of the artisan, the farmer, and the merchant." Unlike his successors – Malthus, for instance – who froze Smith's adaptations into universal law, Smith appreciated the interrelation of economics and historical conditions, according to Seligman. Had Smith lived in 1886, Seligman speculated, he would be in the vanguard of the new economic school. Current times made distribution the central question of the day, Seligman insisted, along with the way in which "private initiative and governmental action" should interact in order to lessen industrial strife.[36]

Arthur Hadley, although more wary of government action, shared Seligman's historicist inclinations. Hadley, for instance, used historical evidence to challenge a concept central to the application of *laissez-faire* principles in late nineteenth-century America – "liberty of contract." "Where two parties to a transaction do not meet on equal terms, free contract may be the surest means of destroying freedom," Hadley argued. Although self-enslavement had been outlawed, there were many contemporary cases that involved the same principle of freely entering into an agreement that denied one party freedom in the long run. Liberty of

[35] Edwin R. A. Seligman, "Change in the Tenets of Political Economy with Time," *Science,* 7, no. 168 (April 23, 1886): 375.
[36] Ibid., 379, 382.

contract, which might have had great meaning in the early nineteenth century, was a charade by the 1880s because of the "rapid concentration of industrial power in a few hands." Concentrated power had eroded the responsibility of the stronger party to the weaker, and allowed the stronger party to shift responsibility to the weaker one. As a consequence, an individual dealing with a large firm could no longer rely on free competition for protection. In fact, his complete freedom to enter into a contract, given the historical concentration of power, might well end up enslaving him.[37]

Hadley stated explicitly that his essay was "not intended as a plea for extension of government activity." He shared a foundational belief, along with other New Liberals, however, in the inseparable nature of governance and the political economy. The very claim to freedom of contract was not derived from natural law. It was the product of a public policy decision. As Hadley put it, "The courts are guided by considerations of public policy in interpreting transactions, and enforcing contracts. A right of every man to make his own bargains, apart from and above such considerations, never has existed, and in a highly organized society it is hardly possible to conceive how it ever could exist." Seligman was equally skeptical of the concept of absolute property rights divorced from the common good. Private property was not "an absolute natural right." On the contrary, the whole conception was a relatively recent construct, an expedient. It was "a question not of right, but of arrangements which will inure to the greatest possible social prosperity."[38]

Hadley proposed holding employers responsible for social outcomes or else subjecting them to the threat of state ownership. As he put it, "Allow the railroad to make arbitrary differences in its charges, and you furnish the most powerful argument in favor of state railroad ownership." But both Hadley's analysis of the "social problem" of the 1880s and his preferred solution acknowledged that the state was already integrally involved in structuring the political economy, and relied on the state to hold corporations accountable for the public trust that had been delegated to them.[39]

---

[37] Arthur T. Hadley, "How Far Have Modern Improvements in Production and Transportation Changed the Principle That Men Should be Left Free to Make their Own Bargains? "*Science,* 7, no. 161 (March 5, 1886), 221, 224.

[38] Ibid., 221, 224; Seligman, "Change," 381.

[39] Hadley, "How Far," 224.

Historical sensitivity to national cultural traditions, particularly as reflected through the way that legal systems shaped political economies, was another hallmark of the new school of economics. For Henry C. Adams, just "as the stroke of the shuttle was limited by the framework of the loom, so the industrial movements of men were bound by the liberties of law and of custom." Continuing the metaphor, Adams insisted that the "industrial weaving of society is largely determined by its legal structure." In explaining the political economy, the "'lego-historic' facts," as Adams called them, were just as important as theories about the economic nature of man.[40]

Although embracing history united new liberals at the same time that it provided the ammunition to break out of the straight jacket of *laissez-faire*, it also imposed considerable constraints. That times and conditions changed did not mean that they did so quickly. Most often they changed in evolutionary, not revolutionary, ways. Cultural proclivities endured and shaped the options available to social reformers. Adams, who leaned toward statist solutions where possible, delivered the following sobering advice in his discussion of economics and jurisprudence: "It may be proper in Germany, where the principles underlying the juridical system are quite different from those that determine either English or American law, to advocate constructive socialism; but it is absurd for one who claims to be a disciple of the historical school of economy to adopt German conclusions in this respect. Our entire juridical structure is against it, and it is easier to bring our industries into harmony with the spirit of our law than to re-organize our society from top to bottom, industries included."[41]

Like other new liberals, Richard Mayo Smith agreed that the economy, political science, and jurisprudence were integrally related. Every state action, every law passed, had economic consequences. And understanding the history of these actions was the best way to approach the study of economics. The historical study of political economy, Smith was pleased to report, paved the way for acquiescence to change. History recorded that even key institutions had changed over time. But despite Smith's plea for greater state intervention – in the guise of better data collection – he issued a cautionary note about the obligations of history. Despite the progressive lessons to be learned from history, the

---

[40] Seligman, "Change," 375; Henry C. Adams, "Economics and Jurisprudence," *Science*, 8, no. 178 (July 2, 1886): 15.
[41] Adams, "Economics and Jurisprudence," 18.

new method was " even more conservative: for it teaches us that social institutions and arrangements are the result of long growth and evolution; that they are intimately connected with civilization, and, when once established, are not to be lightly overthrown. History shows this: for it reveals how slow a growth real civilization is, and by what hard struggles we have attained to our present state." History offered the possibility of progress, but only if the constraints of history were appreciated and properly attended to.[42]

***

The concerns expressed by social reformers in late nineteenth-century America reopened a debate that had been foreclosed by America's embrace of the exceptionalist myth in the second half of the nineteenth century: how best to reconcile individual interest and the common good. In doing so, they challenged the radical and historically exceptional chasm that had been constructed between the public and the private during the Gilded Age. This should not be confused, however, with a return to republican ideology. To be sure, the fear of corruption and distant rule remained and continues to influence American attitudes toward a centralized national state even today. But the positive conception of citizen as disinterested was no longer available to those who would merge public and private concerns. It remained for those who understood "individual" to be socially constructed, and "private" to be dependent on public protection, to forge a new institutional infrastructure that accepted the contingent nature of public-private relations in an interdependent world. That new liberals insisted that the democratic will be consulted in order to discover the "true" answer to this challenge, made the task all the more formidable.[43]

By the 1890s, those who sought to intervene in public life in order to improve the condition of mankind faced a dilemma. The growth of industry, the emergence of a national market, and the effect of a national communications and transportation system, convinced many that there was a single system of cause and effect that could only be controlled and improved by national action. These trends were brought into bold relief by the universalistic tendency of scientific research to find "root causes"

[42] Richmond Mayo Smith, "Methods of Investigation in Political Economy," *Science*, 8, no. 181 (July 23, 1886): 85–87; quotation from 85.
[43] Kloppenberg, *Uncertain Victory*, 170.

and "scientific solutions" that ignored political jurisdictions. That an economically integrated and heuristically consistent basis for national programs existed hardly ensured a straightforward path to a national administrative state.

Ironically, the social knowledge that diverted attention to national problems and solutions was one of the few media that could cross "the boundaries of conventions and roles separating the public world of officialdom from the private world of church, family, school, work, and philanthropy," as two intellectual historians put it. Politics in America still channeled problems and their solutions into state and local venues. And public sentiment about government still tended toward the more visceral attachments of place, region, and party, rather than nation. Local governments, of course, had been able to resolve problems in the past by blurring the distinction between public and private, by recognizing that private interest could serve public purposes. As America's social problems became more apparent, and more visibly national in scope, the extraordinary division that had been forged at the national level between public and private, and the long-standing political distance of the national government, precluded the simple extrapolation of time-tested local problem-solving techniques to the national jurisdiction.[44]

Thus the ideas that undergirded new conceptions of the interdependence of man, and that revived concerns about the egalitarian future of a rapidly industrializing nation, were far more significant in expanding those sectors of the public sphere that did *not* require centralized state administrative capacity. Associative action would not have been possible, indeed, would not have occurred to anybody, if the late nineteenth-century landscape had not been festooned with organizations – ranging from corporations to fraternal groups – that increasingly operated across local and state jurisdictional boundaries. We have already seen the ways in which the national government husbanded the growth of corporations and the national markets that they served. By the dawn of the twentieth century, a broad array of associations operated on a national scale and often exercised authority, albeit

---

[44] Lacey and Furner, "Social Investigation," 14. I am indebted to Barry Karl and Stan Katz for their insights about the economic and heuristic contributions to nation-building, and the gap that yawned between these conceptions and the political mechanisms for realizing them. See "The American Private Philanthropic Foundation and the Public Sphere, 1890–1930" *Minerva*, 19, no. 2 (Summer 1981): 256–60.

narrowly and functionally defined, on a national scale. It just made sense to take advantage of this capacity, especially if it was culturally embraced, as opposed to creating such authority from scratch. As with corporations, much of the public nurture received by national associations began at the state level. But by the first third of the twentieth century, in most instances the associative relationships that transcended public, private, and voluntary boundaries were enmeshed with the national government as well.[45]

It is only in conjunction with institutional developments in the rest of the public sphere that we can begin to understand how and why the administrative national state grew in twentieth-century America. Many of these nongovernmental institutions – like the charitable organization, or the autonomous profession – are seen as predecessors or quaint adjuncts to the national administrative state. Corporations and interest groups are perceived to be driven solely by material interest or the desire for social control – untouched by the intellectual ferment that swirled about them. In fact, they were all forms of associative action directed toward managing a society that had begun to acknowledge the need for national collective action, and even imbued private and voluntary associations with public authority, yet remained wary of central state administration and only relied on it in those rare, "special" circumstances where there were few other alternatives.

Richard Ely concluded the debate in *Science* by noting just such a range of options. "Shall certain functions be performed by co-operative methods or by individual methods? for the state is only a certain kind of co-operative institution," Ely wrote. Should that decision favor cooperative methods, the next question was whether the task should be left to "voluntary co-operation, possibly that of a corporation," or the "compulsory co-operation of the state?" Ely did as much as any new liberal to ensure that the last alternative was considered. But like other new liberals, Ely put his faith in history. "Experience," Ely concluded, "sooner or later, teaches the people many wise things." In their turn to experience, and, more specifically, to history, new liberals liberated America's rich history of public/private relations from the stranglehold of *laissez-faire*. In doing so, they laid the groundwork for a wide range of associative

---

[45] Ellis W. Hawley, *The New Deal and the Problem of Monopoly: A Study in Economic Ambivalence* (New York, NY: Fordham University Press, 1995); Hawley, "Herbert Hoover, the Commerce Secretariat, and the Vision of an 'Associative State' 1921–1928," *Journal of American History*, 61, no. 1 (1974): 116–40.

action over the course of the twentieth century, even if much of it turned out to be less than special.[46]

Treating these institutions as crucial components of associative action – the building blocks of twentieth-century progressivism – instead of impediments to the construction of a centralized state, unlocks the mystery of public authority in twentieth-century America. Placing this development in a far longer history of the ways in which Americans have demanded some kinds of action from the national government and resisted other forms opens the door to constructive solutions to the problems we face in the twenty-first century.

[46] Richard Ely, "The Economic Discussion In Science," *Science,* 8, no. 178 (July 2, 1886): 6.

10

Conclusion: Sighting the Twentieth-Century State

By drawing together countercurrents in the literature – eddies in what is otherwise a torrent of popular and scholarly interpretation that ignores nineteenth-century national authority, *A Government Out of Sight* addresses some of the questions raised in the introduction. That nineteenth-century Americans did not want the General Government involved in their lives, that they preferred to leave things to state and local government and a free market unencumbered by government intervention, and that they got their wish – a national government that did not do anything important – has informed interpretations of the nineteenth century. It continues to frame twenty-first-century political debate, with partisans dividing over the battle whether to resurrect or bury America's *laissez-faire* tradition. The alternative narrative sketched in the previous pages suggests that the fundamental historical premise upon which progressives and conservatives have waged war for the past one hundred. Years is flawed. The battle between "big" and "small" government is grounded in a false historical premise.

The mystery of national authority in nineteenth-century America can be resolved once we recognize that although the United States did indeed govern differently than its industrialized counterparts, it did not govern *less*. Americans did, however, govern *less visibly*. The key feature that distinguished the United States in the nineteenth century was the preference among its citizens for national governance that was inconspicuous. Americans preferred to use the language of the law, the courts, trade policy, fiscal subsidies – supported by indirect taxes – and partnerships with nongovernmental partners instead of more overt, bureaucratic, and visible interventions into the political economy.

Capitalizing on this state-centered conception of nineteenth-century history has important consequences for the way we interpret the *twentieth century*. Why have historians of the twentieth-century and our twenty-first century political leaders failed to get the memo?

The simple answer is that nineteenth-century historians – for good reason – have concentrated on state and local public policies. That is where the preponderance of government authority lay in the nineteenth century. Looking for evidence of *national* authority in the late nineteenth century, in order to recount the origins of *national* state-building in the twentieth century, scholars of modern America are confronted with a story that appears to be largely local.

That is also why I have concentrated on the *national* aspects of governance in the nineteenth century. I have sought to make this story accessible to my colleagues who study the twentieth century because it provides a history of an "associative state" that, until now, has largely been confined to the work inspired by Ellis Hawley, who centered his efforts in the 1920s and 30s. My laser-like focus on the *national* story has provoked howls of protest from nineteenth-century specialists – the very scholars whose work I am indebted to, and without whom, I could not have written this book. Their anguish is grounded in their appreciation for and commitment to context. To tell a purely "national" story of political development in the nineteenth century is to ignore a good part of that history and, because it inevitably neglects context, to leave the reader with a distorted conception of the balance between local and national influence on the lives of Americans. This is a price I have chosen to pay in order to identify some of the enduring patterns of interaction between citizens and the national government established over the course of the nineteenth century. These patterns should be familiar to readers by now, but it is worth summarizing them and the institutions that were crucial to their persistence.

First and foremost, Americans eschewed visible, centralized, national administration by the General Government. That citizens resisted a national bureaucratic state does not mean that they did not ask the national government to do a lot for them. But Americans rebuked Hamilton: they responded far more favorably when the General Government was inconspicuous, or at least hidden in plain sight. Combining national resources and private initiative proved to be a consistent formula for political success in policies ranging from land distribution to internal improvements. Subsidizing a communications system that provided access to newspapers in remote locations stimulated national political debate in a polity that was highly decentralized. The General Government was instrumental in constructing a national market – a contribution soon washed from memory in a torrent of congratulations for America's exceptional stature among supposedly far more statist industrialized nations. Briefly, during the Gilded Age, the federal judiciary labored mightily to separate public from private action. It failed to do so, opening the door to the integration of public and private endeavors on a national scale in the twentieth century.

Americans consistently supported a more energetic, even bureaucratically empowered state, whenever they perceived their security to be threatened – a second long-standing pattern that continued through the twentieth century. During the nineteenth century the Civil War serves as the primary example of this – especially the Confederacy. We encountered the same phenomenon with the War of Independence and, to a lesser degree, the wars of 1812 and with Mexico. But we also witnessed the kind of naked power Americans were willing to grant the federal government when Indians threatened security and economic development. The Trail of Tears was forged by an extraordinary mobilization of federal resources and the naked use of force.

A third pattern that prevailed was resistance to visible forms of national taxation. This, of course, was one of the reasons that Americans went to war against Great Britain. The threat of British functionaries violating the civil liberties of British North Americans was as unnerving to the colonists as the financial consequences of such taxes. Unable to avoid national taxation entirely, Americans settled uncomfortably on the tariff. The discomfort, however, had more to do with the inequitable distribution of costs and benefits from the tariff than the manner in which this tax was imposed. Almost all Americans agreed that this indirect form of taxation was preferable to direct taxes such as excise taxes.

The fourth pattern that endured was the continued use of the law to shape the political landscape. In the second half of the twentieth century, the federal judiciary shifted its gaze from reshaping the political economy to reconstituting the social landscape. Decisions like *Brown v. Board of Education* and *Rowe v. Wade* were highly contested and visible. But in far less apparent ways – by continuing to expand the kinds of fundamental rights that Americans could expect from their government – and by broadening through class action suits the standing of groups that had not previously organized – the courts completed what they had begun with corporations in the late nineteenth century. This "rights revolution," combined with the equally revolutionary expansion of administrative law sanctioned by the federal judiciary, broadened participation in policy formulation to a wide array of groups that matched their growing participation in the electoral process across the twentieth century.

Far more quietly than the high profile battles fought between those who worked to expand the national bureaucratic state, and their opponents who sought to impose an idealized conception of Gilded Age *Laissez-Faire* on state-society relations, these nineteenth-century patterns of interaction between state and society were advanced during the twentieth century through national associations working in conjunction with the federal government. Some of these associations were public – states and local governments. Some were voluntary organizations, like Blue Cross and Blue Shield. And some were profit-making corporations that ranged from defense contractors to the trade associations that served corporate masters. These groups, working in conjunction with the national government, constituted an associative order. Consummated on a national scale at the end of the nineteenth century, this associative order operated within the contours of political patterns established over the course of the nineteenth century.[1]

Engaging the associative order meant that over the course of the twentieth century crucial portions of the national government continued to operate largely out of sight. The rich associative landscape that emerged at the end of the nineteenth century underwrote the return to many of the nineteenth-century political patterns outlined above. State and local governments developed the capacity to act in concert on a national scale. Professions developed powerful national organizations, and universities emerged as national centers of expertise. Voluntary organizations adapted their agendas to national needs, while interest groups and trade associations flocked to Washington, D.C. Corporate social policy competed with voluntary organizations and public agencies to promote welfare. By targeting their appeals through national organizations that worked

[1] For an overview of the ways in which pluralist politics changed over the course of the twentieth century, see Balogh, "Making Pluralism 'Great': Beyond A Re*cy*cled History of the Great Society," Sidney Milkis, Jerry Mileur, eds., *The Great Society and the High Tide of Liberalism* (Amherst: University of Massachusetts Press, 2005): 145–182 and Elisabeth Clemens, "Lineages of the Rube Goldberg State: Building and Blurring Public Programs, 1900– 949," in Ian Shapiro, Stephen Skowronek, and Daniel Galvin, *Rethinking Political Institutions: The Art of the State* (New York, NY: New York University Press, 2006): 187–215. For a penetrating analysis of the strengths and weakness of the American Medical Association, see Christy Chapin, "The AMA and the Institutional Intersection of Political and Market Power, 1945–1957 (paper presented to the Institute for Applied Economics and the Study of Business Enterprise, Johns Hopkins University, October, 2008).

in conjunction with the national government and often administered its policies, Americans demanded support and services from the national government at the same time that many continued to rail against big government. Filtered through the associative order, such federal support seemed less threatening – even traditional.[2]

With this set of nationally organized associations serving as intermediaries between national government and the individual, Americans could preserve their sense of individual initiative and personal control. Individually oriented rights and choice provided the essential link between classical and new liberalism. The associative order capitalized on the collective impulse inherent in the commonwealth tradition without abandoning the classical liberal commitment to individual rights. Blended in localities, and even states, through much of the nineteenth century, this amalgam served individual self-interest by harnessing collective ends. It tapped public sector resources, nationalized through the rich range of organizations that emerged by the early twentieth century. This associative order held open the possibility of achieving on a national scale what proponents of the commonwealth ideal had hoped to accomplish locally in the mid-nineteenth century.[3]

A history of twentieth-century political development that is informed by our revised understanding of Americans' quest for governance out of sight alters the traditional story. A number of scholars, many of them political scientists, have already begun to pull back the curtain and reveal the twentieth-century "hidden" welfare and carceral states, or the "contractual" national security state. Others have chronicled the powerful way in which the national government has responded to waves of moral

---

[2] For a sophisticated discussion of the way in which the voluntary sector adapted to the rise of New Deal social service provision, see Andrew J.F. Morris, *The Limits of Voluntarism: Charity and Welfare from the New Deal Through the Great Society* (New York: Cambridge University Press, 2009). Kathleen Jill Frydl effectively demonstrates how prodigious spending for veterans was obscured by the institutional mechanisms through which it was delivered (in this case, the states, and private contractors) at the very time it expanded federal authority in *The G. I. Bill* (New York: Cambridge University Press, 2009).

[3] Daniel P. Carpenter argues "The unprecedented multiplicity and diversity of civic and voluntary associations during the period 1880–1920 enabled bureaucratic officials to enter and occupy these unique positions." *The Forging of Bureaucratic Autonomy: Reputations, Networks, and Policy Innovation in the Executive Agencies, 1862–1928*, (Princeton, NJ: Princeton University Press, 2001), 365; See also, Ellen M. Immergut, *Health Politics: Interests and Institutions in Western Europe* (New York, NY: Cambridge University Press, 1992). Immergut argues that what matters is not the power of the groups involved in making a decision, rather the country's structure of representation. [11]

impulses. Many of these scholars explore the deep historical roots of such policies. However, few have recognized the degree to which this tendency to delegate national authority and, in some instances, disburse huge sums of taxpayer dollars through intermediary institutions, accelerated a long-standing American tradition forged over the course of the nineteenth century. A quick review of a few of these "hidden" networks of twentieth-century national authority underscores the continuity of nineteenth-century state-society relations. Framing twentieth-century development in longer-term historical patterns accomplishes something else as well: it connects submerged and inconspicuous realms of national authority to a broader interpretation of the evolution of American politics that offers an alternative to the reigning perspective that pits small government against big government. It confirms that Americans have always turned to the national government to solve certain problems, and that they were the most successful when they crafted solutions that did not rely exclusively on that national authority.[4]

RELOCATING TWENTIETH-CENTURY GOVERNANCE

Much of the Progressive Era's effort to shape the social environment should be viewed in the context of restoring some of the traffic across the artificial boundary that Gilded Age jurists, theorists, and some politicians sought to erect. Coordination in response to problems that were national in scale and scope was eased by the wealth of associations that were organized along national lines. While new liberals were eager to intervene in ways that reshaped the environment and leveled the playing field for individuals, they feared that any bureaucratic structures developed by the national government would soon be captured by partisan, or even worse, corrupt field marshals. They did not have to look far for examples, citing the Pension Bureau as exhibit A. Progressives hedged their bets, treating national administrative capacity as one form of many kinds of associative actions required to solve the nation's problems.[5]

---

[4] Citations to the literature on the hidden welfare state, the carceral state, and the contractual states are in subsequent notes. On the state-building impact of moral impulses, see James A Morone, *Hellfire Nation: The Politics of Sin in American History* (New Haven, CT: Yale University Press, 2003).

[5] As Stephen Skowronek has reminded us, a number of institutional logics are in operation at any given time, each of which usually owes its origins to a distinct period of political development. This is the normal state of affairs, a condition that political modelers and historians alike have been too eager to flatten into the regularities of one dominant regime

At first glance, the Progressive Era certainly appears to signal the rise of the administrative state. The traditional story turns on impressive examples of state-building at the national level. To cite just a few, Teddy Roosevelt and his chief forester Gifford Pinchot used the President's executive authority to add tens of millions of acres to the forests managed by the national government. By the time Pinchot left office in 1910, the federal government managed 200 million acres. The 1906 Pure Food and Drug Act and the Meat Inspection Act subjected food and other products to testing by national inspectors for the first time. Each of these important actions either increased the size of the national bureaucracy or significantly expanded existing authority.[6]

Placing each of these federal interventions in an historical context that accounts for the ways in which nineteenth-century Americans governed, new liberal demands that history be taken seriously, and the national associative order that emerged at the end of that century, explains these developments more effectively than does the idea of a sudden infatuation with national state-building or bursts of inspired presidential leadership. One of the themes we have stressed is that the national government acted far more directly, and powerfully, at the margins of the nation. Many of Roosevelt's and Taft's conservation programs could never have been imposed in the East. That the national government remained the largest landholder in the West was one crucial reason for its authority. Many Westerners demanded a federal presence, for the same reasons that nineteenth-century Americans had demanded internal development and territorial governance: it was crucial to their economic and political development.

While Gifford Pinchot lashed out at corporate greed, he worked closely with the largest livestock associations to craft a grazing policy for the

---

or another. Thus, "the incorporation of ancient, common law rules of work relations into the liberal, market-oriented constitutions of the post-Revolutionary era; the incorporation in the Constitution of protection for the institutions of slavery within a regime of individual rights; the promulgation of a regime of individual rights in the context of the primordial norms of the patriarchal family; the development of a mass-based party system around a pre-democratic republican Constitution hostile to the very notion of political parties"; and the development that Skowronek has studied in great detail, "the emergence of a national economy based on the corporate organization of capitalism within the context of a decentralized system of economic regulation rooted in state judiciaries." Stephen Skowronek, "Order and Change," *Polity*, 28, no. 1 (Fall 1995): 95–6.

[6] Brian Balogh, "Scientific Forestry and the Roots of the Modern American State: Gifford Pinchot's Path to Progressive Reform," *Environmental History*, 7, no. 2 (April 2002): 198–225.

national forests. The American National Live Stock Association shared Pinchot's vision of managed grazing in the national forests. Pinchot even appointed a stalwart in the Arizona Wool Growers Association to head up the Grazing Division. By insisting on managing the nation's forests "scientifically," Pinchot emulated the policies of the largest lumber interests – such as Weyerhaeuser. That the Forest Service claimed to be self-financing from the sale of lumber in the national forests – in the same manner as when the Post Office claimed to be self-sufficient by subsidizing newspaper distribution – was an important element of the conservation program, often overlooked by historians. Taking millions of acres of forest out of circulation undoubtedly increased the value of forest held by large corporate interests, pushing up the price of lumber. Rather than displacing the market, federal intervention into forestry shored up that market on a national scale. It did so in conjunction with corporate partners in lumber and agribusiness, and by blending public and private efforts. Newly empowered professionals were a key ingredient in this mixture. These experts supposedly could transcend partisan and parochial interests. Produced by graduate programs, like the Yale School of Forestry, these professionals stood as crucial intermediaries in the new associative order.[7]

The movement for pure food and drugs was another policy area where such experts were in evidence. Here, the key government official was Harvey Wiley, the Chief Chemist in the Chemistry Bureau. Wiley's initiative – Progressive muckraking journalism, the publication of Upton Sinclair's *The Jungle*, which described in graphic detail just what went into processed meats, and public furor over the safety and the quality of its food – were all important components of the drive for legislative action that resulted in federal legislation. But it was Wiley's ability to draw upon a broad range of associations – from the National Food and Drug Congress – which included professional groups, public health agencies, and grocers – to the American Medical Association and the General Federation of Women's Clubs who provided the political staying power to push through the pure food and meat inspection acts. More importantly, the largest meatpackers were already inspecting. They had to do this in order to serve an international market that

---

[7] Karen R. Merrill, *Public Lands and Political Meaning: Ranchers, the Government, and the Property Between Them* (Berkeley, CA: University of California Press, 2002), 48, Chap. 2; For an excellent discussion of the U.S. Department of Agriculture as a "university," see Carpenter, *Forging*, Chap. 7.

demanded as much. National legislation imposed costs on smaller operators that were already being borne by the corporate first movers in the associative order, and shifted the responsibility and cost of coordinating this effort to the national government. As was the case with forestry, the national government worked in tandem with large corporations to stabilize the market and ensure a continuous supply of quality product.[8]

One of the crowning achievements of Progressive Era state building was the Federal Reserve Act of 1913, which created a federated central banking system for the nation. The system was grounded in twelve district banks, supervised by a loosely organized Federal Reserve Board. Housed in Washington, D.C., the "Fed" was composed of five men appointed by the president along with the secretary of the treasury and the comptroller of the currency. Heavily weighted toward the private banking system at the district bank level, balanced by only two government officials at the Fed, the system neatly reflected the tug of war that had been waged over the past twenty years between those who distrusted the ability of private bankers to forego self-interest in managing the nation's money supply and those who feared putting partisan politicians in charge of the nation's money supply. Both sides acknowledged the pressing need for a stable, flexible, centrally guided monetary policy. The Federal Reserve Act provided the tools to achieve these ends. The Fed had the power to establish reserve requirements for member banks. It had the authority to set interest rates for borrowing, and it could buy and sell government securities. But the decentralized nature of the Board itself and the history of powerful private banks, who had served as *de facto* system stabilizers in the absence of a central bank, hindered the Fed's ability to set a clear policy over the subsequent twenty years.[9]

Although it constituted an important moment in the history of federal administrative expansion, the Act formalized the national government's role in national monetary policy by accommodating the full range of new liberal approaches to governance and embracing the associative order. It built upon a system that relied on a set of associative mechanisms to deal

---

[8] Carpenter, *Forging*, 261–70. See also Gabriel Kolko, *The Triumph of Conservatism: A Re-interpretation of American History, 1900–1916* (New York, NY: Free Press, 1963).

[9] Galambos and Pratt, *The Rise of the Corporate Commonwealth: U.S. Business and the Rise of Public Policy in the Twentieth Century* (New York, NY: Basic Books, 1988), 67–68. See also James Livingston, *Origins of the Federal Reserve System: Money Class and Corporate Capitalism, 1890–1913* (Ithaca, NY: Cornell University Press, 1986), Chap. 8.

with the inevitable credit problems created by the business cycle. One such network was the New York clearinghouse. During normal times, the clearinghouse did just that – it settled accounts between banks, assuming its members to be creditworthy. But 1893 was not a normal year. As the economy spiraled downward and over one hundred national banks collapsed, the clearinghouse issued "loan certificates" to help stem the credit crunch between banks. The clearinghouse took it upon itself to suspend payment in cash – which was in short supply – and accept quasi-legal notes in interbank business. The banks, in turn, could use whatever cash remained to make emergency loans. Missing from this formula were national countercyclical mechanisms to deal with financial panics and recessions. When the panic of 1907 hit, the financial sector once again had to turn to private and associative action to stem the tide. This time it was the venerable J.P. Morgan who rode to the rescue, personally reviewing the books of key financial institutions, determining which were worth saving and which were not.[10]

In the wake of these recurring scares, it was not just agrarian interests that demanded a national solution. Sectors of the corporate economy weighed in as well. They were prepared to take action even if Congress would not. In a series of privately funded commissions and conferences attended by a broad array of businessmen and civic leaders, the business community lined up behind sound money and the gold standard. It took the new liberal belief in the power of public opinion seriously. Businessmen sought to form broad public opinion on the money question, going so far as to sponsor cartoons in an attempt to reach a less literate constituency. Explicitly, the movement for sound money sought to emulate the style and appeal of one of the most effective critiques of "hard" money – *Coin's Financial School*. Once the gold standard was secured, advocates of monetary stability set their sights on a centralized mechanism backed up by the credit and authority of the national government. After interviewing directors of central banks in Europe, the Currency Committee of the New York Chamber of Commerce warned the entire Chamber in 1906 that "under our present system of independent banks, there is no centralization of financial responsibility, so that in times of dangerous over-expansion no united effort can be made to impose a check which will prevent reaction and

---

[10] Livingston, *Origins*, 72–73; Robert F. Bruner and Sean D. Carr, *The Panic of 1907: Lessons Learned from the Market's 'Perfect Storm'* (Hoboken, NJ: John Wiley and Sons, 2007).

depression." The Committee advocated a "central bank of issue under the control of the government."[11]

Even after the Fed was established, associative networks, especially the relationships forged between district banks and their local members, continued to serve as an important part of a system that sought the right balance between public control and private initiative. Given New York's historical significance in the field of finance, it is not surprising that the New York Reserve Bank, led by Benjamin Strong, emerged as the driving force behind Fed policy. Of equal importance, the trade groups and individuals who had mobilized to shape public opinion and lobby Congress, continued to exercise influence over the course of the twentieth century.[12]

The examples of "special" associative action – "special" because they did expand the administrative capacity of the national government – were a small fraction of associative action in the first third of the twentieth century. Most relied less heavily on federal capacity. New liberals turned to a range of nationally oriented organizations as *alternatives* to federal administration. One political scientist has aptly labeled these alternative regimes "parastates." They ranged from loosely organized women's groups to hierarchically organized corporations. The degree of federal involvement also varied from minimal to extensive. But the trajectory in all cases was similar – toward a more active federal role in coordination and funding and, in many instances, toward increased administrative capacity.[13]

Women who organized around issues of special concern to their sisters constituted one such parastate. For decades, women were instrumental in forging voluntary networks that provided social services to the indigent, especially women and children. Even without the vote, these women soon turned to state and local governments – and eventually, the national government, lobbying for the Sheppard Towner Act – to finance these efforts. Ultimately, the Women's Bureau established a beachhead in the national government for programs directed at women and children. Whether financed at the local or the national level, however, many of the actual

[11] On privately funded commissions and conferences organized by business leaders, see Livingston, *Origins*, 90–91, and Chaps. 3–4 generally; *The Currency Report of the Special Committee of the Chamber of Commerce of the State of New York* (New York, NY, 1906), 9–11, quoted in Livingston, *Origins*, 161.
[12] Galambos and Pratt, *Rise of the Corporate Commonwealth*, 68.
[13] Eldon J. Eisenach, *The Lost Promise of Progressivism* (Lawrence: University Press of Kansas, 1994), 18.

services were delivered by a diverse array of voluntary groups, making these programs more palatable to a broad range of Americans. Contrary to the scholarly truism that women were more powerful politically *before* they had the vote, women leveraged their votes, to hold elected officials accountable. True to a tradition that preferred the national government to play a supporting role, many women demanded that services be delivered through the voluntary, state, and local outlets that constituted the associative order, not directly by the national government. Thus, funding health services in the states actually increased after the Sheppard-Towner Act – which had delivered federal support for such activities – expired.[14]

Universities also constituted a crucial parastate. Perhaps their most important contribution to the associative order was to create and certify professionals. Universities helped professionals, like doctors, establish control over an exclusive body of esoteric knowledge that allowed these professions to distinguish their members from competitors. Of equal importance, universities limited access to the professions, reducing competition within the profession itself. Through state licensing, the professions were granted a remarkable degree of autonomy over their own practices. Delegating life and death decisions on healthcare to groups like the American Medical Association, for instance, had important public policy implications. True to the patterns of other parastates, the professions and universities soon dramatically increased the support that they received from all levels of government, while retaining a great deal of their autonomy. Although state legislatures, on occasion, intervened in highly visible fashion, and even though the national government eventually demanded more accountability, for much of the twentieth century, vast sums of taxpayer money, public authority, and crucial policy choices were delegated to the professions and to the universities that created and renewed these professions.[15]

---

[14] Women were more prone to seek government assistance at the state and local level than other members of the associative order. Elisabeth S. Clemens, *The People's Lobby: Organizational Innovation and the Rise of Interest Group Politics in the United States, 1890–1925* (Chicago, IL: University of Chicago Press, 1997); Lorraine Gates Schulyer, *The Weight of the Their Votes: Southern Women and Political Leverage in the 1920s* (Chapel Hill, NC: University of North Carolina Press, 2006); Brian Balogh, "'Mirrors of Desires': Interest Groups, Elections and the Targeted Style in Twentieth Century America," in *The Democratic Experiment*, ed. Meg Jacobs, William Novak, and Julian Zelizer (Princeton, NJ: Princeton University Press, 2003), 222–49.

[15] The work of Christopher Loss has changed the way we think about universities in relationship to the state. Breaking out of the more traditional university research-military complex, Loss considers the ways in which universities reshape American citizenship,

Universities also served as coordinating mechanisms for state and federally sponsored public programs. The best example of this is the farm experiment stations and the extension service that worked hand-in-hand with them. The 1887 Hatch Experiment-Station Act provided federal funding for agricultural research at the state land grant colleges created by the Morrill Land Grant College Act of 1862. These laboratories were established to generate new knowledge and, more importantly, to apply that knowledge to the needs of farmers. Land grant colleges created, and the national government eventually subsidized, an extension service that translated science into productive agricultural practice. A series of demonstrations in the early twentieth century met with great success and ultimately received Congressional blessing through the Smith-Lever Act of 1914. This legislation provided federal matching funds for the extension service. Significantly, the local "match" could come from a combination of public and private funds. The focal point for this outreach was the county agent. By 1935, there were 3,300 county agents across the land. These were far from federal functionaries. Because federal and state funding could be matched with private funds, many of the county agents literally received a portion of their salary from one of the era's most powerful interest groups – the American Farm Bureau Federation.[16]

Until the New Deal, the federal government subsidized the dissemination of knowledge through this mechanism. With the passage of the Agricultural Adjustment Act, however, the extension service became a key mechanism for carrying out the nation's seminal agricultural policy, not to mention disseminating billions of dollars. Under the AAA allotment plan, county agents decided how much acreage individual farmers had to take out of production, which in turn determined the federal payment these farmers would receive for fighting overproduction. Agents were also responsible for enforcing these production quotas. Secretary of Agriculture Henry Wallace shrewdly decided to carry out this controversial policy through familiar faces – extension agents – rather than creating a new federal bureaucracy. As the savvy Wallace put it in 1935, "Fortunately, we had the extension services with their corps of ... county

from 1920s through the end of the Cold War. Christopher Loss, *Between Citizens and the State: The Politics of American Higher Education in the Twentieth Century* (unpublished manuscript, forthcoming).

[16] Loss, *Between Citizens* Chap. 3, 12–14. See also Wayne D. Rasmussen, *Taking the University to the People: Seventy-Five Years of Cooperative Extension* (Ames, IA: Iowa State University Press, 1989), and Carpenter, *Forging.*

agricultural agents and a background of 20 years of experience with which to contact farmers."[17]

The New Deal state dramatically expanded its reach into the political economy, but did so through a mechanism that blended state, local, and private associations, all under the umbrella of higher education. By the end of the 30s, a broad array of federal agencies operated through the extension service, from the TVA to the Rural Electrification Administration. Small wonder that Wallace could inform Congress by the late 30s that "by decentralizing the responsibility ... and using the full facilities of the Cooperative Agricultural Extension Service ... it has been found practical to carry through operations involving from hundreds to millions of individual farmers." This would not be the last time the national government effected sweeping change through the friendly and nonthreatening auspices of higher education. The national security state was wedded to the research carried out largely through elite universities. More significantly, as one astute student of state/university relations has argued, the federal government soon turned to universities to adjust citizens' conceptions of just what it meant to be an American.[18]

Even when Americans were forced to construct new national bureaucracies in response to the economic crisis of the 30s, long-established patterns prevailed. There is no better example of this tendency than the legislation that many consider to be the crowning accomplishment of the New Deal state – the Social Security Act. There were highly visible and even intrusive elements of that social insurance program. Franklin D. Roosevelt, for instance, worried that assigning numbers to working Americans would smack of totalitarian government – he was concerned that these numbers would be labeled "dog tags." Yet social insurance – which did assign social security numbers – was the *only* title of this omnibus legislation that was administered at the national level. Welfare, unemployment compensation, and several other key social programs included in the Act were administered at the state and local levels. FDR was keen to spin off administration of social insurance as well, but even his brains trust could not figure out a way, in an age before comput-

---

[17] Loss, *Between Citizens*, Chap. 3, p. 12; Henry Wallace, "A Message to All County Agents," *Extension Service Review* 6, (July 1945): 97, quoted in Loss, *Between Citizens*, Chap. 3, p. 14.

[18] Loss, *Between Citizens*, Chap. 3, p. 25; Henry Wallace, as quoted in Loss, *Between Citizens*, chap. 3, p. 23. For a penetrating overview of New Deal agricultural policy, see Sarah Phillips, *This Land, This Nation: Conservation, Rural America, and the New Deal* (New York: Cambridge University Press, 2007).

ers, to keep track of Americans who were likely to move between states over the course of a lifetime. Keeping track was essential because the Social Security Administration and the Democratic Party claimed that retirement benefits were akin to personal savings accounts that would be there when most needed.[19]

It was the contributory element of social insurance that Roosevelt liked most – even if it did require national administration. The program's supporters labored to maintain the image that workers got back what they put in, even as the program itself became an engine for fiscal redistribution from younger generations to the elderly. It lifted several generations of the elderly out of poverty at the expense of future generations of retirees. Three-quarters of a century later, "social security" remains one of the few nationally administered income maintenance programs and is sharply distinguished from locally administered "welfare" programs by the perception that those collecting social security benefits are merely getting back what they contributed *individually*. The Social Insurance formula hit the trifecta in this regard: individuals felt that they had their own private accounts; employers (and the individuals) contributed to a trust fund that specified what these revenues could be spent on, and the government – as inconspicuously as possible – subsidized the first several generations of beneficiaries.[20]

Individualist rationale or not, Social Insurance linked the national government directly to a broad cross section of its citizens and, ultimately, created a sizeable national bureaucracy – one that even cropped up in Hollywood films like *Tin Men* by the 1980s. Far more characteristic of the New Deal response were two programs that took aim at the heart of the political economy, but employed the associative order to do so. The National Industrial Recovery Act deployed federal authority to cajole key industries – working through their trade associations – to voluntarily limit production that was deflating prices for all. Section 7A of that legislation

[19] For a fascinating account of what the Social Security Administration was able to do once they *did* acquire computers, see Andrew Meade McGee, "'Please, Mr. Machine, Give this to a Human to Read': Electronic Data Processing, Systems Management, and Great Society Idealism in the Social Security Administration, 1965–1974," (University of Virginia, August 2007).
[20] For analytical histories of early Social Security and its administrators, see Martha Derthick, *Policymaking for Social Security* (Washington, D.C.: Brookings Institution Press, 1979), and Edward Berkowitz, *Robert Ball and the Politics of Social Security* (Madison, WI: University of Wisconsin Press, 2003); *Mr. Social Security: The Life of Wilbur J. Cohen* (Lawrence, KS: University Press of Kansas, 1995).

protected organized labor, and sought its assistance in maintaining wage levels. The Agricultural Adjustment Act also sought to curb overproduction, in this case working through one of the most powerful agrarian interest groups – the American Farm Bureau Federation.[21]

As in the past, Americans did empower the national government to expand its administrative reach (and suspend civil liberties) when national security was threatened. World War II and the ensuing Cold War leaps out as the most illustrative example, although the most sweeping reorganization of the executive branch of the national government since the Cold War Era occurred in the wake of the attacks on the World Trade Center and Pentagon on September 11, 2001. Like British North Americans or Americans in 1860, mid-twentieth-century Americans jettisoned their concerns about standing armies and quickly embraced a central government with considerably enhanced powers. During the Cold War, they went even farther, constructing what I have labeled a "prominstrative" state, which combined professional expertise with federal administrative capacity to wage this twilight struggle.[22]

Even during the Cold War, however, Americans avoided what Harold D. Lasswell labeled the "Garrison State." They did so by constructing a "contract state" – taking a page out of the nineteenth-century Post Office's play book and the nineteenth-century Army's procurement handbook. The military-industrial complex thrived in the American setting by outsourcing to the private sector and to academia some of its most vital functions, ranging from weapons development to psychological warfare. That vast portions of this national security state were literally placed out of sight eased acceptance. Large portions of it were classified top secret. Like the national government's actions in the West during the nineteenth century, much of the national security state was physically located beyond the boundaries of the nation or in sparsely settled (and now restricted access) regions, which also eased acceptance.[23]

[21] Ellis W. Hawley, *The New Deal and the Problem of Monopoly: A Study in Economic Ambivalence* (New York: Fordham University Press, 1995). The classic work on the Farm Bureau is Grant McConnell, *The Decline of Agrarian Democracy* (Berkeley: University of California Press, 1953).

[22] Brian Balogh, Joanna Grisinger, and Philip Zelikow, "Making Democracy Work: A Brief History of Twentieth Century Executive Reorganization," (Miller Center of Public Affairs Working Paper, July 2002); Brian Balogh, *Chain Reaction: Expert Debate and Public Participation in American Commercial Nuclear Power, 1945–1975* (New York, NY: Cambridge University Press, 1991).

[23] Harold D. Lasswell, "The Garrison State," *American Journal of Sociology* 46, no. 4 (January 1941): 455–468. On "contract state," see Aaron L. Friedberg, *In the Shadow of*

The classified, contractual, national security state is merely one of several vast regimes that remain hidden and, consequently, insulated from careful scrutiny. The other regimes do not rely on security clearances. Rather, they are hidden in plain sight, obscured only by our failure to appreciate long-standing patterns of American governance. While the list of such regimes is long, the hidden elements of the welfare state, the carceral state, and the federally subsidized infrastructure for suburban growth epitomize America's ability to ignore the national government's influence when it is delivered in a manner that does not create visible national bureaucratic structures. The great irony is that this is precisely how Americans prefer their governance.

Management guru Peter Drucker, writing in the 1970s, referred to proliferation of private pension plans that dotted the corporate landscape after World War II as an "unseen revolution." In Drucker's opinion, this was an "outstanding example of the efficacy of using the existing private, non-governmental institutions of our 'society of organizations' for the formulation and achievement of social goals and the satisfaction of social needs." Drucker got one thing wrong: the nongovernmental part (although he was correct to deny the presence of visible national institutions). As one of the charter scholars of the "hidden welfare state" school put it, "Quite the opposite: Private pensions have been encouraged by public policy both directly and indirectly – through tax and labor law, through targeted regulatory interventions, and through the structure and reach of Social Security itself." Healthcare provision has traveled the same path – shaped by federal tax policy that subsidizes "private" healthcare benefits to the tune of billions of dollars of tax deductions to the employers who provide them. The taxes forgone (or expended) on pensions and health benefits neared $200 billion, by 1999, approximating the cost of Medicare.[24]

---

the Garrison State: America's Anti-statism and its Cold War Grand Strategy (Princeton, NJ: Princeton University Press, 2000).

[24] Peter F. Drucker, *The Unseen Revolution: How Pension Fund Socialism Came to America* (New York: Harper and Rowe, 1976), 46, quoted in Jacob S. Hacker, *The Divided Welfare State: the Battle over Public and Private Social Welfare Benefits in the United States* (New York: Cambridge University Press, 2002), 82; Hacker, *Divided*, 11, 83. For other key interpretations of the hidden welfare state, see Chris Howard, *The Hidden Welfare State: Tax Expenditures and Social Policy in the United States* (Princeton, NJ: Princeton University Press, 1997) and Jennifer Klein, *For All these Rights: Business, Labor, and the Shaping of America's Public-Private Welfare State* (Princeton, NJ: Princeton University Press, 2003). For an excellent example of the political culture that limited the kind of

With a higher proportion of its adult population incarcerated than anywhere else in the world, one might assume that the American public policies that produced this outcome were the product of intense public debate. Yet an influential scholar of this phenomenon finds just the opposite: "the construction of the carceral state was not presented as a package of policies for public debate. The carceral state was built up rapidly over the past thirty years largely outside of the public eye and not necessarily planned out." The reasons range from physical placement – prisons are housed in out of the way places – to the incremental growth of federal capacity to deliver on its rhetoric. Always subject to moral crusades, a federal government that had expanded its national security responsibilities was better able to deliver on political promises. The associative order played a hand in this outcome as well. Well organized progressive groups, who might have checked these tendencies, actually gave the carceral bandwagon a push when they weighed in on behalf of victims of abuse and rape. Contracting out the construction, and in some cases, the actual administration of prisons added to the invisibility of the carceral state.[25]

Another submerged constellation of post-World War II federal policies has profoundly shaped seminal social and political tendencies that continue to this very day. Phenomena as disparate as suburbanization, land use, the location of new industry, and race relations share a set of federal policies that range from home mortgage deductions to highway construction policy. What the policies and outcomes they produced share in common is a substantial federal incentive to white suburban middle-class homeowners. As one scholar has recently pointed out, awareness of federal largesse has been erased, if not eradicated, through a powerful populist ideology of equal opportunity. In the meantime, more visible interventions that provide similar benefits to those not fortunate enough to be white or middle class in the three decades following World War II are labeled "big government" by advocates of "equal opportunity."[26]

taxation and its extent, see Julian Zelizer, *Taxing America: Wilbur D. Mills, Congress, and the State, 1945–1975* (New York: Cambridge University Press, 1998).

[25] Marie Gottschalk, *The Prison and the Gallows: The Politics of Mass Incarceration in America* (New York: Cambridge University Press, 2006), 2; Bruce J. Schulman, "The Privatization of Everyday Life: Public Policy, Public Services and Public Space in the 1980s," in *The 1980s: Gilded Age or Golden Age*, ed. Gil Troy and Vincent Cannato (New York: Oxford University Press, forthcoming), and "The Reagan Culmination," in *The Seventies: The Great Shift in American Society, Culture and Politics* (New York: Free Press, 2001), 218–252.

[26] Kenneth Jackson, *Crabgrass Frontier: The Suburbanization of America* (New York: Oxford University Press, 1985); Tom Sugrue, *The Origins of the Urban Crisis: Race and*

As this last example suggests, and as virtually all of the scholars who write about modern iterations of government regimes hidden from sight insist, the decision to delegate national treasure and administrative capacity to the associative order has had significant consequences. Pensions and healthcare delivered through private mechanisms, regardless of the billions of federal dollars that subsidize them, are skewed toward the middle class and upward. While the United States spends no less on social provision than other industrialized nations, its benefits go disproportionately toward those who need them the least. Conversely, the brunt of America's hidden carceral state falls most heavily upon communities already under economic and racial assault. No wonder that progressives are wary of hidden states. No wonder that to the extent progressives acknowledge these regimes hidden in plain sight, they call for alternatives.[27]

This is where I part ways with most progressives. I do so for two reasons, grounded in lessons drawn from my historical understanding of American political development laid out in the preceding pages. The first lesson is that history endures. In spite of a Herculean effort to distinguish sharply between public and private spheres in the Gilded Age, the long-standing pattern of melding the two persisted in America. In fact, it soon thrived at the national level like never before – aided by the emergence of an associative order and connective institutions like the American Farm Bureau Federation and the American Medical Association. Second, governance out of sight "works" in the sense that Americans accept it. Indeed, they demand it. That is why I urge progressives to embrace this historical tendency, rather than fight it. Progressives must concentrate on the ends – redistributive, just, representative – rather than bogging down in battles over the means – "statist," conspicuous, and centralizing.

DEMYSTIFYING CONTEMPORARY POLITICS

Reorienting the contemporary debate from big versus small government to a discussion about how best to solve pressing problems through means that Americans historically have embraced – means that *include*

Inequality in Postwar Detroit (Princeton, NJ: Princeton University Press, 1996); Matt Lassiter, *The Silent Majority: Suburban Politics in the Sunbelt South* (Princeton, NJ: Princeton University Press, 2006); Kevin Kruse, *White Flight: Atlanta and the Making of Modern Conservatism* (Princeton, NJ: Princeton University Press, 2005).

[27] Hacker, *Divided*. On subsidies that have favored white middle-class constituents, see Ira Katznelson, *When Affirmative Action was White: an Untold Story of Racial Inequality in Twentieth-Century America* (New York: Norton, 2005).

national governance – offers a great opportunity to break a stalemate that historically has only been resolved during times of crisis. Conservatives should concede that Americans have always turned to the national government to solve problems. In fact, conservatives – whether Gilded Age jurists or businessmen eager to establish national markets – have often been the first to advocate energetic national governance.

For their part, progressives should break their lockstep assumption that cooperative partnerships between public and voluntary, or even private, organizations are inherently regressive. Progressives should also master the art of turning the legal and fiscal resources of the national government toward redistributive ends. In short, they should learn how to make government work toward progressive ends, through less visible means. While this is no easy task, it is far more promising than reverse engineering the mechanisms through which Americans have governed for much of their history.

Leading intellectuals, on both the left and the right, have begun to challenge the false dichotomy between small and big government. George Will, for instance, reacted to President George W. Bush's second inaugural address by underscoring that the "core of conservatism" had been updated for Republicans, "who think of themselves as a party of governance rather than of opposition to government and who have come to terms with this fact: Americans talk like Jeffersonians but expect to be governed by Hamiltonians." For Will (and Bush), landmark legislation like the Homestead Act of 1862, the Social Security Act, and the GI Bill support an "edifice of character." For public intellectuals on the left, such legislation provided material sustenance that gave middle-class Americans a leg up. Melvin L. Oliver and Thomas M. Shapiro, for instance, insist that past government policies promoted what "was experienced as self-sufficiency." Writing in *The American Prospect,* they argue that "this long and rich history includes the Homestead Act of 1862 and the land-grant colleges of the 19th century, Federal Housing Administration loans, Social Security, and the GI Bill, as well as the continuous benefits of tax codes that subsidize homeownership, property, and wealth."[28]

The alternative historical narrative charted by *A Government Out of Sight* places America's much vaunted antistatist tradition in its proper

---

[28] George F. Will, "Acts of Character Building," *Washington Post,* January 30, 2005, http://www.washingtonpost.com/wp-dyn/articles/A45993-2005Jan28.html;   Melvin L. Oliver and Thomas M. Shapiro, "Creating an Opportunity Society," *The American Prospect* 18, no. 5 (May 2007): A27.

historical context: as an *ideological* strain that harnesses powerful symbols – whether fear of "consolidation" or warnings about welfare queens – in order to engage in political battle. Perhaps the most persuasive element of this symbolism is the assertion that such values carried the day for the vast majority of American history.[29]

It is time to challenge the deeply held conviction that, historically, Americans have eschewed government intervention at the national level. That is why history matters. Americans must reclaim the national government's critical role in enabling nineteenth-century American expansion, stimulating economic development, and managing international relations. We must better understand the range of cooperative mechanisms that connected state and society. Today, as for most of our history, governmental authority relies on a series of compromises brokered between central authority and local administration; it continues to rely on a host of private and voluntary partners that blur the line between public and private spheres. Although instances can be found from the Gilded Age that correspond to the strict division between public and private spheres inherent in a view of the world espoused by conservative ideologues and progressive pundits, those who seek to ground America's future in that vision of the past should be aware of the extraordinarily narrow and precarious sliver of history upon which it stands.

---

[29] Jill S. Quadagno and Debra Street, "Ideology and Public Policy: Antistatism in American Welfare State Transformation," *Journal of Policy History* 17, no. 1 (2005): 52–78; Garry Wills, *A Necessary Evil: A History of American Distrust of Government* (New York: Simon and Schuster, 1999), 17–18.

Index

Gentleman in Philadelphia, 88
Geological Survey, 357, 358
George III, 59
George, Henry, 321, 365
Georgia, 123, 181, 206–7, 209, 210
Germany, 360, 370, 374
Gerry, Elbridge, 72, 78
GI Bill (Servicemen's Readjustment
  Act (1944), 398
Gibbons v. Ogden (1824), 257
Gierke, Otto Friedrich von, 337
Gilded Age, 2, 5, 14, 17, 220, 300,
  309, 315, 316, 317, 321, 322,
  332, 336, 339, 344, 350, 355,
  361, 375, 381, 382, 384, 397,
  398, 399
Gladden, Washington, 352
Godkin, E.L., 300, 301
gold standard, 286, 345, 344–47, 346,
  347, 344–47, 388
Gould, Jay, 334–36
Governance Act (1804), 188
Governance Act (1805), 189
Grand Army of the Republic, 290,
  296
Great Awakening, 47
Great Awakening, Second, 231, 282
Great Britain, 35, 36, 42, 43, 45, 54,
  56, 62, 65, 74, 85, 86, 132, 147,
  161, 162, 163, 164, 166, 175,
  176, 200, 205, 220, 263, 360,
  381
Great Society, 1
Grenville, William Lord, 162
Gresham, Walter, 335

Hadley, Arthur, 372–73
Hall, John H., 213–14
Hamilton, Alexander, 3, 4, 42, 46, 47,
  51, 52, 56, 57, 58, 65, 67, 76, 79,
  81, 82, 83, 84, 93, 94, 96, 97, 98,
  99, 100, 101, 102, 103, 104, 109,
  110, 111, 115, 116, 117, 125,
  127, 128, 129, 137, 151, 157,
  161, 163, 191, 203, 205, 217,
  218, 226, 252, 264, 380
Hammond, George, 87

Hampton, Wade, 296
Harden v. Gordon (1823), 146
Harlan, John M., 343, 349
Harper, Robert Goodloe, 103
Harrington, James, 22, 27, 30, 178
Harrison Land Act (1800), 180
Harrison, Benjamin, 74
Harrison, William Henry, 181
Hartford Convention (1814), 144
Hatch Experiment-Station Act (1887),
  391
Hawley, Ellis, 380
Hayes, Rutherford B., 346
Haymarket incident (1886), 316, 366
Head v. Providence Insurance Co.
  (1804), 248
Henderson, Gerard, 338
Henry, 391
Henry, Patrick, 63, 83, 100
Higginson, Henry Lee, 297
historicism, 311, 355, 366, 369, 372
Hoar, George, 299
Holmes, Oliver Wendell Jr., 328, 331
Homestead Act (1862), 286, 287, 398
Hopkinson, Francis, 85
Hoyt, Henry, 356
Hume, David, 23, 81
hybrid institutions, 102, 104, 146, *See
  also mixed enterprise*

Illinois and Michigan Canal, 270
Illinois Central R.R. Co. v. Illinois
  (1892), 322
impost. *See under taxation, external*
independent regulatory agencies, 365
indian removal, 4, 205–11
Indiana, 163, 181, 267, 274
Indians, 11, 37, 153, 154, 158,
  163, 167, 178, 179, 186, 189,
  194–200, 205, 213, 215, 217,
  257, 283, 381
injunctions, 209, 318, 319, 322, 350
Innes, Harry, 238, 240
Institute for Government Research,
  138
interest groups, 17, 66, 287, 289, 323,
  350, 351, 355, 377, 383, 391, 394

Turgot, Robert Jacques, 66
Twain, Mark, 300
Tweed, William Marcy "Boss", 300

unintended consequences, 309, 310
Union Bank of Georgetown, 229
Union Pacific Rail Road, 287, 288, 301
United Brewery Workers, 317
United States v. E.C. Knight Sugar
   (1895), 343
United States Military Academy, 211
United States Mint, 103
United States Sanitary Commission,
   290, 302
United States v. E.C. Knight Sugar
   (1895), 348, 349

Van Buren, Martin, 143
Van Rensseler, Stephen, 208
Vermont, 273
vigilance, 18, 21, 23, 24, 42, 85, 106,
   116, 119, 149, 182, 234, 309,
   328
Virginia, 34, 36, 63, 67, 75, 83, 84,
   99, 100, 122, 124, 186, 190, 213,
   251, 258, 348
Virginia Resolution, 106
voluntary associations, 355, 377, 383

Wabash decision (1886), 334, 337
Wade, Benjamin, 292
Waite, Morrison R., 331
Walker, Francis A., 297
Walton, Charles W., 324
War Department, 151
War for Independence. *See American
   Revolution*
War of 1812, 104, 128, 176, 179, 181,
   195, 200–205, 214
Ward, Lester, 359–60, 360
Ware v. Hylton (1796), 160
Warren, James, 79
Warren, Mercy Otis, 88
Washington, D.C., 112, 151, 171, 201,
   264, 383, 387

Wayland, Francis, 283
Wayne, Anthony, 163, 186
Webster, Daniel, 13, 148
Webster, Noah, 70
Welton v. Missouri (1875), 340, 343,
   344
Wentworth, John, 270
West, 11, 66, 69, 70, 75, 130, 132,
   143, 144, 161, 166, 167, 177,
   179, 182, 184, 186, 190, 191,
   197, 205, 211, 221, 228, 262,
   269, 270, 272, 297, 306, 314,
   341, 343, 357, 358, 385, 394
*Western & Atlantic R.R. CO. v.
   Bishop* (1873), 328
Western Herald, 256
Western territories. *See territories*
Western Union, 305, 331
Whig Party, 148, 176, 244, 283
Whigs, 13, 50, 148, 177, 244, 245,
   246, 270, 274, 280
Whiskey Excise Tax (1791), 87
Whiskey Rebellion, 145, 200, 226
Whiskey Ring scandals, 301
Whitefield, George, 47
Whitman, Walt, 280
Whitney, Eli, 214
Wiebe, Robert, 8, 369
Wiley, Harvey, 386
Wilkinson, James, 12, 66, 191
Will, George F., 398
Wilson, Henry, 301
Wilson, James, 75, 76, 107
Wirt, William, 209
women, 5, 14, 18, 26, 37, 78, 95, 115,
   119, 120, 230, 283, 324, 389
Women's Bureau, 389
Worcester v. Georgia (1832), 210
workers, 121, 147, 237, 238, 307,
   315, 316, 317, 320, 328, 350,
   351, 363, 393
World War I, 297
World War II, 394, 395, 396
Wortman, Tunis, 107, 120
Wright, Carroll D., 352